The Story of North Texas

FROM TEXAS NORMAL COLLEGE, 1890, TO THE UNIVERSITY OF NORTH TEXAS SYSTEM, 2001

James L. Rogers

Foreword by Chancellor Alfred F. Hurley

1890 Texas Normal College
1894 North Texas Normal College
1901 North Texas State Normal College
1923 North Texas State Teachers College
1949 North Texas State College
1961 North Texas State University
1988 University of North Texas
1999 University of North Texas System

Denton, Texas
University of North Texas Press

Printed in the United States of America.

10 9 8 7 6 5 4 3 2 1

Permissions:
University of North Texas Press
P.O. Box 311336
Denton, TX 76203-1336

The paper used in this book meets the minimum requirements of the American National Standard for Permanence of Paper for Printed Library Materials, z39.48.1984. Binding materials have been chosen for durability.

Library of Congress Cataloging-in-Publication Data

Rogers, James L. (James Lloyd), 1926–
The story of North Texas : from Texas Normal College, 1890, to the University of North Texas system, 2001 / James L. Rogers ; foreword by Chancellor Alfred F. Hurley.
p. cm.
Includes bibliographical references (p.) and index.
ISBN 1-57441-128-4 (alk. paper)
1. University of North Texas—History. I. Title.
LD5312.R64 2002
378.764'555—dc21
2002000561

Design by Angela Schmitt
Cover photograph by Angilee Wilkerson

Contents

Illustrations

Illustrations (continued)

Foreword

by Chancellor Alfred F. Hurley

Any university would be fortunate to have Dr. James Rogers, the author of this administrative history, among its people. Jim Rogers has already given North Texas much: forty-three years service as a faculty member in the Journalism Department with long periods in important administrative assignments; and, the authorship of the first history on the years 1890-1965. Now, he has generously focused virtually all of his retirement years to date on preparing this new history that strengthens the coverage between 1950-68 and brings the North Texas story through its 1990 centennial year and into the year 2001.

All associated with North Texas will join me, I am confident, in applauding Dr. Rogers' efforts to help his readers better understand how the past has shaped the university of today. Those readers will find in this edition more evidence of what one of my predecessors, Dr. J. C. Matthews, characterized in his preface to the seventy-five-year history as an "up hill" story. Just the same, he accurately forecast that "myriads of helpers will assure continued ascent" for this institution.

Many such helpers have materialized in the remarkably committed groups of faculty and staff members, increasingly reinforced in the last twenty years by alumni and friends, who collectively have enabled the realization of long standing goals repeatedly sought by several administrations.

Rogers identifies those achievements by the university as national recognition for certain academic programs; steadily increasing national scholarship and fellowship awards; and a far more prominent and better received role in the Metroplex as the hub of its only local system; the evolution of a second institution, with the University of North Texas name, the Health Science Center at Fort Worth; a timely UNT campus master plan responsive to enrollments projected to exceed 37,000 and already highlighted by new and renovated facilities worthy of the quality of the programs they house; success in private fund-raising achieved during the first Capital Campaign during the Centennial and the launching of a second campaign with the help of a highly professional development staff, a stronger Foundation; and a revitalized Alumni (or North Texas Exes) Association; and, even, a better defined entryway to the University.

Future histories of North Texas will record, I believe, the accomplishment of significant goals unrealized at this writing; status as a top-tier university with steadily increasing funded research and private support that will enhance and expand existing achievements. In short, we have a lot more to do, but Dr. Rogers' labors have shown us how far we have come.

ALFRED F. HURLEY
Chancellor
UNT System

Acknowledgments

The primary credit for successful completion of this book must go to Sue Walker Rogers, my wife of fifty-five years. She encouraged the work, tolerated my disappearance into a work cubicle for long hours, and actively assisted in developing concepts for presentation and in reading each version of the manuscript to suggest changes, additions, and deletions.

On the North Texas campus, the greatest thanks go to Richard Himmel, University Archivist. He spent many hours locating thousands of documents and files that constituted the raw material for telling the story of North Texas. His review and suggestions over several years were invaluable. The photographs in this book could not have been presented without his work in maintaining voluminous photo files and in locating those seen here. Many of the photos are repeated from the first edition of this book. Others are reproduced from the photo history of the university that Richard co-authored (Robert S. La Forte and Richard L. Himmel, *Down the Corridor of Years: A Centennial History of the University of North Texas in Photographs, 1890*, University of North Texas Press, 1989).

For outstanding recent photographs, special credit is extended to Angilee Wilkerson, photographer in the UNT Public Affairs and Information Services.

Dr. Richard Wells, chairman of the UNT Journalism Department, offered constant encouragement and provided the basic logistic support of office, equipment, and supplies over more than five years. Also in the journalism office, a great debt is acknowledged for continuing assistance from Nelia Smith. I had hoped to complete this second edition for the Centennial Year in 1990; when that proved not possible, Chancellor/President Alfred F. Hurley encouraged me to continue the work and suggested that financing would be possible in the future. Thanks are also extended to Dr. Norval Pohl, who as executive vice president and provost assured me of his support. That support arrived in a timely manner with the completion of the manuscript in 2001 just as Dr. Pohl was being inaugurated as president.

Thanks also to staff members of the University Library and the Public Affairs and Information Service and to the many faculty and administrative colleagues who encouraged this work.

James L. Rogers
Denton, Texas
May 26, 2001

part I

The Private Normal College

1890–1901

It will be our aim to become leaders in the education of the young men and women of Texas, fitting them to creditably fill the most important positions in business and professional circles. We desire the cooperation of all who believe in higher education and who want to see our state in the very front of intellectual as well as material progress.

J. C. Chilton

chapter 1

A City in Search of a College

You are to erect a building on a ground place similar to one exhibited to your citizens 64 x 90 feet, two stairs high, with belfry tower and good substantial roof, the whole building to be plastered, seated, and ready for occupancy by Sept. 8, 1890.

You are to secure to me exclusive control of said building for the use of the Normal College for the term of eight years.

At the end of eight years successful conduct of said college you are to transfer to me, my heirs, executors, or assigns, by deed for use of school purposes only the college buildings and campus.

J. C. Chilton
1890 agreement with City of Denton

The traveler would need an extraordinary imagination to visualize the Denton of 1890 as the setting for a campus. It was, says one historian, "a good small town almost lost in the deep sand of the cross timbers. . . still in the middle of the horse and buggy days."[1] With a population of 2,558, the town had eight saloons, no sidewalks, no bridges, but lots of shanties, mud, and sand. Yet to come were a waterworks, electric lights, telephones, streetcars, a new courthouse, a chatauqua, and an opera house.

Public schooling had existed for only six years, but since 1858 there had been numerous one-teacher private schools, some open as little as a month or two a year. One "professor" opened a school in the Masonic Lodge Hall in 1868 and gained local fame for "Professor Bell's Male and Female Academy." Denton historian C. A. Bridges notes that in the 1870s, Denton "was definitely school conscious."[2] Public agitation led to the creation of a public school in 1884. By 1890 the school had ten grades and was well established.

THE NEED IN TEXAS

There were four state-supported institutions of higher education in Texas in 1890 and forty-five smaller private and church-related colleges. The year before, the University of Texas (founded 1883) had enrolled 307 students and the Sam Houston Normal Institute (founded 1879) 313, the latter the largest enrollment yet reached by any state school.[3] Texas A&M and Prairie View Normal were the other state schools. Public schools were also underdeveloped. Terms were short, teachers were poorly qualified, few high schools existed for the predominantly rural population, and there was no compulsory school attendance.

Advanced public education had come with the establishment of the Sam Houston Normal in Huntsville in 1879. This was stimulated by the efforts of the Peabody Board, which was created in 1867 to help former Confederate States to establish free public schools. The Peabody agent concluded that the Peabody funds could serve best by assisting in the establishment of a good normal school. Some dissatisfaction arose when the legislature located the new institution at Huntsville, but if the city had not donated the former Austin College buildings to the state, the bill might not have passed.[4] Within a few years, this fact would offer a significant lesson for Denton.

The "normal" name for teacher preparation was imported from France, derived from the Latin *norma*, meaning "standard" or "rule." In the early nineteenth century, private normal schools were set up in Vermont and Massachusetts. This led to a lasting institution for teacher education. The first public normal school was opened in 1839 in Lexington, Massachusetts, through the work of Horace Mann. By 1875 most states had passed laws creating normal schools.[5]

In 1886, seven years after the founding of the Sam Houston Normal, State Superintendent B. M. Baker called for the creation of two more normals for white teachers, one in West and one in North Texas.[6] In 1888 State Superintendent Oscar H. Cooper told the legislature that another state normal was a necessity.[7] In 1890 Cooper warned that the great mass of new teachers had "no educational advantages beyond those afforded by country schools." He said that if Missouri could support five normals, Texas should have at least three for white teachers.[8] Also in 1890, the Superintendents' Association and the State Teachers' Association recommended that two more state normal schools be established, "one in North and one in Central Texas." Some Denton citizens were aware of this recommendation; a member of the executive committee circulating it was E. F. Comegys, Denton's school superintendent.[9]

Denton was the site of a summer normal institute in 1885. (These summer training sessions were used as a quick and inexpensive way to provide certified teachers.) State examinations led to the issuing of twenty-seven teaching certificates from an enrollment of seventy-four. Among those receiving first-grade certificates was Denton Superintendent Comegys, who the next year conducted a summer normal at Cisco.[10] Denton also had the example of ambitious neighboring towns. In northeast Denton County the Pilot Point Seminary advertised a collegiate branch[11] and to the east, citizens in 1889 established McKinney Collegiate Institute "to rank with the best colleges as a source for higher learning for the boys and girls of the county."[12]

In 1890, then, Denton had this background:

1. Citizens were conscious of the need for more and better educational facilities.

2. Higher education in the state was underdeveloped, and there was only one state school whose sole purpose was the training of teachers for the public schools.

3. The Denton leadership was fully aware of a statewide effort for the establishment of more state normal schools, especially one in the North Texas area.

4. Experience with summer normal institutes and the example of neighboring towns in trying to establish colleges gave further impetus to Denton's desire for higher education.

A VISITOR FROM THE NORTH

In March 1890 the neighboring *Pilot Point Post-Mirror* observed that "the business men of Denton have at last moved to secure much that is good for the town" by organizing a board of trade of 120 members.[13] Into this setting came Joshua Crittenden Chilton of Detroit, Michigan, searching for a setting for a normal college. He was drawn to the area because his brother, Dr. Robert H. Chilton, was a physician practicing in Dallas. After visiting several towns in the area, Chilton came to Denton.[14]

He arrived with a letter from the Indiana superintendent of public instruction, recommending Chilton as "a gentleman of culture and character and an experienced and successful educator and a thorough scholar, an admirable instructor, and an excellent superintendent."[15]

Chilton was invited to Denton by John A. Hann, a merchant and member of the City Council.[16] Chilton persuaded the mayor to call a meeting of the City Council to discuss the normal college idea.[17] Chilton addressed a meeting of citizens at the courthouse on April 18, 1890. His proposal for establishment of a normal, termed "rather steep" by a reporter present, was received "with tremendous enthusiasm."[18]

Chilton left Denton to discuss his idea in other nearby towns but was back for another mass meeting on the night of May 7.[19] Speeches by Chilton and his supporters won endorsement of the normal, and a committee of lawyers was appointed to study whether the city could legally issue bonds for the construction of buildings for such a school. The five committee members (J. W. Jagoe, A. C. Owsley, J. T. Bottorf, H. C. Ferguson, and T. M. Davidson) reported to a called meeting of the City Council the following day, May 8, that the city could take such action, with a limitation of $20,000 on the amount of bonded indebtedness.[20] Chilton then outlined the conditions under which he would locate the normal college in Denton:

1st - I will employ and pay a faculty of teachers, well-trained for the departments to which each member is assigned and will guarantee to keep employed a teaching force sufficient to accommodate all students who matriculate at the college increasing the number of teachers as the college grows.

2nd - I will advertise the Normal College diligently by the most approved means both personally and by circulars and other printed matter; and I will continue to advertise, and make known the merits of the institution.

3rd - You are to erect a building on a ground place similar to one exhibited to your citizens 64 x 90 feet, two stairs high, with belfry tower and good substantial roof, the whole building to be plastered, seated, and ready for occupancy by Sept. 8, 1890.

4th- You are to secure to me exclusive control of said building for the use of the Normal College for the term of eight years.

At the end of eight years successful conduct of said college you are to transfer to me, my heirs, executors, or assigns, by deed for use of school purposes only the college buildings and campus.

5th - The College buildings to be erected on a lot not less than six acres in extent and agreed upon by both parties.

6th - If the attendance shall reach six hundred students before the end of eight years, then you are to make additions to the college to accommodate the students with class and chapel rooms, said addition to cost not less than three thousand dollars. And you are to allow me to erect at my own expense on the campus such buildings as may be deemed needful to advance the interest and efficiency of the college.

7th - You are not to seek, aid, or encourage the location of institutions of similar scope or character in Denton.

8th - That the 4th clause (above) shall be so construed as to mean that the average matriculation in said school shall be two hundred students for each scholastic year of the last three years of the first five years such school is conducted. That if the average fall below two hundred each of said three years, then at the request of the City Council of the City of Denton, Texas, the said J. C. Chilton agrees to surrender the possession of said buildings to the City of Denton.[21]

The City Council accepted this proposal and asked a finance committee to take the steps necessary to provide the funds. Council members Hann, G. B.

Collins, and T. W. Abney were appointed to a committee that also included Denton residents Judge F. M. Davidson and W. J. Parker to meet with Chilton to make plans for the college.[22]

Within a month, however, dissatisfaction arose over parts of the agreement. The City Council on June 10 appointed a three-man committee to confer with Chilton. This led to revisions that were presented at a special session of the council on June 14. Chilton promised to keep the college in session at least nine months each year but lowered from 200 to 125 the number of students he would guarantee in the third, fourth, and fifth years of operation. His guarantee of 200 students per year was extended to the sixth, seventh, and eighth years. The penalty clause—surrender of the college property to the city—was further hedged with a waiver for any year or years in which there occurred "failure of crops or other providential hindrances."

But Chilton lost the feature of the original contract that would transfer the property to him or his heirs at the end of eight years. In its place the new agreement provided an eight-year lease from the date of completion of the new building, with a renewal for a term of eighteen years if Chilton met the other terms.[23]

In the meantime, a correspondent reported in late May, "Prof. Chilton . . . has now in press large quantities of advertising matter and he will take the field right away to advertise the Texas Normal College."[24] But Chilton couldn't wait to get in the teacher education field in Denton and didn't spend all his time "in the field" advertising the new college. He joined the faculty of a summer normal conducted in Denton's public school building for three weeks in July by a "Prof. Pitman" with a "Miss Terrill" on the faculty. Forty students attended the summer institute, which was authorized by the state superintendent of public instruction to include "a School of Methods and a School of English."[25]

CREATING A CAMPUS

Historians of North Texas agree that a bond election for the normal college building was passed on favorably by Denton citizens.[26] None, however, cite any record of this election. The first official record is action by the City Council on May 28, 1890, instructing the finance committee to have the bonds authorized, registered, and sold.[27] Historians also agree that attorneys discovered that the sale of bonds for a normal school was outside the legal powers of the city, whose bond-issuing authority was limited to free public schools. Two corrective measures appear in the city's records. One on September 3 repealed the council's actions of May 28 and substituted an ordinance providing for the erection of public school buildings in Denton as authorized by the Texas Legislature.[28] And on December 8 the council ordered its minutes corrected so that wherever the word "Normal School Building" appeared it should read "Public School Building."[29] When the normal building was completed, it carried above the door the legend, "Public School."[30]

The city agreed to have a building ready for the opening of school in September 1890, but it was nearly five months after that date before a building site was selected. On July 10, four locations were proposed to the City Council. One of them, identified as Hann Hill, was on Sycamore Street just north of the IOOF Cemetery. Another was ten acres west of the Fair Grounds outside the city limits. These two were to figure most strongly in the ensuing controversy. The backers of the Hann Hill property reported on July 10 that they had $650 subscribed as a donation, but lacked a guarantee of the balance needed for its purchase. The council quickly agreed that a majority of the seven members present would determine a site, but eight ballots failed to produce a majority—and Hann Hill never got more than a single vote. Two days later the councilmen were called together and told that E. C. Smith now guaranteed Hann Hill as a donation to the city. On a 4–2 vote with one abstention, this was chosen for the normal college campus.[31] But time was lacking to complete a building by September. Thus it was that the grand opening ceremonies took place on the courthouse square and the first classes met in a downtown store building. As it turned out, the permanent campus site was still not fixed.

Later accounts[32] suggest that the proximity of the proposed campus to a cemetery was a source of great unhappiness to some citizens. But those who favored the acreage west of the Fair Grounds encountered the protest that no one wanted a college way out in a rural area. On December 8, 1890, an extra session of the City Council was called "for the purpose of considering the erection of the public school building." The July 12 selection of the Hann Hill site was canceled 4–3. That afternoon a three-man building committee was authorized to purchase material and contract for building the school house. The council placed $5,000 at the committee's disposal and also ordered that bills for the school's desks be paid.[33] All this on the same day, with a campus site of five months' standing eliminated and no action taken to secure a new one!

It remained for W. A. Ponder to provide an acceptable site without cost to the city. He and nine men formed what came to be known as "The Syndicate" to buy the remainder of the Eugene Puchalski Survey west and slightly south of Denton. Ten acres of this survey were offered as a campus. Joining Ponder in this group were Mayor J. A. Carroll and Aldermen John A. Hann, and T. W. Abney, along with G. B. Collins, Robert Hann, Daniel Head, H. F. Schweer, M. S. Stout, and B. H. Deavenport.[34]

On January 2, 1891, the Ponder donation was presented to the City Council, along with Hann Hill and four other site proposals. After balloting thirty-three times without a choice the council adjourned until 7:30 that night. The night session produced more ballots (forty-two rounds) but no more results. The morning session of January 3 went through eleven ballots without a choice, so the aldermen turned to other business. Upon returning to the question, five ballots were unproductive. Finally, on the sixth round of voting (the ninety-third in two days), the Ponder donation received six of the eight votes. Mayor Carroll then named a committee of one alderman from each of the four wards to select the lot from the land offered by the syndicate.[35] The ten-acre tract selected was bounded by Hickory on the north, Sycamore on the south, Avenue A on the east, and Avenue B on the west. The rest of the survey of about 240 acres was platted and soon annexed into the city as the College Addition.[36]

As soon as the Ponder site was selected, the council approved plans and specifications for the school building as drawn by "the Architect of Dallas."[37] Bonds for building construction were sold September 8, 1890.[38] A contemporary newspaper reported the sale on December 13, 1890.[39] A city finance committee statement later showed that $15,000 in school house bonds had been sold, less ten percent commission for a net of $13,500 received.

AT LAST, A BUILDING

Construction began in January, and West Denton, especially Hickory Street, took "a majestic leap" with improvements to be seen everywhere.[40] The laying of the cornerstone was purposely delayed until Washington's birthday, but actually held on February 21, 1891, presumably because the twenty-second fell on the Sabbath. The walls of the first story of the building were nearly completed by that time, but the northeast corner was left down to leave room for the cornerstone. The ceremony was conducted by the Masonic Grand Lodge of Texas.[41] One early historian writes that "A great concourse of people assembled at the City Hall and marched to the grounds, led by the Masons, the city officials, and Professor J. C. Chilton's school. The ceremonies were very impressive."[42] A small boy's view was recalled seventy-two years later by a man who wrote, "The whole town was out for the ceremonies. I was 7½ years old and marched in the parade from the square out to the building. And I enjoyed it immensely."[43]

Unfortunately, the city's joy could not last long. After discount, the bond sale had yielded only $13,500, which proved insufficient. On June 8, 1891, the City Council meeting considered ways and means of raising $3,000, the balance due on the new building. The aldermen voted to accept the offer of two Denton banks to subscribe for $3,000 worth of city script bearing ten percent interest.[44] Later, the same procedure had to be followed to settle labor claims against the building.[45] Faced with bills for desks and supplies, the council issued two notes which went unpaid until January 30, 1893.[46] Nevertheless, the City Council formally turned the normal school building over to Chilton in accordance with their contract on July 29, 1891.[47] Thus was completed the city's series of steps to bring higher education to Denton: the issuance of bonds for "Public School Building No. 2," a deception that deceived no one, and the erection of a building with public money for a purpose which had no authorization in state laws.

One other step was involved in the creation of the new college on a formal basis: the issuance of a charter to a group of private citizens who formed a corporation to operate the school. This was filed in the office of the secretary of state in Austin on June 21, 1891. The normal was formally designated as "Texas Normal College and Teacher Training Institute." Its authorized capital stock was declared to be $10,000, divided into 400 shares of $25 each. Three men elected by the stockholders served as a board of trustees. Those named in the charter for the first year were J. C. Chilton; his brother, Dr. R. H. Chilton of Dallas; and H. F. Schweer, a member of the real estate syndicate. The charter also provided for a board of regents to be elected every three years by the stockholders; this was an advisory group to meet annually with the board of trustees to advise on matters "touching the material interests of the institution," but lacking any voting power. Three syndicate members and a city alderman were among those named regents in the charter. The group for the first three years consisted of J. W. Bailey, Gainesville; W. A. Squires, Henrietta; and, from Denton, W. W. Deavenport, T. W. Abney, J. W. Cook, W. A. Ponder, John A. Hann, F. E. Piner, and A. C. Owsley.

chapter 2

"A Much-Praised Man in our Midst"

The Normal College is simply booming. Prof. Chilton and the faculty are very much elated and say that they will have a hundred in school by the end of the first month, there being over eighty now. The patrons of this new institution of learning are highly pleased with the management of the college, and Prof. Chilton is a much praised man in our midst. . . . Denton is destined to be the educational center of North Texas.

Pilot Point Post-Mirror, 1890.

On July 14, 1872, Joshua Crittenden Chilton sat down and penned an elaborate pledge to himself and his future:

> Today is my twentieth birthday.
>
> Youth, and boyhood have nearly fled, and manhood rushes on with its cares, and disappointments.
>
> Farewell youthful days, farewell.
>
> Though cares, and disappointment await me, I am determined to do my duty.
>
> I desire to make my mark in the world and by the assisting grace of God I will make it.[1]

As he donned his long Prince Albert coat and high silk topper on September 16, 1890, Chilton must have felt that at last he would have the chance to make his mark in a big way. After graduating from the National Normal University at Lebanon, Ohio, he was teacher and then principal of the Orleans (Indiana) Graded School and Training Institute.[2] He obtained a favorable letter of introduction from the Indiana state superintendent. In this unlikely Texas setting there must have seemed great promise, as a local correspondent wrote that "the name of Chilton and the name college are on the lips of all" and referred to Chilton as "Denton's great college president."[3]

The promise of a great educational future couldn't have been seen in the physical surroundings as "Prof. Chilton" greeted citizens and students at opening-day ceremonies on the northwest corner of the courthouse square. After reading a psalm and delivering a prayer, the president discussed the establishment of the institution, which he called by its shortened name, "Texas Normal College."[4] He described the struggle of the English-speaking peoples for higher education since the time of Alfred the Great as "one of the grandest efforts of the human race." His tributes to great American universities included Brown University, and he noted that "the institution beginning its initial session here this morning numbers in its faculty one of the honored sons of Brown." (The reference was to J. Q. Dealey.)

Chilton also lashed out at the attitude that women needed to be taught "reading, writing and fancy work only." He praised the move to coeducation, declaring: "So from our educational horizon are the cobwebs of superstition and prejudice being swept, and this institution joins in the advance guard by admitting ladies to all its classes on equal terms with the other sex." His speech also bowed to the impact on pedagogical practice of Pestalozzi and the growth of normal schools and normal colleges "all over the civilized world." Chilton concluded with his view of the role of the new normal in Denton. Some normals, he pointed out, are:

> under the patronage of the state or government, others independent of either state or church, and to the latter class Texas Normal College belongs; its badge the ascendant star of Texas, and lamp of learning; in character, independent, original and progressive.
>
> The scope of the college will include broad courses of study, with abundant opportunity to students to elect or choose such studies as will best fit them for their prospective businesses or professions.
>
> Our aim will constantly be to foster the broadest culture and the highest scholarship. In methods the institution will keep fully abreast the times with due regard to the economy of the time of the student.
>
> It will be our aim to become leaders in the education of the young men and women of Texas, fitting them to creditably fill the most important positions in business and professional circles.
>
> We desire the cooperation of all who believe in higher education and who want to see our state in the very front of intellectual as well as material progress.[5]

The ceremonies continued with speeches by Mayor J. A. Carroll and County Judge F. M. Davidson, and then enrollment for the first term got under way. That afternoon recitations were heard in classes on the second floor of the B. J. Wilson hardware store building. That week about seventy students registered, including some transfers from such schools as Baylor University, Winchester (Tennessee) Normal, and Ward's Seminary in Nashville.[6]

No solution was in sight on the problem of a campus and building, so the city in the meantime began paying rent of $32.50 a month for the use of the downtown building.[7] President Chilton had no minimum enrollment figure to meet his first year but would have to average 125 students by the third year of operation. He had a supporter in the correspondent for the Pilot Point paper, who reported during the third week of classes:

> The Normal College is simply booming. Prof. Chilton and the faculty are very much elated and say that they will have a hundred in school by the end of the first month, there being over eighty now. The patrons of this new institution of learning are highly pleased with the management of the college, and Prof. Chilton is a much praised man in our midst. . . . Denton is destined to be the educational center of North Texas.[8]

The enrollment reached 131 in early December, but not without some extraordinary student recruitment measures. Not the least of these was the importation of twenty-eight Creek Indians from the Indian Territory across the Red River just north of Denton.[9] Later printed sources tell of thirty Indians in the normal student body and of their misadventures with firewater in the local saloons. These later versions assert that the federal government paid the expenses of the Indians, but contemporary records are lacking. Perhaps the normal authorities arranged to be paid for educating the Creeks from the permanent school fund of the Creek Nation, which was started in 1890, or from the educational funds of the Muscogee Nation.[10] The Indian students appear to have been brought in for the second ten-week term starting November 25, 1890. The Indians are not associated with any other time period in any existing record. Enrollment records are not available for the entire forty-week school year, which was divided into four quarters from September 16 to June 21, 1891. Estimates in later years by students then enrolled have placed the figure variously from 150 to 185.

PROMOTING THE NORMAL

Chilton faced strong obstacles in creating a student body of any size. There had been only 300 students at the state university the year before. The main clientele of a normal were teachers and prospective teachers, who were not then generally prepared with any form of higher education. Of 10,120 certified white teachers in service in the state in 1890–91, 8,392 were certified by examination, outside of any formal educational process. Only 623 held college diplomas and 809 normal diplomas or certificates. Another 297 had high school diplomas or certificates.[11] In older sections of the United States the state normal had become an established institution for teacher education. But even there the normal was subject to abuse. As Henry William Shryock, president of Southern Illinois Normal, once wrote:

> Between 1870 and 1880, the success of Holbrook's Normal School at Lebanon, Ohio, led to the establishment, all over Ohio, Indiana, and, to some extent, Illinois, of privately owned and operated schools called Normal schools: but Indiana was the happy hunting ground for the man who had a few thousand dollars, and who wanted to be at the head of a school.[12]

Shryock referred to these as "little individual, half-academic, half-collegiate, half-teacher-training institutions." And it was from this very movement in Indiana that Joshua C. Chilton had received his start. He faced the question: could he develop an institution with good standards and draw enough enrollment to fulfill his contract with the City of Denton?

Chilton's first announcement bulletin tells much of his aspiration for high ideals but suggests that the normal was in the hands of a highly impractical man. It appeared with the endorsement of nineteen prominent citizens, dated May 24, 1890.[13] The bulletin described the advantages of Denton, which it credited with a population of from 3,500 to 4,000 people, although the U. S. Census that year listed it at 2,558. And even though the cornerstone of the first building would not be laid until February of the following year, the bulletin proclaimed that "The Normal College buildings are erected on a magnificent eminence overlooking the entire city." The as yet nonexistent building was described as a magnificent one of nearly 6,000 square feet, containing "large assembly halls, recitation rooms, library, laboratory, college office, toilet rooms, etc." Chilton described the grandeur of the structure this way:

> The exterior presents the triumph of the architect in combining utility and beauty; a majestic belfry tower rises seventy-five feet over the main entrance, which is a massive archway of Denton stone, supported by granite shafts; an abundance of arched windows, relieved at the top by

stained glass, combine with the other features to render the exterior one of beauty and symmetry.

The normal was advertised as a low-cost center for education. Tuition for one term of ten weeks was $18.50, and the entire forty-week school year could be paid for at $48. Room and board was advertised at $2.50 per week. By choosing the lowest priced facilities, the bulletin pointed out, one could stay an entire school year for $148. Chilton even warned of the dangers of excessive wealth: "Let no student or parent imagine that it is necessary to expend a large sum of money in order to get through. It is a fatal mistake. Thousands of good *boys have been ruined* by too liberal allowances of money at college. Students do not come here to spend money." Instead, he pointed out, "intellectual progress and manly and womanly bearing are the passports to recognition with us."

It was repeatedly pointed out that classes were arranged to enable students to enroll at any time during the year so that no student would ever be turned away, a common practice in colleges of that time. The school was intended to meet "the public demand for a more practical education." "Examine the want columns of the daily papers, and then say which would stand the better chance, a student with a four years' course in Greek, or one with practical training in the sciences, and in mechanical or civil engineering?"

Furthermore, the health of students was under constant surveillance by the faculty and a matron, and there were to be no overworked students.

> In view of the fact that in some institutions students break down and must leave before the close of the session, our faculty and matron exercise vigilant care and adjust lessons to meet the capacity of students. Bright and willing students are never taxed to "show off," but on the contrary, they are cautioned against overwork.

Chilton viewed the college as designed to meet the wants of virtually any prospective student. He intended it for (1) students who wanted thorough training in any of six liberal and comprehensive courses of study, (2) school teachers and those preparing to teach, (3) those who couldn't afford a full college course, but who could benefit by staying four to eight months, (4) those with very little education who needed the elementary principles of grammar and arithmetic but who would be embarrassed to enter the primary department of a public school because of their age and (5) special students who wanted to take one or two studies and do original work and independent investigations.

"NINE FULL COURSES"

Front and back cover sheets of Chilton's first bulletin advertised nine full courses:

1. Optional, or Preparatory
2. Teachers' Training Course
3. Scientific Course
4. Full Classical Course
5. Engineering Course
6. Course in Elocution and Literature
7. Business College Course
8. Conservatory Music Course
9. Fine Arts

Of these, numbers six and nine are not described inside the bulletin. But the others are far-ranging enough to appeal to almost any potential student. The Preparatory Department or School of Common Branches offered work at the level of the lower public school grades to students of all ages who could enter at any time and study for an indefinite period of time.

The Teachers' Department or Training Course ran for one year, after which diplomas and certificates were to be granted. Those who didn't remain long enough to complete the course would receive certificates only. This was to prepare teachers for the county schools and for the city schools below the high school. Taken in connection with scientific and classic courses, this course would prepare for high school teaching and for city and county school superintendencies. Applicants were advised that "Students are not required or expected to get an education elsewhere before coming to this institution for methods and principles of teaching."

The degree-granting section of the normal was the Collegiate Department or College of Science and Liberal Arts. The Scientific Course, of unspecified length in the first announcement bulletin, would lead to the bachelor of science degree "for those who wish to become practical business and professional men" and in addition for high school teachers and superintendents. The bachelor of arts would go to Classic Course graduates, "who hold their own ground with graduates of other first-class Classical Colleges and Universities." The Scientific Course emphasized a number of natural sciences and mathematics, but included literature, history, and Latin (with French or German as an elective substitute). The Classic Course stressed philosophy, literature, Greek, Latin, and history, with some mathematics, but no modern language.

The Business Course or Commercial College would require no more than twenty weeks, and some students were presumed to be able to complete the work in half that time. Diplomas were awarded at the end of any term without waiting until the annual commencement. Chilton advertised that "Pupils educated in the district schools are prepared to enter our business course, as our conditions for admission are quite easy." Studies included commercial arithmetic, bookkeeping, grammar, banking, commission, commercial law, shipping, penmanship, spelling, and letter-writing. Optional studies listed were phonography, typewriting, and reporting.

Especially ambitious was the listing of the Engineering Course. This included surveying, architectural engineering, structural engineering, field engineering, geodesy, mechanics, chemical analysis, blowpipe analysis, mineralogy, geology, mining, construction, tunneling, railroad construction, and many others. According to the faculty listing, this material would be taught by the man who also taught all mathematics courses.

This same man, John M. Moore, was also listed on a later page on the faculty of the Conservatory of Music as teaching voice culture and harmony. Chilton himself was assigned classes in the history of music and the theory of sound. Piano, organ, and voice were the fields listed, all to be studied by private lessons at extra rates. A special bargain offer was also advertised:

> The full course in Music, embracing both Voice and Piano, 44 weeks, four lessons a week, and practice, together with two studies selected from our literary course, for only $200, *in advance*. This includes, 175 private lessons, 175 vocal lessons, full chorus drills, elocution, theory, class recitations and two extra branches in the College.

Hall[14] analyzed this offering and that of Chilton's alma mater, the National Normal University of Alfred Holbrook. He found that five of the courses of study listed in Chilton's first announcement coincided with those of the Ohio school. Texas Normal College added one feature, the business course, but lacked the courses in law, medicine, theology, and pharmacy advertised by the National Normal. Holbrook was quite successful in attracting students to his school, with 1,584 students enrolled in the teachers division alone in 1887. Hall concludes that the influence of Holbrook's philosophy of "Independent Normalism" was the major influence in Chilton's formulation of the courses of study for the new Denton school.

THE FIRST FACULTY

The typical normal faculty of 1890 was made up of people with a devotion to the cause of education, experience in teaching, and a formal education of less than bachelor's degree level.[15] Chilton himself fit that description, having normal school training but no college degree. But he did open his school with at least three teachers who were college graduates, one of whom had a master's degree. The latter was Charles E. Sargent, who was listed in the first announcement bulletin as the teacher of natural science, botany, physics, chemistry, geology, and zoology. A student enrolled at that time later recalled that Sargent became poet laureate of New Hampshire.[16] The bulletin listed three bachelor's degree teachers, but apparently only two actually began teaching. They were John M. Moore, B. S., A.B., mathematics, engineering, and surveying, and James Q. Dealey, A. B., ancient and modern languages. Moore later received Ph.D. and D. D. degrees from Yale and became a bishop of the Methodist Episcopal Church South in Dallas. He returned to the campus for the fiftieth anniversary baccalaureate services in May 1940.[17]

W. N. Masters, who visited the new normal that year and who later became a faculty member, reported that he, Chilton, and Moore were all former students of the National Normal University in Ohio.[18] Also destined for a distinguished career was Dealey, who had worked for his family-owned newspaper, the *Galveston News,* for six years before going to Brown University, where he received a bachelor's degree in 1890 just before coming to Denton. He later earned a doctorate and served for thirty-five years as a professor at Brown before becoming editor-in-chief of the *Dallas Morning News* in 1929 until his death in 1937.[19] One of his sons, William L. Dealey, was on the education faculty of the Denton college from 1929 to 1931.[20]

An 1890 newspaper account mentions Dealey, Moore, and Sargent and refers to a "Mrs. McKisig" as a music teacher.[21] This was Mrs. E. J. McKissack, sometimes referred to as director of the Normal Conservatory of Music. During the year, J. A. Sanders joined the faculty to teach the business courses. These are the only members of the teaching staff of 1890–91 on which all printed sources agree. However, some evidence suggests that these people were soon added: O. C. Charlton, natural science; Miss Nettie Sheppard, English and American literature, elocution, and physical training; Miss Pearl Eddleman, stenography and typewriting; Mrs. F. J. Gates, telegraphy; and Miss Ruby L. Chilton, librarian.[22] Unfortunately, the next catalog available today is dated 1893–94, although printed references indicate that a second catalog of 1890–91 was printed, as well as those for 1891–92 and 1892–93.[23]

THE STRUGGLE FOR EXISTENCE

Enrollment was counted cumulatively for four quarters, so it is hard to know how many students were in attendance at the normal at any given time. Catalog lists show 294 students enrolled at some time during 1892–93 and 151 in 1893–94. The bulletins list nine commercial graduates as receiving diplomas at the end of the first year; nine teaching certificates, eleven commercial diplomas and four bachelor of science degrees in 1892; no teaching certificates, thirteen commercial diplomas and five B. S. degrees in 1893; and thirteen teaching certificates, three commercial diplomas, and twelve bachelor's degrees in 1894.

National economic conditions were certainly not favorable for development of the new school. The Panic of 1893, a national economic crisis, slowed the city's business development and economic conditions were generally depressed until 1898.[24] In 1893–94, J. C. Chilton encountered continual financial difficulty. By 1893, not one faculty member remained from the original group, and only two were listed as holding any type of college degree.

Chilton had withdrawn from his original "Nine Full Courses." His 1893 catalog listed college preparatory work, studies toward teaching certificates, the scientific course for the B. S. degree, the classic course for the A. B. degree, the commercial department, and the conservatory of music. Gone was the program in engineering and surveying, which apparently never got any further then the pages of Chilton's first bulletin.

The 1893–94 catalog increased emphasis on teacher preparation, advertising that the college had been authorized by the legislature to issue life and first grade teaching certificates good anywhere in Texas. The Teachers' Department had added a "Model Department" with a critic teacher, presumably using the college preparatory classes as a training school. The course of study listed four meetings a week of "Training in Model School" in one term of the first-grade certificate course. The life or diploma course required one term of "Theory and Practice" in addition to psychology, science of education, and history of education in the professional education courses. A degree of bachelor of pedagogy could be obtained by additional work. None are recorded as having ever been granted.

The collegiate department continued to offer the B. S. degree for two years of the scientific course and the A. B. degree in one more year in the classic course. "From this course," the catalog says, "we graduate students, who hold their own ground with graduates of other first-class Classical Colleges and Universities." To this was added the thought of graduate-level instruction. The final sentence of the section on the classic course says, "The degree of A. M. is conferred on graduates of the A. B. course who do two years of successful home study after graduation."[25]

President Chilton, his catalog makes obvious, was struggling hard to entice students to Denton. He wrote, "We have no examinations on entrance. The president after a friendly talk with the applicant, finds what he needs and wants, and the student begins work." The student could still enter at any time he chose. Yet Chilton still boasted that "this is the foremost Normal College in the South."[26]

ENTER J. J. CRUMLEY

Chilton had to give up the struggle. John Jackson Crumley, who had joined the faculty in September 1892 to teach ancient languages and literature, recalled how it came about:

> Before Christmas of that year [1892], Prof. Chilton broke down completely, both financially and physically. He was practically unable

> to do any work in the school the last half of that year. The tuition had been collected, much of it in scholarships, and had been spent and [O. C.] Charlton, W. F. Moore, and I were certainly left stranded, not even with fuel to heat the building. During the latter part of the winter, 1893, we three men went into the dense stand of young post oak timber just south of the College building and cut wood to burn in our stoves. Charlton was so thoroughly discouraged that he lost all interest in the school.[27]

Crumley said that at the request of Chilton, he agreed to see the 1892–93 year through, and in the spring the trustees asked him to continue the school, collect the tuition, and be responsible for teachers' salaries. (The Chairman of the Board of Trustees was Dr. R. H. Chilton of Dallas, brother of the normal president.) The 1893–94 catalog, for which a publication date is not indicated, lists J. C. Chilton as president and carries the name of J. J. Crumley as vice-president. However, Crumley wrote that "There are several features in this adopted catalogue that I did not like, but did not have the funds to reprint the catalogue entire."[28] The other two men mentioned by Crumley, O. C. Charlton, and W. F. Moore, did not return for another winter of wood-cutting, and their names disappeared in the 1893–94 catalog.

Minutes of the Denton City Council confirm that Chilton was unable to manage the normal college.[29] Spurred on by a citizens' petition, the council on June 26, 1893, appointed a committee "to investigate and inquire into the management and conduct of the President of the Texas Normal College to ascertain if he has complied with his contract with the City of Denton." Some softening hand intervened, for in just three days the investigative order was replaced by a gentler resolution that asked "to examine in and report upon the management of the Denton Normal College."

City Council records regrettably fail to show what became of this investigation. By some process, it led to the calling of a special City Council session on November 4, 1893, to consider "ways and means to have the Normal School continued." Action came rapidly within the next two weeks. On November 8 the council voted to ask President Chilton "whether or not they could procure a release from him to all his interests in the Texas Normal College." On November 18 the council offered $264.50 to Chilton for a release of his title and interest in the school, this amount representing his expenditures for furniture. A committee was appointed to request Crumley "to receive tuition for students for the following term, and to open school on November 21, 1893." Thus J. J. Crumley was the legal chief administrator of Texas Normal College for the bulk of the 1893–94 school year, by action of the Denton City Council. There is reason to infer that, by action of the trustees headed by President Chilton's physician brother, he had become the *de facto* president with the title of vice president sometime before that. No publication survives to show what title Crumley was given, but the 1894 diplomas carried his signature as president.

Though his tenure with the institution was only two years, his contribution cannot be minimized. A later president, Dr. J. C. Matthews, stressed this fact in a letter to President Crumley's son when he wrote, "For every institution which lives, several die in infancy. This would have been the fate of this institution if it had not been for your father. That fact we intend to keep before the minds of the people throughout the generations as this institution becomes greater and greater, as we assume that it will."[30]

President Crumley was the son of John Anderson Crumley, a Tennessee and Texas farmer who believed in education.[31] Of his ten children, eight went to college, six became school teachers and two received the Ph.D. degree. John Jackson Crumley was sixteen years old when the family moved to a farm near Denison, Texas. From 1882 to 1885 he attended college in Maryville, Tennessee, and in 1888 received the bachelor of arts degree from National Normal University in Lebanon, Ohio, J. C. Chilton's alma mater. For the next two years he served as principal of the Chilhowee Academy in Tennessee. In the fall of 1890, as Texas Normal College was opening in Denton, Crumley was advertising the Pilot Point Institute, a "first-class graded school for boys and girls," of which he served as principal.[32] He later recalled[33] that he visited the Texas Normal College in its first home on the northwest corner of the Denton square. The presumption, although not supported by existing records, is that Crumley remained in neighboring Pilot Point for two years until September of 1892, when he began teaching in Denton at the age of twenty-nine.

President Crumley will also be remembered as the man who helped put the "North" in North Texas. State Senator Emory C. Smith of Denton introduced a bill that passed the legislature in 1893, authorizing the school to issue state teaching certificates. When Crumley sent a Texas Normal College diploma to Austin for counter-signing by state officials, State Superintendent J. M. Carlisle responded that the enabling law referred to "North Texas Normal College at Denton, Texas." This he held to be entirely different from the Texas Normal College, and he refused to recognize the diploma as lawful. President Crumley had to get a new state charter under the name specified in the certificate law, and it was this name that served the private school in its remaining years.[34]

THE FATE OF TWO EX-PRESIDENTS

President Chilton's boyhood ambition "to make my mark in the world" died with the forfeiture of his contract for the normal in Denton, and he himself did not long survive the illness that came with his troubled years in Texas. After living in Minnesota, he moved to Bryantsville, Indiana, in May 1895, "knowing that he could not live long, and wishing to die with his four children around him." Death came February 12, 1896, "after an illness of three years duration," at the age of forty-three.[35]

In contrast, former President Crumley had a long and eventful life after he left Denton, where his last official business was teaching in a summer normal institute in 1894. He became president of Holbrook Normal College in Fountain City, Tennessee, for two years, earned the doctor of philosophy degree in Latin at John Hopkins University, and from 1904 to 1909 was professor of Latin at Antioch College. In 1912 he began a twenty-six-year career as associate in forestry for the State of Ohio. After his retirement in 1938, Dr. Crumley continued to lecture on forestry each year at Ohio State University. He was struck and killed by an automobile near his home in Athens, Ohio, on January 2, 1952, just five weeks short of his eighty-ninth birthday.

chapter 3

"Our Work Shall Prove Our Worth"

I vote "no" because the establishment of another normal school will entail a perpetual expense upon the State, and I believe our expenses are great enough now. We have schools now in every portion of the State that provide just as good instruction as this normal would do, and the State is at no expense in maintaining them.

House Opponent
of State Normal, 1899.

The North Texas Normal College opened September 4, 1894, under new management and with a complete turnover in faculty. Steps in this direction had been taken at a mass meeting at the county courthouse on the night of January 29, 1894. This was called by anxious citizens who were trying to keep the school from closing. A committee recommended that the college building should be leased as soon as possible to some "responsible and well-qualified man."[1] In the committee's view, this man was Prof. J. A. Sanders of Milwaukee, Wisconsin, who had submitted a leasing proposition for the school. This is the same man who had earlier served briefly on the faculty of J. C. Chilton as a teacher of business subjects. The City Council took no action, leaving the school in the hands of President Crumley. In the meantime, a significant vision was expressed by the council in appointing a committee "to open correspondence for propositions to lease the building for a term of years subject to an act of the legislature making it a State Normal School." This expression of state support as the salvation of the school was to dominate thinking on the normal's management for the next five years.

THE TERRILL ADMINISTRATION

On March 26, 1894, the City Council leased the Public School No. 2 property to Menter B. Terrill of Decard, Tennessee, for the operation of a college-level nonsectarian school. The contract could be canceled if the state legislature established in its place a state-supported institution for the education of teachers. The Board of Regents retained Colonel T. W. Abney as its president and Alvin C. Owsley as secretary and kept two of its nine members: J. W. Cook and Judge F. E. Piner. The number of regents was jumped from nine to fifteen. On the Board of Trustees, H. F. Schweer continued as secretary, but the two Chilton brothers dropped out. W. A. Ponder moved from the Board of Regents to become president of the Board of Trustees and President Terrill became treasurer of the trustees. The new management opened with a faculty of seven, three of them members of the Terrill family: President Terrill, who taught logic, ethics, and higher mathematics; Mrs. Terrill, English and science; and the president's sister, Miss Ada Terrill, primary and intermediate grades. Others were Sanders, treasurer and teacher of mathematics and commercial branches; Bruno Boezinger, modern languages; Mrs. Sallie Thomley, vocal and instrumental music; and Miss M. L. Hann, art.[2]

The Terrill catalogs indicate that no teacher had received a bachelor's degree from any institution, although Terrill himself attended Yale University *after* his years in Denton. The staff continued with family connections: Miss Hattie Terrill appears in 1897 as teacher of ancient and modern languages and as librarian, and the name of Miss Lutie Terrill in 1900 as shorthand and typewriting teacher.

Menter B. Terrill had come to Denton from a teaching position at Terrill College, Decherd, Tennessee, a school founded and operated by his father.[3] He had been described in newspaper accounts as a successful publicist, an excitable man, and one who was musically inclined. Both he and his wife played in the school orchestra. Mrs. Terrill was referred to as one of the greatest teachers ever serving at the normal.[4] From his father's example, President Terrill had learned the problems of management of a small private school. One of his approaches at Denton was to make the teachers' income dependent upon tuition rather than contracting with them for a fixed salary.[5] Regular college course tuition was lowered from $18.50 to $13.50 per ten-week term, and the subcollege grades cost only $6.50.

Recollections of contemporaries, previous histories, and the few surviving student body photographs reveal that Terrill's formula for financial success relied upon a heavy enrollment of young people below the college level. He advertised that one of the greatest needs of the time was *"true teaching in the lower grades"* and that "no pains have been spared to secure to our patrons the very best instruction in the Primary and Intermediate Departments."[6]

This emphasis shows up in the commencement records of the Terrill school, particularly in its early years. With fifty-three students in September and with 169 students enrolled during the 1894–95 year, no bachelor's degrees were awarded. Only six received state teaching certificates, nine were commercial graduates, and one was given an English diploma. It was 1898 before the first A. B. degree was awarded under Terrill's administration, and that was the only one given that year. Enrollment increased steadily, however, and for several years the number of teachers' certificates awarded rose rapidly. In the second year of the new management, enrollment was mentioned casually in the catalog only in round numbers as 200. The following year one can add up 210 different names in the catalog list, and the 1899–1900 roster has 437 names on it. The commencement records during these years went this way:

Year	State Certificates	Commercial Graduates	English Diplomas	AB. and BS. Degrees
1895	6	9	1	6
1896	13	6	3	0
1897	55	2	2	0
1898	60	12	2	1
1899	134	10	6	5
1900	no listing	9	11	7
1901	no listing	0	36	11

The recollections of one who was enrolled as a youngster in the North Texas Normal College give this picture of how students of all ages fit into the school year pattern:

> During the Fall term each year—until cotton picking was over—the Normal. . . had a good many school teachers enrolled carrying on their studies. When the little country schools opened these student-teachers dropped out and went to teaching. They taught till plowing time came in the Spring when the country schools closed and then they came back for the Spring term and continued their studies.
>
> During all the rest of the year. . . enrollment was principally local girls and boys whose parents thought they could get a better education there than in the public schools. . . . However, there were a good many out-of-town students from over the State and Oklahoma.[7]

"Claims for patronage are based upon our ability to give value received in each and every department of work mentioned in this Catalogue," President Terrill advertised in 1894. "Our work shall prove our worth. Try us." He was making a sincere effort to increase standards. The delay in the awarding of any more bachelor's degrees is explained in part by spasmodic student attendance and in large measure to the lengthening of the course of study for college degrees. Terrill made no drastic change in the kinds of courses that were offered in the Chilton and Crumley years. Whereas in the former years one could get a B. S. in the Scientific Course in two years and an A. B. in the Classic Course in one more year, each of the bachelor's degree courses now required four years of work. For those who wanted more than the minimum required for a teaching course, three years of work could take them to the English diploma—in the time formerly required for both the B. S. and A. B. degrees. The Commercial Department's work could be completed in two ten-week terms on the average. The Teachers' Course led to a first-grade certificate in two years and a life certificate in three years. Terrill's course of study showed no provisions for a model training class or any type of practice teaching. Work outside these sequences was offered in a Music Department and an Art Department. By 1900 President Terrill was referring to a School of Music, a School of Art, and a School of Elocution although there were still no degree programs offered.

WHO SHALL OWN THE NORMAL?

Although President Crumley saved the normal from an early death, and President Terrill put it in an improved financial condition, Denton leaders throughout this period remained fixed on one goal: the location of a state-supported college in Denton. State-wide agitation (by persons outside Denton) for a public normal in the North Texas area had begun even before the creation of Texas Normal College. And a member of the first faculty, O. C. Charlton, said that J. C. Chilton himself, even while in the process of establishing his private school in May 1890, declared that the school would someday become a state normal.[8]

The first overt move in that direction came in February 1893, when State Senator Emory C. Smith introduced a bill in the Texas Legislature to create a state normal school in Denton and appropriate $20,000 a year for its support. The bill "attracted favorable attention but did not pass."[9] This favorable attention included a laudatory editorial in the *Texas School Journal,* the official organ of the state teachers association. It praised Chilton as an indefatigable worker and congratulated the citizens of Denton "upon the flattering prospects of their securing the location of the State Normal."[10] In January 1895 an equally unsuccessful effort was attempted by Denton County's state representative, R. Lee Ragsdale.[11]

For the first four years of the Terrill contract with the city, no mention of the normal college is found in the minutes of the City Council. On February 9, 1898, Terrill, Sanders, "and associates" proposed to purchase the normal college building and grounds. For reasons not explained in surviving records, they withdrew the offer three days later.[12] Two months later, on April 11, the City Council conferred with Terrill and Sanders to "learn if they want to lease the Normal College and if so on what terms."[13] No agreement resulted and the normal continued as usual. However, on April 25, the council voted to sell the normal college for $7,000 "for the purpose of maintaining a high-grade non-sectarian school, and when they fail to run a high-grade non-sectarian school, then the college building and grounds shall revert back to the City without charge."[14] This action, too, resulted in nothing. In June a subscription campaign was conducted in Denton on behalf of Terrill and his associates, the money to be paid to the city in consideration of a lease of the normal school property for six years with an option to renew for another six years if the school continued as a success. The subscription document said that the money donated should be used to secure another public school building in Denton and to make necessary repairs on the normal building, not to exceed $250. The donors signed their names, the amounts pledged and the conditions imposed on the donation. Signatures of twenty-one men pledging $945 were obtained, but unfortunately for the normal, all twenty-one men stated as a condition that their money should be used only for a school building to be located in North Denton.[15]

The City Council found it necessary on September 5, 1898, to vote to issue script for $5,000, one half for a new public school building and the remainder for repairs and additions to Public School Building No. 2, the normal building.[16] But even this amount proved not enough. Events in the legislature were to make a further expenditure justifiable in the eyes of the city, however. On January 23, 1899, the council named a committee to draw up plans and specifications for the necessary additions and repairs. The following month the legislature began considering state support for the Denton normal. As this issue approached its final reading, the council on March 27, 1899, let a contract for $5,280 to improve the building that they soon expected to pass from the city's hands.[17] President Terrill's 1900 announcement bulletin, however, reported the development this way: "Its halls have been filled to overflowing with students. . . . An additional building has been erected by the appreciative citizens of Denton." A few pages later he switched his terms of reference to state that there has been an addition erected which increases the original capacity of the building one-half."[18] Another president was to complain three years later that only four rooms were added, with only two of these large enough for use as classrooms and the other two suitable for cloakrooms.

THE LEGISLATIVE BATTLE

Denton's repeated efforts to obtain state support for its normal college reached a climax when Senate Bill 145 was introduced by Senator Charles Vernon Terrell of Decatur on February 9, 1899. Entitled "An Act to provide for the establishment, maintenance, and government of a State Normal school, to be located at Denton, Texas, and to be known as the North Texas Normal School," the bill was introduced, read the first time and referred to the Committee on Education on that same day.[19] This committee reported the bill out favorably on February 18. On Senator Terrell's motion, the bill was recommitted to the committee on February 22 and favorably reported out again on February 23.

On March 2 the regular order of senate business was suspended and the bill was taken up on its second reading. Senator Terrell proposed that an amendment change the name of the school to North Texas State Normal College. This was adopted. Senator Terrell then introduced another successful amendment, this one specifying that the normal college building that was to be given to the state must be sufficient for at least 400 pupils and that the transaction must fully satisfy the governor, comptroller, and superintendent of public instruction, or they should be empowered to locate the normal college at another place deemed most satisfactory and advantageous to the state. At this stage a 15–10 vote delayed further consideration until March 6.

On March 6, regional factionalism broke out in earnest, a series of amendments being proposed to switch the location of the new college away from Denton. The first such amendment called for a location at some point north of thirty-two degrees latitude, to be determined by a commission of the governor, comptroller, and superintendent of public instruction, who were to report such location to "this or the next special or general session of the Legislature." This amendment was tabled. The next up offered a substitute bill creating the "Oak Cliff State Normal School" in Dallas County, provided such a site should be chosen by three commissioners to be appointed by the governor. If the citizens of Oak Cliff failed to make a suitable donation for the school, the commissioners would be authorized to select some other suitable North Texas location. This substitute was tabled on an 18 to 5 vote.

The author of the bill then rose on a point of order to declare that the tabling motion carried the original North Texas State Normal bill with it. The chair overruled; the senator appealed to the floor; the senate upheld the chair. Another senator moved into the fray, moving an amendment to strike out the enabling clause. This was defeated. The same senator then asked for an amendment to strike out the name of the city, Denton, and insert the name of Whitesboro in its place. This failed. Still another opponent stepped forward, this time to replace "Denton" with the word "Brazoria." The amendment lost and the day's business was halted.

Thirty-seven years later, at a Denton ceremony honoring his work in establishing the state school, Senator Terrell recalled this Senate action as a "bitter fight," which was resolved only after a compromise was reached with South Texas legislators to provide for the establishment of another normal at San Marcos.[20] This action, indeed, emerged from the same session as Senate Bill 260 creating Southwest Texas Normal School.

On March 7, the delaying tactics against the Denton bill were resumed for a time. Efforts were made to substitute San Marcos and Beaumont for Denton in the bill. A final gesture was an amendment forever limiting the annual appropriation for the North Texas State Normal to $15,000. This amendment was defeated 17–10 and the bill was ordered engrossed. The bill came up for third reading on March 9 and was passed and sent immediately to the House of Representatives. There, on the same day, it was given its first reading and referred to the Committee on Education. On March 22, Representative E. W. H. Shelburne of Sanger, Denton County's representative, moved the suspension of regular business to take the bill up for its second reading. He was given a 10:00 A.M. special order for March 23.

At this stage the effort was made to tie the Southwest Texas establishment to the Denton bill, but this was withdrawn by the sponsor because his action was being interpreted as unfriendly to Denton. The bill then passed to third reading by a 66–41 vote. One notable exception was entered by an opponent:

> I vote "no" because the establishment of another normal school will entail a perpetual expense upon the State, and I believe our expenses are great enough now. We have schools now in every portion of the

State that provide just as good instruction as this normal would do, and the State is at no expense in maintaining them.

On March 29 the bill was read a third time. The representative from Collin County made one more fight, offering an amendment to put the college in whichever of the following counties offered the greatest inducement in property or money: Fannin, Collin, Denton, Grayson, Hunt, Dallas, Tarrant, Cook, Hopkins, Rockwall, Wise, Kaufman, Ellis, Montague, or Lamar Counties. But this amendment was tabled, and the final vote went 73 to 39 for the bill. It was signed by Governor Joseph D. Sayers on March 31, 1899. (It should be noted that Representative Shelburne introduced House Bill 504 to create the state normal at Denton. This was offered on February 10 and reported favorably out of committee on February 24, but because of the progress of Senate Bill 145 no further action was taken on the house bill.)

As Denton awaited the governor's signature on the bill, the *Denton County News* on March 30 proclaimed that Denton could expect attendance at the state school to be 500 or 600, of whom 400 or 500 would be boarding students. All of this, it was said, would mean a great deal of trade to all classes of business.[21] The day after the signing, on April 1, a "Mass Jollification" meeting was held in the district courtroom to celebrate the occasion.[22] But realization of the state-support goal remained more than two years away—the 1899 legislature failed to appropriate the funds to finance operation by the state. President Terrill stayed on to operate the normal as a private school the next two years, hoping to become president of the state normal.[23] Senate Bill 145 bound the city of Denton to turn over the building and campus to the state and to furnish "an abundant supply of pure artesian water free of cost to the State." On October 10, 1899, the City Council formally accepted these terms.[24]

President Terrill was thwarted in his candidacy to become president of the state normal. In his place was to come J. S. Kendall, superintendent of public instruction, a member of the very board in whose control the new school had been placed by S.B. 145. Terrill went to Yale University when the private normal closed in 1901 and earned the A.B. and A.M. degrees before returning to Texas. He visited the North Texas State Normal in April 1906, conducted the chapel exercise and told of his plans to teach somewhere in the state. That somewhere proved to be his own institution, the Terrill School in Dallas, which he founded as headmaster in the fall of 1906. It was a college preparatory school for boys which opened with forty students and continued with some distinction for many years.[25] Terrill died in February 1931.

DENTON'S COLLEGE AMBITIONS

There may have been mass jollification in Denton on April 1, 1899, but before the state normal even opened its doors, sober reflection led some Denton leaders to worry about the course of the new institution. The state normal in Texas was not of recognized collegiate ranking, and they feared that the normal would draw only students who were interested in becoming teachers and that the city would lose the economic benefits of drawing students who wanted some other type of training.[26] So on March 25, 1901, the city turned to its favorite technique of those times, the mass meeting in the courthouse, to seek formation of another college. With Judge J. T. Bottorff as chairman, the group voted to establish the John B. Denton College and organized a joint stock company to finance and manage the enterprise. A five-man committee led by J. N. Rayzor took charge of the operation. The block of land later occupied by the southern portion of the Denton Junior High School campus was purchased, and a brick building was erected with a basement and two stories. School opened September 10, 1901, eight days before North Texas State Normal went into operation. President of the John B. Denton College was Oliver M. Thurman, who the year before had been science teacher and librarian in the final year of the private normal's existence. On his first faculty was his wife, a sister of Menter B. Terrill. Also drawn from the Terrill school staff was Miss Frances S. Hanson, a music teacher.[27]

Thus the private John B. Denton College and the public North Texas State Normal College started life together in 1901. By 1903 the Denton College enrollment was something over 150,[28] but the educational competition was becoming a bit steep for a nonpublic institution. Also in 1901, Denton's eyes were once again attracted to Austin, where on April 23 the governor signed a bill creating a school for the white girls of the state comparable to Texas A&M for male students. The author of the bill was Judge V. W. Grubbs, whose brother-in-law, J. C. Parr, lived in Denton. Judge Grubbs threw his support to Denton as a site for the State Industrial School for Girls. Some fourteen towns contended seriously for the school. Denton, typically, called a mass meeting to consider its bid. A committee raised a bonus of $30,000 and offered the state locating committee a choice of several campus sites. The decision for Denton came on January 3, 1903, on the seventy-sixth ballot by the selection committee. The school opened on September 23, 1903.[29] Its name was changed to College of Industrial Arts in 1905.

With two state schools in full operation, President Thurman resigned from John B. Denton College in April 1904 to enter the insurance business. Management of the college was turned over to the Church of Christ, which operated it as the Southwestern Christian College from 1904 to 1908. In 1908 the name was changed to Southland University, but it still attracted only a small enrollment. Soon after that the school organization was moved to Cleburne. Denton historian C. A. Bridges says that the institution was later moved to Abilene, so that the Southwestern Christian College which began in Denton may be regarded as an ancestor of Abilene Christian College,[30] but records at Abilene do not support this hypothesis. Several attempts at private business college operations were made, the most notable probably being the Denton Business College, started in 1901 by H. A. Ivy of Sherman. Attempts were also made to use the vacated John B. Denton College building later in the decade for a business college and for a school of elocution, but the property was soon acquired by the Denton public school system. [31]

In all, at least seven distinct institutions can be identified as coming into being in Denton in the first decade of the twentieth century. Citizens were determined to make good on that earlier newspaper forecast that "Denton is destined to be the educational center of North Texas." But private schools proved not to be the answer, and the city's future growth was staked on the development of its state-supported colleges.

part II

The State Normal College

1901–1923

My conception of the work of this institution was the preparation of teachers of all grades of elementary and high schools in the state. It should prepare teachers for all subjects. . . . Graduates from this institution, instead of being admitted to the freshman class in the universities, should be admitted to the graduate work in them.

W. H. Bruce

chapter 4

Building the Three-Year Normal

> This maturity in age furnished, as a rule, maturity of purpose and character to the student body. A more earnest body of workers, as a whole, I never before had under my control. The standard of preparation with a large part of these students was neither high nor thorough, but the strongest desire to get the greatest possible benefit from the school work, was everywhere apparent.
>
> *J. S. Kendall, 1902.*

The appropriation that made state support a reality came in an act of the 27th Legislature February 18, 1901. This amended the 1899 act to provide an annual appropriation beginning September 1901 and to authorize scholarship appointments each year.

The law placed North Texas State Normal College under administration of the State Board of Education, an ex officio body made up of the governor as president of the board; R. M. Love as comptroller of public accounts; J. G. Tod, secretary of state; and Arthur Lefevre, state superintendent of public instruction, as board secretary. After the 1899 act, three Denton citizens had been appointed as local directors to assist the state board. Members were Judge F. E. Piner, E. C. Smith, and A. C. Owsley. In January 1901, W. A. Ponder was appointed to fill the vacancy created by the death of Judge Piner. During May and June the state board chose the teaching staff and designated September 18, 1901, as the opening of the first session.[1]

Unlike the private normal, the new state institution was restricted to a single purpose. The first announcement bulletin made this clear:

> In the language of the statute, this school has been established "for the special training of teachers." Thus limited by law to one department of educational work, the school will be devoted exclusively to the object of its creation. Having the public school branches as a basis, it will deal with and seek to develop the principles which underlie all education. It will not in any sense be a rival of college or university, nor yet will it assume the duties of the high school or academy. In a general way it must partly enter the domain of all these. Texas demands annually for her public schools twelve thousand or more white teachers, and to aid in increasing from year to year the efficiency of this large body of civic laborers, is the special province of the normal school.[2]

An annual session of thirty-six weeks was divided into four quarters, with the school year ending May 27, 1902. The following year the annual session was divided into fall, winter, and spring terms of twelve weeks each.[3]

The state normal program covered three years. Unlike at the private normal, no pretense was made of offering the bachelor's degree. Completion of the senior year entitled one to "the full diploma of the Normal," which authorized one to teach for life without further examination in any public school.[4] There was some question as to whether any part of the state normal program was of collegiate rank. Reports of the state superintendent classified normals under "Higher Education." The first announcement bulletin said graduates of recognized high schools would be admitted to the junior class without examination, suggesting that the junior and senior years were at the college level. One historian says that freshman and junior years corresponded to the last two years of high school, while the senior year was the only one of actual college level. Nevertheless, "no attempt was made to conform to standardized college requirements." [5] Another historian asserts that the level of training approximated that of secondary schools. [6] The entrance requirement for the freshman class was stated to be "a fair knowledge of the elementary school branches." W. H. Bruce, then a teacher of mathematics and later president, recalled in 1939: "Beginning in 1901–02, the course of study was that of a high school. In the first several years graduates were admitted to the freshman class in colleges."[7]

This latter view is amply supported in other publications. A University of Texas bulletin in 1902 declared:

> Holders of diplomas from The Agricultural and Mechanical College of Texas, from the Sam Houston and the North Texas Normal Institutes, from high schools of the State which are affiliated with the University, and applicants holding first grade State teachers' certificates are admitted to the freshman class without examination.[8]

A few years later the university admitted graduates of the four state normals with fourteen high school units plus one course toward the bachelor's degree.[9] As far as transferability of credit was concerned, the early normal diploma was worth at best only one-fifth of a freshman college semester.

Nevertheless, the first student body was of the same age and maturity that one would expect in a collegiate group. Although the 1899 act specified that tuition was to be free to students who were at least sixteen years old, the admission regulations[10] specified that one had to be seventeen years old by September 18, 1901. The average age of the 511 students in the first annual session was 20.18 years. Of these, 173 already held teaching certificates and

166 had teaching experience.[11] More students above the age of twenty-five than below eighteen were enrolled.

The legislature included "college" in the title of the state school, but Kendall viewed this as sailing under false colors. Bruce recalled, somewhat critically, that the first president "said that the school was not a real college, and he wouldn't let the word 'college' appear" on the school's certificates and diplomas. The Main Building, constructed during Kendall's administration, did not use the word in its identification of the school.[12] The announcement bulletin before the school's opening carried "The North Texas State Normal College" on its title page. These practices were quickly changed when Bruce became president in 1906. (The Huntsville school was officially a "Normal Institute" and the one at San Marcos a "Normal School." Only the founding legislation of the Denton school contained the words "State" and "College.")

THE COURSE OF STUDY

The first course of study listed no optional classes. Each of the three grades was assigned work in seven fields: professional, mathematical, Latin, history, English, science, and art. The freshman professional work included primary methods, school methods, and management and civics. History of education was added for the juniors, and the seniors were to study psychology, moral science, and school organization. For the freshman and junior, the four terms of art included music, calisthenics, penmanship, and drawing, while the senior continued classes in music and calisthenics and added form study and drawing. Mathematics meant arithmetic and algebra for the freshman; plane geometry, advanced algebra, bookkeeping, and teaching methods for the junior; and solid geometry, plane and spherical trigonometry, and methods in mathematics for the senior. [13]

Latin studies began with grammar and moved through Nepos, Caesar, Vergil, and Cicero. In three years students were expected to cover U.S. and Texas history, ancient history and geography, medieval history, English history, and modern history. Sciences were listed as geography, physiology, biology, physics, chemistry, geology, and botany. Grammar, composition and rhetoric, and American and English literature were the English subjects.

Each year led to a particular teaching certificate. The freshman year led to a certificate of the second grade, good for teaching in Texas public schools for two years. First-grade certificates, good for four years, came with the junior year. The full diploma of the normal at the end of senior work was regarded as certification for life. The normal announcement carefully stipulated that these certificates represented more than those issued in the county and summer normal examinations.

W. H. Bruce, a member of the early faculty who succeeded Kendall as president, observed in 1917 that this course was "found impracticable after three weeks. It took about three years to crystalize a course of study."[14] From 1902 until 1908, students were offered two courses of study "of equal value."[15] The Latin Course required three years of study of the Latin language. The English-Science Course, substituted for Latin work in natural science and English literature.[16]

FROM SUPERINTENDENT TO PRINCIPAL

The State Board of Education chose one of its members as the first principal of North Texas State Normal College. J. S. Kendall resigned in May 1901 as state superintendent of public instruction effective July 1.[17] This action was not unusual. Previous state superintendents had become presidents of Baylor University and Sam Houston Normal. Two of the next three state superintendents also left their positions for state college presidencies.[18]

The thirteen teachers selected to join Kendall were not distinguished in academic training or college teaching experience. Only six had college degrees and only one had taught at a recognized college. In fact, Kendall himself apparently never attended more than one year of high school or earned any college degree, even though he attended two universities.

Born in Wilkes County, Georgia, November 4, 1849, Kendall received, in his words, "elementary education in the country schools as they existed during and immediately after the Civil War."[19] His high school training came in 1869–70 at Jonesboro, Georgia, under Colonel Allen D. Candler, who was later governor of Georgia. Kendall described the rest of his education to explain his lack of college degrees by saying he had entered the University of Georgia a junior but "from lack of means left before the close of the college year and engaged in teaching a select private school in Brownsville, S. Carolina." He studied at the University of Virginia in 1872–74, doing work in eight departments, which he said counted more than work that was required for the master's degree at Georgia, "but owing to their irregular grouping, no attempt at any time was made to shape them into a degree."[20]

Kendall moved to Texas in 1874 and taught in a country school for four months. Then, as vice principal, he helped to organize the Honey Grove High School in 1875. He resigned this position in 1881 to organize the Walcott Institute, apparently in Honey Grove.[21] From 1884 until 1891 Kendall served as president of Pritchett Institute, "an endowed school of high rank in Glasgow, Missouri." He became superintendent back in Honey Grove and directed several summer normal schools, which was perhaps his first administrative experience with the teacher education movement. He was elected president of the Texas State Teachers Association for 1895–96. These experiences led to his election as state superintendent in 1898.

The 1901 announcement bulletin listed no degrees for Kendall or any staff members. Training of the faculty can be found, however, in a biographical section of the publication. A 1902 catalog listed the initials "A. M." after the name of Kendall, but no school is listed for the degree. In addition, his title of "principal" was changed to "president." This style for Kendall's name, degree, and title appeared in all catalogs during his administration. An obituary story in the *Normal Journal*[22] stated that the president "attended the University of Georgia and the University of Virginia, from both of which institutions he was graduated with honors." Kendall's own biographical notes indicate that this was in error. In 1912 President Bruce ordered a memorial tablet[23] describing Kendall as "A. M. Pritchett College, 1902."

The correspondence about the memorial tablet contains one of the few contemporary references to President Kendall's full name. Bruce indicated that he was not sure of the correct name, since the name appeared in correspondence and official documents as "J. S. Kendall." Bulletins a half-century later list the name as "Joseph Sutton," yet Dr. Bruce's memorial order listed "Joel Sutton" after he had asked for verification from the Kendall family. The *Normal Journal* of October 1906 repeatedly uses the name "Joel Sutton."

Although Kendall changed his title to president, the official designation at all state normals continued to be "principal." Letterhead used by Kendall in 1905 still carried the latter term. Reports of the state superintendent indicated in 1911 that state colleges had presidents and state normals had principals.

The term "president" was, however, in quite common use, including in letters from the state superintendent to Kendall as early as 1902.

THE FIRST FACULTY

Early bulletins did not list faculty members in any discernible order, but the first two names remained constant: Kendall, followed by W. H. Bruce. As the only staff member with a Ph.D. degree, and having come to North Texas from the presidency of John Tarleton College, Bruce from the first was regarded as the number two man on the staff. An undated request from Kendall to the state board in 1903 requested a $100 annual salary increase for his "head teacher of mathematics." Kendall wrote, "Dr. Bruce stands prominent among Texas school men not only as a mathematician of high repute, but as a man possessing broad general scholarship. His all-around attainments make him valuable to the Normal. In my absence at any time from the school, he fills my place, pro tempore."

Other members of the first faculty were J. A. Sanders, the only survivor from the private normal staff, teacher of bookkeeping and penmanship and assistant in mathematics; F. A. Hauslein, teacher of Latin; Miss Emma Mitchell, who taught history; Mrs. Hayden Lewis, assistant in history and geography; L. D. Borden, teacher of physics and chemistry; W. H. Long, Jr., physiology and natural history; Miss Annie W. Blanton, English grammar and composition; Miss Mattie Simpkins, drawing; Miss Minnie M. Marsh, English and American literature; Miss Annie Moore, primary methods; Miss Mary Stuart Butler, vocal music; and Miss Eugenie Burruss Blocker, calisthenics and elocution. Long had taught five years at Baylor and seven years at Burleson College. The others had taught in elementary and secondary schools. Four were normal school products, including Borden, who went on to take a B. S. from Southwestern University and a B. A. from the University of Nashville. Others with degrees were Hauslein, the bachelor and master of arts, Yale; Long, B. A., Baylor, and M. A., University of Texas; Miss Blanton, B. L., Texas; and Miss Moore, M. L., Southwestern, and B. A., University of Chicago.

Appropriations for salaries, however, made it unlikely that an experienced collegiate faculty could be attracted. The legislature had provided $20,000 per year for Sam Houston State Normal, and it continued this at Denton. The amount remained unchanged during the Kendall administration.[24] In 1902–3 the president received a $2,000 salary plus $500 for house rent, and Bruce received $1,500. Part of Kendall's salary for a time was paid from the Peabody fund. At the $1,400 level were Borden, Hauslein, Long, Miss Mitchell, and Sanders. The lowest annual salary, $1,100, went to four of the women teachers.

INHERITED: ONE BUILDING, ONE TEACHER

In his last report as state superintendent in 1900, Kendall gave this picture of the institution he was assigned to remake into a state normal college: "6 male teachers, 8 female teachers, 380 male pupils, 244 female pupils; salaries paid, $11,000; value of building and grounds, $30,000; value of apparatus, $1,000; volumes in library, 500."[25]

The last private normal session ended August 6, 1901.[26] When President Terrill departed, he apparently took with him all of the records, bulletins, and other documents relating to the private normal. It was generally believed that Terrill had worked hard to gain state support for his normal and expected to continue as its president. This was said to create an estrangement between Terrill and his successors, confirmed somewhat in 1911 and 1912 correspondence of Bruce. Replying to a former student of the private school, he wrote that "our records do not show that you ever attended this school. You mention your attendance during the summer of 1900. This school was established in 1901 and its first session began in September of that year."[27] A year later Bruce acknowledged in answering an inquiry that "there was a private institution in Denton known as the North Texas Normal College. . . and it might be that the party about whom you inquire holds a certificate from that school."[28] A similar inquiry brought from him the statement that "I will say that we have absolutely no record here of the school known as the North Texas Normal College before the State established the present institution here in 1901."[29]

The Kendall administration inherited one building, little equipment, few library books, one faculty member (J. A. Sanders), and no records from the Terrill regime. Kendall left the state superintendency on July 1, 1901, and came immediately to Denton to spend "some days. . . examining carefully the building and grounds of the school with the view of ascertaining what changes and improvements were actually necessary in order to begin the work of the session on September 18."[30] A few days later he went to Huntsville to study the furnishings and physical arrangements of the Sam Houston

Normal Institute. He then spent a week in Chicago going through school supply and furniture establishments to draw up cash estimates of purchases for the normal.

With the help of the local board, Kendall outlined an estimate of expenditures for repairs, improvements, and supplies to begin the normal. These estimates totaling $6,500 were relayed to the state board with the request that they ask the special session of the 27th Legislature then in session to appropriate the amount.

He then turned to the task of having the building and grounds put back into shape. The new principal described it this way:

> The ten acre block of ground belonging to the Normal was cleared of the undergrowth of weeds and briers which had accumulated on a considerable part of it, fences were repaired, gates and stile blocks were put in, and a well arranged set of water closets were built. The school building proper, consisting of fourteen rooms, large and small, exclusive of basement, required considerable repairs. The metal roof was overhauled and repainted, the inside walls of the halls and nearly all the rooms were painted, two rooms were papered, curtains and shades for all the windows were provided, the two wooden entrances to the building, which were in a state of decay, were replaced with new material, and several hundred linear feet of recitation seats for different rooms were procured.
>
> The capacity of the college building conveyed by the city of Denton to the State was estimated to accommodate 400 students. As a matter of fact, three fourths of that number of well grown young men and women, such as attend the Normal, could not be comfortably seated in the chapel of this building.
>
> The first estimate furnished your honorable body, included a frame building about 50 x 30 feet, for a gymnasium or calisthenics hall. With an enrollment of 300 students at the opening of the session and that number daily increasing, it at once became evident that the proposed gymnasium building must be enlarged into an assembly room or chapel where all the students could be brought together once each day or oftener if necessary.

> Accordingly the proposed new building was made 70 x 40 feet in dimensions. By the use of ordinary chairs and allowing sufficient space for two aisles, this room can seat between 500 and 600 persons without undue crowding.

Kendall realized that a great deal more would be needed to provide an adequate physical plant for the kind of college that he envisioned. He was the first in a succession of presidents who would struggle to get funds for the building needs demanded by enrollment. After one year he sent the board this plea:

> As already stated more than once, the buildings now occupied by the North Texas State Normal are inadequate because of their limited size and number of the needs of the school, judged by its attendance for the past year and its prospective increase in numbers in the near future. Indeed, it is strictly within the limits of truth to say that there is not to-day within the boundaries of Texas an institution of learning, denominational, private or state, with half the attendance, but what can lay claim to more commodious quarters than are now possessed by the North Texas Normal. Such being the case, I earnestly ask that your honorable body may recommend to the 28th Legislature such measures as will provide the needed buildings.

Kendall's financial statement accompanied this first annual report. It drew him into a correspondence controversy with his successor as state superintendent, Arthur Lefevre. In a five-page letter, Lefevre took Kendall to task for submitting "the confused summary of accounts out of accord with the accounts as sent in from month to month during the year." The superintendent said he had "spared no pains. . . to square the accounts" without putting Kendall "to the trouble of making the statement in the form in which it should, of course, have been made originally." But, he wrote, "all the patient efforts referred to have been of no avail, and I see no way to discover the items that need to be entered upon our books."[31]

Kendall's reply is not preserved, but its nature is indicated in a further response from Lefevre, also five pages in length. The superintendent wrote that "you have filled a long letter largely with justifications of the 'moral propriety' of expenditures, etc., whereas all that I wanted was intelligible accounts. . . . I must respectfully ask that your bookkeeper give sufficient attention to the matter to understand the points involved." Marginal notations were made in ink on this letter, apparently in Kendall's handwriting. One says "This. . . does not refer to facts," and another says "This is false."[32] After this, the president took great pains to give Austin authorities detailed reports on the handling of funds.

Kendall's annual reports emphasize two matters: the need for more buildings and the health of the student body. He wrote great detail on epidemics in Denton and deaths among students, expressing concern with the lack of proper sanitation by boardinghouse owners. In his last years he campaigned among doctors to get a hospital established in the city. President Kendall died October 7, 1906, less than a month before his fifty-seventh birthday. The cause of death was "consumption, with which he had been afflicted for several years."[33]

J. S. Kendall's brief administration may appear undistinguished. The normal's enrollment increased by only seventy-three students; academic standards were not elevated significantly; there was little progress in curriculum development; the quality of the faculty was not altered noticeably. Published reminiscences recall him as a kindly and polite gentleman. The faculty resolution on his death noted that "he was courteous to all, conservative in speech and action, deliberative in counsel, and considerate of the rights and welfare of others."[34]

But if this does not draw the portrait of a dynamic administrator, let it be recalled that he started with a decaying plant and a new school with no intellectual heritage. Kendall worked with inadequate funds, an inadequately prepared faculty, and a poorly prepared student body. The state-wide setting in which the new school was assigned to operate was a backward one: no compulsory school attendance, comparatively little public secondary education, and a general educational framework that lagged several decades behind that of the older sections of the nation. Kendall and his staff worked against these obstacles, got an infant school on its feet, gave it improved physical facilities, and formed the nucleus around which another man was to build. That man was William Herschel Bruce, who stepped into the presidency within a few days of Kendall's death, beginning a seventeen-year administration (one is tempted to call it a reign or regency) that was to give an entirely new shape and direction to North Texas State Normal College.

chapter 5

Dr. Bruce's Vision

One of the first tasks performed by the Board in the reorganization of these schools was that of designating a definite sphere of work, which, while affording professional training for teachers, should correlate with the work of our public high schools and of our State University. The Normal Schools were made to assume a position midway between that of the high school and the college, and practically uniform courses were planned for them all, giving to the Normals two years of high school and two of strictly college work, which plan is in conformity with that of the most progressive States.

State Normal School
Board of Regents, 1915

It was probably with a great deal of truth even if without modesty that Dr. W. H. Bruce wrote in his later years: "No real development or expansion of the college began until 1906."[1] Barely a decade after taking office, he referred to his predecessor as "our first and worthy president, Mr. Kendall, who I am sure did better in organizing the school than I could have done," but then pointedly referred to the areas in which he thought Kendall had failed and Bruce was succeeding:

> When I became president of the school I had some definite purpose; one was to raise the standard of the school and make this institution assist in elevating the work of the schools to a place of respectability. At one time in Texas normal schools were not in the best repute. It was not considered much credit to have a certificate from a normal school. I have heard of City Boards that refused to employ teachers holding such certificates, because normal schools were regarded as below the standard of first class high schools.
>
> I though it was desirable to get the normal schools from under an ex officio board, for so long as these schools were deemed of not sufficient importance to have a board of regents we could not expect them to enjoy public favor.
>
> I wanted uniform entrance requirements in all the normal schools of Texas, and equivalent courses of study in them. . . . I have always felt that the entire field of education belonged to the normal schools as far as the preparation of teachers was concerned.[2]

These remarks were addressed to his faculty while Dr. Bruce was in the midst of his term as president. In later recollections, he described what he told his first faculty meeting:

> I was elected President in October, 1906. At the first meeting of the faculty, I told them I wished them to know my vision. Since the establishment of the first normal school in Texas in 1879, the work had been confined to that of the ordinary high school, graduation from which admitted students to the Freshman class of the colleges and universities, and was devoted to the preparation of teachers of elemen-

tary, graduate, and rural schools. My conception of the work of this institution was the preparation of teachers of all grades of elementary and high schools in the state, and the training of teachers as specialists in subjects, as physics, chemistry, mathematics, etc. It also should prepare teachers for all subjects, as manual training, home economics, and above all we should have a Model Training School, in which students before graduation are required to teach under competent supervisors.

Then graduates from this institution, instead of being admitted to the freshman class in the universities, should be admitted to the graduate work in them. It ought to be so that a man living in the town of Denton could send his six-year-old child to a kindergarten department; then pass through our standard high school, and from it to any college or university in the state or to our college; so that a child reared in Denton could receive here at least a standard bachelor's degree without ever having to spend a night away from home.

At the conclusion of the statement of my dream or vision, Professor Borden of the faculty said, "You must expect to live a hundred years." I replied, "Not necessarily; but even if this should not be accomplished in my lifetime, we could prepare the way for our successors to realize what we plan."[3]

A SEPARATE BOARD

In 1906 Dr. Bruce joined Sam Houston Principal H. C. Pritchett and Southwest Texas Principal T. G. Harris to seek larger appropriations, more grounds, and better buildings.[4] Only token increases were obtained and it gradually became apparent that little progress could be expected under the control of an ex officio board. The normal heads decided they would have to petition the legislature for a separate board of regents.[5] The idea was not a new one. State Superintendent Lefevre wrote in 1905 that

> the governmental business of the commonwealth of Texas seems to have attained a magnitude which renders it unwise to burden the Governor, Comptroller and Secretary of State with the detailed executive administration of the State normal schools. I believe the public interests would be subserved by the enactment of a law directing the Gov-

> ernor to appoint a State normal school board of five members to manage and control the three State normal schools. . . . [6]

In 1909 the Conference for Education in Texas named Bruce to a commission of eleven members to create "a plan for the reorganization of the educational system of Texas." In 1909, the group called for creation of one or more boards of regents to control the state normal schools.[7] At the 1910 conference, Superintendent J. F. Kimball of Temple delivered a stinging attack:

> The State Normal Schools came into existence, orphaned, like the State permanent school fund was, and were turned over to the same stepfathers— or godfathers as you may please to call them. And so we have it that today in Texas the possibility exists that two men, chosen without reference to their knowledge of school affairs, to their attitude on school questions, to their ability to administer school matters, hold, not in the hollow of their hand, but hold on the corner of their desks, the destiny of the normal schools and of the State organization of public schools, so far as the State Board of Education affects it. Said I, two? I will take it back. One man, the Governor of the State, who is to be elected at the next election, can change every feature of the normal school work of this State by a stroke of his pen—by one stroke of his pen—except to remove the buildings themselves. . . . You see the Governor appoints the Secretary of State, and the Governor and the Secretary of State constitute. . . a two-thirds majority in the control of the educational affairs of the State. That such a cataclysm has not happened is rather due to good fortune and the good quality of Texas Governors than to any prevision or provision of our organic law.[8]

In 1911 State Superintendent F. M. Bralley was still making the same plea, with even more specific complaints that the governor, secretary of state, and comptroller were

> compelled to give attention to many of the details of these institutions, such as employing faculties, approving requisitions for the purchase of books and for laboratory supplies, regulating charges for incidental

> fees, passing upon applications for the publication of bulletins and catalogues, and for the purchase of stationery, including pencils, pens, pins, ink scratch tablets, and hundreds of other minor matters.[9]

The effort to obtain a separate normal board became intertwined with the move toward a uniform course of study for the normals. At a 1907 board meeting, State Superintendent R. B. Cousins suggested the idea of the uniform course. The board ordered the normal principals to prepare such a course to be put into effect at once. Before leaving Austin, Bruce got board permission to delay the report until February 1, 1908. Bruce, Harris, and Pritchett met at San Marcos in August 1907 and again in January 1908. Bruce delivered their report on January 14 to Superintendent Cousins.[10]

The proposal retained a single course of study, permitting few student options. Freshmen could choose between Latin and biological science, while juniors and seniors had a choice from among Latin, German, and biological science. Otherwise, the prescribed course for freshmen included arithmetic, elementary algebra, English, geography, United States and Texas history, physiology, music, reading, drawing, penmanship, and professional work (education). Juniors would take algebra, plane geometry, English, physics, civics, general history, music, reading, drawing, and professional work. Seniors were assigned to solid geometry, trigonometry, English, chemistry, history, bookkeeping, music, drawing, and professional work. Physical culture was to be given during two years a student attended.[11]

The North Texas bulletin of July 1909 indicates a curriculum that followed this proposal closely. However, Principal Harris wrote a five-page letter to Superintendent Cousins on April 16, 1908, protesting the change. He said there was "no important reason why these courses of study should be any more nearly uniform than they now are. The Principals of the other Normals agree with me in this Opinion." After detailing the differing language requirements in different sections of the state, Harris said he desired " to protest most earnestly against the adoption by your body of the uniform course reported by the three principals.[12]

The legislature intervened the following year. It made mandatory the teaching of agriculture, manual training, and domestic science in the normal schools. An appropriation of $18,000 was to be divided equally among the schools at

Huntsville, Denton, and San Marcos for this purpose, the work to begin not later than September 1909.[13] At North Texas this led to provision of more elective subjects. Each year required a student to take eight courses. Freshmen had six prescribed courses, sophomores 5⅔, and seniors 3⅔. Subjects on the freshman elective list were agriculture, Latin, literature, music, reading, drawing, manual training, and domestic science. Juniors had the additional options of physics, German, and civics, while seniors had the added options of mathematics, history, and botany.[14]

In April 1910 state normal principals met in Waco. Principals Bruce, Estill, and Harris agreed that "all the normal schools should give equivalent courses of study, that the courses should contain prescribed and elective subjects, and that each school should require the same number of courses for each of the certificates, 8⅔ for the Second, 6⅔ for the first, 25 for the diploma."[15]

Bruce viewed the new curriculum hopefully: "I believe the time has come in the history of Normal schools in Texas when they ought to prepare teachers for the high schools as well as for the grades and the rural schools. With our present system of electives this can be done."[16]

The legislature transferred control of the four state normal colleges in the summer of 1911.[17] The state superintendent stayed on the board as president, and four other members were appointed by the governor. The board had responsibility for general control and management of the normals. Regents were authorized to determine the instructional departments and subjects of study in each. They could also fix the rate of incidental student fees. The law became effective November 30, 1911, and on the following day Governor O. B. Colquitt appointed the first board. With State Superintendent F. M. Bralley as ex officio president, its members were A. C. Goeth, Austin, vice president; Peter Radford, Fort Worth; Walter J. Crawford, Beaumont; and W. H. Fuqua, Amarillo. [18]

At its first meeting on December 11 the group adopted rules for administering the business of the normals. The regents abolished on each campus the office of treasurer of local funds (thus eliminating a $200 salary item) and provided for depositing local funds in a bank. A "more equitable salary schedule" for teachers was approved. The board directed that practice schools be established in all the normals as soon as possible.[19]

"REBIRTH OF THE NORMALS"

On January 31, 1912, the State Normal School Board of Regents created the most significant change made until that time in its four schools—so significant that Bruce told students in chapel that the normal schools had been entirely revolutionized and that January 31 was the date of their rebirth.[20] The board standardized a four-year curriculum, the last two years to be of recognized college grade. Effective in September 1914, the student who graduated would be able to enter the junior year at the University of Texas and other senior institutions.

The board reported in 1915, perhaps with some inaccuracy:

> The Normal Schools were made to assume a position midway between that of the high school and the college, and practically uniform courses were planned for them all, giving to the Normals two years of high school and two of strictly college work, which plan is in conformity with that of the most progressive States.[21]

The new function of the normals was *not* to be restricted to rural and elementary schools, a role advocated by many opponents who wanted only universities to prepare high school teachers. The board emphasized that reorganized courses would "make the standard of graduation from a Texas State Normal School as high as is maintained in the best Normal Schools of other States, and will enable these schools to perform effectively their proper functions in preparing teachers for the one-teacher rural schools, and for the primary, intermediate, and high school grades of our best school systems."[22]

The board abolished the general course and substituted five distinct courses. The student was to select one of the five without provisions for free electives. The change became effective in September 1912. These were the options:

1. The Agriculture Course, to prepare high school agriculture teachers and rural school teachers.

2. The Industrial Arts Course, subdivided into manual training and home economics to prepare public school teachers of those subjects.

3. The Science Course, to prepare science and mathematics teachers.

4. The Language Course, to prepare teachers of English and either Latin or German.

5. The Primary and Art Course, to prepare teachers of grades below the high school and teachers of either vocal music or drawing.

The first year was the same for all, except that for the Language Course one substituted language for science and mathematics. Otherwise, course differentiation began in the second year. Instead of credits in terms of eight courses per year, the new system provided for fifteen units per year, the unit being defined as five recitations per week for a term of twelve weeks.[23] A year later a history-English class was added and the industrial arts was separated into home economics and manual training courses.

Entrance requirements were specified for each class in terms of "the equivalent" of the appropriate number of years of work in approved high schools or colleges. In addition a subfreshman class was authorized for those who failed to meet first-year requirements. Several methods of admission would be "equivalent" to completion of the required years. For example, instead of completing the ninth grade, a freshman could also be admitted by completing the preparatory class of a Texas state normal school, by earning a second-grade teaching certificate and taking certain examinations, or by taking examinations in nine specified fields of study. In each of the years of study, admission could be gained either by presenting the proper teaching certificate or by examination in the work of the previous year.

Thus, while the new system did establish meaningful standards, it left the door open to students who had gained teaching certificates by means other than formal study. Probably not every student was as fully educated as makers of the standards might have wished. Nevertheless, that requirements were regarded as tougher was indicated by a marked increase in the size of the senior classes at all the normal schools during the transition to the four-year course. No three-year diplomas were to be issued after 1914, and large numbers of teachers apparently returned to school to "complete" their formal education before requirements for additional work went into effect. This culminated in 1913–14 in the largest graduating class ever known in any of the schools and in small senior classes in 1914–15.[24]

A constitutional amendment in November 1912 provided for six-year terms for the governing boards of all state institutions of higher education. The legislature followed this in 1913 by providing for the appointment of six normal regents by the governor, their terms to run so that no more than two members would retire at the end of each biennium. This was done to lessen partisan control of the board and assure continuity of policy. The state superintendent of public instruction was no longer ex officio president of the board.[25]

chapter 6

For the Training of Teachers

The recent legislation concerning Normal Schools, the appointment of a Board of Regents from widely different sections of the state to look after the interests of these institutions, the raising of the grade and definitely settling the entrance requirements for these schools ought to popularize them and greatly increase their usefulness and also the number annually enrolled in them.

W. H. Bruce, 1912

The teacher education movement had used the "model training school" concept from its beginning, but it was hard to convince legislators that normal students needed to practice the teaching skills they were learning. Several Northeastern states between 1839 and 1860 developed practice and model schools.[1] Traditional college efforts to prepare teachers were criticized between 1890 and 1910 because they lacked practice teaching facilities unlike the leading teachers colleges.[2]

State Superintendent Cousins in 1906 urged establishment of a practice department in each Texas normal school, "properly equipped for doing primary and intermediate grade work of the highest quality."[3] Cousins asserted that "efficiency could be at least doubled by such a department. . . . It would be a crude college of medicine that would teach surgery by lectures, without clinics."[4] Cousins' successor, F. M. Bralley, renewed the plea in 1911. He said that of eighty state normal schools in the United States, only seven did not offer a course in practice teaching, and "Texas furnished three of the unfortunate seven."[5]

In his next biennial report, Bralley "most urgently" recommended that the legislature appropriate money for special buildings for practice schools at the four state normals.[6] By the end of 1912 West Texas State Normal had a practice school of eight grades with 120 students; Southwest Texas used two public school grades for observation and practice teaching; Sam Houston operated one grade of practice department work; North Texas awaited appropriations. The regents recommended provisions for a practice program at all the schools.[7]

DR. BRUCE PERSUADES THE SENATE

In 1913, Bruce told a senate committee of the need for a training school at North Texas. One member asserted, "I do not think we can make an appropriation for this innovation." Bruce responded that he and other presidents had inspected normal schools in seven other states and that everywhere they had found the demonstration school to be a part of the institution. But the committee voted against the request. What happened next is told in Bruce's words:

> When we had finished discussing my request for increased appropriations, Senator Brelsford of El Paso said, "[. . .] I am convinced that we ought to do one of two things: we ought to grant Dr. Bruce's request for an appropriation for this building and teachers, or demand

> his resignation as president of the school. If he has come here and imposed upon us in starting this innovation that is not needed in the work of the school, he ought to be dismissed as its president. Now, I do not believe he has done this. I believe he knows what he is talking about, and that this addition to the school is a necessity. I therefore move that we rescind this action and grant the appropriation."
>
> His motion being put to the committee, the vote in its favor was unanimous, and the school was started in January, 1914.[8]

Early in 1913, the college bought six and one-half acres of land on Chestnut Street south of the campus. Most of this was used for an athletic field. But on part of it a seven-room frame building was erected for the training school at a cost of $5,426.49.[9] It was intended from the first that this building would later be converted to a gymnasium.[10]

The Training School was designed to have nine grades, but only seven were offered in January 1914, with one hundred pupils, a director, and four teachers. Two teachers were added the following September and the full nine grades were offered.[11] The director, Miss Maud L. Fiero, was a graduate of a state normal in New York and held the bachelor's degree from Columbia University. All the other teachers were products of North Texas State Normal College with public school teaching experience, but none held a bachelor's degree.[12] The purpose of the school was to give normal students a chance to observe "the organization, conduct, control, instruction, and other details of a model public school, and to give students actual practice and experience in teaching under expert direction." Completion of the ninth grade admitted the training school student to the freshman class of the college without examination.[13] Each teacher except the first-grade teacher had charge of two grades. Pupils were admitted from any section of Texas until the limit of sixteen to a grade was reached. No tuition was charged. But neither was a state per capita apportionment received, so the Training School reserved the right to refuse or to dismiss pupils for lack of ability or poor conduct.[14]

INSTITUTES AND SUMMER NORMALS

The Training School was one step among many in the long struggle to improve the quality of public school teachers. County boards of examiners granted certificates to teachers between 1840 and 1871. In 1871 certification power was given to the State Board of Education, and in 1876 county judges received the right to issue certificates.[15] The first formal teacher education came in 1881 with the summer normal institutes supported by the Peabody Board. That year 451 teachers enrolled in such programs for seven weeks in seven Texas cities.[16] In 1883 the legislature appropriated funds for one white summer normal school in each of the thirty-one state senatorial districts and one summer school for African Americans in each congressional district, each to run for four weeks. Enrollment the first year was 1,078. The state appropriation was discontinued in 1886 and summer normals had to rely on tuition fees plus an occasional appropriation from the Peabody Fund.

In 1893 the summer normal certificate gave the right to teach for four years without further examination. By 1900 there were 118 summer normals enrolling 5,100 students. Of this number 2,994 applied for certificates and 1,965 were granted.[17]

Summer institutes were relied on because so few Texas teachers received either normal school or college training. The summer school was to provide both professional teacher preparation and a review of the subject matter to be taught. For a second-grade certificate, for example, the applicant was tested on arithmetic, composition and grammar, American and Texas history, geography, orthography, reading and writing, and school management and methods of teaching.[18] So many summer students were so poorly prepared that "instead of devoting the time to methods of instruction, school government, the application of the schools laws, and the like, the conductors of the normals are forced, by these new recruits, to devote all time to subject matter, the sole purpose of which is to 'coach' those in attendance for the examination coming at the close of the school."[19] The summer normal continued to be a major source of certified teachers for awhile longer.

Still another agency of teacher education was the county institute. State law required the county superintendent to hold annually at least three county institutes of two days each.[20] But only in 1905 did the legislature require teachers to attend and allow them pay for the days spent in attendance. State Superintendent Cousins wrote that the new system was beneficial and met with "practically the unanimous endorsement of school officers and teachers."[21] Faculty members from North Texas commonly served as guest instructors at these institutes over a wide area. Bruce, particularly, was a frequent county institute lecturer.

The state normals, in fact, played a strong role in continuing the two certification programs—summer normals and county institutes—until the time came when their own programs would supplant them. But that would not come until the state demanded higher standards and provided adequate financial rewards. In 1900, for example, the average salary for public school teachers was $260.32 a year.[22] With the length of the public school term at 108 days as the twentieth century opened,[23] the summer normal institute offered the most promising avenue to the ambitious teacher. The problem was viewed this way in 1906 by State Superintendent Cousins:

> Many of the women marry, a few of them leave the schoolroom for other lines of employment that are more remunerative and less wearing on the nerves. In prosperous times the men seek and find more lucrative employment in other professions and in industrial pursuits. The places of most of these are taken by beginners, many of whom have no special preparation for their work, except the scanty preparation guaranteed by a teacher's certificate. Of the 4345 teachers who stood the summer normal examinations in the year 1906, 2000—practically half of them—had neither professional training nor experience in teaching.[24]

Summer normals set the pattern for teacher education for some years, and when the summer institutes disappeared, the normal and teachers colleges were well established in the summer field. By 1900 in other parts of the United States, summer school enrollment at most normals equaled or exceeded their regular enrollment.[25] At North Texas the summer registration figures surpassed the long-session total in 1911. For many years—until the institution had moved away from its single purpose of teacher education—the summer enrollment would continue as the larger.

At the private Texas Normal College, summer institutes had been conducted under supervision of the State Department of Education. From 1894 on President Terrill advertised eight-week summer terms of regular college work, not to be confused with the usual summer normal. Certification was carried out by examination. This pattern was continued for the state normal. Catalogs advertised summer sessions of eight weeks, longer than the typical summer normal, but the work was still not comparable to that of the long session. Classes were designed to provide a review for deficient students, to raise a state certificate to one of higher grade, or to provide instruction preparatory to entering college classes in the fall.[26] The pattern that had existed during this period is reflected in this recollection by Registrar P. E. McDonald:

> the summer session for the first eight years functioned mainly as a "summer normal institute" under the direction of the state superintendent for the benefit of those who desired to prepare for examinations for state certificates. In those days and later, even until the year 1921, the law made no distinction between certificates based upon examination and those issued for work in the normal schools. The idea never seemed to occur to students of the regular session that it was desirable, practical, or possible to continue their work during the summer session. For several years the only attendants of the summer session were the summer normal students and the few students who failed to meet the requirements for the certificates during the regular session. . . . In most cases to register for the summer work was an admission of failure during the regular session.[27]

THE STANDARD SUMMER SESSION

In his first summer, President Kendall tried to begin a standard summer session and keep control of examinations with the normal faculty. However, he again ran afoul of his successor, Superintendent Lefevre, who insisted that students take the examinations given at the close of the summer normals.[28]

When Lefevre left office, Kendall tried to get Superintendent Cousins to give all the state normals a regular summer session. Principal Harris of San Marcos agreed, but Pritchett of Sam Houston refused.[29] It was not until 1909, however, that the college advertised that "Work may be done during the Summer Session and credit given toward a certificate or diploma from this school."[30] The State Normal Board of Regents in 1912 divided the summer session into the summer school and the summer normal. Each lasted eight or nine weeks, with the summer school offering credit work toward certificates and diplomas.

The summer normal provided review for certificates examinations.[31] Bruce began summer school graduating exercises to confer certificates and diplomas.[32] The state normals also required in 1912 that no certificate would be granted for attendance of less than two terms, either summer or winter. The state superintendent, however, required only twenty days at the summer normal to gain eligibility for taking the state examinations.[33] Nor was it possible any longer to renew a certificate. The holder of a state normal certificate could not receive a certificate of the same grade until he had completed at least two-thirds of the work required for a certificate of the next higher grade and had attended the normal school for two full terms of twelve weeks each or two full summer sessions of the school.[34]

The number of teachers certified rose from 286 in 1902 to 770 in 1913, and the proportion increased of those earning certificates of higher grade. In 1902, second-grade certificates accounted for 51.4 percent of the total, while the diploma and permanent certificates were only 9.4 percent. By 1913 the certificates were almost evenly divided in number among those receiving second-grade, first-grade, and diploma certificates.[35] Holders of certificates from North Texas State Normal College had little difficulty in locating jobs. Every recipient of a first-grade certificate or a diploma in 1906, for example, found a teaching position the following fall.[36] And in both 1910 and 1911, Bruce was writing superintendents that the demand for teachers far exceeded the supply.[37] After six years, the North Texas president was feeling optimistic about the future role of his normal in teacher education. He wrote:

> The recent legislation concerning Normal Schools, the appointment of a Board of Regents from widely different sections of the state to look after the interests of these institutions, the raising of the grade and definitely settling the entrance requirements for these schools ought to popularize them and greatly increase their usefulness and also the number annually enrolled in them.[38]

At that time, North Texas had already more than doubled its annual enrollment, from 732 to 1,503. (These figures are for the total number of different students enrolled at any time during the year.) The summer session continued to increase in importance: in 1912 the ratio of summer students over long-session students was 902 to 782, and by 1922 it was 2,449 to 1,376.[39] Although the trend to heavier summer school attendance was clearly established by 1917, it doubtless received further impetus from the legislature, which provided appropriations for summer sessions starting in that year. Before that time summer operations were supported by tuition fees, with the exception of $500 appropriated for teaching agriculture in 1909 and 1910 and a general appropriation of $1,000 in 1916.[40] Each summer the proportion of students in the summer normal division decreased, so that by 1922 the regular summer session had 1,880 students, compared to 569 in the summer normal.[41]

chapter 7

The Move to Four-Year Status

Dr. Bruce suggested some time ago that we should discontinue the habit of speaking of our school as the Normal. It is a College in every sense of the word and let's call it that. When we speak of it at home or when we write to our friends, College is the word, the Normal College. The best and the most effective advertisement our school can have is what we say and how we say it to our own friends back at home.

Campus Chat, 1920

Thus far, we have seen these stages in the evolution of North Texas:

1. 1890–1901: An ambitious private normal, struggling for financial survival and presuming to offer bachelor's and at times master's degrees in many fields.

2. 1901–1906: A state normal college of high school rank whose president refused to use the legislative title of "college" for the institution.

3. 1906–1912: A normal college in the process of staking a claim to the entire field of teacher education through the upgrading of standards and the creation of a uniform program in Texas.

4. 1912–1914: A junior college in transition working to assure its graduates of junior standing at recognized senior institutions.

Texas normals were trailing by a few years the main current of development of teacher education. In 1902, the North Central Association of Colleges and Secondary Schools proposed its first set of standards for accrediting secondary schools, requiring teachers to be college graduates with a minimum of eleven hours of credit in education. This led to the end of the short course in normal schools. Pangburn notes that this situation "created a direct and powerful pressure upon the normal schools to raise their standards. . . and to seek the degree-granting privilege."[1]

New York State in 1890 required high school graduation for admission to normals. Massachusetts followed in 1894 and by 1900 the national average of thirty-eight large schools was about twenty-six percent high school graduates.[2] In its first year as a state school, North Texas came close to this norm with twenty-three percent high school graduates. But for the of the Kendall administration the percentage averaged fourteen.[3] Harper explains further: "The reluctance of many of the normal schools to enforce a rigid standard of high-school graduation for entrance requirements is understood when we consider that many students turned away by this requirement could go immediately into the schoolrooms of the state as licensed teachers."[4]

Pangburn's study cites the increasing tendency after 1900 for normals to require high school graduation. In fifty-one normal schools from 1895 to 1905, the percentage requiring high school diplomas increased from fourteen to twenty-two. The National Education Association in 1908, *Education* magazine in 1916, and the Carnegie Foundation in 1917 stated high school graduation to be the minimum for entering professional teacher preparation.[5] Another writer notes that in general normal schools were secondary schools until 1900, and in some instances until 1910.[6]

THE UNIVERSITY RESISTS

North Texas students were allowed to graduate under the old three-year plan until September 1915. The first in the four-year junior college course graduated in May 1915.[7] This was significant progress but still fell short of Dr. Bruce's "vision" of a four-year, bachelor's degree-granting institution. In 1917, he told the faculty:

> I have always felt that the entire field of education belonged to the normal schools so far as the preparation of teachers was concerned. I think we stulify [*sic*] ourselves in taking any other position, for suppose we say the purpose of the normal school is to prepare country teachers, and that it is the purpose of the University to prepare teachers for the high schools. This is equivalent to saying that education is not a science, or that if it is a science it applies only to the art of teaching younger children.
>
> . . . . Some universities are still trying to keep the normal schools from invading what they claim to be their territory.[8]

President Bruce numbered the University of Texas foremost among those "some universities." In 1902 State Superintendent Lefevre wrote:

> One of the many direct services of the university to the lower schools is supplying properly prepared high school teachers. . . . Under . . . present law, one might have received every degree that the university can confer, yet would be prohibited from teaching in any public school . . . unless examined and approved by persons whose legal qualification is a "first grade certificate." . . . I recommend that all degrees . . . of the University of Texas have the immediate force of permanent State certificates.[9]

In November 1904 W. S. Sutton of the University of Texas pleaded with the Association of Southern Colleges for the establishment of teacher education as a proper function of universities.[10] He said that universities should eventually prepare elementary school teachers, but should first concentrate on "the needs of our high schools for teachers rationally trained in higher institutions of learning."[11]

His speech made clear that normal schools should be kept in an inferior position in this scheme of things:

> Graduates of the normal schools are. . . not prepared for efficient service in secondary schools, being qualified for positions in the rural schools and the primary and intermediate grades in city schools. . . . The university department of education. . . offers to graduates of normal schools tempting opportunities to prosecute higher work of both an academic and a professional character.[12]

The key question to come, however, was not whether the state university should have a role in educating teachers; it was whether the normal schools should educate teachers for all levels of public schools. This question was raised in discussions at the fourth Conference for Education in Texas in 1910. In an address on unification problems, Superintendent H. F. Triplett of Beaumont criticized both universities and normal colleges. He argued:

> The pedagogy courses in most State Universities are of a sky-scraper type, and have but little reference to practical methods in school work; and the pedagogy courses of colleges are taken, in many cases, to evade certificate examinations.
>
> If the leading instructors in Texas normals are not the equals of university and college instructors, their places should be *declared* vacant. . . . The normal instructor should be all that the college instructor represents, and also be well versed in pedagogy. I know the presidents and the heads of departments in the Texas normals fully meet these requirements in high scholarship and professional attainments.[13]

By 1914 former State Superintendent Lefevre had become research secretary for the Hogg Organization at the University of Texas. His reports clearly delineated the university's opposition to normal school development. Lefevre wrote:

> If the state normal schools were to be transformed into colleges, there would ensue a repeated duplication between each of the normal colleges and the university which would truly be extravagant if the work were honestly performed, or be a dishonest travesty if the transformation were only "on paper." There is almost unanimity of expert opinion that any attempt to transform state normal schools into colleges is "most unfortunate."[14]

Lefevre said normals were not competent to offer college work:

> Of course, the question ought never to arise until the normal schools can require high school graduation for admission to the new two-year curriculum, and until their financial basis enables them to get proper faculties for such work. At present, the Texas state normal school merely qualifies its graduates for entrance to the university with a credit of one course of freshman work. Their teachers are paid no more than the better sort of high school teachers.[15]

Remember, too, that Texas did not adopt compulsory school attendance until 1915. Only Mississippi in 1918 was later.[16] In 1900, Texas public school enrollment was 578,418; in 1917, it was almost one million.[17] However, Texas had still not taken sufficient steps to provide qualified teachers. In 1918 there were 28,823 teachers in service. Of this number, 3,219 were college graduates, 6,628 were normal school graduates, 7,592 had completed high school, and 11,384 were graduates of no schools.[18] Texas needed all the college-level teacher education facilities the state could provide; a single state university could not be expected to answer the demand.

THE NORMALS REACT

Harper[19] observed that upward expansion of normals was natural. He wrote:

> The struggle was purely a defensive one. . . . to avoid being sidetracked by the growing power of the state universities. . . . The basic problems involved in the transition from normals to teachers colleges were: (1) enrichment of the curriculum and the addition of one or two

> years to the length of the course; (2) securing the necessary financial means and popular support; (3) gaining the legal right to grant degrees; (4) preventing the colleges and universities from forcing them out of the field of preparing high-school and special teachers; (5) meeting the problems of standardization; and (6) preserving their identity and distinctive traits as teachers colleges.[20]

By 1900 four normals in the U. S. had become full-fledged teachers colleges, the pioneers in awarding bachelor's degrees being at Albany, New York, and Ypsilanti, Michigan. Four Illinois normals gained bachelor's degrees in 1907. The Department of Normal Schools of the National Education Association in 1908 drew up a statement of policy that outlined the pattern for the transformation of the nation's normal schools. The NEA urged that the word "normal" should be changed to "teachers college." The department resolved that high school graduation should be a requirement for admission to state normals, that teachers be educated for all public school levels, that the preparation of elementary teachers take two years and of high school teachers four years, that research become a normal school function, that state normals set the standards of teacher education in each state, that college and university domination should not be allowed to turn high schools into preparatory schools exclusively, and that the normal school curriculum should include any special preparation required by the broadening scope of the public schools.[21]

State universities were using all their prestige and power to monopolize the education of high school teachers. A major weapon was accreditation of high schools, with a reciprocal agreement that the high schools would employ only teachers with degrees from approved colleges. The Organization of the North Central Association of Colleges and Secondary Schools accelerated the pressures for college-trained teachers. The normals could see the trend: accept standards and grant degrees, or be forced out of the field that was their only purpose.[22]

UPGRADING ADMISSIONS

North Texas State Normal College clearly needed improved admission standards. In President Kendall's administration, students could enter at virtually any time; those who wanted certificates from the freshman and junior classes were expected to attend class not less than one-half the year.[23] Even as late as

1910, Bruce advised that "students may enter school here at any time, but, of course, the sooner one enters after the beginning of the session the better."[24] With the elevation to junior college rank, concern grew for admission standards.

The major problem arose from acceptance of credits from a high school of the first class "as determined by the State Department of Education or a high school affiliated with any college or university recognized as first class by the State Board of Examiners."[25] Bruce wrote to the registrars of ten of these "recognized" colleges, asking for a list of the Texas high schools affiliated with their institution.[26] All but one college responding indicated that they recognized the high schools with University of Texas affiliation. That one was Texas A&M College, which sent Dr. Bruce a catalog listing 415 affiliated schools. Bruce was disturbed by that because, he said, he knew that many of the 415 schools had "absolutely no rank as high schools" and that some did not offer work beyond the eighth or ninth grade. Texas A&M, Bruce found, "affiliated schools by simply having the superintendent fill out a form of application." He asked each normal president to request the Board of Regents to direct the normals to ignore the A&M affiliation list.[27]

The 1912 bulletin[28] changed definitions of high schools. "Affiliated" schools were those recognized by the University of Texas, Baylor, Southwestern, Trinity, Austin, and Texas Christian. High schools classified by the state superintendent were called "approved" schools. Admission was allowed to the normal school without examination for graduates of "affiliated" high schools with twelve units of affiliated credits. All others could be required to take entrance examinations.

Before the addition of the junior college years of study, President Bruce professed indifference to a credit-transfer relationship with the university. His view was that, "The work here is not planned to prepare for the University. Our sphere is entirely different. We are not at all concerned about our credits anywhere, we simply try to meet the demands upon us."[29]

At the same time, he was not willing to concede the inferior status to which the university relegated the normal schools. He defended the normal requirements this way:

> Our students in the Senior class have more than is included in the Freshman class of the University. We admit to the Junior class here on the same

> certificate that the University admits to its Freshman class, so that we demand two years work of the student for graduation after he has met the requirements for entrance to the Freshman class of the University.[30]

Nevertheless, Bruce was happy to announce in 1914 that the University of Texas had recognized the reorganized four-year normal diploma as the equivalent of two years of university work. The bulletin that year proclaimed:

> The diploma of a Texas State Normal will hereafter have a larger significance. It will represent two years of strictly college work. . . .
>
> The new regime will operate to bring the Normal Schools and the University in closer relation and sympathy, and will bring the University within the reach of a greater number. . . . Graduates in the four-year course in the Normals will be required to spend only two additional years in the University for graduation, instead of four years as formerly. The cost of one additional year at the Normal School and two years at the University will be much less than that of four years at the University.[31]

ADDING THE BACHELOR'S DEGREE

The Normal School Board of Regents did not wait long to convert the normals to bachelor's degree-granting institutions. The expansion was recommended by the council of normal presidents and unanimously passed by the regents on October 27, 1916. They acted on the basis of the law creating the board, which read, "The Board of Regents. . . shall have authority to determine what departments of instruction shall be maintained in the State Normal Schools for white teachers, and what subjects of study shall be pursued in each department."[32]

The Board of Regents challenged the University of Texas on the role of the normal schools in educating teachers. Paragraph by paragraph, the resolution refuted the ideas presented by Sutton and Lefevre, declaring that "this resolution covers the latest and best development of normal school work in the United States, and that further enlargement of the course of study will not be necessary for many years to come."[33]

Bruce appointed a ten-member faculty committee to prepare a course of study for the two additional years.[34] He asked that the work be completed by February 1, 1917.[35] The following May, the president told the faculty:

> We start in September the first year of the two additional years' course to make the normal schools of Texas standard colleges. In so far as education is concerned, it is not intended by our Board of Regents that we will give any college work in their [the university's] field other than that of the preparation of teachers, but if we forget ourselves and undertake to do otherwise, and go into a territory that is not legitimately ours, we will have trouble. Just so long as we stay in our own territory I think the future for us is bright.[36]

Bruce's vision was fulfilled, and he did not foresee a time when the North Texas definition of "our own territory" would change drastically. Nor did he foresee much more growth in size, for he told the faculty, "Now, since other normal schools have been established, our attendance is nearly as large as it will ever be, if not indeed as large as it ought to be."[37] Enrollment in that year had been 1,503. He did foresee an organizational change that was to come in the following decade:

> Possibly the next advance in the normal schools will be dropping off our present two years of work known as freshman and sophomore, and restrict the work to four years above the high school. . . . It may be five years or longer before we are ready for this step. There must be in Texas more high schools accessible to the country boy and girl before we can debar them from entering a normal.[38]

Establishment of bachelor's degrees did not go entirely unchallenged. Board President A. C. Goeth called a meeting of the board and presidents on December 17, 1917, to confer with an investigating group from the legislature. This group wanted to question the board's use of appropriated money for expenses beyond the itemized appropriations and the board's duplication by normal schools of the work of the state university. Board members and the presidents had long discussions with the committee but "no definite decision was reached."[39] The regents stood firm despite the legislative group's opposition to a four-year program and its suggestion that not more than two state normals experiment for a time with the bachelor's degree program.[40]

"A STANDARD TEACHERS COLLEGE"

The normal began its 1917–18 session without a clear statement of the program for the bachelor's degree. Nevertheless, the July 1917 *Bulletin* appeared with a hopeful new subtitle: "A Standard Teachers' College." Inside was listed "the American college method for the admission of students," using the admission unit system.

A confusing nomenclature was adopted—the "Junior College" consisted of the four existing normal school years, equivalent to the last two years of high school and the first two of college; the "Senior College" included the "Junior College Class" (fifth year of the normal) and the "Senior College Class" (sixth year of the normal, leading to the bachelor's degree). For admission units, North Texas recognized work done at other state normals and at high schools approved by the State Department of Education or given affiliation by the University of Texas. A subsequent struggle led to abandonment of the University of Texas affiliation system. [41]

The 1917 *Bulletin* offered a preliminary statement of bachelor's degree requirements, including an education major, an academic major of twelve units, one academic minor of nine units and another of six units. The academic major could be in English, mathematics, history and social science, language, and the sciences, including physics, chemistry, and biology. All courses required at least six units in English and three in history or social science.

In June 1917 Bruce raised the question of length of recitation periods—whether to continue four weekly meetings of forty-five minutes or to switch to three per week of one hour's time. School opened the following fall with sixty-minute recitation periods—four a week for freshman and sophomore classes and three a week for juniors and seniors.[42]

In April 1918, bachelor's degree requirements were still being debated. At one meeting the faculty voted 39 to 13 against first proposals for foreign language requirements.[43] Two days later, five options were offered on language requirements. Five ballots were required before agreement was reached, 47 to 4, to establish a bachelor of arts with foreign language requirements and a bachelor of science without foreign language required either for admission or graduation.[44] Later that same month the faculty acted on uniform requirements proposed for all the state normals. They voted against allowing less credit per recitation in reading, music, and drawing. They also raised the uniform state requirement of twenty-seven hours of education to thirty-six. The academic major was now defined as thirty-six term-hours.[45]

UNIFORM REQUIREMENTS AT LAST

Finally, in July 1918, the North Texas *Bulletin* carried the uniform requirements of the normal schools. The new statement clarified some confusing terminology and spelled out degree requirements more specifically. Four divisions were created at each of the state normals:

1. Normal Training School, the first nine grades of the standardized school.
2. Normal School Division, the first year and the second year of the normal school.
3. Normal College Diploma Division, the first two years of college curricula.
4. Normal College Degree Division, the third and fourth years of college curriculums.

The six classes in the Normal Schools were designated freshman, sophomore, junior, senior, college junior, and college senior. Two degrees were offered: the B. A. in Education, with language requirements, and the B. S. in Education, without foreign language.[46]

In 1920, labels were changed to divide the Normal School into the first-year and second-year classes and to call the years of the Normal College freshman through senior.[47] At this time, requirements for six numbered curriculums were spelled out course by course, term by term. The six were planned for teachers of kindergarten, primary grades, intermediate grades, rural schools, high school teachers in science or liberal arts subjects, and high school teachers in vocational fields such as agriculture, home economics, manual training, and commerce.[48]

This left the Normal School as the equivalent of the third and fourth years of an accredited high school, designed to qualify the student for college entrance. But for a time it was to continue in its original function as well:

> But it is also intended to serve a very useful purpose. It is intended to prepare students to become teachers in the public schools of the State. Until such time as the State requires a more thorough training on the part of the teachers in the public schools, this will continue to be perhaps the most vital service that the Normal School performs.[49]

There was no immediate rush of students to enter the bachelor's degree program. In its first year of operation, 1917–18, there were nine students in the college junior class.[50] The following year brought twenty-seven at the junior level and six in the senior year.[51] Of this latter number, five became the first students in history to receive the standard four-year bachelor's degree. Four were awarded the bachelor of arts and the other the bachelor of science in a commencement exercise June 2, 1919.[52]

STRUGGLE FOR RECOGNITION

Further steps were necessary before diplomas could be recognized as equivalent to those from established four-year schools in Texas: approval by the State Department of Education, the Association of Texas Colleges, and the University of Texas. Until this came, normal college graduates could face difficulty in gaining admission to graduate schools and in gaining high school teaching positions open to graduates of recognized colleges.

The state agency moved rapidly to add the normals to its accepted list. The college examiner of the State Department of Education studied the curriculums of the state normals and recommended their approval. State Superintendent Annie Webb Blanton, the former Denton Normal teacher, placed the normal colleges on the list of accredited first-class colleges in December 1919.[53] In 1921 the institution was admitted to Class A membership in the American Association of Teachers Colleges.[54]

University of Texas approval did not follow so rapidly. Southwest Texas State Normal underwent an inspection by a visiting university committee in 1920–21. After making requested changes in courses, the San Marcos school received university approval for the fall term of 1921.[55] The other normals followed suit, it being the understanding of the presidents that "the University of Texas agreed to accredit the five Normal Colleges (Alpine excepted) on the examination made of the Southwest Texas State Normal College as a type."[56] North Texas was visited early in 1922 by a four-man group. The visiting committee suggested some curriculum changes, especially a complete differentiation of the high school and college level courses.[57] The *Campus Chat* reported on March 11, 1922:

> This committee has granted the holder of a degree from this College credit for four full years of standard college work and will admit

> such graduates into the class for master's degrees, provided that the student has graduated with five advanced courses to his credit. They have recognized almost all the work above the second year of any one course as advanced courses.

With acceptance by the University of Texas, the next necessary approval came quickly. On December 18, 1922, North Texas State Normal College was officially notified of its election to membership as a senior college in the Association of Texas Colleges.[58]

CHANGING THE NAME

The number of public normals in the nation reached a peak of 270 in 1920, then plummeted sharply to 150 in 1930 and thirty in 1940. In the 1920s alone, sixty-nine state normal schools became teachers colleges.[59] Of 382 teacher-education institutions in 1922, eighty were classified as teachers colleges and the rest as normals. The eighty teachers colleges granted four-year degrees. Even with the normal name, North Texas was listed among the eighty teachers colleges.[60] Only five of the teachers colleges exceeded the North Texas enrollment. The top six were at Cedar Falls, Iowa, 5,390; Detroit, Michigan, 4,730; Terre Haute, Indiana, 4,678; Pittsburg, Kansas, 4,150; Ypsilanti, Michigan, 3,861; and Denton, 3,728. Only Cedar Falls and Detroit had larger faculties than North Texas.[61] The American Association of Teachers Colleges resolved in 1922 that all teacher training institutions should become senior teachers colleges and confer the bachelor's degree.[62]

The final step in the four-year college evolution now seemed almost anticlimactic. Bulletins had called this "A Standard Teachers' College" since 1917. In 1920 a *Campus Chat* editorial recalling that Bruce had asked students to "discontinue the habit of speaking of our school as the Normal. It is a College in every sense of the word and let's call it that."[63] In March 1922 Bruce emphasized in a chapel speech the national movement to change the name of normal colleges to teachers colleges.[64]

In 1939 Bruce recalled that at a 1921 conference of college presidents with Gov. Pat Neff he had suggested that the word "teachers" be substituted in the names of all the normals.[65] A bill to that effect passed, and a state representative said, "This change in the names of the eight Teacher Training Colleges of

Texas is due entirely to the suggestion made by Dr. Bruce at Governor Neff's 'Think out loud Conference'."[66]

Neff signed the bill on April 9, 1923, to take effect ninety days after adjournment of the legislature.[67] Each college was to be named with the city of its location in the title, as "The North Texas State Teachers College, at Denton."[68] The day after the signing, Dr. Bruce explained the choice of names:

> The only change in the names would be the substitution of the word "teachers" for the word "normal," and adding the name of the town in which the institution was located. . . . The addition of the name of the town was made. . . because all the schools are now spoken of in terms of their localities, this local school having been called for many years the "Denton Normal.". . . It will be known, I presume, in conversation, newspaper news notes, etc., as the Denton Teachers' College.

chapter 8

The Struggle for Money

Dr. Bruce was in Austin constantly during the sessions of the Legislature and frequently appeared before committees of which I was a member. He was held in the highest esteem by members of the Legislature, who always accepted what he said without question. No man who appeared before legislative committees in my six years of service was held in higher esteem. He was recognized as an authority on education.

The chief thing in my recollection of Dr. Bruce and his frequent appearances before legislative committees, is that he was incapable of camouflage or deceit. Everything he said was accepted without question. It never occurred to anyone to doubt the truth or accuracy of any statement made by President Bruce.

Representative R. M. Chitwood, 1922[1]

The 1879 act establishing Sam Houston State Normal set aside $14,000 each year for current expenses.[2] That had risen to $20,000 a year by 1901, and the same amount was provided for North Texas.[3] Tuition was to be free. Each student was required to pledge to teach in Texas for the same length of time as he attended the normal. Applicants from other states could not be admitted except by pledging to teach in Texas schools and "thereby become a citizen of the State."[4]

The Peabody Education Fund had provided $8,000 for the Sam Houston Normal in its first year, but the amount dwindled to $1,000 in 1903–4, when distribution ceased. North Texas received $800 in supplementation of the principal's salary in 1901–2[5] and $1,600 in 1902–3, $500 for the principal's salary and $1,100 to add to faculty salaries.[6] In 1903–4 nothing was given to North Texas.[7]

STATE SCHOLARSHIP HELP

In 1901, each member of the legislature could appoint two scholarship students to the Sam Houston Normal and two to the North Texas Normal. Nine scholarship appointments to each normal were given to each member of the State Board of Education, and the lieutenant governor was given six for each school. This provided fifty dollars a year for each student.

President Kendall repeatedly encouraged state senators and representatives to make all their appointments. In November 1901, appointment vacancies totaled thirty-seven.[8] In no year was Kendall able to get full use of every scholarship, with some appointments failing to be made and with some students dropping out. During the first year of the program, with 360 scholarships authorized, 378 different students got partial use of them during the year.[9] In the second year the number of scholarship students attending was 280; in 1903–4 it was 411; in 1904–5, 388; and in 1905–6, 397.[10] Scholarship appropriations were discontinued after 1908. State normal principals agreed in 1910 to drop the pledge by the students to teach in Texas schools.

The only other income available was student fees. In its first year, North Texas charged an incidental fee of two dollars for each of four quarters. Thereafter there were three terms with an incidental fee of three dollars per term. Each student paid a textbook fee of five dollars for the year, two dollars of which would be refunded if his books were properly cared for.[11] The three-dollar balance was used to buy textbooks.[12]

RAISING APPROPRIATIONS

While Kendall was in office, the appropriation remained at $20,000 per year. The legislature provided $40,000 for a new building in 1903 and $10,000 for building improvements in 1905–6. Kendall presented his budget requests to the State Board of Education and relied on board members to present the proposals to the legislature.[13]

President Bruce first appeared before the legislature three months after taking office. He recalled it this way:

> In January, 1907, I asked the legislature to increase our appropriation. . . . I knew it was useless to ask at the time what I felt the college needed; and so I requested a[n] appropriation for maintenance of $40,000. The House of Representatives made an appropriation of $30,000, but the Senate restricted us to the traditional $20,000 per annum. In the Free Conference Committee of the two branches of the Legislature, a compromise was effected, and we were allowed for the next biennium $22,000 per year. This. . . permitted the addition of one member to the faculty of fifteen. . . .
>
> While this $2,000 did not allow us to accomplish a great deal, it did one important piece of work, the abolition of the traditional $20,000 per annum.[14]

On the eve of his very next effort, an editorial in the *Normal Journal* gave him the support of the student body in this manner:

> The President of this institution will go before the legislative committee and ask for another building and many much needed improvements. No man ever asked for a more reasonable or just demand than he will. Our teachers are overworked, classes overcrowded, and societies hampered by the present conditions under which the institution is forced to struggle. Of course, directly, there is little the student body can do, but we are confident that Dr. Bruce, carrying with him, as we will, the hearty support and well wishes of every student of this school, both past and present, will secure the necessary financial means for carrying on and enlarging the great work being done by this institution.[15]

THE MILL TAX PROPOSAL

The biennial process of pleading before the legislature for operating funds for higher education was widely recognized among educators as unsatisfactory. In 1905 State Superintendent Lefevre proposed adopting the practice of other states to levy "a suitable fraction of a mill tax for the maintenance of state institutions." He suggested that six-tenths of a mill tax (six cents on the hundred dollars) would meet the regular needs of all the state schools, with appropriations necessary only on such special occasions as the construction of a new building. This plan would have allocated $54,000 for each of the state normals.[16] Other state officials proposed mill taxes of some sort, but none was levied.

A force for the improvement of all Texas education was the Conference for Education in Texas, which held its first annual session in 1907. Its aim was "to arouse and strengthen educational public sentiment and to encourage all forms of rational education in Texas." Dr. Bruce was an active participant in its five annual sessions through 1912. At the first session, Secretary of State L. T. Dashiell urged the group "to inaugurate a movement in Texas to remove its higher institutions from the uncertainty of biennial legislative action."[17]

Late in 1908 it appeared that the schools were prepared to work together. C.I.A. President Cree T. Work told Bruce he had received hearty approval of a tax for state higher education from President Mezes of the university, the assistant attorney general, state tax commissioner, insurance commissioner, and other state officials. Work proposed levying an ad valorem tax of one-half mill for the state's higher education institutions, to become effective January 1, 1910. This was calculated to yield in one biennium approximately $906,000 for the university, $377,000 for A&M, $209,000 for C.I.A., $174,000 for the three state normals, and $104,000 for Prairie View.[18]

But just one year later, it appeared that the University of Texas planned to go it alone. In January 1910, Dr. Bruce protested to Rep. F. F. Hill:

> Several years ago the "Conference for Education in Texas" undertook. . . to secure support of all educational institutions by taxation instead of by biennial appropriations.
>
> It was my understanding that. . . in such bill provision would be made for all the educational institutions, including the four normal

> schools, they being as deserving in their sphere of usefulness as the University in its sphere.
>
> Prof. Bizzell [of C.I.A.]. . . informs me that the friends of the University have prepared and will quite soon introduce a bill providing for the institution, but ignoring all others, the authorities of the University being unwilling to have the other schools connected with it in the matter.[19]

In a letter to Estill the same day Dr. Bruce said the affair reminded him of the prediction of a prominent Texas school man "that the normals would be used and their friends requested to popularize the sentiment in the State and that when the time should come for legislative action the normal schools would be ignored."[20]

In the annual Conference for Education in Texas, however, University of Texas representatives continued to maintain a public policy of cooperation among the state's institutions. The conference recommended on April 22, 1910, that the constitution be amended to provide for the support of the state's educational institutions by a special tax. This would be no additional tax, it said, but merely a transfer of support from a general to a special tax to remove the institutions "permanently from the domain of politics."[21]

In his biennial report in 1911, State Superintendent Bralley criticized the appropriations system as "necessarily productive of political entanglements in which personal prejudice and political caprice figure." A fraction of a mill tax would, he said, yield sufficient funds for all the state schools and do away with the "biennial scramble and pull" for appropriations. He presented the endorsement of the State Department of Education for an educational tax.[22]

The University of Texas failed to get an exclusive tax in 1910. That led to the inclusion of Texas A&M College in two measures introduced in the 1911 legislature. One was a constitutional amendment for a tax of 4.4 cents on the $100 evaluation of property to support these two schools. Representatives opposed this as an unreasonable limit on the power of the legislature to provide for the institutions. The other measure, legislative rather than constitutional, would have provided a tax rate of 3.7 for the university and of 1.7 for A&M. The bill was passed by the house but died in the senate.[23]

With the failure of the 32nd Legislature to act, Superintendent Bralley in 1912 repeated the call for a special tax for the support of all of the state's institutions.[24] The University of Texas returned to the strategy of organizing all the state's institutions of higher education under one banner. The year 1912 also brought forth *The State Institutions of Higher Education in Texas*, a financial discussion by a committee known as the Hogg Organization. North Texas had no direct representation on the committee, although President Bizzell of C.I.A. was a member.

The report praised the normal schools as "one of the essential and vital parts of the State's system of public education" but carefully restricted its description of their function to that of training teachers for the common schools. It noted that Texas was calling annually for 3,500 new teachers, while the four normal schools were graduating only 350 a year. The group concluded that the state was not meeting the national standards for support of normal schools.

Texas spent far less per normal school student than the national average, and the money provided for building construction was below average, with inadequate and poorly equipped buildings as a result. Even with some increase in both entrance and graduation requirements in Texas normals, their standards were below the prevailing national standards. These needed raising much more, and this would require additional revenue. The teacher load in Texas was 25.6 students per faculty member, as compared to 16.6 for the national average, indicating the need for employing additional instructors. The report concluded that better buildings, libraries, and laboratories should be provided for the normals and that better salaries should be paid to attract qualified faculty.[25]

Just before the legislature met in January 1913, the governing boards of all the state institutions agreed unanimously on the text of a proposed constitutional amendment. It asked for a tax of one mill (ten cents on $100), estimated to yield in the following year about $2,500,000. The largest share, $1,125,000 would go to the University of Texas; North Texas, like the other normals, would receive $125,000. The governor endorsed the amendment. It was introduced simultaneously in both houses and cleared both committees immediately with a recommendation for immediate adoption without amendment. However, a sudden reversal took place. Former State Superintendent Lefevre, who had become research secretary of the Hogg Organization, said the change was triggered by a revolt of students about a hazing incident at Texas A&M College. A bill was introduced in the legislature to relocate A&M to Austin as a branch of the University of Texas. This never came to a vote, but the one-mill tax bill failed in both houses. LeFevre urged supporters "do not fear to try again."[26]

And try again a number of groups did. The Hogg Organization, in a 1914 book written by Lefevre, again urged passage of the one-mill tax. The emphasis, however, was still on the building of a great state university and reflected the fear of the University of Texas that other schools might grow in size and demand a larger share of the fixed apportionment. Lefevre wrote: "Nothing could be more ill advised. . . than an apportionment contingently dependent upon the number of students. Such a law would inevitably tend to corrupt the administration of all the institutions. The number of students is by no means the controlling factor of proper cost."[27]

Governor Colquitt, in a 1914 letter to the *Dallas Morning News,* again urged adoption of the one-mill tax, but cautioned that even its revenue might not be great enough for the needs of higher education.[28] The 1914 report of the State Normal School Board of Regents endorsed the tax.[29] The same volume reprinted the platform demands of the Democratic State Convention held in El Paso in August 1914, demanding permanent support for all the higher education institutions.[30]

As late as 1921 the mill tax idea was still being circulated, but the normal presidents no longer favored it. In December 1921 the presidents' council recommended as a substitute the levying of indirect, special, and severance taxes similar to a Louisiana plan.[31]

DR. BRUCE AT WORK

Plans for financial stability came to nothing, and Bruce spent a lot of time searching for more funds. He would sometimes solicit local businessmen. In 1908 he typed the following statement on college letterhead: "For the purpose of printing 5000 placards, 5000 post cards, engraving cuts, and meeting other expenses in the advertisement of the North Texas State Normal, for which purpose there is no appropriation, we promise to pay on demand the amounts opposite our respective names."[32] The signatures of thirty-six businesses and individuals appear on the sheet, pledging amounts ranging from one dollar to ten dollars and totaling seventy-eight dollars to meet a bill of $65.25 paid in cash by Bruce at the Record and Chronicle Printery.

President Bruce worked hard to establish friendly relations with political sources and in some cases to help establish friendly individuals in office. In 1910, for example, he wrote Governor Colquitt to recommend that a North Texas Normal graduate be appointed secretary of state. When that was successful, he invited the new official to be the commencement speaker.

The limited scope of operations may be hard to visualize when viewed from amidst today's standards. In 1908–9 T. E. Peters served as secretary, treasurer, bookkeeper, and registrar. He recalled later[33] that he and Bruce had to sit up several nights all night long to make out the teachers' certificates—a job made necessary because the president had no secretary. Until 1911, Bruce typed his own correspondence and transferred a copy of each letter into a Japanese copying book. He seemingly answered every piece of incoming mail himself—including advertising circulars. (A good example is his note to a Chicago clock company. In its entirety it read: "Replying to yours of May 4th I will say that we have not a night watchman and therefore have no use for a watchman's clock.") His books in mathematics also brought requests for help, to which he responded like this:

> Replying to yours of recent date, I will say that corn "in the shuck" differs so much in the amount of shelled corn it turns out either by measure or by weight that no rule could be given for determining how much actual corn is contained in a given quantity of unshucked corn. No author would risk his reputation by trying to give a rule for it.

In another letter he referred a request to the chairman of the committee on teachers, observing that his work in August was so heavy "that I am forced to let the various committees take charge of their several departments." A 1910 letter to a friend outlined his dilemma:

> I am really very busy, myself and if the nights were not very long, I do not know how I could get along at all.
>
> These additions [in enrollment], the putting into operation for the first time an elective system here, the installation of three new departments with equipments to buy, power to provide, etc. etc. almost ad infinitum, considering the fact that the school now demands much

> correspondence and that I have no stenographer, typewriter, or other person to write letters—all combine to make me a very busy person.
>
> Even with all that, I have not once a month a night to myself until after the time for all people to be abed, calls of students, ringing of the telephones, etc. almost prevent any consecutive thought or work until after bedtime. It is then that I have done all my work on the solid geometry.

But even Bruce drew the line somewhere, as this letter to a Denton woman indicates: "Replying to yours of recent date. I will say that I have nothing whatever to do with the laundry, the mending, or the clothing of the young men here in school. Each young man attends to these matters for himself."

It is not surprising, then, to encounter a request to the State Board of Education in June 1911 for an office assistant to perform the duties of typewriter, stenographer, and registrar. The president amplified the request in a letter the next day to his friend the normal graduate, Secretary of State C. C. McDonald, outlining his clerical, letter-writing, and telephone-messenger chores. He explained:

> I do not think it in any respect economy on the part of the State to pay me my present salary to attend to so much work that is purely clerical and which might be done as well by a person who could be employed at much less expense.
>
> I have asked for this addition to the force, not because I would shun work, but that I may work more effectively, and because I would attend to the truly administrative work more closely and effectively. I am confident that enquiry here would elicit the information that I am in no sense a shirk, that I am always at my post of duty. . . . I can then devote my time to the work that properly belongs to the office of the President of the school.[34]

The result was a letter from the governor, telling the president to "go and get a stenographer to suit you." By September Bruce wrote the governor that he had found a young lady for the post, stating that "I wish you would kindly see that she is offered the position right away." It is little wonder that the governor of Texas and other members of the state board were happy to see the creation of a separate board of regents the next year.

It was also in 1911 that the North Texas president was stating that "we are very fearful of losing two of our very best men unless there be an increase in salary."[35] That year's budget campaign was successful, and in the fall Bruce wrote Governor Colquitt:

> Our teachers have been greatly pleased by the report brought from Austin by the Local Board, and they appreciate your position that since appropriation necessary to pay more respectable salaries has been made, you and the other members of the Board are willing to pay them.
>
> In behalf of the students who are to enroll here in the future, I thank you for your liberal treatment of this institution.[36]

In 1912, the president still earned $2,500, but there were ten teachers at $1,800, whereas in 1901, the top pay of $1,500 went to Bruce and the next five received $1,400. The low pay in 1901 was $1,100 for each of four women teachers, while in 1912 the lowest salaries were $1,200 each for two teachers and $1,350 each for four others.[37] Continuing annual enrollment increases made further progress difficult. As Bruce told the faculty in 1917, "Just so long as the number of students increases faster than the appropriation, an increase of salaries would be impossible." The only way to raise salaries would be to get a fixed appropriation large enough to pay the number of teachers that would be needed for some years to come, so that future appropriation increases could go into salary increases instead of for hiring new teachers. The legislature had established four more normal colleges, and Dr. Bruce thought that North Texas enrollment would stabilize at its 1917 level and make this possible.[38]

The Board of Regents in April 1917 asked the legislature to raise presidents' salaries from $3,000 to $4,000 and to increase teachers' nine-month pay by $150 to $600.[39] The legislature did not vote the raises, so the board provided an additional $600 for the presidents from "the funds appropriated to be expended at the discretion of the board." Teachers' salaries remained at the same level.[40]

Bruce explained the 1917 prospects to his faculty this way:

> The legislature up to ten years ago appropriated $20,000 for support and maintenance. We are to have next year for support and main-

> tenance $105,000 for the regular session and $23,000 for the summer session, making a total of $128,000; and the year thereafter we get $133,000. Therefore, if we get more money afterwards, we ought to be able to raise all salaries.
>
> The Board has committed itself to higher salaries. . . . I think you ought to know also that they discussed the following items as helping to determine teachers' salaries: (1) Scholarship, as evidenced by his preparation, the courses he took in college, and the degree that he received, whether bachelor, master, or Ph.D. (2) Successful experience: Experience measured only in minutes and hours is not an asset to a teacher. (3) Personality, industry, etc. The question was asked the Board, whether as a policy sex ought to enter into the determination of the salary, and it was agreed, because men more often stay in the profession permanently, become more often identified as citizens of the town in which the school is situated, and more often they have others depending upon them, etc., that sex should be one of the determining factors.[41]

The World War restricted further financial growth. As requested by Governor Hobby, Bruce directed departments not to buy supplies and equipment unless absolutely necessary to avoid impairing institutional efficiency, "so as to leave unexpended as large part of the appropriation as possible."[42]

Meager as they seemed, faculty salaries were often further drained from a variety of sources. Governor Colquitt asked for subscriptions for the "Dining Service Fund" of the battleship *Texas* in 1914 and was sent $39.[43] On a number of occasions teachers bore the expense of bringing the College of Industrial Arts faculty to the normal campus for such events as the program given by violinist Mischa Elman in 1917, which led to an assessment of $1.95 against each faculty member.[44] To help acquire land south of the campus, each teacher was asked in faculty meeting to pledge an amount equal to his city tax for 1917.[45] The same year, $6,000 was subscribed at a single faculty meeting for the Second Liberty Loan.[46]

After a period of postwar stabilization, faculty economic conditions improved, and in 1920 the Board of Regents adopted this salary scale: deans and directors, $3,000 to $3,600; professors, $2,600 to $3,000; associate professors,

$2,100 to $2,500; assistant professors, $1,800 to $2,000; and instructors, $1,200 to $1,750.[47]

Once again, the credit for much of this progress must go to Bruce. Senator A. E. Wood recalled finance committee hearings this way:

> Dr. Bruce presented the needs of the institution in a manner that was very pleasing to the entire committee on each and every occasion. His forceful arguments, his earnestness and his courage won for him the admiration of the entire committee. He had as much influence with the members of the Legislature as any man in Texas and while it was impossible for the committee to grant everything he desired, yet the institution he represented fared extremely well because of the confidence they had in Dr. Bruce.[48]

Unfortunately, the state hit financial difficulties in 1923, creating problems for the next two decades. For the first time in the history of the school it became necessary that year to discount salary vouchers. Arrangements were made to discount them at two percent.[49] Regents lower salaries for the 1923–24 year. The pay ranged from $1,500 in the Training School to $2,600 for directors of larger departments. Other professors got from $2,000 to $2,400. The president got $4,500 for twelve months and the dean $3,300 for nine months.[50] Progress had been made in the life of North Texas State Normal College, but its financial problems were far from being solved.

chapter 9

"The Normal is Sadly Cramped"

One day the superintendent of the water works of Denton called on me and stated that he was going to cut our water off; that we were using too much, and that they couldn't afford it. I told him, "If you are going to do that, I want you to do it at once, because if Denton is going to cancel its contract with the state to furnish the college with 'an abundant supply of pure artesian water for all purposes,'" I wished him to do it at once, because I had a request before the legislature for a new building, and that two very prominent citizens of Oak Cliff had assured me that if the school was moved to Oak Cliff, they would give us sixty acres of land and duplicate with better buildings those we had at that time on the campus.

W. H. Bruce, 1939 Recollections

North Texas presidents were destined to spend half a century without a predictable source of building funds. Kendall had told his board that the school had the least adequate physical facilities in Texas. In 1902 the president printed a circular for the legislature, asking for a building "to provide all needed room for the Normal for many years to come, even allowing for the certain growth in the attendance much beyond the present enrollment and the further increase in the number of teachers."[1]

The original Normal Building had five classrooms of moderate size, three small rooms for office, library, and reading room, and a chapel seating 200 students. In 1899 four rooms were added, two of them of classroom size and two suitable only for dressing or cloak rooms. In 1901, the frame gymnasium had to be converted into a chapel, and the former chapel became a classroom. In 1902 the rear basement of the Old Normal Building was excavated deeper and a concrete floor laid to create a classroom for physics and chemistry.

THE HALLS ARE FILLED

"And now," President Kendall told the legislature, "with every foot of available floor space occupied, the Normal is sadly cramped in its efforts to accommodate the number of students which, for these first two years of its existence, has filled its halls." Including the old chapel, the gymnasium hall, and the basement, there were ten rooms used for class purposes. Only six were large enough for a class of forty or fifty. The other four were so crowded that blackboard work was difficult and satisfactory lighting and ventilation was impossible. Kendall thought some classes were too large and could be divided if more recitation rooms were available. The library was located in a room twelve by twenty feet, shelved on all sides from wainscot to ceiling, with natural lighting available only from a single window. With the gymnasium in use for classes and chapel, nothing but the outside grounds remained for physical exercise and sports.

Kendall asked for a new building to be located forty feet east of the Old Normal Building. He requested eight or ten classrooms, a "commodious, well-lighted" library room measuring at least thirty by forty feet, and a 1,000-capacity chapel. His circular included a contractor's estimate of $40,000 for the building and $10,000 for furniture and equipment. The president noted that twenty-seven counties surrounding Denton contained one-third of the white population of the state and required slightly more than one-third of the white public school teachers. From this region, "so easily reached by railway," the normal could expect its greatest support, although students were at that time enrolled from one hundred additional counties. A postscript on the circular added:

> N.B.—The building asked for in the above statement is the first which the North Texas State Normal has sought from a state appropriation. For while the school is now in its second annual session, having enrolled each year over five hundred students, representing every section of Texas, the ground and buildings (costing more than $25,000) were donated by Denton, without cost to the state, a fact which cannot be said concerning any other of the state educational institutions.

The students' *Normal Journal* in February 1903 earnestly endorsed the building plan so the school could "accomplish the full measure of success which the public school interests of the State rightfully demand of it."[2] The 28th Legislature added $40,000 to the North Texas appropriation and the following November the *Journal* reported exuberantly that the foundation was being laid for the new Normal Building. The old chapel was moved eighty feet east and 200 feet south to make room for the new structure, and it was announced that the chapel would finally be used as a gymnasium as originally intended.[3] President Kendall in March 1904 announced that the new building would be ready for occupancy in time for commencement exercises.[4] It was completed in May, but it was the next September before it could be equipped for use. The 1904 *Bulletin* [5] described it, rather predictably, as "a commodious and well-arranged structure."

This came to be known either as the Main Building or the Administration Building. It extended 194 feet east and west and ninety-eight feet north and south on the site later occupied by what today's student knows as the Auditorium Building. The structure had three entrances on the north and three on the south. On the first floor were offices, a reception room, library, and six classrooms. Two stairways led to the second floor where there were four classrooms and the chapel. This auditorium, ninety-eight by seventy-six feet, was "seated with opera chairs arranged in circular form" so that as many as 1,200 persons could be seated. Each classroom was forty by twenty-five feet. Eight basement rooms corresponded in size and number to those on the first floor, but these were left unfinished until another appropriation could be made, as it was "desired to use the money on hand in putting above the ground as large a building as possible."[6] Four of these rooms were in the center of the building and two in each wing. The basement area was designated for temporary use for storage and furnace rooms.

The furnace room was vacant for more than a year, however, before central heating facilities were added. The October 1905 *Normal Journal* rejoiced that a large boiler was being installed to provide steam heat, signaling that there would be "no more colds from loitering in the halls in wintry weather." An extra appropriation of $10,000 came for the 1905–6 biennium, and work began in December 1905 on the finishing of the basement.[7] The physics laboratory was located there, while the chemistry laboratory remained in the Old Normal Building. Two basement rooms were fitted as cloak rooms and the rest arranged for classroom use when needed. "A sort of rotunda" was made in the first floor to aid in the ventilation and lighting of the basement. The work was finished in March 1906, but the added classrooms weren't needed for the rest of that school year. Space remained so plentiful, in fact, that room was made for forty pupils attending a kindergarten operated in the Old Normal by the Denton Kindergarten Association.[8]

It seemed time to improve the grounds. The *Normal Journal* in December 1904 praised the construction of brick sidewalks around the new building, but by 1906 student dissatisfaction was expressed this way:

> Listen old students? Do you remember how we skated last year, when the ice was on the ground? "Yes, but there is no ice on the ground now, is there?" No, but there is plenty of slick mud, and we just "skoot" around whether we want to or not. We were much disgusted at the condition of some of our sidewalks not long since, when one of the young ladies of the Normal was seen to fall prostrate into the mud. The Normal students endorsed the good advice of the city papers concerning the improvement of our sidewalks. We need much better ones than we have.[9]

A year later, when President Bruce had been in office three months, a sidewalk leading from the Main Building diagonally to the southeast corner of the campus was removed and a new one heading straight to the south entrance substituted—a change lauded by the *Journal* because the baseball and football grounds were no longer crossed by a sidewalk, a factor which "caused the boys to make some bad plays." Another addition brought this editorial praise: "To add to the neatness and beauty of the Normal and its grounds a new fence is being built. . . of iron posts and iron railings. . . put up in an attractive style to remind one of Texas. . . . In connection with the improvements, several hitching posts have been placed along the north side for the convenience of visitors."[10]

OLD NORMAL BURNS

But the luxury of ample space was not to last. On August 24, 1907, the Old Normal Building was struck by lightning and destroyed by fire. The loss brought forth this mournful obituary in the *Journal,* written by J. A. Sanders:

> At the close of school in May, 1907, the "old Building" was in reasonable repair, fit for service, and was expected to last for generations. If it had remained in existence until school opened in September, 1907, every foot of its floor space would have been in use, the assignment of rooms being one for the Girls' Club, the Reagan Society, the Kendall-Bruce Society, physiological laboratory, ladies' rest room, and printing room, and two each for class rooms, chemical laboratory, natural history collections, and kindergarten.
>
> Its destruction caused deep sorrow in the hearts of the people who had built and lived around it, and of the students and teachers who had learned and taught in it.
>
> The actual property loss was about $25,000 with $5,000 insurance. The inconvenience to the school can hardly be estimated. It is hoped and believed that the next legislature will provide funds, with which to erect a building which, in points of attractiveness and usefulness, will at least equal, if not surpass the "old Building."[11]

The October 1907 *Journal* chronicled the damage of the fire to the students. The Reagan Society preserved its records, but "the Kendall-Bruce society was left destitute of all save its name." Cherished collections of pictures and plates were lost by the girls' groups, as were "the Mary Arden girls' greatest inspiration, the bust of William Shakespeare," the modern novel collection of the Current Literature Club, and the music of the Treble Clef and Glee Clubs.

The major emergency step to make up for the fire loss was the erection of a frame building southeast of the Main Building. "Not quite so large as the Gymnasium," it was fitted out by October as a chemistry laboratory.[12] Students applauded another improvement one month later: "The lighting of all the building with electricity is certainly an improvement. A few times last year it became so dark in the class rooms that the teachers were compelled to dismiss their classes. It is, indeed, a relief not to be compelled to strain your eyes on gloomy days. Lavatories are now in order. Will some one make a motion?"[13]

Kendall had sought unsuccessfully for a campus residence for the president, to be built at Hickory Street and Avenue A, the northeast corner of the campus, at a cost of $2,000 to $2,500.[14] He proposed to build it as his own expense, being reimbursed at a rate of $500 per year. The plan was not accepted and a president's home was not provided until 1909, when a $5,000 two-story frame structure was erected on the site of the Old Normal Building.[15]

PATCHING AND REPAIRING

The Main Building at first had not been fully used, but the Old Normal fire put a strain on the new structure, especially for science subjects. Enrollment had risen from 511 in 1901–2 to 670 in 1908–9. Furthermore, the legislative mandate to begin instruction in agriculture, manual training, and domestic science in September 1909 created an unexpected need for physical facilities almost totally lacking at the normal. To add to Bruce's building worries, the construction of the Main Building was unsatisfactory—constant repairing became necessary to keep it in usable condition. Architects in 1909 told Bruce that it was in dangerous condition. A contractor estimated that a broad concrete foundation costing $3,500 might save the building. The president recalled:

> Going to Austin, I reported this to the Governor and asked him for an emergency appropriation for that amount. He answered that these contractors merely wanted a job, and declined to give me the funds required.

> Returning to Denton, I found that the building had spread more than two inches while I was away. I then wrote this letter to the Governor:
>
> "Dear Sir:
>
> Please send someone in whom you have confidence to examine the building—the condition of which I reported to you. Those whose opinions I respect assure me that it is in a dangerous condition and growing worse. Please file this letter as I am filing a copy of it so that in the event of any disaster to the students attending here, the blame will not fall upon
>
> Yours truly,
>
> W. H. Bruce
>
> The next day I received a telegram from the Governor saying "File an application for $3,500, and let the work begin at once."[16]

The foundation repairs were made during the 1909–10 school year, and interior remodeling and the installation of sewage facilities was completed in the fall of 1910. But in spite of this, maintenance of the Main Building remained a serious problem for the rest of its life. The state normal regents complained in 1913 that "on account of defective foundation, and possibly other faults of construction, the main building is a source of constant trouble and expense, requiring repairs from time to time."[17] Two years later the regents again requested money for repair of the building.[18]

Bruce secured appropriations for a Science Building in 1909. In the meantime, however, the three vocational subjects added by the legislature complicated plans. The building was completed in 1910 at a cost of $35,000 plus $5,000 for equipment, but it had to serve many purposes other than science instruction. Although the *Journal* proclaimed that "in this beautiful structure we may read the history of our state,"[19] the faculty could read in it an unhappy marriage of too many functions. It contained six recitation rooms, chemical and physical laboratories, manual training shop, mechanical drawing room, domestic science rooms, model dining room, engine room, an office for teachers, and a large room for lectures in chemistry and physics.[20] Facilities for the agriculture students consisted of a three-acre block of land near the Normal purchased in the spring of 1910 for $750.[21] There each student was required to seed, cultivate, and harvest a one-fifth acre plot.[22]

OUT IN THE COUNTRY

Though the farmland may have been nice for agricultural studies, North Texas was beginning to feel the disadvantage of its semirural location away from the heart of Denton. In 1900 the fairgrounds occupied a great deal of acreage near the normal—an area roughly between Welch Street and Avenue A extending southward from West Hickory to what is now Eagle Drive. A race track was located about where a parking garage stands across Avenue A from the University Union of the 1980s and 1990s. The opening of the state school in 1901 generated a demand for residential lots around the college. A public auction in October 1903 disposed of the fairgrounds property.[23] Several hundred boardinghouses and private residences were built in the campus area. The normal was tied more closely to downtown Denton in 1910 by an electric streetcar line. The tracks came out West Oak from the square to Fry Street, one block south to West Hickory, and thence westward along the northern edge of the campus to Avenue C, where the cars turned south to Eagle Drive (then Mill Street) and then west to the foot of the hill on Highland Park. The car barns were built just west of what became the No. 1 green of the North Texas golf course.[24] Two separate telephone systems operated throughout Denton from 1903 to 1917.[25]

But other utilities were more of a problem. As has been noted, the Main Building was lighted by electricity in 1907, although this was apparently from a self-contained power source. The city of Denton purchased the water and light plant from the Denton Water and Light Company in June 1905, and a $25,000 bond issue was voted to provide for extensions.[26] Nevertheless, Dr. Bruce had problems in providing utilities needed for the new Science Building. After some delay, he and the local board members purchased a gas manufacturing plant in August 1910 to provide gas for the domestic science cooking room and the chemical laboratory.[27] The local board in January 1910 recommended the purchase of electrical generating equipment for the Science Building and Dr. Bruce urged State Superintendent Bralley to approve the expenditure.[28] One year later, though, the normal president sent this plea to the secretary of state:

> The need of the power is now imperative. All probability of our being able to contract with the City of Denton to supply power at any

> rate approximating economy has been despaired of. The City claims that it would cost $2000 to run a line from the power plant to the Normal, and that for only the one patron it could not afford the expense. Even if the Normal should put up that line, and take out the cost in power, the rate to us would be 15 cts. to 10 cts. per kilowatt, while the company proposing the installation of a plant is willing to guarantee that the cost of power and light thereafter will be 2 cts. per kilowatt.[29]

In June 1911 the president reported to the State Board of Education that the power plant recently installed in the manual training department was much more satisfactory than if the department had been left dependent upon the city.[30] By 1913 the city had a natural gas system.[31]

Another utility problem was created by the city over water. The 1899 act creating the state school specified that the conveyance of the private normal property to the state would "bind the city of Denton to furnish for the use of said school an abundant supply of pure artesian water free of cost to the State, for all the purposes of said school." But the construction of city sewer lines in 1909 and the installation of sanitary facilities in the Main Building in 1910 increased the normal's use of water. In 1912, President Bruce met the city threat to cut off the water as noted at the first of this chapter. He further described his exchange with the city water superintendent:

> He replied, "Why, according to that, you could even put in a swimming pool."
>
> I replied, "Yes, and as soon as I can get a suitable place for it, I'm going to put in one."
>
> I will state here that the college now has a very fine swimming pool.
>
> Emory Smith of Denton, who was for several years a member of our local board, told the commissioners that if they tried to abrogate Denton's contract, he would use *his* influence to remove the school. Nothing else has ever been said about decreasing our supply of water.[32]

Dr. Bruce's last sentence, written in 1939, failed to foresee that the water supply clause would became controversial again.

BOOKS, HEAT, AND EXERCISE

The manual training and domestic science departments took up the space in the Science Building that had been intended for the library and gymnasiums for boys and girls. The normal was left with a room twenty-five by forty feet to serve as library and reading room and with inadequate physical education and athletic facilities.[33] In addition, the school needed a central heating plant. These needs, which really had nothing in common, led Bruce to ask the 32nd Legislature for a combined library, gymnasium, and heating plant to cost $50,000. He also requested $7,500 to equip the building and $10,000 for "library, apparatus, repairs, equipment, and improvement." This last item had been given an annual lump sum of $3,000 in recent years, and from it had come all expenses for library books, building repairs, furniture, janitors' supplies, and grounds maintenance. But even though the new building was to be a library, Bruce's requested increase in this fund was not for more books but rather "for more extensive repairs and renovations needed here."[34]

The legislature appropriated $50,000 for the building, and work began in February 1912. It was supposed to be completed by September, but it was 1913 before the building was available. The final cost was $55,000. This was a three-story structure of steel, brick, and reinforced concrete, with the library occupying an entire floor. Students at midcentury knew this as the Historical Building, with the Museum in part of the old library area. After a 1990s remodeling, this became instructional space for business administration and was renamed Curry Hall for the first business dean, O. J. Curry. The gymnasiums occupied the lower (really a basement) floor, and there were classrooms and meeting rooms for the literary societies on the third level.[35] It was January 1916 before the library area was completely furnished with steel stacks for books, reading tables, and chairs. There were then something more than 8,000 books, forty-eight magazines, and two daily newspapers available to the students.[36]

The central heating plant requested by Dr. Bruce was omitted from the Library Building, and instead a small boiler house was specified. The low bid on this was $240. The president was authorized to sell three frame buildings on the campus, and one of these was the old chapel-turned-gymnasium, which had to be removed to make way for the library. Dr. Bruce arranged with a construction company to build the boiler house ten feet longer than specified and take the gymnasium building in payment.[37]

By 1914 the inventory of expenditures for buildings, grounds, furniture, equipment and apparatus made since 1901 totaled $233,682. Most of this was accounted for by the Main Building, Science Building, Library Building, president's home, agriculture ground and tool house, temporary chemical laboratory, janitor's house, fireman's house and lot, garage, boiler house, athletic grounds, and the temporary Model Training School added in time for opening in January 1914.[38] A $50,000 appropriation made possible the next step, the removal of manual training and home economics facilities from the Science Building. Construction on the Manual Arts Building began in January 1914, and it was completed in September 1915. A supplemental appropriation of $15,000 was required for equipment, and the building was not used until September 1916. This structure was later known as the Art Building.[39] Hopes for central heating were realized in 1915 with the construction of the Power Plant at a cost of $35,000.[40]

SITTING IN THE WINDOWS

The lack of a permanent home for the training school remained a serious problem, one highlighted by a long editorial in the *Campus Chat* in January 1917.[41]

> Not only are many students without rooms, but a number of teachers as well have none in which to meet their classes. Some of the teachers have been using the laboratories in which to give their lectures. Others occupy any room they can find large enough to accommodate their excessively large classes. A number of classes are so over-crowded that the students are compelled to sit in the windows, on chairs, and even two sit on the single-desk seats. More than one class with as many as sixty-five students is compelled because of a lack of accommodations to gather in rooms which have seating capacities for only forty-four students.

Concerning the gymnasium, the editorial complained of the lack of space for physical education activities and of the condition that compelled a class of seventy boys to line up for the use of five showers that most of the time delivered nothing but cold water.

The 35th Legislature responded to the need for better training school and education class facilities by appropriating $80,000 in the spring of 1917. The Education Building was supposed to be completed by September 1918.[42] Construction was delayed during the World War, however, and it was January 1919 before it was put into use. The building was located just south of the original campus on ground between Sycamore and Chestnut Streets purchased by the college "assisted by the generous citizens of Denton."

The Education Building much later housed the School of Business Administration and in the 1960s and 1970s, it was known as the Language-Government Building. The first floor contained offices of the education faculty and the training school domestic science laboratory. The second and third floors were occupied by the training school. A special feature of the third floor was a large observation room, designed to give college classes the opportunity to observe demonstration lessons by a critic teacher and his class. This also served as a training school assembly room.[43] This same land purchase also yielded a two-story frame building, the former home of President Kendall, which was used as the Music Hall. At this point the valuation of all buildings and grounds was listed as $367,770, with equipment valued at an additional $91,201.[44]

The old training school had been converted for wartime use as a Student Army Training Corps barracks. In 1919 Coach J. W. St. Clair found few opponents who would schedule basketball games on outdoor courts. He proposed that the barracks-training school building be remodeled. In 1920 the building was widened, the roof raised, and a hardwood floor laid to create what was known as the Men's Gymnasium for many years.[45] In the 1922 report of the Board of Regents, this was listed as an "Improvised Gymnasium" valued at $5,881. The same inventory also noted two frame structures, a domestic science demonstration cottage at $8,643, and a sanitarium at $9,997.[46]

ARMY TENTS NEEDED?

At the opening of the summer term in 1920, Dr. Bruce met all newly enrolled students in the Main Building auditorium. Some 1,500 crowded into a space designed for 1,200, leading to this report in the *Chat:*

> When the enrollment is complete, the student body will have to be present in chapel on the installment plan. The president said that a new

auditorium was needed, and that he would direct his energies toward securing one. He also assured the students that all who come will be cared for, both as to classes and housing, even if he had to erect a miniature cantonment of army tents on the campus and open up a cafeteria.[47]

Bruce asked in 1922 for $300,000 for an administration building and equipment, $160,000 for an auditorium and equipment, and $300,000 for dormitories and equipment. Pointing out that the expansion of the institution to a four-year college made more buildings, teachers, and equipment imperative, he reported:

> The present administration building, constructed in 1903, was inadequate at the time it was built. The school has entirely outgrown it now. The offices in it are too small. They are dark and poorly ventilated. And the smallness of the number of class-rooms, making it necessary for several teachers to use the same room, makes an efficient schedule of recitations impossible.
>
> But were the present building adequate in size, it should be abandoned. Although it has been rodded from time to time to prevent the collapse of its walls, it has steadily deteriorated until during the past session it was found necessary to brace the north walls with huge beams to prevent their falling.
>
> The institution should by all means have a modern fireproof auditorium of sufficient size to accommodate at least the present student body. The present auditorium, which is almost too uncomfortable for use during four or five months of the year, seats about one-half or one-third of the student body. Besides, being on the second floor, it is not accessible enough, it is too small, and it has become dangerously unsafe, and notwithstanding recent repairs, its continued and rapid deterioration is manifest.
>
> By all means the auditorium should be separate from any other buildings. This recommendation is in conformity with the opinions of all college administrators everywhere.
>
> The growing needs of the institution and the inadequacy of living

> conditions here render dormitories and suitable places for the students to secure meals an absolute necessity.[48]

The State Board of Control recommended an appropriation of $500,000 for these buildings, $260,000 less than requested.[49] The 38th Legislature cut this further to $300,000 for an administration building and $10,000 for a temporary building to house administrative offices until the new structure was complete. The temporary unit was constructed largely from materials taken from the old Main Building, and later became the Harriss Gymnasium for women. It was located on the south side of Chestnut Street, east of the Men's Gymnasium.[50]

Bruce announced to his faculty on March 13, 1923, the appropriation for the Administration Building and the passage of a law changing the name of the institution to North Texas State Teachers College.[51] Some two months later he announced his resignation as president. Thus, the State Normal College era and the Bruce administration came to a close. The major building needs had been largely met with one major exception: dormitories. This was to be the subject of a long struggle of the teachers college period.

chapter 10

Life in Dr. Bruce's Normal

We never dismiss a student because he is slow or dull. Experience has taught me that often the apparently dullest boy makes the best scholar, or if he fails to make a good scholar, he frequently makes a good man and good citizen.

W. H. Bruce, 1910

In the early years they called themselves "Normalites." In later years they were likely to say they attended "Dr. Bruce's Normal." They came from farms and small towns in more than one hundred Texas counties. Most of them were either Baptists or Methodists, with a sizable representation for other Protestant groups and maybe half a dozen Catholics and a single member of the Jewish faith enrolled occasionally. Their average age was twenty or more, and for a good many years high school graduates in the student body were in a distinct minority. Men were always outnumbered by women students, usually by better than a 2-to-1 ratio, and the largest numbers were studying to teach in the elementary grades. Well more than half were the children of farmers and ranchers, and the next largest group came from merchants' families. Relatively few were the sons and daughters of teachers and professional men.[1]

Their parents sent them to a school and to a town noted for maintaining a wholesome atmosphere and a stern discipline for the protection of the young people. The normalite either had already been or would soon become a teacher, and he was expected to behave in every way in a manner befitting one of that calling. First President Kendall and then Dr. Bruce served as guardians and enforcers of these high standards. As soon as the state normal and the neighboring Girls' Industrial College were created, the city of Denton voted itself dry, at which time the infant *Normal Journal* congratulated the citizens for their successful effort to remove the saloon and "this, the greatest of all, temptations."[2]

The normalites typically arrived in Denton by train and were instructed to go by buggy or (after 1907) by streetcar to the normal office, where they would be aided in finding a boardinghouse. In the early years they could board for about fourteen dollars a month—scholarship students were expected to get by on ninety dollars for the thirty-six-week long session and nonscholarship students for a little more than $140 per session. By the time of the World War, boarding rates had gone up to sixteen dollars to twenty dollars per month, but then included conveniences such as electric lights, gas heat, and modern plumbing. The opportunities to work one's way through school were limited, and the practice was officially discouraged. Within ten years there were eighty "first-class" boardinghouses near the campus, and the number was to rise to nearly 200. The boardinghouse proprietor became an arm of the normal staff in enforcing regulations governing student behavior. The houses, in turn, were subject to inspection by the president and the faculty to make sure that regulations concerning sanitation and the provision of heating and lighting were observed.

During the Kendall administration the number of long-session students rose from 511 to 584, while summer normal figures went from 270 to 457. (It should be noted that students were counted in the enrollment of a session regardless of when they arrived or left, and regardless of which term or terms they attended.) In the fall of 1908 Bruce told the faculty that he wanted to enroll 666 students during that year. The *Journal* took up the watch cry, "666 students by the close of school." The total figure the year before had been 567, so there was some doubt expressed. But on April 21, 1909, with classes out for the San Jacinto Day holiday, J. N. Simmons, a young man from Mississippi came into Bruce's office and enrolled. The president pinned a tag reading "I am 666" on the student's coat lapel and sent him out on the campus for all to see.[3]

The following year a decline was expected because of poor crops, a bad drought in the state, and the removal of state scholarship appointments—but the enrollment rose to 724. The figure passed a thousand for the first time in 1913–14, when the long session total was 1,030 and the summer figure 1,026. That boom was caused by the rush of students to get diplomas under the three-year system before the new junior-college standards went into effect; the regular session figure sagged to 636 the next year. Summer enrollment continued its upward climb uninterrupted, however, and was never again bested by the regular figure during the state normal period. Between 1917 and 1921, while the long-session registration hovered around 1,100, the number of summer students climbed from 1,700 to 2,406.[4] In the last year of the state normal college era, 1922–23, regular enrollment was 1,713 and summer registration was 2,670. The school was not only by far the largest of the state normals but had become one of the larger summer schools in the nation, ranking itself ahead of such schools as Iowa State Teachers, the University of Minnesota, University of Texas, New York University, Peabody College for Teachers, Ohio University, and Harvard.[5]

THE DISCIPLINE OF THAT BELL

That Normal bell, that Normal bell,
How many hearts with wonder swell,
The boys and girls and teachers, too,
Obey its summons without ado.

Probably nothing better symbolized life at Dr. Bruce's Normal for the students than the class and curfew bell, eulogized in this verse in the *Normal Journal* in 1915. Later university students knew this as the victory bell at football games without realizing the extent to which it once regulated the comings and goings of normal students. The bell began its tolling in the Old Normal Building and was inherited with that building by the state normal. Its weight wasn't suited to the 1891 construction, though, and an architect in 1904 recommended to President Kendall that the bell be removed and placed outside the building, because its rigging had caused defects in the brickwork.[6] This was done, robbing the students of one of their favorite campus tales as reported here:

> No one, not even the bravest of the boys, would go up into the bell-tower of the old Normal building at Denton after dark. The place was supposed to be haunted by a ghost. Whether or not this was true, no one knew, but people living near the school-grounds had often on windy nights heard shrieks and cries of agony issuing from the old tower. Many attempts had been made to discover the cause of this, but no one had been found who would dare ascend to the haunted place after night-fall.[7]

The next location of the bell is recorded by another student verse writer:

> On the campus of the Normal is a platform made of wood
> From it hangs a bell of iron, placed there for a purpose good.
> And at seven in the evening we can hear its kindly chime;
> Gently, it reminds the students that it is now study time.[8]

The bell's ringing dispatched students from class to class and it ordered them to their boarding houses at 7:00 each class night. In 1905 the faculty ordered the sounding of the bell at 5:00 P.M. "as a reminder to us that we should lay aside our books and rest our minds, but exercise our bodies," sending students for evening strolls around the campus.[9] The bell continued these functions from the roof of the newly constructed Heating Plant in 1915. The yearly April Fool prank was to remove the clapper and hide it—it once disappeared for two years until Business Manager J. W. Smith offered a reward for its recovery, after which the clapper was welded in place. The bell rang the call to battle on Freshman Day, when boys rallied around the flagpole to try to raise their class standard. The bell was kept ringing all day and all night on November 11, 1918, to celebrate the signing of the Armistice.[10] But to the normal student this sound remained basically the voice of Bruce, who ruled every aspect of their lives with a firm hand.

The regulations were designed to keep the whereabouts of students known at all times and to keep them at their studies. No student was allowed to leave the city at any time during a term without the president's approval and without reporting to him upon returning. Tuesdays through Saturdays were school days, and any student absent without cause "by that act severs his connections with the school." Except for Saturday and Sunday nights, students were required to remain in their boardinghouses to prepare their recitations between 7:00 and 10:30 P.M. The curfew bell notified them that they had ten minutes to return home for the start of the study period. Students were required to be orderly at all times, to avoid noisy sports during afternoon study hours, and "to refrain from singing or playing upon musical instruments during study hours at their boarding houses." While classes were in session, off-duty students were required to devote the time to studying and were forbidden to assemble in the halls of school buildings. "To be informed at all times as to the boarding places of students" was stated clearly as "the province of the President." The place of residence was to be chosen from an approved list, and no move could be made during the term without prior permission for good reason.

As might be expected, each normal "young lady" was carefully protected by college regulations from undesirable contact with men. The girls were advised:

> Social visits between the young men and young ladies of the Normal School are limited to Sundays, Sunday evenings and Saturday evenings. At those times young ladies are expected to receive their callers in the parlor and not to entertain them in promenading streets or on the porches or the lawns of the boarding premises. Neither are young men supposed to give attention to young ladies or young ladies to receive attention from young men in the library, reading room, class

> room, halls, corridors or on campus during the school days. These days must be devoted to work, and not to society.
>
> At boarding houses where meals are furnished to both men and women, those not rooming at such houses are required to go only at meal time, and to leave immediately after the meal has been served. . . .
>
> The Telephone of the boarding house must be under the control of the proprietor. Students use it only by permission, and then only for the transaction of necessary business. They must not use it for idle conversation, making or accepting social engagements. Young lady students are not allowed to communicate with young men or young men with young ladies over the telephone. Whenever it is necessary for one to send a message to the other, such messages must be communicated to the proprietor of the boarding house, who will deliver the message and return the answer.[11]

There were only two circumstances under which one could attend theaters or other public places of amusement: by permission of Bruce, or in parties in charge of a faculty member. Buggy riding at night was forbidden to all students. Before a woman student was permitted to receive attention or visits from a young man who was not a normal student, she would have to obtain Bruce's permission. This permission had to be received for each separate occasion, and he would grant it only if he had a letter of approval of such practice from the girl's parents. All social visits had to end at 10:00 P.M.; young lady students permitting a violation of this regulation hour were not allowed to receive further attention of young men, either normal students or others, for the rest of that session.

Lest it be thought that these were mere catalog regulations, not enforced in practice, consider the case of C——, a male student summoned before Bruce and W. D. Butler in 1909. The president made these notes during the interview:

> He says that during last session he took liberties with I——, on porch at Mr. Gant's. He tried to kiss her and put his arm around her—she resisted, but still allowed his attentions afterwards.
>
> Says that during the present session he kissed N—— when calling on her at her home—put his arm around her—she kissed him— Went

> out at night with her several times—to Majestic—to church, took no liberties on way. Have been with her several times since kissed her. Have kissed her several times—about six times.
>
> Have been with B——. On two occasions I have put my arm around her and kissed her. Sat. Mar. 6 came from Majestic to Mr. C. Bell's. Stayed on porch until 10:30 P.M. with her—put my arm around her and kissed her—and she kissed me. She did not resent it. Went to church with her on night of Sunday Mar. 7. Stopped again on porch and kissed her, put arm around her—Have not been with her since.

The B—— mentioned last above was summoned to the president's office on the same day, with this statement resulting:

> Miss B—— on being questioned whether any boy had taken any liberties with her or acted in any ungentlemanly manner, voluntarily says that on Saturday night, March 6 C—— went with her to the picture show—when they returned to Mr. C. Bell's she and C—— took a seat on the porch until between 10:30 and 11 P.M.—That he put his arm around her and kissed her—that she kissed him—that she has been very sorry for it ever since—that she knows the conduct wrong—that she has not been with him since—that she will not go with him again—that she is young and thoughtless—that she now sees the wrong of the conduct and will never be guilty of it again.
>
> Says this is the only time in her life that she has been guilty of such conduct and will never again.
>
> The above was told in private office in the presence of W. H. Bruce alone.

These notes, dramatically headed "The Case of C——," were preserved by the president, but he unfortunately neglected to inform posterity of the disposition of the case. Three days later he compiled two typed pages of notes on "The Case of M——," a young lady who stayed out until 2:00 A.M. at an Elks' Hall ball and missed her classes in trigonometry and physics the next day. She also visited the home of a friend on a study night and professed great surprise to Bruce that a party was in progress, although she didn't return home until

11:25, and Dr Bruce noted, "It develops that there was a dance at Mr. M——'s." But here again the records fail to tell us of the end of M——'s story.

Other letters of Bruce, however, make clear the fate that awaited the fallen female. A 1911 letter to a father, for example, said:

> It came to my knowledge that she has been associating with a man of this town with whom it is dangerous for any girl to go with. She has done this in violation of the rules and of course against my advice and without my knowledge. For this reason I could not under any circumstances keep her here longer.
>
> I advise that you write her at once to come home and send her the money with which to pay her fare.
>
> I would not require you to take her away if I did not have absolute proof of what I have written.

Bruce was prepared to take a matter to any authority necessary to correct a situation. In 1911 he wrote to U. S. Senator C. A. Culberson of such a case:

> For some time the authorities of this school have been annoyed by some employees of the United States (civil service men) undertaking, and sometimes succeeding in enticing girl students from their boarding places at night, presumably for immoral purposes.
>
> Will you please direct me how to proceed to report to the proper authorities such parties as I may find in future causing this trouble.

Fifteen days later he wrote the senator's secretary to thank him for his answering letter, saying, "At the time I wrote Senator Culberson I was not sure that I knew the specific person about whom the most recent complaint was made. Since that time I have ascertained the person, but the postmaster at this place has accepted his resignation, so that now there is no need for further investigation."

In a letter nearly 1,000 words long, Bruce wrote a father in 1910 to ask him to quit asking for special privileges for his daughter. The parents had asked that the daughter, F——, be called to the phone anytime she was called by a young man of the town. Bruce advised the father of the telephone regulations, told him how poorly F—— was doing in her class work, and suggested that she not be allowed to receive the company of town boys. If the father persisted in allowing his daughter such freedom, Bruce asked the man "in advance to relieve me from any further responsibility concerning the result of her year's work."

Another coed in 1910 was caught by Bruce sneaking out to meet boys of the town, whom she refused to identify. Bruce wired her brother "Come for W at once. Do not delay." He followed the wire with a special delivery letter of explanation:

> I did this for the reason that her admissions, made voluntarily, and with apparent indifference, even boldness, leads me to the conclusion that as she has now thrown off all restraint and renounced the authority of the school, she may more openly associate with those with whom she ought not to come in contact at any time, or she may conclude not to remain here until you can be informed of the status of affairs, hence the necessity of your coming at once.

Another woman student was sent home by Bruce in 1910 for improper behavior and leading another girl astray with her. Bruce sent the girl who had been "misled" to school at the Durant, Oklahoma, normal school and carried on a long correspondence with her in 1910, encouraging her to reform and make a good record. The first girl, whom Bruce blamed for the episode, wrote to inquire about her grade records. He responded:

> It is useless for me to look up the record to show whether any or all of your Freshman conditions have been removed, for when a student here has been guilty of the grossly reprehensible conduct that you were guilty of, all credits on our books are forfeited, for under no circumstances should we send out in the state as a teacher of young girls one who has acted as you have with our stamp of approval and recommendation as a model for young children.
>
> Of course I wish you well wherever you go, and I have absolutely no feeling in the premises, but I must discharge my sacred duty to the children of this state in protecting them from unwholesome influences.

To the father of the girl who went to Oklahoma, Bruce reported the outcome of his investigations: "This man in question was a drummer, not living here. The other was a clerk in a store here, whom I had discharged." In those days, the president apparently regarded himself as in a constant state of war against the troublesome town boys. In a letter to another father, he explained the problem this way:

> your daughter . . . did not make passing grades in all her work during the first half of the session.
>
> I do not think it best that young girl students receive company of young men of the town while here. Our experience in the past is that by far the majority of those who have such company fail to pass in their work. . . .
>
> I do not think a reasonable amount of company would operate against a student, but even if the girls would wish to be reasonable in the matter, the boys will not permit them if once they are permitted to begin attentions.

It is helpful to remember that during this period there were twice as many women students as men enrolled in the Denton normal; there just weren't enough of the "approved" normal boys to go around on company nights.

A barber presented a written request in 1914 for lady students to be permitted to enter his place of business to secure such services as shampooing, facial massage, and manicuring. He promised that as soon as the business would justify, he would employ a lady attendant and provide a separate room for the lady students. The faculty granted his request on condition that two or more girls enter his place of business while one of them was having work done and that permission be withdrawn if he failed to run the establishment in an entirely satisfactory manner.[12]

Other matters than boy-girl relationships occupied Bruce and the faculty. Upon request he would write a student or even a former student that a merchant claimed an unpaid bill against the individual; if the affair was not settled, Bruce would write the state superintendent concerning the person's fitness to hold a teaching certificate.

Although discipline appears severe, the student was not always treated without mercy. In 1913 a freshman boy admitted stealing money from the telegraph office during the Christmas holidays and asked for permission to remain in school. His request was brought up at a faculty meeting. After full discussion the following resolution was adopted: "Resolved that Mr. —— be permitted to make a public statement at the Chapel period to the student body, and that if such statement is made in the proper spirit, he be permitted to remain in school with the understanding that he will not be given a certificate this session, even though he should make all the work prescribed for his class."[13]

But far less serious offenses also engaged the attention of the full faculty, as shown in this 1914 report:

> ——, a member of the present session was, by motion, invited to appear before the Faculty and show cause why his certificate and diploma should not be withheld. The charge against Mr. —— was that he frequently used profane and indecent language. Mr.—— acknowledged that the charge was true, but promised to desist from the use of such language in the future. By motion, his character was passed, but he was notified that his certificate and diploma would be cancelled if he failed to keep his promise.[14]

Preserved in the archives are crib notes, an examination paper, and the following 1909 letter, apparently extracted as a condition of reform:

> To the teachers of the Normal:
>
> In my History examination I carried with me a paper containing notes on the History. I carried this paper for the purpose of helping me on my examination. I realise now how wrong it was to do such a thing. I am glad Miss Mitchel saw the paper for if she had not, I might have been tempted to have done wrong again. I am sorry I did such a mean act and I would like to prove to the teacher that I can do the work and do it honestly.

The files are full of the president's letters to parents, advising them that it was a waste of their money to keep an indolent child in school. But he left the decision to the parents, as this 1910 letter explains:

> I make it a rule to deal perfectly frankly with students and patrons. Whenever a student fails to make what I believe to be a good effort and is failing to meet the requirements of the school, I tell his parents frankly.
>
> We never dismiss a student because he is slow or dull. Experience has taught me that often the apparently dullest boy makes the best scholar, or if he fails to make a good scholar, he frequently makes a good man and good citizen.
>
> My observation and experience for thirty years has given me great patience with those who are slow. Of course I want them to try.
>
> This school is but eight years old, and still we have found that many who had the hardest time to do the work here have made the best teachers and have won the best reputation.
>
> We never discharge a student unless it is a question of character. Where it is a question of failure to do his work, the parent must assume the responsibility, as he has to meet the expenses. It would be wrong, in my opinion, not to notify a parent that his child was failing to meet the demands of the classroom.

But he would encourage any student to the limit if he saw signs of promise in that student. He wrote one father:

> Your daughter, C——, had become discouraged and was going to withdraw from school and go home, but when she came to inform me of her decision, I found she had no real cause for discouragement, and I have encouraged her to remain. She has decided to stay with your permission.
>
> As our course of study here is hard for those who have not had good previous preparation, very few of those who have not had a first class high school course before coming here, make good grades the first term, or perhaps the first two terms; but our experience has been that boys and girls who come from rural schools, and who hold out, finally make the best students we have, and succeed best as teachers.
>
> Miss C—— has no cause for disappointment because she has found it impossible to make as high grades in the subjects here as she did in

> those she had in the rural school. We must hold here a high standard for we are expected to prepare our students to teach the various subjects.
>
> I think that it is the best thing that you could do to write C——, and encourage her to stay with her work and "dig it out. " I hope you will do this at once.

With the elevation to junior college rank, the college ceased publication of detailed regulations for student behavior in its bulletins in 1914. In its place, a general statement of discipline was inserted, calling attention to separate printed regulations which every student received. This statement, which appeared essentially unchanged during the rest of the Bruce administration, read:

> Those entering a Normal School are expected to be of sufficient maturity and to have come with a purpose so serious and definite that espionage is unnecessary. By far the greater number of students who come here are eager, earnest, and industrious young men and women, who cheerfully comply with all regulations. But experience has demonstrated the necessity of having well defined regulations concerning the conduct at school and at the boarding places, for the guidance of those whose inclination or whose judgment renders proper direction necessary.
>
> Upon matriculation the student is given a printed copy of the regulations concerning the conduct of students and he is requested not to register if unwilling to conform to the requirements. Whenever a student willfully violates the regulations, ignores the efforts of the faculty to assist him in his character building, manifests a spirit of insubordination to authority, or shows himself out of harmony with the school and its ideals, he is advised that he is not in the right school and is requested to withdraw.
>
> Continuance in school depends upon punctual class attendance and obedience to regulations. Students who must continually be admonished, restrained, reprimanded, or denied the usual privileges, are undesirable and they will not be retained in the school.
>
> The purpose of the school is to train teachers for the public schools

of Texas, and it should not inflict upon the children of the State as teachers those whose character, habits of thought, or low ideals unfit them for directors and exemplars of the young.

To all those who are seeking opportunity to work under wholesome influences, favorable conditions, competent and sympathetic direction, is extended a hearty welcome. Those who are merely seeking diversion, change of environment, or increased social advantages, and those incapable or unwilling to lead the life of a student are advised—urged—to go elsewhere.[15]

THE NORMALITES ORGANIZE

Even within the framework of what today seem to be impossibly restrictive student regulations, a variety of activities occupied the student outside the classroom. The dominant social organization—-the literary society—came into being when the school was little more than a week old. "A body of energetic young men" assembled in the chapel to organize the school's first society. The chairman used "eloquent oratory" on his audience, moving a *Normal Journal* reporter to write, "It would have caused Demosthenes to bury his face in his hands, and in tears, proclaim that Grecian oratory sank into insignificance when compared with that of the distinguished Normalite."[16] In spite of this, the group had to adjourn for further study. On September 30, 1901, the second meeting debated a proposed constitution and, unable to agree, broke into two factions. One group moved to another room and formed the Kendall-Bruce Literary Society, thereafter to be known familiarly as the K-B. The remaining boys formed the McKinley Society, soon changed to the Euphonian Literary Society. The following year it was renamed the Minnie Marsh Literary Society, and women students were admitted. It did not survive the second year of school.[17]

The K-B got its strong rival on October 6, 1902, when the Reagan Literary Society was formed[18] with the purpose being "to further our mental, moral and social development, to attain a higher excellency in general composition and oratory, to better fit ourselves for the duties of citizenship, and to create a greater desire for literary purposes, etc." The K-B and the Reagan societies confronted each other regularly in public debates. In their first year the topic was "Resolved, that organized labor, as it exists today, is calculated to promote the best interests to human society."[19] After he became president, Bruce asked that the K-B change its name to the Robert E. Lee Literary Society so that his name would not be associated with the factionalism of the two groups.[20] During most of the normal college years, the young men took part in the Henry W. Grady Literary Society during the summer session.

The Mary Arden Club was organized as a literary society for women on October 12, 1902, under the supervision of Miss Edith L. Clark, who had just joined the faculty.[21] Its purpose was the study of Shakespeare's works. The first term of its existence was devoted to the study of *As You Like It.* A more general organization was the Current Literature Club, founded on October 20, 1901, under the supervision of Miss M. Anne Moore and Miss Annie Webb Blanton.[22] Its subjects of study were *McClure's, Harper's, The Century,* and *Cosmopolitan* magazines, and current events. The C. L. C. sponsored the first "Lyceum Entertainment" on the campus in February 1903—a dramatic reading of "David Harum" in which a man named Edward P. Elliott impersonated twelve characters. This moved the *Journal* to comment, "From the interest shown in these entertainments, and from the packed house that greeted Mr. Elliott, we feel sure a complete course of lyceum lectures would be appreciated by the students, and hope that arrangements for such can be made for thc coming year."[23]

The club presented a second number in April, the "Imperial Hand Bell Ringers." Another social highlight of that first year of women's societies was the open session of the Current Literature Club in February 1903. Seats were reserved for various clubs, draped in their colors. The Glee Club sang, two Denton women delivered addresses, Miss M. Manora Boylan of the faculty rendered several selections including "Little Boy Blue," a student read a book review, a debate was held, and while the judges were deliberating, another Denton woman entertained with instrumental solos.[24]

Other special-interest groups formed 1902–3 were the Simpkins Sketching Club, for young ladies interested in art; the N.T.S.N. Glee Club, a male chorus that gave programs in the chapel every Saturday evening; the Young Men and Young Ladies Glee Club, which attended a singing convention at Garza; and the Treble Clef Club, a musical group for young ladies. Since classes met from Tuesday through Saturday, a great deal of club activity was scheduled on Monday.

The number of clubs proliferated during the normal years. There was the Mandolin and Guitar Club in 1903; the Oratorical Association in 1904; the

Stone-Horn Octette and Trio Club in 1906; the Octette of Strings and Orpheus Octette in 1908; the Band and Orchestra in 1911; the Press Club in 1912; the YMCA and YWCA, and the T-Club for athletic lettermen in 1915; the Lillie Bruce Dramatic Club and the Arts and Crafts Club in 1918; the French Club and a variety of county and regional clubs starting in 1919; the Ellen H. Richards Club for home economics majors; and two veterans' organizations, the A.E.F. Club and the Silver Stripers, in 1920.

THE GREEN AND WHITE SOARS

The debating activities within and among the literary societies quite naturally led the men students to attempt intercollegiate speaking competition. The Reagan and Kendall-Bruce societies arranged a debate with a San Marcos Normal society in 1904, but it was called off.[25] The two groups found their first off-campus opponent at a local school, the Southwestern Christian College, in March 1905. The following month they debated with Decatur Baptist College in the normal chapel.[26]

In 1907 the boys' literary societies at Southwest Texas State Normal challenged the Lees and the Reagans to a debate. The challenge was accepted, and one member from each of the North Texas societies defeated the visitors from San Marcos. The victory was repeated on the Southwest Texas campus the next year, but a string of North Texas defeats began in 1909. The San Marcos school brought along twenty-three men students for the festivities. The Oratorical Association was host to a reception, with music by the band. During the evening program the Trio Club, Orpheus Octette, and Octette of Strings provided music. The day was "a round of dinners, carriage drives, receptions, banquets, etc."[27] The rivalry blossomed rapidly, outdoing anything that athletic competition yet had to offer.

The West Texas Normal College at Canyon wanted to enter the yearly competition, and at a meeting of representatives from San Marcos, Canyon, and Denton in Fort Worth in 1912, the Texas Normal Debating League was formed. Each school would meet each of the other two, all debating the same question, the home team always having the affirmative. The debates were held on the same night at all three of the schools.[28] The new league stimulated debate activity and raised it to a higher level. Of twelve intercollegiate debates in five years, the Denton normal won ten, winning both the affirmative and negative of the question for five years in succession. Normals at Commerce and Huntsville later joined the Texas league.[29]

GETTING THE NEWS

The story of student publications began with the opening session of the Denton normal and the founding of the monthly *North Texas State Normal Journal.* For the first five years it served as newspaper, magazine, and yearbook for the Normalites. It carried short stories, poems, literary criticism, a roundup of national and international news, and sections on clubs, athletics, personals, and other campus news. The final month's issue was given over to each of the classes for class pictures, prophecies, and other features characteristic of school annuals. In January 1906 the *Journal* staff asked for and got a student vote in favor of an annual to replace the usual May issue of the *Journal.* The result was the 1906 *Cotton-Tail,* a 114-page book with pictures of the faculty, classes, clubs, and athletic groups, along with the same type of literary material usually found in the *Journal.* Among the verse was "The Ballad of the Normalite," the story of a love affair between students with a none-too-subtle jest at Kendall, "the wily President." It read in part:

> "I read it that the kissers shall not go to this old school,
> But I will kiss that pretty maid, for I'm no blooming fool."
> Oh, there were words both soft and low, and kisses sweet and long,—
> But they have heard the Prexy's step and he is up and gone.
> Alas! for those two loving ones! they sent her home next day.
> And he was left, but lost out in the finals so they say.

The name of the *Cotton-Tail* survived only one issue. The next year, the *Journal* reported:

> It was announced sometime ago that the name of our annual would be changed. Several names were suggested and the committee appointed to manage the selection of a new name submitted three names from which the student body might make their selection. From the number of votes cast for the "Yucca," it seemed that the greater number were in favor of the name selected.[30]

This would seem like a straightforward account of an ordinary student activity. But there's another story behind that event. It was recalled many years later by Bruce:

> When the college decided to have an annual, I recommended to the faculty that the students should be allowed to vote on the name, and that it should not be changed from year to year. We agreed to let anyone who had a name to suggest, to write it on a card with his signature and place it in our mailbox, and that a committee of three members of the faculty and three students should select among all the names submitted the ten that they thought most suitable, and that we would present them again for a vote. As most of the colleges of Texas had named their annuals after something indigenous to Texas, I offered the name of Yucca, and it was among the number that the committee selected to be voted upon.
>
> I then had Miss Hillyar, one of our teachers of art, to paint me in colors from a picture of a yucca that I found, the plant in full bloom and to put in large script below it, "Vote for the Yucca." I had this hung in one of the corridors. When the vote was taken, the "Yucca" received a majority of all the votes cast.[31]

In the first dozen years of normal publications a student business manager and his assistant were given the entire responsibility for promoting the *Journal* and the *Yucca*. In return they shared all of the net profit, with the result that the student body came to look on the publications as an individual profit-making enterprise, and that each new school year was started without any money in hand. Dissatisfaction arose between the editorial and business staffs of the *Journal* and in 1908 the Committee on Student Publications referred the matter to Bruce for adjustment. He ruled that the editors must be allowed 284 pages during the year, exclusive of covers and advertisements, the number to be allowed to vary between thirty-six and forty-eight pages of editorial matter per issue.[32] But some business managers were unable to meet publishing expenses, so in 1911 Bruce appointed W. N. Masters of the faculty as financial adviser and chairman of publications, the start of a long association for the chemistry teacher. He recalled that the publications had debts of $500, and the president told him never to let that happen again.[33]

The financial situation improved quickly, so much so that the faculty voted in 1913 to change the management system. The action created a board of editors to be made up of various editors and assistant editors elected by the students, a business manager and assistant elected by the faculty, and the members of the faculty committee on publications. Net proceeds from the publications were to go fifty percent to the business manager, forty percent to the publications, and ten percent to the assistant business manager. If deficits instead of profits should occur, they were to be shared on the same percentage basis.[34]

In the person of Masters, Bruce had found the firm direction of financial affairs that he sought for the publications. As the normal grew in size and rose toward collegiate level, the need was felt for a published statement of regulations governing editorial content as well as financial operations. The *Journal* in October 1915 carried this statement:

> These publications shall be non-sectional, non-sectarian, and non-partisan. Hence any and all articles reflecting in any manner on any public official, on the policy or government of the school, on any member of the faculty, on any student, on any other person, on any religious organization, or on any political party shall be eschewed; and all unbecoming personalities shall be prohibited.
>
> Furthermore, for all contributions thereto, each department shall preserve a high standard of literary and artistic merit.
>
> PUBLICATIONS COUNCIL

Despite the ban on articles reflecting on any member of the faculty, the following appeared in the *Journal* in February 1916:

Our Prayer to the President

Our President which art in the office,
Hallowed be thy name, thy students come,
Thy will be done in study hall as it is in chapel.
Give us this day our daily grades,
And forgive us our demerits as we forgive you for demeriting us.
Lead us not into the office, but deliver us from all lectures,
For thine is wisdom, power and authority forever.

A penciled notation by a *Campus Chat* editor on a 1919 copy of the paper suggests the meticulous attention Bruce gave to student writings. The story in question referred to a planned French Club carnival to be held at the home of a faculty member, saying it would be "a masked ball." The words in quotes were underlined, and the marginal comment said "This article caused all kinds of trouble with Bruce. He didn't like the idea of our having a 'ball.' Offensive sentence!!"[35]

As the institution approached degree-granting status in the fall of 1916, the old *Normal Journal* seemed too much a relic of the precollege years, with its quaint mixture of news, stories, verse, and homilies. Its functions were divided between two new publications: the *Campus Chat,* a weekly newspaper, and the *Avesta,* a quarterly literary magazine. The first *Chat* appeared on October 25, 1916, and the first *Avesta* in the winter quarter of that same school year, early in 1917. The *Yucca* continued to fill the yearbook function. The *Avesta* ceased publication in World War I and did not resume publication until 1924.

North Texas was asked to join the "Inter-Collegiate State Press Association" at its first meeting at Baylor University in April 1909.[36] Thus began a relationship that was to be of value and significance to the school for many years to come.

SHALL STUDENTS GOVERN?

Formally organized student government was not characteristic of the state normal college. However, periodic efforts were made to organize the students. The *Normal Journal* in January 1904 called for a mass meeting of students to create a Students' Council, stressing primarily the need for student control over cheating on examinations. At the mass meeting, the *Journal* writer was accused of being "in league with the faculty" by students who said they would not tell on their classmates who were seen cheating. The February *Journal* defended the plan, but confessed to an undue emphasis on the issue of dishonesty in examinations. President Kendall and the entire faculty endorsed the council and between 100 and 200 students joined to elect representatives from every class.[37]

The following year the *Journal* called for another student meeting to reorganize the student council, but found "considerable apathy" among the students.[38] The judgment concerning apathy was apparently correct, for the issue was not mentioned in the student publication again for some years. An organization was "partially effected" in 1911 but died out before doing anything. In 1913 the *Journal* asked for the reconstitution of that group to participate in making regulations governing students, helping students with their school work, regulating social activities, and fostering athletics.[39] But again nothing came of the move, although the November 1914 *Journal* complained that "though the little pupils of the Training School proudly cherish their Honor System, the Normal has none—why should we not have a Students Council?"[40]

Finally, as the state normal college era was nearing its end in 1921–22, a Student-Faculty Council was created to revise school regulations. Students elected one representative from each of the four college classes and one from the normal division; Dr. Bruce appointed the five faculty members. After the rule revision, the president appointed one more faculty and one more student to the group, which was to become part of the permanent organization of the college. The council claimed "to have helped somewhat toward raising the standards of scholarship and toward democratizing the school."[41] A year later, a faculty vote declared that "the system of allowing the students a voice in the government was for the good of the school, and that the general conduct and discipline of the school was good."[42]

CHAPEL EVERY DAY

Students had a formal institution that was in many ways a substitute for student government: compulsory daily chapel period. For the first thirteen years this was held five days a week. Here the president could make announcements, offer advice, and instruct students in his philosophy. Musical and religious programs were conducted. Noted visitors could make speeches. Election campaigns for publications editors were conducted. Daily chapel provided a form of instant communication and closeness among students and faculty that no amount of student government organization or student publications efforts could bring to a larger school in later years. At the suggestion of Dr. Bruce, the faculty passed a formal resolution in 1913 to abandon Thursday chapel exercises to provide additional time for student activities.[43] However, the five-day schedule was resumed for a time until 1917.

William Jennings Bryan was a chapel speaker in March 1916, and "as he mounted the platform the voices of twelve hundred students and visitors greeted him with the national song, 'America'."[44] In 1922 students heard John Dewey of Columbia University.[45] The picture of a more typical week in chapel can be gained from this story, the first review of the exercises to appear in the infant *Chat:*

> Doctor Bruce conducted chapel exercises Tuesday morning, October 31. He gave some excellent thoughts on *seeing*. He also spoke of the different kinds of *blindness*. Among those he mentioned were *ignorance, passion, prejudice* and *selfishness*.
>
> Wednesday morning Doctor McFarland conducted the devotional exercises. He gave a very interesting talk on the influence of Christ.
>
> In response to a call from the Y.W.C.A. secretary, Miss Appleby, a Sunday school rally was held by the students of each of the various denominations during chapel period Thursday. A good attendance was reported from each section. The purpose of the meetings was to get the students to attend more regularly the Sunday schools of the church of their choice. The result of the meeting is only one evidence of the splendid work being accomplished by Miss Appleby.
>
> Friday morning chapel exercises were conducted by the Y.M.C.A. Mr. Wilson, Y.M.C.A. State secretary for the colleges, made a very inspiring address. The young men are to be commended for the excellent work they are doing in the Y.M.C.A.
>
> Saturday morning, as usual, the chapel exercises were given to music, the band furnishing the music. We should be proud of our band, and we are. Under the leadership of Mr. Pender, it has already with only a short time for training, exceeded the average college band. We bid fair to have the best band this year we have ever had.
>
> The student body voted almost unanimously to accept the proposal made by Doctor Bruce in chapel Saturday, to have school Thanksgiving and have holidays Friday and Saturday following. This was done in order to give those who desired an opportunity to attend the State Teachers' Association at Fort Worth.[46]

Chapel period was a time for indoctrination: "Tuesday Miss Clark made one of her inimitable and instructive talks on 'Things a Young Woman Cannot

Afford to Do'."[47] And it was a time to rally student spirit: "The students enthusiastically voted to lease a private telephone line to Abilene in order that they might keep in touch with the football game, play for play. "[48]

Student activities proliferated and with the four-year college plan in operation, the faculty in 1917 reconsidered student activities and regulations. These procedures were adopted: Study nights governed by curfew would continue every night except Saturday and Sunday, but the bell would be delayed on Monday and Thursday night until 7:45 to give students until 8:00 P.M. to return home. The YMCA and YWCA were permitted to meet on Thursday nights and the Choral Club and *Campus Chat* staff on Monday nights from 6:30 to 7:45. The literary societies and all other organizations were required to meet on Mondays. Chapel exercises were scheduled four times a week, with students to be seated by classes alphabetically so that attendance could be checked. Faculty members were "kindly asked" by Bruce to attend chapel. The president read a report from a student committee he had appointed; this was stated to be "emphatically in favor of enforcing regulations concerning study nights instead of abolishing them, and of compulsory chapel attendance."[49] A year later, faculty action reduced the number of chapel periods from four to three a week.[50] The enrollment grew so large that the auditorium could not hold the student body, so Bruce suspended the compulsory feature of chapel in the 1922–23 year. This led to attendance problems, however, and on March 13 Bruce asked the faculty to consider the matter. After a discussion, the faculty voted unanimously for this proposal:

> That chapel attendance be not compulsory; that the members of the faculty pledge themselves to attend and to urge attendance by the students; that the faculty sit on the platform; that the chapel days in alternate terms be changed from Tuesday, Thursday and Saturday to Monday, Wednesday and Friday; and that the chapel programs be largely religious.[51]

This failed to satisfy Bruce, however, because on the very same day he appointed a twenty-four-member faculty committee to study the chapel attendance question. He warned them that "It is my candid opinion that there can never be a successful enforcement of compulsory chapel attendance by the students unless the president has a much better cooperation of the faculty than he has at this time."[52]

The committee report was adopted by the faculty on April 24. These decisions were included: That students be required to attend chapel and each faculty member to make a reasonable effort to attend; that required attendance would not be possible or wise if the faculty did not set the example; that the new Administration Building include an auditorium seating 2,500; that faculty attendance at chapel should be considered in determining salaries; that students not in class in the period before or after chapel be excused from chapel attendance; and finally, that the term "general assembly" be substituted for "chapel."[53]

TRAINING THE ESTHETIC NATURE

The two lyceum numbers sponsored in the spring of 1903 by the Current Literature Club began a long and successful series. A faculty committee secured four programs in 1904–5 for a "Lyceum Course. . . that will hereafter be a regular feature of each session." Tickets were one dollar for the season or fifty cents for a single admission. The first season included the reading of *King Lear* by Professor S. H. Clark of "Chicago University"; an address on the "Sunny Side of Life" by Dr. James Hedley, "one of America's greatest platform lecturers"; a concert by the Amphion Club of Dallas, a thirty-five-man choir; and readings by Miss Ida Benfey, "the American Story Teller."[54]

Nevertheless, Bruce for some time disavowed any official connection between the college and the lyceum programs except in furnishing the place for programs.[55] But the newly achieved college-level recognition evidently changed his public statements on the matter. The 1914 catalog bragged on bringing to the campus "men and women of national reputation, famous as leaders in public life, noted artists, musicians, and writers."[56] Increasing enrollment made it possible to bring even more prominent artists, such as violinist Mischa Elman in 1917 and Mme Schumann-Heink in 1918.

FEES FOR STUDENTS

Starting in 1915 the college had charged each student a fifteen-dollar incidental fee but no tuition. An expansion of fees for student services began as the result of a World War I development, the Student Army Training Corps.

For this military program, the federal government had operated a hospital, starting October 3, 1918, at 194 West Mulberry and expanding within ten days into another building at 196 West Mulberry. After the war, the buildings were taken over by the college. A practical nurse who had been employed for the SATC, Mrs. Adolphine Grabbe, was employed in 1919 as matron of the "college sanitarium." In September 1919 the J. W. Smith residence at Avenue B and Sycamore was converted into a hospital building.[57] That same month Bruce proposed to the faculty that a student-fee system be installed to finance the hospital. (He had asked the Board of Regents in November 1918 to provide money for a health service program but had been refused.) The faculty voted to submit to the student body the question of assessing themselves a fee of one dollar per session for the hospital.[58] When this plan went into operation, faculty members and their immediate family were allowed to participate by paying the same fee.

The Council of Normal School Presidents in August 1919 recommended to regents that each normal college be authorized to collect a student activity blanket tax not to exceed three dollars per term, provided it was approved by a majority vote of students. Each normal college could employ a student life secretary.[59] In October the North Texas faculty called a student vote on a tax of two dollars per term or six dollars for the regular session, the sum to be divided among athletics, the *Campus Chat,* intercollegiate debates, and the lyceum course.[60] The measure passed and three students and three faculty members were appointed as a student activity fee committee.[61]

GETTING THE EAGLES FLYING

The state normal began with no organized athletic program and no way to support one. The boys organized teams in football, baseball, and basketball, seeking help where they could find it. In 1902 football uniforms were acquired with money contributed by Denton merchants, and the normal athletes were matched against the Denton Athletic Club. The game was played on the fairgrounds just east of the campus. The *Normal Journal* carried an analysis of the weakness of the two teams but neglected to mention which team won.[62] That same year, girls organized three basketball teams, with names like the Cardinals and the F.R.O.G.S., and played on improvised courts behind boardinghouses on Monday afternoons.[63] In the spring the boys' baseball team played a team from nearby Roanoke and the Denton Athletic Club. In September 1903 the normal won what may be its first "intercollegiate" athletic contest, a 14-6 victory in baseball over John B. Denton College, the new private school that was struggling to get established in Denton.[64] The next month the football team beat "the Denton boys" and in November took on Polytechnic College of Fort Worth, which won 18-0.[65] For the next two years the football opponents were limited to Denton High School and the Denton Athletic Club, although on several occasions normal students played with the Denton High team against high schools from nearby towns. In 1905 a baseball series was scheduled with Southwestern Christian College, the successor to John B. Denton College.[66]

Makeshift sports events didn't satisfy the normalites, who wanted a formal athletic program with proper supervision and facilities. A *Journal* editorial complained that athletics had not received proper encouragement, urging the provision of playing fields, equipment, and "a systematic course of physical training."[67]

The first athletic contact with another of the state normals came in April 1907, when the Denton normal baseball team challenged the San Marcos team to a game in Denton. The challenge was accepted.[68] But even in 1907 there were faculty anxieties about the evils of intercollegiate athletics. It is interesting to read nearly a century later the views of J. R. Swenson of the normal faculty, who conceded that some form of sports was "as essential to the college as lectures, library and laboratory." Writing in the students' *Journal* on "College Athletics," Swenson warned that "The commercialism of the game and the temptation to graft and extravagance by the irresponsible handling of immense sums of money taken in and paid out are in many institutions sources of moral danger and constitute an unnecessary strain on the unformed characters of undergraduates."[69]

Swenson's words stimulated the student comment in the next month's *Journal* that "never before in the history of the Normal has there been more enthusiasm shown in athletics." A number of new football squads and another basketball team were organized. Great zeal was shown in the pursuit of the idea of intracollegiate competition.[70] Reorganization of the normal to a four-year basis in 1912 again spurred student demands for something more "collegiate." *Journal* writers again took up the cry for intercollegiate sports, complaining that the normal "has never had the rank, even of a first-class high school, in athletics." This being the first year of the new four-year course of study, the paper declared it time for the provision of "college athletics."[71]

In the summer of 1912, a visiting faculty member from the Paris, Texas, schools volunteered to direct the baseball team. He was J. W. Pender. He returned the following summer and coached both boys' and girls' teams. In the fall of 1913 Bruce hired Pender for the regular long-session faculty and gave him in addition the functions of a director of athletics. The first task was to provide better athletic grounds in an area on the south of the campus that was "a waste of trees and briars." Some of the men students interested in athletics, helped by the janitors, cleared and plowed the field to make it usable. A small grandstand was built.[72] The women students got regular faculty supervision for their athletic program when Miss Beulah Harriss joined the staff in 1914.

In keeping records, the school has traditionally regarded the fall of 1913 as the start of its intercollegiate sports program, since the school had arrived at ranking with two college years beyond the high school. The one football game that year was a 13-0 loss to Texas Christian University. In the normal college years that followed, athletic opponents were such schools as Durant (Oklahoma) Normal, Burleson, Terrell, Sam Houston Normal, Decatur Baptist College, Dallas University, Trinity University, East Texas Normal, Simmons University, Austin College, TCU, and other nearby Texas and Oklahoma colleges. North Texas got its first regular coach for men's athletics in 1915, when J. W. St. Clair joined the staff, freeing Pender for his classroom duties. Theron J. Fouts in 1920 became football coach, beginning a long association with the school that would later include duties as dean of men and director of athletics. St. Clair continued to coach basketball.[73] As the normal period drew to a close, North Texas joined the Texas Intercollegiate Athletic Association in December 1921, its first conference affiliation.[74] The basketball team won the conference title in 1921–22. The football team went undefeated in the fall of 1922 in conference play, but as a new member, was not yet eligible to claim the championship.

The state normal had thus acquired most of the traditions usually associated with athletic life and school spirit. The school colors of green and white were apparently first adopted in 1902–3,[75] although the *Normal Journal* made no such reference until 1908.[76] Students and sports writers got along quite well for years by referring to the teams as the "Normal Boys," but in 1922 a student election settled on the nickname and mascot of "Eagles."[77] In 1919 the *Chat* sent a sports writer to cover an out-of-town game for the first time, a meeting with Simmons College in Abilene. At the same time students filled the auditorium in Denton to listen to a report coming over a leased wire from Abilene—going so far as to have a snake-dance through the aisles at halftime. Unfortunately, the sports writer and fans were rewarded with a 23-0 loss in a game called on account of darkness. The *Chat* reported that "Normal played in a dazed, uncertain way absolutely unknown to her in former games." Undaunted, the normal fans chartered a special train the next week to Sherman for the Austin College game. Spirit was high, but the game was forfeited to Austin College in an argument over an official's call.[78]

Still lacking was a school song, something that had been periodically sought over the years. Contests were held during the first decade of the state normal to find a song. In 1912 the *Journal* published its candidate for one, but it was 1922 before the present Alma Mater, "Glory to the Green and White," was adopted by the students. It was the work of two students, the words by Charles Langford and music by Julia Smith, who was later to win fame as a composer.[79]

North Texas, soon to become a teachers college, in 1922 reached something of a crossroads in the management of athletics. Even as early as 1907, Professor Swenson had expressed worry about commercialism in intercollegiate sports. He later became known among his students as an opponent of athletics. In 1922 George M. Crutsinger, chairman of the faculty athletic committee, said that the 1921–22 academic year had been brought to "a near-crisis in the realm of intercollegiate athletics in the United States, which followed soon after the great furor in organized baseball." He declared that the country was about "to run off after strange gods, or possibly to allow strange gods, or their worshippers, to run off with its sports." Crutsinger noted with satisfaction that some of the older Eastern universities were returning to the concept "that athletics exist for the school and not the school for athletics." But he saw dangers facing any school engaged in intercollegiate programs and urged that North Texas uphold these ideals:

> First, that the training is the thing and not the score; that a college which must depend on winning games for its advertising has nothing of value to advertise. Second, that time and money spent on sports can

> be justified only when such expenditure brings the greatest good to the largest number of students. Third, the value and advantage to be derived from athletic contests with other colleges are recognized, as is also the absolute necessity of keeping these intercollegiate relations upon the highest possible plane of sportsmanship.[80]

Crutsinger's statement is an especially significant one in the history of intercollegiate sports at North Texas. At a time when other schools were moving in a variety of undesirable directions, this school was holding to a set of high standards that would influence its operations for decades to come. Crutsinger in the *Campus Chat* a year later said that intercollegiate athletics were a function of the Physical Education Department under direct control of the president of the faculty. A faculty athletic committee supervised all aspects of intercollegiate contests, passed on player eligibility, and approved all contracts and schedules.[81]

KEEPING THINGS IN HAND

In 1917 Bruce decided that student activities were getting out of hand. He called a special faculty meeting in February to suggest a limit to the number of clubs and societies that a student could attend. It was November of 1917 before the faculty voted that curfew be delayed from 7:00 until 7:45 so that students could attend Choral Club and *Campus Chat* staff meetings on Mondays and the YMCA and YWCA on Thursdays. All other groups were required to meet on Mondays.[82] He appointed a committee to investigate after Miss Edith Clark "spoke of the heavy duties of the girls who belong to so many Organizations and of a number of them breaking down nervously."[83] The 1920 catalog announced installation of the point system. This was designed to relieve overburdened students, limiting them to twenty points a term, with points being distributed in such fashion as fifteen points for *Chat* editor, fifteen for YMCA president, ten for athletic team membership, three for choral groups etc.[84] This system became even more elaborate in a revision approved by the faculty in 1922.[85]

chapter 11

"He Has Builded a Monument"

Considering the slow development of education in Texas and the numerous hindrances that have appeared from time to time, the growth of the North Texas State Normal College under the leadership of Dr. Bruce, has been marvelous. His has been a stupendous task, and truly the work of a great man. Through sacrifice of personal advancement, and because of his love of the institution, he has builded a monument that shall stand forever; the material foundation, the scope of which shall widen from year to year. This foundation is not only material but spiritual, and shall live as an eternal influence in the lives of the thousands of students who have attended the institution, and of the many members of the faculty who have labored with him.

Resolution of the Faculty
June 25, 1923

"My chief merit, if I am due any," Dr. Bruce said at the close of his administration, "is the faculty I assembled."[1] That view was shared by his successor, President R. L. Marquis, who wrote:

> It is my belief that Dr. Bruce showed unusual wisdom in the selection of the men and women who made up the teaching staff of this college during his administration. On this account if I must confine my choice to one thing, I would unhesitatingly say the Faculty of the North Texas State Teachers College is his finest contribution to that institution and, I might incidentally say, to the State of Texas.[2]

Only six of the first fourteen state normal teachers held college degrees. When President Kendall died in October 1906, he had increased the number of degree holders to ten of seventeen, including seven with the master's degree. Bruce's big task was to reduce the number of nondegree teachers and increase those who held the bachelor's degree. His long-range "vision," though, would require a significant increase in master's degree teachers.

With conversion to the junior college four-year curriculum in 1914–15, there were thirty-one faculty members. Eight of these had no degrees, fifteen had bachelor's, seven master's, and one doctoral. That showed little change except in bachelor's degrees, which jumped from two to fifteen. When the bachelor's degree began in 1917, there were nine without degrees, twenty-seven bachelor's, eighteen master's, and two doctoral. (The first Ph.D. other than Bruce had been hired the year before. He was L. M. Ellison, an English teacher with a Ph.D. from the University of Chicago.) In 1917, North Texas compared more favorably with the rest of the nation's normal schools than it had in 1905. The figures were bachelor's degrees: fifty-seven percent nationally, forty-nine percent North Texas; master's degrees: twenty-two percent nationally, thirty-two percent North Texas; doctorates: four percent nationally, three percent North Texas; no degree: seventeen percent nationally, sixteen percent North Texas.[3] Master's degree teachers first outnumbered those with bachelor's degrees in 1919–20 (twenty-seven to twenty-five). In 1922–23, Bruce's last year in office, there were five without degrees, twenty-two bachelor's, thirty-three master's, and two doctoral.

The Council of Normal School Presidents in 1917 resolved that the minimum preparation for a normal faculty should be the master's degree and that professional training in teacher education should be required.[4] In 1922 the council followed the standard of the American Association of Teachers Colleges, "which requires that teachers of college subjects hold college degrees and. . . in the college division the minimum requirement should be the master's degree."[5]

The American Association in 1921 approved North Texas for membership but warned Dr. Bruce that one of his chief departments had no one with more than a bachelor's degree. The president recalled:

> When the committee had left, I called a meeting of the several members of the Science Department and told them what the committee had said. I told them, "Now, we must meet that requirement." I started out when I accepted the presidency to make this a senior college, and so I told them at the first meeting of the faculty after my election. I could have supplied each of their places with one who had the Ph. D Degree, but I had some objections to this. The first was that they had helped me to develop this institution. I said, "It is as much yours as it is mine, and I have no more moral right to dismiss you than you have to have me dismissed. A second objection is that you now have your homes and your families, and I have not the heart to force you to look for other positions. But the third reason is that I know how to conduct an institution with men, but I would dislike to undertake to conduct it with degrees. Now, I suggest that each of you get his Master's Degree, so that I will have both men and degrees. You can do this by two of you taking a leave of absence next year, and the others lending them money to pay their expenses; then when they return, let them repay the lenders and let two more go.
>
> They all agreed to this, and within a few years every member of the staff had either his Master's or Doctor's Degree.[6]

President C. E. Evans of Southwest Texas State Teachers College wrote in 1926:

> Dr. Bruce was among the first in Texas to advocate high standards of scholarship in the faculty of the State Normal Schools. His way of

> expressing it was rather unique: "I see no reason why a man who is to teach lawyers and physicians in an abnormal school should have better scholarship and better salaries than an instructor who is to teach teachers in a normal school." When we compare the record of normal schools twenty years ago. . . we can appreciate the hard fight Dr. Bruce has made for the elevation of standards.[7]

It was also difficult to get teachers who were trained in the right specialties. President Kendall based his salary recommendations on the number of subjects an individual could teach.[8] Until the faculty grew large enough to allow greater specialization, maintaining quality instruction would be difficult.

TEACHING LOADS HEAVY

Teaching loads also left a great deal to be desired. The standard load in 1915 was five classes, each meeting five times a week for forty-five-minute periods—in today's terminology, close to a twenty-five-hour load. Two teachers that year were given six classes each, and a combination of recitations and laboratories for six periods per day was common in science and agriculture, Also to be considered were other assignments—committees, coaching, sponsoring student organizations, patrolling boardinghouse areas and campus to make sure that curfew and other regulations were being observed, inspection of boardinghouses, visitation of sick students, chapel attendance, frequent night faculty meetings, etc.

Administrative offices as they are thought of today were unknown in the early years of the state normal. The faculty handled a wide range of nonteaching chores. In 1913, there were twenty-three faculty committees on a faculty of only thirty, some committees having as many as seven members.[9] The committees were in charge of athletics, boarding houses, chapel, chapel exercises, classification, commencement, course of study, discipline, emergency fund, entertainments, intercollegiate debates, literary societies, lyceum, musical organizations, ornamentation, publicity, recommendation of teachers, rules and regulations, schedule of recitations, sick students, student publications, summer schools, and time. In February 1914 the committee on sick students was enlarged to include all the faculty, who were instructed to look after the sick students on their respective boardinghouse lists.[10] One year later six committees were added.[11]

The goal of standard collegiate ranking led to gradual improvement in faculty load. In 1917 the Texas normal presidents agreed that eighteen hours a week would be an average assignment, "but may exceed this amount when necessary."[12]

Bruce felt the need of an administrative lieutenant to act in his absence and assist in academic matters. W. D. Butler filled that role in 1914, when the faculty on several occasions elected him temporary chairman while Bruce was out of town.[13] Butler came to teach mathematics in November 1906 when Bruce became president and in a decade became the first dean of the college.[14] Miss Edith Clark was dean of women in 1916,[15] but there was no dean of men. Butler also filled this role. He served until his death in April 1922.

Summer employment helped identify prospective faculty for the regular session. Of 104 such persons employed in summer during the first twenty years of the state normal, nineteen became members of the regular faculty.[16]

In addition, Bruce recruited at regional teachers association meetings, the Texas State Teachers Association convention, county institutes, and among school professionals. As he wrote one superintendent, "I wish to keep up with the bright, sensible, capable, school men of the State, for there may at any time be a place here to be supplied."[17] His strong moral concern for character overrode his concern for academic accomplishment. In 1910, Bruce wrote for recommendation on a candidate, asking a superintendent to state "what you know of his success as a teacher of this subject, his influence in the school, his habits, morals, disposition, character, and in all the elements that go to make manhood first, ability and scholarship afterwards."[18]

Texas colleges could not produce even a small fraction of the teachers needed by the state's colleges. In 1912, only four North Texas teachers had studied at a Texas college. In 1917, only fourteen of fifty-three were Texas-educated. However, importation of faculty from the East, South, and Midwest brought to the rural student body a more cosmopolitan outlook.

A local product who did make good was a woman with a bachelor's degree from the University of Texas who joined the first faculty in 1901 as an English teacher. She was Miss Annie Webb Blanton. Normal teachers who published books were a rarity, and Miss Blanton was such a one. She wrote a series, *Outlines and Exercises in English Grammar.* In addition to wide use in Texas and in the normal itself, these works were adopted in 150 cities in New York, including high schools in Buffalo and New York City.[19] Miss Blanton became a celebrity on the campus as a result of the women's suffrage movement. When Texas in 1918 permitted women to vote and hold office, she announced as a candidate for state superintendent of public instruction. Miss Blanton carried 251 of the 252 counties in the state to become the first woman ever to hold a state elective office in Texas.[20] The August 8, 1918, lead story in the *Campus Chat* told of a parade from the library to the English teacher's home on West Mulberry, where she was congratulated on her election. Miss Blanton served two terms as state superintendent and then joined the education faculty at the University of Texas, where she taught until 1946. She was the founder in 1929 of Delta Kappa Gamma Society for women in education.[21]

It was faculty effort that led to the development of a standard teachers college, but it is often the unfortunate fate of the teacher to lose his place in history to the administrator who symbolized an era. This story should have left no doubt that this was Dr. Bruce's era and that Dr. Bruce's personality and philosophy were stamped upon the normal far more than was the case of later presidents, who dealt with larger and more complex institutions.

THE WORKS OF A SCHOLAR

Bruce's publications in mathematics deserve special mention. His first was a short monograph, *Some Noteworthy Properties of a Triangle and Its Circles,* published in 1904 by D. C. Heath and Company. This led to his listing in the 1906 edition of *American Men of Science.* While teaching in the University of Texas summer session in 1900, Bruce roomed in the home of Professor W. S. Sutton. They collaborated on a pair of texts, *Arithmetic, Lower Book* and *Arithmetic, Higher Book,* issued in 1906 by D. C. Heath.

With C. C. Cody of Southwestern University, Bruce wrote *Elements of Plane Geometry* and *Elements of Solid Geometry* for the Southern Publishing Company in 1910. Revised editions by Dr. Bruce alone appeared in 1923, 1929, and 1930. Bruce's *The Nine Circles of the Triangle,* published by North Texas State Teachers College in 1932, was described by the dean of engineering at the University of Texas as "one of the most significant and valuable contributions to geometric investigation that has taken place since the Civil War. It bears the stamp of the genius and love of genuine science and a devotee of geometrical pure science."[22]

At the request of State Superintendent W. F. Doughty, Bruce wrote *Principles and Processes of Education,* published in 1916 by the C. A. Bryant Company and prescribed for summer normal institutes in 1916, 1917, and 1918. Bryant in 1923 issued a poem by Dr. Bruce, "The Charms of Solitude." As president-emeritus, he also had a number of poems privately printed.

SERVICES TO THE PROFESSION

Bruce was elected president of the Texas State Teachers Association in 1905 and served as chairman of the Texas State Board of Examiners from 1905 to 1910.[23] From its organization in 1912 until his retirement in 1923, the Council of Texas Normal College Presidents had Bruce as its president and leader. In virtually every educational movement—in the state or nationally—when the Texas normals were called upon to have a representative, Dr. Bruce was chosen.

Other credits would include *Who's Who in America, Who's Who in American Education, Who's Who Among North American Authors, Leaders in Education, Who's Who in the West, Texian Who's Who* and *Texas Writers of Today.* He helped found and was named a Fellow of the Texas Academy of Science. In 1919 Bruce was elected vice president of the American Association of Teachers Colleges.

THE PRESIDENT RETIRES

On May 26, 1923, barely a month past his sixty-seventh birthday, Dr. W. H. Bruce appeared before the Board of Regents in Austin to offer his resignation. He gave as his reason the illness of his wife, who had suffered a serious stroke.[24] The board named Bruce president emeritus and professor of education for the next two years. President R. L. Marquis of Sul Ross State Normal College, a former Denton faculty member, was unanimously elected to succeed Dr. Bruce.[25]

Thus ended the administration of W. H. Bruce—but not his service to North Texas State Teachers College. He took Mrs. Bruce to Opelika, Alabama, where his brother and their daughter and son operated a clinic. She remained there while Dr. Bruce returned to Denton to teach half of each year until her death in September 1937.[26] After that Bruce made his home in Denton most of the time, remaining active until his death December 30, 1943, at the age of eighty-seven. His passing came at the home of his son and daughter in Opelika.[27]

Of Bruce's contributions to the teachers college movement, President C. E. Evans wrote:

> He insisted at all times upon sound standards of scholarship and genuine, thorough professional training. It was his ambition to make the college work of the Texas Normal Schools from Freshman to Senior classes, the equivalent in standard college hours of effort to that of the best colleges in America. The idea of a cheap school with cheap standards did not represent the conception Dr. Bruce had of a normal school. The Teachers Colleges of Texas owe a great debt to him for his consistent and persistent advocacy of high standards of college scholarship; indeed, it is this long period of continuous support that has made the present standards of Teachers Colleges in Texas possible.[28]

Let the story of "Dr. Bruce's Normal" end with the resolution adopted by a unanimous rising vote at the faculty meeting of June 25, 1923. A portion appears at the head of this chapter. Other excerpts said:

> Dr. Bruce began his major educational life work when he was elected President of the North Texas State Normal College in October, 1906. Assuming the responsibility of an institution that had a faculty of 14 members and an annual enrollment of 1028 and that was a Normal School of unstandardized credit, Dr. Bruce had a definite vision of a complete Teachers College that would rank among the foremost of American Colleges. By careful planning and arduous work, he with his loyal faculty has, step by step, developed the North Texas State Normal College into a Teachers College that is now recognized as a college of the first class, that holds membership in the American Association of Teachers Colleges and in the Texas Association of Colleges.
>
> To speak specifically, it is interesting to note that the annual enrollment. . . during Dr. Bruce's presidency, has increased from 1,028 to 4,700; that the annual legislative appropriation has increased from $17,500 to $300,000; that the faculty membership has been increased from 14 to 118; that when the Administration Building shall have been completed, the appropriation for which was made under the Administration of Dr. Bruce, every building now on the Campus shall have been constructed under his direction; and that the original campus of ten acres has been enlarged to an area of twenty-five acres.

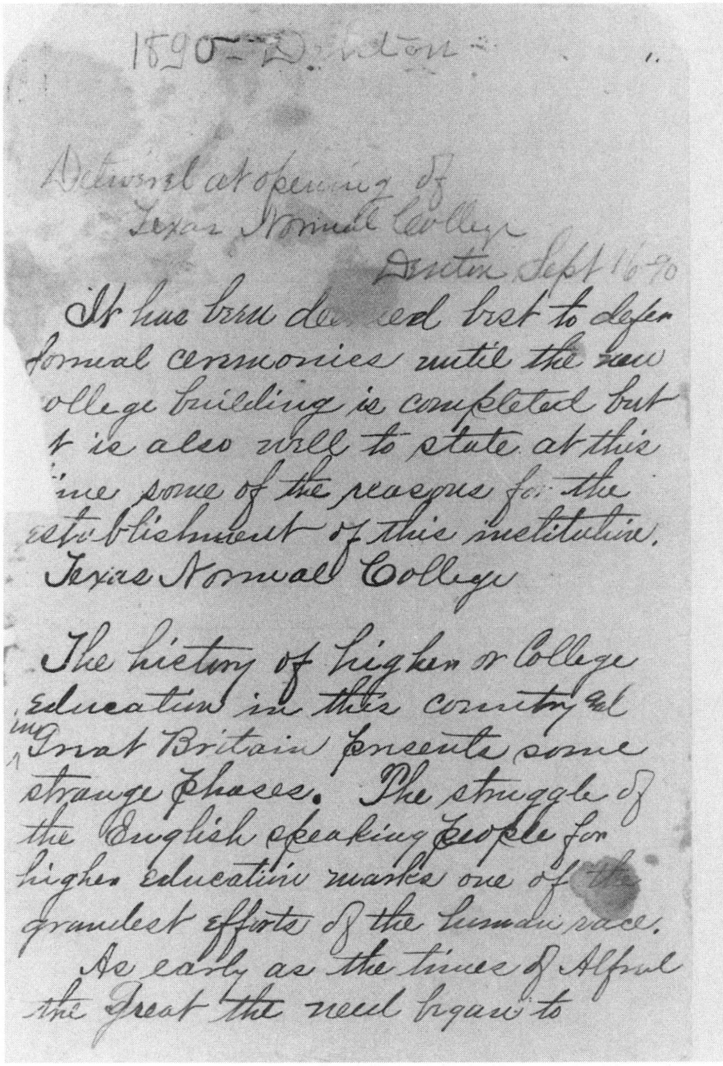

1890—Denton

Delivered at opening of
Texas Normal College
Denton Sept 16-90

It has been deemed best to defer
formal ceremonies until the new
ollege building is completed but
t is also well to state at this
ime some of the reasons for the
establishment of this institution.
Texas Normal College

The history of higher or College
education in this country and
in Great Britain presents some
strange phases. The struggle of
the English speaking people for
higher education marks one of the
grandest efforts of the human race.
As early as the times of Alfred
the Great the need began to

The concluding paragraphs of President J. C. Chilton's opening-day speech at the Texas Normal College on September 16, 1890, reveal his ambitions for the new institution to become a leader in Texas higher education.

Joshua Crittenden Chilton negotiated the contract with the City of Denton that established Texas Normal College and Teacher Training Institute on May 8, 1890.

Disagreement on selecting a site for a college building forced classes to open on September 16, 1890, on the second floor of a downtown hardware store, seen here in a 1931 photograph.

The Normal Building was built in 1891, going into use in the second year of the normal's existence. It was struck by lightning and burned to the ground in 1907.

John Jackson Crumley, President, 1893–94.

Menter B. Terrill, President, 1894–1901.

Students of every age from preparatory grades through collegiate level made up the student body of 1894.

Joel Sutton Kendall, President, 1901–6.

William Herschel Bruce, President, 1906–23.

Student homes away from home at the normal college and teachers college were boardinghouses—dozens and dozens of privately operated enterprises that operated prior to the era of dormitories. Lives of coeds like these were closely regulated in "Dr. Bruce's Normal."

Looking northwest, a 1919 air view shows the Education Building, Manual Arts, Power plant at left; Library, Science, and Main Building at right.

The Main Campus entrance was on Hickory Street with Science Building at left, Main Building in center.

Normal students gathered here daily for chapel on second floor of Main Building.

Auto travel on Avenue A led to problems in front of Library.

part III

The State Teachers College

1923–1934

Notwithstanding the fact that the teachers colleges of Texas are institutions of the first class and hold positions of dignity among the colleges of America, they are rated in the fifth place, so far as maintenance and salaries are concerned, by the Board of Control and the Legislature. Sober thought does not warrant the state's placing the training of its citizens fifth in importance.

R. L. Marquis

chapter 12

The Search for Equality

> Be it resolved, that each President of each State Teachers College in Texas, notify all members of their faculties that they are employed by the State to teach, and are not employed as politicians; and that they should refrain from participating in partisan politics, and that to do so will jeopardize their positions.
>
> *Board of Regents, August 22, 1925*

> In order to establish in the minds of our respective faculties a greater sense of security, and give faculty positions greater dignity, we recommend that the Board of Regents appoint a committee of two to confer with a like committee from the Council of Presidents on the question of tenure for faculty members.
>
> *Teachers College Presidents,*
> *March 19, 1926*

The Denton college opened in the fall of 1923 with a new name, North Texas State Teachers College; a new president, Robert Lincoln Marquis; and a new dean, W. Joseph McConnell. These two men were to be the presidents of the teachers college era, President Marquis for nearly eleven years and President McConnell for the rest and two years beyond. Both men had normal college experience—President Marquis as a teacher at Huntsville, Canyon, and Denton normals as well as president of Sul Ross State Normal from 1920 to 1923; Dean McConnell as a member of the Denton faculty since 1916. The job ahead would continue to be arduous, the difficulties compounded by opposition from other segments of higher education, by the Great Depression, and by a devastating war.

THE PROBLEMS AHEAD

Financial problems underlay most of the other problems. The report of the University of Texas examining committee in1922 laid out the problems:

(1) The library needed building up by setting aside adequate appropriations for each department year after year. Too much money had been spent in the purchase of duplicate textbooks for students.

(2) Summer classes were overcrowded and the teachers were overworked.

(3) The faculty needed a portion of each year free for graduate study and research. Salaries needed to be sufficient for a teacher to go to another institution for this work.

(4) The lack of funds hampered the Denton college "more than any other Texas Normal College which I have examined." The scholastic standing of the faculty was high enough if necessary funds were provided. This lack showed itself in an overworked faculty and a lack of equipment for the number of students taught.

Lack of state financial support was holding back the potential of the Denton campus. The report said, "I was very favorably impressed by the atmosphere of this place. The faculty is young and apparently vigorous and progressive. With proper equipment and encouragement, I believe that this school is bound to develop into a very strong college."[1]

President Marquis announced a slight salary increase for the 1923–24 year, but warned the faculty that this had cut departmental maintenance appropriations in half. Asking each teacher to make small funds serve the greatest purposes, he said "we are forced to choose and leave on the ground of relative values." The new salary schedule provided a maximum of $1,800 a year for instructors up to a maximum of $2,600 for heads of departments. The normal load for teachers was hopefully set at fifteen recitation hours per week with 150 students (except 100 in English composition), but a maximum load of eighteen hours was allowed.

THE EDUCATIONAL SURVEY

In August 1921 the legislature created a Committee on Surveys of Institutions of Education. It was to identify unnecessary duplication and avoidable expense, which it attributed "to the fact that the work of higher education in Texas has not been properly systematized and coordinated." The committee of nine citizens was charged with reporting a method of systematizing higher education and financing it efficiently and adequately. The legislature provided $50,000 for the survey in 1923.[2]

Marquis asked the faculty to respond so as "to make a fair impression upon the people of Texas, who pay the taxes to maintain this school." He said they should show that teachers colleges operate during twelve school months at capacity, six days a week from 8:00 to 5:00, and with teachers carrying a fifteen-hour teaching load.[3]

In 1925, the survey group offered these recommendations:

A State Board of Higher Education of nine laymen should be created. They would approve new courses, determine areas of study, approve the creation of new colleges, and prepare budget estimates.

Graduate work would be restricted to the University of Texas, except for graduate agricultural study at Texas A&M.

North Texas State should not train teachers of home economics or of the trades and industries.

The demonstration schools at all the state teachers colleges should be strengthened. Buildings are much needed at the teachers colleges, especially dormitories. Their location in relatively small towns makes the need for dormitories doubly important.

The teachers colleges should emphasize more largely the training of teachers for rural schools. These colleges need to duplicate work for elementary teachers, but they should divide among themselves the high school subjects to develop stronger specializations and avoid duplication.

The state should assign accreditation to some competent body. The Association of Texas Colleges, which provides for colleges to be grouped in four classes, rates all four-year colleges in Texas as "Class A Plus," the highest rating. Not enough Texas colleges have regional and national accreditation.

At some colleges, it is too easy for students to pass. Examples of the range are CIA, eight percent not passed; Sam Houston State seven percent not passed; and North Texas State, 15.7 percent not passed.

Texas should require four years of teachers college training for a teaching certificate.

Teachers college graduates almost all enter teaching and stay for a considerable number of years. The problem of the teachers colleges is not of cutting out training for any given teaching field, but rather of coordinating programs among the various teachers colleges.

All colleges except the University of Texas are doing poorly in developing faculties with master's degrees. Teachers' salaries are far below the national average, which impairs the efficiency of the institutions.

Teaching loads are too heavy in the state, with the North Texas State Teachers College requiring the heaviest loaded.

Libraries need better facilities than they now have.

Student social life is well supervised, and the standards of student conduct are rather high. Religious influences are splendid in all cases. A tendency is developing to neglect physical training and to emphasize the development of winning athletic teams.

The survey calls for more generous appropriations to raise the standards of educational services.

RESPONSE TO THE SURVEY

The presidents of the state-supported colleges deliberated in 1926 over the major survey proposals. They approved the state board of higher education, endorsed a building program for all state schools backed by bonds for at least $50 million, and supported reorganization of the system of appropriations for state colleges.[4]

The final survey report filled eight volumes. The Legislative Committee of the Survey Commission prepared eleven constitutional amendments and twenty bills designed to provide a statewide coordinated system of education. Yet in 1933 a published survey of Texas teacher training was still recommending that these measures be passed; the survey had led to very little change in the organization or status of Texas higher education.[5]

THE SALARY STRUGGLE

President Marquis fought to see that teachers colleges got a better share of available money. In his first biennial report to the regents he listed among the most pressing needs a salary scale to hire and retain highly trained teachers.

Marquis appeared before the Board of Regents on behalf of teachers college presidents in 1924 to explain the hardships worked by budget cuts made by the State Board of Control. President Cousins of Kingsville spoke of "the absurdity" of $1,600 annual faculty salaries. The teachers college presidents recruited an interesting ally, President W. M. W. Splawn of the University of Texas, who told the board that teachers in the teachers colleges should be paid the same as those in like positions of undergraduate instruction in the University.[6]

At an earlier meeting, Splawn told the teachers college presidents that there should be one "great central graduate University of Texas" at Austin. One of the presidents described the agreement:

> We unanimously joined Dr. Splawn in his second thesis. . . and agreed to support the idea of one graduate university in this State, while he agreed to support our contention for a salary level for our colleges equal to that at the University of Texas, excepting the graduate school. . . .
>
> With the help of the University we ought to be able to secure the passage of the appropriation bill that will adequately remunerate the teachers in the Teachers Colleges.[7]

Comparative salaries were run in the *Campus Chat* on August 11, 1925, to show the continued disadvantage of the teachers college. The presidents of the University of Texas and Texas A&M would get $10,000 that next year, Texas Tech and C.I.A. $7,500 each, and the teachers colleges $4,500. The English department head would get $4,250 at Tech, $3,750 at A&M and C.I.A., and

$3,600 at North Texas. Similar differences were provided in other positions, with the teachers colleges always at the bottom of the scale. At North Texas the department heads who taught all summer would be earning $300 a year more than the president.

UNIFORMITY SOUGHT

President Marquis spoke to presidents of state colleges in January 1926, pleading the case of the teachers colleges. Faculties and buildings should be as good as those of other institutions, he said, because "if the teacher profession is recruited from the lower half, intellectually and spiritually, of our young people, the nation will be imperiled." Marquis recommended that other state institutions "should say to the world" that teachers colleges are the places to prepare teachers.[8]

In March 1926 the teachers college presidents asked regents to let them prepare budget requests on a salary scale equal to the other state institutions for undergraduate work,[9] and the regents unanimously adopted such a request for 1927–29.[10] Presidents wanted to be free to determine individual teacher's salaries from a lump-sum appropriation. This desire was thwarted by an attorney general's ruling that amounts for each teacher must be uniform.[11]

In his biennial report in December 1926 Marquis repeated his call for a salary scale equivalent to that of first-class colleges. He elaborated on this in 1928 in an interview with the *Dallas Morning News,* declaring that Texas teachers colleges were rated in the fifth place by funds provided by the Board of Control and the legislature.[12] In 1929 the Board of Control again denied the request of the Board of Regents for presidents' salaries at the national average of $6,000.[13]

The Depression set back any hopes of economic gain for faculty members for some time. In its May 1932 budget request, the Board of Regents asked for the current amount, but admitted that every state employee "should expect a cut in salary." One year later the board voted that no faculty member should earn in 1933–34 more than seventy-five percent of the 1932–33 salary.[14]

The decade starting in 1923 provided precarious security for some faculty in the teachers college system. In 1923, regents refused to re-employ a teacher of many years' standing because the individual was "a disturbing element in the teaching force." In 1925 a San Marcos professor was dismissed by the board because he "had taken an active part in practically all partisan politics during the seven years he had been at San Marcos." The regents unanimously voted "that each President of each State Teachers College in Texas, notify all members of their faculties that they are employed by the State to teach, and are not employed as politicians; and that they should refrain from participating in partisan politics, and that to do so will jeopardize their positions."[15]

A response was submitted by the teachers college presidents to the regents on the following March: "In order to establish in the minds of our respective faculties a greater sense of security, and give faculty positions greater dignity, we recommend that the Board of Regents appoint a committee of two to confer with a like committee from the Council of Presidents on the question of tenure for faculty members."[16] The board appointed the committee the same day, but later minutes fail to disclose any further action.

The Depression further increased job insecurity. The board told its presidents to give preference to Texas candidates for positions; in 1932, no teachers college could employ more than one member of a family. Finally, in May 1932 the board resolved that:

> in the selection of all persons employed. . . in the State Teachers' College System, the salaries named are the maximum salaries to be paid. . . and may he lowered in the discretion of the Board of Regents from lack of funds or any other reason. . . . The services of any person so employed may be dispensed with during the current year by the President or Board of Regents on giving such person thirty (30) days notice.[17]

UPGRADING THE FACULTY

Nevertheless, progress was made in building a North Texas faculty qualified by graduate education. The new minimum goal had to be at least a master's degree for every teacher, with as many others as possible working toward the doctoral degree. Even though he never earned the doctoral degree himself, President Marquis recognized its necessity for department heads.

In response to the pressure to acquire graduate degrees, some of the Denton faculty commuted to the young Southern Methodist University in Dallas, where they could acquire a newly created master's degree in education, often without taking leave from their jobs.

In June 1925 President Marquis pointedly singled out one department director. He recommended that his salary be made $3,000 instead of $3,600 "as long as. . . he holds no more than the master's degree." By 1927 half a dozen or more faculty members took leave for doctoral study. In 1929 the number was eight.

Over time, academic ranks had been assigned haphazardly, often with no relationship between rank and an individual's salary or academic background. In March 1929, Dean McConnell reported that the faculty had forty-three professors, twenty-seven associate professors, nine assistant professors, and five instructors. Responding to accreditation requirements, the Board of Regents a few months later requested the reranking of the staff in conformity with the salary scale. This resulted in thirty-six reductions in rank and two raises, and the staff for 1929–30 carried twenty-eight professors, nineteen associate professors, twenty-six assistant professors, and thirty instructors. The maximum salaries were professor and director $3,600, professor $3,000, associate professor $2,700, assistant professor $2,500, and instructor $2,000.[18] President Marquis also added administrative assistance. In 1924 he created the office of dean of men, to be filled by J. E. Burk of the English Department; in 1928 he organized a permanent Placement Bureau in charge of E. H. Farrington and an Ex-Student Secretaryship, assigned to Miss Mamie Smith.

Faculty progress led the *Chat* on March 10, 1928, to proclaim a first ranking among the nation's state-supported teachers colleges. "Denton was found to rank first in the qualifications of teaching staff, first in the reduction of percentage of lower degrees during the last ten years, first in the amount of progress made during that decade, and first in the meeting of standards of 'general practice' over the United States."

This report was based on data collected by Dr. A. L. Crabb of the George Peabody College for Teachers and the United States Bureau of Education.

The percentage of teachers with bachelor's degrees dropped from fifty-four in 1917 to 13.3 in 1926–27, and master's degrees from twenty-eight in 1917 to 78.6% in 1926–27.[19] By 1930, one man in four had a doctoral degree. The doctoral degree figure for women teachers, though, was only 4.6 percent. In total, the North Texas State faculty had the highest graduate attainments of the Texas teachers colleges.[20]

chapter 13

The Old Guard Dies Hard

Heretofore its membership has been confined to old-line classical colleges. Teachers' colleges were not eligible. The Texas State Teachers' Colleges might have obtained admittance earlier if they had transformed themselves into classical colleges "which also do teacher training." But this change the authorities of these colleges declined to make. The several colleges had been established expressly as teachers' colleges, and moreover the authorities were proud of that fact, believing it important to advance teaching as a profession.

The vision of the heads of our teachers' colleges has reached the representatives of the old-line classical colleges in the Southern Association.

Dallas Morning News,
December 15, 1925

The teachers colleges of Texas lacked one major recognition: membership in a regional accrediting association. Geographically this meant the Association of Colleges and Secondary Schools of the Southern States. Practically, however, this was difficult because the Southern Association provided membership for colleges and universities, for junior colleges, and for schools, but none for teachers colleges.[1] Yet the North Central Association, whose territory adjoined Texas in Oklahoma and Arkansas, had created a teachers college section and accredited a number of institutions. This led the Texas schools into a dual effort: either get the Southern Association to recognize Texas teachers colleges or align themselves with the North Central group.

NO MORE SUBCOLLEGE

Even in 1923 the "Normal School" or subcollege years were still part of the Texas schools' organization. Yet the Southern Association's standards specified that a college could not maintain a preparatory school as part of its college organization.[2] For this reason, at his first faculty meeting, Marquis announced that subcollege work would be eliminated during the 1923–25 biennium. The president promised to try not to cause any faculty member to lose his job. It would require, he said, acceptance of a heavier load and willingness of some teachers to give up their college faculty classification.[3] This action was opposed by presidents of other teachers colleges, but Marquis prevailed.

This persistence brought the realization of his goal: a standard high school, duly separated from a standard four-year college. To meet the needs of the dwindling number who would have entered the old normal school division, a three-year "Special Curriculum" specified the Demonstration High School senior year plus the first two years of the college to lead to a temporary certificate entitling the holder to teach for three years in the elementary grades.[4]

NORTH OR SOUTH

In February 1923 President Bruce wrote the "Southern Commission of Accredited Schools" and asked how to apply for membership for his college.[5] President Marquis asked the teachers college presidents in July 1923 to consider their relationship to various associations of colleges. The group voted unanimously to investigate affiliation with the North Central Association. They also asked Dr. W. S. Sutton, acting president of the University of Texas, if he would support a teachers college request for affiliation.[6]

President Hill of Canyon was secretary of the presidents' council and wrote to Dr. Sutton in Austin. Hill disclosed that the teachers colleges had "sometime ago" applied to the Southern Association for membership but were "turned down practically without a hearing." The North Central Association wrote Hill that the only course for Texas teachers colleges would be to do as Arkansas had done in 1923: line up all Texas institutions and have Texas annexed to the North Central group. President Marquis at first thought this to be an impossible condition but within a few weeks was urging Hill to seek the cooperation of all Texas colleges in moving to the northern group.

Both the University of Texas and Texas A&M College refused to consider the North Central proposition. (Texas was a Southern Association member; Texas A&M was preparing an application.) However, Dr. Sutton wrote that he would be happy to see the Texas teachers colleges admitted to Southern Association membership. The presidents then sent a membership request to the Southern Association, sending President C. E. Evans of Southwest Texas State to Richmond, Virginia, in December 1923 with formal letters of application. The Texas groups were required to resubmit applications on official forms in January 1924. As a result, the association approved Texas teachers colleges graduates to teach in its accredited high schools.[7]

In January the Texas presidents moved in two directions. They applied to the Southern Association for membership and voted unanimously to proceed with the application to North Central.[8] They received permission of the Association of Texas Colleges to enter the North Central Association.[9] In May the presidents instructed President Evans to continue negotiations with the North Central Association.[10]

The presidents voted to accept membership in the Southern Association if offered, but to transfer that membership to the North Central Association if that were judged desirable.[11] The Southern Association in December 1924 heard a report that "the Texas teachers' colleges are setting a *very* satisfactory pace in the South for schools of their class." Admission of teachers colleges was deferred for a year. Marquis was notified that a report on North Texas would be sent in January by Dean H. D. Campbell of Washington and Lee University, chairman of the Commission on Institutions of Higher Education.

In April, Marquis wrote Dean Campbell to inquire what had happened to the report. Campbell responded that "it would be unfortunate if the teachers' colleges. . . should affiliate themselves with the North Central Association instead of with the Southern Association." Marquis's reply did not disguise his impatience with Dean Campbell: "This matter must be settled at the next meeting of the Association or the Texas group will ask the Southern Association to waive territorial jurisdiction over the Teachers Colleges. . . . We feel certain that the North Central Association would act at once and admit us."

Dean Campbell sent a copy of a subcommittee report that said:

> The Texas State Teachers Colleges. . . show a remarkable example of an effort to work out a Teachers' College of high academic standards. The Committee wishes to congratulate them on setting a pace for the South in this regard. They have established collegiate standards of admission, and are working toward degrees of sound content, without an undue proportion of professional work. Their buildings and equipment are good, their graduates have by work in other institutions attested the quality of their training. The faculties are enthusiastic in their work, and ambitious to improve their qualifications by further graduate study. However, the salaries paid for nine months to heads of departments, \$2,900.00, \$500.00 below our standard, are too low to secure or retain the best training. We recommend, therefore, that action. . . be deferred.

In spite of the statement about salaries, though, Campbell wrote that the cases were postponed largely because the association felt that special standards for the teachers colleges should be prepared. Marquis responded that Texas salaries would meet the association standards in the next biennium. He announced with confidence that "our schools will have a good effect upon teacher-training programs in the other Southern states. We fully expect sympathetic encouragement from your Association."

THE PRESIDENTS PERSIST

The teachers college presidents prepared to apply for membership at the spring meeting of the North Central Association.[12] They learned that this would probably require a waiver by the Southern Association, so they decided in April 1925 to "push to some sort of conclusion" with the Southern Association at its next annual meeting. After that, if necessary, they could conclude negotiations with the North Central Association.[13] In June the presidents voted to press the Southern Association, "demanding either admission or a waiver of territorial jurisdiction," meanwhile continuing negotiations with the North Central Association.[14]

The stage was thus set for the showdown with the Southern Association traditionalists. Marquis heard again from President Payne of Peabody College, who said it was "perfectly ridiculous" that North Texas was not allowed in the association even though "it will lend more strength to the Southern Association than said organization will lend to it." But Payne predicted that "the old guard of the Southern Association will die pretty hard on this matter." The teachers college presidents decided they needed further support from the "old guard" in their own state, particularly the University of Texas. They asked President Splawn of the university to prepare a letter on behalf of the teachers colleges and to have it signed by other Texas colleges and university presidents. Each teachers college submitted a second formal application to the association.[15] The North Texas submission contained a letter of commendation from the University of Texas registrar and statements from other universities on the admissibility of North Texas graduates to graduate study.

The Southern Association met in Charleston, South Carolina, from December 1 to 4, with Presidents Evans, Marquis, and Hill representing all five of the petitioning Texas colleges. (Sul Ross State, Stephen F. Austin State, and the newly formed South Texas State at Kingsville were not involved at that time.) The Commission on Institutions of Higher Education voted to create a division of teachers colleges. Standards for that division were about the same as for other colleges, except that not more than one fourth of the work required for graduation could be in professional education and that adequate facilities for practice teaching and observation must be provided. Minimum salary standards, faculty teaching loads, etc., remained the same as for other colleges. The commission then voted into membership in the Southern Association Division of Teacher Training Colleges the five Texas teachers colleges at Denton, Canyon, San Marcos, Commerce, and Huntsville. No other institutions were admitted that year.[16]

Marquis wrote President Payne of Peabody two weeks later, "the battle for teachers colleges was already won before the session opened." The victory was viewed this way by a *Dallas Morning News* editorial on December 15:

> Heretofore its membership has been confined to old-line classical colleges. Teachers' colleges were not eligible. The Texas State Teachers' Colleges might have obtained admittance earlier if they had transformed themselves into classical colleges "which also do teacher training." But this change the authorities of these colleges declined to make. The several colleges had been established expressly as teachers' colleges, and moreover the authorities were proud of that fact, believing it important to advance teaching as a profession.
>
> The vision of the heads of our teachers' colleges has reached the representatives of the old-line classical colleges in the Southern Association.
>
> They have come to see that the teachers' colleges are entitled to recognition as technical colleges, and that the sole excuse for the existence of the Texas Teachers' Colleges lies in the fact that they were intended only as agencies for the training of teachers.

The victory became even sweeter when Marquis became a member of the Commission on Institutions of Higher Education in 1927 and in December 1928 was elected president of the Association of Colleges and Secondary Schools of the Southern States. It appeared that the teachers colleges had arrived on an equal footing with other four-year institutions in the state. Unfortunately, North Texas State Teachers College, like its sister institutions, faced many more years of struggling for advancement.

chapter 14

"On With the Battle!"

> The North Texas State Teachers College, at Denton, is the largest, and in many respects the best, of the teachers colleges of Texas. . . . If teachers colleges were to be discontinued, one by one, The North Texas State Teachers College should probably be the last to be discontinued.
>
> *The Griffenhagen Report, 1933*[1]

The teachers college, in President Marquis's view, was "a rather modern institution with a brief past, a somewhat uncertain present, but a hopeful future."

DUPLICATION, OPPOSITION

North Texas State was now accredited at the state, regional, and national level; it was prepared to concentrate on educating teachers; it had the agreement of the other state colleges and the University of Texas that all undergraduate teachers in the state should be paid on a like basis. But it had many obstacles yet to face. Continuing from the Texas Educational Survey was a concern over "duplication" and "efficiency" in all institutions. This concern became greater when revenue sources dropped sharply during the Depression.

Marquis in 1925 attacked the State Department of Education for trying to pass on standards for teachers colleges and prescribe courses of study.[2] State Superintendent S. M. N. Marrs contended that laws on teachers' certificates gave his department authority to standardize teachers colleges. Resistance by the presidents, however, led him to instruct his college examiner to stop his examination visits to the teachers colleges.[3]

At the Texas Democratic convention in 1926, Marquis tried to get gubernatorial candidate Dan Moody to accept a plank demanding "a system of teachers colleges as a necessary part of the public school system, which will furnish to every school in the state well trained, cultured teachers." Marquis was told that Moody would include a plea for all education.[4] President Estill of Huntsville later wrote the teachers college presidents, enraged by the platform statement that said, "In the rapid strides Texas is making for leadership among the states of the Union it is important that we shall have places of learning for our future statesmen, scientists, men and women of arts, farmers and stockmen in Texas, under her control and jurisdiction."

Estill declared, "The unjust discrimination in the platform declaration is merely another evidence of a situation that continually confronts us, a persistence of the old notion of the insignificance of the teacher's calling and ignorance of the modern development of the standards and standing of the profession. . . . On with the battle!"[5]

Marquis went on a mission to Dallas after a teacher wrote that her assistant superintendent was ignorant of the advances made by the teachers colleges and that "we have been told time and again that graduates of *first class* colleges will be shown preference in every way and the Teachers Colleges are not included." Marquis talked to Dallas administrators and was assured that "no further discrimination would be made" against the Texas teachers colleges.[6]

THE REGENTS SPEAK OUT

The question of duplication arose again when the presidents of the University, A&M, and Texas Tech sought a bill to would eliminate duplication in colleges. The teachers college presidents asked the Board of Regents to adopt some countermeasure. The board distributed to the press a statement on duplication. It was long, involved, and unsympathetic to the "technical schools." The regents responded with a counter-attack:

> It is. . . against public policy to attach a department of teacher-training to schools whose main purpose does not include the teaching of education as a profession.
>
> If the schools that are established and maintained as industrial or technological institutions will cut out their departments of teacher-training that are now used as a mere incident in the accomplishment of another purpose and that seem to be used to catch public favor and patronage and to increase their budget appropriations by this increased enrollment, there will not be much reduplication left among the higher institutions of learning in Texas.[7]

This statement, more than anything that had gone before, ended the polite cooperation between the state teachers colleges and the other state colleges. It revealed a basic assumption: that there wasn't enough money and enough students to go around, and that the advancement of one institution, rather than advancing the cause of education in general, served to damage the other institutions. This basic assumption produced much bitter fruit yet to be harvested.

INVOLVING THE PRESS

President Marquis went to Fort Worth in 1928 to discuss with an editor "misstatements of facts" in an editorial in the *Star-Telegram*. Marquis reported to the teachers college presidents that the editorial writer confessed that he was wholly uninformed on the subject:

> I was assured that the *Star-Telegram* hereafter would not refer to the Teachers Colleges as normals and that the *Star-Telegram,* further, would no longer be guilty of assuming and implying that these institutions are anything other than colleges of the first class. The fact is, I saw the order written for the reporters and due notice given by the editors. I think the interview will result in a decided change of tone whether the items carried are news items or editorials.[8]

Presidents Marquis and Whitley had even greater success with the *Dallas Morning News* the same year. They persuaded the *News* to do a series of articles on the teachers colleges. Fifteen articles appeared from November 11 through November 25, 1928. They had been read and checked in advance by the presidents from Denton and Commerce, and the type was provided for reprinting at the college print shop in Denton. The reprinted bulletin, *How Texas Trains Its Teachers,* was distributed widely throughout the state. This was highly favorable to the teachers colleges—in fact, completely uncritical. Much of the material reflected the Board of Regents statement of 1927: other institutions had invaded the domain of the teachers colleges; the legislature and the State Board of Control discriminated against the teachers colleges in appropriations; the teachers colleges were of high quality as measured by state and national standards.

Teachers colleges had been making real progress in upgrading teacher education. In 1919, only forty-six percent of all teaching certificates were based on college credits, the rest on examination. Ten years later, in 1928, ninety-five percent of the certificates were based on college credits. Of these, 47.6 percent came from teachers colleges, 20.9 from private senior colleges, 14.3 percent from other state-supported institutions, 7.5 percent from junior colleges, and 9.7 percent from African-American colleges.[9]

Times were about to change, however, and the Depression was to give birth to an attempt to destroy much of the teachers college system.

THE GRIFFENHAGEN REPORT

Surveys of Texas higher education seemed to come due every decade. The Hogg organization reported in 1914 and the Texas Educational Survey Commission in 1925. Still another appeared in December 1932 as part of a larger investigation by the Joint Legislative Committee on Organization and Economy. Staff work was done in less than ten months by the firm of Griffenhagen and Associates, "specialists in public administration and finance." The work was created by the legislature in 1931 to eliminate unnecessary expense and duplication in government agencies, prompted by the Depression, lowering property values, and the need for new tax sources.

The committee proposed that a Bureau of Higher Education be established, headed by a chancellor of higher education. The various boards of regents would be eliminated. A drastic reorganization of the entire higher education system was recommended. Three schools would be abolished: the School of Mines and Metallurgy in El Paso, North Texas Agricultural College at Arlington, and Southwest Texas State Teachers College. Four teachers colleges—East Texas, Stephen F. Austin, West Texas, and Sul Ross—would become junior college branches of the University of Texas, as would Texas A&I College and John Tarleton Agricultural College. Sam Houston State and Texas Tech would become four-year liberal arts colleges, the latter to become known as West Texas State College.

The committee found the idea of two state colleges in Denton intolerable and recommended that the College of Industrial Arts be merged with North Texas, the new school to be known as North Texas State College. Freshmen would be housed and educated on the CIA campus, while all others would meet classes on the North Texas campus.

The committee attacked inadequate qualifications of state teachers college faculty members, noting that while North Texas had twenty-three teachers with doctoral degrees, the largest number at any other school was seven. It praised North Texas as being "superior as an institution, academically, professionally, and in general organization and administration," this being true because the college encouraged its faculty to secure training at larger universities by increasing salaries when they earned higher degrees.[10] The report said that North Texas was the only teachers college that sought faculty with the best qualifications. The Denton college was praised because it "encourages its faculty members to take leaves of absences and spend their time and savings, in securing specialized training for their work."

The economy axe would eliminate as many faculty members as possible. This was to be done by combining departments into a few large divisions (for example, placing agriculture, biology, chemistry, physics, mathematics, and geography in a single sciences division), by eliminating classes of fewer than fifteen students, and by cutting out fields of study that lacked an "efficient" number of students. "The tendency in all institutions is to have far too many instructional departments," the report said. "The North Texas State Teachers College drops departments for which there is little demand by students. The others continue to build up departments."[11] Praise for North Texas was prompted by discovery that the college discontinued agriculture even though the law still made its study compulsory.

North Texas was cited for having the best distribution of professorial ranks[12] and for its "exceptionally effective placement service."[13] But because CIA held a monopoly on the Denton public schools for student teaching, the report held that practice teaching facilities at North Texas were inadequate with only the Demonstration School available. The report held that men's physical education had "degenerated into athletics" at all teachers colleges, but noted that North Texas had instructors in physical education with master's degrees and was able to grant degrees with majors in the field.[14]

The committee wrote that North Texas "abides by these rules for admission but definitely attempts to maintain scholarship standards by increasing the number of failures of inefficient and poorly prepared students. The result of this policy is indicated by the low percentage of failures of graduate students, from this institution, who attend the University of Texas."[15] But the committee urged that a better method would be to raise entrance requirements. However, the group wrote, "Until admission standards are raised, the policy of maintaining high standards at the expense of a fairly high percentage of failure, as followed in The North Texas State Teachers College, should be continued."

Griffenhagen and Associates conceded that North Texas had a grossly inadequate library building,[16] but were appalled by a "waste of library funds in the purchase of books that are unusable." They discovered that a number of technical books had been on the library shelves from four to seven years and had been used by only three or four students in that time.[17]

But the big savings would come by eliminating small classes and light faculty loads. At North Texas, this would mean that seventeen teachers, or twenty percent of the faculty, could be eliminated. The library could dispense with four, including the reference librarian, loan desk librarian, and reserve librarian.[18]

The Griffenhagen group advocated a single board to replace all boards of regents. Until that happened, the report declared, "there can be no coordinated program of higher education in Texas and waste and inefficiency will continue to be the rule."[19]

The report severely criticized the Teachers College Board of Regents as ineffective, reporting that it indiscriminately authorized programs and graduate degrees at all the colleges regardless of need or of capability to handle them. It said that the regents nearly always acted to save teachers colleges from the encroachments of other state institutions or to provide for their expansion.[20]

The Griffenhagen group called for a severe cut in appropriations in all state agencies. North Texas expenditures for 1930–31 totaled $545,997.90; the request for 1933–34 was $561,003.53, but Griffenhagen recommended $375,845.[21] The survey group nevertheless gave North Texas the encouraging endorsement that appears at the head of this chapter.

A STRONG REACTION

Despite the more favorable treatment, the report prompted a strong negative reaction from NTSTC. Marquis had established his position while the studies were still being made. The time had come, he said, "for us to make it perfectly clear to the people of Texas that a large number of state-supported schools enjoy the privilege of operating as teachers colleges but prefer to sail under an ensign of a different designation."[22] At the next student convocation after the report appeared, Marquis said that North Texas would be "unalterably opposed" to the destruction of any state school but would favor budget cuts made necessary by the state of the economy.[23] Students organized on their own and sent a letter to the legislature asking that North Texas State continue as a teachers college rather than as a liberal arts college, that the teachers college system be retained, and that the entire system of higher education be continued except for modifications warranted by economic conditions.[24]

The faculty also opposed conversion to liberal arts colleges, arguing that "the teachers colleges should instead become still further professionalized until a well-trained teacher is available for every class room in Texas."[25] A month later the Board of Regents issued a formal statement, stating that all colleges and state agencies should share in any reduction in expenditures. If changes in the educational system were needed, the regents asserted, they could be made more calmly at a later and more propitious time.[26]

The controversy once again caused concern over newspaper attitudes. The *Star-Telegram* in Fort Worth considered that the abandonment of some teachers colleges would be no loss and, to the chagrin of President Hill of Canyon, championed the advancement of Texas Tech.[27] The *Dallas Morning News,* which just five years earlier had so vigorously praised teachers colleges, endorsed the abandonment of teachers colleges or converting them to junior colleges. Presidents Marquis and Whitley went back to the *Dallas Morning News* office to see what could be done. They conferred for an hour with Dr. J. Q. Dealey (who had taught at Denton in 1890), Managing Editor John E. King, and Lynn Landrum. Whitley complained of "bitter, stinging things" being said about teachers colleges in *News* editorials. Both presidents stressed the willingness of the Board of Regents to achieve financial economies without destroying the system. They left hoping for "a slightly different attitude at least."[28]

STATE BOARD TROUBLES

The State Board of Education, newly reconstituted in 1929, soon decided to try to extend its sphere of influence into college affairs. The result was in many cases a duplication of the Griffenhagen study's efforts and a multiplication of worries for the teachers colleges. The board set out in January 1932 to integrate the teachers colleges and other colleges with the work of the university, to consider abolishing nineteen sets of overlapping and duplication on nineteen campuses, to eliminate duplication of the teachers colleges with one another in their courses of study, and to see if "the state has about twice as many teachers colleges as there is any excuse for."[29]

The state board summoned college presidents and other administrators to meetings for interviews, asked colleges to fill out questionnaires and produced a report on December 17, 1932, almost simultaneous with release of the Griffenhagen report. The State Board of Education recommended to the governor and the legislature that:

1. Matriculation fees in all state colleges be increased to $50.

2. There be no duplication of a public school system and a demonstration school in the same town.

3. Some teachers colleges offer only two years of college work.

4. Various special fields, such as art, home economics, music, library science, architecture, agriculture, and engineering be offered at very few schools.

5. CIA be merged with North Texas State Teachers College, provided that the existing CIA buildings be used so far as possible exclusively for the instruction of girls.[30]

The board recommended a drastic cut in the number of major fields in the teachers colleges. The number of majors would be North Texas fifteen, Southwest Texas and East Texas seven each, Sam Houston five, Stephen F. Austin and West Texas four, and Sul Ross four. This led the president of Stephen F. Austin State to write the president of the Board of Regents that "the Denton school is the only one that is left with a real college program."[31]

The Teachers College Board of Regents included a response to the State Board of Education in the same statement it made for the Griffenhagen report. The regents politely disagreed with the "drastic proposals" but suggested that they would provoke "general consideration and discussion" that would result in the permanent improvement of tax-supported higher education. Without saying so outright, the regents challenged the authority of the State Board of Education to act in this area, writing that "whatever changes in our educational institutions are desirable in the interest of efficiency and economy can be best effected by those charged with the responsibility of administering them."

The teachers college presidents did recognize that they had a problem with their demonstration schools. In March 1932 President Marquis asked other presidents to join him in two moves for greater practice teaching opportunities: (1) to make greater use of surrounding public schools and (2) to change the academic calendar to the two-semester plan to conform to that of the public schools. In May of that year the presidents recommended and the board adopted the semester plan to replace the quarter system effective in September 1933.[32]

The economic reform efforts resulted in the Anderson-Hughes-Metcalfe Bill, a bill which a *Dallas Morning News* writer predicted would not be opposed by the teachers colleges since it would not abolish them entirely but merely limit their activities "by preventing them from realizing their ambition to be splendid universities." As amended, the bill would create a single governing board for all state higher education institutions and continue graduate work at the University of Texas and Texas A&M. The bill did not pass.

REPEAT PERFORMANCE

The Associated Press suggested in a story in August 1933 that the State Board of Education would let higher education institutions alone and study the public school system instead. The story reported:

> An exhaustive inquiry was made into administration and courses at the state-supported colleges prior to the last regular session of the legislature.
>
> The reports of the board of education and of the legislative committee on efficiency and economy aroused so much opposition that the advisability of reorganizing the system was magnified into a major issue during the session.
>
> "The board had so much difficulty as a result of its investigation of the teachers colleges and other state schools that I believe it would be wise to steer clear of them for a while," W. A. Morrison of Cameron, member, said.

But just seven months later, in March 1934, the State Board of Education announced new findings on higher education. The board recommended that every freshman or sophomore class must have at least ten pupils and no junior or senior class have fewer than six. The board interpreted this ruling to mean that only three or four state-supported colleges would qualify as four-year schools. The board also recommended that graduate work be dropped at every school except the University of Texas.[33]

The State Board of Education in 1934 also asserted that Texas had a large oversupply of teachers, for which the teachers colleges were to blame. The teachers college presidents answered that there was a shortage of *fully qualified* teachers, even if there were untrained teachers out of work at that time. The Board of Regents in November used the State Board of Education's own standards to show the need for four-year teachers colleges. Of the 41,000 teachers in Texas, from 12,000 to 15,000 had less than two years of college training, below the minimum preparation specified by the State Board. In addition, the regents pointed out, the state needed about 4,000 teachers trained each year as replacements, most of whom would have to be educated in the teachers colleges. The board statement read:

> The Legislature in the acts creating them charged them with this duty. It is their only function. The Board of Regents think therefore that instead of reducing them they must be enlarged, instead of weakening, they must be strengthened. This, not because of institutional pride but because Texas can never have an adequate system of education until there is a good teacher in every school room.[34]

The board thereupon further defied the State Board of Education by unanimously directing the presidents of all the teachers colleges to maintain a minimum of eight major departments in order to maintain their recognition throughout the nation as standard senior colleges.

chapter 15

More Students, Less Money

[F]unds spent for the summer school in 1928 ($88,228.33) were not sufficient to give our students the sort of instruction they are entitled to have. We had many classes that were too large, and we employed too many student-instructors. We actually need $100,000 for our summer school, and I am asking for $60,000 to supplement the $40,000 allowed for 1929. In this connection I might say that we actually enrolled more students than the University last summer, and the University spent approximately $130,000 on the summer school. I feel that $100,000 is a modest request.

R. L. Marquis, 1929

The teachers college story to date has made clear the impact of financial crisis on faculty development, college standards, and the very survival of some of the colleges. North Texas State Teachers College was not hit by the threat of extinction, but it encountered especially severe handicaps in two areas: the development of adequate buildings and the maintenance of its summer school.

When Marquis took office in 1923, that year's appropriation had been $233,569. He saw appropriations rise to $418,735 in the year ending August 31, 1926, sag slightly before climbing to a peak of $435,200 in fiscal 1929, hover around the $400,000 level for the next three years, and drop to $340,370 in 1933. As Marquis started his last year in office in the fall of 1933, appropriations for the next twelve months had plummeted to $286,183.[1] Most of the appropriated funds went into salaries. Local funds, principally student fees, had to provide much of the operating expense for many items that failed to get appropriated allotments. Even this source was further restricted by the Pollard Bill of 1927, which limited matriculation fees to thirty dollars for a nine-month session and prohibited the charging of compulsory student activity fees.

NECESSITIES DENIED

Perhaps in no area would President Marquis feel greater frustration than in his attempts to secure buildings. The new Administration Building secured by Bruce was constructed during Marquis's first year in office. But in spite of repeated requests, he would never see another major building go up in the nearly eleven years of his presidency. Marquis saw no net increase in long-session enrollment during his term, but summer enrollment showed significant gains, and it was during this time that the classroom need became most evident. In two other areas the need was independent of class enrollment: library improvements demanded a new building, and the college lacked any facilities for housing or feeding its students. In addition, the old training school had become an eleven-grade Demonstration School, creating added space demands.

In his first report to regents, Marquis listed as pressing needs the acquisition of more land, the completion of the athletic fields and recreation grounds, added wings for the Library Building and the Education Building, a large dormitory for women, and a large commons or cafeteria. Two years later (in December 1926) he repeated these same needs, adding that students were living in more than 300 boardinghouses and that the college should have dormitories provided at least for freshman girls. In 1928 Marquis called for the doubling of the size of the Education Building, for the addition of a second story on the Power Plant for increased manual arts training space, for two good gymnasiums, for more land, for dormitories and a cafeteria, and for a library, which "is no longer a need; it has become a necessity." In 1930 the president observed that "Since no material improvements have been provided by the legislature, our recital of needs remains the same."

The requests were transmitted by the Board of Regents, but they were cut by the State Board of Control and were not restored by the legislature. The unfairness of this procedure was pointed out to the regents in 1926, when the Board of Control approved $780,000 in buildings for Texas A&M, $200,000 for CIA, and $655,000 for Texas Tech. The building money allotted to North Texas at that meeting was $10,000 for repairs to the Education Building.[2] In response to a letter from the state legislative chairman of the Texas Federation of Women's Clubs in 1928, Marquis complained that "This College is second in size only to The University of Texas, yet its buildings have cost to date only $580,000."[3] In 1931, the legislature did provide appropriations for a building at each teachers college, but this was vetoed by Governor Ross Sterling.[4]

THE CAMPUS CHANGES

Nevertheless, the campus did undergo changes in appearance. The southward movement that had begun with the construction of the Education Building and the closing of Sycamore Street between Avenues A and B was to become more pronounced. In 1923–24 there was located from east to west on the south side of what had been Sycamore Street: Kendall Hall, the former private home of President Kendall being used for music; the Education Building, known in later years under the names of business administration, language-government, and psychology; a two-story frame building, the Demonstration Cottage for home economics girls; and another frame structure, the Sanitarium. South of these latter two houses and facing on Chestnut Street was a frame house known as the Music Hall. (In the fall of 1931 another house next door to that one was also put in use for music instruction.)

Already across Chestnut Street to the southwest were the men's gymnasium (former Training School and World War I barracks) and the ballpark. The development of this area into a Recreation Park of significant proportions began in August 1923 with the purchase of the half block directly east of the ballpark. With this acquisition, the portions of Avenue B and Prairie Street that separated it from college property were closed, and ditches were filled in and graded to a level. Also at this time the old Main Building was being torn down, and material from it was used to build what a student writer called "the new temporary administration building." This was also south of Chestnut Street but east of what had been Avenue B before its closing. It was to become the girls' gym, later known as Harriss Gymnasium. But while the new Administration Building (today's Auditorium Building) was under construction in 1923–24, the temporary building was partitioned into ten classrooms and put to instructional use beginning with the winter quarter in January 1924. The next year the partitions were torn out and hardwood floor and bleachers were installed.[5] Removal of women's physical education from the gymnasium located in the basement of the Library Building made possible the creation of six new classrooms in that location.

The first campus post office substation was located on the campus on November 1, 1924, with the college providing quarters, equipment, utilities, and janitor service for Teachers College Station of the Denton Post Office for one dollar per year.[6] It was located in the Library Building. A legislative appropriation in 1925 made possible an addition to the Power Plant. Power machinery of the woodworking department was moved to this site from the basement of the Manual Arts Building. This helped create space in that basement for the Teachers College Print Shop, which opened in 1925 with two Linotype machines, two printing presses, a paper cutter, and a folder. Also in 1925, the college had bought a residence at Avenue A and Sycamore east of the campus. This was remodeled and opened in 1926 as the College Club House. Also opened in 1926 was the swimming pool that had been constructed in the recreation park.[7]

Marquis asked B. B. Harris, head of the biology department, to lead a committee in charge of landscaping and beautification. One of the products was reflected in a *Campus Chat* headline that read, "ARTIFICIAL LAKE ON CAMPUS PLANNED." The reference was to the small body of water later known as the Fishpond in the old campus area. This was completed in October 1927. Economics and government classes and offices were moved to the Manual

Arts Building, making room for the top floor of the Library Building for observation work in Demonstration School classes.

Another 1927 project was the construction of steel stands to seat 2,200 persons on the west side of the athletic field. The football playing area was lengthened to correspond to new rules of that year, and the fence was moved toward Avenue A to encompass some newly purchased land. The park had been expanded with the construction of the swimming pool east of the stadium in 1926, and east of that an open-air theater that was dedicated in the summer of 1928. A 1930 map of the Recreation Park shows six tennis courts at its northwest corner (now the site of School of Music buildings), a practice field to the southwest (later covered by the Laboratory School and still later by music expansion), and in the northeast corner a group of croquet and volleyball courts and an archery range (on ground now covered by the Student Union Building). The southeast quadrant is shown that year as "shaded playground," but was later developed as a miniature golf course.

DREAMS OF A TOWER

When Ezra Cornell described his dream of the university that bears his name, he wrote of one special feature, "a lofty campanile—a clock tower looking proudly down the slope. . . and bearing a deep-toned peal of bells." In the 1960s, when architect Edward Durell Stone presented his model of a new state university campus in Albany, New York, school officials were surprised to find a tall tower placed on the central mall. Stone's explanation was this:

"Every school must have its bell."[8]

North Texas had lacked this kind of symbol, even though its curfew bell survived on the Power Plant roof from the Old Normal Building that burned in 1907. Acting on the "every school must have its bell" philosophy, ex-students of the teachers college early in 1928 announced a fund drive to construct a memorial tower dedicated to veterans of the World War. They planned to locate the tower south of the library, with construction to start on November 11, the tenth anniversary of the Armistice. Plans for the monument were drawn by O'Neil Ford, an ex-student then working with an architectural firm in Dallas. The tower was to be 130 feet high with a winding staircase leading to the top, where there would be two electric clocks with chimes to replace the curfew bell. At the base would be the offices of the Ex-Student Association.

The alumni hoped to raise $60,000 in their campaign for its construction.[9]

The tower plans did not succeed, but in the summer of 1931 an audience in the open-air theater heard a description of expanded plans. Architect Ford had incorporated the memorial tower into a student union building expected to cost about $100,000, and a group of ex-students had accepted the plan in November 1930. The summer meeting launched the campaign to raise the $100,000.[10] The Depression proved to be too much of an obstacle however, and it would be another quarter century before the school could get its tower and "bell."

A MUSEUM GROWS

In the spring of 1925, the students of the Criddle Society voted to sponsor a museum in memory of E. D. Criddle, the history department head who had just died. The first few exhibits were quartered in the history offices in the Administration Building. A year later the Board of Regents named Dr. J. L. Kingsbury of the history faculty as curator of the Historical Collection, which was given one room on the third floor of the Library Building. Two more rooms had been taken over by 1929. In March 1930 the legislature designated the college museum as a State Historical Collection. Dr. Kingsbury by 1931 had developed a collection of manuscripts and documents, arms and weapons from 1840 through the World War, articles representing American economic and industrial development, foreign items, and archives of the college.[11]

Three other structures were built during the Marquis administration, all going into use in 1933. These were a college hospital, a one-story brick veneer building on the southeast corner of the campus at Avenue A and Chestnut; a dressing and equipment room built under the stadium stands; and a small greenhouse for botany laboratories.[12] Marquis used local funds to remodel the frame building formerly used as a hospital to house speech classes and a drama laboratory.

THE SUMMER SLASH

North Texas, like all schools, suffered from cutbacks by the State Board of Control, and the situation became worse for summers. Summer school appropriations were cut from $80,000 to $40,000 for 1928 and 1929, despite a pledge from the Board of Regents to fight for "proper legislative support."[13]

These were cut on the grounds that "those who attend the summer session . . . should pay all or a part of the cost of operating the summer schools." Since 11,000 of the 15,000 summer enrollment at that time was at the state teachers colleges, they were penalized most heavily.[14] North Texas had the greatest problem of all, as indicated by a 1926–27 long session enrollment of 1,473 and a 1927 summer enrollment of 2,724.

Marquis in 1929 asked the House of Representatives for special assistance in these words:

> Find enclosed a copy of our request for emergencies covering the summer school for 1928 and 1929. I believe the analysis speaks for itself. I wish to say, however, that the funds spent for the summer school in 1928 ($88,228.33) were not sufficient to give our students the sort of instruction they are entitled to have. We had many classes that were too large, and we employed too many student-instructors. We actually need $100,000 for our summer school, and I am asking for $60,000 to supplement the $40,000 allowed for 1929. . . . I feel that $100,000 is a modest request.[15]

That same year the presidents of the state-supported institutions presented their summer budget requests on the per capita cost of the enrollment of the preceding summer. This, again, placed the teachers colleges at the bottom of the financial ladder, since these costs were determined to be fifty-five dollars per student at the University of Texas and CIA, fifty dollars at Texas A&M and forty-five dollars at the teachers colleges. The amount paid by the summer student, ten dollars, was deducted from these amounts to determine the appropriations.[16]

THE IMPORTANCE OF SUMMER

Summer normal institutes were no longer important for teacher certification by 1925. Marquis told the state superintendent that "we should declare that the summer normal is no longer a useful part of our educational system."[17] Catalogs carried no mention of summer normals after 1927, but summer became more important in the education of teachers. In August 1929, more than 3,300 of 3,527 students enrolled at North Texas had signed a contract to teach that year. This supported Marquis's argument that "the summer schools of the state-supported institutions of Texas have contributed more to the increased efficiency of our public schools than any other factor that has operated during the last fifteen years."[18]

The presidents of all state colleges asked for 1931 summer session emergency appropriations at the same levels they had requested for 1930 (when they were allowed exactly half the amount requested). The scope of summer work at North Texas is seen in the figures agreed upon by the presidents: $65,000 for the Denton teachers college as compared to $40,000 for the University of Texas, $25,000 for Texas A&M, and $20,000 for CIA, all of which drew far larger appropriations for the regular session.[19] The North Texas enrollment that summer proved to be 3,504. President Marquis was fighting for the state's largest summer school and largest teacher education program when he appealed in 1931 to the chairmen of the senate and house finance committees in this manner:

> The summer schools have been the first, if not the sole, means of raising the standards of our public school teachers during the past years. . . . The salaries paid at this time do not attract the best young people in our states and we do not have them going into teaching in large numbers, nor do their salaries enable them to leave all their teaching for a year and attend school. They can, however, spend a summer in one of the state institutions and materially increase their professional fitness, and they have been doing this by tens of thousands during the past ten or fifteen years.[20]

The legislature dealt more sympathetically with North Texas State Teachers College in that session, but in June 1931 Governor Ross Sterling vetoed many items in the appropriations bills, including $257,850 allocated to North Texas. Lost were all summer appropriations for the second year of the next biennium, which amounted to $75,000 for Denton, a library building allocation of $175,000, and various other items for maintenance and operation.

In January 1933, Governor Miriam Ferguson sent word through her husband, former governor James E. Ferguson, that all colleges were to cut their budgets twenty-five percent across the board. This was followed by proposals from the State Board of Education, the Committee on Economy, and various legislators that summer schools be abandoned altogether. The teachers college presidents and regents insisted that summer schools must run in 1933 "in some manner."[21] All state college presidents agreed to ask the legislature for seventy-five percent of the amount received for the summer of 1932.[22] The solution to the summer school finance problem was presented at a faculty meeting in January 1934. Teachers were advised that they would earn twenty-five percent less in each summer month than they did in the long session months, at the direction of the Texas Legislature.

TUITION INCREASE SOUGHT

Another area of financial struggle came in a 1933 proposal to increase the student's share of costs through higher tuition. At North Texas, students had been paying ten dollars per quarter as a registration fee, five dollars for student activities, and one dollar as a health fee. Presidents of denominational colleges came before presidents of state colleges in March 1932 to complain about the low charges being made at the tax-supported schools. The president of Simmons University, acting as chairman of the church-related schools, requested that student fees be increased at all state colleges.[23] Bills were introduced in the legislature in February 1933 to increase the teachers college fees to $150 and the fees at the University of Texas and Texas A&M to $175 for the school year.[24] The measures failed, but a new tuition charge was levied as the colleges converted to a semester basis in the fall of 1933. Students began paying twenty-five dollars tuition in each of the two long-session semesters, with local funds to be used in lieu of laboratory fees and hospitalization charges. Student activity fees were left up to each institution since they could not be required of students.[25] At North Texas the activity fee was set at $7.50 per semester. Thus, under the quarter system a student paid a total of forty-eight dollars in fees for the long session; the new scale raised total costs to sixty-five dollars.

chapter 16

Toward a Graduate School

It [North Texas] is the only faculty of teachers colleges that has any considerable number of members who have an adequate conception of what constitutes graduate work. The North Texas State Teachers College is the only institution of the teachers colleges that is qualified to give graduate work, leading to graduate degrees. For the others to attempt to give graduate work, or to grant the degrees for additional under-graduate work, is to cheapen graduate work in the State of Texas.

The Griffenhagen Report, 1933

We have been dealing with the school's gains as a standard four-year teachers college during the administration of President R. L. Marquis. The next section, Part IV, will carry through the transition of the teachers college to an institution of broader purposes in the presidency of Dr. W. J. McConnell. But many of the threads of that transition were first woven into the teachers college pattern during the period currently under consideration.

Once again North Texas rode a national movement, not in the vanguard but at a stage when preparedness rather than expediency could dictate the timing of developments. Three teachers colleges in the United States had the right to grant master's degrees before 1920; three started programs between 1920 and 1925; nine added the degrees by 1930; and three more by 1935. By 1939, thirty-one of the 150 teachers colleges belonging to the American Association of Teachers Colleges were offering master's degrees.[1]

FIRST EFFORTS IN TEXAS

Presidents of some of the Texas teachers colleges began seriously considering the addition of graduate work around 1927. President J. A. Hill of West Texas State exhibited the most enthusiasm. Regents F. A. Martin of Fort Worth and J. O. Guleke of Amarillo spent a day in Canyon in June 1928, at which time Hill urged them to create master's degree programs at Canyon, Denton, and possibly Huntsville. The three agreed that the board had the authority to do so, and Hill told them that graduate work could easily be started for an additional $20,000 at each college. The Canyon president thought that this should be done by the summer of 1929, at which time he expected one hundred graduate students to enroll at his institution. He wrote this in a letter sent only to President Marquis, rather than to all teachers college presidents as was the custom among members of the group.[2]

President Marquis responded favorably but with caution. He noted that the matter had been discussed quite a bit at Denton and that the teachers colleges would feel an increasing pressure to do graduate work. He wrote that Hill's suggestion that the board authorize graduate work in three institutions "meets my approval." Marquis observed that in ten years North Texas had granted more than a thousand degrees, having started with a class of five, and predicted that 1,500 more would be conferred in the next five years. He wrote that North Texas planned to have twenty faculty members with doctorates in the next five years and that by that time "graduate work would be the next logical step for us."[3]

It did not take long for second thoughts to strike Marquis. Ten days after writing the foregoing words he told President Hill that he should not like to undertake graduate work at North Texas until a number of conditions were fulfilled. These included at least ten or fifteen percent of the faculty with doctoral degrees and an even larger percentage in the Department of Education; improvement of the staff of the Demonstration School; employment of some outstanding faculty members "who would grace the faculties of any college"; and improvement of library holdings and the library staff. Even with these conditions, Marquis added, "I am not so sure now as I was some months past that a college needs to put on graduate work in order to survive. I am coming to believe that it is worth a great deal to be known as an outstanding undergraduate college. To be perfectly frank, I believe I am not quite so enthusiastic for graduate work as I was a year ago."[4]

THE PRESIDENTS DISAGREE

The question reached the Board of Regents for discussion on October 8, 1929, being raised on the grounds that the better high schools were demanding that teachers hold M. A. degrees and that teachers colleges were thus obligated to meet that need. The presidents were asked to write their views and recommendations, together with data on probable enrollment, cost, etc., to President Marquis, who was asked to digest the material for a report at the next board meeting.[5] This assignment for the North Texas president led to a misunderstanding on his part and protests from at least three other teachers college presidents. Marquis did not submit a report for the presidents or for himself when the board met on February 10, 1930. He did forward to the board the report of a committee of North Texas faculty members appointed by Marquis, and it was this document that touched off the controversy. Relations were not improved three years later when the Griffenhagen study group on the state economy used the North Texas committee report as a weapon against all the other teachers colleges.

Members of the committee were Dr. L. W. Newton, history department director, chairman; Dr. W. J. McConnell, dean of the college; Dr. B. B. Harris, director of the biology department and later to become dean; Dr. L. A. Sharp, professor of education and later to be named chairman of the Graduate Council; and P. E. McDonald, registrar.

The group began by pointing to the hard-won recognition that had come to the bachelor's degree programs of the state teachers colleges, declaring that they "would not look with favor upon any policy that might impair the esteem in which these colleges are held." To the committee, this meant that any master's degree to be conferred by any one of the colleges must be "predicated upon such sure foundations as to command early recognition anywhere." Otherwise, the report said, one could turn out an inferior product that could involve the teachers colleges in another ten-year struggle for a respectable standing. A step by one or all without full preparation would "subject this class of colleges to such unfavorable criticism as to endanger the standing of even their bachelor's degrees before the better graduate colleges and universities of America."

With this caution, the committee asserted that one, or perhaps two, of the state teachers colleges should now be made ready to confer the master's degree. This was because of the demand for high school teachers and administrators with the master's, individuals who had to attend liberal arts colleges or out-of-state teachers colleges for graduate work. From this point on, the North Texas committee report was even more certain to arouse the ire of other presidents:

> Nothing could so easily establish a reputation for mediocrity as would the inevitable suspicion that would follow the announcement of the entry of seven state teachers colleges into the graduate field. But the assignment of this field to one or two of them, with definite preparation for the task, would produce not only a sense of assurance of high standards but also a reputation for conservation on the part of the entire state teachers colleges group. With a spirit of cooperation among these colleges, this function exercised by only one or two of them could be made to stimulate the activity and progress of all. By such cooperation a great number of the graduates of all of these colleges could be diverted into the graduate teachers college.[6]

The committee did not name which schools should offer the master's degree. However, it suggested that the selection should be made with regard to the number of bachelor's degrees granted by the various teachers colleges (North

Texas had the most), to the number of students already enrolled in advanced classes (North Texas led the group), and to those departments which have an adequate number of teachers with standard doctoral degrees (again, North Texas was the leader). It is not surprising that some presidents objected when this written report was given to the Board of Regents.

ESTILL PROTESTS

President Estill of Sam Houston State protested that Marquis had misled his colleagues. He said that Marquis was supposed to make a digest of data submitted by the other presidents, as indeed the board minutes of October 8, 1929, showed. Marquis responded that he was guilty of not reading the minutes and of assuming that each president was sending a copy of his own report to the board. He told Estill that his statement to the board on behalf of all the presidents said "that I could not codify the reports; they were too varied to reconcile so that they would constitute a recommendation." Estill further objected because Marquis had led everyone to believe that he was opposed to the installation of graduate study at that time. Marquis's defense was that the committee statements could not be interpreted as a report from the president of North Texas, since all had heard him oppose the graduate program, not just in all the colleges but even in only one or two. Marquis wrote Presidents Estill, Hill, and Evans that he would not oppose board action authorizing some other school to begin graduate work, "but I am not ready to begin the undertaking here." President Marquis concluded his defense this way: "I do not always agree with the judgment of individuals, nor am I always convinced by majority votes. I seem to be in the minority on this graduate study question, and I am, therefore, probably wrong, but I have seen nothing so far that is convincing enough to keep me from holding the opinion I now have."[7]

Marquis did, indeed, hold a minority viewpoint, for on October 16, 1930, the Board of Regents resolved that in view of the rising standards of public education and the demand of public schools for teachers with more advanced professional training, and in view of the responsibility of the teachers colleges for the preparation of better teachers for the public schools, all seven state teachers colleges in Texas be authorized to offer the master of arts degree.[8] Apparently the only recognition in public print on the North Texas campus was one erroneous sentence in the *Campus Chat* of January 17, 1931, which stated: "Beginning this summer a Masters degree, a special kind for teachers, will be conferred." The faculty minutes show that President Marquis appointed a temporary committee to study the master's degree matter, but North Texas was not to become one of the teachers colleges offering graduate work at this time.

OTHER SCHOOLS BEGIN

Other teachers colleges, in fact, encountered financial difficulties in trying to start graduate courses. The State Board of Control disapproved of the graduate program in its budget and recommendations. Trying to counteract this, the Board of Regents arranged a joint meeting with the State Board of Education and some members of the Board of Control in January 1931 to discuss graduate work. The outcome was the authorization by the regents for those colleges that so desired to begin graduate work on their own resources in the summer of 1931.[9] West Texas State Teachers College acted at once and showed forty graduate students enrolled in the summer of 1931, nineteen in 1931–32, fifty in the summer of 1932, twenty in 1932–33, seventeen in the summer of 1933, and none in the following year. Sul Ross State started at the same time, but recorded figures only of twenty-one in the summer of 1931 and forty-one in the summer of 1932. Sam Houston State made a single venture into the field with thirty-one graduates students reported in the summer of 1932. No other teachers college joined this group.[10]

Nevertheless, the Canyon and Alpine actions stimulated further pressures in Denton. The faculty voted January 1932, favoring the giving of graduate work by thirty-three to twenty-five. Looking around him at the forces being marshaled in the attack against teachers colleges, President Marquis still resisted, declaring that "the teachers colleges have undertaken this expansion at an unfortunate time, and we are thus laying ourselves open to attack at a point where we are little able to defend ourselves."[11]

Marquis found an ally in President Sam H. Whitley of East Texas State Teachers College, who argued that "our problems have been greatly agitated by introducing graduate work into the teachers colleges at this time." He was sorry that the North Texas faculty had voted in favor of graduate work and that Huntsville had announced its plans to begin the program. He was not in favor, President Whitley said, "of agitating the public mind in this period of depression, non-payment of taxes, and general era of bad feeling by making additions to our curricula."[12] H. W. Morelock, president of the smallest teachers college, Sul Ross State, took personal offense at these views and drafted Presidents Hill and Estill to help push the master's degree cause. Estill agreed heartily, stating that the matter involved the welfare of the teaching profession and the recognition of the institutions that represented the profession in the education of teachers. "If we back down at this time," he declared, "we shall make an ignoble surrender to the liberal arts colleges, state and denominational."[13]

THE ECONOMY WAVE

Soon, however, the general movement toward tax-cutting made graduate study appear to be a luxury none could afford in the face of attack. Of the two schools that had started fifth-year programs, one was threatened with extinction and the other with reduction to junior college level. President Whitley of Commerce was chosen for a committee to report to the State Board of Education on programs for all state-supported colleges. He secured the agreement of the other teachers college presidents (given somewhat reluctantly in one or two cases) that graduate work should be limited "in the main" to the University of Texas. President Marquis asked for the addition of the words "at present" to this statement. President Hill at Canyon said he was willing to accept this principle so long as Texas Tech and the College of Industrial Arts were kept out of the graduate field. At the same time, President Whitley was to make the effort to persuade all state colleges other than the teachers colleges to abandon the field of teacher education except in the form of minors offered in the junior and senior years.[14]

This tactical withdrawal by the teachers colleges that had started graduate courses did not save the entire group from an attack by the Griffenhagen Committee. Its report asserted that the teachers college authorities "fully recognize their unfitness to give graduate work. . . but this does not deter them."[15]

The report then moved to the North Texas State faculty report of 1930, which argued against giving more than one or two teachers colleges the right to grant graduate degrees. It stated that in this report "The unfitness of the teachers colleges for the giving of graduate work was presented by President Marquis." This doubtless increased antagonism toward Marquis, as did its statement that North Texas State Teachers College is the only institution of the teachers colleges that is qualified to give graduate work.[16]

In this area, however, as in most others, the Griffenhagen recommendations were not followed. All the teachers colleges were in the graduate business within two years of the report's publication in 1933.

chapter 17

Big Saturday Night

To all those who are seeking opportunity to work under wholesome influence, favorable conditions, and competent and sympathetic direction the College extends a hearty welcome. Those who are merely seeking diversions, change of environment or increased social advantages, and those who are unable or unwilling to lead the life of a student are advised to remain away.

The North Texas Catalog, 1930.

The teachers college student of the 1920s had no Student Union Building, no night football, no ready transportation to his hometown or to nearby cities. The result was the development of a Saturday tradition that lasted through several decades.

An early approach to "what to do on Saturday night" was a Saturday evening open house, introduced in the last year of the normal college. The student life secretary and the ladies of the faculty invited students to spend two or three hours on Saturday nights in the Library Building reading rooms. This offered "some place to go and an opportunity to meet friends informally, under conditions of safety and propriety."[1]

THE SHOW BEGINS

In 1925 a moving picture machine was installed in the auditorium, with pictures shown every Saturday night. The *Campus Chat*[2] proudly announced the acquisition of this equipment, with two machines installed in an asbestos fireproof booth in the balcony, providing no interruption during the process of entertainment for the changing of reels. "A screen with a gilded face" was installed on the stage. The *Chat* observed that only outstanding pictures would be presented, remarking that "no story that is simply commonplace will be shown."

The silent pictures of the time required the addition of music locally. A young music faculty member named Floyd Graham gathered some young men to provide a pit orchestra for the motion pictures at CIA and NTSTC and to play for some college dances. The latter were first allowed on the campus in 1924–25. Many of the orchestra members were students. Graham's major concern, he said, was to help young musicians work their way through college.[3]

The end of the usefulness of the pit orchestra was signaled in 1929, when the first full-length, all-talking motion picture feature was shown.[4] The film starred George Jessel in *Lucky Boy*. The Floyd Graham pit orchestra was transformed into a stage band to provide a show before the movie. A one-reel comedy and a newsreel were also usually shown.

The Saturday Night Stage Show had begun. It became a beloved tradition of the teachers college period and beyond. The North Texas State Teachers College stage band for seven consecutive years beginning in 1928 performed at the annual convention of the West Texas Chamber of Commerce.

Several students began entertainment careers on the Saturday night show. One was Joan Blondell, known on the campus as Rosebud. She was enrolled in two speech courses while in school in the fall of 1927 and appeared with the Dramatic Club in George Bernard Shaw's *Candida*. She left then for New York and appeared in several Ziegfield productions and began bit parts in the motion pictures in 1930. A brother, Edward Blondell, returned from Hollywood in 1932 to direct a Saturday Night Stage Show production entitled "1932 Follies."

The *Campus Chat* in March 1933 reported that the stage band would present that hot Harlem torch song "Going Going Gone!" It was "to be featured by none other than Clara Lou Sheridan and her big-little voice." In July Miss Sheridan won the district "Search for Beauty" contest held by Paramount Studios and was later signed to a Paramount contract.[5] In 1933, seven-year-old Nancy Jane Gates, billed as a "diminutive star deluxe" did a specialty song and dance number, "Lazybones." The stage band, which soon became known as "Aces of Collegeland," selected Miss Gates as its sweetheart, and she appeared for a number of years while in public school in Denton. At fifteen, in 1941, she signed a contract with RKO Studios, beginning a motion picture and television career that was to extend into the postwar years.[6]

The official status of Saturday Night Stage Shows was indicated by President Marquis, whose two sons were members of the stage band. In an assembly speech to students on "Your College" in 1929 Marquis said: "Saturday Night Stage Shows are given to keep the students out of trouble or from wandering downtown or to other houses. The equipment is the best that can be bought for the shows, but when better is made we will buy it."[7] The stage shows survived for more than a decade after World War II, but eventually fell casualty to the automobile, greater student mobility, and a diversity of new interests.

ANOTHER NEW MEDIUM

Radio arrived in Texas in the 1920s. It became part of a reunion of 800 ex-students at the Texas Hotel in Fort Worth at the convention of the Texas State Teachers Association in December 1923. The teachers college banquet was broadcast for one hour and a half by WBAP, the *Fort Worth Star-Telegram* station. A telegram to President Marquis from the wife of the president of Iowa State Teachers College in Cedar Falls, Iowa, reported that the teachers college program had been listened to in that city. Among those speaking to the gathering on radio were Governor Pat M. Neff of Texas, President Marquis, Dean of Women Edith L. Clark, Miss Mary J. Byrne of the Class of 1914, president of the Texas Grade Teachers Association, and President Emeritus W. H. Bruce, who had traveled from Alabama to attend the banquet.

Later that month the college presented a program over the *Dallas Morning News* station, WFAA, aimed at students and ex-students who were home for the Christmas holidays. Dean W. J. McConnell spoke, and music students performed. A loudspeaker was hooked up on the roof of the Manual Arts Building so the program could be heard by Denton citizens. In January 1924, the teachers college again broadcast musical programs on WFAA and WBAP. Students gathered to listen to the loudspeaker on the Manual Arts Building. The *Dallas Morning News* reported that responses from friends "in all parts of the English and Spanish speaking world" had come in.

STUDENT ORGANIZATIONS

The normal college clubs and societies continued into at least the early years of the teachers college period. Four literary societies continued active: Mary Arden and Current Literature for women, the Reagan and the Lee societies for men. The men's organizations did not thrive well. In the last year of their existence, 1928, the Reagans dropped to fourteen members while the Lees had thirty-five. The Current Literature Club was continued for a good many years before suspending activities. The Mary Arden Society remained active into the 1970s.[8] The men's literary societies were replaced by social organizations, starting in 1927 with the formation of the Talons with forty members. This organization is not related to the service group formed more than thirty years later. In 1930 two other men's groups, Geezles and Pi Phi Pi, began. Still others appeared during the 1930s. Women's social sororities didn't develop until the latter half of that decade.

The Press Club continued its activities. The *Campus Chat* and the *Yucca* maintained publication, and the *Avesta* came back to life again in 1925 and was published as a literary magazine for another half century. In 1926 the *Chat* began printing on the campus by students, with L. R. Woodson as their instructor. At this time the paper enlarged from a six- to a seven-column format and became more thoroughly departmentalized.

Campus Chat and *Yucca* offices moved to the new Administration Building in 1924. With the opening of the Print Shop in 1925 and the resumption of the *Avesta* magazine, two of the three publications printed on the campus for the first time. In April 1927 North Texas journalists again joined the Texas Intercollegiate Press Association, bringing to twenty-one the number of member schools.[9]

In 1930, the *Yucca* received an All-American honor rating from the National Scholastic Press Association. This publication, edited by Ralph Houston, was the first of many that would be named All-American.[10] The Ex-Students Association began publishing in 1930 the *Ex-Students' News*.[11] Similarly, there was recognized the need for some organized means of getting news about the teachers college to professional newspapers off the campus. County clubs on the campus had been asked to approach their hometown editors with news of North Texas, and a student had been employed in 1929 to do part-time publicity work. In 1930, President Marquis realized that rumors about the summer school appropriations difficulties could be damaging enrollment. No summer school announcement bulletin was published, and it was rumored there would be no summer school or at best for only six weeks. Marquis asked students to write friends and to ask their local papers to print reports that the college would maintain a full twelve-week session.[12] By 1934 the school had established a News Service to handle publicity of its activities. It was conducted by J. D. Hall, Jr., who also taught journalism, directed the Print Shop and was one of the student publications sponsors.[13]

The Green Jacket Club was formed in 1926 with thirty-five members. Active musical organizations of this time were the College Choral Club, Girls' Glee Club, Men's Glee Club, along with College Band and College Orchestra. The Lillie Bruce Dramatic Club continued under that name until 1928, becoming known for five years starting in 1929 simply as the Dramatic Club. Afterwards it took the name College Players. The Debate Club was organized in 1929 and remained active thereafter. By 1931 a *Campus Chat* writer could report that the college debate team had achieved the most successful season in the history of the school, winning fifty-three of seventy-four debates. The top-ranking team was composed of Charles Brooks and A. A. White, who lost only five times in thirty-seven debates, winning first place in two of five tournaments. The top honor was their first place in the Southern Tournament in

Atlanta, Georgia. The women's team took first place at an invitational tournament in Arkadelphia, Arkansas.[14]

Departmental clubs were the Kindergarten-Primary Club for education students, the Cottage Cousins and then the Ellen H. Richards Club in home economics, and an Industrial Education Club. The W. H. Bruce Scholarship Society, a scholastic honor group started in 1924, was known just as the Scholarship Society for four years and then became Alpha Chi. Kappa Delta Pi was organized as a scholastic honor group in 1926. Delta Psi Kappa for women in physical education was organized in 1928. The 1929 year saw the start of Pi Kappa Delta, a forensic society; Pi Omega Pi, national commercial teachers fraternity; and Pi Gamma Mu, national social science fraternity. Continuing as local groups were the E. D. Criddle Historical Club from 1925 on, and the W. N. Masters Chemical Society, started in 1927. The Young Men's Christian Association survived through 1928, and the YWCA until 1931.

In January 1925 the Women's Forum started up. This group created a Forum Council with officers representing all women and with representatives from each class. The Council took up topics that might normally have gone before a Student Council: honor on examinations, health, boardinghouse improvements, and other school problems, which were brought before students in assembly programs, *Campus Chat* editorials, and posters.[15]

NO STUDENT UNION

With no student union building, the *Campus Chat* in July 1925 pointed out that "meet me in the auditorium" had become a campus slogan. This was the gathering place for studies, the *Chat* noted, also recognizing that "in spots far removed from curious ears sit pairs more assiduously interested in each other than in the books which lie neglected in their laps."

Dean of Women Edith Clark and Dean of Men J. E. Burk placed a letter on page one of the *Campus Chat* in 1925 reminding "young men are to stay away from the boarding houses of young ladies." This regulation applied except to Saturday evenings after six and Sunday after four. The letter said that "young ladies are not to stand in front of boarding houses, talking to young men. . . . Young men who accompany young ladies to functions at the college, except on off-nights, will take their leave promptly on returning to the young ladies' boarding places."[16] In the same issue, the *Chat* reported that the regents agreed that students who married during the term would automatically be dropped from school. The *Chat* story said "the reasons are obvious."[17]

What had been the Lyceum Series became first the Artists' Course and then the Fine Arts Series. By the fall of 1923 references to "chapel" had disappeared and in the future students attended "assembly programs." In September 1927 Colonel Charles A. Lindbergh gave students "the Lindbergh thrill" by circling low over the campus three times in his monoplane, *The Spirit of Saint Louis*.[18]

Students occasionally manufactured their own excitement. An eighty-foot flagpole in the campus center was dedicated on November 11, 1925, in honor of Armistice Day. It was called the largest flagpole in the state except for one at a Fort Worth ballpark. Skirmishes among students took place around the flagpole, mostly on Freshman Day. In 1927, upperclassmen flew their flag and defied freshmen to take it down. They greased the flagpole with axle grease containing chipped glass and the freshmen fought all day to get the flag down but never succeeded. That night upperclassmen rang the curfew bell every thirty minutes to summon aid from more upperclassmen when it looked as if the freshmen might get the upper hand. The *Campus Chat* wryly noted that the dean of men "has relegated such affairs as these to the vicinity of vacant lots."[19]

SAFETY, CONVENIENCE, COMFORT

A modern problem appeared in print in 1930, when Marquis inserted a front-page notice in the *Campus Chat* headed "Safety, Convenience, Comfort," asking students to avoid parking on Hickory Street in front of the campus. They were invited to go to Avenue A or Avenue B.

Still lacking a dormitory or a union building, the teachers college in 1930 offered the Community Clubhouse, a two-story frame residence at the northeast corner of Sycamore and Avenue A. (Later students became acquainted with it as the Men's Building, housing the athletic department and the dean of men.) Tables, hot and cold water, and a gas supply were furnished for students who brought their lunches. The clubhouse quartered the YWCA and was presided over by the student life secretary. In 1930, the office of the dean of freshman girls was located in the Clubhouse, and she scheduled meetings there for student organizations and served as hostess. Next door to the north on Avenue A, the Mary Arden Club erected the Mary Arden Lodge, which served for many years as its meeting place and as a site for teas and other social activities.

STUDENT CONDUCT

The rigid restrictions of Dr. Bruce's Normal didn't disappear abruptly during the first years of the teachers college. For boardinghouses in 1930, for example:

> Musical instruments or radio may be played from 12 to 2 and from 6 until curfew. Students who violate this rule forfeit the right to keep portable or ukulele.
>
> Telephones are to be used only for business and no social engagements are to be made over them.
>
> On school days students are expected not to waste their time or make themselves conspicuous by going to the picture show too often or loafing in the stores on the streets or on the campus.[20]

A series of moral questions occupied the attention of the editorial page of the *Chat* in 1930. One editorial was headed "Is Dancing a Sin?" The writer stated that dancing was no sin, but that it was a source of much immoral practice and thought and "some young people who go wrong may justly attribute the cause of their downfall to the dance."[21]

The student editorialist also attacked the problem of smoking. He recalled that about two or three years earlier President Marquis had made a gentlemen's agreement with men students that there would be no more smoking on the campus. The writer regretted that "we find cigarette butts scattered promiscuously about on the walks and among the shrubbery." The editorial asked, "Does it look well to pass to and from buildings on the campus through a maze of cigarettes with fire on one end and suckers on the other?"[22] After a survey of Eastern college students showed that a majority claimed to be drinkers, the *Chat* attacked those who would openly violate the Prohibition laws and the moral code in the habitual use of liquor. Such students should not be kept in college, the editorial declared, and no student should receive a diploma "who has shown by his conduct that he often deliberately violated the law of the land."[23]

STUDENT GOVERNMENT

As the teachers college period opened, it still had the Student-Faculty Council, composed of six students and six faculty members. Marquis appointed committees in 1924 to draft a proposed constitution for student participation in college government. A joint student-faculty group submitted the constitution for a student election to create the Students' Association. It provided a council to include a president, vice president and secretary elected by the general student body, a man and woman elected from each college class and the subcollege department, and the dean of men and dean of women. It provided for student participation in discussions and recommendations on many student activities, excluding academic matters. After "heated debate" in several chapel periods, the election was set for December 5, with students voting by secret ballot as they left the auditorium. Marquis had required that a favorable vote by a majority of students enrolled would be required for passage. This would require at least 803 favorable votes for the acceptance of the constitution. However, the proposal not only lacked the necessary majority of those eligible to vote, it also failed 538–402 among those who did cast ballots.[24]

The only change in the Student-Faculty Council for a number of years was in the increase of the number of representatives to eight students and eight faculty members, rather than six of each group. A 1930 view of council functions was described in a news story this way: "The Council holds monthly meetings at which time questions concerning the welfare of the student body are discussed and recommendations made to the President and to the Dean of the College."[25]

Students made another try in 1932 for a "Constitution of Cooperative College Planning." This effort led to a favorable student vote in April 1934, 275-168, to create a charter for the group. The death of Marquis intervened, however, and this plan was never implemented.[26]

OTHER STUDENT SERVICES

Miss Adolphine Grabbe, a practical nurse, was made superintendent in September 1922 and held the position until August 1930. The teachers college had no regular college physician, calling in Denton doctors as the need arose. In February 1929 the Board of Regents authorized Marquis to arrange with a doctor for two hours of work a day in the hospital at one hundred dollars per month. Dr. M. D. Fullingim, who had been the army physician on the campus in 1918, served in this capacity until September 1930. At that time Dr. L. O. Hayes became the school's first full-time physician and Miss Nina L. Preuss became the first registered nurse at the hospital.[27]

Placement of students in teaching positions was handled by a faculty committee, until 1928, when Marquis announced that he had created a Placement Bureau to be directed E. H. Farrington of the history faculty, who had been chairman of the faculty committee.[28]

ATHLETIC EVENTS

North Texas joined an athletic conference for the first time in 1922, affiliating with the Texas Intercollegiate Athletic Association. Against other members of the TIAA that year, the North Texas football team was undefeated but lacked a full schedule and was ineligible for the title. The Eagles finally won first-place in football in 1931. The 1923 football schedule was fairly typical of the decade. It included Southern Methodist University, Baylor, Grubbs Vocational School, Trinity, Austin College, and three other state teachers colleges, Sam Houston State, West Texas State, and Southwest Texas State.

Each year from 1923 to 1936, the season began with either Southern Methodist or Texas Christian University, almost always with a loss. The only opening victory came against Southern Methodist in 1933, 7-0 in a year that was relatively undistiguished otherwise.

Coaches during this period were Theron J. Fouts, 1920–24, later to become athletic director; John B. Reid, 1925–28; and Jack Sisco, 1929–41, later to become a member of the Board of Regents. All three were Baylor graduates. In fact, every North Texas football coach between 1913 and the end of World War II was a product of Baylor.

Intercollegiate basketball began in 1916, when SMU edged the normal school, 25-23. Basketball was coached during this time by J. W. St. Clair, Fouts, Reid, and Terrence Myracle. In the first two years of the Marquis administration, another basketball tradition, that of girls' intercollegiate athletics, became the center of disagreement between the athletic committee and the Board of Regents. The result was that after 1925 there was no further intercollegiate competition in basketball or track for women students. The girls' basketball team, coached by Miss Beulah Harriss, had played three undefeated seasons in 1918–20, to be recognized as the champions of the State of Texas.

THE MARQUIS PHILOSOPHY

President Marquis expressed his philosophy of intercollegiate athletics in a 1924 letter to a representative of the National Collegiate Athletic Association.[29] He stressed that no effort was made to attract athletes from high school or other colleges, and that no inducements were offered athletes in either money or student labor: "The coaches are simply required to take the material which they find at the opening of school and turn out the best teams possible under the circumstances." Marquis opposed the hiring of coaches *per se* by a college. The president concluded with this commentary on athletic recruiting:

> In my opinion, one of the most unfortunate conditions now existing in the schools is the tendency to spoil boys who are playing in the high schools over the state. The boys are in no sense to be blamed if they get an entirely incorrect idea of their importance and a distorted conception of relative values. . . . I am really very much opposed to the practice that some colleges are guilty of scouting around among high schools, offering inducements for the various football stars to enroll in this or that institution. I am thinking of the harm done to the boys rather than to the college.

Football, basketball, track, tennis, and baseball, along with intramural activities, could not be considered a major expense in the 1920s. Most support for athletics came from the optional student fee, which was divided this way: debate and oratory, 7.5 percent; athletics, 37 percent; fine arts, 27.75 percent; and publications, 27.75 percent.[30] In 1923–24 the student activity fee yielded $3,900. Guarantees received for playing games away from Denton amounted to $2,501.50. Local gate receipts contributed but $641.85 during the year and a special fund yielded $400. Total income was $7,443.35. The money was not spent for scholarships or coaching salaries. For cash guarantees to visiting schools and expenses of game officials, the school spent $2,889.40; for athletic equipment, insurance, telephone calls, and supplies, $1,831.13; and for traveling expenses, $2,730.82, making a total of $7,451.35 and a deficit of $8.00 in the athletic fund for the school year.

THE CONFERENCE PROBLEM

Disagreements arose among members of the Texas Intercollegiate Athletic Association. Within six years, two new athletic conferences were formed by members who split away from the TIAA. In part the split was caused by disagreement over the kinds of athletic standards that ought to be imposed, and in part by the geographic separation of the members.

A principal problem was Marquis's insistence on enforcement of the prohibition of freshmen participation in intercollegiate varsity sports. In a letter to the *Dallas Morning News* on March 23, 1925, Marquis said that not only should freshmen be banned from intercollegiate athletics, but schools should in addition enforce the rule that barred a student from intercollegiate contests during the first year after he had transferred from one school to another. Marquis argued further that no man should be allowed to participate in athletic contests after he had played one year on the varsity team—the purpose being to distribute playing opportunities among more of the men students.

Marquis had a strong ally in Roy Bedichek, chief of the Interscholastic Bureau of the University of Texas Division of Extension. Bedichek wrote Marquis that he, too, favored limiting a boy to playing one year. He confessed, however, that he had not been able to find any teacher who agreed with that position.

The first open split came in May 1925 when five institutions announced they would resign from the TIAA and form the Texas Conference. The departing members were Southwestern, Trinity, Howard Payne, Simmons, and Austin College.[31] Each of these institutions was church supported, and the five had agreed to ally themselves "along denominational lines." After North Texas efforts to dissuade them, the five Texas Conference schools agreed to stay in the TIAA for the 1925 football season but would start Texas Conference basketball play in 1926.[32]

Kern Tips, a sports writer for the *Houston Chronicle,* wrote President Marquis to ask for his views of the impending split and the "proportion of the apparent dissatisfaction."[33] Marquis responded with a lengthy explanation.[34] The North Texas president wrote that the TIAA had been formed to rid college athletics of "objectionable influences and to put college sports under complete control of the college authorities." He credited the TIAA with abolishing the offensive evils of the professional athlete and the gambler that were widespread in Texas before the TIAA was formed. He expressed the hope that all institutions involved would have second thoughts on the matter and that the TIAA membership would remain unchanged.

EAST vs. WEST?

On July 28, Marquis wrote to the president of each of the five Texas Conference schools. He asked that each do what he could to reverse the plan and to keep his institution within the TIAA. He proposed a geographical east-west split among the members with an annual championship playoff between the top teams in each division. These letters produced some interesting answers. The president of one university wrote: "Due to the pressure of other things and due to a lack of native interest in athletics, I have given the question to which you refer no thought at all." Another answered: "I have not interested myself particularly in the situation and have no definite views. . . . I suppose I will have to let the matter rest as it now stands."

But the strongest response of all came from President Thomas Stone Clyce of Austin College. He wrote:

> I must say frankly to you that the state teachers colleges are responsible for the movement by the new conference. They came into an old organization and proceeded immediately to dominate, or attempt to dominate everything. I know that when I attended one meeting of the TIAA in the interest of a condition that existed in regard to Austin College I was scarcely treated with courtesy. . . . Some of the other institutions that are pulling out of the TIAA have long been members of the organization. They do not appreciate the fact that those who have so recently come into the organization should attempt to take things in hand and run them according to their own ideas. So rather than to have any additional unpleasantness, they decided to pull out and form a new conference[35]

Marquis responded that he was greatly surprised at the charges against the teachers colleges.[36]

Just before the December TIAA meeting Marquis attended the meeting of the Southern Association at which the five teachers colleges were admitted to membership. This particular meeting, it developed, was devoted especially to the development of more stringent academic regulations concerning intercollegiate football. President Marquis was quick to attempt to turn this new development to his advantage. He was interviewed by a Dallas reporter the day before the conference meeting. He declared that the Texas Intercollegiate Athletic Association would have to keep freshmen off its football teams. He said that resolutions unanimously adopted at the Southern Association meeting would lead to some action by the TIAA. Furthermore, he said, the Southern Association ruling specified that no institution could remain or become a member of the association unless it belonged to a qualified athletic conference—a conference composed of athletically and scholastically related institutions. The news story continued:

> "The fifth resolution is the one that has a kick in it." Dr. Marquis said. "The Texas colleges have been saying that they were grown up. Now here is their chance to prove it. The TIAA must adopt these rules and enforce them. The freshman regulation is just. Spoiled high school athletes should be allowed to cool their heels a year before getting on a collegiate team."[37]

Nevertheless, the five denominational colleges went ahead with their plans to withdraw from the TIAA and form the Texas Conference.

George M. Crutsinger, chairman of the NTSTC faculty athletic committee, and some other teachers college faculty representatives, finally brought the freshman rule to a successful conference vote at the December 1927 meeting. However, there was little success for some time in getting the actual enforcement of the freshman rule. Marquis turned to the Southern Association for help, but the chairman of the Commission on Institutions of Higher Education of the Southern Association responded sympathetically but reported that it was hard to get Southern Association members to apply athletic regulations stringently, particularly where association member schools were aligned in conferences with schools that were not members of the association.[38]

The TIAA in 1927 applied the freshman rule only to its schools that were members of the Southern Association. A year later the rule was changed so that it applied to all schools effective December 1, 1929. The problem remained with schools in the Texas Conference. TIAA members complained that recruiters from Texas Conference schools told high school seniors that they could not play football that fall in the TIAA, but that they could play in the Texas Conference schools. This produced further friction among the Texas colleges.

LONE STAR FORMED

By 1930 the TIAA had expanded back to eleven members. These were the teachers colleges at Nacogdoches, San Marcos, Commerce, Huntsville, Alpine, Canyon, and Denton, along with Texas A&I College, Daniel Baker College, Abilene Christian College, and McMurry College. Marquis resumed his efforts to create an east-west zone split with championship playoffs in the TIAA but was unsuccessful.

Finally in May 1931, five schools formed a new association, the Lone Star Conference. Members were Stephen F. Austin, Sam Houston, East Texas, Southwest Texas, and North Texas State Teachers Colleges. Competition began in 1932 with Trinity University (formerly of the Texas Conference) as a sixth member. North Texas was to remain a member of the Lone Star Conference for fourteen years before moving on to other athletic affiliations.[39]

chapter 18

Best People, Best Water

We are fully cognizant of your achievements in behalf of this college, such as the beautification of the campus, the general improvement of scholarship in the faculty, the raising of our collegiate standards, and the gaining for this institution a high and secure recognition by the best accrediting agencies in the country. We are gratified at the place of leadership yielded to you in all movements for the betterment of teachers colleges. What touches our hearts most is the consciousness that while you have been very, very busy with all of these accomplishments, you have never once lost those human qualities that proclaim you the friend of each member of the faculty.

Petition from the faculty
April 1931

When Robert Lincoln Marquis assumed the presidency of North Texas State Teachers College at the age of forty-three, he told his friends, "I have found the best people and the best water on earth; when a man finds that, he there builds his home. I have settled here and have started negotiations for a lot in the cemetery."[1]

His jest in retrospect has tragic overtones, for he died in less than eleven years at the age of fifty-four. That they were not easy years has been made clear in the foregoing chapters; that they were gratifying years for him seems evident in his speeches and in his writing.

TEACHERS COLLEGE MAN

President Marquis regarded himself above all else as a teachers college man. His career brought him into association with four schools in the normal college-teachers college system of Texas. On several occasions it appeared he might move on from the Denton presidency, but he never did. He was the president of two—probably three—Texas colleges.

Marquis was born January 4, 1880, in Goliad County (as he jokingly told a student reporter) in "the middle of a big ranch in a log house, and destined, therefore, to be a great man."[2] He received the A.B. degree from Texas Christian University in 1901, the B.S. from the University of Texas in 1902, and the M.S. from the University of Chicago in 1903. He taught one year at Jarvis College, four years at John Tarleton College and one year at Sam Houston State Normal. That brings his academic career up to the 1909–10 year, which is omitted from his official biographical listing.[3] However, a historian of Texas education says that Marquis spent that year as first president of Midland Christian College, a small collegiate venture that survived from 1909 to 1921.[4] Nothing in any Denton records ever mentions this presidency. Marquis taught at West Texas State Normal College in Canyon from 1910 until 1918, when he moved to Denton to teach biology. He was chosen from this post to become president of Sul Ross State Normal from 1920 to 1923, the year of his return to Denton.

With this background it is not surprising to read in the new president's first Denton address the assertion that "the principal task in view for us is to make the world recognize the business of teaching as a profession and treat it as such." Speaking to an overflow crowd in the college stadium at an evening chapel period late in June 1923, Marquis declared:

> Frankly, I am in favor of placing all the snares, traps and pitfalls possible in the way of those who come to Teachers Colleges for a lark or to prepare to teach merely as a "stepping stone" to "higher things." But I have usually found that those who use it as a stepping stone have found it, rather, a "stumbling block." I favor raising the admission requirements of the College, making the requirements in grades and health so high that only those who are determined to teach will be able to qualify themselves. [5]

At the end of the 1924 summer session, the president told students that the term was the most successful in history—successful not because of the largest enrollment on record but "because of the amount and quality of work done." He voiced what was to become a recurring theme in remarks on the role of teachers colleges:

> I see in the summer school of the Teachers College a system that encourages industry and ambition and at the same time eliminates the shiftless and lazy from the profession of teaching. It is a machine that encourages one group and discourages another, thus giving us a sifted and selected product. . . . Of all vocations, teaching should be the last to utilize the anemic and ne'er-do-well. If people can not stand the pace set by the summer school group, let them drop out and go into something less strenuous. As I see it, the summer school is a blessing as a selective draft.[6]

In May 1925, two years after taking office, Marquis was formally inaugurated as president of the teachers college. Twelve days later, the North Texas president was given the honorary doctor of laws degree by Austin College at Sherman. The *Campus Chat* thereafter referred to him as "Dr. Marquis," a practice more common then than now for holders of honorary degrees.[7] The *Chat* story that reported the honorary degree also told of the receiving of the doctor of philosophy degree by the college dean, W. J. McConnell, who had studied at Columbia University.

INTEREST AT A&M

Shortly thereafter, Marquis became involved in the search for a new president at Texas A&M College. That vacancy was first mentioned in connection with Marquis's name in newspapers in June 1925. Marquis was approached directly on July 3 in a letter requesting a list of references. Marquis responded with the names of the Teachers College Board of Regents, the presidents of most of the other public and private colleges and universities in the state, a number of public school people, Texas State Teachers Association officers, and members of the State Board of Control.[8]

He followed the advice of his own regents: let the A&M regents ask for information or references as needed, but don't mount a campaign that would flood the A&M regents with unsolicited mail. In this manner, Marquis acquired the endorsement of the immediate past governor of Texas, Pat M. Neff, and Attorney General Dan Moody, who would become governor the following year. He was also supported by the president and the dean of the School of Law at the University of Texas, a number of leading judges of the state, college administrators, and many attorneys and bankers.

On August 3, however, a writer for the *Dallas Journal* advised President Marquis that the A&M Board of Regents had settled on another candidate. Marquis replied this way:

> What you say concerning the prospective choice of the A&M Board is no surprise to me. I have believed for some time that the choice of the Board has been settled for weeks. . . . You are aware, of course, that I am tremendously interested in the whole question of teacher training. I am perfectly willing to dedicate my entire life to this work and I see no better place than Denton and the Teachers College where I may work.

AND SAN ANTONIO CALLS

Illness kept Marquis from work several times. The regents granted him a thirty-day leave "for benefit of his health" in 1926.[9] Five years later, in early April 1931, he was again at home with illness when a news story from San Antonio created a major stir. Newspapers reported that Marquis was about to be elected school superintendent in San Antonio at more than twice the salary he received at North Texas. He issued a statement saying that "he had nothing to say about the report, that it was unofficial, and that he did not know its source."[10] The reports proved true, and Marquis was offered the superintendency at $10,000 a year. The news brought forth a petition from the faculty, part of which appears at the head of this chapter. The petition also said:

> The honor done you. . . prompts the members of this faculty to attempt to express to you, in the most sincere manner, our sense of your value to this institution, and to convey to you our desire that you remain with us. . . .
>
> Our strong and sincere attachment to you induces us to hope that our best interest will prove to be your best interest, so that you will remain for many, many years our honored and beloved president.

Marquis declined the offer of the San Antonio job. His response to the faculty indicated that two factors had influenced his decision: dedication to teacher training and happy associations in Denton. He also said, "If the Board of Regents grants me a leave of absence in its June meeting, I shall be away from the campus for two or three months.[11]

The June meeting of the regents found Marquis present but not taking active part. Dean McConnell presented the budget for the following year. Marquis was granted leave of absence with full pay for such time as was judged best by the president and his physician.[12] Correspondence to President Marquis during his convalescent period referred to his condition as high blood pressure. Others of his contemporaries describe the 1931 condition as a heart attack. He did return to work after that summer and completed nearly three more school years in office.

On the morning of Thursday, April 12, 1934, President R. L. Marquis was stricken by a heart attack that was regarded as critical from the onset. His condition worsened on Sunday, and offices in the Administration Building remained open to keep students, faculty members, and other friends advised of the president's condition. Early that night, April 15, he died of a coronary occlusion. He was survived by his wife and twin sons, Robert Lincoln, Jr., and Richard, both of whom pursued careers as college professors.[13] On Tuesday the body of the president lay in state in the college auditorium prior to the services that afternoon. Among those speaking were Henry Paulus of Yoakum, member of the Board of Regents, and President J. A. Hill of West Texas State

Teachers College. In the large group of out-of-town educators attending the services were the presidents of the state teachers colleges, President H. Y. Benedict of the University of Texas, and faculty members and administrators from many other colleges.

Hundreds of messages of tribute were, of course, written at that time. In a resolution from the faculty, these statements appeared:

> The College, which he has helped to expand into a great institution, has lost a head whose influence will continue to live, not only in its material development, but in the shaping of its policies and ideals. The state is deprived of a valued educator, and the teaching profession has lost a far-visioned idealist, whose work has been a mighty national force in strengthening and dignifying his profession. He believed that no king was ever anointed to holier service than the schoolmaster; that the highest calling was to prepare young people for better, happier, nobler living. . . .
>
> But, although the loss of our leader is deep, the loss of our friend is unfathomable.[14]

part IV

Teachers College in Transition

1934–1949

Teachers Colleges were established to prepare teachers. With this uncommon singleness of purpose and in spite of inadequacies of material advantages, the Teachers College system of Texas. . . has attained distinction that is regarded as signal throughout the nation. One of the institutions of the Texas system [North Texas] enrolls annually more students, records more credit hours, and confers more degrees than any other state teachers college of the nation or than any other institution of higher learning in Texas except the State University.

W. J. McConnell

chapter 19

The Foundation is Laid

The progress which has been made by the Texas system of teachers colleges has been achieved in spite of the fact that the colleges of this system have been faced with obstacles not encountered by other educational institutions of the state. Among these are inadequate plant facilities, discriminating salary schedules, and lack of teaching laboratory facilities. Tolerance of such obstacles on the part of the state is all the more unforgivable when it is apparent that for teachers colleges the quickness of conversion of monetary outlay into citizenship values in the democracy is without a parallel in educational expenditures. Every dollar, wisely spent, on teacher preparation forthwith begins to bear dividends to society.

W. J. McConnell, 1937

On the surface few major changes appeared at North Texas State Teachers College between 1923 and 1934. No change in fundamental purpose or structure was made. Financial difficulties made it hard just to maintain standards, especially in the maintenance of summer schools. Little progress in campus expansion or building development was possible. Enrollment figures for the long session show a loss rather than a gain. In 1923–24 there were 2,101 students. This number sagged to 1,473 in 1926–27 when subcollege work was moved from the teachers college. It climbed to 2,018 in 1932–33 and then fell to 1,704 the following year, well below the 1923 level.

Several factors are concealed by these figures, however. For one, they do not account for the significant development of the summer school in contrast to the old summer normal. In 1924 the summer total was 2,756 and in the summer of 1934 it had gained to 3,273. These people had become predominantly standard college degree-seeking students. In 1924 in two commencements North Texas conferred a total of ninety-four bachelor's degrees; in 1934, in two commencements, that figure had risen to 423.

THE STUDENT BODY

The students themselves were no different in their background during the 1923–34 period. Women were still in the majority. Nor were the family backgrounds of the students very much different in 1933–34. The occupational listings of parents showed that by far the largest number, 499, were farmers. Next in order of frequency in this Depression year was the unemployed, with 319 parents having no occupation at that time. Following on the list were ninety-eight teachers. The nonagricultural occupations included bakers, barbers, bookkeepers, brick masons, butchers, carpenters, clerks, cobblers, county officials, druggists, filling station operators, grocers, laborers, lumbermen, mail carriers, mechanics, ministers, oil field workers, printers, railroad employees, sheet metal workers, teletype operators, truck drivers, and the like.

Nor was there much change in student religious backgrounds. Baptists were most numerous with 575 students, Methodists second with 471, and no church affiliation, 261. There were 123 from the Church of Christ, 120 from the Christian Church, and 118 Presbyterians. There were only seven Catholics, no Christian Scientists, one Mormon, two of the Jewish faith, and no Unitarians.

Only a slight change could be detected in geographical origins of the students who came to Denton. At no time during this period were Dallas County and Tarrant County significant contributors of large blocks of students. In 1923–24 there were thirty students from all of Dallas County, 1.6 percent of the total enrollment. Tarrant County accounted for thirty-nine, 1.9 percent of the total. Denton County, on the other hand was represented by 688 students, thirty-three percent of the total student body. The beginning of an increase in the two nearby cities could be seen slightly in 1933–34, when Dallas County sent 4.6 percent of the student body to North Texas, and Tarrant County accounted for 4.2 percent. Denton County had dropped slightly to thirty percent.

The level of advancement of the long-session student was further below the summer student by 1933–34. Of 1,704 long-session students 1,447 held no teaching certificate and ninety held certificates but had no teaching experience. In the summer, however, of 3,273, only 789 held no certificates and 107 held certificates but had no teaching experience. All of the rest had teaching experience, including several hundred each year in years of experience from one through nine. There were sizable numbers with as much as twenty years of experience and even a scattered few with thirty-five, thirty-six, and thirty-eight years of experience as teachers.

There was also an increase in the number of major fields in which degrees were conferred. In 1924, forty students received bachelor's degrees in seven majors. In the commencements of 1934 there were twelve bachelor's degrees in art, ten biology, thirty business administration, nine chemistry, twenty-one economics, eighty-two education, fifty-one English, three Latin, seven Spanish, eighteen geography, nineteen government, fifty-seven history, twenty-eight home economics, fifteen industrial education, twenty mathematics, nine music, nineteen physical education, two physics, and nine speech. It was also in this year that the institution conferred its first bachelor of music degree. In such diversity may be seen the basis for the development of the liberal arts in the years just ahead.[1]

THE NEW PRESIDENT

Death took President R. L. Marquis from the campus just as the public institutions of Texas began to emerge from the worst effects of the Depression and into a period of unprecedented growth. Leadership in this period fell to the man who had been dean of the college during the entire Marquis presidency. In April 1934, one hundred instructors and college employees signed a petition to the Board of Regents urging that Dr. W. J. McConnell, dean of the college, be chosen as next president.

Seven of the nine members of the Board of Regents met in Austin May 14 to consider the selection of a president. Formal applications had been received from only two individuals. No presidents or members of the faculty of any of the state teachers colleges had applied. The name of Dean McConnell was presented and no other nomination was made. One vote was taken, with Dr. McConnell being unanimously elected as president.[2] The following week Dr. McConnell selected Dr. B. B. Harris, head of the biology department for thirteen years, to become his successor as dean of the college.

The new president and his faculty faced a series of major challenges intensified by the retrenchment during the worst years of the Depression. Lying immediately ahead were such issues as these:

1. Beginning graduate study.

2. Deciding the function of a teachers college in a society whose educational demands were changing.

3. Staffing an institution that had developed graduate work of a more complex nature and of organizing itself to fulfill its assignments more effectively.

4. Providing a physical plant for expanding enrollment, part of which was making up for the failure of the State of Texas to provide any dormitory facilities up to that time.

In less than three years McConnell was able to point out that North Texas State Teachers College enrolled annually more students, recorded more credit hours, and conferred more degrees than any other state teachers college of the nation or than any other institution of higher learning in Texas except the University of Texas.[3] He compared many of the teachers colleges favorably with "what I regard as the best institutions of the United States" in strength of faculties, in soundness of instruction, in scholarship of graduates, and in contributions to "the social, economic and governmental on-going of the nation."

W. Joseph McConnell was born April 12, 1883, in Batesville, Arkansas, the son of a minister. The family moved to Alvord, Texas, when he was three years old and it was from this high school that he graduated in 1902. On June 19 that year in Boyd, Texas, he married Miss Clara Bradford. For the next five years the young McConnell taught in a rural school in Wise County, and in high schools in Boyd from 1907 to 1910, and at Van Horn, Texas, from 1910 to 1912. The 1912–13 school year was his first venture into higher education as a student, and that was in Denton at the North Texas State Normal College. McConnell began teaching at Petrolia, Texas, and served as superintendent there between 1912 and 1916. When school was not in session, he attended the University of Denver, receiving the bachelor of arts degree in 1915. He joined the North Texas State Normal College faculty in 1916 as a mathematics teacher and continued in summer sessions at Denver, receiving his master of arts degree in 1918. In 1919 he became professor of economics and director of that department, retaining the directorship when he became dean of the college in 1923. He received a Ph.D. from Columbia University in 1925.

Dean McConnell was elected president of the Association of Texas Colleges in 1927 and served on the executive council of the American Association of Teachers Colleges from 1940 to 1945. From 1942 to 1944 he was president of the Council of Texas State Teachers College Presidents. In 1945–46 he served as president of the Southern Association of Colleges and Secondary Schools. President McConnell was elected a fellow in both the American Association for the Advancement of Science and the Texas Academy of Science.

Mrs. McConnell joined the normal college faculty in 1922 and served as director of the home economics department in the teachers college until 1932.

chapter 20

Graduate Work Begins

I do not subscribe to the implication that all professional work is in the Department of Education. I do not regard our courses in history, English, biology, et cetera as the mere content equivalent as what is offered in these departments in many institutions . . . . No amount of professional work apparently thought of by you as work in the Department of Education can remedy the defect of a lack of knowledge of the field taught.

President W. J. McConnell
January 30, 1936

It will be recalled that President Marquis stood firm against too early an introduction of graduate study. The North Texas faculty insisted that certain high standards be met and that only one or two of the state teachers colleges should be authorized to enter graduate study. After the attack on the unsuccessful graduate attempts by the Griffenhagen report, the state Board of Regents moved more carefully when graduate study finally began.

In June 1935 the regents authorized North Texas and West Texas State Teachers Colleges to begin offering graduate work in September 1935. Other schools were to "get in shape to offer graduate work" in the summer of 1936, "or as soon thereafter as they are qualified to do such work with credit to the system."[1] This was interpreted to mean that teachers colleges other than Denton and Canyon were to restrict their courses to a summer term. However, in February 1936 the regents asked all seven presidents to report in March on the demand for graduate work, the ability of the schools, and the requirements for such work.[2] The presidents reported that many public schools then had as great a percentage of master's degree teachers as did many college faculties fifteen years earlier. They requested a full five-year program for all of the state teachers college system.

INSTANT RESPONSE

North Texas graduate studies met with instant success in enrollment. In 1935–36, there were sixty-five long-session students and 604 the following summer. Long-session enrollment in subsequent years went to 104, 120, 181, and 206 before the effect of the war slowed down enrollment. Summer graduate enrollment went to 636, 778, 906, and 937 in the period ending in 1940.[3] The first graduate majors authorized were biology, chemistry, economics, home economics, physical and health education, English, government, history, mathematics, Spanish, and education in three fields: elementary education, secondary education, and school administration. The master of arts degree called for the language requirement of the bachelor of arts degree from North Texas. The master's degree was a thirty-semester-hour program of which the thesis would require either three or six semester hours of credit.[4] Twenty-seven master's degrees were conferred in the summer of 1936, eight in the spring of 1937, and forty-two in the summer of 1937.[5] By 1944 President McConnell reported that North Texas had granted 812 master's degrees, nearly double the number awarded by the next largest graduate program, that at Southwest Texas State Teachers College.

When the North Texas graduate bulletin was published, President C. E. Evans of San Marcos protested the master's degree being offered in a subject matter field with only six hours of work in education. "If the teachers colleges decide to follow this policy," he wrote in January 1936, "we cease to become standard state teachers colleges, are no longer professional schools, and the teachers of the future must be trained in the arts colleges which have departments of education." Evans suggested that North Texas violated the policy of the Southern Association.[6] Without revealing its authorship, McConnell asked members of the Graduate Council for their immediate reaction. He wrote Evans that the Board of Regents was not asking for a uniform graduate course in each teachers college. He wrote:

> Am I to believe from your letter that you think English literature, nature study, correction of speech defects, the teaching of history, training in auditorium activities of schools and the training of school librarians are not professional courses, whether they are denominated education or not? To devote a fifth year chiefly to the Department of Education would, in my opinion, be the equivalent of returning to the old Normal set-up. . . .
>
> Of twelve teachers colleges accredited by the American Association, only three, I believe, offer a master's degree with a major in the Department of Education only. We had already decided upon our course long before we knew this was a fact.[7]

OPPOSITION DEVELOPS

In reporting to the Board of Regents in March 1936, McConnell showed awareness of the need to justify the quality of graduate studies. He listed forty-three faculty members who held doctoral degrees and ten others who were added to the staff in summer, when graduate enrollments were heavier. The regents discussed possible opposition at their meeting in October and to a committee with Presidents Whitley and Hill to draft a resolution citing the demand for teachers college graduate work, results accomplished to date, and setting forth the regents' approval of the work.[8] The resolution was to be used in case of a fight before the legislature. On the same date as the board meeting, McConnell told a faculty meeting that the State Board of Education had asked schools whose graduate work had not been approved to come before the board and give reasons why the institution should offer this work.

The state board met on November 19. McConnell outlined the facilities, faculty, and enrollment at North Texas and told the board that the number of students during the first years of the master's degree program had no parallel at any other institution.[9] Upon his return to Denton, Dr. McConnell told a *Campus Chat* reporter that the board's familiarity with the demand for graduate work in the teacher training field and with the plant and the high standing of the North Texas faculty would get their support. He pointed out that ten state-supported colleges agreed to remain at the master's degree level, leaving higher graduate work to the University of Texas and Texas A&M. The schools were the state teachers colleges, Texas Tech, Texas A&I, and TSCW.[10]

McCONNELL ATTACKED

The matter was to be considered by the legislature early in 1937. McConnell's presentation to the state board in November and North Texas actions to win the legislature drew the wrath of President Hill of Canyon. Hill wrote McConnell an angry letter, accusing North Texas of "taking care of her own interests regardless of its effect upon sister institutions." Hill especially feared that legislators were going to compromise by agreeing that one teachers college would be permitted to offer graduate work, and that one would be at Denton.[11]

McConnell wrote a long response noting that Hill's letter sent him "through the day with a heavy heart." Nevertheless, McConnell refuted the accusations, stating his interest in talking about the strong points of all state teachers colleges to work to the best advantage of the entire system.[12]

Restrictive legislative efforts, however, did not succeed, and graduate study was permitted to continue in teacher education at all the colleges. With the outbreak of war, long-session graduate enrollment at North Texas State sagged to eighty-one in 1942–43 and to seventy-five in 1943–44. The summer figures dropped from a high of 937 in 1940 to a low of 213 in 1943. The graduate enrollment, as did the total enrollment, resumed its upward climb with the end of hostilities in sight, reaching 205 in the 1945–46 long session and 513 in the summer of 1946.

chapter 21

The Goals Expand

In view of the strongly expressed wishes of the people of certain areas of Texas that the State Teachers Colleges liberalize degree requirements so that students may obtain a college education of the first class without taking subjects especially designed for teachers, and in view of the fact that in many cases the State Teachers Colleges may offer such instruction to the youth of the respective areas without additional cost to the State of Texas:

It is the sense of this Board of Regents of the State Teachers Colleges of Texas that the President and proper officials of each college, within their discretion, be authorized to accept students and offer courses leading to a degree without requiring formal courses in education. However, no Teachers' Certificate may be granted such student until required formal courses prescribed for Teachers are completed.

Board of Regents, State Teachers Colleges
November 25, 1937

The teachers college entered the 1930s under heavy attack. The response was at first to defend the institutions as they were known. Then came a constructive response in developing the teacher education function even more strongly. Before the end of the decade, this was followed by expansion beyond that single purpose for which the institution had been founded.

A member of the Demonstration School faculty, H. B. Masters, wrote Marquis in 1933 to recommend a teacher training program that would be far-reaching in service to the public schools. He suggested that the president appoint a committee of five members to begin extensive research work to begin drawing up a teacher training plan for the next ten years.[1] Dean W. J. McConnell and President Marquis appointed a committee with Masters as chairman, the other members being Dr. J. C. Matthews, Dr. Sam McAlister, Miss Cora Stafford, and Dr. Harold Brenholtz. The appointment letter said, "it is known to all of us that the teacher training phase of education is on trial." The committee was asked to study the problems of the institution, undertaking "any type of research that may appeal to you."[2]

"COURT OF REASON"

Two and one-half months later the committee on research in teacher training reported to the president and the dean on the charges against the existing teacher training program.[3] The committee noted that normal schools undertook the curriculums of the liberal arts colleges in order to gain recognition, some students entered them for a general education or to prepare for other professions, and the teachers colleges staff "allowed their sentiments and training to become divorced from public school problems." At the same time the liberal arts colleges were adding education courses and demonstration schools for the preparation of public school teachers. The committee noted it was "difficult to distinguish between a teachers college and a liberal arts college. . . . Thus, the teachers college finds itself on trial at the court of reason." The committee asserted "There is only one method of attack: organize a continuous functional curriculum building program and direct every nerve and fibre of our being to serving the public schools of the state."

The research committee cited such accomplishments as faculty acquisition of higher degrees, progress toward a uniform grade curve, modern and extensive equipment to simplify teaching, growth in the library, and in addition:

The beginning of a system whereby student teachers can do their practice teaching in public schools.

A teacher-placement bureau that has established a record for dependability.

A plant that is an example of how public buildings should be kept.

An extension department that has established a valuable contact with the public schools.

Educational conference.

For students, the panel recommended compulsory enrollment in the placement bureau, an improved testing and advisory system, and more work in the Demonstration School before entering student teaching. More service to teachers in the field was suggested through publications of the faculty, establishing a loan library, and offering extension lectures.

There then followed a list of suggested policies. Virtually every one spelled out that every course should be oriented toward preparing public school teachers. Every college course should build familiarity with the bibliography to be used in teaching that subject in public schools. The report asked that "every college course shall make every possible effort to adapt the activities to the needs of the public schools of Texas." It declared that every teachers college teacher should develop public school units for teacher training in seven fields: fine arts, vocational arts, health and physical education, citizenship activities, language arts, science and mathematics, and education.[4]

TEXAS STANDARDS RISE

In 1934 state rulings required teachers to have at least two years of college and hold at least a six-year elementary or a four-year high school certificate. Teachers who didn't meet this standard could continue teaching if they attended a state teachers college or other college each summer until meeting the standards. School systems with four-year high schools were directed to employ only teachers in their entire system from elementary on up who were graduates of colleges, universities, or state teachers colleges. Principals and superintendents were required to have at least a bachelor's degree and have completed at least eighteen semester hours of credit in educational administration.[5]

E. H. Farrington, director of the Placement Office, indicated that these regulations materially increased the demand for teachers. At the same time, Farrington said, schools were restoring positions that were cut out with the advent of the Depression. In 1935 he reported that there had been more calls for teachers than the college could supply. Demand had been steadily declining, and in 1935 it became the heaviest since 1928.[6]

The illness and death of Marquis had delayed implementation of the committee on research in teacher training. In the spring of 1935, McConnell asked that curriculum study activities be started with Matthews as chairman of a nine-member committee.[7] Seven faculty groups were organized along departmental lines, with each to have subcommittees to write out general objectives for the teachers college, bibliographies on curriculum construction in their division, and bibliographies on materials used by public school children and in college courses in the division. In a letter to the faculty, Matthews wrote:

> This is a crisis in thought as well as economy. Public school people in the State of Texas are undertaking to meet this crisis in thought through a statewide curriculum building program. A normal amount of effort in building teacher training curricula will keep us up with the program of the public school people. It will take more than a normal effort if we are to lead in the movement. It behooves us, then, to put forth every possible effort in order to maintain a position of leadership in the public school system of the state.[8]

In October 1935, Matthews took a leave of absence to join the State Department of Education as director of textbooks and curriculum. In this capacity he returned to the campus to work with the teacher training program on several occasions.

A CONCERN WITH PURPOSE

The first bulletin of North Texas State Normal College in 1901 declared, "In the language of the statute, this school has been established for the special training of teachers. . . . The school will be devoted exclusively to the object of its creation." In 1917 the bulletin emphasized that the new bachelor's degrees were designated in education. Starting in 1920, bulletins referred again to the creation of the school as a teacher training institution and reported: "All its energies and activities are directed to this end." This statement last appeared in the 1928 bulletin. For several years after that, the annual catalog made no direct reference to educational purpose. It was a 1936 pictorial bulletin rather than the annual catalog that next referred to institutional purpose. This stressed the teacher training function but made clear that liberal arts subjects were basic in college organization. This bulletin stated:

> Although the North Texas State Teachers College maintains the standards of the senior liberal arts college, its executives have always kept in mind the essential fact that it is primarily a professional school devoted to the training of teachers. The academic courses, therefore, while they cover a field parallel to that covered in other colleges, attempt to present materials of a special value to teachers in elementary and secondary schools, and to school administrators.[9]

This statement no longer says the college is devoted *exclusively* to this purpose but rather *primarily*. A prospective student could read this and learn of availability of academic courses parallel to those in senior liberal arts colleges.

The Board of Regents in 1937 recognized the pressures toward a broadening of the teachers colleges. It voted unanimously that the teachers colleges no longer had to require education courses for a bachelor's degree and also opened the door to dropping the world "teachers" from the name of the schools. "It is the sense of this meeting that we have no legal authority to change the official name of the State Teachers Colleges—that we recognize the need and value of shorter titles, and have no objections to the current usage of shorter names as is being done so long as the identity is not changed."[10]

North Texas did not drop the use of the words "teachers college" nor did its bulletins for the next few years carry any overt indication of changes authorized in the 1937 board policy statement. Nevertheless, the first catalog after that board meeting dropped from its bachelor's degree requirements "a minimum of twelve semester hours in education."

A request from the American Association of Teachers Colleges induced the next overt move away from the single-purpose concept of the teachers college. The association asked that its Standard VII be met in part with a statement of aims and objectives of the college. A committee of five faculty members proposed a new statement in October 1941. It read, "North Texas State Teachers College is primarily concerned with the preparation of men and women for happy and effective citizenship. Its purpose is twofold: to develop educational leaders and to cause students to acquire an appreciative understanding of the broad liberal culture basic to a democratic society."

These two sentences did not constitute any radical clarification of purpose. In fact, their wording suggests considerable compromise in their selection. Dr. L. A. Sharp, professor of education and chairman of the Graduate Council, moved the adoption of this statement at a 1941 faculty meeting. Another committee member, also a professor of education, objected. He was Dr. G. A. Odam, director of the Education Department. He complained that the statement "gets away from what he had always thought of as the specific aim of the institution, namely, the training of teachers." Dr. Odam proposed a substitute motion to allow the president and others selected by him to word a statement of aims and purposes to be submitted at once to the American Association of Teachers Colleges. Dr. Odam's motion was voted down and the faculty approved the committee's statement of purpose.[11]

This led the student newspaper to declare, "'Horse and Buggy' Aims Discarded as Faculty States New Purposes." The *Chat* writer said these aims were replaced with a broad statement that set the preparation of men and women for effective citizenship as the primary goal. The *Chat* account said that the new statement was voted after "rather spirited debate." Noting that Dr. Odam asked for the emphasis of teacher training as a primary reason for the existence of the college, the story then said:

> "In a changing world the aims of an institution designed to serve the state were of necessity changed from time to time, but the primary purpose of the institution has always remained the same, the preparation of educational leaders," President W. J McConnell commented this week on the faculty's action.
>
> "Out beyond the service to the students who register from year to year are the needs of the youth of the state to be taught," the president added, in pointing out that the statement adopted retaining this task of training teachers as fundamental.

"The college has, however, gone beyond its original purpose and in point of fact is serving the state in at least three ways," Dr. Sharp said at Friday's faculty meeting in explaining the wording of the statement of the aims prepared by his committee.

"North Texas," said Dr. Sharp, "is now training teachers, is offering to many of its students who do not plan to enter the teaching profession a broad cultural education, and is offering to many others pre-professional training in such fields as medicine."

"A statement of aim was sought which would be descriptive of the educational program at North Texas as it actually is today, rather than of what we thought it should be," Dr. Sharp declared.[12]

MORE ACADEMIC RATINGS

During this period three major academic rating associations approved the NTSTC programs. Graduates became eligible for membership in the American Association of University Women beginning September 12, 1939. The first accreditation in a field other than teacher education came with admission to the National Association of Schools of Music as an associate member on December 27, 1939. During 1939–40, representatives of the Association of American Universities visited the campus to study the standards and achievements of the college. In the fall of 1940, the association membership voted approval of North Texas State Teachers College, making it the third teachers college in the nation to receive this recognition.[13]

Just days before American entrance into World War II, Dean B. B. Harris announced a committee to evaluate the teachers college curriculum, aiming to eliminate course duplication and to improve programs. All faculty members were to be involved. A syllabus was to be made available to a course of study committee for approval before a new course could be added. The committee also emphasized the phrase *teacher education* rather than *teacher training*, suggesting a new cooperative attitude in all departments in the education of teachers and the general education of all students.[14]

On December 8, 1941, the faculty was called together to discuss the impact of the war on the teachers college. But some business went on as usual: President McConnell told of the emphasis of the Southern Association on curriculum studies throughout its membership. He encouraged exhaustive studies on the effectiveness of the teachers college curriculum in meeting the aims of the school. He also said that the aims of education were changing daily and that the statement of aims for North Texas as adopted by the faculty at the meeting of October 17 could be changed at the will of the faculty.[15]

GENERAL GRADUATE WORK

In 1942, McConnell asked the Board of Regents to make education courses optional in the master's degree, just as they had been in the bachelor's degree for several years. The board ruled that this policy could not be instituted for one school and asked Dr. McConnell to withdraw his request until the matter could be given more study.[16] Six months later the council of presidents endorsed the request, and the board agreed that education courses would be optional for a master's degree.[17]

REORGANIZATION

In 1944 McConnell told the faculty that he wanted a study of possible reorganization of the college to meet changing postwar conditions. In the spring of 1945 he appointed three men to coordinate suggestions for reorganization and asked them to present a plan for discussion and for adoption, modification, or rejection. Members of this central committee were Dr. Floyd Stovall, director of the English Department; Dr. L. W. Newton, director of the History Department; and Dr. O. J. Curry, director of the Business Administration Department. The committee submitted a preliminary report to department directors for a meeting on May 21, 1945. The report was approved in general with some changes, and the committee was asked to prepare a final reorganization plan. This was submitted on November 6, 1945, and discussed at a faculty meeting on November 12. McConnell told the faculty that the reorganization carried with it no intent to hamper the work of teacher training but declared that the institution had earned enough recognition for its general liberal arts college work to make some new approach desirable.

The principal objection at the first meeting was raised by Dr. G. A. Odam, director of the Education Department, who felt that his department was being treated unfairly by the curriculum for prospective teachers. He proposed a rewording which included this sentence: "It shall be the responsibility of the School of Education to designate and approve all course requirements for the degree Bachelor of Science in Education."[18] Three days later the discussion was continued and Odam's comment was included in the report.

Miss Cora Belle Wilson of the history faculty objected to the removal of the word "teachers" from the name of the school. McConnell explained that this would merely be giving a more accurate picture and "that the college was training people for professions other than teaching, but that many students were kept away from the college because they thought it was a teacher training college exclusively." Dr. Newton and Dr. E. S. Clifton supported this viewpoint, stating "that many advantages accrue to a university or college which are denied to a teachers college and yet the university or college retains the privilege of training teachers." Dr. Odam responded that the institution would gain more students if it were made "a very strong institution for training teachers only." The plan came to a vote at this meeting on November 15,1945, and passed with but one negative vote.[19]

The Board of Regents approved the plan on November 23. This began informal use of the title North Texas State College in a number of contexts. However, the Board of Regents instructed that the formal name of the institution was established by the legislature and that all bulletins must carry the full legal name of the teachers college on the front cover.[20]

The change in name was the first recommendation of the committee in its section on organization. The plan created the College of Arts and Sciences and "as many schools as the expanding scope of the institution may require." Those originally established were the School of Music, the School of Business, the School of Education, the School of Home Economics, and the Graduate School. In the first subsequent catalog the unit labeled the School of Business by the committee was designated the School of Business Administration, the title that remained the official one thereafter.

The College of Arts and Sciences was divided into three divisions: science, incorporating biology, chemistry, mathematics, and physics; social sciences, including economics and sociology, geography, government, and history; and humanities, including art, English, foreign languages, journalism, library service, and speech. Recommendations were for geology to be added to science, psychology to be added to social science, and philosophy to be added to humanities. The original report asked for health and physical education to be included in the College of Arts and Sciences but was unable to determine a division in which it belonged. The final result was to place a Department of Health, Physical Education and Recreation in the School of Education.

The committee asked that the reorganization not be used as a device for the proliferation of administrative offices. Nevertheless, it recognized that the creation of the new units would require additional officers. It recommended the following officers: dean of administration and the deans of the College of Arts and Sciences and the Schools of Music, Business Administration, Education, Home Economics, and the Graduate School. This plan was carried out. The committee wording then established an Administrative Council made up of ex officio officers including deans, chairmen of the divisions in arts and sciences, plus six elected members from the faculty. In the next year's catalog, however, the term for this organization is Faculty Council, not Administrative Council.[21]

chapter 22

The Campus Grows Again

Buildings are used to approximately 100 per cent capacity during desirable hours of the day, and quarters are being used for instructional purposes which were never intended for such. Mezzanine floors have been provided in storerooms for supplies which require attendants to stand in a stooped position while working. Some $50,000 worth of equipment is now set up in corridors where adequate protection is not afforded. Rooms have been divided by running partitions which should not have been built but which were necessary to a maximum utilization of space.

W. J. McConnell, May 16, 1938

Teachers college regents voted unanimously in August 1933 to authorize the use of federal money for buildings. This made it possible for North Texas to plan for new kinds of buildings: housing, food service, and recreation.

A DORMITORY AT LAST

In 1933 President Marquis submitted an unsuccessful proposal for a student union and dining hall to be financed under the National Recovery Act at a cost of about $150,000.[1] Then, just before his death, he developed plans for a women's dormitory for Public Works Administration financial assistance. At a February 1934 meeting, the regents learned of a federal requirement for assurance of occupancy of a dormitory to capacity. The board authorized the presidents to require students to live in dormitories constructed with Public Works Administration funds.[2]

An architect's plan for a women's dormitory was approved by the board in May 1934. A loan application was submitted under terms of Texas Senate Bill 9 passed on February 16, 1934. This authorized state colleges to borrow federal funds to build dormitories, kitchens and dining halls, and hospitals without cost to the State of Texas.[3] The legislature then had to amend the act to authorize the boards to pledge revenues from the use of the buildings to the payment of bonds or notes.[4]

North Texas received a federal loan of $160,000 and an outright grant of $50,000 to build a dormitory with PWA funds. The building was to be located on Avenue B west of the existing campus between Sycamore and Mulberry Streets. The Board of Regents in November 1934 awarded contracts for $189,443 for the new dormitory, which would be known as Marquis Hall in memory of the late president.[5] In December 1934 dormitory revenue bonds for $163,000 were issued. Construction began on Marquis Hall in April 1935, and the building went into use in 1936, the first college-owned dormitory in the forty-six years of its history. When completed, Marquis Hall required an additional PWA allotment of $22,000 for fixtures.[6]

MORE PWA AID

In June 1935 the regents approved federal loan requests for these buildings: women's dormitory, $310,000; men's dormitory, $262,000; recreation building, $175,000, the loan to be repaid from student activity funds; library building, $225,000, to be paid with fee of one dollar per semester of the regular term and one dollar for the summer session; little theater and speech building, $40,000, to be financed by a charge of twenty-five cents per student from the student activity fund; and an addition to the hospital, $10,000.[7] The recreation building would occupy the site of the Men's Gymnasium in the recreation park. It would include a men's gymnasium to seat 2,500 and an indoor swimming pool and bowling alley.[8] Plans were for a women's dormitory to house 250 and a men's dormitory housing 196. Under the PWA program fifty-five percent of these funds came as loans and forty-five percent as an outright grant.[9] In November 1935 the board approved the architect's plans for the Library Building. The *Campus Chat* had reported in September 1935 that President Franklin D. Roosevelt had approved WPA projects including $40,000 for a speech building and $12,000 for a hospital addition at North Texas. The speech building was not to materialize in spite of this announcement. The hospital addition, however, went up for bidding and on December 12, 1935, the regents let a contract for $10,999 for the hospital wing.[10]

The Library Building became a joint project of state and federal funds. The regular session of the Texas Legislature in 1935 appropriated $25,000 toward a library building. The first called session in October was asked to appropriate an additional $112,000. This bill was passed contingent upon a grant of at least $100,000 from federal funds. The final result was the two sums of $25,000 and $112,000 from the state, plus an allocation of $117,000 from PWA, providing $254,000 for the library.[11] Frame buildings, including the two houses used for the orchestra and music hall, were moved out to clear the site for the new library to be located on the east side of Avenue B, facing west just north of Chestnut Street. (When a new library was opened in 1971, this structure became known as the Information Sciences Building.)

At about this same time campus improvement projects totaling more than $20,000 were being carried on with about three-fourths of the support coming from the WPA. One of these was the construction of concrete steam tunnels from the Power Plant, one to the old Library Building, one to the Education Building, one to Manual Arts, and another to the Science Building. Another project involved the laying of sanitary sewer lines in the section of the campus where Sycamore Street once ran. These were to connect to the new Marquis Hall and Library Building.[12] Construction contracts were let for the library in

February 1936 for $194,040. The architect estimated that the equipment and fixtures and additional fees would run the total cost to approximately $251,000.[13]

LIBRARY DEVELOPMENT

The library in the first years of the state normal had been nothing but a small collection of books in a small room adjoining the president's office in the old Normal Building. When the Main Building was constructed in 1904, the books were moved into the southeast room of the first floor. President Kendall had employed Mrs. Pearl C. McCracken as an instructor of English and mathematics but asked her, when she arrived in February 1903, to oversee the collection of library books and the textbooks, which were loaned to students.

The first Library Building opened in 1912. This was located on Avenue A and was later called the Historical Building and later Curry Hall. One of its three floors was devoted to the library, but equipment for properly storing and handling books was sadly lacking. In 1913 the librarian was relieved of the custody of textbooks. The next year a full-time library assistant was employed.[14]

Mrs. McCracken's annual report for 1923 showed that the state teachers college began with library holdings of 13,724 volumes. By 1934, this had increased nearly fourfold to 52,100.

THE NEW LIBRARY

With the move to the new building in 1937 and with graduate programs in effect, continual improvement was needed in the quality of library services as well as growth in the number of acquisitions. President McConnell asked the librarian, Mrs. McCracken, and Miss Mary Patchell, chairman of the faculty library committee, to work on means of developing better conditions in the library. In December 1938 the Carnegie Corporation announced that North Texas would receive an award of $9,000 over three years for purchase of books for general reading. Of twenty-nine teachers colleges selected for the grants only seven received $9,000, and the others received $3,000 or $6,000.[15]

After thirty-six years of service at North Texas, Mrs. McCracken retired as librarian in August 1939. Her successor was Dr. William Stanley Hoole.[16] As Mrs. McCracken left office there were 82,779 books in the library, a great contrast with the tiny roomful of books she had inherited in 1903 as a part-time assignment. Of this number, 7,705 were located in the Demonstration

School library.[17] The holdings reached 100,000 in May 1940. The annual budget for books and periodicals was $16,000, aided in each of three years by the $3,000 from the Carnegie Corporation. Carnegie also donated phonographic equipment and 1,000 of "the world's best records." This was placed in the soundproof room of the Music Building under the direction of the library and was open twenty-five hours weekly. A weekly concert of recorded music with commentary by a member of the music faculty was open to the public. The Carnegie gift brought the record holdings of the library to 2,500.[18]

In 1941, the library was organized into six units: the Museum Library, the Demonstration School Library, the Teacher Training Library, Music Library, Phonograph Records Library, and Main Library, as well as the College Bookbindery, which from its establishment in 1934 until 1939 had been an adjunct of industrial arts. In the statistics of Southern Colleges and Universities Libraries for 1940–41, the library collections of seven institutions from Texas were listed. The largest by far was the University of Texas with 673,888 volumes. Others in order were Rice 157,100; SMU 125,109; and North Texas 111,453. Others listed with fewer than 100,000 at that time were Texas A&M, Baylor, and TCU. Money expended for books that year was largest at the University of Texas followed in second by NTSTC.[19] In February 1942, Dr. Hoole reported that "our college library is the third largest teachers college library in the world." He listed ahead of it Teachers College, Columbia University, and Indiana State Teachers College at Terre Haute.[20]

BUILDINGS DEDICATED

In February 1936 PWA officials allocated $30,909 to North Texas for construction of a band and orchestra hall. This included an outright grant of $13,909 and a loan of $17,000. The loan portion was financed by an unusual arrangement for a classroom building. Student members of the band and orchestra were to live in rooms on the top floor, which was to be fitted as a dormitory, the income from the room rent to pay for the bonds on the building.[21] Thirty-six men students took up residence in the new Orchestra Hall in November 1936.

Governor James V. Allred proclaimed April 21, 1937, as Teachers College Day in Texas. This recognized San Jacinto Day in 1879, when Governor O. M. Roberts had signed the bill appropriating money for the establishment of

Texas's first teacher training institution at Huntsville. NTSTC used the occasion to dedicate the four new buildings erected under the Public Works Administration: Marquis Hall, the Library, Orchestra Hall, and the new wing of the College Hospital. The four represented a cost of $568,000, of which $380,000 had come from federal grants or loans. The dedication program was conducted in two sections. The first in the auditorium included an address by Robert Lee Bobbitt, an ex-student of the college who was then chairman of the State Highway Commission; remarks by J. J. Taylor, editor-in chief of the *Dallas Morning News;* and formal presentation of the buildings by Walter A. Koons, head of the legal division of the Public Works Administration in Texas. At 11:30 the ceremonies switched to new broadcasting studios located in the Library Building, and a two-minute segment of the program was broadcast over Station WFAA in Dallas. The audience in the auditorium listened to the broadcast. The orchestra played, President McConnell spoke, and the buildings were dedicated by Dr. James G. Ulmer, vice president of the Teachers College Board of Regents. The opening of the radio studios portended the initiation of a regular weekly radio broadcast over WFAA under the direction of Floyd Graham.

DORMITORY LIFE

With the opening of Marquis Hall to 114 women students in the spring of 1936 and with thirty-six men moving into Orchestra Hall in the following November, the college for the first time faced the task of supervising student dormitory life. Students accustomed to boardinghouse traditions were reassured by McConnell in January 1936. He said the dormitory would not be a place of "reform for incorrigibles" but "a happy, most completely wholesome and satisfactory place for the young women."[22] Marquis Hall residents were allowed to entertain young men from 5:00 until 7:00 on study nights and until 11:00 on Saturdays and Sundays. The women dined at either a lunch grill or in the main dining hall.[23]

In October 1937, the college opened a new $10,000 grandstand, doubling the existing capacity of Eagle Stadium. This put seating facilities on the east side of the playing field, bringing capacity to about 7,000. Only students, ex-students, and faculty members could sit in the new stands, the object being to create a concerted Eagle rooting section.[24]

McConnell announced in 1938 the renaming of the Men's Gymnasium as the Recreation Building. It was repaired in the summer to provide the center as a six-night-a-week winter play and dance program designed to mark the teachers college as "one of the undoubted leaders in college recreation." McConnell said this step was taken in part as a result of demands by students who were familiar with the "unique summer play program" of the college. Dr. McConnell said "the college has long pioneered in college recreation work, and its summer program particularly has placed it ahead of other schools in the United States.[25]

EXPANSION PROBLEMS

By the end of 1937, North Texas again needed to purchase more land for expansion. McConnell complained to the board that property owners were asking exorbitant prices for property. The board responded that it was "time to let the people of Denton know that the college and state would not be held up in their efforts to enlarge the college, and that condemnation proceedings be had by the attorney general, or the proper authority, against certain properties desired in the expansion program." The president was authorized to purchase property that might then be had at reasonable prices. He was authorized to go to Washington to try to secure federal funds of $310,000 as a direct loan to construct a second unit of Marquis Hall.[26]

At their next meeting the regents instructed the presidents to include the purchase price of land in PWA loans and grants.[27] McConnell was directed to apply for federal aid for a home management house for home economics students. He was authorized to use $13,750, if necessary, to match funds from the Public Works Administration.[28]

McConnell next moved to plan dormitories, one for men and one for women, under the PWA program. PWA made a grant in June 1938 for forty-five percent of the cost up to $257,727, and by issuing bonds the total could reach $315,000 for the women's dormitory.[29] A similar provision was made for the men's dormitory, and on August 17, 1938, contracts were let for both dormitories at a combined construction cost of $464,020.[30] The women's residence was named Terrill Hall, and the men's became Chilton Hall after the early presidents. Terrill Hall reached a total cost of $313,000 and Chilton Hall a figure of $257,727.[31]

Dormitory construction led to the moving of frame residences to be used as student housing. From the Terrill Hall site went two frame houses that had been known as the Marquis Hall annexes. They were relocated on Avenue A, next to another house bought by the college, and the group became known as the College Tri-Houses. The men's dormitory, Chilton Hall, was built on the west side of Avenue C facing east between Chestnut and Prairie Streets. Frame houses there had served as cooperative living units. They were moved to a site on Highland Street just across from a college warehouse. A central dining hall was moved to the same block. The boardinghouses thus created were used in many cases to house teachers college athletes.

By the fall of 1939, five college boardinghouses for women were ready, along with a dining hall to accommodate 150 girls. The halls were named for former governors of Texas: Coke, Throckmorton, and Hamilton Halls on Avenue A, Murrah and Bell Halls on Highland Street, and Runnel Hall, the dining hall, located centrally to all five. The office, Roberts Hall, was also located on Avenue A.[32] Room and board ranged from $26 to $27.50 a month in Marquis and Terrill Halls, $22.50 a month in Chilton Hall. In the cooperative boardinghouses, with students staying four to a room, the room and board charge per month was $12.50. Boardinghouse fees in the approved zone surrounding the campus were in the range of $22.50 to $26.50 a month.[33]

OTHER BUILDINGS

In September 1938, the PWA approved financing for the Home Management House at Avenue A and Chestnut Street. Of the $30,000 cost, $11,250 was in the form of an outright grant. The brick veneer building replaced a two-story frame house that had been used by home economics students.[34]

The college turned to a new source of funds to provide a United States Post Office on the campus. The Hogg Memorial Loan Fund lent the Board of Regents $10,000 to build a post office. The college would then rent the building to the federal government. Contracts were let in June 1939. It was located on the west side of Avenue A north of the College Hospital.

On May 18, 1939, the *Campus Chat* noted a five-year anniversary date in Dr. McConnell's presidency and reviewed the physical development of the college, which in that time had increased in long session enrollment from 1,704 to 2,889, a gain of almost seventy percent. In 1934, buildings were valued at

$716,200.95. In 1939 they were worth nearly three times this much, $1,845,429.59. The six major buildings in this expansion were Marquis, Chilton, and Terrill Halls, Orchestra Hall, the Library, and the Home Management House. Other physical expansion had included the hospital addition, the new athletic stand, and a brick entrance to the athletic park.[35]

MUSIC GROWTH

In May 1940 regents voted to issue bonds for $50,000 and allocate $20,000 from local funds to construct a combination music building and residence hall for men. When construction bids came in, the loan authorization increased from $50,000 to $65,000.[36] Construction proceeded in 1940 on Music Hall, adjoining the existing Orchestra Hall on the east. The three-story brick veneer building was occupied in March 1941 with fifty-two men living in the third-floor dormitory. The first two floors were devoted to classrooms, practice rooms, and a broadcasting studio, which until that time had been located in the Library Building.

This enabled the moving of piano practice rooms from the clubhouse, but the Music Department still occupied in addition to Music Hall and Orchestra Hall a music annex on Avenue B, a practice house on Sycamore, a studio building on Sycamore , and a frame structure known as the Education Annex. The old home of President Kendall, known as Kendall Hall, formerly music department headquarters, was taken over by the Speech Department. The speech classrooms and offices in the Manual Arts Buildings were assigned to business education, which also moved into the area used by the college News Service. This latter moved to the ground floor of the Manual Arts Building. [37]

One more dormitory for women was completed before war halted construction. In November 1940 McConnell sold property that he owned to the teachers college, stating that with an addition costing about $40,000 the building could accommodate about one hundred girls. The board paid McConnell $12,000 for the property and sold $60,000 in bonds for the dormitory to be known as Oak Street Hall.[38] This brought to more than 1,000—nearly one-third of the student body—being housed in college-owned property. This included 700 women in three dormitories and nine school-owned boardinghouses and more than 300 men in Chilton Hall and the dormitory floors of Music Hall and Orchestra Hall.[39]

In 1941 the college planned a $270,000 Science Hall to be constructed on the west side of Avenue B, between Sycamore and Chestnut Streets. Money was appropriated by the 47th Legislature, but the project was canceled when it was learned that defense needs—even before the actual outbreak of war—would prevent the school from getting any kind of priority rating for such building.[40]

STILL NOT CAUGHT UP

The college dispensed entirely with an assembly hour because that provided facilities for an additional fifty classes or so in that period. Dr. McConnell reported that scheduled hours during the long session were 8:00 until 5:00, and during the summer 7:00 until 5:30. During both sessions, he said, some evening classes were necessary. The chairman of the committee on scheduling classes, B. E. Looney, estimated that at least twenty-five additional classrooms were needed in 1938.

Representatives of the State Board of Education and the Boards of Regents of State Schools met in Dallas in May 1940 to consider building needs for all of Texas higher education. McConnell told them that the need for buildings at North Texas State Teachers College was acute. He attributed this to several factors. The first was that with the exception of $137,000 provided by the 44th Legislature to match a federal grant for a library, no state appropriations for buildings had been given to North Texas in nineteen years. During those nineteen years, Dr. McConnell said, the enrollment had increased from 597 to 3,371. He reported the reliance on old frame buildings (originally boarding-houses) to provide classrooms with no fire or equipment theft protection. He listed a need for buildings for science, education, physical education, and industrial education at a cost of more than a million dollars.[41] Of these requests, only that for the Music Hall was achieved before World War II halted construction activity.

chapter 23

From Depression to War

> When the North Texas State Teachers College, Denton, begins construction of a new three-story brick music building this fall, it will mark another step in the growth of the Department of Music, a growth that has been one of the outstanding developments in music education in Texas during the past two years. . . .
>
> That this ambitious program. . . is already being realized in part is shown not only by the increase of music students and music majors in the department but also by the fact that among these are some of the most brilliant young students from the Southwest, many of whom are regional and national contest winners, and that working with these students NTSTC directors have built up at least two musical organizations of near professional quality, the NTSTC A Cappella Choir and the College Symphony Orchestra.
>
> *Dallas Morning News, September 1940*

The period under discussion opened with a steady climb from the last of the Depression-related enrollment drops. Long session enrollment sagged from 1,805 to 1,749 in 1929–30, climbed again to more than 2,000, and fell to 1,704 in 1933–34. Similarly, the summer of 1933 showed a drastic enrollment reduction in one year, from 3,130 to 2,432. This loss was more than recovered in the summer of 1934, when the figures climbed back to 3,273. From here on a new pattern was to develop. The long session enrollment climbed steadily, starting at 1,807 in 1934–35. Annual figures thereafter were 1,984; 2,230; 2,448; 2,891; 3,377; and a peak of 3,581 in 1940–41.

At the same time summer session enrollments hovered just above the 3,000 mark for five successive years. In the summer of 1940 the number of students sagged below 3,000 for the first time to 2,977. It was also the first time since 1910 that the long session enrollment had exceeded that of the summer session. This was to be the pattern from that time forward, although both long and summer session enrollments began a decline in 1941–42 because of World War II, a decline that was not arrested until the summer of 1945. The lowest summer enrollment was 1,452 in 1944, and the long session low was 1,886 in 1944–45.

FINANCIAL IMPROVEMENT

Fortunately, the fiscal affairs of the teachers college were taking a turn for the better. Appropriated funds went up steadily throughout this period, rising from $281,243.45 for the 1935 fiscal year to $749,262.00 in 1945–46. The total budget, including local funds, student fees and so on, climbed from $485,146.32 in fiscal 1935, passed $1,000,000 for the first time in fiscal 1940, and by fiscal 1946 reached $1,576,437.94. Much of the increase was required to take care of the increased enrollment and the operation of new dormitories. However, the faculty was able to realize some genuine salary gains. Those at full professor, for example, earned in the range of $2,400 to $2,880 in 1936, between $3,000 and $3,600 from 1938 to 1945, and $3,150–3,900 in 1946. During the same time periods, associate professors earned $1,920–2,200, $2,400–2,700, and $2,625–3,150. For assistant professors the growth steps were $1,650–1,800, $2,200–2,400, and $2,310–2,640. Those at the instructor's level were earning $1,350–1,650 in 1936, $1,800–2,100 between 1938 and 1946, and $1,980–2,310 in 1946. However, the problem still existed with summer school appropriations, and in most of these years the faculty was paid at the rate of either eighty-five percent or ninety percent of their regular monthly income for service in these months.[1]

FACULTY QUALIFICATIONS

In 1935 the regents said that faculties should be selected "with due regard to holding degrees which are recognized as evidence of scholarship." A board resolution said that new faculty must meet higher academic standards, that if faculty members do not improve their scholastic standing they cannot be considered for promotion and that, furthermore, faculty members may expect "the probability of not retaining their positions" if they fail to obtain higher degrees in their profession.[2]

Summer Employment Changes

The Board of Regents also required faculty members to take one summer term or its equivalent off each three years starting in 1937.[3] When the fall enrollment became larger than summer in 1939, regents responded with a new policy, that no longer could any teachers college faculty member assume that summer appointment would be automatic.[4]

A New Factor: Research

The job of the faculty during this period was still regarded almost exclusively as that of teaching and public service. However, there were some small beginnings of the concept of research as a desirable faculty function. Dr. J. K. G. Silvey, who joined the faculty in 1935, was interested in water purification research. In May 1939 regents approved a contract of Dr. Silvey and Dr. B. B. Harris with the City of Dallas, paying them $1,800 each per year for scientific advice in the purification of the Dallas water supply, the contract also to provide for payment to four graduate students at twenty-five dollars per month. At the same time McConnell recommended that Dr. J. L. Carrico of the chemistry department be permitted to accept funds for analysis work from outside sources in addition to his regular salary, such services to be rendered outside his regular hours.[5]

At about the same time the college began promoting a course in chemurgy, a branch of applied chemistry dealing with the industrial utilization of farm products. A survey course started in the summer of 1939 was advertised as the first ever to be taught in the United States. The college employed Gilbert Wilson, a White Oak High School teacher and graduate of the college, who had won wide attention with his yam dehydration machine. At North Texas, Wilson continued his research on dehydration of the sweet potato and on uses of the buckeye ball as a source of pure protein for cow feed. The chemurgy program was endorsed by the agricultural editor of the *Dallas Morning News* and by *Dallas Morning News* editorial writers. The program became another of the casualties of World War II.[6]

PRACTICE FOR TEACHERS

Teachers in training needed to observe professional teaching and to practice their intended profession. In Denton, TSCW used the public schools for this purpose. North Texas had grown to a size where the Demonstration School could not provide professional experiences for the number of teachers in training. A move toward expanding outside Denton was noted in 1932, when the Board of Regents authorized purchase of two automobiles for transporting students to teaching centers.[7] A week later President Marquis wrote to three members of the education faculty to ask them to work with the Dallas County superintendent in placing student teachers. [8]

Space Needed Elsewhere

In 1931–32, the college had 245 sophomores doing observation and some elementary-grade student teaching. In advanced student teaching there were four elementary teachers and forty-three high school teachers. They were placed this way: Demonstration School, twenty-two; laboratory assistants at the college, ten; Denton High School, ten; and Ponder High School, five. The cost of transporting the students to Ponder was twenty-five dollars a month. That year, L. A. Sharp, director of the Demonstration School, pointed out that North Texas was not meeting the minimum standards of the American Association of Teachers Colleges for the number of hours of student teaching required in a year. He suggested that the best arrangement would be to enlarge the Demonstration School, the feasibility of which he doubted. His report then suggested sending students out to do student teaching in nearby public school systems for an entire quarter or semester.[9]

Both Marquis's proposal for sending student teachers into Dallas County and Sharp's proposal to send out a student teacher for an entire term were premature. Nevertheless, they did point the way to what was to become a major part of the student teaching program of future years.

Building Expansion Sought

President McConnell also sought a great increase in facilities for student teaching. The Demonstration School building accommodated 320 pupils. McConnell asked for a building to house 1,000 pupils. He observed that the Denton Public Schools offered no opportunities for expansion because the State College for Women "entered them several years before Teachers College did. We are using three cars to transport our student teachers to nearby towns and villages, and one man is supervising regularly employed teachers in a number of schools, some of them many miles from Denton."[10]

In 1937 McConnell declared that the college would be stopped from any further expansion unless more adequate teaching facilities could be provided. He said that the crowded condition in the Demonstration School was "virtually intolerable at this time." He renewed his plea for a building to house at least 1,000 students.[11] In a 1938 report, McConnell quoted J. C. Matthews, director of teacher training, on the inadequacies of the Demonstration School. Matthews said the present building was inadequate for the number enrolled and "supposed to be a model, is inferior to literally hundreds of school buildings in the state." He also said that facilities for 2,000 children, both on and off the campus, were necessary to meet the standards of the American Association of Teachers Colleges.[12]

The correction of this inadequate situation, too, would have to await the recovery of a postwar period, when both a new Laboratory School and a widespread system of student teaching in the public schools could be developed.

SPEECH, MUSIC DEVELOP

In the first fifteen years of granting bachelor's degrees North Texas graduated 2,893 students. The most popular major through June 1934 was English with 637 majors. Others were history 283, elementary education 250, home economics 233, business administration 152, mathematics 123, industrial education 116, foreign language 113, chemistry 113, physical education 110, government 66, geography 56, biology 51, music 40, art 37, physics 31, and speech 20.[13] Speech arts was started in 1930, dropped after one year, and reinstalled in 1932.

A Promising Future: Music

President McConnell announced in September 1938 that an enlarged and combined Music Department was being created with Dr. Wilfred C. Bain as the department head. The president described it as a "unique program of inexpensive music education." Dr. Bain had been on the summer faculty and in the summer of 1938 organized the institution's first A Cappella Choir, which was heard on WFAA in Dallas. Several instructors were added. Five degrees were offered under the department arrangement: bachelor of science in music education, bachelor of music in music education, bachelor of arts in applied music, bachelor of arts with a theory major, and a band master's certificate.

Campus music organizations that year included the A Cappella Choir of forty voices, a fifty-piece Symphony Orchestra, sixty-five-piece College Band, the stage band ("Aces of Collegeland"), a radio ensemble for the regular broadcast over WFAA, the College Chorus, and a number of instrumental and vocal ensembles. The schedule that year included three major concerts by the Symphony Orchestra, three band concerts, a spring band festival, tours by the stage band and the A Cappella Choir, and the presentation of an oratorio and several shorter cantatas by the College Chorus.[14] One year later Dr. McConnell reported that college enrollment jumped from 2,891 to 3,377 for the fall of 1939. He pointed out in a faculty meeting that the Music Department led the institution with an increase of 109 percent.[15]

World Premiere of Opera

On February 16 and 17, 1939, the world premiere was presented of the opera, *Cynthia Parker,* written by a graduate of the school, Julia Smith. Principals of the production were a former Metropolitan star, Leonora Corona, and two Texas singers. The production drew 1,400 special guests from the city and from out-of-town, leaving only about 700 seats for students. The second performance the following night was scheduled primarily for students. The Texas State Network broadcast the first night's performance through Station KTAT, Fort Worth, and twenty-three other Texas stations.

Several choruses were combined to form a Great Chorus to perform the Beethoven Ninth Symphony with the Dallas Symphony Orchestra in Dallas in February 1942, the first of many such performances with major symphony orchestras. In 1942 two A Cappella Choirs were formed to accommodate the number of singers. For the first time girls would march with the sixty-five-piece marching band for football games. The schedule for the symphony band, the concert version of the marching group, was also expanded.[16]

National Accreditation for Music

North Texas was awarded associate membership in the National Association of Schools of Music in 1939 and two years later was made an institutional member. It was the second teachers college to be so designated by the organization, the only accrediting agency for schools of music in the United States. Dr. Bain was re-elected national vice president of the organization and was appointed to a three-member committee to re-evaluate the music education curriculum for the 150 member schools in the United States. The Music Teachers National Association elected Dr. Bain as a member of its national executive committee.[17]

STUDENT LIFE

Teachers college students in 1934 looked forward to the 1936 Texas Centennial by staging a Texas Centennial Pageant in the college stadium for students, the Texas Centennial Committee, and other state dignitaries. Eight episodes used eight elaborate stages twenty by twenty feet. In the center of the field a stage forty-five by sixty feet carried the main action of the pageant. The production made big theatrical news in Texas daily newspapers.[18]

It was a time when President Roosevelt's secretary of labor, Frances Perkins, came to the campus to declare that "no magic thing has happened yet to end future depressions." In a speech in the Main Auditorium, she advocated compulsory unemployment insurance and old age pensions as a means of social security and promised that a definite program would be placed before the next congress to achieve these ends. She urged the retention of much of the national recovery program as a permanent part of Federal governmental machinery.[19]

In February 1935 seniors raised funds for a memorial bench for President Marquis to be located facing the fish pond. It was dedicated on May 29, 1935. Nearly a year later, however, the bench was moved to the south side of the new Marquis Hall on recommendation of a Houston landscape architect.[20]

The Saturday night stage show and movie continued as a big entertainment feature, but some students wanted more. Students in 1936 agitated for the showing of motion pictures on Sunday at the commercial theaters in downtown Denton. The question was put to a public vote, and the *Campus Chat* soon began carrying advertisements for Sunday shows at the movie theaters.[21] The Fine Arts Series continued, with programs like that of violinist Albert Spalding in 1937.

As the 1938 school year opened, the *Campus Chat* added a new line to its nameplate: "Largest State-Supported Teachers College in the United States—49 Years of Continuous Service." The same issue announced six attractions for the year's Fine Arts Series including the United States Navy Band; John Gurney, bass-baritone of the Metropolitan Opera; the Ballet Caravan; and the Martha Graham Dance Company.[22] In February 1939 the *Chat* recorded the first-place ranking of the top North Texas debate team at the Baylor University tournament, regarded as the largest and most important competition in the Southwest. But the debaters' performance was subordinated to the account of a modern miracle in assembly, "an actual demonstration of transmitting and receiving of television." The apparatus was constructed at a cost of $12,000, the *Chat* story said, and quoted David Sarnoff, president of the Radio Corporation of America, announcing that commercial production of television sets for home use would begin soon at a cost within reach of the majority of homes.[23]

PUBLICATIONS WIN

Among academic subjects gaining increased attention in the late 1930s was journalism. The result was soon made evident in college publications. In the 1937–38 school year the *Campus Chat* was entered in the college newspaper competition sponsored by the Associated Collegiate Press. Judges gave the *Chat* the second highest honor rating, first class, in the competition. Cosponsors of the paper were J. D. Hall, Jr., and C. E. Shuford. Editor of the prize-winning newspaper was Alonzo Jamison, who many years later became the state representative from Denton County.[24] After that year the *Chat* abandoned its traditional appearance, giving up the old style typefaces, the formal headline patterns and balanced makeup in favor of a cleaner sans serif type with modern flush-left headlines and a cleaner overall appearance. In April of 1940 the *Campus Chat* was awarded its first All-American rating by the National Scholastic Press Association. This proved to be the first of dozens of such honors that were to become almost a tradition with the staffs. The first All-American paper was edited by Ray Edwards.[25] The *Yucca* of the same school year later received an All-American rating, the only college yearbook in the state to do so. North Texas was one of eight schools in the nation to have both yearbook and newspaper in the All-American class.[26] The *Avesta,* which had begun as a quarterly magazine and converted to three issues a year under the semester system, in 1941 switched to two issues a year, one for the fall semester and one for the spring semester.[27]

HOMECOMING AGAIN

The 1930s also saw efforts of the students to revive a Homecoming tradition on the campus and stimulate more life in the Ex-Student Association. Homecoming had been tied to commencement or some spring event almost since the beginning of the college. In May 1934 the first Homecoming since 1928 was scheduled. Special efforts were made to bring back the big class of 1914.[28] However, the Homecoming in its second year of revival was held at the end of May honoring students of the private normal college, 1890 to 1901. Dr. J. J. Crumley, the second president of the normal, returned as speaker, and Mrs. M. B. Terrill, widow of the former president, also attended. A Homecoming banquet was held at night at the Southern Hotel. Joining former President Crumley and Mrs. Terrill was Dr. J. Q. Dealey of the *Dallas News,* a member of the 1890 faculty.[29] Later that week the baccalaureate speaker was Bishop John M. Moore, also an 1890 teacher. In November 1935 about seventy-five delegates attended a conference to discuss ex-student organization, particularly at the local level, and to attend the football game with arch rival East Texas State Teachers College.[30]

Two years later a two-line banner head in the *Campus Chat* announced an event that was labeled "Open House" for ex-students. The event opened with "a rip-roaring pep rally climaxed with a huge bonfire at the end of Chestnut Street," Friday night. The committee in charge was headed by Dr. J. C. Matthews, president of the Ex-Student Association. Dean B. B. Harris announced that the open house would probably be a biennial event on the occasion of the game with East Texas State at Denton.[31] In 1938, with no game scheduled in Denton with the Commerce teachers college, the Ex-Student Association scheduled an annual Re-assembly Week between October 10 and 15. This time was set aside for the reorganization of county clubs throughout the state and for exes everywhere to assist the association in bringing addresses and records of ex-students up to date.[32]

The big rivalry with East Texas was to resume in Denton the following year. And another event helped to make it an even bigger occasion. The college scheduled its Semi-Centennial Homecoming for ex-students on the campus November 18. The Homecoming was a part of a series of what was called Golden Jubilee Year activities at the college.[33] By 1941, Homecoming Day was beginning to take on the air of a campus tradition. In addition to the Commerce football game, there was scheduled a morning meeting of the Ex-Student Association, a luncheon, a coffee by the Green Jackets, and a number of programs by North Texas organizations serving as hosts to visiting East Texas State organizations. Evening activities included a Homecoming stage show and an all-college dance.[34]

THE FIFTIETH YEAR

The school year of 1939–40 was set aside for the observation of the Fiftieth Anniversary of the teachers college. October 6, 1939, was declared McConnell Day in appreciation of the leadership of the president. The program in the Main Auditorium featured a speech by Dr. James J. Ulmer, president of the State Teachers College Board of Regents, who accepted four new buildings added to the campus that year. The structures were Chilton and Terrill Halls, the Home Management House, and the College Post Office. In all, the *Campus Chat* noted, the teachers college physical plant had grown from an evaluation of $1,586,422.93 to $2,931,203.86, an increase of about eighty-five percent. The day's program also included the first of the "Golden Jubilee" series of the Teachers College weekly broadcast to be heard over WFAA each Saturday.[35]

The Golden Jubilee ended with "Culmination Week" April 18–21, 1940. The *Campus Chat* said that 10,000 visitors and exes returned to the campus for the various programs, with former president W. H. Bruce as the honored guest. Capacity audiences attended two presentations of an operetta, *El Tor*, by Mamie Smith of the English faculty. A Friday morning Jubilee Assembly featured a speech by Robert L. Bobbitt, chairman of the State Highway Commission. T. V. Smith, professor of philosophy at the University of Chicago and Congressman-at-Large from Illinois, spoke Saturday morning. That night the feature was an 1890–1940 college stage show. The Sunday schedule included concerts by the A Cappella Choir in the morning and by the College Symphony in the afternoon. The guest artist for the latter program was Julia Smith, ex-student and composer.[36]

LONE STAR HEYDAY

Formed in 1932, the Lone Star Athletic Conference was almost exclusively a state teachers college enterprise until the war suspended intercollegiate competition after 1942–43. Trinity University, a church-related college, competed unsuccessfully for three years before dropping out, leaving a five-member field of Stephen F. Austin, Sam Houston, Southwest Texas, East Texas, and North Texas State Teachers Colleges.

The Eagles dominated the football scene during this period, coached throughout by Jack Sisco except for the final 1942 wartime season under Coach Lloyd Russell. North Texas teams won the conference championship seven times during these eleven seasons and fell to third place only twice. North Texas found its biggest national football publicity after the 1936 season, when the *Campus Chat* was able to gloat in a headline that "Not a Single 'Big' College Star Named on Real All-America." The occasion was the selection of Eagle halfback Johnny Stovall to "The Real All-America Team" in the magazine, *Sport Pictorial.* Big universities were banned from consideration in the balloting by Stanley Woodward, president of the Football Writers' Association, and sixty-five coaches, professional scouts, and sports writers.[37] Coach Sisco, who in 1959 was to become a member of the college's Board of Regents, compiled a record of seventy-four wins, thirty-seven losses, and ten ties as football coach from 1929 through 1941.

It was in track, however, that North Texas State Teachers College gained national athletic recognition. Two sets of identical twins captured the nation's fancy with their running performances. Delmer and Elmer Brown and Wayne and Blaine Rideout established a world record of 7 minutes 27.5 seconds in the indoor mile and seven-eighths medley relay at the Thirty-first Annual Millrose Games in Madison Square Garden in New York City on February 5, 1938. In April of that year the Rideout brothers were joined by Alvin Chrisman and Henry Morgan at the Forty-fourth Annual Penn Relays, where they set a world record of 9 minutes 59.4 seconds for the outdoor two and one-eighth mile medley relay. On June 18, 1938, at the Princeton Invitation Meet, Wayne Rideout became the first Texan ever to set an individual world track mark by running the three-quarter-mile race in 3 minutes 0.3 seconds.[38] By 1940, North Texas track men had won seven Lone Star championships and held the conference record in ten events, including every running event except the hurdles. The teams of this period, coached by Choc Sportsman, also succeeded regularly in the Texas Relays, Border Olympics, Penn Relays, and Kansas Relays.[39]

In basketball the Eagles encountered more difficulty in conference games, but climbed to a Lone Star championship in 1938 under the tutelage of Coach Henry G. "Pete" Shands. Shands, who was to coach at North Texas from 1935 until 1959, in that 1938 season also took his team to the semifinals of the Oklahoma City Invitational Basketball Tournament. Coach Shands also coached the tennis team to ten Lone Star Conference titles. Intercollegiate competition began in golf in 1939, but it was not until much later that the Eagles gained prominence in this sport.[40]

AIDING ATHLETICS

The Southern Association granted permission to the Lone Star Conference in the summer of 1937 to use freshmen in athletics, but a 3–3 tie vote by the conference schools blocked any action. The measure came up again at the 1938 spring conference meeting, and athletic representatives voted in favor of freshman eligibility provided the academic authorities of the colleges gave their approval. So it was that for a good many years North Texas teams followed what was generally regarded as a small-college practice, soon to be disallowed by the National Collegiate Athletic Association.[41]

More concern was arising in colleges about financial aid to athletes. Whereas North Texas had once renounced assistance to players and financial inducement to persuade a high school student to attend the college, by 1937 it was recognized that if a player was promising, he could be offered "a maximum of board, room, and fees by way of work." The players were selected by the coach. While there was no alumni aid or control, the Denton Chamber of Commerce was called upon to assist in locating jobs for players.[42]

In the fall of 1942, a war-curtailed football schedule of eight games was played. One of the opponents was a military team from Camp Hood. The regular coaching staff had left the campus and temporary coaches took over for one year. Intercollegiate competition and the Lone Star Conference went into a three-year wartime suspension from 1943 to 1945.

THE APPROACH OF WAR

The Board of Regents in August 1940 ruled that a student who was drafted into military service should have fees refunded to him for all credits not earned. They further voted to hold open the positions of any faculty members who might be drafted. The board offered full facilities of the teachers colleges to the preparedness program and invited the federal government to utilize the colleges for ROTC, National Guard, or other training units whenever practical.[43]

The regents also asked the presidents to work out a "course of Americanism" to be given in all the colleges. A board vote ruled that no employee of a teachers college should receive any funds from the college unless he was a citizen of the United States or had declared his intention to be one, nor could he be paid if he would not take the oath of allegiance to America. All presidents were charged to check "carefully, but privately," into the records of any out-of-state students or those from foreign countries, if any, "to the end that the teachers colleges shall not be used in assisting any subservise propoganda [*sic*] from any source."[44]

Part of this concern may be traced to reports from the Dies Committee (the House Committee on Un-American Affairs) intimating that communism existed in Texas teachers colleges. The board action is recorded this way:

> The Presidents were questioned at length as to whether or not any subserviseness [*sic*] existed in their schools, with the result that nothing was found substantiating any charges of that nature, and the President of the Board was requested to write a letter to Hon. Martin Dies, Chairman of the Investigating Committee to the effect that an investigation had been made by the Board, and no evidence was found of the existence of communism in the colleges, but to assure Mr. Dies that the Board stood ready at any time to cooperate thoroughly and heartily with his committee if any information tending to show the existence of any communism in the Teachers College was obtained in his investigations at any time, and to aid and assist in every means possible in its eradication.[45]

The first defense-related unit established at North Texas was a Civilian Aeronautics Authority flight training unit, which went into operation in the fall of

1940. College staff members taught some of the ground courses such as meteorology and navigation, while flight instruction was carried on at an airfield constructed for the purpose north of Denton.[46] McConnell worked with the War Department and with the commander of the Eighth Corps Area in San Antonio in an effort to get an Army ROTC unit on the campus. This effort proved unsuccessful.[47]

By the summer of 1941 enough men had been mobilized so that entertainment of soldiers from nearby bases became an important college social function. An example was a Saturday party for men from Camp Wolters, Mineral Wells, at which they swam and played games at the recreation park, were served a barbecue supper, were saluted by Floyd Graham and the Aces at the Saturday Night Stage Show, and attended a girls-tag dance on the recreation park slab.[48]

As winter approached, the *Campus Chat* reported the results of a student poll under the headline, "American-Japanese War Is Due, But U. S. Should Win Struggle." The story said that fifty-five percent of students questioned thought that war between Japan and the United States would come, and quoted one coed as predicting that "I believe we will be fighting Japan in a few days." The *Chat* issue was dated December 5, 1941.

THE WARTIME CAMPUS

The day after the attack on Pearl Harbor, Monday, December 8, students and faculty members gathered in the Main Auditorium to hear a radio broadcast of President Franklin D. Roosevelt's speech to Congress asking for a declaration of war against Japan. McConnell told the assembly that he had notified state and national authorities that the college would do everything possible as an institution during the emergency. The president said he had absolute faith in the wisdom, judgment, and training of faculty and students to enable them to "go through this period and retain the equilibrium that educated men and women are supposed to have." McConnell said, "It is a time for sober thinking and not a time for emotional outbursts. The world is going through a struggle, an agony, today that we hope will be the last of its kind in history."[49]

One week later, representatives of patriotic and service organizations of Denton County joined students and faculty members in the teachers college Main Auditorium for a morning county-wide Bill of Rights Day Rally. The following day coed students, house mothers, and faculty wives were called to a meeting in the auditorium to plan five kinds of work they could do to help in the defense effort—knitting, first aid, nutrition work, sewing, and ambulance driving. McConnell appointed Registrar Alex Dickie chairman of an advisory council for campus civilian defense activities, other members being the dean of men, dean of women, and dean of the college. They were assigned to work on extension courses for military inductees, camp morale and recreation, civilian defense courses, and deferment and postponement of inductions. Plans were announced to establish a Women's Volunteer Ambulance Corps on the campus.[50]

In January 1942 President McConnell attended the National Conference of College and University Presidents on Higher Education and War in Baltimore and reported that the most significant decision was one to maintain existing academic standards for graduation even while seeking means to accelerate the four-year college course. Regular staff members of the college, who already owned more than $28,000 in defense bonds and saving stamps, pledged a monthly purchase of $2,150 at a special faculty meeting that same week.[51]

North Texas State "defense shops"—a new designation for the industrial arts laboratories—were placed on a twenty-four-hour-day schedule at the request of the state employment office to make room for 200 out-of-school youths. The program started in January 1942 with night classes for forty-five students. The schedule included ten-week courses in auto mechanics, woodwork, metalwork, welding, forging, and electricity.[52] For the spring semester of 1942, thirty courses were scheduled to emphasize defense training for college students who were planning to go into military service or defense industries. Departments involved were industrial arts, mathematics, physics, physical education, home economics, government, and business education.[53] To further accelerate the educational progress of students, a three-week intersession was scheduled for the period between the close of the summer session and the start of the fall semester. In March the first of several programs to permit men to enlist in reserve programs and continue in college was approved. The Navy Department authorized participation of North Texas State in the V-1 Accredited College Program. Freshmen and sophomores were permitted to enlist as apprentice seamen and enroll for two years while seeking to qualify for Naval V-5 or V-7 officer training programs that would carry them through to bachelor's degrees.[54]

THE WAR EFFORT

By the fall of 1942 the campus was immersed in the war effort. Six Navy reserve programs were in operation, along with a Marine Corps Officer Candidates' Class, two Army reserve programs, and the Coast Guard Reserve Cadetship. The college was approved by the federal government as a sponsoring institution for Engineering, Science, and Management War Training programs in chemistry, physics, and mathematics. Civilian Pilot Training continued, with the students now being assigned to the college by the Navy instead of enrolling on an open, voluntary basis. The federal government also financed courses in preflight training. A course was added to prepare teachers of civilian defense classes at other schools. The State Director of Vocational Agriculture directed a course for out-of-school youth, with more than 300 students being trained; it was the first of its kind in Texas to include women students.

Another project, going under the name of the Number One Defense Program, was supervised by the State Director of Vocational Education for War Industries and the North Texas Department of Industrial Arts. Courses were offered in radio operation and repair and in aircraft sheet metal work. The college was one of eight centers in the state designated to train sheet metal workers for the Consolidated Aircraft Corporation in Fort Worth. Classes also continued in Red Cross first aid teacher training and nutrition. The home economics staff, with the cooperation of the Office of Price Administration, conducted one-week sessions on consumer education for all students. The Federal Security Agency designated the teachers college library as a War Information Center to receive and display information that governmental agencies wished to make available to the public. But one effort, organization of a uniformed Women's Defense Corps, failed to develop well, and President McConnell reported, "sustained interest in this activity has not been marked."[55]

In September 1942 the Navy moved twenty V-5 cadets to the campus for two months of basic training. They were housed at 109 Avenue B in the Corona House.[56] But the largest group of men in uniform on the campus were not enrolled in a college program. They were army men sent to a glider training center in Denton. The only connection to the college was the contract by which the government rented Chilton Hall to house and feed the men, whose number according to the contract could range between 200 and 500 cadets. As a result, male civilian students had to be moved out and housed elsewhere in the campus area.[57] This contract also called for the Army Air Corps to use portions of two adjacent blocks, together with an option of using a one-hundred-acre tract for drill purposes and the partial use of two classrooms. There was a turnover of about 250 to 300 men every four weeks, none of them enrolled in the college and none instructed by any North Texas faculty members. By contrast, the CAA flight program added an enrollment of twenty-five to thirty men in the college every eight weeks. This required two full-time and four part-time faculty members and displaced two classrooms and Orchestra Hall from regular use.[58] The CAA program came to an end July 31, 1943.[59]

ASTP ARRIVES

Just as the CAA program ended, McConnell announced that 250 Army students had arrived on the campus in preparation for the activation of an Army Specialized Training Unit on August 9, 1943. Members of the unit were housed in what had been cooperative housing for women. The ASTP men were taught by the regular faculty, and the Army reimbursed the college for hospitalization, tuition, food, and housing.[60] The program ended in March 1944, however, when the general war situation led to the closing of most Army Specialized Training Units throughout the country.[61] In the meantime, the glider-pilot training unit had been converted into a liaison-pilot training school when the need for glider pilots decreased, but a corresponding decrease in the demand for liaison pilots led to cancellation of the contract for Chilton Hall as of December 31, 1943.[62] Enrollment figures for 1943–44 showed that military programs had contributed 352 men to the campus, while there were only 297 civilian males enrolled.

Fluctuations in enrollment created problems in staffing, especially since an appropriations bill rider in 1943 specified that because of the war and the need of strict economy, the state institutions of higher learning "shall offer only such courses and teach only such classes for which there is such a demand that each fulltime instructor shall have a teaching load of not less than fifty students in all courses below the graduate level."[63] The teachers college presidents tried to keep all faculty members possible, issuing a statement that it would be shortsighted to discharge faculty members for a temporary emergency that would probably result in their permanent loss to the colleges. They declared that since the younger faculty members had entered military or defense service in large numbers, it would be the teachers with long service to the colleges who would be displaced in any cutback. The presidents said that inflation had in effect cut salaries thirty-five percent, that war had increased the duties of faculty members, that there was a serious teacher shortage, and that veterans would be returning in large numbers to colleges after the war. The implication was clear that the presidents would do everything they could to hold their faculties together during the war.[64]

The enrollment hit its low point in the 1944 summer session with 1,452 students, the smallest number for either long term or summer since 1921–22. With no military programs left on the campus, the long session figure in 1944–45 was 1,886, the smallest since 1934–35. The male enrollment of that year was 330, the lowest number of men since the 1917–19 period of World War I. But during that year the war in Europe was brought to a close and the problems of the returning veteran began to occupy the teachers college staff.

chapter 24

Postwar Boom

They asked that specific measures be taken to consider these factors:

a) An adequate and equitable salary schedule.

b) An adequate and dependable income for building purposes.

c) A procedure by which the various agencies now directly concerned with problems of education can be brought into closer cooperation.

d) An effective plan of publicity.

e) A plan for securing from candidates for state office commitments, in advance of election, to policies agreed on by the previously mentioned meeting.

Board of Regents
Texas State Teachers Colleges, 1945

The war ended with the surrender of Japan in August 1945. Full demobilization would take awhile, but the impact on the North Texas campus was immediate in 1945–46. Enrollment jumped from 1,886 to 2,936 in a single year, the largest gain being from 330 to 1,201 men. The stage was set for an enrollment surge all over the state. This was not due entirely to the return of veterans and to federal assistance to them. Texas college enrollment had for some time been increasing faster than in the nation as a whole. Between 1929–30 and 1945–46, enrollment in Texas increased eighty-four percent, half as much again as the fifty-two percent in the United States.[1]

By the summer of 1946, 1,051 of 2,926 students were veterans, and in the fall most men were former servicemen, as 1,642 veterans enrolled of a total of 3,803 men and women. This was the largest enrollment for any semester in history. For the first time ever, men students outnumbered women, a condition that was to prevail until 1979. The fall 1946 ratio of sixty percent men to forty percent women established a pattern for most of the long sessions for the next two decades.

The war produced economic changes and rapid growth in the metropolitan areas of Dallas and Fort Worth. North Texas State Teachers College began to draw students from a more concentrated area. Shifting populations and changes in the employment patterns in Texas also produced a different type of student body. By 1949, Dallas County, which in the early teachers college years provided a negligible proportion of students, had become the leading source for North Texas students. Tarrant County gradually increased its supply of students, although it was not to climb above Denton County into second place until ten years later. Fall semester enrollment reached 4,677 in 1947 and 5,133 in 1948. Summer enrollments were 2,926 in 1946, 3,491 in 1947, 3,118 in 1948, and 3,784 in 1949. This was soon reflected in number of degrees in three commencements each year, the total being 444 in 1946, 779 in 1947, 1,027 in 1948, and 1,413 in 1949. After 1948 the number of graduates was never again below the 1,000 mark. The prewar peak of 882 had been reached in 1940.

CRITICAL SHORTAGE

In the fall of 1945, McConnell described the housing situation at the college as "critical and alarming." Dormitories had been filled three months before the opening of the fall semester, and every room in private homes listed with the college had been filled by August 1. McConnell estimated that one thousand students were turned away because they could not find places to live.

Classroom space was also inadequate. Upper floors of Music Hall and Orchestra Hall were still dormitories, the income being pledged to bond retirement. The Board of Regents resolved in 1945 that an emergency condition required the use of this space for classrooms. This authorized the school to liquidate the bonds by paying $28,000 from local funds. The board issued $335,000 in bonds for an annex to Oak Street Hall. Another expansion move was addition of another stack level in the library.[2] Also in 1945, the first fifty prefabricated hutments were acquired through a federal lease. These were moved from McGregor, Texas, to a site on Bradley Street, north of Oak Street, and rented to GI married students for twenty-five dollars per month. This housing area, known as Vet Village, eventually doubled in size and, like most of its kind on other campuses, outlived the postwar emergency period.[3]

In the fall of 1946 steps were taken to stretch classroom space. Classes were scheduled in previously unacceptable periods. Regular assemblies were abolished so that no regular period was lost. Classes were scheduled during the noon hour, the dining rooms being opened an hour longer to make this possible.[4]

SEARCH FOR ADEQUACY

The 49th Legislature had cut back requests for appropriations because many items were regarded as unnecessary in wartime. The collapse of Japan came just before the 1945–46 school year with appropriations already pegged at the wartime level. Students poured into Texas campuses, creating expense without providing sufficient revenue. Faculty recruitment became difficult. The supply of staff members had been reduced by the wartime absence of men and by the fact that virtually no salary adjustments were made in Texas. Long waits for payments from the Veterans Administration for student veterans left the college without payment of tuition and fees. In November 1946, the Veterans Administration made no payments to the teachers colleges for the fall semester but was in arrears for $450,000 for 1945–46. The amount owed to North Texas State alone was $130,000. Regents had to authorize McConnell to borrow $75,000 until federal payments could be received.[5]

A state teachers college committee headed by McConnell called a meeting of representatives of all boards of regents, faculties, and presidents of state institutions. They set as goals an adequate salary schedule, dependable building income, closer cooperation among educational institutions, an effective publicity plan, and support commitments from candidates for public office.[6]

In 1947, Dr. S. B. McAlister of the government faculty told a faculty meeting that for the first time all college presidents had agreed on a formula for making requests to the legislature. The appropriation for a school was to increase in the same ratio that 1947 enrollment increased over 1937 enrollment, with an increment added for a cost-of-living increase.[7] The 1947 legislative session did produce an increase in funds for North Texas. The 1946 fiscal year had operated with appropriations of $743,634.08 plus local funds for a total expenditure of $1,334,841.88.[8] The college opened the 1948 fiscal year with appropriations of $1,279,451 and estimated local revenue to make $1,897,451.[9]

NORTH TEXAS LOW

The formula was supposed to provide salary increases averaging twenty-five percent, but at North Texas the average for 1947–48 was 17.5 percent. Because he had been able to carry from the previous year a cash balance of $150,000 with accounts receivable of $50,000, President McConnell got board approval to add about $200 to each instructional position for an average increase just under twenty-five percent. Faculty members making between $2,100 and $3,321 would now earn between $2,500 and $4,000. Deans were at $5,200 and $5,300, and the president's salary advanced to $9,500 for twelve months.[10]

Deans and department directors in February 1948 were unanimous in blaming inadequate salaries for failure to meet competition from other colleges, government, and business. Most departments turned to part-time instructors to fill the void. In the Biology Department, thrity-seven percent of the budget went to temporary staff. Of the 1,100 students in the department there were 450 "who never see a permanent staff member." Recruiting efforts at a large national convention in December 1947, brought a report that the salary base at North Texas was about seventy percent of that of most institutions in the East, Midwest, and Far West. One administrator said "the pay schedule has made it difficult, if not impossible, for us to secure adequately trained staff." Adding to the financial problem, another dean said, "our need for classroom and office space becomes increasingly desperate."[11]

Appropriations requests for the 1949–51 biennium were prepared in the spring of 1948 on the basis of a formula agreed upon by the presidents of the state colleges. Requests were calculated on the basis of $281 per student of freshman and sophomore standing, $361 per student in the junior, senior, and graduate levels, and $40 per student enrolled in technical courses. President McConnell wanted twenty percent more than this because of what he considered its inadequacy but did not present the request to the board.[12] Some relief came from the legislature, which provided a fifteen percent cost-of-living adjustment for all state employees, effective April 1, 1949.[13]

TEMPORARY BUILDINGS

The fastest additional housing and classroom space came by using temporary government surplus buildings. Four two-story barracks structures came from Camp Barkeley, Texas, to house 240 single veterans, moving and set-up costs being paid by the federal government. They were located south of Chilton Hall, future site of the Quadrangle Dormitories. Two bachelor's office quarters were moved from Eagle Mountain Lake to the west end of the campus. Regents issued $90,000 in bonds to place these buildings at West Chestnut and Avenue E. The dormitories, which housed 294 men, were named Legett Halls. Other buildings came from Camp Howze for a thirty-two-bed hospital annex, a 300-capacity cafeteria for the temporary men's dormitories, a temporary journalism building in the center of the campus, a music building just south of Orchestra Hall, and a classroom-office building just east of the library (the Education Annex). These were erected on the campus without cost to the college.[14]

The administration made plans for two more women's dormitories. Instead, one large dormitory was authorized in February 1946 as Bruce Hall. A bond issue of $1,300,000 was approved.[15]

Sale of $75,000 in bonds provided a clubhouse on the hill where an eighteen-hole golf course was developed. The student activity fee was raised from eleven dollars to fifteen dollars per semester, backing a bond sale of $150,000 to construct a "students memorial union building." However, the application for construction materials was twice denied in Washington.[16] Plans were drawn in early 1947 for the first wing of the student union, but construction was delayed to await lower prices. A $15,000 metal building was located north of the hospital to house a $100,000 gift of equipment for the Industrial Arts Department. Surplus property acquired by the college was valued at between $180,000 and $225,000.[17]

The Oak Street Hall annex finally opened in February 1947, and two wings of Bruce Hall were occupied in September. The rest of the rooms were occupied in February 1948, but the kitchen did not open until a month later, even then being unfinished.[18] College labor crews used materials given by the government to build a service center to provide a garage, carpenter shop, paint-electrical-plumbing shop, central supply building, lumbershed, and warehouse.[19]

Revenue bonds provided the next source of construction. The original plan provided a gymnasium by moving a building from Camp Wolters and brick veneering; rebuilding an army service center from Camp Bowie as a student union building; and constructing a press and publications building, a post office, and a book and supply store. Contracts totaling $513,429 were awarded in July 1948 for the gymnasium, the Student Union Building, and the Journalism Building. The post office and bookstore were incorporated in the Union Building.[20] In November the $125,000 portion of a contract for the gymnasium was abrogated. The architects were asked to design for $300,000 a building to be completely new, rather than a rebuilt war-surplus structure.[21] At the same time the board authorized development of seventy acres of land in the southwest portion of the campus purchased from legislative appropriations the previous year for athletic and recreational facilities.

THE BUILDING AMENDMENT

In the 1945 legislature there was much interest in finding a building fund for colleges other than the University of Texas and Texas A&M but several bills failed.[22] College presidents developed a constitutional amendment to be submitted to the legislature in 1947. Fearing bills that would force them to share their permanent fund revenue, on January 13, 1946, the Texas A&M and University of Texas boards supported comprehensive building funds for other state-supported colleges.

A committee of ten from the other colleges proposed an amendment that would allocate the unused portion of funds from the present seven-cent levy for the Confederate Veterans Pension Fund. Institutions covered were the teachers colleges, Texas Tech, TSCW, the College of Mines, Texas A&I, John Tarleton Agricultural College, North Texas Agricultural College, and Prairie View A&M.[23]

The 1947 legislature called an election on this amendment for August 23, 1947. McConnell told the faculty that only $137,000 had been appropriated to North Texas by the legislature for buildings in the past twenty-five years. He declared that the five-cent tax could change the course of the building history of the state colleges.[24] The plan was approved by a vote of 102,531 to 97,318.[25] This authorized boards of the fourteen colleges to pledge ad valorem tax funds to secure bonds for "acquiring, constructing, and initially equipping buildings or other permanent improvements." This power was expressly limited to thirty years, with the five-cent tax to expire when bonds were repaid. Each college received percentage allocations based on student enrollments of the ten-year period ending January 1, 1948.[26] Reallocations were to be made not later than June 1 of each succeeding ten-year period based on average long-session full-time student enrollment for the preceding five years. No other funds were to be received from the general revenue for buildings or improvements except in cases of fire, flood, storm, or earthquake.

THE OPPOSITION SUES

The closeness of the balloting on the constitutional amendment suggests a strongly organized opposition. This there was, most of it in West Texas, where it was argued that Texas Tech should share with the University of Texas and Texas A&M rather than join the "smaller colleges." Four Lubbock men and one from Dallas filed suits against the attorney general and secretary of state, contesting the legality of the election. The district court combined the suits for trial eight months later, in April 1948. Sixteen of the seventeen colleges entered the litigation as contestants or partisan interests. Only Texas Tech did not.[27] The district court trial came after months of effort by attorneys to reach an agreement on the facts in the case. Once an agreement was reached, the trial itself lasted only one hour.[28] Having lost that suit, the challengers appealed to the Third Court of Civil Appeals. The appeals court ruled that the election was valid.[29]

The opposition appealed to the State Supreme Court, which on January 5, 1949, dismissed the appeals, saying it had no jurisdiction.[30] In reporting the first division of ad valorem funds, the *Dallas Morning News* headlined its story, "Texas

Tech to Benefit Most From Bill It Fought." The Lubbock school was awarded a percentage of 16.54877 each year of the collections from the five-cent tax. North Texas was the second largest beneficiary with 12.64522 percent.[31]

In the meantime construction had continued on the Student Union Building and the Journalism Building. The Union Building was dedicated on the fiftieth anniversary of the legislative act establishing North Texas as a state institution, March 31, 1899. A bronze plaque with names of 147 former students who died in military service was erected in the main foyer. The dedication speaker was Major General Roger Ramey of the United States Air Force, a North Texas graduate and later a member of the Board of Regents. The ceremonies began an annual program series that was to last until 1961 as North Texas Day.

Building amendment bonds sold in the summer of 1949, yielding for North Texas $2,195,000. Buildings first planned were a science building, named Masters Hall, at Avenue B and Sycamore, and a men's gymnasium. Revenue bonds and local funds provided the first two units of the Quadrangle Dormitories and the Women's Gymnasium. In the fall of 1949, plans were under way for a $2,700,000 building program.

THE WATER CONTROVERSY

Growth of the campus and the city led to the problem of an adequate water supply for the campus. The result was a dispute of several years' duration that involved the state attorney general, state courts, and the legislature. The source of the disagreement was the 1899 act transferring the city normal property for creation of a state school. This bound the City of Denton "to furnish for the use of said school an abundant supply of pure artesian water, free of cost to the State, for all the purposes of said school. . . ." On October 16, 1945, City Attorney Earl Coleman wrote to McConnell that the City Commission could not legally enter into such a perpetual contract, so the City of Denton is furnishing water to the college without any authority to do so.

President McConnell obtained an opinion from the attorney general holding that the City of Denton was legally bound to furnish water free of cost.[32] The *Denton Record-Chronicle* on January 22 declared that "one of Denton's oldest controversial questions was settled officially by the action." That statement proved to be erroneous.

On March 7, 1947, Mayor J. L. Yarbrough notified the City Commission that it was "imperative and a public necessity" that water bills from the two Denton colleges be paid. Hot weather and a water shortage brought the matter to a critical stage. On July 27, Yarbrough informed McConnell that water for the college swimming pool, athletic field, and outside grounds would be cut off on July 29. President McConnell was out of town, but Board of Regents chairman William L. Kerr sent instruction to tell the city that the matter had been referred to the attorney general and that the college could take no further action.[33]

The water cutoff to the athletic field and swimming pool was halted when it was learned that the action would also cut off water to several instructional buildings. On July 31, the City Commission advised the attorney general that it felt obligated to force the issue. The commission then ordered that all water used by North Texas State Teachers College be cut off on August 28, 1948, and remain cut off "until such time as the courts of the state shall judicially determine, temporarily or permanently, that the City of Denton is obligated to furnish free water to such institutions in the future." Attorney General Price Daniel prepared an injunction proceeding leading to a suit against the city,[34] but the case was never heard. In 1949, House Bill 6 authorized the Board of Regents to contract with the city to furnish water to North Texas. The city attorney stated that the city would bill the college for water at commercial rates. This ended the struggle over Denton water.

THE COLLEGE CHANGES

The 1946 reorganization plan had given a new shape to the academic structure of what was in all but name a state college. The influx of veterans and changing population in the region had produced a different kind of student body from that of the prewar teachers college. The first large construction programs in many years gave a different appearance to the campus. Perhaps at no other point in its history had the college seen an alteration in character and purpose so marked.

More Research Needed

After the war, research grants began to appear more frequently. In February 1946, Cities Service Oil Company provided $1,200 to Dr. Price Truitt for research in hydrocarbons, chlorination, and nitration, and the Texas Company gave $1,500 for research by Dr. J. L. Carrico in hydrocarbons. Three months later, the Research Corporation of New York City gave $4,500 for one year of research on "Stereoisomerism of Synthetic and Natural Polyenes" by Dr. R. B. Escue, Jr.[35]

A small beginning in state support came in 1945, when the legislature appropriated $14,000 for research. A faculty research committee recommended its allocation.[36]

At the request of McConnell in February 1948, Dr. J. K. G. Silvey, professor of biology, offered these views:

> It is imperative that a progressive science staff be afforded opportunities to do scholarly and creative work. One of the *musts* of this institution is to recognize this need in its staff and to place at their disposal the equipment, time, and money that they may produce original work. Fundamentally, research is the tonic that keeps a teacher alive. The absence of this tonic results in the loss of vitality, interest, and a final decadence of high-caliber instruction.

The problem in 1948, of course, was financial support. In an accompanying memorandum, Dr. E. H. Hanson, director of the mathematics department, wrote:

> But there is another benefit which the people of Texas should expect from an institution such as this, and that is the benefit to be derived from programs of research and scholarly study carried on by the various departments. In this latter phase, I believe that we are definitely below the desirable standards. . . . Our salaries do not compare favorably with those paid elsewhere. In my opinion, it will be most difficult to attract to our staff persons of recognized research ability.

McCONNELL RESIGNS, BRIEFLY

Dr. W. J. McConnell presented to the Board of Regents on May 5, 1948, his resignation as president of North Texas. Minutes state, "the resignation was so unexpected that the board took no action except to express their sincere appreciation, admiration and respect of Dr. McConnell and his record as an educator."[37] At a faculty meeting in May the Council of Deans presented a letter expressing the "warm feelings of gratitude, affection and esteem" of the staff of the teachers college for President and Mrs. McConnell. The faculty approved the letter by a unanimous standing vote and in June decided to purchase a retirement gift for the McConnells.[38]

However, in July the board unanimously asked McConnell to reconsider his resignation until August 31, 1949. McConnell agreed. In November 1948, the regents created the position of vice president and invited three faculty members to appear before the board. They were Dr. S. B. McAlister, chairman of the division of social science; Dr. Floyd Stovall, dean of the College of Arts and Sciences; and Dr. J. C. Matthews, dean of the School of Education. After the interviews, it was unanimously ordered that Dr. Matthews be elected vice president of the teachers college.[39]

INDEPENDENCE FOR NORTH TEXAS

Postwar changes were affecting all teachers colleges in the Texas system. On March 1, 1949, the Council of Presidents recommended that the regents ask the legislature then in session to change the names of the seven colleges to *state college* from *state teachers college* except for San Marcos, which would be called Southwest Texas State College of Education. The presidents also asked that the new designation be for the Board of Regents of the Texas State Colleges.[40]

North Texas did not stay with this group movement, however. On March 10, 1949, a bill was introduced to create a separate board of regents for North Texas State College. This was introduced by Senator R. L. Proffer of Justin with a companion bill by Representative Hal Jackson of Denton, cosponsored by seven other representatives, all ex-students of the college.

In Denton, President McConnell said, "There are problems peculiar to the institution because of its enrollment, now more than 5,700 for the regular session, and because of its great expansion in services, plant, and faculty. Concentration of population in this area has called for specialized training in many fields, creating a demand for a multipurpose institution." He observed that North Texas was then the largest college in the state not administered by a separate board, being more than twice the size of any other teachers college.[41]

The new Board of Regents would have nine members but only one member could be from any one state senatorial district, and no member could be a resident of Denton County. North Texas State College continued with the same scope of work, "said work and activities to be increased or diminished, altered or changed in any manner deemed by the new governing board to be conducive to the betterment of the services offered, or which may be offered, by such institution to the people of Texas."

The change originally was to be effective September 1, 1949. However, it was feared that the college might lose its funds under the college building amendment. The state attorney general drew up a substitute clause to guarantee these funds by making the change immediately after the governor signed the bill, declaring that "the fact that the enrollments and appropriations for the North Texas State Teachers College, at Denton, have increased rapidly in the last several years to the point that said College is now one of the leading educational institutions in Texas and the great Southwest" created an emergency so that the rules could be suspended and put the act in full force immediately. The amended bill passed the Senate by a vote of 21 to 3 and cleared the House 116 to 0 on May 10. The bill was signed by Governor Beauford Jester on May 23, 1949.[42]

STUDENT LIFE ALTERED

Changes in the student population became evident on the postwar campus. A dean noted early in 1948, "the student body is mobilized in spite of the general shortage of automobiles." There were far more married students, and Dean of Men William G. Woods worried that neither college-owned nor off-campus housing was designed for them. Responsibility for emergency postwar housing shifted from the veterans' home communities to the college towns. As a result, Dean Woods said, "living arrangements such as are provided by temporary makeshifts are tolerated but not welcomed, either by students or the college." Men students were scattered over a wide area, and it was no longer possible to require all students to live in dormitories or approved campus homes. Men students were advised that they could be admitted only if they could take care of their own living arrangements.[43]

Most prewar student organizations continued—to be joined in 1945 by Mu Phi Epsilon, national music sorority; Beta Beta Beta, national biological society; Alpha Rho Tau, art organization; Gamma Iota Chi, or GIX, for former service men and women; Delta Sigma Delta, chemical research; Future Teachers of America; the K-O-E-D Klub, radio broadcasting; the League of Women Voters; the Modern Writers Club; Political Economy Club; PreLaw Club; and Phi Alpha Theta, honor society in history. In 1949, the catalog listed sixty-four student organizations. In addition there were thirteen social organizations, some with Greek letters. Although not called sorority or fraternity, they became a nucleus in another few years of chapters of national Greek-letter social fraternities and sororities.[44]

In the spring of 1948 a student election created the United Students of North Texas State College. The purposes of the organization were stated:

> To further coordinate student activities with the programs of the faculty and administration; to develop among the student body a greater and more enlightened interest in those matters affecting the students and the college; to provide a means of discovering student opinion; to provide means for making known to the college administration the thinking and feeling of the students; to encourage a more reasonable participation in government functions and student activities.

Officers were elected in the spring to serve for the following school year. A student senate was elected in the fall by each class.[45]

STUDENT RECREATION

The first postwar recreation center was the college golf course and clubhouse. Buses were run by the Denton bus lines daily from 3:00 to 6:00 P.M. from the campus to the clubhouse. On all-college nights the buses ran from 3:00 to 9:00 P.M., with the final bus returning to the campus at 10:30 P.M. A recreation room and snack bar were provided, with hopes expressed this way by Athletic Director and Dean of Men T. J. Fouts:

> This clubhouse will greatly reduce student attendance at roadhouses, beer joints, and public dance halls in our surrounding territory. It provides clean, wholesome recreation with supervision for all students. It should help eliminate many of our discipline problems. A manager and his wife will live on the premises and will at all times maintain strict supervision over all activities in the building.[46]

Intercollegiate athletics, too, experienced a postwar resurgence with some wanting something closer to "big-time" sports. The first postwar football season opened with a new coach, Odus Mitchell, and with an overwhelming 47–0 loss to Texas A&M. The rest of the year, however, brought seven victories, including a 14–13 defeat of Amos Alonzo Stagg's College of the Pacific team in the Optimist Bowl in Houston. The following year, the sports editor of the *Dallas Morning News* wrote:

> For a number of years recognition as the strongest team in this section outside the Southwest Conference has been accorded either to Texas Tech at Lubbock or to Hardin-Simmons at Abilene. This season is different.
>
> North Texas State's Eagles of Denton now hold this position and they're not likely to be pushed off their pedestal. They're long-odds favorites to walk off with the Lone Star Conference crown and they may be better than some of the teams in the Southwest loop.
>
> [The writer pointed to a narrow 12–0 loss to Arkansas and a surprising 20–12 victory over the University of Florida.]
>
> Odus Mitchell has come up with an outfit that on the record looks like one of the strongest in this section.[47]

The Eagles did win the conference title, won ten games, lost only to Arkansas during the regular season and went to the Salad Bowl in Phoenix, Arizona, where they lost 13-6 to the University of Nevada. The event brought much newspaper publicity from Nevada along the lines of "Whoever heard of Denton Teachers?"

Golf became an important intercollegiate sport under Coach Fred Cobb. His first team won ten dual matches and lost four, his second had an 8-5 record, and in 1948 the Eagle squad went undefeated in eleven matches and won three tournaments. The 1949 teachers college team won the national (NCAA) golf title, a feat that was to be repeated for three more years.

Growth in enrollment and athletic success created unrest among some of the Lone Star Conference schools and led to a division of interests within the league. Negotiations were conducted in 1948–49 for North Texas, the University of Houston, and Trinity University to withdraw from the Lone Star

Conference and be joined by Hardin College of Wichita Falls (later Midwestern University) in the formation of the Gulf Coast Conference. Thus as NTSC left the teachers college system, it also ended athletic league association with the other teachers colleges. The Gulf Coast Conference, unhappily, never matured, although it survived for eight years until North Texas withdrew.

END OF AN ERA

As the teachers college era prepared to end in 1948–49, campus life still showed many of the smaller teachers college ways. Much student activity still centered on "The Corner," where as the *Yucca* noted, "business and pleasure meet. . . where a meal, a prescription, or a haircut or finger wave is just around the corner." Students could still ride buses to the square on movie dates or to the College Clubhouse for dancing, but publications began listing lake parties and "jaunts to Big D" as regular recreation events. The mobile student population was pushing outward on the perimeter of the campus community.

The student yearbook pictured "the family man" among students as a normal part of campus life, and the student wife was no longer a rarity. The graduate student was becoming a long-session fixture as well as a summer phenomenon. Social notes began referring to the Greeks and the Independents as major campus forces. The *Yucca* openly pictured a page of "the weekend spirit," which displayed a variety of beer-drinking males (but no females) out for a Saturday night in "the greener and wetter pastures of Dallas and Fort Worth." In the spring the "long-awaited dreamhouse. . . a new and ultramodern center. . . the elegant structure. . . made 1949 a great year"—the students moved into the Student Union Building, created from a former Army service center.

The first USNT Senate went into action, acclaimed by student writers as "its youthful members, full of ambition and initiative, found a new outlet for political talent that had long searched for betterment in campus affairs." During the year "a near-professional approach to school problems demonstrated the maturity and conviction" of the student politicians. Intersorority Stunt Night packed the Main Auditorium as five Greek groups competed to entertain the students. Debate continued to be a major activity, as student speakers tried to match the men's 1948 record of winning the national debate trophy at West Point.

Alpha Phi Omega, intended to be a service organization, made a start at a brief life on the campus and introduced the Ugliest Man Contest to North Texas. Students lined up in the afternoon to get seats for one of two shows by Vaughn Monroe, his orchestra, and variety acts. One of the programs was broadcast on a national network. The big attraction was Monroe's "Moonmaids," three of whom had performed just a few years earlier as student members of the Swingtette on the Saturday Night Stage Show. Homecoming was a big-time show now, with bonfire, parade, queen, two dances, many bands, but still featuring the traditional football clash with East Texas State. Sadie Hawkins Day in the Li'l Abner tradition was still "big" on campus. Booths, concessions, entertainment shows, and dancing were a feature of the Halloween Carnival in Harriss Gymnasium—and a historic first was noted when films of the carnival and the coronation of the King and Queen were shown on television station WBAP-TV, the first campus event ever seen on the broadcast screen. Later that year, the touring student Opera Workshop cast of *Carmen* was also seen on WBAP-TV.

As the *Yucca* observed on its title page, "5,000 of us came and each of us played a part in making it a great North Texas Year." It was the last year of North Texas State Teachers College.

Robert Lincoln Marquis, President, 1923–34.

Avenue B runs south through the center of this picture to the recreation park, a major campus addition of the first teachers college decade along with the 1923 Administration Building (top, center).

Teachers College students gathered in the Main Auditorium every Saturday night to attend a movie and the stage show by 'Fessor Floyd Graham and the Aces of Collegeland.

Miss Beulah Harriss (left) founded the Green Jackets spirit organization, shown here a year later at a 1926 football game. The group survived until the 1970s.

W. Joseph McConnell, President, 1934–51.

The Teachers College at last acquired spacious library facilities with this new building in 1937.

These four Eagle runners gained a distinction in 1938 that still stood in 2001: the only two sets of identical twins ever to hold a world record in track and field. The team of Elmer Brown, Delmer Brown, Wayne Rideout, and Blaine Rideout set a world record in the indoor mile and seven-eighths medley relay at the Millrose Games in Madison Square Garden in New York.

A patriotic effort as war approached in 1940 was the civilian flight training program conducted by the Teachers College with the federal CAA. Flight operations took place at the Denton Municipal Airport and ground instruction was offered on the campus. About twenty-five students were trained at a time, and the classes continued into the first years of the war.

part V

Building a University for a Metroplex

1949–1968

All the factual evidence indicates that by all odds North Texas State University is the public institution most logical for adoption by the region in its search for the greatly needed expansion of public higher education programs. North Texas State University brings to the task 75 years of experience in higher education. It presents a strong, established graduate program with 30 years of development and experience behind it. It offers doctoral-level operations that have been building for 15 years. It enters the last quarter of its first century with the designation as the institution for the North Texas area with the assignment of conducting doctoral programs in the sciences, mathematics, the humanities, social sciences, teacher education, business administration, and fine arts.

J. C. Matthews

Author's Foreword to Part V

From the 1965 Edition

The Story of North Texas has arrived at the point where it seems more like current news than history to this writer. The situation reminded a colleague of the debate by Dr. Samuel Johnson and Oliver Goldsmith as to whether an author should continue his history of England to the present day. As recorded by Boswell, Goldsmith said that he should. Dr. Johnson replied, "No, Sir; he would give great offence. He would have to tell of almost all the living great what they do not wish told. . . . It is laudable in a man to wish to live by his labours; but he should write so as he may *live* by them, not so as he may be knocked on the head. I would advise him to be at Calais before he publishes his history of the present age."

In this case, the writer has no fear of telling the untellable about the living, of writing so as to be knocked on the head or of having to flee to Calais before publishing the story of North Texas State College and North Texas State University. He does, however, recognize that events are too recent to permit objective analysis; that for most of these years he would be writing of events in which he was personally involved; that in effect a detailed chronicling of the period could constitute an assessment of a faculty and administration of which the writer has been a part. So Chapter 25 will review only in broad outline some of the major trends since 1949. The detailed story is left to some future historian, perhaps one who will in the One Hundredth Year enjoy the task as much as this one has in the Seventy-Fifth Year of North Texas.

The View from 2000

At the time the previous two paragraphs were written, the author was just starting a brief administrative career as vice president, administrative affairs, and then as director of university planning and analysis. He served on the staffs of President J. C. Matthews, John Kamerick, and C. C. Nolen, between 1964 and 1978. It thus remains true that he is writing of events in which he was personally involved; what follows this page is no less than a detailed chronicling of a period in which the writer has had a part. Nevertheless, the reader is left to conclude that "some future historian" mentioned above is the same individual who wrote what went before.

This writer devoted the period of 1978 to 1996 full-time to teaching in the Department of Journalism. Retired in May 1996 after forty-three years on the North Texas faculty, he embarks on the task of writing a factual and, he hopes, fair-minded chronicling of the years since J. C. Matthews took office as president in 1951. Chapter 25 goes back into the seventeen years of the presidency of Dr. Matthews to record the contributions, the successes, and the problems that he met at a volatile period in the growth of North Texas.

chapter 25

A Life Devoted to North Texas

> To be a moral man is to obey the traditional maxims of your community without hesitation or discussion.
>
> *Charles S. Peirce*
> *Collected Papers*

After fifteen years as president of North Texas State Teachers College, W. Joseph McConnell welcomed the new Board of Regents of North Texas State College to the campus on June 4, 1949. The nine new regents assembled at the call of Governor Beauford Jester. After a motor tour of the college grounds, the regents met in the Student Union Building, adopted bylaws and elected officers: Ben H. Wooten of Dallas, chairman; S. A. Kerr, Jr., of Huntsville, who had been on the teachers college board, vice chairman; and Robert Caldwell, business manager of the college, secretary.

Although he had announced his retirement in May 1948, Dr. McConnell stayed on for two more years of service with the new state college board. His final retirement became known after an executive session of the Board of Regents on January 24, 1951. The eight regents present announced that they had voted unanimously that McConnell's resignation be accepted effective August 31, 1951; that J. C. Matthews be elected president effective September 1, 1951; and that McConnell be made president emeritus on that date at reduced pay. Even after he retired from the paid position, McConnell continued as president emeritus until his death at the age of seventy-two on November 24, 1955.

McConnell's contributions were summed up by Wooten at the dedication of the McConnell Memorial Tower of the new Administration Building on December 16, 1956. He said:

> From 1934 to 1951 this institution grew from a small single-purpose Institution to a large multipurpose college of national prominence.
>
> It changed from a physical plant evaluation of approximately two million dollars to one of more than twelve million dollars—six times as much.
>
> It grew from a library of 50,000 volumes to more than 200,000 volumes—four times as many volumes.
>
> It enrolled 1,700 students in 1934 and 5,100 in 1951—three times as many.
>
> Its faculty increased from 86 to 230—nearly three times as many.
>
> Among other things, graduate work was initiated, a separate Board of Regents was provided, a university-type organization was established, and the school became a member of the National Association of Schools of Music and was approved by the Association of American Universities. . . .

> The Board of Regents thought it was fitting that this tower, standing as it does at the center of the campus overlooking the 22 major buildings which were built during his administration and representing the culmination of a dream of students, ex-students, faculty, and Board of Regents, should bear his name.

THE NEW PRESIDENT

James Carl Matthews had already devoted the larger portion of his life to North Texas when he became president on September 1, 1951, the first and only graduate of the school to hold the office. He was born near Gordonville, in the Rock Creek Community of Grayson County, Texas, on October 16, 1901, the oldest of nine children. After schooling in West Rayland and Thalia, he passed teacher certification examinations in order to be admitted to North Texas State Normal College in 1920. He wanted to become a teacher and interrupted his education to serve as principal at Rayland, Texas, in 1921–22. For six months of his senior year he was employed as a student teaching assistant, receiving the bachelor of arts with a major in history and minor in English in 1925. That August, Carl Matthews married a fellow student, Miss Rena Mae Waggoner of Denton.

Matthews taught history in the North Texas Demonstration School until 1932 with periods of leave for study. He received the M.A. degree in 1928 and the Ph.D. in 1932, both from George Peabody College for Teachers. In 1932 Dr. Matthews became professor of education and then served as director of student teaching from 1933 to 1935. At that time he took a two-year leave to serve as director of curriculum and textbooks for the Texas Department of Education. He returned to NT as director of the Demonstration School and of student teaching and in 1938 assumed the title of director of teacher training. In 1946, Matthews became the first dean of the School of Education, a title which he retained upon being named vice president in 1948.

The three children of Dr. and Mrs. Matthews, two sons and a daughter, are all graduates of North Texas, as are many other members of the families.

Dr. Matthews died November 9, 1996, a few weeks past his ninety-fifth birthday.

A MATTER OF STYLE

When J. C. Matthews retired from the presidency in August 1968, it had been forty-eight years since he entered the state normal as a freshman. He taught for several years in the higher education program in the College of Education and then occupied an office as president emeritus until 1978—thus his time on the campus extended nearly sixty years. Except for time at graduate school and on leave to the State Department of Education, his entire career had been spent on the campus. He was to be the last of the old school of college administration; it was no surprise that just after he left office, some of the most dramatic changes in operating procedure occurred almost immediately.

The "old style" of administration was characterized by the concentration of power in the president and the absence of widespread participation in decision-making. President Matthews, who had been the college's first vice president, did not fill that position until he had been in office for two years, at which time he made a popular appointment of Dr. A. M. Sampley. He was a noted poet, a highly regarded teacher, and a successful director of the NT Library.

The terminology for the chief administrator in academic departments was not "chairman" or even "head." Each of these was known as a "department director," and in most departments decision-making power was concentrated with the director. Some directors were able to organize faculty committees to help in the decision-making process, but there was no sign of faculty personnel committees to review progress toward tenure and promotion.

While there were many active faculty committees, most of the members were appointed by the president, possibly on recommendations from others. The election of members of any committee was a rarity.

Hiring of Personnel

Although searches for prospective faculty took place in the department, the president usually interviewed each candidate and controlled the final approval. A similar procedure was followed for support personnel, some of them well down in lower echelons of staff. There was no organization known as a "Personnel Office" during the Matthews tenure. For clerical and secretarial positions, the job applications were filed with the secretary to the president, who helped departments locate and interview applicants.

Control of Expenditures

The details of budget preparation were handled by President Matthews personally. While he respected recommendations from department directors on many personnel matters and budgetary needs, the final entry into the budget draft was made by him. He was fond of explaining that the chief business officer should be responsible for preparing the income budget but nothing more; the president should be responsible for the expenditure budget.

Managing Details

The president paid great attention to the minute details of building and maintenance projects. When the Library Building was being planned in 1967, Dr. Matthews wrote this as part of a long letter to the architect in Houston:

> In the brick I would use three, maybe four colors nonconspicuously contrasting, and I would eliminate altogether the pink ones. I think the texture of the brick on the Biology Building is probably superior to the texture of the others which have been used, and that type should be examined as a likely one to turn to. It has better possibilities of not weathering with freezing and expanding of ice in crevices and it probably has more adhesive qualities than ones they used earlier.[1]

Student conduct also came in for close scrutiny. For most of this president's tenure, there was no position called "dean of students." The dean of men and dean of women usually reported directly to the president, and he quite often set the rules and specified the punishment for violations. In many ways, the student code could be traced back to Dr. Bruce's Normal, which specified strict behavioral standards for students. Women students were required to live in dormitories. Since most of the dorms were for women, only freshman men were required to live in university facilities and then only until the available spaces had been filled. The week-night curfew for women was 10:50 P.M. and midnight on Saturdays. Those who came in late faced an immediate trip to the office of the dean of women. When panty raids became a collegiate fad in the 1950s, men who were caught participating in these were dismissed from school. And one of the major reasons for disciplinary dismissal of women students was being discovered to have visited the residence of a male.

Much of the onus for these actions was placed by students on Dr. Imogene Bentley (later Dickey and then Mohat), who was indeed the person who dealt directly with discipline of women students. She worked closely with the president, however, and it was reasonably clear to observers at the time that she sometimes acted out of loyalty to Dr. Matthews rather than out of her own conviction that a particular action or policy would be of her own choosing. She was a close friend of President and Mrs. Matthews and was one of the influential counselors on many topics in the Matthews administration.

The Civic Fund: A 1967 Case Study

One focal point of faculty resentment was the Civic Fund, a means of collecting faculty contributions for charitable groups, the Denton Chamber of Commerce, and the statewide Committee of Governing Boards. The problem lay not in the concept of organized faculty giving but in the lack of voluntary participation. Particularly galling to some was the agreement found at the bottom of the annual employment contract. Here's an example from the contract in 1953:

> The faculty by vote has adopted a cooperative system of discharging a part of its charity and civic responsibility through payment by each staff member of ½ of 1% (or less) of the nine month salary to a committee of the faculty for distribution to the faculty floral fund, Crippled Children's Society, Red Cross, Chamber of Commerce, Salvation Army, Red Seal, Infantile Paralysis, Boy Scouts, Girls Scouts, and others. Staff members will be asked to leave signed checks covering the amount in the Business Office when they get their salary warrants on November 3 and March 3.

What is not clear in the records is how "the faculty by vote" adopted this system. After years of agitation, some faculty members registered protests about this with some regents and with state officials in Austin. This is indicated in a letter from Matthews to State Representative Alonzo Jamison in February 1967: "With reference to our discussion yesterday on the civic fund, I would like to state that it will be our policy to make the fund optional and to have it handled through the departments. . . . There will be no mention of the fund in any contractual arrangement. If I can answer any further question, I shall be pleased to do so."[2]

This took place a year and a half before the president's retirement. A fairly predictable result was that in the first semester, voluntary contributions totaled about eighty percent of the amount that would have been required.

RELATIONS WITH THE BOARD

President Matthews began office as the clear choice of the regents, strongly endorsed by Dr. McConnell, who had been rather evidently grooming his vice president for the job. Matthews enjoyed a close personal relationship with Chairman Wooten. Wooten recalled later that he had been a supporter and friend of President McConnell and this feeling was transferred to the next leader. He put it this way: "Dr. McConnell, a great friend of mine, was very strong for Dr. Matthews and naturally that had something to do with my opinion."[3]

The bylaws of the Board of Regents were based on statutes that vested all power in the board. The regents delegated operational powers to the president but retained approval of funds expenditures, travel expenses, hiring of employees, naming of department directors, and changes in academic programs or standards. Given this background, it was to be expected that the board, and especially its chairman, would continue to have strong, centralized presidential powers. Again, Ben Wooten's later recollections of Matthews spell this out:

> It was a period of great growth. I liked his policies very much. He was an individual that did not ask everybody in the country what ought to be done. Some people seemed to think that he did not get enough advice from other people, but I place results over method. I was very favorably impressed with him, and our relationship developed into a friendship that I cherish very much.[4]

Up from the Pine Bur Club

Wooten and Matthews shared similar backgrounds—both grew up in rural settings at the start of the twentieth century, both came to the North Texas State Normal College, and both found the girls they would someday marry as normal students. Benjamin Harrison Wooten came out of the Panola County piney woods of East Texas and took up residence with some others from his home area in a house north of the campus. There the young students kept a cow to provide milk for their own table and for sale to others to provide money for some of their expenses. He earned a teaching certificate (there was as yet no bachelor's degree awarded) and then volunteered for service with the Army in Europe for World War I. The postwar years took him into a banking career, and when Governor Beauford Jester named him to the NTSC board in 1949, he had become president of the First National Bank in Dallas.

A Two-Man Committee

In effect, board members through most of his term trusted Chairman Wooten to act on their behalf. Many of the day-to-day policy decisions were made during telephone conversations between the board chairman and the president—a good many longer-term policy plans could be accomplished by a trip to Dallas to the bank office of Mr. Wooten.

A Problem With Federal Aid

However, by the late 1960s one political issue divided the regents—the seeking of federal funds for the construction of buildings and for support of instructional programs. It was not that this was a new issue. Aided by special authorizing acts of the Texas Legislature, North Texas in 1935 and 1936 built a Library Building and its first two dormitories with the aid of funds from the Public Works Administration. At about the same time, funds from the Works Project Administration helped fund the construction of steam tunnels and sanitary sewers on the campus. But the mood of the 1960s was not the same and some regents strongly opposed the Higher Education Facilities Act of 1963.

A Struggle Over the Facilities Act

On February 14, 1964, Matthews reported that there was a one-third matching rate for federal dollars and that North Texas was expecting about $1.3 million from the state constitutional ad valorem tax fund. He told the board that "we could have an additional $645,936 added to it which would give us $1,937,800 for classroom building. . . in place of $1,291,873. We need a recommendation from the Board of Regents on this matter before we can proceed with any of the steps necessary in regard to new classrooms."[5]

The board responded with all nine members voting for a motion from Regent Joe Nelson to ask the president to have its attorney study the act to "determine whether or not it contains provisions which are inimical to the best interests of the university." The president was back at the October meeting to suggest that federal funds be sought for the biology building then being planned. Three key regents were absent: Paul Cates, Ray Cowan, and Berl Godfrey. The board voted 6–0 in support of the president's suggestion but delayed final action pending study by a special committee. In the meantime, the administration was authorized to begin the application process based on preliminary drawings for an additional 24,000 square feet in the biology building.[6] Wooten appointed a committee of Carroll Sullivant, Godfrey, and David Kimbell.

A February Showdown

At the board meeting February 18, 1965, Regent Nelson asked that the question of the federal application be made the first order of business.

Regent Kerr moved that the president proceed to seek the federal funds. Several regents argued that it was not proper for federal tax money to be spent to support state institutions. Two members (Cowan and Sullivant) were absent that day, so with the chairman not voting, the resolution failed 4–2. It appeared that the building plans would have to be delayed.

Near the end of the meeting, Chairman Wooten asked if there were any further business. Regent Paul Cates of Amarillo said he wished to address his fellow regents. His comments included the following concepts:

> I will be leaving in a few weeks to devote a year in Japan in missionary work for my church. Since my term of office as a regent expires in a few months, that means that today's actions will be my last as a regent of North Texas State University.
>
> Now you all know me as a true political conservative—I know that some have described me as being well to the right of Attila the Hun. I am strongly opposed to the idea of federal aid to public universities. But since I am leaving today, and since I know that these dollars will be spent at some university in Texas, I cannot bring myself to use my own political beliefs to deprive students of the opportunity to have this building. Since I voted against the original motion, I therefore move to reconsider the proposal.[7]

Chairman Wooten called for a vote on the motion to reconsider, and the vote was 3 to 3. The chairman exercised his privilege to vote and recorded an "aye" to pass the motion. Nelson, seconded by Godfrey, moved to oppose the acceptance of a federal grant for the biology building and another 3–3 tie resulted. Wooten cast the deciding vote and the application was approved, establishing the precedent for a succession of applications for many varieties of federal program funds in the years just ahead.[8]

PLANNING CAMPUS DEVELOPMENT

President Matthews carried almost single-handedly much of the thinking and projecting about the physical growth of the campus. The automobile had not been a major problem in earlier years. However, as enrollment climbed, more students began to live away from the campus in Denton or other cities and began to drive to class. With no parking lots available, students parked on city streets. This created friction with the many individuals living in homes adjacent to the college. It created problems for the City of Denton, whose officials had to deal with complaints.

Problem: A Campus on City Streets

The normal began in 1890 with only ten acres of campus. As land was needed for expansion, the college had to buy private property. The campus became a mosaic of city blocks interlaced with city-owned streets. By 1960 traffic signals dotted the college area and parking meters lined the streets right next to classroom buildings. Students walking from class to class often had to cross streets filled with cars.

The city also sought more thoroughfares running north and south in the areas of both NTSC and TSCW. Denton officials announced plans to cut through a residential block to open Avenue C between Hickory and Oak to connect northward to Highway 24 (later University Drive/U.S. 380). Matthews vigorously opposed this plan to create a traffic thoroughfare through the campus. TSCW President Guinn objected to a similar plan for Bell Avenue, but Denton built both thoroughfares over the objections of the two colleges.

Reaching for the Interstate

In the mid-1960s, the Texas Highway Department had begun construction of a new highway, one that became Interstate 35 East to Dallas and connected northward to Oklahoma City. This had cut off the northeast corner of the North Texas golf course, requiring the relocation of the first green. The highway split the athletic zone of the campus, separating the golf course and its clubhouse from Fouts Field and the Men's Gymnasium. Preparations were also being made to build an Interstate 35W to Fort Worth, which would join Interstate 35E right at Fouts Field.

The highway construction would provide an obvious physical linking of the North Texas campus to the Dallas-Fort Worth metropolitan area. President Matthews envisioned a southward move of North Texas across Mill Street (later Eagle Drive). The area along the interstate service road between Avenues A and D would join the campus to the freeway, adjoining the athletic portion that already abutted the interstate from Avenue D to Avenue I (later Bonnie Brae). He knew this would require the purchase of a lot of land, most of it covered with single-family houses, for which he had virtually no funds.

Big Problems: Buying Land, Closing Streets

NTSU and TWU joined the city in an ill-fated attempt in October 1962 to pass an urban-renewal ordinance to get federal funds to buy lands for expansion of both campuses. This was defeated decisively in a city election, and it left NTSU with little land-purchase money. The ad valorem tax for building funds could not be used to buy land. Sale of bonds against tuition income and a few auxiliary enterprise funds financed a limited land purchase. By policy, North Texas negotiated land purchases rather than condemning property. Eminent domain had never been used until 1967, when some landowners chose not to sell at appraised prices.

Board members grew concerned over receiving requests from the president to purchase land at a variety of locations near the campus. Regents wanted a land-use plan showing the need for the land. The architectural firm that had designed most of the buildings for NTSC drew up a proposed campus map, following suggestions on building placement given them by Matthews. This did not satisfy the board.

Bring in Some Experts

The concern became greater in July 1964 after board discussion of sites for three new buildings. The regents voted 8–0 to ask the building committee to survey firms that made master plans.[9] Chaired by Regent David Kimbell of Wichita Falls, the committee worked with the administrative staff to develop a list of prospects. The following April, the board approved a planning contract with Caudill Rowlett Scott of Houston.[10]

Involving City Leadership

The CRS team and university representatives met during the next year with the Denton city staff, City Council, and Planning and Zoning Commission. On November 4, regents approved basic planning assumptions for university development. The board added a campus building design study to the CRS contract and asked them to design a speech and drama building.[11] This served as a pilot project for the design study, defining elements to be used in future buildings. The university thus abandoned its long commitment to neo-Georgian architecture.[12]

During December 1965, Vice President James L. Rogers appeared before the Planning and Zoning Commission and the City Council to show the general plans, property purchases, and street closings being considered. In February 1966 the president told the regents that:

> The master plan activities have been presented to the Denton City Council and the Denton Planning and Zoning Commission, and both groups responded enthusiastically. In a year-end statement for the *Denton Record-Chronicle*, the mayor described the start of NTSU master plan studies as the most significant happening of the year in the City of Denton.[13]

The Denton paper on February 14 published a report on property-purchase plans for a university planning district and the news that the Coordinating Board had authorized the purchase of the land. In the fall, Rogers conducted small-group meetings with faculty and students to show slides and discuss the plans. Responses and suggestions were relayed to the planners. Caudill Rowlett Scott delivered the final plan on May 8, 1967, and copies were distributed widely on campus, in the community, and elsewhere in the state.[14] Maps and other plan graphics appeared in the *Denton Record-Chronicle*, the *North Texas Daily*, and the alumni magazine.

The campus plan and an accompanying CRS study for buildings and landscape development led to construction that greatly altered the appearance and feel of the campus. Whereas regents of the old school had favored the traditional Georgian-inspired architecture, the new policies freed designers and landscape architects to adopt a contemporary adaptation of campus tradition.

Destination: 20,000 Students

Enrollment neared 14,000 as CRS began its studies, and it based the primary campus plan on serving 20,000. The Coordinating Board projected that NTSU would reach that figure in 1972-73. (North Texas did not surpass 20,000 until 1983, more than a decade after expectations.) CRS recommended that the university establish these planning boundaries:

- Hickory Street on the north
- Bernard Street on the east
- Eagle Drive on the south
- Avenue E on the west

Some exceptions were made, most notably the exclusion of the business block on Avenue A at Hickory and the block east of that.

Caudill Rowlett Scott based its work on four basic concepts: a sense of entrance, perimeter identity, unity, and orientation. Automobiles were to be moved to the perimeter to create a pedestrian-oriented campus. Many blocks of streets would need to be turned over to the university for redevelopment as landscaped walkways and open spaces. From this arose major problems in coordinating planning with the city and in displacing occupants of private land.

The City of Denton at that time had a problem-filled election to close one downtown block of Austin Street to develop a civic center. President Matthews sensed that this was not the time to bring university street-closing requests before city officials. That task was left to the administrations of Kamerick, Carter, and Nolen. However, in 1968 the first two buildings were completed under the campus plan and design study: the Language Building and the Speech Building. Both faced on Avenue A, an area that became a center of protest on street closings.

RELATIONS WITH THE FACULTY

With a number of older faculty members, Matthews enjoyed friendly relations that had been built up over his years as a colleague. His personality could not be described as extroverted but rather "reserved." His efforts on behalf of program development, faculty salaries, and institutional growth earned respect from the older, more traditional members of the faculty.

Faculty Development

Two major faculty goals drove this administration: increasing the percentage of faculty with earned doctoral degrees and raising faculty salaries to be more competitive with larger Texas universities and, especially, with universities elsewhere. The Texas Legislature did not bring Texas salaries up to the national median and beyond; this would have required major tax increases. So North Texas relied upon two major strategies: increase faculty salaries by transferring funds from other sources and attract former North Texas students to their alma mater after study for the doctoral degree.

Appropriations provided a line item, "teaching salaries only." This money could not be transferred to cover any other cost, but other funds could be moved into teaching salaries. Matthews turned to the fund group known as auxiliary enterprise. This included student service fees and income from dormitories, cafeterias, the Student Union Building, and bookstore. The strategy was to hold down expenses in the auxiliaries to acquire a surplus that could be moved into teaching salaries.

For example, in 1967, $200,000 in housing revenue was transferred to educational and general funds.[15] During most of Matthews's tenure, the amount for salaries was at least five percent greater than that appropriated. This varied from year to year, ranging from $75,000 to $350,000 more than appropriations.

Working on Faculty Salaries

The visiting committee for the Southern Association self-study in 1962 did not regard such progress as adequate, stating that "[w]hile above the requirements, the salary scale is appreciably below what is required to build a. . . growing university of this kind. Particularly urgent is the need to increase the salary level in the upper ranks to retain able research men and to attract yet others to this campus."[16]

Here are median salaries by rank for three academic years: the first year of the Matthews presidency, the year of the Southern Association Self-Study (1960–61), and the final year of the Matthews tenure:

Rank	1951–52	1960–61	1967–68
Professor	$5,600	$8,000	$15,560
Associate	$4,600	$7,000	$12,973
Assistant	$4,100	$6,300	$10,714
Instructor	$3,600	$5,200	$ 8,313

Another measure came in a report to the faculty and regents. It compared AAUP grades for salaries for 1962 and 1967. For average salaries, North Texas moved from E to C for professor, D to B for associate, C to A for assistant, and B to A for instructor. In the minimum-salary category, NTSU changed from E to B for professor, D to A for associate, D to A for assistant, and C to A for instructor.

The legislature appropriated the salary for the president as a line item. The Board of Regents did not supplement Matthews' salary for fourteen years of his term. At many other colleges, the appropriated president's salary served to establish a ceiling on all other salaries. But when more funds became available, Matthews budgeted more money to others than he himself could earn. In 1964 and 1965, the vice president, deans, and some department heads were paid more. In 1966 the appropriation for the president rose to $16,500—and President Matthews budgeted more than that amount to forty-six faculty members in fourteen departments.

In Fiscal Year 1966, the Board of Regents relented and authorized a supplement of $5,000 for the president's salary, the first year for such an action.[17] Not surprisingly, when it came time to hire a new president in 1968, the regents authorized a salary of $35,000, $21,000 being the appropriated amount and the supplement being $14,000.[18]

Doctorates for the Faculty

In 1962, of 326 faculty members, 150 or forty-six percent had earned doctoral degrees. Unfortunately, that was no better than the 1951 figure of 45.9 percent. (This was, however, second in Texas only to the University of Texas, which had the highest percentage at 57.8.) Fortunately, the 1973 Southern Association report showed that sixty-seven percent of the faculty held doctor's degrees.[19]

WHAT SHALL BE THE ROLE OF THE FACULTY?

The Southern Association, the administration, and the faculty were in accord on the need for more doctorates, better salaries, better fringe benefits, and lighter teaching loads. But the issue of faculty participation in academic governance exposed the growing disagreement between president and faculty leadership. The 1966 report and follow-up actions from the Southern Association increased the pressure to open the campus to more faculty responsibility.

Seeking Faculty Participation

More colleges in the nation were developing faculty senates to help determine academic policy. North Texas had a Faculty Council presided over by the vice president. The body considered degree programs, course offerings, academic standards, regulations for academic standards, admission requirements, academic load, and registration procedures. Of the twenty members of the council, thirteen were ex officio administrators and seven were faculty members elected from the various schools and divisions. The faculty generally did not regard the council as a democratic organization.

The major efforts to increase the faculty role were made by the local chapters of the American Association of University Professors and the Texas Association of College Teachers. In 1959 a Joint Committee on Faculty Participation in College Administration recommended a major restructuring for faculty participation in academic affairs. On February 8, 1960, the two chapters voted to recommend "the establishment of a true faculty senate, that this senate operate within a clearly defined charter, that all faculty committees operate under the mandate of such a senate, and that this senate be composed of faculty members elected from the various schools and divisions of the college."[20]

The AAUP and TACT chapters then formed a new joint committee to develop specific recommendations. Perhaps sensing that reference to "participation in administration" was unduly threatening, this group was called a Joint Committee on Faculty Organization. In its report in April, the committee made extra efforts to present a cooperative attitude:

> The committee would first like to commend the present Administration for its successful efforts and capable leadership in building the professional environment which the faculty at this college now enjoys. The President has been very helpful and cooperative in this committee's

> study of present and potential faculty contribution to the development of the college. The Administration and the two organizations are not working at cross-purposes. Our mutual purpose is to encourage means and procedures through which the Faculty can render additional assistance in the formulation of college policies. . . .
>
> The. . . recommendations in. . . this report are governed by three major principles. . . .
>
> (1) The changes recommended should be instituted in a gradual manner. . . .
>
> (2) Increased participation by the Faculty should be in policy formulation and not in administration. . . . The authority and responsibility for administering policy rests properly with the President of the college.
>
> (3) The major emphasis of faculty participation in policy determination should be in the area of academic affairs.[21]

The committee suggested three means of gradually enlarging the Faculty Council to make it more representative of the faculty and then outlined new areas of responsibility and authority for the enlarged Faculty Council. The report asked that these proposals be submitted to the president by the TACT and AAUP presidents. Committee members were H. W. Kamp, chairman, William F. Belcher, Horace R. Brock, Mary E. Evans, Hiram Friedsam, Joel T. Howell, Robert W. Ottman, Robert C. Sherman, and Paul Smith.

This did not draw a quick response from Matthews, so the chapter presidents arranged a meeting with the president on May 11, 1961. They were Jack Scroggs of the history faculty and Kendall Cochran of economics. That meeting is preserved in a memorandum written by Dr. Cochran describing the meeting:

> 1. President Matthews was at first rather negative, pointing out that the document. . . was too radical, that it called for too much, that could interpret too many powers to be delegated by the President of the College to a faculty.
>
> 2. We then pointed out to him that it was not intended to be a final plan or delegation of authority—quite the contrary, it offered several

> alternatives in some cases, and spelled out long-run goals to work toward, in others. And if he approved of the idea of greater faculty participation in principle, then the next correct step would be for him to appoint a committee of his own to work closely with him in drafting the kind of a plan that was feasible and practicable.
>
> 3. When this was clearly understood, he then neither agreed or disagreed with the general principle, but did state emphatically that because of the current attitude of the Board of Regents, this is not a propitious time to begin such changes. He also stated that the statements he made on this matter to the General Faculty last fall still hold to an even greater degree. . . .[22]

In the 1962 self-study, faculty members were asked if the university was structured for effective cooperative planning and implementation of policy. Of those responding, sixty-nine percent said they had no opportunity to participate in developing and implementing general university policy. Similarly, eighty-five percent reported they had not been afforded an opportunity to evaluate the institutional organization and its effectiveness.

The self-study report did not deal with faculty participation specifically, choosing instead to write diplomatically of differences between the faculty and the administration. "There is no formal organization or body representative of the faculty as a whole," the report stated. This was followed by a cautiously worded recognition that significant numbers of the faculty would like to have a role in decision-making. Referring to the AAUP-TACT effort, it said, "Although the suggestions have resulted in no concrete progress, there is hope that a beginning has been made in the examination of the problem of formulation of faculty opinion and its proper presentation for administrative consideration."[23]

This report was circulated to the faculty in December 1961. One might speculate that the president would maintain a conciliatory posture on this issue pending the arrival of the visiting committee in March 1962. Instead, Matthews chose to present his views at a very public forum: the January 1962 commencement.

A Public Prescription for the Faculty

The president customarily presented brief remarks at each commencement, there being no commencement speaker. The *Denton Record-Chronicle* on January 29, 1962, headlined its report, "Matthews Challenges University's Profs." The resultant uproar illustrated the width of the gulf between Matthews and much of the faculty. He told the audience that he was "departing from my usual practice of making a personal farewell statement to you and devoting the major portion of these remarks to university policy."

The remarks outlined the responsibility of students, faculty, and administrators. The stage for antagonism was set by a reference to industry's "rule-of-thumb practice to discard a machine when it fails to measure up to 66 percent of its capacity." This was followed by the statement that the university should see to it that the student "measures up to this 66 percent bench mark," outlining the necessity of class attendance, thorough work, academic honesty, and achieving full potential. This led to the section that angered the faculty:

> Staff members. . . too, should operate up to at least 66 percent of their capacity and high on the list of measures of their effectiveness are:
>
> unselfish devotion to duty as contrasted to faculty welfare projects;
>
> preparation of their own lessons as contrasted with long hours spent in criticizing administration and students for their shortcomings;
>
> staying on the subject at hand as contrasted with visiting with the class about the items in the news or the gossip on the campus;
>
> realizing that academic freedom is for the purpose of aiding the teacher in freeing the mind of the student and not a cloak for the professor to hide behind while he engages in surreptitious practices not open to other citizens;
>
> conducting himself in such a way that the students will do well to be in his classes even if they do little more than try to be like him instead of insisting upon having no other responsibility than to teach his classes and then be allowed to do as he pleases afterward;
>
> and finally, make a genuinely significant contribution to the community of scholars which is so often talked about but which so often means the existence of a faculty clique to decide what policies the administration and board should adopt.
>
> A teacher's time should be freed for teaching. And he should gladly teach just as the student should gladly learn.[24]

Southern Association Response

The visitors' evaluation of the governance issue was much more direct than that in the self-study committee report:

> By all odds the dominant concern among the faculty at present is that related to the absence of any widespread faculty participation in the establishment of academic policy for the University. There is extensive complaint against the Faculty Council on the grounds of its exclusiveness, its administrative coloration, and its general ineffectiveness. Such dissatisfaction extends to the University Committee system, which is entirely appointive and generally inactive.
>
> Chief morale issues among the faculty include this desire for some sort of Faculty Senate; a hope for greater decentralization of administrative control; and a strong wish for greater clarification of the University's purposes, particularly as these relate to its supposed broadening of scope and liberalization of objectives.[25]

The AAUP chapter on May 17, 1962, unanimously voted to "recommend and urge that the president take early and favorable action upon these recommendations." Another resolution urged that a merit system be installed to determine faculty promotions, salaries, and salary increases. Another asked for official recognition of the distinction between violation of tenure and termination of contract of instructors on probationary appointment and the establishment of due process under which probationary appointments could be terminated without embarrassment or injury either to the individual or the institution.[26] Dr. Martin Shockley of the English faculty urged stronger AAUP action. In a memorandum to the executive council, Shockley wrote:

> The major function of the Council, as the institution passes through this time of troubles, should be to provide through the chapter a faculty voice, to serve as channel and as spokesman for an inchoate, repressed and voiceless faculty. . . .
>
> As a chapter and as a faculty, we have, I conclude, exhausted methods of tactful persuasion, long suffering patience, and humble supplication. Circumstances beyond our control have pressed upon us the

> necessity of adopting a more positive tone in discharging our responsibility as spokesman for our voiceless faculty. It may be that we can forestall further deterioration; should deterioration continue at the present rate, some sort of institutional catastrophe is inevitable, and it may be imminent.[27]

Accreditation Follow-Ups

A Southern Association committee on December 1962 recommended a report of "satisfactory completion" of the accreditation process. However, a letter stressed that "The Committee on Standards and Reports was especially concerned that steps be taken to give the faculty a feeling of greater participation in policies affecting the instructional program" and that improvements were needed in the graduate program and student personnel programs.[28] The letter further noted that the university would be asked in September to "describe all actions which have been taken in regard to areas of need as pointed out in the self-study and the visiting committee reports."

Matthews gave that follow-up response in a five-page document in September 1963. Referring to the "case of the participation of the faculty," he said "there have been a number of steps." These steps were:

1. An invitation by the AAUP chapter to meet with the president, at which meeting the president spoke for 30 minutes followed by a 45-minute question-and-answer and opinion-sharing period. "The meeting was referred to over and over in the course of the year," the report noted.

2. A Council on Teacher Education was established to represent a cross-section of all departments and to free the Faculty Council from detailed matters and give it more time to deal with policy.

3. More frequent meetings were held with department heads to make them more aware of policy and matters connected with administration and teaching.

4. The North Texas chapter of TACT was the largest in the state and was used as a vehicle for a stepped-up contact with the faculty on its activities in many areas—"legislation, policy, etc."

5. The president met with the Faculty Tenure Committee for two hours after a study of the existing tenure document and "it was concluded that the tenure statement was in order and that it would be continued."

6. A faculty policy committee on the use of the Computer Center for instruction and research was established as a result of the visitation.[29]

The Commission on Colleges was dissatisfied and asked for details on faculty participation, improved campus communication, reorganization of the university, and improvements in the structure of the College of Arts and Sciences. This led to another Matthews report on September 30, 1964. Concerning "faculty participation in academic policy," this new response reported that

> this is a subject for special study during the university's 75th Year now in progress. Faculty, staff, administration and Board have been called upon to make the 75th Year activities in 1964–65 center around topics which would naturally follow from concerns for widespread faculty participation. In approaching this question, our plan has been to find out in which areas participation would be most valuable and then to formulate steps in light of the needs—rather than to create a formal structure and ask it to seek out a useful function.[30]

Gordon Sweet responded in January 1965 that "The Committee on Standards and Reports for Senior Colleges. . . found this second report to be satisfactory."[31] Nevertheless, in November, Dr. Sweet asked for a report on progress in delegating authority and providing faculty participation in academic matters."[32]

The Matthews response consisted of three pages and an organization chart. The main item was this:

> Membership in the Faculty Council has been restructured to bring about greater faculty representation. In its membership as previously reported, the Council had one representative from each division of the College of Arts and Sciences and one from each school. . . . The faculty now elects two members each from [each division and school]. It is felt that this increase in faculty representation is more appropriate for the size of the respective academic units, and that this step will encourage greater faculty initiative in the improvement of the academic functions.[33]

Dr. Sweet's December response said, "The Committee found this special report to be satisfactory and requests no further reports at this time on the program."[34] A twenty-five-page follow-up report from NTSU in 1967 did not deal with faculty participation issues.[35]

Concerns About Tenure

In the 1950s and 1960s, some American universities were placed on probation by the AAUP for violation of tenure policies. The North Texas chapter of AAUP sought the creation of a formal tenure policy with written procedures for awarding tenure and stated guidelines for due process in cases in which nonrenewal of contract or outright dismissal were being considered.

The climate of the 1950s was colored by national inquiries into "un-American activities." Texas students were required by law to sign a loyalty oath certifying that they were not members of any subversive organizations, and state employees had to sign a similar oath. The list of subversive groups was updated regularly by the Texas Department of Public Safety. In 1967 the legislature removed the requirement for the student loyalty oath, but the state continued to require state employees to sign the oath.[36]

Faculty members would probably have been more concerned had they known of some of the private expressions from some board members about the faculty. Some regents were vigilant to see that undesirable ideas and activities not be sanctioned on the campus. In private, they asked to see textbooks used in courses such as economics. In one case described by President Matthews, a newly appointed regent handed the president a sheet of paper with the names of several faculty members written on it. According to Dr. Matthews's oral account, the regent said that he wanted these individuals to be removed from the faculty. And, the president reported, he explained to the regent that this action would be a violation of established procedure and could not be done.

Nevertheless, the Southern Association accreditation team found that academic freedom and tenure were in strong shape on the campus—a strong president had shielded the classroom and the faculty from external intervention. The committee report said in 1962:

> There seems to be general agreement on this campus that academic freedom in the classroom is scrupulously respected. The tenure policy is strong and clear and honored in the observance. There is evidence, however, that timidity prevails in the behavior of faculty respecting activities outside the classroom, especially in areas of so-called "controversial" issues and matters affecting university policy and administration.[37]

Major Goals for the Faculty

Five other recommendations of the visiting committee represented goals that the president had also articulated and worked toward. A great deal of continuing joint faculty/administrative effort would be seen:

1. Increased pay levels, especially in higher ranks.
2. Increased Ph.D. proportion.
3. Greater recognition of research and scholarship in faculty advancement.
4. Widened geographic area of selection of faculty personnel.
5. Improvement in fringe benefits.

THE ADMINISTRATION EXPANDS

In transferring funds to teaching salaries, Matthews showed a commitment to holding down the size of the administration. For years, there had been only one vice president: Matthews from 1949 to 1951; Dr. A. M. Sampley from 1953 to 1959; and Dr. J. J. Spurlock from 1959 forward. Matthews named an assistant to the president and a comptroller in 1961. The assistant was Dr. Wayne Adams, who supervised physical plant operations as his major responsibility. The chief accountant, John L. Carter, Jr., was named comptroller to become the chief financial officer.

During the first decade of the Matthews presidency, there were no administrators named for these functions: dean of students, personnel, physical plant operations, public relations, research, sponsored grants, development, housing, planning, institutional research, attorney, instructional and media services, student financial aid, student employment, facilities planning and construction, police department, student activities, and legislative relations.

Visitor Reaction

The Southern Association visiting committee saw this lack of administrative delegation as a problem. It learned of possible plans to consolidate fiscal and business affairs under a new vice president. The visitors endorsed this move, saying it would reduce the number of people reporting to the president. They suggested a similar move in the area of student personnel.[38]

The committee also expressed serious concern for the internal organization of the College of Arts and Sciences, which lacked "the centralization of control and coordination of effort usually found in such units of a university." The report was especially critical of limitations on the arts and sciences dean, who did not "participate responsibly in the hiring of new faculty" nor in "recommending promotions and pay increases," and who appeared to exercise little if any "guidance in curricula changes or course additions." This was not an attack on the person who served as dean. Rather, it criticized a structural failure that "inevitably hampers the kind of long-range planning required for the steady growth, flexibility, and responsiveness of an undergraduate program."[39]

Board and President Respond

In the second follow-up report in September 1964, Matthews advised that reorganization of the administrative structure was nearly completed:

> This proposes creation of the offices of a vice president of academic affairs, vice president of fiscal operations, vice president of plant and nonacademic personnel, and a fourth division dealing with development, planning and institutional advancement. Another area marked for further refinement in organization involves the various student services.[40]

The regents in the Seventy-Fifth Year worked on plans for a new table of organization. In December 1963 Dr. Matthews added a second assistant to the president, naming the director of the News Service, James L. Rogers, to that post. The board also elected him secretary to the Board of Regents. The board then instructed the president to develop a new administrative organization for the regents' consideration. This was accomplished in the summer of 1965 and announced in the first faculty newsletter that fall.

President Matthews thus went through his last three years with three vice presidents: Spurlock as academic vice president, Carter as fiscal vice president, and Rogers as administrative vice president. Instead of occupying a separate division, student affairs were assigned to the administrative vice president, along with news and publications, planning and development, alumni relations, and intercollegiate athletics. A director of student personnel was named to handle student housing and employment.

The arts and sciences problem was addressed by naming new people as chairmen of divisions of humanities, science, and social sciences, posts that had been filled by department heads. These were to work with the faculty in their divisions to develop improved instructional techniques, research activity, and interdisciplinary coordination.[41]

The budget for general administration rose by $44,313 for Fiscal Year 1966, but as a percentage of total general revenue appropriations, it fell from 7.4 percent to 6.4 percent. In the last budget prepared by Matthews for 1969, that percentage was still held to 6.7 percent.

THE END OF AN ERA

It was J. C. Matthews's wish to go out of office on his own schedule, on his own terms. In the last years of his tenure, a minority group of regents began to oppose the more traditional positions of the president and of Chairman Wooten and his board allies (see, for example, the account of policy on federal aid above).

Forcing the President's Hand

Matthews picked August 31, 1968, as his retirement date, the end of seventeen years in office, two months before his sixty-seventh birthday. Partly in jest but also with some apparent seriousness, he explained to friends that he didn't want to be remembered as the president who had served the longest in office—both W. H. Bruce and W. J. McConnell had served for seventeen years. He shared his schedule with the Board of Regents some twenty-one months ahead of time and asked to be able to make a public announcement at the start of his final year in office. He thought that the regents agreed to this. At the board meeting of August 17, 1967, however, this schedule was unexpectedly disrupted by one regent.

In the final minutes, Regent Nelson moved "that the chairman at the proper time appoint a committee to make recommendations to the board concerning the selection of a successor to President J. C. Matthews whenever that might become necessary." Matthews appeared (to this writer, at least) to be angered by the unexpected development and said that he had not planned to make any statement but that under the circumstances he wished the following remarks to become a part of the record:

> Last November I notified the members of the Board that I wished to be relieved of the duties of chief administrative officer of the Uni-

> versity effective August 31, 1968. I would like it made clear that this action was mine alone and that the motion brought up today does not constitute an action to force my retirement, as it might appear to me who did not have the full background. In talking with the Board in November I observed that the question of any future assignment was subject to an arrangement agreeable to the Board and to me. This is still my position.[42]

The regents agreed that a special committee would be needed, and Chairman Wooten said that he would appoint one soon. Wooten later confirmed that "there was no pressure, whatever," for the president to retire, and that Matthews stated that he did not want to play a part in the choice of his successor.[43]

The retiring president resumed his title of professor of education and was named to the newly created J. C. Matthews Chair of Higher Education. He continued in this role until May 1972, at which time he became president emeritus, with an office in the Administration Building, where he continued to write and to advise doctoral students in higher education until August 1978.

The 1968 *Yucca* staff asked the president for a letter to be printed on the occasion of his retirement. He showed his realism about progress that had been made:

> Accumulate the volumes through the years and the image of the University emerges. . . reminding you of how long a problem has gone unsolved, and suggesting that all worthwhile progress is slow to come.
>
> In 1890 President J. C. Chilton wished "to see our state in the very forefront of intellectual as well as material progress." He must have thought of "forefront" as being not less than second or third, and here we are 78 years later, rated somewhere in the thirties among the 50 states in many measures of our educational progress. Worthwhile progress is indeed slow to come, but it will never come without effort.[44]

Worthwhile Progress: Slow and With Effort

Nevertheless, James Carl Matthews could see a great deal of progress in the previous seventeen years.

Faculty Development

Average salaries for full professors went from $5,000 to $15,000. A minority of the faculty held doctoral degrees at the start; a majority did by 1968.

Doctoral Programs

Doctoral enrollment began as he took office in September 1951. He conferred the first doctorate in August 1953. Dr. Matthews oversaw addition of Ph.D. degrees in biology, chemistry, physics, and business administration. He stimulated development by faculty and administration of other doctoral areas that would be added soon: art, English, history, mathematics, political science, psychology, and sociology.

Major Growth

He led the university through a major growth program.

Enrollment went from 4,300 students to nearly 15,000.

The library grew from 187,000 volumes to 700,000.

The annual budget increased from $4 million to $15 million.

Physical plant value went from $15 million to more than $50 million.

Campus Master Plan

The campus of 2000 was shaped by a master campus plan that was brought into being from 1964 to 1966 and implemented in large measure in the following six years. This effort produced a pedestrian campus with perimeter parking, a new concept of building design, and construction of seventeen buildings.

The Seventy-Fifth Year

J. C. Matthews knew first-hand forty-five years of the North Texas story when he called for a major Seventy-Fifth-Year observance in 1964–65 that would set many new directions for North Texas. As that year began, he described his faith in the people who built the university: "Institutions depend upon people; dedicated, hard-working people; just, fair, thinking people; moral, dependable, yes, God-fearing people; people with humility and strength. These are the qualities that have brought North Texas State University to this good hour."[45]

Bringing Integration

In his fourth year, President Matthews persuaded the Board of Regents that a Black man should be admitted to the doctoral program in education. In his fifth year, he was faced with preparing the university to open the campus without legal restrictions to all people.

Cooperation and Coordination

This president led the state and region in cooperation and coordination in higher education. The governor named him chairman of the committee that planned creation of the Texas Commission on Higher Education. He also:

• chaired the presidents' advisory committee that worked with the new commission.

• was elected and re-elected for six years to be chairman of the Council of Presidents of State-Supported Colleges and Universities.

• was one of the founders of the Inter-University Council of the Dallas-Fort Worth Metropolitan Area.

• headed the IUC committee that developed a major cooperative library program for the area.

In the summer of 1968, this tribute was sent to the NTSU president from the Inter-University Library Committee:

> The Committee is especially grateful for your leadership during the first year-and-a-half of its activities. . . . It was during this period that the foundation was laid for nearly all of the ventures that have proved of inestimable value to the several libraries of the Council Colleges and Universities. In all of our discussions you gave us impartial guidance. . . .
>
> For all of its success during the past four-and-a-half years, so largely resultant from your leadership and steadfast interest, the Committee salutes you, Sir, and wishes you Godspeed.[46]

As the NTSU president prepared to leave office, so, too, did Dr. Jack K. Williams, the Texas Commissioner of Higher Education, who was leaving to become president of the University of Tennessee. The writer of this book was sent to Austin to talk with Commissioner Williams on August 1, 1968, about the state master plan for higher education. Dr. Williams made these comments:

> Dr. Matthews knows more about the state system and needs for cooperation than any man in the state. He was talking cooperation long before anyone thought of creating the old Commission on Higher

Education or the present Coordinating Board. He stands above all college presidents in ethical conduct and the high principles which higher education should always embrace.[47]

The Era Ends

Forty-eight years after the young freshman Carl Matthews came to Denton to be met at the depot by President W. H. Bruce, J. C. Matthews left the office of the president. He returned to a faculty office in the Education-Home Economics Building, a structure that was later to be named Matthews Hall. Presiding at his final commencement on August 23, 1968, he told the graduates:

> So as you leave us tonight, I hope you go with some sense of greatness, with some lasting friendships, with a feeling that there is something noble in the human race, and with the knack of looking at the positive side of things. I hope you know that; worthwhile things are hard to achieve and are slow in coming and that hard work comes before celebrations of success.
>
> But I also hope that you have learned to dream.[48]

For one group of students, the editors of the student yearbook, the impressions of the dominance by this one man of the major course of events at North Texas led them to conclude their retirement tribute to the president with this bit of hyperbole:

"J. C. Matthews *is* North Texas State University."[49]

chapter 26

Growing Toward Seventy-Five

And finally there is a point which may not have occurred to you. Your diploma will become more and more valuable with the years. For just as you have helped to raise the standards of the school, so will those who come after you continue to raise these standards and you will be the recipients. They will be serving you. We are North Texans all—normal school graduates, teachers college graduates, college graduates, and university graduates.

You have had the opportunity to see history in the making.

J. C. Matthews
Commencement Remarks
June 2, 1961

When J. C. Matthews became president in 1951, North Texas State College was sixty-one years old. He was aware that in fourteen years his Alma Mater would have completed seventy-five years, and he began thinking of that year as a planning milestone for the development of the college.

WHERE DO WE WANT TO GO?

Had a list of planning goals been published in 1951, it might have looked like this:

1. Adapt to the growing urbanization pushing toward the campus from the south and expand the enrollment base.

2. Build a faculty composed mostly of holders of doctoral or other recognized terminal degrees. Recruit young faculty from a wide geographic area.

3. Develop doctoral degree programs for most academic areas in which master's degrees were already offered. Add master's degrees to meet regional needs.

4. Build major research in all doctoral program areas and in as many others as possible.

5. Become recognized as one of the four major higher education institutions in the state and earn corresponding legislative financial support.

6. Modernize and expand the physical plant for larger enrollments and programs of greater complexity.

7. Develop a good college library into a major graduate and research library.

WHERE ARE WE COMING FROM?

The normal college and the teachers college for sixty years had served rural and small-town Texas. This was more a reflection of the state's population distribution than of the appeal of teacher-education colleges. In 1890, only 15.6 percent of Texans lived in towns of at least 2,500 population.[1] Just after the first bachelor's degrees were granted in 1919, that figure had risen to 32.4 percent. As the teachers college faculty broadened the bachelor's degree function beyond preparation of teachers, the urban percentage rose to 45.4 percent. When North Texas State College arrived with a separate Board of Regents in 1949, urban residents were sixty percent of the population. And when it became North Texas State University in 1961, three-fourths of all Texans lived in urban centers.

THE METROPOLITAN INFLUENCE

The sprawl of the Dallas-Fort Worth region made the once-sleepy frontier town of Denton part of what was at first called a Standard Metropolitan Statistical Area. Later, in 1983, a new classification placed Denton in the nine-county Consolidated Metropolitan Statistical Area with a population of 3,143,000, tenth largest in the nation. At this time, eighty percent of the state's people lived in MSAs.[2] The region became known as "the Metroplex," a designation that was made official by the Comptroller of Public Accounts.[3]

These population shifts can be traced in the county of origin of North Texas students. Dallas County, for example, accounted for three percent of the student body in 1930, for 7.4 percent in 1940, and for 7.9 percent in 1950. Not until 1956 did Dallas County become the college's leading county of origin with 707 students, 11.4 percent of the total. Denton County was second with 628 and Tarrant County was third at 361.[4] Tarrant County, represented largely by Fort Worth, moved into second place by eight students in 1963, but has come in third behind Dallas and Denton in most subsequent years.

WHO SERVES DALLAS AND FORT WORTH?

The rural, agricultural Texas established its public colleges in the protective atmosphere of smaller towns. Before the 1960s, the largest cities had no state-supported four-year colleges: Houston, Dallas, San Antonio, and Fort Worth. The two largest cities with state-supported institutions were Austin, with the University of Texas, and El Paso, with the College of Mines of the University of Texas (later Texas Western College). In 1927, Houston created a junior college that became a city four-year institution in 1934. The two-year San Antonio College was founded in 1945. Neither Dallas nor Fort Worth had a junior college before 1965, although Arlington State College operated as a freshman-sophomore unit of the Texas A&M System until 1959.

In the first half of the twentieth century, these cities had not grown to the size of most major U.S. cities; all of public education was segregated; the rate of high-school graduation was low; and the rate of college attendance was lower still. In Texas the college-going rates of eighteen-to-twenty-four-year-old residents was nine percent in 1940 and 14.3 percent in 1950.[5] Dallas had Southern Methodist University after 1910. Texas Christian University moved to Fort Worth in 1911. Residents of these two cities exhibited pride in their hometown private universities. Widespread concern about the lack of state-financed colleges or junior colleges in Dallas and Fort Worth had not yet developed.

This was all to change. The primary forces were these:

- Rapid metropolitan population growth
- Awareness of the lack of significant graduate and research programs
- Recognition of the value of a major doctoral university to economic development and growth
- Recognition by the University of Texas system that its traditional legislative support would be threatened by the rise of an urban-dominated legislature.

To this list might well be added a developing national fascination with the voluntary higher education consortium to improve use of resources and to resist creation of larger state super-systems of universities. Leaders of both public and private colleges and universities had been listening when the Texas Legislature began showing an interest in mergers or closing of campuses to reduce costs.

GROWTH YEARS

The newly named North Texas State College opened the 1949 fall semester with a record enrollment of 5,282 and followed with a record summer enrollment of 4,088 in 1950. The veterans' boom ended, however, and registration dropped to 5,093 in the fall of 1950 and a low of 4,318 in the fall of 1951 as Matthews became president. The summer session low was the 2,481 figure recorded in 1953. Fall semester enrollments climbed steadily thereafter up to the end of the Matthews tenure (1967–68):

1952 4,449	1957 6,213	1962 9,921
1953 4,592	1958 6,779	1963 10,802
1954 4,952	1959 7,035	1964 11,878
1955 5,515	1960 7,494	1965 13,343
1956 6,185	1961 8,844	1966 13,973
		1967 14,589

Summer registration stayed somewhere in the 3,000s until 1960, then shot up to 4,109 in 1961, 4,536 in 1962, 5,212 in 1963, 5,791 in 1964, and to 6,586 in 1965.

Most of the degrees granted by North Texas in its first seventy-five years came after 1949. In the few normal college years that degrees were offered and in all the teachers college years, a thirty-year span from 1919 to 1949, degree recipients numbered 12,891. In the next sixteen years an additional 25,207 graduates were recorded, bringing the total to 38,098 in June 1965. The teachers college awarded 1,353 master's degrees, and another 5,474 master's recipients were added to the list from 1949 to June 1965. All of the doctoral degrees of the first seventy-five years—140 of them—were conferred by the state college or the state university. After 1960, graduate enrollment became an increasingly larger percentage of the total. In 1961, when graduate students surpassed 800, President Matthews secured membership in the Council of Graduate Schools in the United States.

In 1962, graduate head-count enrollment first surpassed 1,000 and again constituted more than ten percent of the total. Here are the fall-semester figures:

Fall	Enrollment	Grad. Enrollment	Percent Grad.
1951	4,318	431	10
1952	4,449	472	10.6
1953	4,592	373	8.1
1954	4,953	400	8.1
1955	5,515	463	8.4
1956	6,185	530	8.6
1957	6,213	505	8.1
1958	6,779	578	8.5
1959	7,036	580	8.2
1960	7,480	738	9.9
1961	8,835	829	9.4
1962	9,921	1,002	10.1
1963	10,802	1,294	12.0
1964	11,878	1,476	12.4
1965	13,343	1,789	13.4
1966	13,973	2,097	15.0
1967	14,589	2,432	16.7

Another index of growth was the annual budget. The figures, taken from minutes of the Board of Regents, are as follows:

1949–50	$ 3,736,594	1958–59	5,478,811
1950–51	4,155,193	1959–60	6,735,124
1951–52	4,303,498	1960–61	6,935,774
1952–53	4,272,301	1961–62	8,179,952
1953–54	4,175,361	1962–63	8,767,965
1954–55	4,218,801	1963–64	10,350,210
1955–56	4,579,493	1964–65	11,300,036
1956–57	4,511,340	1965–66	13,735,316
1957–58	5,352,049	1966–67	15,029,841
		1967–68	17,930,270

These include educational and general expense and auxiliary enterprises, but do not include building construction. The increase is obviously a function of enrollment, since appropriations, tuition income, and auxiliary enterprise revenue rise with the number of students; but the rising figures also indicate a qualitative advance for improvement of faculty salaries, the library, etc.

When President McConnell retired, physical plant evaluation had reached more than $12 million. Much of this was construction completed in his final years in office with the constitutional building fund. That began a building program that would bring physical plant investment in August 1965 to $32,514,991. The rest of the first constitutional building decade yielded three more buildings in 1956. The second decade brought a flurry of classroom building construction from 1959 to 1961 and the bond fund balance would produce the most expensive classroom building in the institution's history—a Biology Building—in 1966–67. Federal loans produced a men's dormitory in 1957, but the North Texas financial structure was so sound that after 1960, dormitories and a new Union Building were handled by bond issues without federal support. These buildings were added during the state college and state university period through 1965:

INSTRUCTIONAL BUILDINGS		
Laboratory School Education	1950	$ 530,670
Men's Gymnasium	1950	340,755
Masters Hall (Biology, Chemistry)	1951	1,229,683
Women's Gymnasium	1951	323,076
Administration Building	1956	846,260
Laboratory School Gym	1956	175,936
Physics-Mathematics	1959	908,461
Industrial Arts	1959	703,982
Business Administration	1960	1,369,607
Education-Home Economics	1961	1,210,308
Music	1961	1,137,392

OTHER BUILDINGS		
Quadrangle I (Dormitory)	1951	$ 221,609
Quadrangle II	1951	221,609
Quadrangle Cafeteria	1951	129,852
Stadium	1952	764,981
Quadrangle III	1952	275,822
Quadrangle IV	1952	275,822
Kendall Hall	1952	783,682
President's Home	1956	67,944
West Dormitory	1957 and 1960	1,308,561
Hospital	1958	427,642
Crumley Hall	1961	1,066,290
McConnell Hall	1961	1,067,207
Graduate Apartments	1961	307,163
Maple Street Hall	1964 and 1965	2,252,606
Student Union Building	1964 and 1965	1,079,292

STATEWIDE COORDINATION

The Texas Legislative Council asked its staff to study statewide college coordination for a report to the legislature in 1951. *Public Higher Education in Texas* appeared in November 1950. It listed advantages and disadvantages of types of statewide organization. These included voluntary coordination, a division of higher education within the Texas Education Agency, organization of all colleges under one of the three existing systems (University of Texas, Texas A&M, Teachers College System), a single integrated system with a single board, or a single central agency with separate boards.

Move NTSC to Arlington?

The study described the Dallas and Fort Worth areas as the only ones in Texas "which do not now have a state-supported institution of higher learning." One solution suggested a "cooperative arrangement of schools, faculties, facilities, and credit." A more drastic suggestion provided that North Texas State College be moved to Arlington to combine with Arlington State College to form a new college. This was to be a commuting college without dormitories, with a night education program and a technical institute. The Denton campus might be used for some other state purpose such as a state hospital.[6]

This proposal was surprising in light of other sections of the staff report. It showed North Texas to be the fourth largest among nineteen public colleges and one of only five accredited by the Association of American Universities. In the number of equated full-time graduate students, the University of Texas was the leader, followed by North Texas.

The report showed that many teachers in state colleges were teaching in fields in which they had no degree. The percentages of such teachers ranged from a low of 7.5 percent at North Texas to highs of 47.8 percent at the University of Houston and 52.1 per cent at Arlington State College. The closest figures to those of North Texas were 15.5 at East Texas State and 19.7 at the University of Texas.

NTSC Next to UT in Faculty Degrees

Of the state total, 34.4 percent held doctoral degrees. The University of Texas had the highest proportion, 57.8 percent, with North Texas next at 45.9 percent. There were 292 bachelor's-degree college teachers in the state, but only three taught at North Texas. None of the forty-one nondegree teachers were at North Texas.

PROGRAM EXPANSION

The North Texas State College Board of Regents on August 10, 1950, voted unanimously for the college to start offering the doctoral degree in education and music starting in the first summer term of 1951. On January 24, 1951, the regents approved degree requirements for the doctor of education and for the doctor of philosophy in music. The first date became especially significant after the legislature met in 1951.

Rather than follow legislative council proposals, the legislature instead "froze" course expansion at all colleges. Each college was required to certify that it had not established a department after October 1, 1950. North Texas regents voted that "the administration has certified to the Board that the courses of study for the doctorate were in operation in September, 1950." Because the "administration and the Board have acted in good faith in taking each step in initiating the doctorate program," the chairman and secretary of the Board of Regents would certify that North Texas was in compliance with the legislative resolution.[7] This legislative freeze on course expansion continued while means of state coordination were sought.

THE SIXTH NAME

In February 1961 an NT graduate, Representative Joe Ratcliff of Dallas, introduced a bill to change the name of NTSC to "The University of North Texas." Eight other ex-students cosigned the bill,[8] which won approval of the house, 126–17, on April 10. The major dissent was from Representative Maud Isaacks of El Paso, who said, "It has always been a teachers college and is one today."[9] The bill was unanimously reported out of the Senate Education Committee on April 18, with immediate passage expected. On the floor of the senate, however, opponents organized to make some bitter accusations. Senator Charles Herring of Austin, arguing that the bill would damage the University of Texas, called it "a fraud on the public" and said it was ridiculous to think there could be two universities "in a little town the size of Denton." Senator Herring said, "That school is nothing but a teachers college and that's what it's going to be for years to come."[10] Senator Hubert Hudson of Brownsville charged that "Half of the courses taught at North Texas can't be transferred to half the leading colleges in the nation. All you have there is courses in education, methodology, and physical education."[11]

On April 26 Senator Herring prepared to filibuster against the name change. But when Herring suggested the name be changed to North Texas State University, the bill's Senate sponsor, Senator Tom Creighton of Mineral Wells, accepted the revision, and the bill passed to third reading.[12] The house accepted the NTSU designation on May 1, and Governor Price Daniel signed the bill on May 8, 1961, in the presence of President Matthews, Senator Creighton, Representative Ratcliff, Representative Alonzo W. Jamison, Jr., of Denton, and Jack Wheeler, president of the United Students of North Texas. May 10 was set aside as a day of celebration—the first University Day that launched an annual event—and in the words of the *Denton Record-Chronicle*:

> The victory bell on the old power plant rang and rang. And the carillon chimed and chimed.
>
> There was good reason. For, as one person put it, Wednesday was the greatest moment in the long history of NTSC. . . .
>
> Much of the cheering came at a 1 P.M. assembly when 2,400 persons filled the Main Auditorium to capacity. It probably was the first assembly in more than a decade for the Main Auditorium to be filled.
>
> Although the assembly was intended to be an hour of serious discussion on the responsibilities of a university, it turned out to he more than that. The speakers were interrupted by applause so many times that the event more closely resembled a political rally.
>
> But no one seemed to mind, for it was a day of celebration too.[13]

President Matthews recognized the disappointment of May graduates, who were unable to receive diplomas bearing the university name. He said in his commencement remarks, "some day the fact that you were here on University Day will loom much larger in your mind than the fact that the word university is not on your diploma. You will feel a bit sorry for those who are only recipients of the goal and not participants in the quest."[14]

THE 1962 SELF-STUDY

University status arrived just as the faculty began the institutional self-study for the Commission on Colleges and Universities of the Southern Association of Colleges and Secondary Schools (see Chapter 25). The study restated institutional purpose, saying that "the university proposes to maintain undergraduate and graduate programs in depth and completeness rather than to offer them in boundless assortment." The faculty steering committee judged the university to be fulfilling its mission in many respects, with a sound fiscal program and expenditures per student having risen twenty-five percent in ten years. Significant gains were noted in library holdings, fewer than two percent of the faculty held only bachelor's degrees, and nearly half held doctoral degrees.

The committee urged continuation of legislative appropriation based on enrollment, along with formulas which recognize changes in the costs of higher education. The big handicap had been that enrollment gains ran ahead of the figures on which appropriations are based. Because of the ten-year base period employed, the ad valorem tax for building purposes was even less responsive to needs caused by enrollment changes.

The steering committee did not address wishes by many faculty members for a faculty senate with a policy-making role, instead suggesting greater effort by administrators to keep their staff members informed. The study suggested that salary increases were most needed in the upper echelons of the faculty. The self-study report urged major changes in emphasis on research, writing:

> The faculty apparently does not realize the importance of the research function of the university. Specific, tangible research incentives originating at the departmental level are the exception rather than the rule. The relationship among the three basic university functions does not govern much staff thinking in regard to research, and the role of research in the functions of instruction and public service is far from being as significant as it should be. The role of research as a university function has not been adequately emphasized.[15]

ORGANIZING FOR COOPERATION

The North Texas region needed a major effort to increase the supply of doctoral graduates from local universities. In February 1964, the five doctoral-level public and private institutions organized the Inter-University Council of the Dallas-Fort Worth Area. Charter members were SMU, TCU, NTSU, TWU, and the University of Texas Southwestern Medical School. An IUC Library Committee in 1964 arranged for libraries of the five schools to be connected with a private-line Teletype system to help locate materials for graduate study and for research.[16] In 1965, more than 6,300 Teletype messages were handled. At midyear, the Teletype service was offered to twenty-seven industrial firms that maintained their own libraries, and eleven accepted and were connected to the system. Faculty and doctoral students were given courtesy cards permitting them to use all IUC libraries.

Library Cooperation Successful

The year's experience indicated the poverty of library resources. Of items requested for doctoral and research programs, only forty-eight percent were available in any IUC library, and only sixty-eight percent were to be found in any Texas library.[17] Further, 14,000 scientific and technical serials were received in Texas libraries, but only half of them in the combined academic, public, and independent libraries of the Dallas-Fort Worth area. This led to IUC cooperative acquisitions of journals and books—one that assigned purchases to one university library and made them available to all.

Within two years the council added as associate members the four-year colleges (University of Dallas, Bishop College, Arlington State College, Texas Wesleyan College) and the Baylor College of Dentistry. Still, the IUC emphasized doctoral programs—between fall 1964 and fall 1965, the number of doctoral students in the five schools rose from 540 to 740.

GRCSW Becomes Controversial

The Graduate Research Center of the Southwest was created in 1961. Corporate donors at first sponsored it to promote scientific research and postdoctoral studies. However, one major factor aroused suspicions on existing campuses: the charter authorized the center to award academic degrees. The GRCSW was located on a 1,245-acre campus in Richardson, just north of Dallas. Physicist-engineer Lloyd Berkner was the president for the center's first five years, having come from the presidency of Associated Universities, nine eastern schools that cooperated in running the Brookhaven, New York, National Laboratory for the Atomic Energy Commission. In 1966, Berkner described the initial emphasis on research and postdoctoral study as necessary for building a strong faculty. He left at that time, and his successor, Gifford Johnson, announced that the center would move to graduate education.[18] Thus was born controversy and distrust that would divide, rather than unify, higher education in the region, what many came to regard as "the Dallas problem."

GRCSW became the focal point of yet another consortium. The Inter-University Council had barely organized when some of its members joined in August 1965 the chartering of The Association for Graduate Education and Research of North Texas (TAGER). Much of its planning was the work of GRCSW Vice President Bryghte D. Godbold. Its seven private institutions agreed to combine faculty and other resources to help expand graduate programs. Members were GRCSW, SMU, and TCU as participating institutions, and four predominantly undergraduate institutions as associate members. These were Austin College at Sherman, Bishop College, the University of Dallas, and Texas Wesleyan College of Fort Worth.[19] In December 1965 the Ford Foundation awarded TAGER a $112,000 planning grant. North Texas was invited several times to join the consortium but declined to do so.

TAGER Builds Support

Lay leaders, especially in the business sector, supported the TAGER plan. It aimed to expand doctoral education in eight areas: physics, chemistry, biology, materials, applied mathematics, mechanical engineering, electrical engineering, and geography. TAGER hoped to combine the best teachers from the seven institutions to form a "respectable" faculty for the eight disciplines and to create some "truly distinguished faculties" by recruiting leading scientists in industry as adjunct faculty.[20] Gifts provided microwave connections for one-way television and two-way audio to each campus and to cooperating industrial plants.

SEEKING GOALS FOR DALLAS

In Dallas, leadership came from business leaders in the newer high-technology industries, notably Texas Instruments. Many had been active in creating and financing the Graduate Research Center. One, Erik Jonsson, was elected mayor, and became a major force in efforts to reshape Dallas. His 1964 proposal led to creation of the Goals for Dallas program, sponsored by the Graduate Research Center of the Southwest and the American Assembly. After six months of study, eighty people met in June 1966 in Salado to ratify a voluminous mimeographed document of community goals and essays to guide planning.[21]

Goals for Higher Education

One of twelve goal areas dealt with higher education, declaring, "Dallas and the North Texas area. . . can and must become one of the greatest educational centers of the nation. . . . All should be of high quality with our graduate programs reaching to become steeples of excellence."[22]

Eight supporting statements followed, paraphrased here in brief:

1. Expand private support, insist on significant increases in state support, and supplement both with federal funds.

2. Pool teaching resources for costly science and technology graduate programs.

3. Seek a state effort complementary to that of TAGER.

4. Seek increased cooperation between state and private institutions.

5. Enlarge and strengthen postgraduate basic research and education.

6. Develop an outstanding junior college system, including vocational-technical programs.

7. Provide excellent libraries for all colleges.

8. Coordinate all area libraries, with facilities available to all.

Build a Great University?

The first Goals for Dallas report in 1966 tackled the higher education question that would occupy the region and the state for the next decade. It recognized a major difference of opinion on a vexing question: is there already a basic foundation in present institutions for a greater education effort or is an entirely new "great university" needed? Many business leaders argued for a new super university, but most educators saw no reason for this, pointing out that "such efforts would have to start from scratch, adding one more immature school to those already here."[23] The essayist suggested that "Another possibility is to combine ASC, NTSU, and TWU."

At NTSU, President Matthews said in an interview, "Another state university in the area would cause cleavages. We are all really one big community now. Dallas ought to quit thinking about the Dallas city boundaries or the Dallas County line."

Build It in Dallas!

An essay on graduate education goals suggested even more strongly the major support for a new state-supported campus in Dallas.

> Many Dallas industry leaders feel passionately that the State of Texas ought to build in or near Dallas a first-rate state university with strong

> doctoral and master programs. . . . Only a state-supported school can command the financial support to build superior doctoral programs in engineering and science. . . .
>
> The Chamber's education committee has made overtures both to Texas A&M and the University of Texas in the past few years, trying to demonstrate the need for a strong state-supported graduate school here.[24]

MATTHEWS AND THE METROPOLITAN MISSION

No Texas higher education leader had demonstrated a stronger commitment to interinstitutional cooperation than Matthews. The North Texas president served as chairman of the Council of Presidents of State-Supported Colleges and Universities in Texas from 1952 to 1960. In 1952 he was also appointed to the Texas Board of Examiners for Teacher Education. Matthews was elected in December 1954 as chairman for public institutions of higher learning in the Southern Association. He served in 1955 on the steering committee to plan the Texas Conference on Education. In 1954 he became one of nine regents of Texas Education's Hall of Remembrance. The Association of Texas Colleges named Matthews as its vice president in 1957–58 and as its president for 1959–60.

Matthews Chairs the Coordination Effort

But the major role of President Matthews came during the legislative "freeze" on course expansion. Governor Allan Shivers appointed a committee of sixteen, with Matthews as chairman, to find a means of state coordination of higher education. This was a temporary Commission on Higher Education, which led to the formal creation in 1955 by the 54th Legislature of the Texas Commission on Higher Education. The commission was told to develop appropriation formulas, uniform reporting systems, and a continuing study of all phases of public senior higher education. No new department, degree program, or certificate program could be added at any state-supported college or university without approval by the commission.[25]

North Texas program development was largely unaffected in the early years of the commission. In 1959 regents agreed to a commission recommendation to discontinue graduate work in home economics.[26] The first program addition was the master's degree in speech and drama in 1962, followed the next year by commission approval to convert a five-year bachelor's degree in library service to a master's degree. President Matthews and the board insisted that new programs require readiness in faculty, library resources, and known demand in the field. He articulated this during the Seventy-Fifth year: "Perhaps one of the most consistent traits of North Texas State University through its 75 years of history has been its humility—not getting the claims in advance of the facts; letting the facts constitute the claims."[27]

Persuading the Metroplex

North Texas faced two major problems in perception in the metropolitan area: persistence of the "teachers college" image, and what Matthews called "the county-line syndrome," referring to the difficulty in getting the Denton campus recognized as part of the concerns of the area. Matthews and the regents knew they had to forestall the creation of another university in "our territory." One step in the strategy was to place the word "university" in the name. But far more was needed.

A Question of Role and Scope

North Texas had to solidify its position in the region as a doctoral institution. In November 1962 requests for Ph.D. programs in biology, chemistry, physics, and business administration were transmitted to the Commission on Higher Education. A year later, the commission chairman appointed a three-member ad hoc Study Committee for Graduate Programs in the Dallas-Fort Worth area. In meetings with business and educational leaders of the area, the committee found that two factors were significant in its deliberations:

1. The formation of the Inter-University Council of the Dallas and Fort Worth Metropolitan Areas to cooperate for graduate programs of eminence to avoid needless overlap and duplication.

2. Presentation of *Industry Report to the Texas Commission on Higher Education* by representatives of business in Dallas and Tarrant Counties. This report asserted that the North Texas region had been neglected by the state in graduate education, "it is the region whose industrial characteristics give it the Southwest's greatest demand for highly trained minds."

NTSU: "One of the Five"

Yet another study came from the Governor's Committee on Education Beyond the High School. North Texas provided a statement of role and scope to that group in August 1963: "Texas has the size, the resources, and the need to justify the development of five universities as focal points in its program of higher education. It seems logical for the role and scope of North Texas State University to be developed with the thought that it would be one of these five."

In August 1964 the Governor's Committee agreed, listing North Texas State as one of the five state-supported universities in Texas.[28] The others were the University of Texas, Texas A&M University, the University of Houston, and Texas Tech.

Matthews and staff were delighted. A Seventy-Fifth Year bulletin proclaimed, "The growing needs of the vast Dallas and Fort Worth metropolitan area have brought North Texas State University to the brink of its greatest period of service."

More NTSU Doctoral Programs

In 1964 a Commission on Higher Education report endorsed the Inter-University Council and urged adequate support for existing graduate programs. For North Texas State University specifically, the commission approved doctor of philosophy programs in biology, chemistry, and physics (which started in September 1964) and a doctor of philosophy in business administration starting in September 1965.

The report classified North Texas as "a multipurpose doctoral level university." It was designated as the institution whose role in the region would be to develop doctoral programs in the scientific fields other than engineering and medicine, and in the fine arts, humanities, social sciences, and mathematics. That designation, as President Matthews stressed at every opportunity, taken with existing doctoral programs in education and music, embraced all the areas in which graduate work was then offered at the institution. The university goals for role and scope had earned recognition from the appropriate state agencies.[29]

A Setback From the Coordinating Board

In 1965 the new Coordinating Board, Texas College and University System (see below) asserted that only four state-supported schools in the future would award Ph.D. degrees. North Texas was being dropped as "one of five" in Dr. Matthews's listing. The only exception was to be that NTSU and TWU would be permitted to continue "certain" doctoral programs already in operation.

Arlington State College might be included in joint Ph.D. programs with the two Denton schools. The Dallas dilemma was restated by a *Goals* essayist this way:

> Many Dallas Chamber of Commerce leaders fervently hope the Board will see fit to provide more doctoral training [in] the populous Dallas-Fort Worth area. Some believe this should be a brand new state school. Others would like to see NTSU, TWU and ASC combined under one chancellor. Such an arrangement, these men believe, should give the chancellor the authority and the responsibility to mold the schools into one strong system, to discard, to innovate, to build graduate programs of excellence to meet imperative needs of this part of the state.[30]

The Community College Factor

Metropolitan areas in Texas were late in starting junior colleges. The Tarrant County Junior College District opened two campuses in Fort Worth in 1965, and the Dallas County Community College District started classes in a converted downtown department store in 1966.

As expected, North Texas freshman and sophomore enrollment soon dropped. In fall 1965, enrollment included 7,185 lower-division students, 53.9 percent of the total, and in 1966 the percentage was 52.7. The percentages of North Texas freshman-sophomore students declined steadily: 45.4 in 1967, 42.6 in 1968, and a low of 34.3 percent in 1975. This, of course, impacted the classes offered, the demand for dormitory rooms, and the number of faculty members needed in departments that offered courses required of all students.

Wooing the Metroplex

North Texas sought to bolster its position both as the largest and as the dominant force in higher education in the metropolitan area. This became the dominant theme of the university's Seventy-Fifth Year in 1964–65. Board Chairman Ben H. Wooten noted that enrollment of 11,878 students made North Texas the fourth largest university in the state and that for three years NTSU had been Texas' second largest source of university graduates. He wrote that North Texas:

> is the largest of the higher institutions serving the state's greatest concentration of people—1,878,000 in the Dallas and Fort Worth metropolitan areas. Recent approval of new doctoral programs and the assignment of other doctoral fields to be developed place North Texas State in a position to be of major service in meeting the needs of the region for advanced graduate study.[31]

As the Seventy-Fifth observance neared its end in 1965, President Matthews made a report on the May 8 anniversary of the signing of the university bill. He asked for a study of the possibility that North Texas should enter the field of engineering in response to the demands of the metropolitan region. The president declared:

> It is clear that the region relies heavily on North Texas State University: it is the largest school, it has the largest graduate enrollment, it grants the most degrees each year, it has 30 years of experience as a graduate center. It offers doctoral-level operations that have been building for 15 years. All the factual evidence indicates that by all odds this is the public institution most logical for adoption by the region in its search for the greatly needed expansion of public higher education programs.[32]

COORDINATING TEXAS HIGHER EDUCATION

We have seen repeated state efforts to create a state system of higher education and a mechanism for coordinating it. One more was introduced in 1965. Governor John Connally sought the passage of two major bills to alter the structure and governance of Texas higher education. His proposal to place each four-year college under one of three governing boards did not pass. Legislators did, however, pass House Bill 1, creating the Coordinating Board, Texas College and University System with greater power than the Commission on Higher Education. The state's colleges came under authority of the Coordinating Board in September 1965. In just fifteen years, then, North Texas had been influenced by all of these measures:

1950	Texas Legislative Council	*Public Higher Education in Texas* published
1951	Texas Legislature	Freeze on degree programs
1953	Governor	Temporary Commission on Higher Education named
1955	Texas Legislature	Commission on Higher Education created
1963	Commission on Higher Education	Study Commission on Graduate Programs in Dallas-Fort Worth created
1963	Study Commission	*Industry Report to the Texas Commission on Higher Education*
1963	Commission on Higher Education	North Texas designated doctoral institution
1964	Governor's Committee on Education Beyond the High School	Five major universities designated for Texas
1965	Texas Legislature	Coordinating Board, Texas College and University System created

A COMPULSION FOR COOPERATION IN DENTON

The two Denton schools continued under pressure from state agencies to move closer together—in cooperation if not in actual consolidation of activities. The two universities presented a joint document to the Commission on Higher Education on March 12, 1964. This was a twelve-point program outlining plans for graduate program expansion at each university, demonstrating that the two universities had planned complementary programs committing each school to full cooperative endeavors in all future graduate school developments. [33]

President Guinn and others at TWU feared more proposals to merge the two Denton campuses. They wanted to show enough cooperation to eliminate that threat without sacrificing the academic autonomy of TWU. While Dr. Jack Williams remained as Commissioner of Higher Education, TWU's role as an independent graduate school remained very much in question. In

1968 Dr. Williams maintained that the Coordinating Board staff would never again submit a graduate program proposal from TWU to the board unless it was a joint submission with NTSU. This, he said, was established policy. Even the board member who was the strongest advocate of TWU independence agreed with this position, Williams said.[34]

WANTED: AN M.I.T. OF THE SOUTHWEST

The Graduate Research Center was the first effort to create a major research-oriented scientific and engineering institution. When the GRC was transformed into the Southwest Center for Advanced Studies, existing universities were certain that SCAS would try to become a degree-granting institution, particularly at the doctoral level.

SCAS, its business colleagues, and the Dallas Chamber of Commerce proposed to donate the SCAS property to the state and convert it to a campus of the University of Texas System that would be regarded as "The M.I.T. of the Southwest." This proposal was viewed cynically by President Matthews and some others in state-supported universities in the area. To them, the offer to donate SCAS facilities was an effort to bail out of an unsuccessful philanthropy; keeping land around the campus was seen as a move to increase land values. The donated property was labeled a "white elephant."[35]

The Texas House of Representatives on May 27, 1967, asked the Coordinating Board to:

> plan, develop, and recommend for the North-Central Texas area a state-sponsored program to provide regional university facilities of the first class, making available adequate doctoral programs in the sciences and technology, and expanding and initiating complementary graduate programs compatible with private institutional efforts and utilizing to the fullest extent existing public and private educational institutions in that area. . . and to study and recommend how the resources of the Southwest Center for Advanced Studies may best be utilized, from the standpoint of the state. . . .[36]

A staff draft in May 1968 considered enrollment forecasts by the three state schools in these counties plus East Texas State University. The staff made forecasts for 1972, and proposed enrollment limits through 1980.[37] Growth at these schools would be left unregulated until September 1972, when recommended limits would be imposed. By 1980, UTA would be held more than 10,000 students below its forecast enrollment, NTSU nearly 6,000 below, TWU 7,000 below, and ETSU 6,000 below. Some of the difference was to be taken up with enrollment at a new campus in the area. The staff put it this way:

> That there be authorized in 1969, for an initial enrollment in September, 1973 of 1,800 students, an upper-level senior institution to be located in the Dallas metropolitan area, primarily to serve commuter students and offering programs only for juniors, seniors, and graduate level men and women. The college is to be in direct support of the Dallas and Fort Worth County Junior College Systems and is to be for commuting students.[38]

This did not involve the Southwest Center for Advanced Studies in the Coordinating Board's area plan nor did it mention the University of Texas System beyond the consideration of UTA.

THE UNIVERSITY OF TEXAS IN NORTH TEXAS

The University of Texas System had maintained a presence in Dallas since 1949 with the Southwestern Medical School. It made a second significant move by arranging the transfer of Arlington State College from the Texas A&M University System to the University of Texas System in 1965. Later name changes were to the University of Texas at Arlington, the University of Texas Southwestern Medical School, and subsequently to the University of Texas Health Science Center.

The Texas Legislature was changing rapidly because of the explosion of metropolitan population and court-mandated one-man, one-vote procedures in apportioning population to legislative districts. Matthews perceived University of Texas strategy as an "invasion" of every possible populous area so that home-district support could be marshaled from a majority of legislators. This, he believed, explained the move to naming a "University of Texas" for Tarrant County (Fort Worth) and creation of similarly named campuses in Dallas, San Antonio, El Paso, Midland-Odessa, and possibly Houston.[39]

To the Coordinating Board 1968 Dallas plan, University of Texas System Chancellor Harry Ransom said the board should have made the university system the heart of Dallas development. At a Coordinating Board hearing on June 21 the chancellor first made public mention of a relationship between his system and SCAS.[40] Then in August in an extended memorandum, Chancellor Ransom spelled out the system's precise intentions.[41] Internal studies of coordinated efforts by the system in Dallas and Tarrant counties had been continuous since 1965. Affiliation with the Graduate Research Center-Southwest had been under joint consideration by the two governing boards since March 1967. Ransom stressed that plans were final for the system's move into Dallas:

> Proposals by the Office of the Chancellor, University of Texas System were approved by the Board of Regents in their meeting at Midland, Texas, on July 26, 1968. Both the proposals and the approval clearly stipulated that the next official steps were to be submissions to the Coordinating Board and to the Sixty-first Legislature.
>
> The principles for the establishment of the University of Texas Center for Advanced Studies, approved by the Board of Regents of the University of Texas System on July 26, 1968, were finally approved by the Board of Governors of Southwest Center for Advanced Studies on August 20, 1968.[42]

The University of Texas System proposed to establish in the Dallas-Tarrant area "an urban university organization." It would have three "geographically separate but functionally integrated campuses collectively providing a full range of undergraduate, masters, doctoral, and professional programs," meeting the increasing demands of the region for a "complete urban university." UTA would develop a full range of academic areas through the doctoral level and the medical school would expand into major professional graduate studies in biological, physical, and health sciences. The Center for Advanced Studies would be devoted at first to physical sciences but would expand "to fill the need of future facilities for additional educational opportunity in the region."[43]

The Board of Governors of the Southwest Center for Advanced Studies, in turn, agreed to convey to the University of Texas Board of Regents 250 acres of land, including buildings, facilities, and equipment, the combined gift being valued by them at $11 million.[44]

THE COORDINATING BOARD RESISTS

Commissioner Williams and his staff opposed further involvement of the University of Texas System in Dallas and Fort Worth; yet they recognized the political pressure on the political appointees on the Coordinating Board and on the Texas Legislature from UT System supporters, the Dallas Chamber of Commerce, and the city power structure.

In the spring and summer months of 1968, Dr. Matthews, Dr. Williams, and others in the area discussed a union stronger than a voluntary consortium of existing campuses in North Texas. Some advantages could be found in having one board of regents for NTSU, TWU, UTA, ETSU, and the SCAS property in Richardson in a single university system. In midsummer 1968 the North Texas president arranged for the commissioner to have an extended discussion with Vice President Rogers.[45]

Commissioner Williams advised NTSU to stick to a positive approach. Even if Dallas support were totally withdrawn, he said, North Texas would continue to flourish as "the first-class institution it has long been." Rather than cry hurt, the North Texas view should stress the needs of the area and the great possibilities available through joint ventures. "If the Dallas-Fort Worth leadership would turn to existing institutions and say 'How can we help you?', there would be no limit to the great things possible," Williams said.

The commissioner said he believed that the need to get rid of SCAS was the central motive of the Dallas people—"If SCAS hadn't come into the picture, this Dallas effort probably wouldn't be made." He rejected as "unfounded philosophical speculation" the myth that affiliation with the University of Texas would aid any school.

His forecast was that only two or three of the eighteen Coordinating Board members would support the University of Texas proposal for UT-SCAS, but that a major political fight in the legislature was inevitable. Commissioner Williams said he was preparing a statement for the Coordinating Board meeting of September 16, even though he would be leaving the job on September 1.[46]

That statement was drafted on August 5. It called for the creation of a new, multicampus urban university for the Dallas-Fort Worth area under a single governing board.[47] It remained as a staff document for study by board members, who were preparing for a public hearing on the question in Dallas on September 16.

NEW LEADERS FOR NTSU, COORDINATING BOARD

Jack Williams and J. C. Matthews left the scene on September 1, barely more than two weeks before the Dallas public hearing. Dr. Bevington Reed was promoted to succeed Williams as commissioner. At NTSU, new president John Kamerick had just moved from Ohio (see Chapter 27). He faced a major confrontation with the powerful university system during his first month in office. Commissioner Reed was known to support fully what he called "the Williams plan" for Dallas-Fort Worth-Denton. President Kamerick reviewed a position paper prepared for him to present at the hearing, asking that the University of Texas plan not be accepted.

Dallas Chamber Seeks Delay

However, as the NTSU delegation arrived in Dallas on September 16, they learned that the Dallas Chamber of Commerce representatives sought postponement of the public hearing and a new hearing date was scheduled for October 11 in Austin. The stack of twenty-page handouts of the North Texas position was taken back to Denton and never was made public.[48] Reed released the text of the Dallas plan staff paper on September 26. Dallas Chamber of Commerce leaders attacked the plan for failing to accept the $11 million gift of SCAS. The *Chat* editor used a page-one editorial to attack both the Coordinating Board and the University of Texas plans.

> Texas educators appear determined to take from North Texas State University that intangible thing for which it has striven during its 78 years—its identity. . . .
>
> They would take from North Texas State University its advanced programs. . . that have brought NTSU national recognition.
>
> They would take from North Texas State University the governing board that has so successfully handled the difficult job. . . .
>
> They would do these things in an effort to overcome "an indefensible deficiency" in the production of master and doctoral degrees. . . .

They would do these things in an attempt to unload an $11 million white elephant (the Southwest Center for Advanced Studies). . . to be supported by taxpayers' money.[49]

A Single Board and Chancellor

Under the Coordinating Board plan, a new university would have a single board and a chancellor and staff to work with NTSU, TWU, and UTA, each to award bachelor's degrees in its own name. But graduate degrees would be awarded by the urban university. An educational services contract would give the Southwest Center for Advanced Study sponsored research as a major activity, while its staff would teach in the university-at-large, especially at the doctoral level.

The governing board would contract for educational services with private colleges and universities. And the new board would plan to open a new upper-level senior campus in the Dallas area by no later than 1973.[50]

POLITICAL MANEUVERING, CONCILIATION EFFORTS

Dallas-Fort Worth-Arlington leadership secured a further delay in the Coordinating Board hearing date to November 11.[51] The University of Texas strategy called for a common Dallas-Arlington-Fort Worth position, one that would exert great political force on the Coordinating Board and on the Texas Legislature.

President Kamerick discovered that friends were hard to find. The Dallas group went all out for the University of Texas approach. Some Tarrant County forces were upset at the prospect of enrollment limitations at UTA and the possible subordination of UTA. No one in Tarrant County, however, wanted UTA under the same board of regents as the two Denton universities. The North Texas president wrote a conciliatory letter to the UT chancellor.

> I have a completely open mind with respect to the University of Texas proposal for the Dallas-Fort Worth region. We may end up by opposing the proposal although I doubt that our opposition would be of very much consequence. . . .
>
> I would hope that the ultimate position assumed by us would not be motivated by anything as petty as parochial self-interest or academic imperialism.[52]

Ransom responded in an equally friendly manner: "Most particularly I am grateful for your position on the variant 'North Texas' plans. Each of us knows that your first responsibility is to advance N.T.S.U. None of us has the slightest intention to 'compete'—much less obstruct—your plans."[53]

Commissioner Reed's forecast of strong Coordinating Board support for the Williams plan was being undermined. In October 1968 Reed and a staff associate, Dr. Jack Cross, explored possible counter-moves with the two Denton university presidents. As a result, Presidents Kamerick and Guinn brought in President D. Whitney Halladay of East Texas State University to discuss a formal alliance to be approved by the Coordinating Board. This generated the idea of a federation of the three universities to strengthen graduate education in the North Central Texas area. Kamerick perceived this federation idea as politically expedient, although it did not represent his true wishes. These were summarized in an unusually frank letter to TCU Chancellor Moudy on November 1:

> We are not against all changes in the Dallas-Fort Worth Area; however, it is my personal opinion that great hopes are being nurtured on the weakest of foundations. It is self-deception or deception of the worst sort to propose the possibility of an instant first-rate university.
>
> We are still in the process of formulating our position and when we have finished all our conversations I shall share the paper with you. I do regret the Coordinating Board is apparently receding from its support of the Coordinating Board Staff Proposal, and I do believe education in the area will be the worse for the political settlement of an educational problem. Nonetheless, we are prepared to live with the outcome.[54]

As the hearing date approached, the North Texas strategy called for one presentation to be made by each president (NTSU, TWU, and ETSU) and one to be made jointly on behalf of a new federation of all three schools.

NO CONSENSUS BEFORE THE COORDINATING BOARD

At the November 11 hearing, Kamerick represented North Texas State University as a school far removed from its teachers college beginning, one just now blossoming as a graduate school.[55] He portrayed the doctoral programs as rapid in enrollment growth, slow to develop the necessary state support. "The most rapid and economical way to increase doctoral productivity would be to build upon the strengths that already exist," he asserted. Speaking to the proposals before the board that day, he declared, "we are not convinced of any particular merit in either plan. We would suggest that a more definitive study is needed. It is too loosely assumed that by some magic of organization or through the patina of a famous name, an instant first-rate state university can be produced. This is deception, or self deception, of the worst sort."

In summary, Kamerick made four points:

1. We doubt the need for drastic reorganization measures.

2. We worry about demolition or destruction of our own resources built up in response to demand.

3. The quickest way to achieve the goal desired is to pour resources into existing institutions.

4. While an upper-level undergraduate institution might be needed in Dallas-Fort Worth, this is quite different from building an enormous new graduate school. Given these conditions, the North Texas president proposed that:

> the Coordinating Board define the roles to be assumed by each institution in the area, particularly the roles in the development of doctoral programs. If this is done we will not at this time object to the Southwest Center for Advanced Studies becoming a part of the University of Texas system, provided that it can truly serve an educational function for the universities in the area. We agree to this with the understanding that the Southwest Center for Advanced Studies would continue to be what it is now, a group of specialized institutes for advanced studies, not a university.

The joint statement of the three universities[56] proposed a federation of public universities in Dallas, Fort Worth and adjoining counties. There were to be four members: NTSU, TWU, ETSU, and the new upper-level senior campus recommended for Dallas County by the Coordinating Board. UTA was "welcomed and invited" to join. The new Dallas campus could have its own governing board, or it could be placed under the NTSU Board of Regents or under the Board of Regents, State Senior Colleges.

The presidents would try to contract with the Southwest Center for Advanced Studies to continue sponsored research and provide staff to federation members. The federation would emphasize cooperation and coordination of graduate efforts, primarily doctoral. The consortium would be governed by a group composed of two board members and the president from each school. Any member would be free to present special requests to the Coordinating Board even if it had been screened negatively by the governing body of the consortium.[57]

At this hearing, Ransom proposed that SCAS be added to a unified University of Texas program, which would support appropriate doctoral programs for UTA as resources could be developed. The Ransom statement on the SCAS facilities began by suggesting that it could provide immediate assistance to other academic programs. Then it came to the essence of the Dallas battle:

> Apart from the proposed transfer of facilities to the U.T. System, the larger site provides open-ended development of educational cooperation in:
>
> 6.3.1 *Undergraduate Programs.* The U.T. System concurs in the Coordinating Board staff's emphasis upon future educational needs in the region. The U.T. System is prepared to undertake *such additional undergraduate responsibilities at the site of the Center as the Legislature may approve for the University of Texas at Dallas.* [Emphasis added]
>
> 6.3.2 *Graduate studies and post-doctoral research.* This is the area of greatest present capacity at the Center. It also assures future cooperative development. [58]

The other shoe had been dropped. The hearing included a presentation from the Chambers of Commerce of Arlington, Dallas, and Fort Worth. It recommended unrestricted growth at UTA, NTSU, and TWU, noting that this would still leave major deficiencies. The concluding recommendations called for these steps:

1. Leave Arlington within The University of Texas System, with no predetermined limitations on its enrollment or programs.

2. Approve the creation of additional future capacity. . . within The University of Texas System.

3. Accept the SCAS gift, for placement within The University of Texas System, as a base upon which to develop a distinguished institution emphasizing graduate education.

4. Plan for optimum continued development of North Texas State and Texas Woman's Universities at both under-graduate and graduate levels.

5. . . . explore means [to] extend some type of support to private colleges and universities. . . .[59]

The hearing adjourned without formal action by the Coordinating Board, and the participants had to await a December 3 meeting to learn of the recommendations of the board's committees on undergraduate higher education and on graduate and professional education and research.

THE COORDINATING BOARD GOES AGAINST UT

In December the Coordinating Board adopted its committee recommendations. One conciliatory move approved UT to receive the SCAS campus and programs as the University of Texas Center for Advanced Studies at Dallas. However, it was not to be a degree-granting campus, nor was it to become the upper-level college sought for Dallas. Instead, the new upper-division and graduate college was designated to come under a separate governing board.[60] This campus would be authorized in 1969 to open in 1973 with an enrollment of 1,800 students, then grow to 8,300 by 1980.

The Council of Federated Universities would be formed at the first of the three petitioning schools; other public and private members could be added later. Each school was assigned a role and scope as follows:

NTSU: A full spectrum of master's degrees plus certain top quality doctoral programs as approved by the Coordinating Board in the basic arts and sciences, teacher education, business administration, and the fine arts. Cooperative doctoral programs could be undertaken in other fields with federation members if approved by the Coordinating Board.

TWU: Maintain its present master's programs and limit doctoral programs initially to those already established. It was to continue primary responsibility for home economics, women's physical education, radiation biology, and radiation chemistry for the region.

ETSU: Maintain programs through the master's level in the basic arts and sciences and offer the doctor of education degree in five areas.[61]

THE LEGISLATURE DECIDES

The scene shifted to the 61st Texas Legislature convening in January 1969. Representative Jack Blanton of Carrollton introduced HB 303 establishing the University of Texas at Dallas as a "university of the first class," with courses and degrees at all levels. The battle lines had the UT system backers and the Dallas leadership ready to bypass the Coordinating Board and create the new university at Dallas, while federation universities' backers campaigned for the Coordinating Board plan. Again, Tarrant County legislators could play a decisive role.

Senator Don Kennard of Fort Worth led the vocal opposition to the UT Dallas bill, arguing that the new campus would damage UT Arlington and the Denton universities. Chancellor Ransom tried to reassure opponents that the system would not harm existing institutions. However, one Dallas senator provided ammunition to Kennard against the UT bill. Surprisingly, that senator was a former student of North Texas, Ike Harris. He told Station KRLD in Dallas on April 2:

> There is opposition based on the fact that it would cost too much money. However, in the long run it will be less financial burden on the taxpayers because we can focus our attention in the North Texas area on the University of Texas at Dallas and then devaluate our advanced degree-granting programs at the other state-supported schools in the area.[62]

This and other moves from Dallas supporters strengthened the hand of Senator Kennard and lent some credence to the report that Governor Preston Smith was considering vetoing the Dallas bill if it passed. President Kamerick wired all of the North Texas regents on May 24 asking them to communicate with the governor immediately to express support of a veto. When the veto came to appear unlikely, Kamerick sent a telegram to the governor on May 29: "Strongly commend your support of Coordinating Board planning for Dallas-Fort Worth area."

Senator Kennard could not defeat the legislation, but the bill that emerged did follow Coordinating Board policy to limit new universities to undergraduate work at the junior and senior levels only. This was reflected in a letter to the governor from Kamerick that said:

> we at North Texas State University are very grateful to you for the modifications which have been introduced into the bill creating a University of Texas at Dallas. From the beginning, we have believed there was a place in the University of Texas System for the Southwest Center for Advanced Studies. We did not believe that it was desirable for the State to create a new major State university in Dallas, at this time. The changes which have been introduced, as a result of your action, go far toward meeting the specifications of the Coordinating Board which coincide with our own convictions in the matter.[63]

On June 13, Governor Smith signed the modified bill creating the University of Texas at Dallas as an "upper-level institution."

chapter 27

Free of Violence

Whenever a public school or a college or university has been integrated, either by court order or voluntary action, the students and the faculty, the community and individuals of both pro and con views, have all gained when the step was taken with a minimum amount of discord. It behooves all of us to make a special effort to stand behind the board in this step, as we never have stood behind it in any other.

J. C. Matthews
Remarks to a Faculty Meeting, 1956[1]

"Cultural diversity" and "multicultural," words so common on university campuses at the end of the twentieth century, would have meant little on the campus at the midcentury. The year 1954 marks the event that ended a relatively homogeneous student population at North Texas. On May 17, the U. S. Supreme Court ruled in *Brown v. Board of Education of Topeka, Kansas,* that racial segregation in the public schools is inherently unequal and, therefore, illegal.

SIXTY YEARS OF SEGREGATION

In 1954, the term "foreign student" rather than "international" was standard, and it could be applied to only eleven students, 0.24 percent of the student body of 4,953 students. Only 122 came from other states, so that 97.3 percent of North Texans were from Texas. For more than half a century, North Texas had been legally segregated. No records showed whether any Spanish-speaking students had enrolled. Civil rights categories were not reported before 1970.[2]

Statutory limitation to "white students of the state" did not appear in the founding legislation of North Texas State Normal College. However, in 1911, the legislature stipulated that a new normal school board was for "all state normal schools for white teachers."[3]

The policy of "separate but equal" schools for white and black had been regarded as the law of the land. In Dallas, the Dallas Colored High School opened in 1892; St. Peter's School in 1910 as a boarding and day school for Negro students; Booker T. Washington High School in 1922 to serve all Black students in the Dallas district. Following *Brown v. Board of Education,* in 1954, thirty-two Black parents filed a petition to end Dallas school desegregation.

A Note on Nomenclature

From 1950 to 2000, we have seen many changes in the terminology applied to members of ethnic groups. Foreign students became international students. Orientals became Asians. The "polite" word for the black population was taught to be "Negro," although some North Texans borrowed from the National Association for the Advancement of Colored People to speak of "colored." In the '60s and '70s, the "Black Power" movement brought the term "Black" into currency. One of the first organized support groups at NT called itself the Afro-American Student Union. Wide usage developed later for "African-American."

For the Spanish-speaking population, the reference had been "Mexican." With greater group awareness, the term became "Mexican American." This was often replaced by "Latin American." The two terms appear in names of the League of United Latin American Citizens (LULAC), and the Mexican American Legal Defense Fund (MALDEF). Use of "Chicano" in the '60s and '70s proved unacceptable to many elders. At North Texas for a time enrollment data was collected for "Spanish-Americans" and later for "Hispanics." But many resisted being tied to Spain by such words. Another term, "Latinos," became widely used.

Which terms to use? The dilemma becomes greater as one moves across half a century of concerns over the status of minority groups. This book tries to avoid value-laden or pejorative terms but does use in context a word or phrase appropriate to the time being described. At any point in the story, however, the generic terms likely to be used are "Black, Hispanic, Asian."

The President's Background

In his early experiences and in his educational career, J. C. Matthews had little experience in working with Negroes. In the Grayson County area of his childhood, he recalled, "There was not a Negro." At age eight he moved to Foard County, which was "all white."[4] He attended segregated public schools, he earned his bachelor's degree at a segregated North Texas, and he completed two graduate degrees at George Peabody College for Teachers in a segregated Nashville, Tennessee. A product of his times, he faced desegregating NTSC as unfamiliar territory.

FIRST BLACK STUDENT ENROLLS

When he had been in office two years, Matthews wrote Texas Attorney General John Ben Shepperd on September 3, 1953:

> I need some advice in advance of registration, September 21, which I believe you are in position to give me without elaborate study on your part.
>
> A colored teacher in Fort Worth has been taking courses at Texas Christian University as I understand it to be applied toward the doctor's degree. I assume that she already has the master's degree. She has been told by Texas Southern University that her work will have to be done

> in an institution which offers the doctor's degree in order to be transferred to apply on the degree. . . .
>
> She has conferred with our Dean of the School of Education relative to attending Saturday classes here in the fall. She has said she does not want to make a test case of the matter, and she has been told that no colored person has enrolled at North Texas State College to date. As you know, we offer work toward the doctor's degree.
>
> We should like to have your advice on this matter. Perhaps you could telephone me collect upon receiving this letter.[5]

The files do not record what response was received from Shepperd or what was communicated to the potential student. Marcello says "she never applied for admission."[6]

Sweatt Case Impacts NTSC

One case had impacted higher education even before the Brown judgment. In 1946, a Houston mail carrier applied to the University of Texas Law School and was rejected because of his race. Heman Marion Sweatt sought help from the NAACP and filed suit. The Supreme Court on June 5, 1950, ruled 9–0 for the plaintiff. The key point was that the law school for Negroes was not equal, and thus no "separate but equal" program was available. Sweatt registered for classes at the University of Texas in September 1950.

Matthews was aware of that case, which soon became relevant in Denton. Tennyson Miller, forty-one, had been principal of "the Negro high school" in Denton but had just become principal of Lincoln High School in Port Arthur. His wife operated a beauty shop in Denton and had continued to live here. In 1954, he was spending the summer in Denton. He had a master's degree from the University of Wisconsin and was eligible to work toward the doctorate. President Matthews learned that Miller was interested in taking a course at North Texas in school law. Matthews told Miller he would find out about his status. As Matthews recalled:

> I went to Dallas and talked to Mr. Wooten. . . . We called board members, and I told them that I thought there was no question but what this meant. According to the Sweatt case decision in all particulars he was eligible to take doctoral work. Doctoral work was not of-

> fered at a Black institution. . . . It was decided by telephone that I should go to Austin to check with the attorney general.[7]

Attorney General Concurs

An attorney general staff member advised that admission in this case would be routine, and the Board of Regents authorized it. Matthews had been putting Miller off until he got this clearance. Miller wrote from Port Arthur to ask for favorable endorsement from the president:

> It is my conviction that my entrance now would contribute much to the successful, inevitable integration of Negroes into the school. My every effort would be toward the quality of deportment and performance that would dispel much of the apprehension that some may be harboring at this time. Knowing even in my own work the burdened seriousness of making an unusual decision, I understand why any caution may be yours. Yet there are decisions to be made, and we cannot be without the courage to make them.
>
> . . . .I am asking that you and the graduate committee favorably consider my application, and, if I am admitted, accept, support, and guide my efforts as a student at NTSC. . . .
>
> I will make another trip to Denton this coming Saturday as a final follow-up to this letter.[8]

Matthews responded with a telegram: "Administrative approval meant necessity of checking with Board of Regents. Now seems possible for you to enter North Texas upon completion of health blank and graduate admission blanks provided you are planning to pursue doctorate program. Saturday trip unnecessary unless you have further questions."[9] Miller enrolled for the second summer term in 1954. An Associated Press story made clear that admission of the "first Negro student" was restricted to doctoral students. It quoted Matthews, "our policy on Negro undergraduates or Negro students working on master's degrees is not changed. They will not be admitted to North Texas State at this time."[10]

Miller was apparently the second Black individual to enroll in Texas under the Sweatt order, four years after Sweatt began his studies in Austin. Forty years later Miller reminisced, "I think the administrators wanted me not as a token but as the first to open the doors to other Black students."[11]

LAWSUIT FILED

It is interesting to note that Thurgood Marshall (later a Supreme Court justice) was the attorney in both the Sweatt and the Brown cases. After *Brown* came to prominence in 1954, President Matthews began informal conversations with board members about its implications here. He recalled it this way:

> I said, "We are going to have someone appear some day and want to enter." . . .
>
> At this time we didn't have a specific issue, so we were visiting in light of a principle. . . . I was saying I thought it was better if we had a person admitted without any necessity of a court order. I thought that . . . when you [have] to do something, you are in worse position than you would be if you did it on a voluntary basis. There was no debate, as I recall, then. I don't think there was even a show of attitude. The situation was not critical at that moment. But I was taking the prior step. . . anticipating that this was going to happen.[12]

Nevertheless, Matthews was well aware that the admission of one Black doctoral student did not indicate that the NTSC Board of Regents was ready to approve full desegregation of the college. Furthermore:

> During the period immediately before and after the arrival of the first African-American undergraduate at North Texas, Matthews also had to consider the strong and unyielding opposition to desegregation being waged by high state officials, particularly Governor Allan Shivers and Attorney General John Ben Shepperd. Both men condemned the Supreme Court's decision in *Brown* and attempted various legal ploys to circumvent it. As an employee of the state, Matthews found himself caught between the Shivers-Sheppard forces, who chose to defy the courts and fight the NAACP, and the NAACP, which had the courts on its side.[13]

Joe L. Atkins Applies

The administration and the Board of Regents were forced to take a final stand with the arrival of a Dallas man, Joe L. Atkins, on the campus on June 13, 1955. The best account of these events, and others related to the desegregation story, has been provided by Ronald E. Marcello, a member of the North Texas history faculty and director of the Oral History Program.[14] The following descriptions are drawn from Marcello's work, from the author's recollections as a participant in the process, and other sources that are documented in the endnotes.

Atkins came to the campus on June 13 to seek enrollment, accompanied by his mother and by Mrs. Juanita Craft. Mrs. Craft had been a member of the NAACP since 1935 and sponsored the NAACP Dallas Youth Council. Atkins had graduated from Lincoln High School in Dallas and attended Philander Smith College in Little Rock in 1955–56. Marcello gives this account:

> After his freshman year, Atkins returned to Dallas determined to enroll at North Texas. His parents were supportive, although his mother had some misgivings. "It was basically because of all the turmoil going on in the country at the time, so she had a little fear," Atkins later recalled. Mrs. Craft encouraged him to apply because Denton was essentially a college town. . . and no widespread racial hostility existed in the community. Atkins was also aware of Tennyson Miller's favorable experience at North Texas.

The Atkins group first talked with Registrar Alex Dickie, who brought them to talk with Vice President A. M. Sampley. Sampley was required to defend a state law and a regents' policy with which he seemed quite uncomfortable. A kind and gentle man, Sampley was widely respected as a former Poet Laureate of Texas, director of libraries, and arts and sciences dean at North Texas. Atkins later recalled that it was a "long, very cordial conversation."[15] Sampley informed them that NTSC was planning a program for gradual integration over a four-year period, starting with seniors in the first year and working down to admitting freshmen in the fourth. Mrs. Craft reminded Sampley of the legal ramifications of the Brown ruling and advised him not to delay the desegregation process. She insisted that Atkins receive an application form.

Atkins wrote Sampley three days later to report that he had applied and had requested a transcript from Philander Smith. Sampley replied that he had placed the admission application in the files "pending further clarification of your status."[16] President Matthews asked for a meeting of the Board of Regents to consider the application.[17]

> When the board met a few days later, its initial mood was one of defiance. Chairman Wooten. . . opposed Atkins's admission, and none of the other members favored integration at the undergraduate level. One [Matthews recalled] responded, "Let 'em sue!" The attorneys on the board, Ralph Elliott of Sherman and Berl Godfrey of Fort Worth, advised, however, that the college would lose if a suit were filed.
>
> . . . . They decided to deny Atkins admission while accepting the fact that the college would lose a resulting legal challenge. Nevertheless, they could then explain to white parents that the federal courts, not the college, were responsible. . . , Wooten later recalled. . . .
>
> At the same meeting, the board also completed an alternate plan to full and immediate integration that it had been contemplating since the admission of Tennyson Miller [the four-year phased-in plan described by Sampley].[18]

Matthews later recalled that he "hoped that they would have said, 'Let's do it the way we did with Tennyson Miller.' In fact, I recommended that, but I knew then that I was probably going to be representing a losing cause."[19]

Having confirmed that the regents' ruling would not change, Sampley wrote Atkins on July 18:

> In accordance with the agreement made in a conference with you, we are reporting the present status of your admission. . . . It has been the policy of the Board of Regents to admit only those members of your race who are candidates for the doctor's degree, and that policy has not been changed. Since you are not a candidate for the doctor's degree, we are not authorized to admit you at this time.[20]

The Dallas regional NAACP attorney, U. Simpson Tate, recommended that Atkins file suit. Joe L. Atkins was a minor, so his father Willie Atkins filed for an injunction to require his admission to NTSC. They filed on August 11, 1955, in the United States District Court of the Eastern District of Texas, Sherman division, naming as defendants Matthews, Sampley, and the nine regents. Tate told the Atkins family that if they could not get a temporary injunction, he could attend Texas Western College in El Paso, which had already been ordered in July to desegregate. That way, Atkins would not lose a semester of schooling.[21]

The Atkins Court Case

On September 10, 1955, the judge did deny the temporary injunction and set a date for a hearing Friday, December 2, in Sherman. President Matthews and Vice President Sampley were present. An assistant attorney general, Billy E. Lee, questioned Matthews to elicit from him the board's proposal for the gradual admission of Negroes over four years, leading to admission of freshmen in 1959. After the Sherman hearing, Matthews wrote regents of his testimony and of the sympathetic remarks by Judge Joe W. Sheehy, who nonetheless said that he had no choice but to enjoin the college to admit Atkins and all others of his race. The regents were given thirty days to file an appeal, but Matthews advised them that both Lee and the judge thought that an appeal would be futile.[22] On December 17, Matthews wrote Lee that there would be no appeal.[23]

Policy was changed from then on by the judge's order that "the defendants, their successors in office, their agents, servants and employees, and each of them be forever restrained and enjoined from refusing admission to the minor Plaintiff or any other Negro student of the same class as Plaintiff to the College solely because of their race or color."[24]

WHO WILL BE FIRST?

When Atkins applied for admission, only two four-year state colleges in the former Confederate States were offering admission without reservations to qualified Black undergraduate candidates. Both were in Louisiana: Southwestern Louisiana Institute (since September 1954) and McNeese State College (February 1955). As the Atkins case proceeded to trial in the fall, seven other colleges joined that list for the fall semester of 1955, including Texas Western College at El Paso. The others were Southwestern Louisiana College, University of North Carolina, University of Arkansas, Arkansas State College, and Henderson State College in Arkansas.[25] Atkins chose the only Texas college available to him, Texas Western, and thus did not enroll at North Texas.

Mrs. Cephas Arrives. . .

Instead, the first undergraduate Black student was a forty-one-year-old woman, Mrs. Irma E. L. Cephas, who would commute from her home in Fort

Worth. Her first day on the campus was February 3, 1956, by unhappy coincidence the same day on which another Black woman, Autherine Lucy, began classes at the University of Alabama. Stones were thrown at the new student in Tuscaloosa, Alabama, and after three days of rioting, she was forced to flee the campus, and the Alabama Board of Trustees barred her from the campus. When the court on February 29 ordered her readmission, the trustees expelled her from the university.[26]

This was the stuff of major network television news. News directors quickly saw the contrast in Mrs. Cephas's arrival in Denton without violence. President Matthews was alarmed by this pairing of the two news events—his prescription for a peaceful campus was to say little and have as little news attention as possible. He wanted Mrs. Cephas to be treated like any other student. He told some of his staff, "If the national television news shows rocks being thrown in Alabama and none being thrown in Denton, this is an open invitation to some trouble-makers to say, 'Hey, let's go to Denton and throw some rocks.'"

The news of successful desegregation at NTSC was carried on all three national network news shows and on local news in Dallas and Fort Worth. Since Mrs. Cephas lived in Fort Worth, Station WBAP-TV (Channel 5), the NBC affiliate in that city, was especially interested in her enrollment. A reporter interviewed her at her home and then came with a technician and sound camera, prepared to enter a classroom and question her classmates. Matthews told the reporter there would be no cameras inside any classroom. Instead, the crew did a stand-up interview of Mrs. Cephas outside. Matthews refused a sound interview but agreed to silent film footage of him at his desk. That pose ran on Channel 5's local news while the voice-over narration criticized Matthews for trying to censor the news.[27]

After the first flurry of news coverage, the lone Black student was able to attend classes in comparative calm and obscurity. Marcello evaluated it this way: "The administration of North Texas was proud that desegregation of the college had been free of violence. Pragmatic, decisive leaders and fortuitous circumstances in Denton prevented a repetition of the scene in Tuscaloosa. On the other hand, North Texas never encouraged African-American enrollment."[28]

. . . and Others Follow

NTSC had become an island in an ocean of segregated communities and institutions. No other four-year public college in the northern half of the state had yet admitted Blacks. Public schools remained segregated in spite of the *Brown* case. Public facilities in Denton were for whites only. A Black student from NTSC would not be permitted to eat in a restaurant near the campus or downtown. A Black student could not attend movies in Denton. A Black student was not welcome in many retail establishments. For a time, at least, he or she would be expected to worship at one of the "colored churches" in Denton.

President Matthews counseled everyone to treat all students just alike in the classroom and educational activities. Football Coach Odus Mitchell asked if Black athletes would be eligible for his team. The answer: if they show up, give them a uniform and treat them like the others. What about music groups? All students were to be allowed to participate but with a special proviso: if you take a musical group on tour, you should try not to take Black students into segregated towns with segregated audiences. To do so, the president argued, would be to put the Black students in a potentially hazardous position.

What About Housing?

In one of the most controversial of his "proceed with caution" decisions, Matthews ruled at first that no dormitory rooms would be available for Black students. They had to commute from their homes or live in private homes in the "colored part of town." However, the Denton paper noted that in the first summer after Mrs. Cephas enrolled, two Black women students lived in a women's dormitories.[29] This procedure was relaxed gradually with the admission of some older women school teachers in the summer and with the eventual housing of a few Black women in a special section of Oak Street Hall. It was even longer before men could be integrated in a dormitory.

What About Academic Abilities?

The first Black students who entered North Texas faced a daunting environment. They came from a segregated high school that lacked the facilities, staffing, and programs of most all-white Texas high schools. They had to live off campus. There were no Black faculty members or administrators. The only Blacks visible to them were service personnel—custodians, groundskeepers, cafeteria workers. The college was not equipped to provide formal counseling or assistance in adapting to new surroundings. It was generally assumed that they would not be educationally equipped for college studies. Nevertheless, Matthews asked the faculty at the fall 1956 meeting to treat them well, to treat them fairly, to treat them like any other student—and not to grade them sympathetically. He meant that it would be no favor to give a higher grade than earned, that the student would need to know the standards to be met if the integrated education was to be of value. In the view of this writer, who was on the faculty at the time, a large majority of the faculty was supportive of the new Black students, recognized the educational handicaps they might have had in the past, and was willing to extend extra personal assistance in the class setting to help. Some, however, appeared to err in prejudging Black students as doomed to failure at NTSC.

A 1994 magazine review of integration at North Texas included the views of several students of those first years. Recollections were described this way:

> Several of UNT's first African-American students recalled incidents of prejudice by their professors. [An administrator said] all African-American students were automatically placed on academic probation. . . . "Faculty in some departments were more accepting of integration than faculty in other departments."
>
> [Another alumnus] remembers faculty who had a difficult time pronouncing "Negro." "It was pronounced many different ways but always came out as a derogatory term."
>
> For the most part, however, UNT's faculty welcomed integration. . . . Several of UNT's African-American alumni speak fondly of the support they received from administration and faculty.[30]

ATHLETICS AS CATALYST

For many, two young men became symbols of North Texas integration and ambassadors of good will for the entrance of Blacks into campus life. The two symbols were Abner Haynes and Leon King, who came to Denton just after graduating together at Lincoln High School in Dallas. They came under the oral instructions Matthews had given to Coach Odus Mitchell: any Negro who comes out on his own should be given a fair chance. The tension felt on the first day was recalled later by Haynes in an oral history interview with

Marcello, who described the events as Haynes and King arrived at the practice field in a taxi:

> They could see clumps of players standing around on the other side, and all eyes seemed to be on them. Then the tension mounted when the two blacks observed that no coaches were yet present and noticed these three players coming toward them. As Haynes remembered, "Here these guys are coming toward me. . . . I have no idea what's going to happen . . . ." In the lead was Garland Warren, a junior from Denton, who extended his hand and said, "I'm proud to be playing with you. Welcome to the team." About the same time Charlie Cole and his brother Vernon, the blonde, did likewise. The blacks were stunned. As Haynes remembers "I wanted to kiss them. I never expected that. . . . It blew our minds because we sure needed a friend." Shortly afterwards, about twenty more came by, almost like a procession. . . . Not everyone came forward, but the welcome was much more than they expected.
>
> President Matthews attended the first practice to ensure that no incidents took place.[31]

Credit to Vernon Cole

Coaches, players, and President Matthews were alike in crediting the leadership of Vernon Cole. In 1956 freshmen played on a separate team and were not eligible for varsity competition. Freshman Coach Kenneth Bahnsen told Marcello that Cole "was the leader that made it work. . . because he had the respect of every player that ever played with him." A classmate who grew up with Cole in Pilot Point, G. A. Moore, said, "He made integration perfect, because if Vernon said it was all right, then it was all right, as far as I was concerned."[32] Other doubters were converted once the athletic talents of Haynes and King showed up on the practice field. Haynes was challenged early on by a player from East Texas who later admitted, "As far as I was concerned, he was a nigger, and I was a white. Not a Negro but a nigger." During the 1956 season that man's views changed, and he credited Haynes for showing him the way: "I guess I grew up more on the racial barrier thing in a month or two months of the football season. . . than all the other times put together. . . . He [Abner] was a friend of mine by that time, not just an acquaintance. I considered him a friend."

The Corsicana Incident

The freshman team in 1956 (like the varsity teams of the following three years) would encounter serious problems at games away from the campus. The pivotal event captured by Marcello came in the second road trip of the year for the freshmen. The team traveled to Corsicana to play Navarro County Junior College. The game was significant, Marcello wrote, because the players "had one of the most frightening experiences in their young lives there, but at the same time that experience brought the team together as perhaps nothing else could." The first episode came at the pregame meal in a Corsicana restaurant. A waitress told the two Black players they would have to eat in the kitchen, but Joe Mac Pryor, a 300-pound lineman, said, "Wait a minute! Ma'am, they're with us. They'll eat with us." Bahnsen sent for the manager and told him the entire team would walk out without eating if all could not be served. The manager backed down.

Events at the football field were more serious and alarming. Four men told Bahnsen before the game that if he played "those niggers . . . may die." When the team entered the field for the kickoff, some in the crowd chanted, "Get that nigger boy! Get that nigger boy!" The Corsicana players resorted to name-calling, biting, and spitting to try to humiliate the North Texas team. In spite of this, Haynes ran for four touchdowns to put his team ahead 35-14 in the fourth quarter. This increased the crowd's hostility and led Bahnsen to call a time-out to take the two Black players from the game. He asked the bus driver to move all the clothing from the locker room to the bus, turn the bus around, and be ready to leave immediately at the end of the game. Bahnsen told the players to keep their helmets on and run for the bus at the final gun, with Haynes and King protected in the middle of the group.

Marcello declared that the mob in Corsicana solidified and unified the nineteen young freshmen, not one of them willing to see their teammates abused. Team reaction on the bus on the way home was that "We showed 'em!" One player later reminisced that "When they were hollering all those insults at Abner and Leon, they were hollering them at the rest of us, too." Haynes later recalled:

> "The challenge brought us together. They had to decide in Corsicana where they were coming from. . . . These were special human beings,

> not your run-of-the-mill human beings. They weren't brought there to assimilate with a black. They were brought there to be educated and play football and were thrown into something they had no control over, and they handled it. That's how I know they were special, because something was dealt on them that they were not prepared for, and they handled it."[33]

Upon fielding an integrated varsity team in 1957, North Texas lost lucrative contracts with the three public Mississippi universities, whom they had played for several years. Hazards were encountered in several cities where integration was not an accepted practice. For a game at the University of Houston in 1959, no hotel would accept the Black players with the team, and the players refused to be separated. So an ingenious solution was found: the team traveled on a chartered train to Houston and spent the night aboard Pullman cars in the railroad yards.

By the time King and Haynes were seniors, in 1959, the Eagle football team finished with a 9–1 record in the Missouri Valley Conference and played in the Sun Bowl on December 31. Haynes was drafted to play for the Dallas Texans in the new American Football Conference and was named rookie of the year and player of the year in the AFC for the 1960 season. He moved with the team when it became the Kansas City Chiefs. King earned bachelor's and master's degrees from North Texas and a doctorate from Nova University and enjoyed a successful career as a public school administrator in Dallas. Marcello's account sums up the reasons for successful athletic integration this way:

> There was a college town without a history of racial turmoil. There was a college president who was bent on obeying the letter of the law and preventing interruptions in the education process. There were coaches who worked out practical tactics to keep the team together. There was a highly respected team leader who befriended two blacks at a time when they needed friends. There was a special group of young men who rose to the occasion when confronted with a situation not of their own making and, most important, there was a personable black super star who was instrumental in winning games and who was able to maintain discipline and composure in the face of adversity.[34]

MAKING THINGS WORK

As the quotation that opens this chapter indicates, Matthews's greatest concern was to keep "a minimum amount of discord." He preferred not to have public statements about desegregation, especially if they referred to "how well things are going." He asked the editors of the *Campus Chat* not to write editorials in praise of the success of integration at North Texas. He also arranged constant vigilance by staff members in physical plant operations to prevent any indication of protest from being seen. If a cross was placed on the lawn of the president's home, it was removed at dawn. If a hate slogan was chalked or painted on a building or sidewalk, it was obliterated before the school day began. If a poster or sign was put up, it was torn down immediately. The prevailing mood was to be "business as usual."

A Problem in Accounting

In the fall semester of 1956, a popular question was, "How many Negroes have enrolled?" Paradoxically, it was a question that wasn't supposed to be answered. Printed admission and registration forms did not provide for a student to indicate "race." Furthermore, the university was advised that federal agencies would regard it as evidence of discrimination if that question were to be asked. Officially, no one could know how many Black students had registered.

Anyone acquainted with the president, however, would know that he wanted some indication of that number and some method of tracking their academic progress. Matthews arranged to have an assistant registrar place inconspicuous coded pencil marks on registration forms so that he could have a count. Such numbers are not preserved in any official records, however. The best public records of the extent of minority enrollment were collected by Richard Morehead of the Austin bureau of the *Dallas Morning News.* After the early enrollment at UT Austin and at NTSC, other public four-year colleges slowly began admitting Negro students. Morehead wrote Matthews in March 1958 as part of a survey of Texas colleges. Matthews responded in a Western Union message: "Fall [1957], 181. Did not re-enroll in spring, 77, subtotal 104. New students in spring 29. Total in spring, 133. This means that 43% dropped out after one semester. Total student enrollment in the fall semester was 6212."[35] Subsequent reports to Morehead showed 203 Negroes in the fall of 1958, 247 in 1959, 160 in spring 1963, 220 in 1964, and "approximately 300" in 1965.

That last approximation came after Morehead wrote Matthews, "We know that racial records are not kept at most institutions," and the president responded, "You are right in assuming that we do not keep a record that would reveal the race of the student."[36]

Official published mention of enrollment by "civil rights category" came after the federal policy was changed to require such reports. The first *Fact Book,* published in 1978, indicates for the first time data by "civil rights category" for the fall of 1970, showing 640 undergraduate and 129 graduate students in the category then labeled "Afro-American." That was 775 of an enrollment of 13,996, or 5.5 percent.

Other State Colleges

Five years after the first undergraduate enrollment at North Texas, the Southern Regional Council reported the names of Southern colleges that had desegregated. In Texas, forty-two were listed, many of them junior colleges and church-related colleges. Five state-supported senior colleges were on the list: Lamar State, North Texas State, Texas A&I, Texas Western, and the University of Texas. Others in the Dallas-Fort Worth metropolitan area were Dallas Theological Seminary, Brite College of the Bible at TCU, Southwestern Baptist Seminary, SMU, and the University of Dallas. North Texas thus remained the only geographically convenient integrated state campus for Blacks living throughout North and Northeast Texas.[37]

The Spanish Speaking Few in Number

Only seventy-five Mexican-American children enrolled in Dallas schools in 1915 and still only 1,500 in 1925. The Spanish-speaking population resided primarily in South Texas, a condition reflected in North Texas enrollment in the 1970s. Comparisons of North Texas undergraduate students showed 646 Black and 74 Hispanic in 1970, 703 and 162 in 1971, 847 and 239 in 1972, 881 and 256 in 1973, 1,040 and 272 in 1974, 1,172 and 329 in 1975, 1,244 and 359 in 1976, 1,252 and 369 in 1977, 1,283 and 288 in 1978, and 1,323 and 440 in 1979.

The number of undergraduate Hispanics passed 500 for the first time in 1986 at 531, and that number shot up rapidly by the centennial year of 1990 to surpass a thousand at 1,022. By 1997 the undergraduate number was 1,346, compared to 1,608 Blacks. At the graduate level, Hispanic enrollment didn't reach 200 until 202 enrolled in fall 1992. In 1996 and 1997 the Hispanic graduate students outnumbered graduate Black students for the first time, 288 to 249 and 299 to 263.

Tracking Success Rates

If enrollment data was tabulated outside of official channels for a decade or more, records of retention and academic success were even more nebulous. One of the reports to Morehead showed that in the fall of 1958, forty-three percent of Negroes dropped out after one semester as compared to twenty-two percent for all other students. What is missing here is any indication of probable reasons for withdrawal; some of it could be attributed to academic problems, other to personal dissatisfaction, lack of financial means, etc. The author recalls that President Matthews in the early years of integration told faculty members that percentages of Negroes placed on academic suspension were far higher than for other students.

Civil Rights Compliance

After a decade, North Texas needed to demonstrate that equitable participation was occurring. The president asked all heads of budget units for reports of Negroes enrolled and of those active in student clubs and extracurricular activities. In the fall of 1967, all student financial aid other than athletics went to 882 whites, 143 Negroes, and 25 others. Others included Indian, Asian, and Spanish American.[38] Athletic scholarship grants at that time went to 142 white, 33 Negro and 5 other.[39]

"Gradualism" continued to be the pattern in providing dormitory space for the Black student. The pattern of women graduate students being assigned space in summer was the entry point in 1956. In 1957 the senior women's dormitory director sent a memo to the president headed "SPECIAL STUDENTS (assigned for summer term)," followed by the names of nine women. At the top of this file is a note in Matthews's handwriting: "File: Joe L. Atkins."[40] This was the code method of recording the extent of desegregation of dormitories. Nothing had changed by 1961. The president answered a Houston principal who wrote the graduate office for information about dormitory space for "Negro women teachers who want to attend the graduate summer school." His answer said:

> We have had a few Negro women in the dormitories in the summer. Because of the physical facilities available we have never had more than seven in any one term. I assume that since we have not had any change in the facilities which are to be used in the summer of 1961 that this will be the case for us for the summer.
>
> Applications are filled on a first come first served basis.[41]

At the same time, a memo from the president's files suggests that there was at least one Negro male assigned to West Dormitory in the summer of 1961.[42]

Increasing Participation

Success in football led to the addition of Black players to the basketball team and the track squad in 1957–58. The alumni newspaper, the *North Texan*, in 1994 traced the increased role of Black students in student life as recalled by several alumni. An Austin attorney, Joel Bennett, class of 1968, said the success of integrated sports helped the campus and the community accept integration as a whole. He recalled:

> The black athletes set some high standards of good character, and that made it easier for whites to accept them and other black students. Some of the administration had fears and uncertainty about what would happen if you threw these races together, and when they saw that the athletic teams gained by having black athletes, it paved the way for other blacks to become involved in campus organizations.[43]

Bennett was one of those involved: he was one of the first Black senators in student government. Another, Dr. Mickey Burnim, class of 1970, became the first Black student senate president. He also was vice president of the student body, president of both the junior and senior classes and one of the first Black residents of West Hall, the first men's residence to be desegregated. The *North Texan* pointed out:

> He also helped break the racial barrier of the Talons, a men's spirit group, at the same time that the Green Jackets, a women's spirit group, took its first African-American members.

> "My statement in coming to a predominantly white university was to show that blacks could be competitive and do well in any kind of environment if given the chance," says Burnim, now provost and vice president for academic affairs at North Carolina Central University in Durham, North Carolina. "The success that I enjoyed while at NT was because I was given the chance."[44]

Others who broke barriers were Nicki Wilson, first Yucca Beauty in 1969, Rosalind Johnson, first Black Homecoming Queen in 1973, and the first cheerleader and band majorette in the early 1970s. In pointing to these cases, the *North Texan* noted that the racial barrier remained in social sororities and fraternities: "Because of this, African-American students formed their first sorority, Delta Sigma Theta, and fraternity, Omega Psi Phi, in 1968." The following year saw the establishment of an NAACP chapter.

Living in Denton

The crisis point with the Denton community came with organized efforts of groups of white and black students and their sympathizers to gain for Blacks the rights to attend movies at the Campus Theater. In the fall of 1961, lines of members of this group would form and attempt to buy tickets for all. The manager had others form a second line and told the cashier to sell to whites in that line. The situation threatened to turn uglier, and there were rumors of violence and of some individuals coming into town with rifles. Several concerned community leaders, foremost among them the publisher of the *Denton Record-Chronicle*, Riley Cross, kept working behind the scenes with various parties concerned to keep the peace. Ultimately, agreement was reached to admit all to the theater. Similar problems were encountered in opening restaurants, even those around "The Corner" of the campus, and of boardinghouses and apartment houses near the campus. In a number of cases, it took the prospect of federal intervention in student housing to provide integrated apartment houses.

James Carl Matthews, President, 1951–68.

(below) With a new name and a university-type reorganization, North Texas State College began an emphasis on research. With a new biology-chemistry building, Masters Hall, in use in 1951-52, these administrators posed for this picture to call attention to the research potential. Shown are President J. C. Matthews, J. K. G. Silvey, chairman of the division of science; B. B. Harris, dean of the college; and President-Emeritus W. J. McConnell.

The expansion toward university status brought doctoral programs to the campus. Harold Hitt receives the first NTSC doctoral degree in August 1953 from President Matthews and is hooded by Dr. A. Witt Blair, dean of the School of Education.

An Air Force ROTC unit was established at North Texas in 1951, in part a response to the Korean War. Here, 1951 cadets parade at Homecoming past "The Corner" at Hickory and Fry Streets.

(left) A young journalism student from Marshall, Bill Moyers, (second from left) began making a name for himself in 1952–54 as a writer for the *Campus Chat* and as a class president and student leader.

(right) Moyers wrote a feature story about a young singer from Tennessee who became an instant success on the Saturday Night Stage Show in the spring of 1954. He was Pat Boone, who while an NT student won national TV spots by winning competition on Ted Mack's Amateur Hour and Arthur Godfrey's Talent Scouts.

The biggest national sports attention at North Texas since the 1930s track teams was provided by Coach Fred Cobb's golf teams, who won four consecutive NCAA championships from 1949 to 1952. Don January and Billy Maxwell went on from those feats to gain further national golf recognition.

With admission of a Black doctoral student in 1954 and a Black undergraduate in 1956, NTSC began the process of desegregation. Eagle halfback Abner Haynes was one effective symbol of the campus change starting in 1956. Haynes was an NTAll-American and later starred for the Dallas Texans of the American Football League.

Cheerleaders and the Concert Band lead a student rally in front of the Student Union Building on May 10, 1961, to celebrate the signing of the bill in Austin two days before changing the name of North Texas State College to North Texas State University. The *North Texan* called it "a day that thousands would remember for the rest of their lives."

Debate was a major activity in the normal and teachers college years, and in 1948 the men's team won the national trophy at West Point. In May 1962 John Swaney and Ann Hodges took NTSC debating national and international on the NBC television network, winning the championship debate of a TV series in May and defeating a team from Oxford University in a prime-time contest in July.

The 1923 Administration Building had provided offices, classrooms, and a large auditorium. An enlargement of administrative functions was facilitated by construction of a new Administration Building, shown here in March 1956. The tower and its carillon were dedicated as the McConnell Memorial Tower.

J. C. Matthews had been the first North Texas vice president, then named Arthur Sampley as his vice president, to be succeeded by J. J. Spurlock. With urging of the Board of Regents, Matthews for the first time expanded his administration by adding more vice presidents. Shown in 1966 are Matthews; James L. Rogers, administrative affairs; Spurlock, academic affairs; and John L. Carter, fiscal affairs. Carter was also acting president in 1970–71 and 1979–80.

(above) Members of the Talons spirit organization move the old Curfew/Victory Bell from the roof of the Power Plant to a trailer in 1962, converting it to a portable football spirit symbol. After the bell cracked, the Talons dedicated it to the university and placed it in the University Union in 1982.

(photos above and bottom right) A popular student gathering place from the late 1920s onward was the water fountain, shown here with the Science Building in the background. When that building was demolished to make room for the Language Building in 1968, the gazebo from the water fountain was saved in the same location to preserve tradition.

This structure faced Chestnut Street and heavy auto traffic when it opened in 1965, replacing the former Army Service Center that was moved to the campus as a union just after World War II. This 1965 structure was surrounded by new construction to create the University Union of 1976.

Dr. Imogene Dickey Mohat came to the faculty in the summer of 1943 as Imogene Bentley and became dean of women in 1944. Known to students as "Big Red," she served as one of the campus's major administrative forces in that post until 1968, when she returned to teaching English full time.

Probably the most widely known unit of the School of Music for many years was the Lab Band. Dr. Gene Hall founded it in 1947 as the laboratory for a "dance-band program," which he directed until 1959. The many jazz bands in this program performed in Europe, North and South America, and Australia over the years. Here the One O'Clock Lab Band Director Leon Breeden and band leader Stan Kenton prepare for a thirty-minute performance introduced by Kenton and televised in Los Angeles in 1966.

(middle and bottom right) The old-style training in business brought images of training of typists. An IBM 1620 arrived on campus and was installed in the Business Administration Building, signaling the start of a major technological change that would reach the entire campus within three decades. Dr. C. L. Littlefield, shown here with the IBM 1620, chaired the first computing group in 1962.

part VI

Changing the Guard in Changing Times

1968–1971

chapter 28

A Time of Rapid Change

a large number of problems were carried over from the past at North Texas State University. Obviously, not all of these can be solved in one or even two year's time. To an extraordinary extent, however, President Kamerick has moved, in conjunction with the faculty, to make the decisions and to create the structures to solve these problems. Because of his evident ability, his sincere concern for faculty members as individuals, and his transparent goal of fairness for all, there is no man on the campus who evokes even a small fraction of the confidence that both faculty members and students have in President Kamerick. Last year we said, in effect, that his credentials were excellent; this year we can add that his relationship with the faculty has been superb.

NTSU CHAPTER, AAUP, 1969

The decade of the 1960s had started calmly enough. There was little on the Denton campus to suggest that turbulence lay ahead. North Texas State College got its new name in 1961. Metropolitan-area population growth provided no future for the quiet rural model of the normal school and the teachers college. But few were looking ahead to the kind of turbulence that would come in 1968, the kinds of events in the world, in the nation, and on American campuses that led *Time* magazine to label it "the year that shaped a generation" and "a knife blade that separated past from future."[1]

Faculty dissatisfaction with inability to participate in academic decision-making grew steadily. Student leaders, especially those elected to office in the United Students of North Texas, sensed that student activism was on the rise and that they had few prospects of following the trend.

THE IMPACT OF A RETIREMENT

Plans for the retirement of Matthews were made public in August 1967. This news set off a flurry of activity among faculty members anxious to find a role in the process. Their concerns were recognized within two months by the report of the board's Special Committee on the Selection of a President. Wooten appointed Regents E. C. Pannell, Fort Worth, chairman; Dean Davis, Austin; David Kimbell, Wichita Falls; and A. M. Willis, Longview. The board chairman automatically served as a member.

The committee reported to the full board on October 19, 1967. They announced the creation of an advisory committee of eleven faculty members, the president of the student body, and the alumni president. They asked this group to "appraise the nature of the presidency of the university and to suggest the desirable qualities and qualifications in potential candidates."

Four committee members were appointed by President Matthews: John Carter, fiscal vice president; Robert Sherman, chairman of the Division of Science; John Carrell, School of Business Administration; and Dwane Kingery, dean of the School of Education. Faculty elections named Kendall Cochran, economics; Silas Griggs, English; C. L. Littlefield, business administration; Paul F. Smith, education; Ellen Wright, home economics; and Miles Anderson, physics. Ex officio members were Charles Dixon, United Students of North Texas, and H. G. Wells, alumni representative.

Dr. Anderson was elected chairman of the group. In an oral history interview,[2] he revealed a process that began with considerable distrust: faculty members distrusted the president and the board, the board distrusted a faculty that was prone to express unpopular views. An early friction point was a vote by the NTSU TACT chapter asking that regents restrict their search to persons not then on the NTSU faculty or staff. This generated resentment by some board members, but it became clear to all that the regents would search as widely as possible throughout the nation.

Anderson also revealed some early hostility by arts and sciences faculty toward candidates from either education or business administration. Many of the early fears faded as the committee began describing what the university president does and what major priorities for the future should be. Anderson's account and the written report of the committee[3] show the needs judged to be of major importance:

1. Provide comprehensive and systematic planning of educational programs to stress unity, so that the arts and sciences could develop much of the strength that had been developed independently in the professional schools: music, education, and business administration.

2. Improve the image of the university, which is still widely regarded as a teachers college even though having developed to the point where the quality and breadth of the university's academic programs are underrated.

3. Open channels of communication among the units of the university, providing more involvement for faculty and students in the life of the university. Provide more communication with alumni, with metropolitan area leaders, and with "men of national eminence in diverse fields."

4. Overcome funding limitations by clear representation of the university's stature before state funding authorities, by searching for funding from widely diversified private and public sources, and by enlisting the alumni in financial support of the university.

With board acceptance of this report, Committee Chairman Pannell asked Anderson to choose two other faculty members to join the board committee to screen candidates. Anderson named Cochran and Smith. Regents' inquiries and faculty suggestions provided seventy-five potential candidates for screening.

Committee deliberation reduced this list to ten names, three of those having been selected by all eight panel members. In this group was the name of Dr. John J. Kamerick, academic vice president at Kent State University in Kent, Ohio. He was the first of nine candidates to be interviewed.[4] Anderson described the final procedure: "the booklet from ACE had suggested that the next step was to visit high-ranking candidates in their own home grounds, their own home territory. . . it was unanimous to visit Dr. Kamerick at Kent and then maybe a couple of others after that. But we'd wait and see what happened."

Pannell, Kimbell, and Anderson visited the Kent campus, spending two days talking to those who knew Kamerick's work. After their return, the decision took form: "Invite him and his wife to come down, and if they can be sold, let's stop the search."

On May 8 a press conference was held in the president's office to introduce the president-designate to news reporters and photographers. A University Day Assembly had already been scheduled for that morning, and Dr. Kamerick was introduced to the student and faculty public at that gathering.

This process was of considerable significance in the development of the university. It involved regents and faculty representatives in a joint effort in a way that had never been done before. Each group gained a greater understanding of the role of the other group than had been possible previously; there was greater respect and less suspicion than before. These factors doubtless facilitated the tasks that would face the new president starting in September 1968.

John Kamerick's education, his teaching experience, and his administrative career took place in the Midwest—in the states of Iowa and Ohio. He thus brought a fresh perspective to the North Texas campus. But he also faced a political environment quite unlike those in which he had worked.

Kamerick received the bachelor's degree in general science and philosophy from St. Ambrose College and his master's and doctoral degrees in history from the University of Iowa. He joined Kent State in 1956 as assistant dean of the College of Arts and Sciences after teaching history at the State University of Iowa and Marycrest College in Davenport, Iowa. In 1960 he became dean of the College of Fine and Professional Arts, and was named vice president and dean of faculties in 1963. He became vice president and provost in 1966.[5]

A NEW ADMINISTRATIVE STYLE

The presidency of John Kamerick would be brief, but his impact would prove to be out of all proportion to the time he spent at North Texas. Three revolutionary changes occurred: a change in administrative style marked by greater delegation to other administrators, a change in philosophy of the faculty role in university governance, and a new approach to student life that was greatly influenced by societal turbulence of the times.

THE CABINET CONCEPT

Nine days after taking office President Kamerick assembled the three vice presidents he inherited from the Matthews administration and organized them into the President's Cabinet. Members were John L. Carter, fiscal affairs; James L. Rogers, administrative affairs; and James J. Spurlock, academic affairs. The new president advised them that he wanted to meet at least biweekly and would use the cabinet as his principal structure for communication and decision-making at the top administrative level. An Administrative Council would be formed soon to include administrators who reported to vice presidents.

But above all, Kamerick said, the group faced "the need for developing machinery for greater faculty participation in the decision-making process."[6] In rapid-fire order he listed some other early goals of his administration:

• Membership in the National Association of State Universities and Land Grant Colleges.

• A North Texas chapter of Phi Beta Kappa.

• Improvement of communication on campus, including a single newsletter sent to all constituencies.

• Recognition of faculty achievement by selecting a faculty speaker for winter commencement.

• Creation of awards for good teaching.

• Student participation in curriculum planning.

• Creation of a student discipline review board.

• End of mandatory faculty attendance at commencement, replaced by attendance of ten percent of faculty on a rotating basis.

• Consideration of the proposal to create a University of Texas at Dallas, which he asked Rogers to discuss at the fall's first faculty meeting.

He also asked for a different pattern of involvement for the three vice presidents, whom he asked to attend all board meetings, assume approvals (formerly presidential) for items such as travel fund requests, sit on the stage at the fall faculty meeting and at commencements, and in general take over routine paperwork processing and approvals from the president.[7]

At the second cabinet meeting two weeks later, still more targets for early action were listed.[8]

• Faculty election of a group to plan faculty participation in institutional affairs.

• Collection of regulations by the vice presidents for a faculty handbook and an academic policy handbook.

• Establishment of a university press.

• Improvement of Union Building facilities and services.

• Thorough attention to a campus security plan.

• Programs for keeping regents informed.

• A minority student counseling program.

• Attention to discrimination in off-campus housing.

The new president was listening attentively to large numbers of faculty members and students, seeking to show responsiveness to suggestions and complaints. The list of ideas for changes, improvements, and new methods grew rapidly. By October, this administrative wish list included these ideas:[9]

• Investigate adding physical education facilities to the Coliseum.

• Move classes out of the Union Building.

• Review the fate of the Laboratory School and plan alternate use of its buildings.

• Establish a committee for academic space planning and nonacademic space use.

• Use stadium parking lot during class days.

• Improve condition of golf course and clubhouse.

• Establish policy for creating endowed chairs.

• Seek board action to establish a foundation for receiving gifts to the university.

Old-timers who needed definitive evidence that the winds of change were blowing strongly needed only to read one sentence from the cabinet minutes for that third session: "The use of nude models in life drawing classes in art was approved by President Kamerick."[10]

KAMERICK AND THE FACULTY

The establishment of faculty governance called for the faculty to elect a Committee on Faculty Participation, which was named in November.[11] Members were Hershel Anderson, Sam Barton, Kendall Cochran, John Douthitt, H. W. Kamp, Gerald Kirk, vice chairman, C. L. Littlefield, James Mahoney, David McGuire, Clovis Morrisson, Jack Scroggs, Paul Smith, chairman, Harry Snapp, and G. R. Vela.

The committee was asked to produce an organizational charter for board action in February and election of members before the end of the 1968–69 academic year. A proposed charter for a Faculty Senate was, indeed, ready for consideration at the board meeting of February 6, 1969.

Three other committees brought policy documents before the board at the same time. These were a faculty tenure statement, a policy on recognition of campus clubs, and a code of student conduct. Such substantial changes proved too much for the board to act upon at a single meeting. Action on all four documents was deferred for consideration on March 7 by a special board committee that would report to the next board meeting on March 14.[12]

The tenure statement was based on a set of Coordinating Board guidelines.[13] A faculty vote approved it and it was adopted by the regents with several amendments by the regents' special committee. It was a standard approach to tenure policy, following standards of AAUP and the Association of American Colleges.

Regent Dean Davis proposed an amendment to stipulate that adequate cause for faculty dismissal would include not only incompetence, moral turpitude, or neglect of professional responsibilities but also "actions or statements by a faculty member which demonstrate a lack of academic responsibility as imposed by Section II hereof."[14] The amended statement was approved 6–0.

A similar vote approved the Faculty Senate Charter as recommended by the board committee. Two changes had been made in the approval process that reserved more clearly the powers of the university president and of the Board of Regents. One change said actions of the Faculty Senate were not final until approved by the president, subject to the regulations of the Board of Regents. The regents also added a stipulation that their approval was necessary for any amendment to the charter or its bylaws.[15]

The senate was empowered to decide and promulgate academic policy except tenure and review policy. President Kamerick added one qualifying sentence to this power: "Such policies become official when published in the President's Bulletin," a statement that gave him added control. The senate could consider all other "matters of general welfare to the university," with the actions not final until approved as stipulated above. Membership was to be forty-eight voting senators, forty elected from groupings of the instructional units and eight elected by and from the faculty at large, apportioned by academic rank.

The first senate was elected in May, just before the close of the 1969 spring semester, and the historic first meeting came on May 28. The charter designated the university president as the senate president, so the presiding faculty officer was known as the vice president. Dr. Jack Cross of the education faculty was elected to this post.

Kamerick described the senate as "the primary voice of the faculty in expressing convictions or opinions on a wide range of topics of campus-wide significance," enabling individual representatives to consider the health of the entire university community when making decisions instead of merely the health of one department or division. "The walls can be high in the departments," he told a student writer. "One of the great things I hope for is that the Faculty Senate will move people out of their tight shells into wider circles of association. The old idea of the university held together by the heating system has to go."[16]

The senate named a University Committee as an executive committee to carry on senate business between meetings. Shortly after the first meeting, Kamerick wrote to the University Committee suggesting a policy-setting agenda for the senate.[17]

> I have deliberately avoided the creating of policies which are properly academic until the Faculty Senate could be organized and create the necessary committees for appropriate work.
>
> This partial listing is intended to indicate areas in which some policies may be necessary.
>
> 1 organization of instructional departments
> 2 consultative process for appointment of new faculty members
> 3 class absences
> 4 admission

5 field trips
6 credit by examination
7 procedure for curricular change
8 promotion criteria
9 definition of rank and titles
10 cheating
11 fund raising and sales
12 academic dismissal
13 library policies
14 probation status for students
15 research policy, including patents and copyrights
16 transfer from one college or school to another within the university
17 outside employment
18 conflict of interest in government sponsored research.

STATUS OF THE FACULTY

Problems other than governance faced the faculty. Questions of salary, work load, and fringe benefits were also of concern. The report of salaries according to the AAUP grading scale for 1968–69 portrays the status:

No.	Rank	Salary	Compensation	AAUP Grade
144	Professor	$15,776	$16,119	C
114	Associate	$13,017	$13,360	B
202	Assistant	$10,726	$11,069	A
131	Instructor	$8,403	$8,746	A
All ranks average		$11,884	$12,227	

Salaries were improved by the following year, and the AAUP compensation grades rose accordingly. For 1969–70 the compensation averages by rank and the AAUP grades were professor, $17,620, C; associate professor, $14,381, A; assistant professor, $11,991, A; and instructor, $9,536, AA.[18] The higher grades for compensation were based on the Texas Teacher Retirement System and Social Security contributions. Group insurance payments, sabbatical leaves, and lighter teaching loads had not yet been achieved. A committee created by President Kamerick in June 1969 reported in April 1970 a group of recommendations for improvement of faculty fringe benefits, noting that many of these would require legislative authorization and appropriation:

1. Establish responsibility in the Personnel Office to administer fringe benefits.
2. Provide transferability of retirement annuities from other schools under new optional retirement program.
3. Create a Faculty Club.
4. Provide a recreation area on Garza-Little Elm Reservoir.
5. Provide state financing of:
    a. Health and life insurance
    b. Money for sabbatical leave program
    c. Free parking
    d. Free tuition for faculty families
6. Office space for retired faculty.
7. General legal counseling for faculty.

The Texas Legislature in 1967 had authorized a program of faculty development leaves but declined to appropriate funds for that purpose. Regents approved the broad authorization for such a program in May 1970, and the president announced that "a modest number of development leaves will be available to the faculty in 1970–71," with leaves having to be funded by adjustments in scheduling and in class and section size, and employment of temporary personnel at less than full faculty member replacement cost.[19] A committee developed leave operating policies, and these were endorsed by the senate.[20]

President Matthews had helped hold down administrative costs by assigning many support duties to the faculty. Probably the most dreaded of these was working for several days of registration each semester. This included the mechanical tasks of signing up students for classes, assessing tuition and fees, and general clerical staffing. It took a year for the budget to be adjusted, but relief came in October 1969, when Vice President Spurlock announced the hiring of one hundred individuals to handle registration duties, freeing faculty members for departmental counseling.[21]

MORE ADMINISTRATIVE STRUCTURES

As promised in the first cabinet meeting, Kamerick created an Administrative Council of fifteen members: the president, vice presidents, student deans, academic deans, registrar, business manager, and others who reported to vice presidents. The first agenda included discussions of campus security, dormitory fire drills, longer library hours, extending dormitory curfew hours past 10:50 P.M. on weeknights, security of registrar's records from fire, starting a campus mail delivery service, the need for a new student union, code of student conduct, new dormitory regulations, handling of student hot checks, and proposals to create a University of Texas at Dallas.[22]

Kamerick assigned the dean of students in January 1969 to report directly to the president, assuming responsibility for the deans of men and women, guidance, health service, placement, Union Building, and student activities. While President Matthews had kept close supervision of physical plant administration through an "assistant to the president and resident engineer," Kamerick separated himself from such details. The man in that office, John Matt Howard, became simply "resident engineer" reporting to the fiscal vice president.

Kamerick found no clear role assignment for the three division chairmen in the College of Arts and Sciences. He asked that one become an associate dean in the Graduate School for research and sponsored programs and that another become an associate dean in the College of Arts and Sciences. At the same time, the Department of Economics and Sociology was divided into two departments after Coordinating Board approval.[23] In August 1969 Dr. Miles Anderson of the physics faculty was named associate vice president for academic affairs.

A classified personnel office was created to recruit nonfaculty employees and to develop a fair compensation system. Joseph L. Mitchell was named director of the unit.[24] The Personnel Office was given oversight of equal employment opportunity and of compliance reviews for the U.S. Department of Health, Education, and Welfare. Concern for fire safety, especially in dormitories and the hospital, led to creation of a Fire, Safety, and Sanitation Department. The earlier proposals to install an IBM System 360 mainframe computer led to establishment of a University Computing Center for both academic and administrative uses.

The Placement Office, traditionally concerned with teacher placement, was merged with the Business Employment Service. The business offices were authorized to close on Saturday morning. Offices of registrar and admissions closed on Saturdays when an information center was set up in the Administration Building foyer. Cafeterias in some dormitories were scheduled for closing, with residents assigned to eat in other halls. Twice-daily deliveries and pickups of intracampus mail and of outgoing U. S. mail were instituted. New freshmen were scheduled for two-day summer orientation conferences preparing for the 1969 fall semester.

The state Coordinating Board forced another change by adopting a statewide uniform academic calendar. North Texas was the last school in Texas to adopt it, beginning in the fall of 1970. The fall semester began in late August rather than in September and ended before Christmas rather than in mid-January. The spring semester started in mid-January rather than in February and ended in mid-May rather than about June 1. The summer session was cut from twelve to eleven weeks, with class periods running for ninety rather than eighty minutes daily. As one consequence, winter commencement ceremonies were abandoned.[25]

POWER TO THE DEANS

Kamerick's experience as provost at Kent State predisposed him to depend on deans to work directly with the academic vice president. The position of the deans remained cloudy during 1968-69. They were members of the Administrative Council, a group concerned mostly with coordination and communication. The charter excluded deans from membership in the Faculty Senate, and their ability to influence academic activities was fairly restricted. In June 1969 Kamerick wrote to Vice President Spurlock to suggest a remedy. The wording of the memo is rather revealing of the president's approach to working with his vice presidents.[26]

> When the Committee on Faculty Participation took the action of excluding deans from membership in the Faculty Senate, it seemed to me at the time it would be necessary to have an advisory committee to you so the administrative voice would not be ignored. While I shall leave this to your judgment, it would seem to me at the minimum a council could be formed which operated under your chairmanship and included all of the academic deans for the discussion of administrative

> procedures and policy questions. On the other hand you may believe this can be achieved through the existence of the Curriculum Committee.

The deans began meeting with the vice president in the fall of 1969, directed by Spurlock that "for the time being the role of the council relative to Faculty Senate actions will remain unofficial. The council will review senate legislation, and will provide the president with a copy of the summaries of its meetings."[27] Kamerick wrote two days later to Cross as "cochairman" of the Senate.

> The Faculty Senate. . . will be dealing with many matters. . . of vital importance to. . . academic administrators. . . . I believe the University would benefit as well as the faculty Senate from a joint cooperation between. . . academic administrators and members of the Faculty Senate; therefore, it would seem most desirable that the Faculty Senate in making recommendations secure the opinion and enlist the cooperation of academic administrators prior to final actions.
>
> While it may take longer for final actions to be achieved, I do believe in the long run the result will be much better.[28]

In January the president announced the creation of the Council of Academic Deans. Spurlock was chairman and the associate vice president was secretary. Kamerick's statement of duties for the council made clear that the Senate was expected to share academic power with this administrative body. His charge said it would have these duties:[29]

> 1. Interpret academic policy concerning admission, academic standards, and degree requirements.
>
> 2. Advise the president and academic vice president on academic matters.
>
> 3. Develop uniform administrative practices for implementing academic policy.
>
> 4. Serve as an appeals board on academic questions.
>
> 5. Serve as an advisory and resource group for senate committees studying academic legislation.

6. Cooperate with the senate to draft academic policy and make policy recommendations to the president.

7. Initiate research on academic matters.

The senate continued to worry about possible loss of privileges to either the academic vice president or the deans. The University Committee responded to Kamerick that it agreed with the need for mutual cooperation and exchange and suggested that the deans' meetings be open to observers from the senate or even that the senate could elect one of its members "to insure efficient liaison between the two bodies."[30] Kamerick, in turn, wrote the Council of Deans to suggest the possibility that the council could exchange liaison members with the senate. "It might indeed be possible to invite the Co-Chairman of the Faculty Senate to sit in as a member of the Council of Deans and designate some member of the Council of Deans to be liaison with the Faculty Senate. These are only suggestions, however."[31] Ultimately, this proved to be a workable procedure.

At one point in this running struggle (in late April), the president wrote the deans, "I know many of you are also concerned about the larger question involving areas of jurisdiction, particularly of the Deans Council and the Faculty Senate. As I am responsible for the creation of both, I recognize my obligation. In a subsequent, rather lengthy document I shall address myself to this matter."[32]

Apparently this document was not produced, but the president did meet with the Council of Deans just four days after sending that memo. On May 1 Kamerick told the deans he would prefer that the role of the council evolve rather than be defined in advance. He did say that the deans' council should be a major source for policy creation, "operating on an equal footing with the Faculty Senate." He also asked that more policy-making authority be delegated to the level of the college. Kamerick expressed a hope that the Council of Deans could initiate structural changes, listing as examples:

1. Establishment of an honors unit.
2. Creation of new academic units.
3. Possible division and/or realignment of existing units.
4. Initiation of new programs (and perhaps deletion of old ones).

"The influence of departments in some matters is too great. . . there is a need for restoring a greater degree of unity to the University, strengthening its more universal features, probably at the expense of departments," Kamerick was quoted as saying.[33]

SALARY, EQUITY, AND ADMINISTRATIVE POWER

Among many faculty members who had chafed under strong presidential powers, the question of peer review of promotion, salary, and tenure became paramount in planning their new-found participatory roles. For some, it heightened the resistance to perceived intervention by dean or vice president between faculty action and presidential approval.

Even before Kamerick arrived, an AAUP committee urged reform in setting faculty salaries. Its report suggested that in place of a merit system, faculty salaries and promotions were based on personal and subjective evaluations by selected administrators.[34] The AAUP group recommended placing a salary budget in the library and electing departmental committees to recommend promotions and salary increases.

In October the president of the AAUP chapter, Dr. Harry F. Snapp, transmitted two resolutions from the AAUP chapter. One urged the president to establish a policy to inform a faculty member of any negative criticism "in writing at least one week prior to any discussion or use of it that the director or the departmental committee might make relative to promotions or salary raises."[35]

The second AAUP resolution urged that a faculty member who "openly advocates for consideration a policy at variance with that of his department director or dean" shall not be accused of being uncooperative, and for some director, chairman or dean to do so would be "prima-face [sic] evidence of the violation of the faculty member's academic freedom."

President Kamerick replied to the resolutions quickly, turning the AAUP governance principles back at them: "The president should make as little policy unilaterally as possible. I am anxious for the policy to be created by faculty bodies, by student bodies, by administrative groups, or by mixtures of all three."[36]

In January 1969, the Committee on Faculty Participation asked for election of an interim review committee. This was chosen in February from the various academic units "to review questions concerning salaries, promotions, and related matters that any faculty member might bring before it."[37] The temporary committee insisted that it should report its recommendations directly to the president, but Kamerick responded that the academic vice president must be "a part of any adjudication arrived at by the committee."[38]

A permanent review committee charter was adopted in January 1970, dedicated to "more equitable allocation of salary and rank, and to more just decisions on other faculty matters."[39] One of its early actions was to recommend the basis for actions in setting faculty salaries for the next year. In this case the committee agreed with the deans but was opposed by the president. The review group and the deans' council both wanted salary recommendations based on merit and adjustment of inequity. Kamerick wanted to start with a base increase reflecting years of service and inflation but conceded to the recommendations.[40]

Committee-administrative friction continued. Review Committee Chairman Sam Barton complained in May that faculty appeals directly to the academic vice president

> are more numerous and the settlements more generous than for cases appealed to our committee. . . . we are concerned with the possibility that the penurious and inadequate settlements frequently made to cases submitted through our Committee were necessitated by the reportedly numerous and more generous settlements negotiated directly with the Vice President.[41]

It was two months before Kamerick answered the complaint. The response offers a good view of the presidential effort to walk the tightrope of participatory governance:

> I have discussed this matter with Vice President Spurlock and he is in agreement with me that the work of the University Review Committee is absolutely essential. . . . He views the Committee as a place for faculty members to go when they have been unable to obtain satisfaction in any other way. . . .
>
> I believe, then, rather than viewing the matter competitively, an adjustment can be made which would view the work of the Committee and the academic vice president as cooperative and complementary.[42]

Its first annual report showed it had held forty-five meetings concerning sixteen cases. Three went to formal hearings and settlements were obtained without hearings in others. The committee became defensive at one point:[43]

> Contrary to reports circulated by some members of the faculty, the Committee does not begin with the assumption that the appellant is always right but that the appellant always has a right to a fair hearing . . . . The U.R.C.'s judgment is based on the preponderance of documented facts developed in our investigation and our recommendations to the administration are supported by the information developed.

COMMITTEES, COMMITTEES, COMMITTEES

Based on a committee he had chaired at Kent State, Kamerick appointed the four cabinet officers, the resident engineer, five faculty members, and three students to a Space Planning Committee, chaired by Rogers. The group recommended assignment of space to academic and administrative departments.[44] Rogers was also assigned to lead another committee to study improving and expanding the union.

It took longer, but in March 1970 the Academic Master Plan Committee was formed as recommended by Vice President Spurlock. It included eight faculty members, three students, one regent, one alumnus, and four administrators, plus the academic vice president as chairman.[45]

In July Kamerick asked an administrative assistant to compile for him a list of committees he had established in his first year. This list included for 1968–69 the Cabinet, Administrative Council, Faculty Senate, Graduate Student Council, and committees on academic standards, disciplinary review, disciplinary readmissions, admission of culturally disadvantaged students, student conduct, establishment of a code of student conduct, admission charges to students for university facilities, communication, convocations, faculty participation, freshman orientation, interim review, recreation and leisure facilities, space planning, university press, and University Store. Thirteen of these showed student membership.

THE SENATE AT WORK

The senate opened its first academic year in September 1969 by creating an

Academic Standards Committee, a Curriculum Committee, a Committee for Compensation and Fringe Benefits, and a Faculty Research Committee.[46]

These were followed in October by the University Election and the Alumni Citations Selection Committees and in April by Committees on Student Recruitment, Faculty Salary Study, Scholarship, and University Tenure.[47] The Graduate Council in March 1970 was made a creature of the Faculty Senate.[48]

University committees were usually appointed rather than elected. In 1969 the Committee on Committees named members for committees on Charter and Bylaws, Faculty Load, Honors Program, Sabbatical Leave Policy, Student Publications, Student Activities, Promotion Criteria, Alumni Citation Selection, Graduate Council, Faculty Salary Study, Faculty Participation in Departmental Governance, Student Recruitment, Scholarship, University Tenure, Academic Standards, Criteria for Promotion, Athletics, Fine Arts and Lectures, Campus Clubs, Curriculum, Compensation and Fringe Benefits, University Election, and Faculty Research.

Kamerick asked the senate to name Spurlock as ex officio chairman of the committee studying faculty load ("of greatest importance, at least financially") and to work with the vice president as a consultant to the committee on criteria for promotion.[49] Kamerick also wrote the Faculty Election Committee in May 1970 to require that a faculty member with rank in a department retain voting privileges in all elections even though he might have an administrative position.[50]

POWER WITHIN THE DEPARTMENT

Faculty usually objected to concentration of decision-making power in a department director or dean as much as they did for a president or vice president. The Committee on Faculty Participation created interim guidelines for faculty participation while still working on the senate charter. This provided that "department director" should become "chairman."[51] Each department was to have at least five elected committees plus an executive committee. Chairmen's duties were to be carried out "with the advice and counsel of the departmental faculty." Appointment of chairmen was to be made from nominees submitted by the departmental faculty. Deans would be appointed after "advice and consultation with the appropriate faculty."[52]

A pattern of division of authority began to emerge: university wide, the faculty gained control of much academic policy, especially that affecting salary, tenure, and promotion. The Council of Deans also emerged as a new power center, exerting considerable force in its own right, often exercising more real and immediate control over academic affairs than the Faculty Senate. Within the department, faculty influence made its strongest gains. No longer would there be a group of powerful chairmen, each with virtually a life contract for the position.

PROGRAM CHANGES

The new governance pattern led to the creation of some new units and organizational changes in others. In the School of Education, the Department of Education in 1969 created divisions of elementary education, secondary education, educational leadership, counselor education, interprofessional studies, and higher education.[53] That action was preceded by one of the more controversial moves: removal of psychology from the education department to the College of Arts and Sciences.[54] The School of Business Administration was changed to the College of Business Administration in 1970, and its degree fields became separate departments: accounting, finance, insurance and real estate, marketing, communication, international business, personnel management, industrial relations and law, business education, and management and decision sciences.[55]

Also in 1970 the Department of Library Service was designated an autonomous School of Library and Information Sciences.[56] In April 1970, the government department became the Department of Political Science.

BUILDING FOR THE FUTURE

"We have time to build North Texas into the graduate center of this area," President Kamerick told a TACT dinner meeting in February 1969. "We already have a higher percentage of graduate students than any other school in the state, including the University of Texas."[57] This would require both major curriculum additions and expanded campus construction.

Matthews worked on the details of planning and construction; Kamerick preferred that these be delegated under his very broad supervision. He supported the campus plan implementation, and it fell his lot to be in office when the first major street closings became necessary. He did not enter personally into negotiations with the city nor did he appear before the Planning and Zoning Commission and the City Council.

In May 1969, the university asked the city to close Maple Street between Avenue D and E for construction of a coliseum. The mayor of Denton was Zeke Martin, a former Eagle quarterback and strong backer of athletics. He endorsed this closing as vital to the athletic program, and the City Council voted to close the street that summer.

Who Owns the Streets?

That summer the issue of major street closings came to full public attention. The May 1967 campus plan emphasized the importance of a pedestrian-oriented campus:

> The circulation plan is based upon maximum reduction of pedestrian-vehicle conflicts and the development of a comprehensively planned system of walks for pedestrian traffic, and to unify the many outdoor spaces on the campus.
>
> Cross traffic must be eliminated by closing campus streets as shown on the plan. Several stages of "auto withdrawal" could be planned to coincide with the development of new buildings. . . .[58]

NTSU in July asked the Planning and Zoning Commission to abandon these streets:

- Chestnut Street, Avenue A to Avenue C,
- Avenue B, Chestnut to Mulberry and Maple to Highland,
- Sycamore, B to C.

Under Texas law, for the university plan to function, the university had to own land on both sides of a street to be closed. The problems came, however, from property owners who believed that a closed campus might damage public access to their property. At public hearings, protests came from owners of businesses on Avenue A, Hickory, and Fry Street, and from those on Highland Avenue and southward who feared the loss of access from the north.

Faced with such vocal opposition, the Planning and Zoning Commission tabled the NTSU request on September 3 and then on November 21 denied the request. The university appealed to the City Council on December 9, referring to three years of joint planning with the city. The university said, "We will be asking that many more blocks of streets be abandoned in the years ahead in order to create the final form of the campus that you see in the master plan."[59]

The City Council approved the street closing on April 28, 1970. This came near the end of Kamerick's term and left the problem of Avenue A to the acting presidency of John Carter.

NEW SOURCES OF MONEY

The major changes of 1968–70 greatly increased costs over the spartan standards of the Matthews administration. Matthews had often said that he believed state-supported schools should be fully funded from public funds, either state or federal, that private fund-raising should be left to private schools. He had also opposed the extension of any form of tax-generated funds, whether state or federal funds going to private and church-supported colleges and universities.

Seeking Private Money

It wasn't surprising that pressures for change facing Kamerick included the demand for formal organizational steps to solicit private funding.

The new president perceived that enrollment-driven state funding would lag still further with major shifts in enrollment patterns. New junior college districts in Dallas and Tarrant Counties immediately impacted NTSU. As late as 1966, the enrollment at North Texas was fifty-six percent lower division (freshmen and sophomores). By the spring semester of 1969 that percentage had dropped to thirty-seven. Kamerick said, "As the mix shifts to upper level and graduate work, education becomes more expensive. A different type of faculty is required. North Texas is spending less per student than any private school in the area. We spend roughly 70 to 75 percent as much to educate as do the private schools. This produces internal strains. We will turn to all possible sources of revenue—federal, alumni, and private sectors. "[60]

In his second month, Kamerick asked for the creation of a foundation to receive gifts and in January he showed an organization plan to include development, community relations, and alumni relations. In January 1970, he assigned work on a North Texas State University Foundation, to be proposed to the June meeting of the regents.[61] In March, a consulting firm, Frantzreb and

Pray Associates, was hired to study the fund-raising needs and potential of the university. The company presented a development planning audit in June.

Results of the audit were not surprising. The consultant called for an immediate change in institutional attitudes toward private fund development. Major recommendations included:

1. Create a foundation for fund-raising activities for annual, capital, and deferred gifts from individuals and businesses.

2. Create a foundation board of trustees.

3. Create a case for philanthropic support for all levels of giving.

4. Create an experienced professional staff.

5. Centralize all volunteer relations: fund-raising efforts, records, acknowledgments, and reporting procedures.[62]

The project led to the employment of a director of development for the fall of 1970, the creation of an educational foundation and board of trustees, and some very slow beginnings into the philanthropic support area.

Increased Federal Emphasis

Washington programs had become vital to all colleges and universities. NTSU sought legislation to increase or to add interest subsidies on college housing loans, graduate programs for "developing" institutions, grant and direct loan funds for academic facilities construction, grants for science education, Korean and Cold War veterans assistance, and strengthened doctoral programs.

This led to a contract with a Washington consulting firm to assist in "securing, expediting, developing, or directing" more federal funds into programs that would help NTSU. Kamerick described the group as "the Washington office of the university."[63]

But Don't Forget Austin

The Texas Legislature remained the primary support for basic university programs, and it was in Austin that most developmental activity had to be concentrated. As a Midwesterner, Kamerick faced formidable obstacles in developing appropriate governmental acquaintances and in familiarizing himself with the state bureaucratic machinery.

The 1969 legislative session was the new president's first Texas experience. For basic appropriations requests, he continued to rely upon John Carter, who had become widely known and trusted among most personnel in the state capital. The appropriations campaigns continued to rely heavily on cooperation through organizations of state university governing boards, presidents, and business officers.

After one of his first steps in the appropriations process, Kamerick described recommendations from the Legislative Budget Board as disappointing, noting that North Texas had lost more than $2 million in one year and $3 million in another from the amounts requested by the university.[64]

"DEAR GOVERNOR"

The governor appoints state boards and can wield great influence on campuses in his appointment of one-third of the nine-man Board of Regents every two years. In September 1968, when Lieutenant-Governor Preston Smith had won the Democratic Party primary, the just-installed NTSU president sent him North Texas football tickets and invited him to dinner.[65] Smith took office as governor in January 1969. Kamerick wrote him a congratulatory letter on January 7, complimenting him on his interest in Texas college students. On February 27 the president reported to the governor the steps he had taken to "promote the active participation of students in roles of responsibility."[66]

With the May appointment date for North Texas regents approaching, the new governor would soon reappoint three board members or appoint new regents who were not a party to the selection of Kamerick. In March Kamerick wrote the governor about the make-up of the board, but such a letter is not found in the University Archives. An often-told story at that time reported that the new man from Ohio had written to ask Governor Smith to consider the appointment of three "more liberal" regents. This was said to be a political blunder that alienated both the governor and the regents whom he told. The story may be apocryphal, but Kamerick's letter did draw a response from the governor:

> Dear John:
>
> I do appreciate your concern over the make-up of the Regents and want you to know that I share your concern. I will work with you in every way to see that we secure the services of the most qualified people available.
>
> I am keeping an open mind on possible appointees and will be happy

> to visit with you concerning same at any time. However, I would prefer to postpone a meeting until after my tax problems are solved.[67]

Within a few weeks the governor did see Kamerick in Austin to discuss board appointments.[68] The following fall, when the regents were finally selected, Kamerick wrote Smith that "North Texas is most fortunate that such outstanding men have been asked to serve and have accepted."[69]

The new appointees were Berl E. Godfrey of Fort Worth, a former board member, Davie James Lawson of Dallas, and Gus F. Wortham of Houston. The group's organizational meeting was significant: Ben H. Wooten of Dallas retired from the board, having served for twenty years as the only chairman since North Texas was placed under its own governing board in 1949. To replace him as chairman, the board elected A. M. "Monk" Willis of Longview, a board member since 1965 and an active participant in the search for president in 1968.[70]

It was sometimes observed that President Kamerick's major problem was his inability to understand Texas politics. One faculty member reported to this writer that Kamerick met with the committee that had been elected to find his successor in 1971 and told them he "blew it" when he made it a practice to court Lt. Gov. Ben Barnes rather than Gov. Preston Smith. "I backed the wrong horse," he told the committee. "I thought Ben Barnes was the future of Texas politics."

THE RETURN TO IOWA

There was speculation at the time that frustration with the state political system would lead the relatively new president to move on. Campus rumors began in his second year of office to report that he was seeking a presidency back in more northerly, more familiar, academic climes. It was not a surprise for many faculty members to learn of his resignation. The political frustration shows in his letter of resignation to the Board of Regents in May 1970:

> This is a difficult letter for me to write. I hope, therefore, that you will excuse its brevity.
>
> Not too many days ago I was offered a position as President of a university in my home state of Iowa. Although there have been other

> opportunities to move this year, none were quite as attractive as this. After giving the matter very intense thought for several days, weighing the advantages and disadvantages to the institution and to me, I eventually accepted the offer.
>
> Many factors entered into my decision, as some of you will know. Perhaps none of them need to be mentioned but I will say that I did weigh the probability that someone else might be able to do more for North Texas State University with State Government than I.[71]

Relations with the faculty probably didn't influence his decision to leave, for most evidence showed favorable response to the new president. In October 1968, the regional conference of the AAUP sent to the Board of Regents a resolution of appreciation "for the outstanding leadership and example provided by President John J. Kamerick in implementing faculty participation in the governance of North Texas State University."[72] In the following year, the same group endorsed the action of the NTSU chapter of AAUP in nominating President Kamerick for the Alexander Meiklejohn Award for "the establishment and maintenance of an atmosphere of academic freedom."

After the first year of the Kamerick administration, AAUP officers wrote Wooten to express the great faculty satisfaction with the new president. They said:

> a large number of problems were carried over from the past. . . . To an extraordinary extent. . . . Kamerick has moved, in conjunction with the faculty, to make the decisions and to create the structures to solve these problems. Because of his evident ability, his sincere concern for faculty members as individuals, and his transparent goal of fairness for all, there is no man on the campus who evokes even a small fraction of the confidence that both faculty members and students have in President Kamerick. Last year we said, in effect, that his credentials were excellent; this year we can add that his relationship with the faculty has been superb.[73]

SEARCH FOR A SUCCESSOR

The president's resignation was announced on May 26, 1970. The executive councils of AAUP and TACT on May 27 rushed a memo to the Board of Regents stating that they

> wish to call to your attention the high esteem in which President Kamerick is held by the Faculty of N.T.S.U. and the faculty-wide as well as student approval of his conduct of University affairs, particularly his advocacy and implementation of faculty and student participation in framing University policy.
>
> Because of the success of President Kamerick's administration . . . we respectfully urge that . . . the Board of Regents follow again the same general policies and guidelines as those employed in the selection of President Kamerick.

At an executive session on May 28 the board accepted the resignation of Kamerick, who was to become president of the University of Northern Iowa. Chairman Willis then made this statement: "Mr. John Carter will be named as acting president at such time as Dr. Kamerick leaves. Mr. Carter shall serve in this capacity with the understanding that Mr. Carter does not aspire to the presidency of North Texas nor will he be considered when a president is finally determined."[74]

The board agreed to follow the procedure that had been used in selecting Kamerick, asked the president to call for faculty election of their representatives, and named as the regent members Willis, Dean Davis, Bruce Street, Davie James Lawson, and E. C. Pannell. The faculty chose ten members to serve on an advisory committee with five regents, two elected staff members, the president and vice president of the United Students of North Texas, and the president of the Alumni Association.[75] The faculty group elected a subcommittee to represent them in meetings with the full group. These were Jack Scroggs, chairman, Franklin L. Elder, Clifford Hutton, and H. W. Kamp.

A Board of Regents resolution cited Kamerick for becoming "nationally renowned for his administrative ability, his organizational insight, his unparalleled ability to engender admiration from faculty, students and board alike."[76]

chapter 29

Voices of Protest

Nineteen sixty-eight was a knife blade that severed past from future, Then from Now: the Then of triumphant postwar American power in the world, the Then of the nation's illusions of innocence and virtue, from the more complicated Now that began when the U .S. saw that it was losing a war it should not have been fighting in the first place, when the huge tribe of the young revolted against the nation's elders and authority, and when the nation finished killing its heroes.

Time 1968: The Year That Shaped a Generation

This was 1968, a year when the public watched as:

- Presidential candidate Robert Kennedy was assassinated.
- Civil Rights leader Martin Luther King was shot to death in Memphis, and in 125 cities across the nation Blacks turned to violence and rioting that lasted for a week.
- Chicago police battled young demonstrators outside the Democratic Convention as the nation watched on television.
- Unarmed civilians were shot to death by U.S. troops sweeping through the South Vietnamese village of My Lai.
- Lyndon Johnson announced on TV that he would not seek another term as president.
- Columbia University students staged a six-day occupation of university buildings; San Francisco State students carried on months of strikes, demonstrations and clashes with police; at Berkeley, student rioting led to a campus curfew.
- Richard Nixon was elected president on November 8, and at Christmas time the astronauts of Apollo 8 circled the moon.

The North Texas Board of Regents supported a new president in bringing greater involvement of the faculty; they also wanted the involvement of students in activities affecting them, but they feared an invasion of an alien "counterculture."

There was no unanimity among students or faculty about the spreading student activism in the country. There was no unanimity about many of the major issues, including the war, the selective service, and the civil rights movement.

STUDENT DEFIANCE UNWELCOME

Moving from Ohio into a politically, economically, and socially conservative state, John Kamerick was aware of the conflict between student agitation for change and Texans' fear of student violence. A Texas Poll revealed that eighty-one percent of Texans said students who defied college authorities should be expelled from school. And eighty-two percent said colleges and universities "should not give in to Negro leaders' demands that more Black students be admitted to these institutions whether or not they meet academic requirements."[1]

To deal with this, Kamerick sought commitment from regents, administrators, faculty, and students to a set of principles by which problems of student behavior could be judged. He had the dean of students, assistant to the president, and director of security meet with the Denton police chief "to formulate plans for insuring security of the campus." They proposed that the dean of students would deal with any "student disturbance, sit-in, lay-in, picketing, or any other student action that interferes with the normal operation of North Texas State University or interferes with the rights of other students."

The dean of students would first request students to disband and invite them to the office to discuss grievances. If students refused, the dean would "announce to participants that they have been suspended and will be removed by force," and ask the police chief to remove them from the campus.[2] Kamerick advised regents that this was as an interim measure.[3] Kamerick also asked the cabinet and other administrators to consider a recommendation to commission campus security staff as police officers with authority over traffic and public safety in the campus area.[4]

INVOLVE THE STUDENTS

In his first month in office, Kamerick promised changes. He planned a code of student behavior but it would not be aimed at curtailing student activists. "Although I condemn the extremes of student activism, I honestly must say that I think students have a lot on their side. I think it is proper for students to have more of a voice than they have had at many institutions in the past," Kamerick said.[5]

He asked the United Students of North Texas to help bring students into decision-making roles. His letter to Troy Phillips, the student president, was reprinted in full in the October 18 *Campus Chat*:

> I wish to enter into serious discussions on the role of the students in the University community. . . . we should in all universities move toward more formal institutionalized modes of student participation. . . .
>
> . . . in some matters students should have the dominant role in making decisions and determining policy; in other matters students should share authority equally with the faculty and/or the administration; in

> still others probably the major role must be assumed by the faculty and/or the administration. . . .
>
> [We] will need to know from USNT. . . how the students desire to participate in the governance of the University. . . .
>
> May I urge you to move quickly on these questions I have raised, not at the expense of thorough consideration, but quickly nonetheless.[6]

Students should have the dominant role in decision making, Phillips responded, in establishing Union Building policy, control of student publications, and the complete autonomy of USNT. Strong student sharing with the faculty was recommended in policies and programs of the Student Activities Committee, housing regulations, and student discipline decisions. He also asked for a "definite voice, but not total, or equal, control" in determining curriculum, admission requirements, and tenure of faculty.[7]

For reviewing policy, the president turned to William Lindley, the retired Air Force general whom President Matthews had named dean of students. Kamerick asked Lindley to review residence hall regulations, perhaps forming a committee to recommend on- and off-campus regulations and examine student involvement in disciplinary procedures. He wrote, "I am much concerned that our students be protected from discrimination in housing.[8]

He also asked Lindley to work with others on a policy for student groups inviting speakers to the campus. Because he wanted a written policy in place immediately, Kamerick supplied an interim policy for the dean of students to follow.

A CODE FOR STUDENTS

Kamerick also created an interim disciplinary review committee.[9] This was drafted at the president's request by John Carrell, faculty member in business law.[10] Lindley was asked to draft a proposed code of student conduct as soon as possible.[11] The dean of students provided the draft on November 26, explaining ,"at this stage it has been. . . approved by the USNT Senate Committee, as well as by Dr. Rogers."[12] The president circulated it for review by the President's Cabinet, the USNT Senate, and the Committee on Faculty Participation.[13]

The Lindley draft was not well received by the students or the faculty committee. Phillips wrote Kamerick with two pages of suggested changes that weren't reflected in the code draft. The faculty committee response was even more vehement. Chairman Paul Smith said that the fourteen members of the committee had unanimously approved seven pages of objections. He asked that the code be thoroughly rewritten by a committee that would include two faculty members and two students.[14] As first written, a faculty subcommittee wrote, the code "will alienate many reasonable students in that it will ultimately result in a student body existing in a state of fear and intimidation."[15]

On December 20 the president wrote to the faculty committee, "I am asking Vice President Rogers to convene the committee just as soon as possible after school reopens. I hope we can move rapidly to solve some of the differences which have appeared.[16]

The committee produced a new code rapidly. Members were B. J. Brabham and J. B. Smallwood (faculty); Lindley and M. C. Sutton (administrative); Ben Kressman, Troy Phillips, and Ellen Stricklin (students); and Rogers, chairman. The first portion defined misconduct subject to discipline:

1. Dishonesty such as cheating, plagiarism.

2. Forgery, alteration, or misuse of university documents.

3. Obstruction or disruption of university activities.

4. Physical abuse of any person on university property.

5. Theft of property or damage to property of the university or a member of the university community.

6. Violation of published policies or regulations.

7. Use, possession, or distribution of illegal narcotics or dangerous drugs.

8. Disorderly conduct or lewd, indecent, or obscene conduct or expression on university property.

9. Failure to comply with reasonable directions of university officials acting in the performance of their duties.

10. Discrimination against any person (race, color, religion, sex)

11. Conduct which adversely affects the student's responsibility as a member of the university community (first offense, admonition only).

The discipline code section defined the role of the dean of students, possible penalties, set up a committee on student conduct, and provided for hearing appeals.[17]

This document was part of the major policy package accepted by the board on March 14. These were the Statement on Faculty Tenure, the Faculty Senate

Charter, Policy on Recognition of Campus Clubs, and the Code of Student Conduct. The board added one feature: findings of the committee on student conduct could be appealed not just to the President's Cabinet but also to the Board of Regents.[18] The first committee was selected in April with John Carrell as chairman. One of the faculty representatives was Dr. Mary Evelyn Huey, who later became president of Texas Woman's University.[19]

WHO MAY GATHER HERE?

Recognition of campus clubs was an especially sensitive matter in the regents' perception. The basic issue was control over what activities could take place on the campus, that is, "on state property." They wanted to find legally enforceable means to prevent violence and to punish those who engaged in it. They did not want national groups like the Students for a Democratic Society or the Black Panthers openly active at North Texas. The key to control was right of access to campus facilities, and the way to control that was to limit access to recognized organizations. When the clubs policy reached a board committee, it recommended addition of a key paragraph reading, "The Campus Clubs Committee may consider the performance of a national organization in considering the application of a local unit of such an organization on this campus."[20]

The existence of any club recognition policy had been opposed by the AAUP, the USNT Senate, and the *Campus Chat.* A technique for circumventing the new policy appeared even before its approval. A group calling itself "Communications Unlimited" scheduled a concert in the Main Auditorium to raise money for people arrested on marijuana charges. To gain use of the auditorium, the Young Democrats' president offered sponsorship "to get around school regulations."[21] But members of the Young Democrats forced the resignation of the president in a dispute over the action, and the *Chat* attacked the YDs editorially for the proposed sponsorship.[22]

COMMUNICATING WITH STUDENTS

The president wanted to forestall student demonstration rather than confront it. He asked a speech department faculty member to organize a forum for exchange of views among students, faculty, and administrators. Dr. Don Beck formed a Communication Committee, selecting six other faculty members, who in turn chose several "articulate and representative" students to help plan a biweekly program that was billed as "FORUM!" Early topics in the 1969 spring semester were registration procedures, police/student confrontation, and a series on Black-White issues. Two counselor education professors, Dr. Bob Berg and Dr. Garry Landreth, helped organize the programs.[23] At the end of the semester, Kamerick wrote two of the committee members that he was "disappointed with attendance this year at FORUM, which was designed as an opportunity for students to air their grievances before faculty and administration." Nevertheless, the series resumed the following November with a Forum on "The Black Experience at NT."

At an April cabinet meeting, Lindley reassured the group that the Code of Student Conduct covered the situation adequately so that a separate policy on demonstrations would not be needed.[24] Nevertheless, Kamerick asked Lindley "to investigate the techniques that would be involved in securing a court order in case of such disturbances as the occupation of a building and to determine what would be involved in the injunctive process."[25]

Lindley felt the need for a stronger position if disturbances should arise. In May the dean wrote to Kamerick to request a change of title.

> The executive officer of student affairs should be designated the Vice-President for Student Affairs. This removes him from constant direct association with students and places him in the main stream of the entire student affairs program. It frees time for regular visits to facilities and consultations with the Directors concerning their problems. It also provides a feeling among the Student Affairs personnel that they have a voice at the same level as the academic, financial, and development divisions.

At the same time he asked that campus security be transferred to his division from fiscal affairs.[26] Kamerick agreed and the Board of Regents approved it for the following fall. M. C. Sutton became dean of students, and the dean of women, Nancy Dickens, became associate dean of students for women.

ABANDONING *IN LOCO PARENTIS*

Latin was a dead language for most Texas students, but few were unaware of the phrase, *in loco parentis.* It was an epithet used to demand the end of university administrative intrusion into private lives of students, including actions on the campus.

Immediately after Kamerick took office, Lindley recommended the end of three practices: university approval of off-campus housing, the ban on political speeches on campus, and forbidding women students to enter a man's apartment, subject to expulsion.[27] Women's housing regulations were modified almost immediately to relax curfew hours and standards for "appropriateness" in dress. Minor discipline problems were heard by a dormitory standards board or by a university-wide Women's Standards Board rather than by the dean of women.[28] The age at which women would no longer be required to live in a dorm was lowered to twenty-two, and one dormitory was set aside for graduate students. A new dormitory, Kerr Hall, had two separate tower wings, and one was set aside for men and one for women, providing in effect the first "coeducational dorm" on the campus.[29]

Between 1968 and 1970 a variety of other student-oriented changes were made, some trivial, some significant. Formal action was taken to ensure the confidentiality of student records. The cabinet approved a USNT request to place soft-drink machines in some campus buildings. A student radio station, KNTU-FM, received a license and began broadcasting in 1970. At Kamerick's insistence, the *Campus Chat* changed from semiweekly publication to four days a week in the spring of 1970, adopting a new identity as the *North Texas Daily.* The USNT Senate launched a program, FACE (Faculty Analysis Controlled Evaluation) to evaluate the faculty and publish the results as a guide for students in registration. In the fall of 1969 a group related to student religious centers adjoining the campus began "The Free University," a program of noncredit short courses taught by students or others who proposed them. In the following year sorority women were allowed to relocate their "houses" from the university-owned Chilton Hall to the privately owned College Inn.

BRING ON THE OMBUDSMAN

In the 1960s the Scandinavian concept of the ombudsman, a people's representative, was adopted at several universities. Kamerick saw in this an opportunity to build more student confidence in their university environment. Probably no effort at smoothing out student-administrative-faculty relations occupied so many hours of labor by so many individuals as Kamerick's interest in an ombudsman.

This represented study by the Faculty Senate, the USNT Senate, and the Board of Regents and many meetings and joint sessions. The Faculty Senate recommended a plan, approved by the president with some modification, and adopted in principle by the board on January 29, 1970. Kamerick described the task of the ombudsman as helping students get informal and fast settlement of their problems. He wrote, "The power of the ombudsman will include the duty of determining the gravity of the grievance, the authority to acquire information, the opportunity to give advice, and the right to make the findings public."[30]

The ombudsman selection process quickly bogged down because of lack of responsiveness from student government representatives. Dr. Jack Cross told Kamerick in May that at all three meetings of an ombudsman selection committee, the three USNT student appointees failed to attend. Kamerick advised Cross to proceed without the students, and the committee submitted three nominees for the post.[31] The president forwarded these to the chairman of the Board of Regents. By that time Kamerick had announced his resignation, and he left the file behind for his successor to act upon.[32] In effect, that spelled doom for the whole ombudsman process.

"WE DEMAND. . ."

In the fall of 1968, Black students made up five percent of undergraduate enrollment and 1.8 percent of graduate; Spanish surnamed students were 1.2 percent of undergraduate and 1.1 percent of graduate enrollment; Asians made up 0.4 percent of undergraduates and 3.1 percent of graduates. Blacks received 32.2 percent of undergraduate student financial aid and 10.1 percent of graduate financial aid.[33]

North Texas fared poorly on employment of minority groups. Black employment was professional zero, semiprofessional and clerical zero, domestic three, personal service (cooks) seventy-four, building service forty-four. For what was then called "White with Spanish surname," the figures were professional two, clerical four, and personal service four.[34]

The *Campus Chat* reported a protest by pickets in front of the Union Building on September 26 and carried a photograph of a young Black man carrying a sign saying, "College Inn unfair to Black people."[35] Within a week the student paper had another photo of Black pickets, this time in front of the Denton police station carrying signs saying "Billy Club Justice Must End" and "Police Brutality Must Stop." The protest was called at a meeting of about thirty-five Black students the night before, the *Chat* said, after a junior from Houston claimed he was beaten by a jailer after being arrested on a charge of being drunk in public.[36]

Kamerick needed to work with organized groups of Black students who had not yet gained official recognition. His dilemma in early months was that the policy for approving student groups had not been set by regents. He identified one moderate group of Black students that sought to work through the National Association for the Advancement of Colored People; another, more militant group, sought rapid action through the Afro-American Student Union. As a first step, the president got the existing Campus Club Committee to approve the NAACP student group in October.[37]

That left the problem of an application from the Afro-American group for approval. Kamerick instructed the Campus Clubs Committee that "no action is to be taken on requests. . . pending before the committee until the regents have approved a policy statement."[38]

The union had appeared on campus early in the fall semester. A representative asked David A. Webb, director of libraries, to add certain books to the library for the Afro-American collection. Webb told him that they should have the collection added to the Browsing Room soon. The same representative, Willie Rowlins, also asked for creation of a special collection in the new Library Building (then under construction) to be named the Malcolm X Memorial Collection.[39]

On January 14, 1969, faculty members found in their campus mailboxes a mimeographed sheet titled "End University Complicity With Racism." A preamble stated, "North Texas State University is a racist institution. We demand that the administration take an official position on these existing practices. Afro-American Student Union, Students for a Democratic Society." Kamerick asked Rogers to prepare for him a response to be sent "at least to the Afro-American Students." The practices for which an official position was demanded included these:

- Housing discrimination in approved apartments and rooming houses.
- Support of a campus organization (Kappa Alpha fraternity) that "exhibits

racist attitudes and practices by praising America's slave-master class who subjected Blacks to centuries of cruel oppression."

• Lack of Black faculty or administrators, employing Blacks only as kitchen workers and maintenance men.

• No courses offered in contributions of Black people to society.

• No concern for "Black ghetto dwellers" in Denton and elsewhere.

• Failure to solicit low-income students and to inform ghetto dwellers of financial assistance available.

• No university board or rules concerning sanctions against racist faculty or administrators.[40]

The response prepared for the president commented on each statement and attempted to explain the university record and position on each. A summary suggested that the mimeographed paper was based on misinformation and stated, "The University expects that any individual who feels that racism is being practiced will make a complaint about such practice; each complaint will be given careful attention."[41]

The next day, Kamerick wrote to Frank Wyman, using his student post office box address but not his title as head of the Afro-American Student Union. He told Wyman that as he understood his requests, "I believe all of them are changes which I would favor, too." He invited Wyman to discuss them with him.[42]

About a month later, the Afro-American group issued another one-page document of demands. Nine general points were listed, beginning with "We demand that. . . ." That listing included:

• Refuse to approve housing where Blacks were discriminated against.

• Make dormitory rooms available to Blacks on the basis of date of application.

• End discriminatory hiring practices.

• Establish a biracial board to hear cases of Blacks accused of misconduct and to hear complaints of racial prejudice in administrative or faculty relations with Blacks.

• Provide Black counselors for Black students in the dormitories.

• Establish more effective scholastic counseling for athletes.

• Make allowances to compensate for admission standards for minority groups and Blacks in particular.

• Actively recruit low-income Blacks and take advantage of available scholarship funds for minority students.

• Involve the university in relieving the plight of Denton ghetto-dwellers and "serve as a political recourse base to the residents who are at the mercy of a racist city council."[43]

The rest of the document was a list of demands for Black studies programs, including the hiring of Black faculty and special courses relevant to Black students. These demands were the subject of a February 19 meeting of the Administrative Council. Members sought to list ways in which they could respond to the concerns of the Black students. Student personnel deans reported their plans to drop approval of off-campus housing. They recommended that dormitory rooms be assigned by the director of housing rather than by dormitory directors. Deans and department directors were urged to intensify efforts to recruit Black faculty. Admissions and recruitment of Black students was assigned to a committee for study. Departments were asked to see how they might implement Black studies programs if appropriate to their discipline.[44] Two days later, President Kamerick again wrote Wyman, this time writing, "When you have time, I would like to tell you what we are doing, and will do, to meet many of the requests stated by the Afro-American Student Union."[45]

A mimeographed "newspaper" headed "Afro-American Student Union, Vol. I, Leaf. II" soon appeared, announcing an April 24, 1969, meeting to review the list of demands and the responses. The paper wrote that some demands were unanswered, some unsatisfactorily answered, and others showed promise.

WORKING FOR IDENTITY

In the spring of 1969 the campus observed its first Negro History Week. James Brown, Jr., national NAACP youth director, spoke to an audience of 300 at the opening program. The student NAACP chapter presented certificates of achievement to "outstanding Negro students." An indication of a degree of general campus acceptance was indicated by the list: Joe Greene, the first consensus football All-American in North Texas history; Nicky Wilson, the first Yucca Beauty; Marva Hunt, first Negro cheerleader; Mickey Burnim, USNT vice president; and Black students who had been North Texas Relays Queen, Homecoming Queen runner-up; and several USNT senators.[46]

The publicity for this event shows that many NAACP members were still routinely using the term "Negro" as a racial indicator. Not so with students active in the Afro-American Student Union. After the group held a rally to demand a number of changes, the *Chat* editorialized that the matters should have been "requested" rather than "demanded." One of the leaders wrote the editor that this word was appropriate "in the only language the white system understands—power. . . . You. . . are still looking at the Black movement as a civil rights movement. As Blacks we have redefined it. It is not a matter of civil rights (with the overtones of courtroom legalities) but is a matter of human rights due by nature to each individual at birth."[47]

Another view of racial terminology came in February from Dr. James Farmer, new assistant secretary of the Department of Health, Education, and Welfare, who told a capacity crowd of 500 in the University Theater that "A few years ago, a man would have been insulted if he was called Black. Now it is an honor."[48]

The following month the Afro-American Student Union promoted a Black Arts Festival. Muhammad Ali, former heavyweight boxing champion, spoke to 1,300 persons in the Main Auditorium, telling them that the NAACP, the Congress on Racial Equality, and other civil rights leaders had failed the Black man "in getting what we all want—freedom and equality for all men." But, he warned, "Forget violence. Violence is only inviting slaughter."[49]

And as academic year one of the Kamerick administration ended, newspapers carried the story in June 1969 of the employment of the university's first Negro administrator, Dr. T. R. Lee, Jr., as associate dean of students.[50] (But the August 7 *Chat* told of his resignation to return to a public school job.)

By the following fall, relations had improved to the point where the Afro-American Student Union was recommended by the Campus Clubs Committee and approved by the President's Cabinet in accord with the board-approved policy.[51]

MEETING FEDERAL REQUIREMENTS

The university was a long way from satisfying federal examiners in the regional Office for Civil Rights. A series of deficiencies were reported in June 1969 by Clarence Laws, deputy director of the Dallas office. These included the following mandates:

> The university must keep full records, advise within 30 days of action taken, and have detailed information, names and dates, to show integration efforts.
>
> No less emphasis can be placed on the recruitment of Negro students than white students.
>
> All contacts with prospective students should include information regarding financial assistance programs.
>
> The University must assure itself that assignment to dormitories and other housing facilities is done on a non-discriminatory basis. Specifically, Negroes and other minority groups will not be segregated. . . .
>
> Comparable recruiting efforts should be made for Negro and white faculty members. The compliance review revealed that there were no Negro faculty members. . . .
>
> During the compliance review. . . there was no evidence found that any Negro student seeking membership in predominantly white Greek letter social organizations had ever been successful.[52]

The letter was circulated to members of the cabinet, the Administrative Council, department directors, and others. The president asked for a reply from each about possible responses to the report. Kamerick wrote that the university could lose its $1.6 million annual federal aid if it were found to be in violation of the federal act. [53] In his response to the Office of Civil Rights, Kamerick was able to report that North Texas had just hired its first Black faculty member, Dr. Wayman T. Dever, as professor of education.[54]

ISOLATE THE RADICALS

After a demonstration on October 25, 1968, to protest the presence of Air Force recruiters in the Union Building, armed forces recruiting was moved from the Student Union Building to the Business Employment Service in March 1969.[55]

The SDS group returned on November 3 and 4 with an all-night sit-in at the union. A student reporter noted the presence of ex-Marines, who differed with the protestors' views of the Vietnam War. President Kamerick was quoted as saying peaceful demonstrations that did not interfere with the operation of the university and did not involve violence were within the constitutional rights of students.[56]

In November 1968 Kamerick sent the regents a number of clippings from the *Chronicle of Higher Education*, one concerning SDS involvement in a proposed two-day national strike that might take the form of occupation of campus buildings, another describing rapid growth of the group on campuses, and yet another describing the probable undesirable effects of SDS presence. Kamerick then got more specific about the Denton situation:

> Earlier we had learned that North Texas State University was to be a prime target because the SDS believed last summer it was a good university at which to capitalize on faculty and student unrest.
>
> Many of the actions taken this fall have been designed to insure that SDS could secure no substantial following among students or faculty members. It is my firm believe that had we not taken some of these steps, the SDS effort to organize on Monday, November 4 would have been far more successful. Actually I think it is correct to say that the demonstration was a failure.[57]

USNT President Troy Phillips criticized police for arresting nine SDS members in Denton for distributing obscene material "that wasn't obscene," and said that the Administration Building had been locked early after rumored attempts of an activist takeover and the doors of the Union Building were wired together from the inside.[58]

ATTACKING THE STUDENT PRESS

An AAUP committee in November 1968 recommended giving greater control over the *Campus Chat* to university students. Possibilities suggested were:

> 1. Transfer editorial authority to a university-wide publications board.
>
> 2. Journalism faculty members might continue to check copy in advance, but they would be allowed to make only stylistic, not substantive changes.
>
> 3. One edition of the *Chat* per week could be produced by journalism students; the other or others by separate staffs, free of advance approval of copy.
>
> 4. One page of each issue of the *Chat* could be the responsibility of

journalism students and the journalism department; the rest of the issue could be written by a separate staff.

Opposing the plan were C. E. Shuford, department director, and editor Jerry Smith.[59] A *Chat* editorial on November 20, signed by the entire staff, labeled the AAUP plan hasty and not soundly based and called for its rejection.[60]

Members of SDS moved in to start a petition drive demanding that the editorial page of the *Chat* be turned over once a week to anyone who wishes to submit a signed article "presenting any opinion whatsoever." Dean of Students Lindley told the protesters they could not conduct the drive since SDS was not a recognized organization.

Two members of the Young Democrats took over the petition. The *Chat* identified Joe Lemming, a journalism major, as one of the SDS members. Lemming attacked Shuford and the paper's faculty adviser, Martin L. Gibson, for stifling student expression and suggested that the group needed to get Gibson's job. "If we can get control of the *Chat,* we can make the whole activist cause move," the paper quoted Lemming as saying.[61] Young Democrat members disavowed the two students who continued the SDS petition, but the USNT Senate voted 18–11 to endorse the YD petition.[62]

Activism turned violent as well as strident in one more outbreak before the end of the 1969 spring semester. On May 11 an early morning fire was discovered in the Air Force ROTC supply room in the Men's Building. The fire was attributed to a Molotov cocktail thrown through the second-story window. Damage was listed as $27,000. Kamerick said he did not believe any student was involved, but the responsible individual or group would suffer the full penalties of the law.[63]

In a year-end interview, the president revealed his thoughts on campus unrest: "First, I believe that as long as we have the Vietnam war continuing we will have serious disruptions. And second, I am concerned about extreme repressive measures against legitimate dissent. I do think there will be a stiffening resistance to giving into demands backed by force."[64]

ANOTHER ENEMY: DRUGS

Terms such as "hippies" and "street people" were being used more frequently about some of the young people who hung out on one block of Fry

Street just north of the campus. "Head shops"—purveyors of drug paraphernalia, underground newspapers, and the like—appeared on Fry.

The *Chat* devoted nearly a full editorial page to a feature, "POT: Grass Grows Well at North Texas," examining student drug use. A Denton police captain said the use of marijuana among NTSU students "is becoming more widespread. . . . The evidence is that a good number use it." A sociology faculty member who had done a sample survey estimated that forty-five percent of male students and fifteen to twenty percent of females used marijuana. The tenor of the story was that drug use was significant, that sellers would be prosecuted, but that students were unlikely to be detected or arrested.[65]

One marijuana arrest that spring led to a protest march and a counter-protest march. A North Texas freshman man charged that an officer struck him in the face while questioning him at the police station. The chief of police suspended the officer pending investigation. Three days later about 300 students marched to the police station to protest the incident. Sponsors were listed as Students for a Democratic Society, the Afro-American Student Union, and the Radical Caucus of the Young Democrats. The next week, fourteen other student organizations sponsored a National Law Enforcement Day March along the same route in support of the Denton Police Department.

The governor wrote periodically to state university presidents to express his concern about the drug problem. Early in 1970 Kamerick wrote to Governor Smith, noting "full support for your campaign against drug abuse." At North Texas, he wrote, drug abuse was punishable by suspension under the Code of Student Conduct.[66]

ATHLETICS IN THE MIDST OF TURMOIL

The search for increased recognition in the metropolitan area and the state contributed to the desire to expand the athletic program. After joining the Missouri Valley Conference in 1957, the Eagles soon moved into the "major college" classification in football, basketball, and track. National exposure in games with basketball powerhouses like Cincinnati, Bradley, and Drake led to a desire for similar stature in other sports.

The emphasis to be given to athletics didn't earn consensus among faculty, students, alumni, or administrators. The basic athletic budget came from the student service fee, which also supported student activities, student publications, the Health Service, and the Fine Arts Series. Broadcast fee income was negligible. Ticket sales income was slight—large numbers of nonstudents seldom came to football games at Fouts Field, and the number of seats available for sale to nonstudents in the Men's Gymnasium was restricted. Occasionally, a sizable football guarantee could be obtained by playing at a large university. Such opportunities were limited. Coaching staffs were not large, and coaches were required to teach physical education classes to provide a share of their salaries. The tennis coach and the golf coach doubled as football assistants. For many years, one man was both athletic director and director of the physical education department.

The student newspaper and the *Denton Record-Chronicle* undertook periodic campaigns each fall to "Fill Fouts Field Full," but never accomplished their goals. Fouts Field had not been designed to bring spectators close to the playing field or to provide good sight lines. "Big-name" teams could not be attracted to play in Denton because of the low attendance and the limit on potential ticket sales of a 20,000-seat stadium or of a 4,000-seat gymnasium. One possible solution to this problem came as construction began on Texas Stadium in Irving for the NFL Dallas Cowboys. The Faculty Athletic Committee in August 1969 explored the budgetary hopes and problems associated with a change, then suggested that "such a step is necessary if North Texas is not content with its 'intermediate' status in the football world."[67]

Athletic Director Jess Cearley and Vice Presidents Carter and Rogers met that month with Clint Murchison, Jr., owner of the Dallas Cowboys, and reached preliminary contract agreements.[68] The Board of Regents approved a contract to play in Texas Stadium from 1970 through 1974, starting with a December 5, 1970, game with Memphis State.[69] Construction was not finished in time, so the Dallas venture was delayed until the fall of 1971.

In November 1968 the football, golf, track, and tennis coaching staffs sent to the athletic director a three-page report of recommendations for improvement. Among the suggestions were these:

- As the highest priority, build an athletic dormitory.
- Assume that the Missouri Valley Conference is breaking up. North Texas should apply immediately for membership in the Southwest Conference.
- Improve the quality of the athletic physical plant.

• Increase size of coaching staffs or relieve coaches of teaching duties to give them more time for recruiting and for coaching athletes.

• Increase the recruiting budgets and the number of scholarships in each sport.

• Improve the quality of competition in a given sport, especially football, by playing more games away than at home.

• By improving the quality of the intercollegiate athletic program, we can improve the public image of the university as a whole.[70]

In January 1970 a prepared news statement announced the separation of intercollegiate athletics from physical education, calling the demands too great to require of one man. Football Coach Rod Rust was named athletic director, and Dr. Jess Cearley continued as chairman of the Department of Health, Physical Education, and Recreation.

For Eagle sports fans, 1968 was a good year. Joe Greene, a defensive tackle, led the Eagles to a winning season in 1968 and was named to the consensus All-American football team as Coach Rod Rust's team won eight and lost two. In basketball, the university approved the televising of all home basketball games on UHF Channel 39 for the 1968–69 season. Coach Dan Spika used the talents of a pair of fast guards, Joe Hamilton and Creston Whitaker, to take the team to the best record they had ever achieved in the Missouri Valley Conference. That spring, Winton E. (Pop) Noah, who had coached twenty-one years at North Texas and forty-two years in all, was presented a plaque of appreciation from the student body at the eighteenth annual North Texas Relays in the spring of 1969.[71]

chapter 30

Carter: Act One

With your help and cooperation, we hope to keep this university moving toward the attainment of its role and scope as a major university until a president has been selected.

John L. Carter Jr.
Speech to the Faculty, August 1970

The Kamerick term in office—only two years—represented the most radical change in governance in the history of North Texas. His departure created an abrupt break in the rapid transition toward increased faculty participation and student involvement in administrative affairs. The sudden loss of leadership came just one year after another major transformation: Gov. Preston Smith's appointment of three new regents and the replacement of Ben H. Wooten as chairman by A. M. "Monk" Willis in May 1969. When Chairman Willis announced on May 28, 1970, that John Carter had been named acting president, it launched another period in which one man would become dominant in many of the most significant affairs of the university: Chairman Willis himself.

The acting president was a mild-mannered fifty-four-year-old accountant, an experienced fiscal officer with a state-wide reputation for financial integrity, but a man whose professional background had not called for him to develop the personal skills of dealing with various university constituencies, either internal or external. The board asked him to keep things on an even keel but put him on notice that he was not eligible to be given the responsibility permanently.

John L. Carter, Jr., graduated from the University of Texas at Austin in 1946 and attended Texas Christian University on the way to becoming a certified public accountant. He joined NTSU in 1955 as the chief accountant after working as the college branch auditor for the University of Texas System and as an assistant state auditor. Carter was named university comptroller in August 1961 and was promoted to vice president for fiscal affairs in 1965.

Before Carter began his acting role in September, the machinery for seeking a new president was in motion, as noted in Chapter 28. Board Chairman Willis also served as chairman of the search committee, joined by Regents Dean Davis, Davie James Lawson, E. C. Pannell, and E. Bruce Street. Student representatives were Jimmy Deming, president, and Andy Kupper, vice president, of the United Students of North Texas. Alumni were represented by their Association president, James Martin of Arlington. The faculty election named Jack Scroggs as chairman of their group, along with Miles Anderson, Don Beck, John Douthittt, Franklin L. Elder, William Glaze, Clifford Hutton, H. W. Kamp, James Lee, and David McGuire. Staff employees elected John Matt Howard and G. A. Robason as nonacademic representatives. A subcommittee named to meet with the regents' committee comprised Professors Elder, Hutton, Kamp, and Scroggs. By July 23, 1970, the committee had published selection criteria that closely resembled the document used in the selection of Kamerick.

It became clear that even with the published standards, there was not a unified agenda for the process. Regents feared that the role of the faculty in governance had grown too large; many in the faculty feared that the next president would not share the Kamerick philosophy of faculty participation; and a number of active students saw the opportunity to increase the importance of their roles. As a result, participation in campus affairs by regents, both individually and collectively, began to increase.

THE BOARD OF REGENTS AT WORK

Before 1966 the North Texas Board of Regents did not hold open meetings. The only nonregents to attend were the president and the staff member who served as secretary to the board. No news personnel were admitted. Results of the meetings were given by the president to the News Service director, who distributed news releases to the press. In 1965 the *Denton Record-Chronicle* sent a reporter to a meeting unannounced, and the board members, although taken by surprise, nonetheless invited the reporter to attend the meeting. This practice became a regular one; it preceded the passage of the Texas Open Meetings act in 1967.

Not surprisingly, though, regents began relying even more heavily on their established practice of discussing and deciding many issues during the course of an informal dinner meeting the night before the scheduled regents' session.

President Kamerick had invited faculty representatives to attend board meetings as observers or to discuss an agenda item. Regents appeared to welcome the opportunity to hear faculty views. Willis told the Faculty Senate in December 9, 1970, that he would like for some members of the faculty to meet informally with the Board of Regents before board meetings. As board chairman, Willis extended this idea even further and began making rounds of offices on the campus to visit with a number of administrators and faculty members.

In a March 1971 interview with the *North Texas Daily,* Willis said, "We work through the leadership of the president." He described the process this way: "'I talk to the people I trust about the problems facing North Texas,' he said. 'Then I can find out where the problems really are. One of my jobs, as I see it, is, without going in and stirring up people, to try and ascertain as much knowledge as I can and make my questions known so organized procedure can follow these alterations.'"[1]

Regents as Administrators

Willis became an active participant in many routine activities. Various memos in Carter's files showed that Willis intervened in matters concerning admissions regulations[2] and student housing.[3]

Intervention in these areas might be regarded by an acting president as a necessary annoyance. But two major areas of regent concern brought direct action that in more normal times would have been delegated to the president to handle with his staff, the faculty, and students. One involved selection, retention, granting tenure, and promoting faculty. The other concerns were triggered by the national spread of student activism and violent student protests. Some—but not all—regents developed passionate views on these topics. They sought to limit faculty participation and to hold student activists in check.

The Governor, the Regents, and the Faculty

A mechanism for board activity in faculty selection became apparent in a memo sent by Carter to Vice President Spurlock in December 1970:

> I have received a request from Regents Street and Godfrey to provide them with a list, by name, of those individuals who will be recommended for tenure for the next fiscal year. They have also indicated that they would like to have a list of any new faculty members to be added to the staff and also a roster of the students who have been nominated to be teaching fellows next year.[4]

A Spurlock memo shows that he reluctantly provided the desired lists to Carter. The following month, Carter wrote Spurlock of even further regent activity: "As you know, Mr. Willis appointed a Regent's committee to look into employment and tenure. Mr. Godfrey is chairman of the committee. The chairman of the committee has asked that we select five faculty members to meet with his committee on February 1 in Fort Worth."[5] In March Spurlock sent a collection of material on faculty members requested by Godfrey and Street after a meeting with women faculty members. Spurlock wrote that he was concerned about such a document being sent directly to the regents but said, "I really don't see any other alternative."[6]

The Governor's Role

Concern over faculty attitudes and political beliefs in the state extended into the Texas Legislature and the Office of the Governor. In January 1971 Governor Smith called a meeting of regents of all state colleges and universities. He advised them to enforce state laws and reasonable codes of conduct for both students and faculty—or not serve on the boards. The governor said that disruption and violence do not have to be tolerated on any campus. Statutes exist, he said, to enable administrators to discipline or expel students, to regulate "freedom of expression" without violating the First Amendment, and not to tolerate conduct that interferes with its normal activities or the protected rights of other members of the college community.

The tenor of the meeting is well indicated by a story in the *Fort Worth Star-Telegram*.[7]

> Smith said he believes the college "is not a law unto itself and that boards of trustees must reassert their prerogatives."
>
> . . .The governor drew two vocal "amens" from the audience when he said: "High respect for faculty tenure should not be projected to a system of protection for incompetents or an implied grant to professor of freedom from reasonable responsibilities and restraints."

Regent Godfrey Assails Faculty Control

One of Governor Smith's appointees to the North Texas board, Fort Worth attorney Berl E. Godfrey, followed up with an interview, telling a reporter that the people had lost control of their schools. His views were described this way by the *Star-Telegram*.[8]

> Yesterday in Austin, Godfrey lashed out at what he described as "two unions"—naming the Southern Association of Universities and Colleges [*sic*] and the American Association of Universities [*sic*]. . . .
>
> Godfrey said he believes that Texas colleges should withdraw from these associations. . . .
>
> He told about one Texas school at which committees made up of faculty members from the various departments present the administration with what salaries certain professors should receive.
>
> "They are telling the administrations what their salaries will be," said Godfrey, "and this isn't right."

The Confirmation of Godfrey

In Texas, the governor had occasionally risked having a board appointee rejected by the Texas Senate if that individual was not regarded as sufficiently conservative. But with the conservative Governor Smith in office in 1970, this equation had changed. A November 29, 1970, "Austin Report" in the *Dallas Times Herald* declared that there were nine liberal or anti-Smith senators who looked forward to letting Smith know "they think his choice of state agency board members do not represent the cream of the crop."[9] The report said close senate scrutiny would include Godfrey, credited with "leading a movement to sack Dr. John Kamerick as the college's reform-minded and popular president."

Sen. Don Kennard of Fort Worth announced that he was seeking support to block the appointment of Godfrey. Kennard told reporters Godfrey's "attitude toward professors and teachers is indefensible" and "I don't think he should be on the board."[10] The senate voted on March 25 to deny confirmation. Godfrey told the Associated Press, "My philosophy has been that the control of the schools ought to be returned to the regents as contemplated by our statutes, and that we should have the right to discharge any faculty member that we think is tending to cause impressionable young men and women to lose confidence in his country and respect for the democratic principles for which you and I stand."[11]

PHASE BLUE AND A CONCERT IN THE PARK

On July 20, 1970, the Coordinating Board adopted regulations for stricter treatment of disruptive students. State colleges and universities were directed to make "full use of the general law and of available administrative regulations, including expulsion" to prevent disruptions and to penalize those responsible for disorders.[12] A *Dallas Times Herald* writer reported in October 1970 that North Texas State "this summer bore the brunt of criticism from Gov. Preston Smith for student troubles."[13]

Two events during the Carter interregnum focused attention on the North Texas campus, brought letters of protest, aroused the governor and legislators and moved the Board of Regents to call for sterner measures to suppress student activism. The regents adopted a tougher policy on use of campus facilities and expanded a campus security department into a full-fledged police department.

Rallying in the Park

Both moves were triggered by a series of unauthorized rock music concerts and student protest speeches in July and August of 1970, just after Kamerick had left for Iowa. Some student activists took Berkeley, California, as a model and renamed the old-campus area behind the auditorium as "the People's Park," usually shortened to "the Park." This became the rallying point for student protests.

Students identified by the student newspaper as "the campus radical activist group" timed concerts in "the Park" to coincide with the arrival of freshmen (and some of their parents) for summer orientation. They passed out literature as the new students gathered for a meeting in the Music Recital Hall. On the night of August 3, 1970, as about 400 people listened to a rock concert in the old-campus area, a campus security officer told the concert leaders that they would have to stop using amplified music. He said they were disturbing the peace and accused them of breaking and entering a campus class building to plug in their amplifiers. The musicians continued to play. After conferring with Vice President William Lindley, security chief Bob Wallis told concert organizer Brian Kelly that the concert was disturbing the peace and interfering with other organized freshman orientation activities. The concert ended.

But the repercussions came from a speech made by a young woman graduate student who urged the crowd to join the coming revolution and who attacked the members of the Board of Regents in a variety of derogatory terms, applying some choice four-letter words to them.

Betty Ann Duke Is Fired

When that incident was reported the next morning, Regents Chairman Willis happened to be on hand. The woman who had attacked the regents was Mrs. Elizabeth Ann Duke. She was employed as a teaching fellow to teach freshman composition classes. President Carter that morning issued a directive that Mrs. Duke be dismissed from her teaching position. It did not take long for the Duke case to become a *cause célèbre.*

Freshman orientation brought further public notice, as Editorial Director Dick West of the *Dallas Morning News* wrote a column on August 30, "A Shocking Start for a Freshman." He focused on a young freshman woman and her mother who received a printed leaflet from "students of the radical left." This, he wrote, preached communism and world revolution.[14]

Phase Blue Erupts

About two-thirds of the column was devoted to a second item, a volume of freshman English readings called *Phase Blue.* West attacked the book because of its inclusion of selections by Black activists Eldridge Cleaver and Angela Davis, and of articles with titles such as "Why Students Seize Power," "The Pill and Modern Woman," and "God Is Dead in Georgia." After detailing his objections to the attack on Anglo-Saxon justice, he asked, "Are we to rip and sever, little by little, that civilized fabric so carefully stitched for us by great minds of the past?" [15]

A good many irate Texans wrote the regents, President Carter, or the English Department. West, himself, said he received voluminous mail running 90–10 in support of his position. At Carter's request, the chairman of freshman English, Dr. Jack White, wrote a long letter challenging West's interpretation of the text, and much of it was published in the *News.* The English Department chairman, Dr. Ernest Clifton, told the *North Texas Daily* that "West is a bigoted man whose editorial was marked by an inclusion of facts supporting his point of view and omission of facts supporting the total balance of the book." Clifton had received eight letters criticizing the book and Carter had received thirty letters about the book. On one day West printed thirteen letters to the editor, all of them except one agreeing with West's views.[16]

Regent Godfrey wrote the board secretary, enclosing a copy of the West column, stating, "At the next meeting of the Board of Regents I would like a full and complete explanation of who determines what courses are required and particularly why this course and this book was selected as required reading for freshmen." [17] Regent E. Bruce Street of Graham answered a complaint letter to say he wanted "a new, hard re-appraisal of the standards used in text book selection, as well as regulations governing the activities of students and non-students for non-university approved operations."[18]

On September 4 Carter wrote to Willis that Vice President Rogers and Roy Busby, director of public information, visited with West and found West to be unresponsive to requests for a more balanced presentation. Carter's letters on the subject pointed out that distribution of the student leaflet at orientation was stopped as soon as it was detected. On September 9 Carter wrote each regent at the request of Willis, sending to each a copy of the textbook, the White letter, a report on all the other U.S. schools that used the text, and a statement of the method used to select texts in the English Department.

Other complaints came directly from parents who had attended freshman orientation. One father wrote to the president, enclosing a copy of the handbill that had helped trigger the West column. He suggested that constitutional laws were available "to you to forestall these anarchists and unless they are used to the fullest degree possible, not only our colleges, but indeed our nation can well be destroyed. Disturbing the peace, trespassing, vagrancy, inciting to riot. . . are some of the possibilities."[19]

Carter responded that he shared the writer's feelings about the leaflet, that the university had those responsible removed from the premises, reporting that "Our security halted the park concerts and those responsible are being dealt with according to University rules and regulations."[20]

Controlling Use of Facilities

The board executive committee met August 20 to pass an interim policy, "Use of Physical Facilities of the University by Registered Student Organizations." This was to serve until the regular board meeting in November. Registered organizations could use building or grounds for events for students, provided that such events could not be attended "by any person who is neither a student nor employee of the institution." A group that violated the policy was to be removed from the registered list by the university president. The North Texas chapter of the Texas Association of College Teachers objected to the interim policy, suggesting that if a statement was necessary, to have two faculty members who were attorneys to draw up the document.[21] The board adopted a more detailed policy on November 19, noting that it had been reviewed and endorsed by the Council of Academic Deans and reviewed and endorsed by individual members of the University Committee, who stressed that this was not an action by the Faculty Senate.[22]

Building Up a Police Force

Regents also sought greater campus police strength to prevent violent protest activities. Street met in Austin on September 15 with four Department of Public Safety staff members and wrote to his fellow board members on September 21. Col. Pat Speir urged Street to maintain a close liaison with Denton police and emphasized that if DPS troopers were called to the campus, they would be in complete charge and would do whatever they felt needed to be done. He also suggested the name of an FBI agent in Fort Worth who could be helpful in recruiting for a university security force.[23]

Just two days after Street's letter was sent, a group of students staged a demonstration to protest the dismissal of Mrs. Duke, leading to a confrontation with Denton police outside the Administration Building. This triggered further regent concern, culminating in a letter sent by Street on October 21 to regents, Carter, and Vice President William C. Lindley. Looking to the November board meeting, he recommended a stronger statement of policy, a reevaluation of the tenure policy, more effective screening of prospective employees, and changing the security division to "The University Police Department." He further urged improved communications among administration, faculty, and students to gain student understanding and cooperation. [24]

In November, regents changed the budget request to the 1971 Texas Legislature for police from $117,023 to $350, 658 for 1972 and from $122,430 to $360,703 for FY 1973. Regent Street accompanied Carter to Austin to make personal pleas for the money.

THE CASE OF BETTY ANN DUKE

Reaction to the concerts in the park focused on one individual—Mrs. Duke, who was pursuing a Ph.D. degree in English. She had taught one section of English 131 in 1969–70, and the department recommended that she teach two sections in 1970–71. President Carter notified her by letter on August 25 that he had rescinded the offer from the English Department "at the direction of the Board of Regents. . . for use of obscene language and conduct unbecoming an instructor in front of students and others on the university campus."[25] In response, Mrs. Duke requested a hearing. She also wrote on August 27 asking the North Texas chapter of the American Association of University Professors to help her regain her appointment.

Carter obtained four written statements from complaining witnesses. The Denton chief of police, Wayne Autrey, stated that she used obscenities in a speech at the National Guard Armory in Denton on May 6, 1970. A university security officer alleged that she had charged improper conduct by administrators and used obscenities in a speech in the park on July 30. Another witness said she urged women students to conduct a dormitory strike. Yet another charged the use of obscenities at the August 3 speech. Copies of these statements were sent to Mrs. Duke with a letter from Carter on September 9. This time, Carter's charges were more detailed. He said her fellowship offer was rescinded because of these factors:

1. The use of profanity.

2. Encouraging the violation of published university rules and regulations, especially those relating to housing.

3. Participating in a meeting on the campus that was not sanctioned as provided for in the Code of Student Conduct.

4. Obscene descriptions of administrators and the governing board, attempting to discredit these officials, thereby reducing the effectiveness of their administration.

5. Accusing the faculty and administration of immoral acts.

6. The exercise of professional integrity by a faculty member includes a recognition that the public will judge his profession and his institution by his statements. The statements in question discredit the concept of academic responsibility as established and recognized by the faculty of North Texas State University.[26]

The letter also granted her request for a hearing to be held September 23 before the President's Cabinet (Carter and the three vice presidents).

On September 14 the local AAUP president, Roland Vela, appointed a special committee to investigate the case. Clovis Morrisson of political science served as chair, with two English faculty members also on the committee: Robert L. Hughes and James M. Linebarger. The committee met with President Carter and went to Longview to meet with Chairman Willis. The members were denied their request to attend the hearing before the cabinet, so they "concentrated. . . on trying to convince Mr. Carter and Mr. Willis to follow procedures of academic due process" and to change the hearing body to "a committee of the faculty, preferably of the English Department, but possibly the Faculty Tenure Committee." The committee did not succeed in these efforts. Their report gave the group's interpretation of the early events:

> We can understand why the case was handled as it was initially. The Acting President has been in office for only a few days when the case came to his attention; he had nothing in his background to prepare him for such a case; and there were no established procedures for such cases involving Teaching Associates. The committee has the distinct impression that much of the early decision-making in the case was done by some members of the Board of Regents.

> If our assessment is correct, however, there is still no justification for later excluding the faculty from handling what was essentially a faculty matter. Consequently, our committee is of the opinion that a serious and unnecessary breach of academic due process has occurred in the Betty Duke case.[27]

The *North Texas Daily* asked Mrs. Duke in an interview, "Your dismissal was brought on by the Board of Regents rather than the administration?" She gave a one-word answer: "Yes." Then, when asked to expand on the views that led to her dismissal, she gave this explanation:

> in the speeches that I made during the summer and last spring I talked about the oppressiveness of this system for students on this campus, for black and brown people across the nation, for the colored peoples of the world. . . . I exposed this system which operates here. . .at the university and also on the national and international levels as a system which is based on the accumulation of wealth by a few people.
>
> These people make most of the important decisions about what happens in this world. The system is based on white racial superiority. The system is based on male supremacy. The system is supported by military strength. I also talked about who has the power in this system and used them as an example at the local level—the Board of Regents, who are all white men of some wealth who run this university in the interests of business rather than in the interest of the community.[29]

The Cabinet Hearing and Its Aftermath

The hearing began at 10:00 A.M. on September 23. Carter presided, with legal counsel by an assistant attorney general from Austin. Mrs. Duke was represented by two Dallas attorneys with established reputations in civil liberties cases. The questioning of Mrs. Duke focused on determining whether she had indeed been the person who made the statements on the occasions outlined in Carter's letter. She stipulated that she was, indeed, that person. She and her attorneys stressed that the First Amendment protected her right to make such critical comments and that she should therefore be permitted to continue in her teaching position.[29] At the request of the Duke attorneys, a court reporter was brought in to record the proceedings. At the conclusion,

Carter announced that the cabinet would deliberate on the matter once members had studied the hearing transcripts.

During the morning, a group of students came to the Board Room on the second floor of the Administration Building, where the hearing was held. A *North Texas Daily* reporter wrote that they were there to give the cabinet a petition demanding the reinstatement of Mrs. Duke. About seventy students were present, and one said the petition had 500 signatures.[30]

At 1:00 P.M. those students rejoined a larger crowd outside the Administration Building. The larger group then returned to the Board Room, seeking to present the U.S. Constitution and Declaration of Independence. They were told that if they would go outside, a cabinet member would talk to them. They did, and Vice President William Lindley went outside to talk to them. The *Daily* reporter described the next events this way:

> After [Lindley] left, the crowd decided to re-enter the building. They were headed back to the second floor when they were met by campus security officers. The officers were lined up across the landing, stopping anyone from going up to the second floor. The students sat down on the first floor and on the stairs, where they stayed until the Denton Police arrived.[31]

Lindley told cabinet members that he had called the Denton Police to help university security personnel and that officers from the State Department of Public Safety were gathered at the edge of the city awaiting call if reinforcements were needed. The situation was growing more tense.

> The police were called after the group of students who occupied the entrance and main stairway were given 10 minutes to evacuate the Administration Building.
>
> "I suggest you vacate the building in 10 minutes," Vice President Lindley told the crowd of about 250. Some students and faculty members tried to get the group to disperse but were unable to do so. When the police arrived, Lindley came down onto the landing and told the group. "You've been given ample time to clear the building. You are now in violation of the law."

> [Denton Police Chief Wayne] Autrey shouted that everybody left in the building would be arrested. This was not enforced, but everyone cleared the building and gathered in front.[32]

The scene outside had the ominous look of a riot about to happen. A crowd of perhaps a thousand students stood around. Denton police dressed in riot gear and holding shotguns at the alert were lined up in opposition to that crowd. A peace-maker emerged in the person of Jack Wheeler, an associate dean of students. He circulated among the students, talked with Chief Wayne Autrey, and then reported to the cabinet that if they would send the police away, the students would leave the Administration Building area and confine their meetings and protests to the "Park" area. This was satisfactory for Chief Autrey, and over objections by Lindley, the other two vice presidents joined Carter in approving this move. The police left and the student crowd gradually dispersed. The campus had escaped violence and possible injury.[33]

On the following day nine students representing different campus factions met for two and a half hours with the President's Cabinet to explore possible actions to follow the student demonstrations. The lead story in the *Daily* the next morning quoted some of the students and gave administrative viewpoints from John Carter and Jack Wheeler. The story left the impression that little had been accomplished.

Disciplinary Action

On October 9 three students revealed to the *Daily* that the dean of students had suspended two of them from school and placed the third on disciplinary probation. Subsequently it was learned that two other students had received similar treatment. At its next meeting, October 13, the USNT Senate gave a vote of confidence to the five students and asked for their unconditional reinstatement.[34] The next day, the Faculty Senate declined to act on the USNT bill. The five disciplined students, three of whom were suspended and two placed on probation, appealed the action of the dean of students to the Committee on Student Conduct. After seventeen hours of testimony, the committee announced on October 21 that it had found that all five students had violated the Code of Student Conduct but in all but one case found extenuating circumstances and lessened the penalties.[35]

The Board of Regents met on the same day that the committee judgment was announced and moved quickly to ratify the interim policy on use of facilities by nonstudents. The president of the USNT, Jimmy Deming, spoke to regents urging them to include a student advisory committee on board actions and to work toward the statutory inclusion of a student member of the board. He expressed fears of violence on the campus because there "are no outlets for frustration here." Deming complained that "Vice President Lindley has lost his ability to communicate with students. . . something has got to change."[36]

The Faculty Seeks to Open Communication

The Faculty Senate, through its University Committee, on October 21 sent Carter a two-page letter. It reviewed the disarray on the campus and offered to help restore a more normal, orderly state of affairs. At the same time it was clear that the regents were being condemned for acting alone in the first stages of the Duke case. The University Committee spelled out its "reflections on the state of the university" and asked Carter to transmit them to members of the Board of Regents. The committee letter asked for a move to better communication between regents and faculty. Adverse reaction to the Duke case and facilities use policy "could have been averted had the regents, administrators, faculty members, and students understood more fully the facts and procedures employed." A concern for the university's future was presented this way:

> We should like to record our concern also for the repute this university has in the public eye. Recent journalistic treatment and some political oratory portray the faculty as proselytizing radicals and the students as victims of our extremism. In fact, such charges are far from true. . . . [The] facts belie the notion that this university is endangered from within by radicalism. We should like to see information disseminated which will represent us accurately, not as threats to individuals and to society, but as hard-working people loyal to the best of American culture. Favorable publicity becomes even more imperative with the growth of competition in our region by other institutions of higher education.
>
> Finally, we wish to indicate our willingness to help alleviate causes for such concerns. . . . We see in this crisis opportunity for creative change—not destructive disorder only; for responsible action—not for explosive rebellion and reprisal only; for sustained growth—not for loss and damage only. We believe we can seize these opportunities best

> when all branches of the university have means for open exchange of thought and opinion.[37]

Carter did transmit the letter to the Board of Regents. This led to a meeting between Willis and the University Committee on the day of the November 19 board meeting. Cross wrote to thank Carter for bringing this about and added a tribute that doubtless gave the acting president a much-needed morale boost:

> We hope that our conversation with him [Willis] will begin to improve the mutual understanding and communication which we believe should characterize the relationships between various parts of the university.
>
> May we add a more general expression of respect and appreciation for the quality of your administration? We know some of the problems which attenuate an interim presidency, and everyone familiar with university life today can see some of the difficulties of administrative responsibilities. In spite of all these adverse circumstances, you have, we believe, guided the university wisely; and for this leadership we and our colleagues on the faculty are in your debt.[38]

Questioning the Regents

After the October 21 regents' meeting, the USNT Senate unanimously endorsed five questions to the Board of Regents and a proposal for a student demonstration to be held outside the Administration Building on November 12, a week before the next meeting of the regents. The questions asked for removal of the facilities use policy, elimination of archaic dormitory regulations, the employment of a student ombudsman, student and faculty representation on the Board of Regents, and the replacement of Vice President Lindley by "a reasonable administrator to reign over the student affairs office."[39] Later action added student parking problems as the subject of a sixth question. Carter asked the board secretary to transmit these questions and some related documents from a group identifying themselves as the Committee on Popular Expression.[40] The spokesman for that group was Joe Burgoyne, who had been president of USNT the previous year, was then a member of the USNT Senate, and who had identified himself publicly as one of the students disciplined after the demonstrations in support of Mrs. Duke.

Burgoyne, the Committee on Popular Expression, and the USNT senators made Lindley their target. The student senate had voted on September 29 calling for "commander-in-chief Lindley" to resign and now the list of questions charged that "the General is unfit to act as a college administrator under circumstances which demand rational behavior" and stated that most of the group agreed that the proper action was for the board to remove Lindley from his position.[41]

The *North Texas Daily* devoted the editorial page on November 12 to two long "dialogues," one with Lindley and one with Burgoyne, and to an editorial in support of the rally scheduled that day by the Committee on Popular Expression. It supported five of the proposals but said "the proposal to remove William C. Lindley, vice-president for student affairs, is quite dubious at the best. It is a personal attack on the man and is not an attempt to better the students' situation on campus."[42]

On the appointed day at 10:00 A.M., a carefully orchestrated series of committee demonstrations began as students assembled in front of the Administration Building. As promised by COPE leaders, none of the activities resulted in any confrontation or any violence. Some of the events were described in the *Daily*'s lead story the next morning:

> Demonstration activities began with a silent march by the demonstrators through the front doors of the Administration Building, up the main staircase, then down the east stairway and out of the building. . . . A procession of six students bearing a gray coffin led the assembly to the Main Auditorium. . . .
>
> Standing before an estimated 400 students in the Main Auditorium,[Acting President John] Carter accepted the proposals and said he would present the questions to the regents for their consideration. He also said he felt sure some response would be forthcoming from the board after their discussion of the points.[43]

The Regents Respond

On November 19, the regents met in relatively quiet surroundings as a lone protester sat outside of the Board Room with a sign reading, "superpig." The significant responses to students were the passage of a revised, less stringent facilities use policy, the naming of a four-member committee of regents to meet with student groups after each board meeting, and conducting a forty-minute closed meeting with USNT President Jimmy Deming.

Chairman Willis later commented on each of the points raised by the COPE questions:

> Housing: This board knows that it needs to be restudied. We are studying that matter, and some changes will be made.
>
> Ombudsman: Former President Kamerick didn't include the position on this year's budget or in the planning for next year's. We are sincerely trying to find the money and find the right individual.
>
> Parking: We are making some studies of parking facilities available . . . and some improvements [will] be made.
>
> William C. Lindley: The board feels the hiring and firing of administrators is not an area of student responsibility. It will remain with the regents.
>
> Student representation on the Board of Regents: The regents are appointed and have no power to appoint [other members]. The new committee is a start.[44]

Students Seek More Power

The Student Senate and the ad hoc committee tried to use the perceived unrest to obtain more participation in the decision-making process. A bill passed by USNT on November 3 declared, "The legislation passed by this body must be acted upon by the administration within three weeks and wherein said administration does not act on or vetoes our legislation, that one representative of the administration defend its action before this body while it is in session or a written explanation of the administrative decision be presented before this body." The President's Cabinet reacted on November 23 by writing Lindsay Keffer, the USNT adviser, that the cabinet had voted to continue its policy of having the appropriate vice president "respond as rapidly as possible to any bills or requests for information from the senate."[45]

THE DUKE CASE: LATER STAGES

Appealing the Dismissal

After the President's Cabinet had upheld Mrs. Duke's dismissal, she asked for a hearing before the Board of Regents. The regents granted the hearing and chose to conduct it in the law offices of Regent Berl E. Godfrey in Fort

Worth on February 19, 1971. About twenty-five students and nonstudent supporters crowded into the small conference room. Mrs. Duke and her attorneys, Ed Cloutman and Sylvia Demarest, spoke to the board, arguing especially for her right to speak under the protection of the First Amendment. Chairman Willis later announced that the regents upheld the withdrawal of her teaching fellowship for "conduct unbecoming a faculty member." Her attorneys announced that they would file suit seeking reinstatement as a teaching fellow and a doctoral student and back pay and damages.[46]

Organizing Another Demonstration

Mrs. Duke became involved in a campus "strike" two days before she spoke to the regents, and that put her in court before she could institute her own lawsuit. She teamed with David Haylon to call a rally or strike on February 17 "to educate the people as to the purpose of U.S. involvement in Southeast Asia." The USNT Senate voted 12–7 to call for the student strike and rally. USNT President Jimmy Deming vetoed that bill and Vice President Lindley said that nonstudent speakers at the rally would violate campus security regulations. The USNT Senate voted 14 to 12 to sponsor the rally, hoping that this would bring the proceedings within the scope of the facilities use policy.[47]

The morning of the rally, however, the President's Cabinet voted to apply for a temporary restraining order to block the appearance of Haylon and Mrs. Duke as unauthorized persons not affiliated with the university. The order was granted by District Judge Bob Scofield and served by a deputy sheriff a few minutes after the rally began at noon. About 400 persons attended to hear both Haylon and Mrs. Duke continue with attacks on U.S. policy in Southeast Asia and on suppression of women and Blacks in the United States.[48] The next morning Sheriff Wylie Barnes arrested the pair on charges of violating the court order. In a preliminary hearing before Judge Scofield at 3:00 P.M., Mrs. Duke was released pending a formal hearing, but Haylon was held on a previous charge of passing a bad check.[49] An informal poll of students and faculty members by the *Daily* on February 23 showed little support for those in the rally, and two *Daily* editorials denounced the demonstration and the speakers.

Judge Scofield presided over a hearing starting on February 24 to consider making the temporary injunction permanent and to determine if Haylon and Mrs. Duke should be held in contempt of court. On March 4 the judge held both of them in contempt, sentencing Mrs. Duke to one day in jail and Haylon to three days in jail. Judge Scofield also issued a permanent injunction against them.[50]

A Suit Against NTSU

Mrs. Duke and Haylon filed suit on March 4 in the U. S. District Court in Tyler, seeking \$150,000 from the State of Texas. They claimed that legal action taken against them for their alleged participation in the February 17 rally was unconstitutional. They also sought an injunction to bar any further proceedings against them as a result of the rally. Their attorney, Michael Whitten, said that the size of damages was based on allegations of false arrest, false imprisonment, and denial of freedom of speech.[51]

At a preliminary hearing in Sherman March 10, U. S. District Court Judge William Wayne Justice granted a request to sever the injunction action from the damage suit, sending the latter to a later civil trial. He delayed the injunction hearing until April 5.[52] After two days of hearings, the judge took the case under advisement. On June 1, Justice ruled that the state court's contempt citation and restraining order were unconstitutional. His ruling also wiped out the North Texas policy concerning off-campus speakers, which he said violated the 1st and 14th amendments; that campus security regulations barring "undesirables" from the campus and the state statute which authorized that regulation were unconstitutionally vague and too broad; and that the Texas Penal Code that allows injunctions against individuals who constitute a "clear and present danger" was unconstitutionally applied because no danger was showed at the February 17 rally.[53]

Mrs. Duke felt vindicated and filed yet another suit in the federal court. She received a July 20 hearing date for her plea for reinstatement as a teaching fellow.[54] On September 2, the federal judge ruled that Mrs. Duke must be reinstated under the terms of her original contract and be subject to the terms of that contract. C. C. Nolen, who had just become president, said that the university was complying with the order and reinstating Mrs. Duke.[55] Mrs. Duke talked to student reporters:

> she said she will continue to perform as she did prior to her dismissal.
>
> "I don't think I need to make any promises to the university and I won't take the classes back on their terms," she said. "I shouldn't have been fired in the first place.". . .

"I still believe in revolution by any means necessary. I think this case shows you can work through the system sometimes, and I guess you ought to give the system a chance, but if there is no other means available, violence may be necessary," she said. "And when violence comes, I'll be ready for it."[56]

A Tragic Aftermath

Those 1971 quotes in the *Daily* proved prophetic. She moved to Austin, where she continued radical movement activities for about a dozen years. By one newspaper biographer's 1988 account, Mrs. Duke told her family in 1983 that she felt her life was in danger from the Ku Klux Klan and the FBI and "went underground." As part of an extensive review of Duke's career, reporter Doug J. Swanson wrote in the *Dallas Morning News*[57] of her arrest by FBI agents near Philadelphia on May 23, 1985, driven by a physician colleague and carrying two loaded handguns:

> A search of the car revealed two more guns, $9,000 in cash and the keys to a garage she had rented. . . nearby. . . .
>
> Agents who raided the garage discovered. . . 162 cartridges of dynamite, 1,000 feet of detonating cord, dozens of boxes of ammunition, an Uzi semiautomatic rifle, instructional booklets on the use of explosive and 275 counterfeit Social Security cards. . . .
>
> "Alan Berkman [her physician companion] and I are revolutionary anti-imperialists," Ms. Duke said at her arraignment in Philadephia. "We've done the most that we could to resist the crimes of United States imperialism. . . . There needs to be more active military resistance."
>
> Awaiting trial on charges that could have resulted in a sentence of 52 years, Ms. Duke was released on bail—over the vehement objections of prosecutors.[58]

The objections proved to be well-founded, for on October 12, 1985, Mrs. Duke disappeared from a home in a woods near Philadelphia. But that didn't end the story of her rebellion. Three years later, the federal government added another offense to the list for which she was sought—wishing to prosecute her for setting off a bomb in the U.S. Capitol. Elizabeth Ann Duke and six others were indicted in May 1988 for that bombing. The indictment also alleges that "as part of a radical left-wing group called the Armed Resistance Unit, they detonated seven other bombs in Washington and New York." Six of the seven defendants in the Capitol bombing case were brought to a Washington federal court on May 25, 1988, for arraignment. All pleaded not guilty. One of their number was missing: Mrs. Duke. A long-time friend from Austin, Lori Jo Hansel, told the Dallas reporter: "I hope she's well. I hope she's healthy. I hope they never catch her."[59]

THE CARTER YEAR ENDS

Announcement of the election of a new president was made on May 7, 1971. The *North Texas Daily* that morning quoted Carter as saying he hoped he would not be remembered as the president in office during the Duke-Haylon incident.[60] The case still had a distance to go in court, and it seemed that Carter would be unable to escape having the events of this case serve as one of the significant events of his year in office. He was, however, sent back to his fiscal domain with a ringing vote of confidence from the regents as articulated by Willis at a meeting called to introduce the president-elect to the faculty and staff:

> your Board of Regents wants to. . . publicly testify to our gratitude for the faithful and effective service of this man during a most difficult time. His loyalty and devotion and dedication to this institution has been an inspiration to all who serve it. . . . John Carter is a living example of a man that does his duty and has done it at North Texas. He puts North Texas first and John Carter second. And in the accurate annals of any history of this university in the future, there must be reserved an imperishable page for the faithful service of this good and decent man.[61]

part VII

Reaching Outward in Troubled Times

1971–1982

The need for private support of state-assisted universities is absolutely essential in providing that margin of greatness. Today, every public university we associate with greatness at the national level receives generous private financial support. It has been rightfully said that "Legislatures build basically sound universities, but *great* public universities are built by private gifts, grants and bequests." If North Texas State University is to achieve this greatness in all its academic programs and continue to increase its relevancy to the economy of North Texas and the Metroplex, it, too, must secure a larger share of the philanthropic dollar during the next decade.

Community Service Bureau, 1975

chapter 31

A New Team Arrives

After I was announced as President on May 7, I felt the need to bring together a top-level administrative team involving individuals whose energy, initiative and zeal would be harnessed in a compatible manner which would allow me to operate in the role of President as I see it. Change is a common characteristic of all large enterprises—universities in particular—and so I present to you now a new administrative team.

C. C. Nolen
Speech to the Faculty, August 1971

The Board of Regents emerged from executive session at 10:00 A.M. May 7, 1971, to announce that the seven regents present had elected forty-six-year-old Calvin Cleave Nolen as president effective August 1 at a salary of $37,500 per year. At 11:30 all but one of the board gathered on the stage of the Music Recital Hall to present their choice to an audience of faculty and staff. Chairman A. M. Willis spoke at length in tribute to Acting President John Carter, to the faculty-staff committee elected for the presidential search, and especially in praise of the regents' choice, C. C. "Jitter" Nolen, vice chancellor for development at Texas Christian University.

> Now, my friends, with all my heart I believe that this is the greatest day in the history of North Texas State University. In making this statement, I am not unmindful of the solid achievements of the past nor do I underestimate the challenges of the future. Your committee and your regents believe that your new president can meet that challenge. Make no mistake about it, this man has the 100 percent support of the board of regents, and he will be the boss.
>
> This man is a man of abiding honor and unquestioned integrity. He possesses keen intelligence, boundless energy, and broad vision. He understands the true meaning of academic excellence because he has been exposed to an academic community all his working life, and he is an acute observer. He is a fair man, a reasonable man, a responsible man, a tough man, and a compassionate man. He is a good communicator because he truly cares about people. He listens and he can make a decision.
>
> He has an intimate knowledge of the Dallas-Denton-Fort Worth triangle and is highly regarded in that area and in Austin and in state government and with state public officials. And he understands the vital importance to North Texas of building a public image that will deserve and maintain public confidence. . . .
>
> Put your trust in this man. Put North Texas first and yourselves second. Give this man your hand and your heart and your help, and if you do I promise you that he will give you the inspiration and the leadership and the direction to make this university be what it can be and must be—the pride of Texas and the envy of the Southwest.[1]

Regent Willis might be forgiven the elaborate language of praise, for he doubtless was extremely concerned about the nature of this faculty's reaction to the selection of Nolen. And a number of faculty members might have been showing concern at least as great in inspecting the president-elect, for he was chosen in spite of the lack of the first two of the eight qualifications stipulated by the document prepared by the faculty-staff search committee and approved by the Board of Regents. That list began this way:

- He should have a distinguished educational and academic background with an earned doctorate from a well-established university, recognized by his peers and experience as a college teacher.
- He should be broad in his academic outlook and have demonstrated an appreciation for the intrinsic values of disciplines other than his own.[2]

Even the concerns of Willis and the faculty about this new administration could not have anticipated the tragic events that would come in the next eight years. An immensely personable man, Nolen nonetheless proved to be unable to unite faculty support for his goals, managed to alienate a number of powerful regents, found himself accused of professional misconduct and misuse of funds, and in the end resigned under fire from state officials "for the good of the university."

INTRODUCING A NEW BREED OF EXECUTIVE

Nolen's biographical data indicated a twenty-year career in university administration: ten years as director of the student union at the University of Texas in Austin, four years as assistant director and three years as associate director of the UT Development Board, and three years as vice chancellor for development at Texas Christian University. His sole degree was a bachelor of arts in educational psychology received in 1948. He had never taught a class in his life. Apparently Chairman Willis had decided to bank on this man's strong experience in private fund-raising, his wide circle of friends and acquaintances in Texas political and business circles, and on his personality and reputation for devotion to church and service to public welfare agencies.

The image problem associated with the choice was summed up in a Dallas newspaper's Sunday magazine article before Nolen's November inauguration:

> On paper Nolen was not a likely candidate. True, he was familiar with universities, having been on the UT Austin campus for 18 years . . . before going to TCU in 1968. His down-to-earth approach and a broad sense of humor had made him a successful fund-raiser and tub-thumper for higher education. On the other hand, he had earned no degrees beyond his Bachelor of Arts in educational psychology from UT Austin in 1948. North Texas had not had a full-time president without an earned doctorate since 1934. Nolen had no teaching experience; his university jobs had been strictly management positions. Finally, Nolen lacked in the mind's eye a sense of dignity and serenity customarily associated with the office of university president. His nickname was based on a popular comic strip character of the 1930s and 1940s, an energetic, mischievous monkey named Jitter. Nolen was an ex-UT cheerleader who stated unequivocally that his best management decisions were firmly rooted in his experiences as a Boy Scout senior patrol leader. If Nolen were named president, there would be some audible gasps from the more tradition-prone corners of academe.[3]

Nolen Meets the North Texas Family

The Nolen personality stood him in good stead as he faced this new challenge. His background as a student union director and as a fund-raiser for two major universities had honed his personal skills, and he was able to relate quickly to almost any type of individual or audience. His strong church background, a continued dedication to the Boy Scout movement, and even his undergraduate experience as a cheerleader, a member of the Friar Society, and selection as one of four Cactus (yearbook) outstanding students were building blocks for his leadership style. Even his nickname—the only first name ever used—was adopted when he was a youngster at a Boy Scout gathering and someone called him "Jitter." His first public words on the North Texas campus, made in response to that Willis introduction, called for an effort aimed at lifting the reputation of North Texas.

> North Texas State University probably has the greatest potential today for good of any university in our state and perhaps beyond. Here is a university with a strong tradition of the past, the gathered capacity of the future resting in a town with another fine institution and sitting

at the apex of the most golden triangle of the state. It would be a shame if we became anything less than one of the leaders in this state . . . .[4]

Reaction to the Selection

Nolen felt that he had the complete support of all of the regents. The *Dallas Times Herald* quoted Nolen as saying that he had the one hundred percent backing of the regents, who had reassured him that their job was to conduct policy decisions and his job was to see that they were carried out.[5] Ironically, it was conflict with some regents and an inability to get board members to unify behind him that led to some of the university's problems during his term.

Nolen's correspondence just after his selection showed an understandable apprehension. He wrote to Congressman Jim Wright that regents chose him "in the hope that a man who has been dealing with private fund-raising could bring a measure of efficiency to the Office of President that a man of purely academic background might not be able to bring."[6] In May he wrote Logan Wilson, president of the American Council on Education, that he had become involved with the NT board in helping them to attract Bryce Jordan to the post, but Jordan remained with the UT system as president of the University of Texas at Dallas. "After that," he wrote Wilson, "the North Texas board decided they needed a cheerleader and the idea was too fascinating to pass up."[7]

Church and Public Service

Nolen brought the religion of his private life into his public role. He inserted religious references into many actions as president in a way that had not been done at North Texas. While still working at TCU he told a supporter that "All public universities that I know of could do with a little more Christian love and our intention is to carry that with us if we can."[8] That effort attracted much attention and some criticism when he called for public prayer at the first faculty meeting in August. He asked the new academic vice president, Dr. Gus Ferré, to give an opening prayer, commenting on his desire to bring a religious faith to university affairs. Some told him privately that he had overstepped the bounds of accepted practice at a public university, something that appeared to startle Nolen. Yet other faculty and staff members thanked him for the religious concern.

Nolen maintained a major role in the governance of his church, the Disciples of Christ, the group that supports Texas Christian University, and in 1973 agreed to serve as a member of the General Board of the Christian Church.[9] He arranged for NTSU administrators and faculty members to "fill the pulpits" of Denton churches on various Sundays in November. President Nolen, Vice President Ferré, and others gave sermons at many Denton churches.[10]

Even after six years in office, Nolen made forthright statements of personal faith. In his speech to the fall faculty meeting, the president adopted an ecumenical posture:

> Each of us should be able to find ways to witness to our own faith in such a way that we encourage an awareness that all human endeavor stands under the judgment and mercy of God. Our own lives should be an affirmation of hope and promise as we strive to become and to develop fully human persons—for my part as measured by the priesthood of Jesus Christ.[11]

Willis Leads in Search

The presidential search process had not gone as smoothly as the previous one. By November 1970, some dissatisfaction was evident on the campus about the lack of results from the search committee. After a November board meeting, Willis told a reporter, "I could get us a president tomorrow, but I want the best president in the United States. I'll guarantee you I'm on his track."[12] Three months later, the chairman said that the procedure was still in the personal interview stage and no appointment date could yet be named.[13]

What Willis did not disclose was that the committee had offered the position in the fall to Dr. Bryce Jordan, acting president of the University of Texas at Austin. A *Dallas Times Herald* writer later reported that "the hopes of the selection group remained high as Jordan seriously considered the offer for several months. By February he had reached his decision: no."[14] But two years later, Willis was still praising the man who had become the UT-Dallas president: "In my judgment, Bryce Jordan was beyond question the most able man we considered, and we offered him the presidency of North Texas State University."[15]

Records of what happened next in the search process are not to be found in the university archives, a dramatic contrast to the detailed records of the selection of John Kamerick three years earlier. Nolen has written that it was he who nominated Bryce Jordan for the North Texas presidency and that his acquaintance with Willis developed while he, Nolen, was interceding with Jordan to persuade him to accept the job. Willis subsequently asked Nolen to submit a résumé to offer his own name for consideration. Various committee members recall that the Willis technique in promoting the Nolen candidacy was to discuss the possibility individually and in private with faculty or board members.

IMPORTING A "NEW TEAM"

The Board of Regents announced on the morning of May 7, 1971, that it had selected Nolen. In taking this action the Board noted that it had "accepted and endorsed a letter of May 6, 1971, from Mr. Nolen to Chairman Willis."[16] Willis and Nolen had agreed that the four vice presidents would submit resignations effective Aug. 1, 1971, to enable Nolen to choose new personnel. They also agreed to implement quickly a long-range planning process, at least ten years ahead. The board and the president would invest time and money to aggressively attract private funds to NTSU. [17]

On May 7 Nolen met with the four vice presidents as a group and asked each of them to write him a letter of resignation immediately. In choosing Carter as acting president, Willis had stipulated that he must not become a candidate for the permanent position but assured him that he would resume his fiscal vice president's position. In listing his candidates for academic vice president in the letter, Nolen had effectively announced that he would not continue Spurlock in that role. He told Rogers that he intended to abolish the office of vice president for administrative affairs. It was quickly determined that Lindley would no longer be employed at North Texas, Spurlock would return to his post as professor of chemistry, and Rogers would be asked to create and direct an office of institutional research. Several months later, Nolen told the *Dallas Times Herald* that there had been no evaluation: "I simply told each of the vice presidents that I would not be able to get to know them well enough to make the decision properly. I just felt the need to move on with a new team."[18]

Leaders From TCU, UT Austin

Nolen chose new team members from among those he had known at Texas Christian University and the University of Texas at Austin. The first to be announced was Dr. Gustave A. Ferré, chairman of the philosophy department at TCU. He was named academic vice president on June 16. Ferré, fifty-four, had served as chairman of the Faculty Senate at TCU. Most of his experience had been at small church-related colleges such as Cotner, Rio Grande College, and Alderson-Broaddus College. A native of Sweden, he earned a bachelor of arts from Boston University, bachelor of divinity degree from Andover Newton Theological School, and a doctorate from Vanderbilt University.

Two days later, Nolen announced that the vice president for student affairs would be Dr. Rollin Sininger, forty-one, dean of students for six years at Stephen F. Austin State University. Sininger indicated that he had been friends for many years with Nolen, who was director of the UT Student Union while Sininger was assistant dean of students at the Austin university.

Nolen's team-building recognized that his role was that of fund-raiser, not academic leader. His role would be "taking to the stump for the sake of this university. . . in attracting the public confidence and the public support that will be necessary for us to continue," he told the *Times Herald*. "I'm probably not equipped to be the educational leader, so I will have to rely in large measure on Dr. Ferré's. . . leadership in that area."[19]

In moving to activate the fund-raising function in the first week of June, Nolen sought the advice of Art Frantzreb of the consulting firm of Frantzreb and Pray Associates of New York, which had presented a development planning audit for NTSU in June 1970, just as Kamerick was leaving office. Nolen wrote that he was discontinuing the position of administrative vice president "so I can get directly at some of the administrative areas such as Public Relations, Alumni Affairs and Development.[20] He moved Dr. James H. Stewart from director of development to assistant to the president. Named new development director was Jim Reid, development director at Southwestern University in Georgetown.

Also coming from Austin that fall would be Dr. Jim B. Pearson, a historian who was named associate vice president for academic affairs. Dr. Miles Anderson was changed from associate vice president to executive associate to the academic vice president. Ferré, Sininger, and Pearson all received immediate tenure. Nolen worked hard to stress the importance of the arrival of "a new team" that would make a major difference in the operation of the university.

Academic Changes Proposed

Nolen gave Ferré a major role in the first faculty meeting. Ferré made it clear that he came with a mandate for major change. He called for a review of academic programs and their leaders, suggesting that he would not necessarily accept the views of faculty committees, and that as a result there might be efforts made to remove him from office. In essence, Ferré was saying that he intended to evaluate each dean and, if necessary, to replace him—a "new team" at the level of the colleges and schools. He stressed that he would make final decisions by himself.[21]

Ferré asserted that if the goal is great teaching, then faculty rewards would follow accordingly. He called for the basing of promotion, tenure, and salaries on the basis of "research that is worthwhile and teaching that is worthwhile." He suggested looking at the organization of the university in some areas such as dividing the College of Arts and Sciences into three different colleges.[22]

Ferré at Work

Ferré exhibited a new management style that quickly brought conflict with the academic deans, the Faculty Senate, and many of the faculty. He showed determination to extend Nolen's "new team" approach throughout the academic community. He later wrote that his first objective had been to evaluate the leadership quality of each academic dean. He asked each school and college to assess its strengths and weaknesses and to outline goals for five years. The result was described this way:

> After careful study of the reports and long personal inquiry, the Vice President of Academic Affairs found it necessary to look for new leadership at the dean's level for each of the schools and colleges with the exception of the Graduate School. . . . It was understood that after the deans were hired it would be their responsibility to evaluate the leadership at the department level and recommend necessary changes.[23]

The "new team" philosophy was clearly re-emphasized by Nolen in a 1976 institutional progress report to the Board of Regents, in which he listed the number-one achievement of his administration in academic affairs to be "upgrading of leadership positions within academic units, including the vice-president and seven new deans."[24]

The philosophical revolution in faculty participation brought by the Kamerick administration was not acceptable to Ferré. He asserted that "the Faculty Senate and University Review Committee and the Curriculum Committee had been led to believe, by a previous administration, that they had final decision-making roles." He wrote that it was his job to convince the faculty organizations that their functions were to advise and not to decide. "Unfortunately," he admitted, "this continued the adversary relationship between faculty and administration." [25]

ORGANIZING FOR ACTION

The pattern provided by John Kamerick's President's Cabinet was adopted by Nolen. His first cabinet comprised Carter, Ferré, and Sininger. But this left out a number of units that reported directly to the president, giving him a span of control far greater than the size of the cabinet. So he created a formal "president's staff" that would meet independently of the cabinet. Members were the directors of development, of public information, of the alumni office, and of planning and analysis, and an assistant to the president. The president's staff could advise him and conduct activities on his behalf but they were to leave all decision-making powers to the cabinet. Nevertheless, there remained a considerable territorial tension among the vice presidents and staff members.

Nolen continued the concept of the Administrative Council. In December 1971 he named thirty-five members to this council and suggested that it would meet in January. Members were the vice presidents, the president's staff, all academic deans, and first-line administrators who reported to one of the vice presidents. But it was not called upon for any identifiable function, and the Southern Association Self-Study report in September 1973 asserted that "The Council has been inactive since 1971."[26] That self-study identified a pressing need for more effective coordination of the work of the academic, student, and fiscal functions: "For the very good reason that such functions remain loosely defined, the faculty does not clearly understand the functions of the President's Cabinet, the Administrative Council, and the Council of Deans."[27]

Management Problems Arise

Nolen addressed some of these management problems before the arrival of the Southern Association team in early October. In September 1973 he announced the enlargement of the President's Cabinet and the reactivation of the Administrative Council.

The existing cabinet members were called the executive committee (voting members). Three others were added as "nonvoting, full-participation members": Dr. Marvin Berkeley, the dean of the College of Business Administration who served as consultant to the president on interdepartmental affairs; Rogers; and Roy Busby, assistant to the president. Nolen hoped that the nonvoting members would bring less parochial views on issues, but he reserved the decision power for the vice presidents.

Nolen continued to change personnel or duties assigned for members of his staff. In November 1972 he reversed his first instructions assigning responsibilities for planning new buildings and major remodeling to the physical plant administration under Carter. Now the president asked Rogers to resume all of the facilities planning and programming functions. Busby had been director of public information but was moved in May 1973 to the position of assistant to the president after Stewart left to become president of the new Tyler State College. Janice Odom was promoted from assistant to director of public information. The following July Jack Wheeler moved from associate vice president for student affairs to a new position, special assistant to the president, assigned to deal mainly with governmental relations.

Even after two years, in 1973, the organization was still bothered with confusion about some responsibilities and authority. The dean of students complained to Sininger that a student found cheating had been suspended from school by academic officials, whereas the Code of Student Conduct made this a matter for the dean of students to discipline. Sininger in turn wrote Ferré, "In the future, please advise faculty and staff to refer all cases of misconduct to the dean of student's office or let's consider placing the whole system within your area."[28] Two months later Ferré complained to Nolen that a student affairs committee had dropped an academic dean from membership and that "The present committee has no representative from this office, which this office considers regrettable."[29] A little earlier Ferré complained that his academic authority was being undermined by Rogers, who had published for the first time a university fact book containing detailed enrollment and budgetary data for circulation to the entire university community. Ferré told Nolen and Rogers in a conference that deans and department chairmen were "using these data against me" in arguing for their budget requests and asserted that such information should be restricted for his use in decision-making.

Unfortunately, the faculty-administration relationships did not improve with time. The faculty reacted negatively to a number of changes in style. The president's outgoing personality seemed to deflect some of this friction away from his office, but it lodged at the next step down the table of organization, in the office of the vice president for academic affairs. The 1973 accreditation visitors' report dealt rather sternly with what they perceived as a flawed academic organization. In particular, they wrote:

> There does seem to be a vast gulf between the departments and the higher administration in regard to faculty communications and input. The faculty are willing to cooperate with the administration. *One of the key questions seems to be whether the Vice President for Academic Affairs will be able to delegate his authority to the various deans and directors and to utilize their inputs in the decision-making process.*[30]

Nolen called a newly constituted Administrative Council into session on September 6 to charge it with more formal action. He also enlarged the membership in keeping with the recommendations that would appear in the self-study by adding two Faculty Senate representatives, two from the Student Government Association, and the president of the Student Activities Union. He told the group its purpose was "to provide for regular and systematic discussion of university problems, questions of policy, and administrative procedures. Recommendations of this group would be forwarded to the President's Cabinet."[31]

It was no surprise, then, when the report of the Southern Association called for continued efforts to improve organizational communication and coordination:

> *It is suggested that the President's Office attend to coordination at all levels at the earliest opportunity. Specific attention should be directed toward the relationships of the vice presidents with one another and with members of the faculty and staff.*

Finally, *efforts should be undertaken to improve communication between administrators and faculty as well as between administrators and students, especially as regards the flow from faculty and students to top administration.*[32]

Two months later, the president was clearly still expressing frustration at his inability to get a manager's hands on the information he needed. He wrote to each vice president, asking to be "more thoroughly informed about pressing matters over which each vice president has direct responsibility." [33]

The administrative frustration spread to the conduct of meetings of the President's Cabinet. In the spring of 1976 the Board of Regents asked Nolen to bring a progress report to the board to help it evaluate the "efficiency and efficacy of the administrative system in fostering a climate for the achievement of the university goals." This led Nolen and the cabinet to a goal for "improvement of the cabinet procedures for establishing agendas, conducting meetings, and following up on action items." Nolen moved in November of 1976 to change cabinet procedures. He named Rogers as cabinet secretary and asked each cabinet member to work with him in preparing the agenda, furnishing ten copies of each document that needed cabinet discussion or action. He declared that cabinet sessions should concentrate on "discussion and decision on policy, problems, and plans of general university concern, and items of information which will benefit from discussion across lines of vice presidential responsibility." He asked that the vice presidents inform all cabinet members on matters that involved just their areas, serving "the information function and at the same time help us to concentrate cabinet meeting activity on general concerns and matters needing group interaction."[34]

Puzzling Over Physical Plant

Carter's response to the self-study suggested that the pending reorganization of physical plant operations would clear up problems mentioned in that area. His desire for the change illustrated the difficulties that had existed for some time in handling a difficult operation on a very low budget. President Matthews had named Dr. Wayne Adams, an education professor, as assistant to the president in the 1950s and used him as the administrative link to physical plant planning, construction, and management. Later, he hired John Matt Howard from a Fort Worth engineering firm, naming him assistant to the president and resident engineer. When Kamerick became president, he did not like the arrangement and transferred Howard and all physical plant operations to the fiscal vice president.

Correspondence files show that Carter and Howard disagreed frequently, and that Carter was frustrated by some of Howard's manner of operations. When regents such as Bruce Street and Hugh Wolfe began complaining to Carter about the condition of buildings and grounds, Carter identified Howard as the cause of the problems. Accordingly, he secured Nolen's agreement to remove Howard as director of physical plant operations.[35] Nolen reassigned Howard as resident engineer, attached to the Office of Institutional Analysis and Planning. In comments reacting to the 1973 self-study, Carter predicted that the problems would be solved by the reorganized physical plant operations. In fact, however, the split in functions made coordination among divisions even more difficult and created major difficulties for the president that would contribute to his eventual alienation from some board members.

By this time, it was evident that the president did not have effective control of administrative operations.

The New Team Begins to Break Up

In May 1974 it was announced without public explanation that Vice President Rollin Sininger would take a leave of absence for the fall semester and would then accept a spring-semester teaching assignment in the Psychology Department. Sininger was guaranteed an amount equal to his twelve-month administrative salary for the next two years.

For the fall semester, "during Sininger's absence," the associate vice president, Jane Gentry Smith, was designated to represent student affairs at the President's Cabinet and the Faculty Senate, while Dean of Students Ell Sorenson represented the division at the Council of Deans.[36] Smith was named vice president for student affairs ad interim, February 1 to June 1, 1975, and the "ad interim" was removed on September 1, 1975.

By this time, the private Texas College of Osteopathic Medicine had been made a state school assigned to the North Texas State University Board of Regents (see Chapter 34.) This complicated Nolen's administrative/managerial problems. A new dean was to be employed for TCOM, but until that time, Nolen felt the need for an experienced university administrator to report to him in his dual role as president of TCOM as well as of NTSU. That led him to get Ferré to take a year's leave of absence and to become vice president for medical affairs, ad interim, TCOM, for twelve months starting September 1, 1975. Nolen wrote to Ferré, "This means you have the option to return to the office of vice president for academic affairs, NTSU, beginning September 1, 1976."[37] Nolen asked Ferré to serve as chief academic officer at TCOM, to be replaced during that interim as academic vice president for NTSU.

In February of 1976, as Ferré was planning to resume the academic vice presidency at NTSU, Nolen advised Ferré that he would be named consultant to the NTSU president the following year. Ferré told Nolen by memorandum on February 10 that he could not accept that position. Nolen wrote back to Ferré on the same day, stating that "your request to return as Vice President for Academic Affairs cannot be granted."[38]

Ferré continued to work at his TCOM post, and in April Nolen addressed to him another memorandum about his future:

> You will serve as Consultant to the President and will be placed on the NTSU budget. As Consultant you will be responsible for several important matters and will be carried on the budget for 60 percent of his time. . . . You would be serving also as Professor of Philosophy, on leave for the period September 1, 1976, through August 31,1977. . . . However, it is not anticipated that the Consultant position would be carried beyond August 31, 1977.[39]

However, the *Denton Record-Chronicle* on May 30, 1976, reported that Ferré had been named senior minister of Dallas First Community Church and that he would continue as a consultant to Nolen. The writer described it this way:

> Several times Ferré came under fire from NTSU faculty members whose overwhelming opinion in a campus-wide poll last year was that they did not want him to return to NTSU after his year at TCOM.
>
> Ferré said emphatically this had nothing to do with his decision to accept the First Community offer. . . .
>
> The president Thursday. . . said the position of vice president for medical affairs would not continue, with TCOM Dean Ralph L. Willard assuming "operational control."[40]

Enlarging the Team

At the start of 1975–76, the university had two new people as vice presidents: Miles Anderson for academic affairs and Jane Smith for student affairs. The process of enlarging the size of the administrative staff was well under way. In two years as assistant to the president, Jack Wheeler had integrated himself well into the circle of higher education representatives in Austin. In 1975 he was named vice president for public affairs. Wheeler, however, moved on to join the University of Texas system the following year. To fill the Austin lobbying role in November 1976, Nolen turned to a retired vice president from Texas A&M, Tom Cherry. Cherry had been the principal fiscal officer at A&M and had established high visibility and credibility in Austin. Under state retirement laws, he was able to work one-third time for NTSU, continuing to live in College Station but traveling to Denton and Austin as needed.

In November 1976, Nolen created three new vice president positions. Roy Busby was named vice president for university relations. He continued some of his assistant-to-the-president functions, including serving as secretary to the Board of Regents, and began broadened responsibilities for the development office, public information office, and intercollegiate athletics. Nolen persuaded the business dean, Dr. Marvin Berkeley, to serve one year in an ad interim role as vice president for administrative affairs. In reinstituting this position, the president asked Berkeley to devise a system for coordinating the functions of planning and analysis, physical plant, security, legal adviser, and equal opportunity. Dr. Ralph Willard joined Texas College of Osteopathic Medicine as dean of the college and also became vice president for medical affairs and joined the NTSU President's Cabinet. When Berkeley's ad interim year was up, Nolen named to his position Hermas Miller, vice president for fiscal affairs at West Texas State University. Miller had previously been employed in state government in Austin, including service with the Legislative Budget Board. E. E. Stuessy of Austin and several other regents suggested him to Nolen for the NTSU position.

NOLEN AND WILLIS: THE REAL TEAM?

It was evident early that Nolen regarded the university as the responsibility of a Willis-Nolen partnership. The closeness of the two could be seen in their voluminous correspondence, numerous telephone calls, and the frequent presence of Willis on the campus. (In one sense, this was not a completely new situation: we saw in an earlier chapter that President Matthews and Chairman Wooten maintained a close liaison throughout, but this was a formal one and did not involve frequent contact or campus visits by Wooten.)

Working for Willis

When Nolen had been president for nine months, Willis moved to Washington as an administrative assistant associated with Congressman Ray Roberts of McKinney. He continued as NTSU board chairman and still made frequent trips to the campus in that connection. Willis employed a hands-on style in dealing with campus questions, the most striking example being his immediate and direct intervention in the dismissal of Elizabeth Ann Duke. Willis frequently asked administrators to send reports directly to him, especially when he was following up on a negative report.

Perpetuating the Willis Name

Early in 1978, Nolen and Willis began conversing about naming a building for Willis. Long-time board policy stated that nothing on the campus would be named for a living person, stressing that no administrator or board member could receive such an honor. Attitude toward this policy was changed at the insistence of Nolen, who wanted the freedom to solicit large capital gifts that would lead to the naming of a facility for a living donor. The policy itself fell when board members wanted to name buildings for their long-time chairman, Ben Wooten; for another colleague whom they greatly admired, Carroll Sullivant; and for President Emeritus J. C. Matthews, who for a long time sternly resisted Nolen's efforts to name the Education-Home Economics Building for him. Once Wooten Hall, Matthews Hall, and the Sullivant Visitor Center had those names in place, the old naming policy was dead.

Thus it was that on August 24, 1978, the Board of Regents resolved to designate the new structure as the A. M. Willis, Jr., Library. The resolution declared that because Willis "expresses constantly his deep devotion and great respect for the intellectual, social, and human accomplishments of the university, it is appropriate that he be honored for his loyal and devoted service." Nolen joined in, saying, "no one is more worthy of having this particular facility named in his honor. He is the complete board chairman."[41]

The move led to a Faculty Senate resolution on October 11 opposing the regents' action on grounds that it departed from the original policy of the naming of buildings.[42]

WORKING WITH THE BOARD

The furor that surrounded the Elizabeth Ann Duke case had reinforced the desire of some board members to keep a close watch on the campus. Nolen inherited the Duke case and her suit against the university. After just one month in office, Nolen received a federal court order reinstating Mrs. Duke. He sent a copy of the order from District Judge Justice to each regent, reporting that he was in the process of complying.[43]

Regents Stay Involved

During Nolen's eight years in office, regents became more and more directly involved in campus detail, often offering helpful support. Bruce Street of Graham, for example, was interested in art, and his enthusiasm brought him to the campus in November 1971 to oversee preparation for proper landscaping and beautification of the Art Building to be in place at the time of a major ceremony for the opening of the building.[44] Regent Dean Davis in company with Willis talked to John Carter and gave instructions about how much money should be placed on deposit in each of three Denton banks. Nolen wrote Davis to say that he hoped deposits could be placed in a manner that would boost his fund-raising efforts. He wanted more in Dallas and Fort Worth banks and asked Davis's permission to increase the suggested deposit for one Denton bank by fifty percent.[45]

E. E. Stuessy of Austin, a public construction company owner, came on the board in 1973 and was almost immediately named chairman of the board's building committee. He quickly immersed himself in the details of construction activities on the campus. When Miles Anderson asked John Carter for some assistance from physical plant crews on some campus improvements, Carter told him he had to assign more people elsewhere because "Mr. Stuessy has criticized us for the way the window sashes look outside the Administration Building. [46] Stuessy was politically active and closely aligned with Governor Dolph Briscoe, and Nolen often asked him to use his influence with the governor in behalf of proposed legislative programs. In 1976 Nolen sent a check for one hundred dollars to Stuessy for tickets for a dinner honoring Governor Briscoe. In October of that year the president wrote Stuessy to ask him to support a write-in candidate for associate justice of the Supreme Court of Texas in the November election, "my friend, Judge Sam Houston," then a district court judge in Denton County. "I hope you will help me spread the word about this man. More than that I plan to support him with a contribution to his campaign fund and I hope you will join me in doing the same," Nolen wrote.[47]

Willis visited with officers of the Student Association. He asked the acting student affairs vice president, Jane Gentry Smith, in the fall of 1974 to report to him about a list of complaints he had received from Quincy Ollison, the student president. Smith reported to Nolen about her "letter to Monk about Quincy's list." She told Willis that she wished she could assure him that the problems on the list had disappeared but they had not. She gave the board chairman her assessment of the problem source for each and the "progress we may have made." Quincy's list included the Health Center, a Day Care Center, alcohol policy, financial aid, student employment, affirmative action programs, student service fee for fine arts and stadium bonds, assistance programs for minority students, and club sports.[48]

An Accreditation Warning

An outside evaluation of the style of the regents' involvement in the operation of NTSU was provided by the visiting committee for the Southern Association. The committee acknowledged the effectiveness of the Board of Regents in its role as policy-maker and said it had made major contributions to the growth and development of the university. But this was followed by the statement of a major concern:

> While it is frequently very difficult to draw the line between policy and procedure and between actions related to the development of policy and actions related to actual administration, it is essential that members of governing boards studiously avoid even the impression of what might be considered interference in administration. In the case of North Texas State University there is some evidence that well-meaning regents have become more involved in the actual administration of the institution than is appropriate. Since this impression was not a result of complaints by University officials, it is perhaps sufficient, at present, to dismiss the matter by suggesting that *current members of the Board of Regents maintain the traditional separation of powers so vital to the health of North Texas State University.*[49]

Available records for that time don't show a response to this suggestion by Nolen or by the board members. The following summer, Willis wrote to a new board member, Kenneth May of Lubbock, outlining the ways in which he would suggest that May view the responsibilities of a regent:

> One of the great difficulties in our Board is that we do not meet enough times a year to have the full Board briefed on all the things the University is doing. I have made certain suggestions to Mr. Nolen to try to correct this situation. My own view happens to be that one of the things that is wrong with higher education is the failure of the boards to involve themselves with the plans and problems of their individual institutions. I do not mean involving the boards in the day-to-day operations of the universities but they have a right and an obligation to be knowledgeable about the performance of the individual institutions they serve. As you know, educators have a tendency to only want support when they get in trouble or to rubber stamp all their recommendations. They like to maximize minor successes and forget or cover up weaknesses.[50]

After two more years of operating in the same manner (or perhaps with even greater regent participation in administration), the president stood up and cried, "Enough!" On September 11, 1975, he wrote the regents that he had sent a memorandum to members of the President's Cabinet to remind them "of the obligation each has regarding the free flow of information between regents and our key administrators. I trust each regent will appreciate my position in this matter." He enclosed a copy of his cabinet memo.[51] The memo revealed Nolen's sense of losing control and of his need to assert his leadership role. Cabinet members were told to inform the president of any information they received from or sent to board members. He advised them, "It would be impossible to be responsible for the entire administration of the University without having all the knowledge necessary by which responsible decisions and delegation of authority or responsibility can be made."[52]

After four years in office, President Nolen still faced obstacles in organizing for planning and management and for maintaining strong policy relationships with the entire Board of Regents.

chapter 32

In Search of Goals

I am convinced that the university which does not make clear choices about what it will be and what it will not be, will, at the same instant, not make progress and will begin to die at the core.

C. C. Nolen
Speech to the Faculty, August 1974

Nolen had committed to rapid implementation of long-range planning, at least ten years ahead. He had also recognized that short-term goals would necessarily be stated in two-year terms, writing "that at least two years will be required to implement some current projections."[1]

Three years later, in August 1974, Nolen told a faculty meeting that his vague and generic impressions of North Texas had now been refined and fleshed out by his "baptism of fire" with the Southern Association self-study, the legislature, and a constitutional convention. He declared the two overriding goals for the year to be to maintain the North Texas position as the leading university in the region and to be "the very best university of which we are capable." He said "we are fighting very hard to maintain the first but we can do a lot better job of the second." To that end, he outlined four objectives in support of those goals:

1. Good teaching.
2. Take the university to the community.
3. Adequate rewards for the faculty.
4. Student recruiting.[2]

PLANNING IS PARAMOUNT

Evaluation of the president, staff, and faculty was intimately intertwined in Nolen's mind with the planning process. Nolen's navy training had oriented him toward management by objectives, and his work in university development had immersed him in the development of case statements, missions, and the evaluation of results with donated funds.

Step One: 115 Faculty Members Undertake Self-Study

The second ten-year follow-up study by NTSU for the Southern Association of Colleges and Schools should have begun in 1970–71. This, of course, came as an interim president took over during the search for a new president, so the association allowed the school to wait until the next president would have been in office for several months. This provided Nolen with an opportune vehicle to explore recommendations for new directions for the institution.

After consultation with the Faculty Senate, Nolen named to chair the self-study Dr. Miles Anderson, executive associate vice president for academic affairs. After talking to faculty members and department chairmen, Anderson recommended a list to the president, who appointed an eight-member steering committee. This group, in turn, named members of eleven committees to study and report on the areas required by the Southern Association. Each school, college, and department was asked to do an internal study of its operations. As Anderson later reported to the Faculty Senate, of the 118 committee members, only three administrators were involved.[3]

The self-study found several themes occurring repeatedly, deserving immediate attention. They were:

> 1. Absence of apparent long-range, or even short-range planning.
> 2. Lack of clear statements of purpose and goals.
> 3. Lack of administrative policy statements on a variety of matters.
> 4. General confusion about the roles which are or should be played by various constituencies of the institution, particularly with respect to questions of governance.
> 5. Proliferation of administrative structures and positions and rising administrative costs.
> 6. Absence of general understanding of how budgets are prepared and administered. Criticism of what is understood.
> 7. Lack of funds.
>
> All of the above seven items, in fact, could be related in one way or another to the over-all issue of planning. This lack is the most obvious common factor in the entire study; it is also perhaps its most important finding. We believe that the organization of this university for long-range planning on a continuous basis is its most pressing need.[4]

What Is Our Mission?

The last systematic attempt to define purpose of the university was published in the 1962 self-study for the Southern Association. This statement said this was "to fulfill its role through the following functions: Instruction, Research, and Public Service." To provide the goals committee with a starting point, the steering committee administered an Institutional Goals Inventory developed by the Educational Testing Service, giving it to all faculty and administrators and to a sample of 400 students. The goals committee then drafted a statement of purpose but, having done so, immediately declared it inadequate and called for the creation of yet another committee to develop "a more clearly defined statement of purpose."[5]

Seeking a Unique Combination?

Comparing responses to the goals inventory with those at seventy doctoral-level American universities, the steering committee concluded that the North Texas constituency did not want to fit into the mold of the purely research-oriented university or of the institution that placed most of its emphasis on teaching. One major strength the respondents sought to maintain grew out of the institution's teachers college-state college heritage: "a student-oriented concern for intellectual, personal, and academic development, fostered by an environment in which personal relationships among faculty and students are encouraged." In addition, however, the emergence from this teachers college background into a state university is "recognized in a much greater concern for developing graduate study and research programs." The committee concluded this way:

> It may well be that these goal responses constitute a strong call for the planning of an academic community which can blend the following elements without major conflict.
>
> 1. The best of the past: a strong, student-oriented undergraduate teaching mission.
>
> 2. The most successful new programs of the emerging university: strong graduate programs and a vigorous research activity.
>
> 3. The most promising area for future development: continuing education and public service geared to the needs of the surrounding metropolitan community.[6]

Visiting Committee Responds

The Southern Association sent its visiting committee to the North Texas campus October 7–10, 1973, "at a time when the University was beginning to recover from four changes in presidential leadership in a period of five years." Almost whimsically, the visiting committee summarized the situation:

> That the University academic community not only lived through but throve during this period of administrative handkerchief-dropping, is a testimony to the ability of a university to survive administrative deprivations as long as it has its faculties about it. With its present president, the administrative situation has been in the process of stabilizing.[7]

Clarify the Purpose

The visitors asked the president to appoint a representative committee to develop a statement that would "adequately and precisely reflect the purpose of the university." "This would now seem possible in view of the stability of and confidence in the new administration that has been observed throughout the campus during the course of this visit. There appears to be widespread optimism with regard to the future development of the University."[8]

Give More to the Library

Improvements in library procedures were suggested. These included membership in the Council of Deans for the director of libraries, restudy of the formula method of allocating book budgets, systematic weeding of the collection, increased budget for library needs, and extending faculty rank, status, and salaries for the professional staff.

Graduate Studies Come of Age

The visiting committee noted that in the decade since the Commission on Higher Education approved creation of doctoral programs and sanctioned expansion at this level into the humanities, sciences, and social sciences, "the graduate program of this institution may be said to have come of age." Further, the Coordinating Board from 1965 on reinforced the status of North Texas as one of six universities designated for continuing growth in the graduate disciplines. In an italicized cautionary note, however, the report said:

> *It is suggested that before exposing itself to the stresses of expanding activities, the graduate faculty at North Texas should carefully assess its resources and its procedures to make certain that the integrity of present programs is protected and that the development of new ventures has firm footing and adequate financial support.*[9]

The committee expressed some concern over the excessive size of some graduate seminars and the presence of too many students of marginal ability, said by some faculty members to be admitted simply "to fill the quotas of teaching assistants." For that reason, the group recommended that the faculty take leadership in increasing the quality of graduate students and in preparing teaching assistants to handle their teaching assignments.

Encourage Research

The visitors were "convinced that the support of research by North Texas State is substantial" and expressed approval of the president's proposals to develop "pinnacles of excellence" as graduate programs demonstrated their vitality. To the president they wrote that an already strong Mathematics Department should "be encouraged to advance its concerns to even higher levels, both for its own organic development and as a buttress to the already strong research programs in physics and chemistry." The committee further suggested that the humanities, especially English, history, and foreign languages, should be pressed to demonstrate more research activity.[10]

Expand the Planning Effort

The accreditation group noted that the North Texas self-study report provided an excellent analysis of the situation at the university, recognizing areas of weakness and showing commitment to improvement in those areas. Because the new administration had understandably placed high priority on meeting immediate needs, the study gave little attention to future plans and projections. A major recommendation was restated: "Current efforts in the area of planning should be expanded and accelerated to develop short and long range plans for the university as a whole as well as for each division within the institution."[11]

NOLEN AFTER FOUR YEARS

The Southern Association had granted a grace period for a young administration to get oriented, identify needed directions, and propose implementation plans. Concrete action plans were now expected. In notifying Nolen that the annual meeting of the association in December 1974 had reaffirmed the accreditation of NTSU, association executives requested the submission of the first follow-up report by September 1975.[12]

At the same time, Nolen had launched the university into an era of private fund-raising. This needed the base of a "case statement," the development officer's tool for working with potential donors. Further, the Board of Regents sought an instrument for evaluating the president's leadership and accomplishments.

To meet these needs, Nolen and his staff prepared a four-year progress report to appear early in 1976: *President's Report, North Texas State University,*

1971–1975. This was a handsome, expensive document of fifty-four pages, probably the most elaborate promotional publication that had ever been published at North Texas. In it, Nolen introduced a recitation of accomplishments with this statement:

> This administration has seen the enrollment grow to a record, 16,879 students in the fall of 1975;. . . research funds and library holdings have grown at a faster pace; and private funds have increased to further augment legislative appropriations.
>
> But growth has not been the overriding theme of the last four years. From the Institutional Self-Study of 1971–73 to the Statement of Purposes and Goals of 1975, a central concern has been planning for all aspects of the University community—planning for academic progress, planning for student needs outside the classroom, planning for facility requirements for the growing student body, planning to meet fiscal responsibilities, planning to meet the needs of the community.[13]

Another Try on Goals

The president appointed a nine-member faculty committee on purposes and objectives in September 1974, asking for an interim report by January and a final report by May 1, 1975. The chairman was Dr. W. H. Glaze, associate dean of the College of Arts and Sciences. Preliminary work by the group led to the scheduling of a retreat on goals and objectives on April 12 and 13, 1975, at the Tanglewood Country Club on Lake Texoma northeast of Denton. The twenty-two participants included the President's Cabinet, deans, several faculty members, a graduate student, and regents A. M. Willis and Kenneth May. From this meeting there emerged a draft statement of purposes and goals of about 250 words in general terms and a much longer, more specific document entitled "Goals for 1975–85, A Program for Excellence."[14] This program scheduled eight elements, summarized here from the Tanglewood document:[15]

1. Recruit at least ten teacher/scholars of national and international recognition to the permanent faculty.

2. Enroll more students of outstanding potential.

3. Develop four units with financial allocations that would elevate and sustain them at a level of national and international recognition.

4. Demand higher standards of achievement from students, faculty, and staff.

5. Improve auxiliary support services, including a center for instructional media and a center for the improvement of teaching and research skills.

6. Re-evaluate the present admissions policy.

7. Conduct a development campaign to draw additional financial support from external, nonstate sources, with efforts made by all segments of the university.

8. Implement a system of program planning and budgeting at all organizational levels.

A Quick Response

On July 1, 1975, Nolen formed a Planning and Budgeting Task Force headed by Dr. Marvin Berkeley, dean of business administration and member of the President's Cabinet. The president named a representative for each vice president plus the director of university planning and analysis. Nolen charged the group to develop a system for planning and budgeting to lead to rational decision making at all levels of university operation, leading to a final report by May 15, 1976.[16]

On the work of this task force Nolen rested his hopes for achieving that opening pledge to regents to develop rational long-range planning and to respond to the Southern Association's mandate to put such a system into place. The Tanglewood retreat documents led to a role and scope statement for the Coordinating Board. At its November 1975 meeting, regents voted an expression of approval of "the direction, the leadership and the enthusiasm of the President and the administration."[17]

ENLARGING THE ROLE AND SCOPE

Nolen asked Commissioner Bevington Reed at the Coordinating Board in August 1974 for rapid evaluation by the board of the role and scope of North Texas. He noted that a number of changes had taken place in the metropolitan area in the five years, and he sought a more dominant role for North Texas in the metropolitan area. [18] The Coordinating Board the following year started the role and scope review for North Texas. Dr. Charldean Newell, associate academic vice president, coordinated the production of a role and scope statement sent to Commissioner Reed on January 8, 1976.[19]

TCOM Becomes Significant

Development of the Texas College of Osteopathic Medicine is described in more detail in Chapter 35. Bringing that once-private school under the control of the NTSU Board of Regents certainly became one of the more significant actions led by Nolen. After three years of cooperative instruction and research, the two institutions were united under the NTSU board in May 1975. TCOM's first class of eighteen doctors graduated in June 1974; in 1975 twenty-five physicians were graduated.[20]

Use of the TCOM academic programs and its campus location near downtown Fort Worth was perceived by Nolen and staff as a means of leveraging expanded roles for NTSU based on the TCOM affiliation. The extent of this was seen in Nolen's unpublished proposals at the Tanglewood goals conference and in the role and scope statement submitted to the Coordinating Board.

Nolen: a University System, New Campuses, Professional Schools

At the Tanglewood retreat, Nolen offered his own vision for the university. A record of this is found in a handwritten document headed "C. C. Nolen's goals for the next three years" and signed at the bottom "interpreted by Gus Ferré." Three of these were radical departures from the North Texas course. These did not make it into the published program of excellence, but they did influence Nolen's actions in his remaining four years in office. As interpreted by Ferré, he proposed to:

1. Achieve legislative influence commensurate with the top three universities by developing a university system, beginning with Texas Woman's University.

2. Expand the campus to include sites in Dallas, Fort Worth, and Houston, giving resident credit and being served by a transit system. This included Nolen's vision of a university center at the planned Flower Mound New Town just west of Lewisville.

3. Develop a full university to include a medical school (osteopathic), nursing, law, and dentistry.

Enlarging the Role and Scope

The influence of these thoughts on later program development efforts may be found in the role and scope statement sent to the Coordinating Board.

The summary circulated in the *President's Bulletin* noted the rapid increase in graduate enrollment—a twenty-one percent increase from fall 1974 to fall

1975—and proposed degree program requests to the Coordinating Board through 1980. Again, special emphasis was placed on synergistic relations with TCOM for "already emerging health-related programs that cut across a number of academic units at NTSU." Development was envisioned in Denton for biochemistry, clinical chemistry, medical genetics, toxicology, medical dietetics, and health care administration. Joint programs forecast with TCOM included medical aspects of studies in aging, rehabilitation, behavioral studies, community health, health education, communication disorders, biological sciences generally, and on retraining/retooling continuing education programs for health professionals. The document promised continuing efforts to work with TWU in the health sciences fields, especially paramedical training programs. Then came the assertion that NTSU should house any new pharmacy, nursing, or dentistry programs in the North Central Texas area. The summary also suggested strong interest in a school of law and a program of legal studies. [21]

Working with Texas Woman's University

The statement acknowledged the need for cooperative action with Texas Woman's University but only hinted at the possibility of bringing that cross-town campus into a North Texas system. The proposals for joint action were couched in cautious terms, suggesting cooperative developments in health, physical education, and recreation, home economics, and library and information sciences.[22]

Reaching Out to the Metroplex

The role-and-scope statement pointed to almost thirty years of service to the metropolitan area, at first with extension courses and more recently with resident-credit courses. Expansion into the metropolitan area focused on the leasing of the Easterwood Building in downtown Dallas as a major commitment to consolidate programs for graduate students in Dallas County. The document declared that the University would seek immediate authorization of a downtown center as "critical to the natural development of long-existing programs. [23] Less ambitious references were made to the continuation of programs at mid-cities school sites and expansion of existing Fort Worth programs at TCOM. The board went still further, resolving to establish off-campus centers. It said:

> the Board of Regents of North Texas State University instructs the President to initiate procedures to establish official physical locations in the form of Centers, or other appropriate designations, in both Dallas and Fort Worth for the purpose of offering the most cost-effective quality educational opportunity within the capability of the University.[24]

Regents Request Action

Just three months later, on February 27, 1976, the board asked "the administration" to furnish evidence that actions were being taken to implement the goals, prepare a progress report to provide the means for evaluating the administration, and undertake a comprehensive study for board action on policies to strengthen the university and move it toward the desired excellence. The board asked for these steps:

1. Prepare for the next meeting an outline of actions already taken to implement the goals program and of priority steps to be proposed.
2. Propose in April a program for gathering information the board will need to evaluate the administration.
3. Present a comprehensive study in August of ways for the board to strengthen policies to help achieve stated goals and desired level of excellence.[25]

In June Nolen met with the regents' Role and Scope Committee to discuss the presidential evaluation procedure. He gave them an outline on June 3 offering several premises for presidential evaluation.[26] He wrote that presidential leadership would be stronger if the executive could discuss with his board his office's goals and the degree of success being achieved. Of particular interest is this statement: "The explicit assessment of top management personnel provides an opportunity for in-service improvement of performance, and for the mutual education of the Board of Regents and the President. At the same time it affords a President the protection and respect for individual dignity that guards against capricious action."[27]

The president moved immediately to begin the process, asking cabinet members to prepare suggestions for a presidential statement for a June 10 meeting. This would outline the two to five most significant achievements and the two to five most unusual opportunity or problem areas in each of the six major areas of responsibility to be listed in the evaluation document, to be known as the institutional progress report.[28] A draft of this report was to be sent to the

Role and Scope Committee by mid-July, with a final version to be reviewed by that committee and submitted to the full board at its August 26 meeting. The board would then work with the president to agree on institutional and presidential priorities for each of the next two years and beyond and on the evaluation criteria that would be used for those periods. The board was then to discuss the planning and budgeting process that was being developed.

Reporting Progress to the Regents

For the August meeting with regents, Nolen and the cabinet created the Institutional Progress Report for 1971 to 1976.[29] For each administrative division, this offered detailed lists of achievements and future problems and opportunities.

THE PLANNING AND BUDGETING VENTURE

During the 1975–76 year, the Planning and Budgeting Task Force was designing a structure and schedule and planning the involvement of as many faculty and staff as possible. The emphasis on a formal planning process was not a phenomenon peculiar to North Texas. Spiraling inflation and an expanded student base had made "resource allocation" and "accountability" and "program budgeting" buzz words in higher education. A federally funded operation in Boulder, Colorado, the National Center for Higher Education Management Systems, developed many planning tools, including standardized database formats and computer simulation models for analysis. NTSU became an early adopter of NCHEMS systems.

The task force arranged conferences of the heads of all budgetary units in May 1976 and again in September 1976. Including the cabinet and representatives from the Faculty Senate and the student government, this totaled about eighty people. At this stage, budget units were invited to volunteer as pilot departments. Speaking to the September conference, Nolen stressed his role as the liaison officer who communicates the program and policy concerns of the faculty and staff to the governing board and those of the board to the faculty and staff. [30]

The pilot testing of the proposed system was done by twenty volunteer units, academic and administrative. The chairman/director and one assistant from each of the pilot units attended a December 1976 workshop. They received drafts of the planning assumptions statement and mission and goals statement, along with instructions for the next several months. In January 1977 some 900 faculty and professional staff members were given a printed status report summarizing progress on the work and inviting them to comment on the planning assumptions and the missions and goals. Meantime, members of a skills development subcommittee were working individually with the pilot units.

In March 1977 Task Force Chairman Berkeley reported to the Faculty Senate and spoke to their concerns, which were numerous—some feared that the "system" would prove to be a bureaucratic tangle that would transfer power from the faculty to a central committee. Also in March, there was a general meeting with the heads of the pilot units to discuss problems and to answer questions. The vice presidents reviewed the first reports from the pilot units with each unit head. And in April, Dean Berkeley reported to a committee of the Board of Regents on progress made and on a proposed schedule of activities.

In May 1977, pilot units submitted a proposed five-year plan and an annual plan. A mission and goals subcommittee submitted a revised statement. This led to a two-day retreat by the President's Cabinet to evaluate the planning and budgeting process, and identify major planning decisions.

The Board of Regents in August 1977 approved a document, *University Planning and Budgeting: First-Year Report*, August 1977. This included goals and planning assumptions for a five-year period and a statement of university priorities for six major program areas. Copies also went to every department and budget unit on campus for study and suggestions. On February 16, 1978, Nolen put out a call for the planning and budgeting process to be put into action throughout the campus.[31]

Clearly, the president and the board were staking a great deal on the successful development of a new system to improve the operation of NTSU. But President Nolen did not know that he would have little more than another year in office and that most of this planning and budgeting system would vanish with his departure.

A WARNING NOTE: SUPPORT DOESN'T MEASURE UP

For Fiscal 1978 and Fiscal 1979, the legislative news was not good in terms of expanding the university goals for research. The legislative appropriation for organized research for 1977–78 was $793,933 (the same as for 1977) but for

1978–79 it was only half that amount: $396,966.[32] As the 1978 Fiscal Year neared an end (and indeed, as the term of office of President Nolen approached a conclusion), Vice President Miles Anderson delivered a memo to the president that showed how far away from accomplishing its broad goals the university really was in expenditure of education and general funds. He noted that the median education and general expenditure per full-time equivalent student for doctoral institutions in the Southern Association was $3,097 but was $2,254 at NTSU.

Furthermore, Anderson noted, "we expend only a little over one-fourth as much on research as does the median institution in our classification." In spite of substantial emphasis on extramural funding, the university began from such a relatively poor financial position that extraordinary measures would be needed to meet research goals. [33]

chapter 33

How Firm a Foundation?

The North Texas State University Educational Foundation, Inc., exists to promote the growth, prosperity and continuing excellence of NTSU academic programs through contributions of private financial support to the University. The Foundation was authorized by the NTSU Board of Regents in the spring of 1972 and received its charter from the State of Texas in June of that same year. . . .

It is the stated preference of the NTSU Board of Regents that gift funds be received through the North Texas State University Educational Foundation, Inc. This is particularly true of unrestricted gifts since the Foundation has the trust authority to administer gifts, bequests, and devices with a flexibility that assists materially in the execution of the purposes for which the donation was made.

—*Foundation Report, 1977*

Of the factors leading to selection of C. C. Nolen as president, his experience in raising private funds for higher education stood at the top. No previous administrator at North Texas had his level of experience and competence in the area that was becoming known as "university advancement." Chairman A. M. Willis told the faculty that the new leader "has an intimate knowledge of the Dallas-Denton-Fort Worth triangle and is highly regarded in that area and in Austin."[1] His outgoing personality was admirably suited to the basics of public relations and development: personal contacts, effective communication, and "working the prospects" and "making the case."

WORKING NEW TERRITORY—IMMEDIATELY

Nolen began talking and writing more than three months before he was in office. He wrote and phoned the business and civic leaders of the Metroplex whose confidence he had earned as the TCU vice chancellor. He maintained a network of University of Texas contacts that read like a "Who's Who" of chancellors, presidents, development staff, political office-holders, and alumni leaders. He maintained contacts through the Boy Scouts, his church, Austin and Fort Worth civic and cultural groups, state and local political figures, and leaders in charitable organizations. Nolen wrote dozens of such people that summer to establish in their minds his pending relocation to North Texas. He acquired leads to influential and wealthy NTSU ex-students and started them thinking in terms of helping roles they could play.

Asking Denton: What Do You Think?

Just six days after being named, President Nolen invited several dozen Denton residents to a "Town and Gown Meeting" to listen to their positive and negative views about North Texas.[2] Nolen wanted a guide to potential strengths and weaknesses in building community support. These items became part of the Nolen agenda for public relations and fund development:

Some Problem Areas

No place to park.

Sagging employee contributions to the Denton United Fund.

Lack of seminars to help business, industry, and citizens.

Schedule conflicts among NTSU, TWU, and community public events.

Students using the city-county hospital rather than student health service.

Lack of community awareness of NTSU plans.

Undesirable persons hanging out around the campus area.

Faculty and staff must be more involved in the community and should be encouraged by the town people.

People object to the radical, or liberal, element at North Texas. Not enough balance between liberal and conservative elements.

On the one hand, people complain about the division between the two communities: university and town. But when campus personnel participate, people complain that the professors are trying to run everything.

Most of the university radicals or liberals get involved in local elections. Some seem more interested in opposing than in assisting.

The town hasn't really gotten a lot of good community leadership from university personnel. Faculty membership in the Chamber of Commerce has fallen from 200 to 65.

The faculty population is so mobile these days that many don't feel they are a part of the community.

When new professors move into town, they criticize the lack of parks, recreation facilities, etc. Yet they will oppose getting new industry that would provide tax money to help pay for these things.

University Positive Values

The fine arts and lecture series are an invaluable service to the community.

Denton is more stable economically and more recession-resistant than other parts of the country because of having the university in this town.

The largest percentage of the student body is made up of good, solid citizens.

Many businesses use the expertise of a great many faculty members.

City officials have been encouraged by recent visits from regents who have expressed interest in community affairs.

Businesses rely on student employees and most of the student help is very good.

The university forms a base for the kind of industry and commerce we want to attract to Denton.

Our public schools are good because of the universities.

The university gives the people of the city the impetus and ability to adapt to change—and only through change is progress made.

Many business and professional people work elsewhere and could live elsewhere but choose Denton because of its academic community.

BUILDING A DEVELOPMENT PROGRAM

Creating a development program where none had stood before could easily be described with a trite but true phrase: a Herculean task. He could rely on his development office for much of the labor, but the initiative and the spark would have to come from the Office of the President. Nolen recognized this better than anyone. In retrospect, Jim Reid wrote later that the program began in 1971 without any of the basic elements that have made other fund-raising elements successful and with “the added negative effect of previous administrative policies against the active solicitation of gift support.”[3]

Reid spent his first month in office as development director outlining in a September report the needed tasks to organize the development program. He recommended four steps to be announced at the inauguration ceremonies two months hence: creation of a President’s Council, development of a case statement for alumni annual giving, creation of a development board, and the identification of a core of business support.[4]

The NTSU Development Board

At the November 2, 1971, meeting, the board adopted regulations for private fund development.[5] The regents asked for “vigorous efforts to attract private-fund support for meeting these needs,” and charged the president with defining current and future needs of the university for fund-raising purposes.

The board action authorized creation of a Development Board to be “the agency responsible to the president, and through him, to the Board of Regents, for all private-fund development for the university.” This group would have no more than twenty-five members appointed for three-year terms. The Development Board was to be responsible for identifying total development needs of the university, planning support for programs to meet these needs, and developing gift possibilities not related to predetermined projects.[6]

This met the timetable of Reid’s September recommendation—the creation of the board—but it would take several months to identify, evaluate, and approach prospective members of the board. It would be another year, October 5, 1972, before a Development Board would have its first meeting. However, another of the items on the inauguration agenda was more amenable to a fast start-up.

An Inauguration as a Springboard

The inauguration was scheduled for December 1, 1971. Dr. Harry Hunt Ransom, chancellor emeritus of the University of Texas system, spoke at the

10:00 A.M. ceremonies in the Main Auditorium. Many state political figures, both legislative and executive, were in the academic procession. Notable in the platform party were Governor Preston Smith and Lieutenant Governor Ben Barnes.

A noon luncheon for 700 guests became the platform for announcing the first major effort at seeking private money for unrestricted use. Willis announced the chartering of a President's Council to donate private unrestricted funds. He listed twelve persons, including six regents, as charter members.[7] An annual gift of at least $1,000 qualified one for membership, and gifts or bequests of $25,000 or more gave the donor life membership. This event constitutes a landmark in fund-raising efforts at North Texas, as the council endured as a significant force.

Needed: A Private Foundation

Handling private funds for a state university usually requires creation of a tax-exempt educational foundation free from the direction of state agencies. Thus the regents on April 6, 1972, approved articles of incorporation and bylaws for the North Texas State University Educational Foundation, Inc.[8]

This was to be a perpetual nonprofit corporation to provide financial support for research, teaching, scholarship, and facilities. It was organized to receive, hold, manage, and control property acquired by donation, gift, grant, bequest, purchase or other means. The foundation was empowered to transfer or use these assets for the benefit of NTSU. Formal incorporation was received in the summer of 1972. The first three directors were regents, and that group met August 24, 1972, and elected A. M. Willis, president; E. Bruce Street, vice president; and C. Dean Davis, secretary-treasurer.[9]

The foundation could not solicit gifts that by law or regents' policy could be received directly by the university. Further, the foundation would accept gifts only for purposes in keeping with programs and policies established by the regents. The regents on November 9, 1973, resolved that gifts should be received "primarily through the North Texas State University Educational Foundation."[10] If the foundation were to be dissolved, all assets and earnings would be distributed by the foundation board, and in no case would "assets, properties, or the proceeds thereof be subject to appropriation by the Legislature of the State of Texas."[11]

Nolen the Development Officer

A common folk saying could have been originated to describe Nolen: "He never met a stranger." He moved comfortably in any group and never lacked for conversation starters. Some of his ideas about his presidency were delineated in the *Dallas Morning News* after eight months in office, explaining the philosophy of the new president:

> "I have the trust in God that I'm at the right time for all things to come together. . ." Nolen said. . . . "most of the serious problems at NTSU can be attributed to money or the lack of it. . . ."
>
> And raising private funds. . . to go with what the university gets in budget from the state legislature is what Nolen recently told a student gathering is one of the things he'd probably like to be remembered as doing for NTSU. . . .
>
> He believes [his] development experience makes him a better president for Texas' fourth largest university. . . .
>
> As NTSU seeks private funds Nolen believes the university must become more of an influence in the region and the state. At his inauguration he told an audience including state political leaders that "NTSU cannot be all things to all people, but it can be more things to more people."[12]

DESIGNING FUND CAMPAIGNS

The Nolen development program was set in motion in remarkably short time. The foundation legal work, the Development Board activation, and the renewal of alumni activity came about within approximately one year.

The Development Board Gets Going

The fifteen-member NTSU Development Board came to life on October 5, 1972. The chairman was Gordon Carpenter, trust officer of the First National Bank in Dallas, who had been active in alumni support efforts. Former NT regents were represented by Mrs. Grace Cartwright of Weatherford and Berl Godfrey of Fort Worth, and there were three former members of the Texas Legislature plus four Denton community leaders.

Regents charged the board to approve all fund-raising efforts and to seek financial support to be channeled through the foundation. The group would work with alumni, present ideas for improving North Texas, and act politically in suggestions to the governor about appointments to the Board of Regents and action as lobbyists for NTSU.[13]

A Campaign for the Ninetieth Year

After two years at work, Chairman Carpenter and five other members of the Development Board went before the Board of Regents in November 1974 to propose a fund-raising campaign goal of $8.25 million to be achieved by 1980, the University's ninetieth year. This would go for seven endowed chairs, fourteen endowed professorships, fourteen endowed scholarships, and $3 million in construction funds.[14]

Waking Up the Alumni

Nolen and Reid knew that the Alumni Association had not been organized to serve the development function. A university staff member served part-time as the executive secretary of the alumni group and maintained address files for former students. Alumni were encouraged to attend Homecoming, to organize North Texas Day meetings in their communities each March 31, and to work to encourage high school students of their towns to attend North Texas. A tabloid newspaper, the *North Texan*, was published four times a year.

Organizing for More Activity

The Seventy-Fifth Year observance led to creation of an office of alumni affairs with a full-time director, Dr. Wayne Adams, in September 1966. In its first year the main objective was to enlarge and automate the alumni mailing list. In the second year, the office established dues-paying membership in the association at five dollars per person and built an "active" list of 3,700 alumni. However, the record-keeping did not incorporate the type of data that more sophisticated programs used to rate alumni as prospective workers and donors to the university.

Bringing Alumni Into the Development Program

When Adams retired, Nolen brought in the university's first experienced professional director, Tony Gustwick. Reid led a committee to recommend alumni organization and programs. This led to a detailed status report to the Board of Regents in May 1974.[15]

Progress was cited for the program in establishing an alumni loyalty fund through the educational foundation, an alumni club program, alumni publications, awards and recognition, continuing education, and involvement of students in alumni activities prior to graduation. These activities gained momentum and enlarged in scope during the next five years.

FIVE YEARS OF PRIVATE FUNDING

Based on a report of fund-raising counsel, Frantzreb and Pray, in the second year of the Kamerick presidency, a Development Office was established and a director employed for 1970–71. Nolen had discussed the findings of that study with Art Frantzreb. He and the Development Board determined in 1975 that the university would again need the assistance of a firm of development and fund-raising consultants. The board employed a Dallas-based firm, Community Service Bureau, Inc., which began a feasibility study for the university in May 1975.

Service Bureau Report

Normally, the consultants said, a client institution has already defined and documented its own case statement. At North Texas, however, the bureau needed to develop for presentation to the university's various publics a realistic and salable case statement and listing of priority needs.

The Case Statement

CSB prepared a five-page case statement, which it sent out to about one hundred key leaders on campus, in Denton, and over the metropolitan area and state. This was done to provide the basis for extended personal interviews with each individual. The statement said a ten-year master development plan would require an investment of $44 million beyond the annual operating budget, $22.5 million to come from private sources. Phase 1 of this plan would try to secure $10.5 million in donations.[16] About half of that money would go for buildings and endowment, the rest for new programs such as the Dallas Center, Institute of Applied Science, Bureau of Business Research, Center for Economic Education, and others.

Some Discouraging Interviews

The bureau interviewed ninety-seven persons chosen because of a leadership connection to the university or because of their community leadership status. Included were five regents, thirteen Development Board members, seventeen faculty members, and sixty-two external interviewees, mostly from

Denton, Dallas, or Fort Worth but with eleven from elsewhere in Texas. This was obviously not a random sample nor was it large enough to use for inference to a larger population. The answers were, however, both revealing and disturbing. Here are some interview results:

A majority of faculty/staff respondents said the university's public image was not well known, seventy-one percent said NTSU's image was not academically accepted, and fifty-nine percent said that NTSU is still thought of elsewhere as a teachers college.

Of those interviewed in Dallas, sixty-seven percent said the public is not knowledgeable regarding activities at NTSU; eighty-nine percent could not identify firms, foundations, or individuals of wealth who might support an NTSU development program; sixty-one percent predicted that a major development program would not be successful; and sixty-one percent said they would not make a personal pledge or contribution to an NTSU development program. Answers were somewhat more optimistic among Fort Worth respondents, perhaps because of the sense of identification of NTSU with the hometown TCOM.

"Serious Weaknesses"

With these many negative conditions facing the university, Community Service Bureau cited a fund-raiser's axiom, that favorable factors must outweigh the unfavorable that would affect the outcome of a project. The consultants said their study indicated "serious weaknesses in NTSU's ability to mount an all-out Development Program for $10,500,000 in the immediate future." A limited program could be attempted, they wrote, in Denton and on the campus, but cultivation and organization would have to precede a later campaign for Dallas and Fort Worth. Interest was found in support for some of the centers listed in the case statement, and there appeared to be support in Fort Worth for TCOM.[17]

Unhappily, the unfavorable factors appear to support the consultants' report of "serious weaknesses" in NTSU's development prospects. They cited opposition to private contributions to a state university, a weak public image, doubt as to the economic impact of NTSU on the region, limited fund-raising appeal of the best-known programs, and absence of a strong alumni association.

What could a consultant recommend in such an unfavorable environment? CSB chose to advise the university to put its efforts into developing a persuasive case that would encourage and inspire faculty and volunteer workers and to persuade prospective donors that this was an institution deserving of support. The positive factors, in other words, would not be documented by empirical evidence but rather by persuasive case statement. These were the statements that were outlined to provide the positive stance for a development campaign:

1. NTSU *is* a major university—although largely unrecognized—providing comprehensive education for a large number of students in a variety of fields.

2. NTSU *is* a growing university.

3. NTSU *is* recognized as providing above-average training in certain fields and is beginning to be recognized in others. Additional areas of specialization, unrecognized at present, can be promoted, which will further add to the prestige and appeal of the University.

4. The financial need. . . can be proven and shown to greatly exceed anticipated state allocations.[18]

Development Board Says "Not Now"

When the bureau recommended an immediate start of a Phase I public relations and fund-raising program, the goal was no longer the $10.5 million outlined in the original case statement. It instead suggested a target of $1 million. Instead of going to all possible constituencies in the state, the report recommended that the first phase must concern itself with the solicitation of the university family—the Board of Regents, the Development Board, faculty and staff, and Denton businesses, industries, and residents. While this was going on, the consultants said, the administration would have to continue with preparations, cultivation, and key enlistments for the following phases. The CSB report then concluded by recommending that the university immediately implement the program.

The Development Board reacted by accepting the CSB findings as valid, but declined to take any further action, instead voting to table action. What brought this response? To the surprise of Nolen and Reid, it was not anything in the findings to date or in the development activities to date. Instead it was a fear that an ongoing conflict with the City of Denton would kill any hope of success.[19]

That conflict had to do with the university's steady progression toward creating a "closed" pedestrian campus according to its 1966 campus plan, a goal that was being achieved by asking the Denton City Council to close city streets running through the campus. Many blocks of streets had already been closed, but the real crisis arose when the request came to close Avenue C and D, which appeared to threaten community access to a large shopping center between Eagle Drive and Interstate Highway 35E just south of the campus. (See Chapter 34)

What Results Were Achieved?

Eight months after the CSB report hit a roadblock on the streets of Denton, and at the end of five years of the Nolen administration, Jim Reid reported results in obtaining gift funds. This is the five-year tabulation from that document[20], which included the prior year as a base for comparison:

1970–71	$246,500.00
1971–72	$361,768.00
1972–73	$516,271.00
1973–74	$541,727.00
1974–75	$598,106.00

Progress was being made, but it was a long way from the multimillion-dollar enterprise that had been envisioned in the service bureau case statement. To make matters more discouraging, there were still more serious questions to be raised about the educational foundation in the years just ahead. These questions triggered the actions that led to the resignation of Nolen as president.

chapter 34

New Issues for Students

At first it appeared that student apathy had melted away; activism had triumphantly returned. . . . Gradually the dream vanished. . . . A new administration and a possible revival. The idealists hoped 1972 would be the year of great and beautiful changes, while conservatives waited cautiously. Real and phony radicals were not convinced, but a hopeful mood was evident.

The Yucca, 1972

The student yearbook had trouble in categorizing the "student movement" of the late 1960s and early 1970s. Some North Texas students became activists and protesters. Many more did not. Paradoxes abounded:

Controversy over the Duke case continued into the 1970s, but much of the campus became excited over the naming of NTSU students as Miss America twice, in 1971 and 1973. On the Johnny Carson television show, Miss America Phyllis George exhibited a 150-foot congratulatory telegram signed by 5,300 students.[1]

Students made serious observances of the end of the war in Vietnam and expressed concern for the status of Blacks and of women on the campus, but they showed far more activity on behalf of a successful football team and an effort to join the Southwest Conference.

The United Ministries sponsored Free University courses in yoga, macrame, and Israeli folk dance. Major student efforts were directed against a parking system that they said had empty faculty parking spaces next to classroom buildings while students had to walk in from Fouts Field.[2]

NEW ISSUES FOR STUDENTS

Issues that had appeared on other American campuses continued to make their way to Denton. Students asked for a staff attorney to help students, for official approval of an organization for homosexuals (now becoming known as "gays"), for international groups such as Iranian students to organize protest marches under university protection, for the sale of alcohol in the University Union, for formal student evaluation of faculty members, and a number of others.

Concerns With National Affairs

The outside world continued to move into students' lives. The right to vote was lowered to age eighteen in time for the November 1972 elections, but student yearbook writers bemoaned the futility of the student liberal mood:

> It has always been a disgrace to many to be labeled a hippie, but in '72 it was even more indecent to be labeled a liberal. . . . If you were a North Texas student, whether hippie or not, you probably voted for liberals Frances Farenthold and George McGovern and left yourself wide open for ridicule. . . .

> Out of the 31 precincts in Denton County, McGovern carried only one—Precinct 5, the one in which North Texas students voted. . . . As a student, your vote did not make that much difference.[3]

The energy crisis impacted student lives with full force in 1973–74. Gasoline shortages were hard on commuters. Carpool listings were publicized. Student bus service from Dallas was stepped up by Transportation Enterprise Inc., and service was added by TEI for Fort Worth and the mid-cities area. The university considered remodeling a dormitory for commuters, going to a four-day class week, and closing some buildings on the weekend to save fuel.[4]

The Vietnam War ended officially on January 28, 1973, with limited reaction from student groups. A Free University class in nonviolence was formed to "bring the peace home." A group from the United Ministry Center conducted a "peace vigil" in front of the Union. Some aligned themselves with the War Resister's League.[5] Black students began participating more actively in special organizations. Each year a Women's Emphasis Week was held—in February 1974 speakers included two television personalities, gubernatorial candidate Frances "Sissy" Farenthold, women deans from two other colleges, attorneys, and counselors on divorced women and women and the law.[6]

Helping International Students

In October 1972 a group of students started meeting as the "International Club" and later in the year changed the name to International Students Association. Harve D. King, assistant dean of students who was the second Black administrator after Dr. T. R. Lee stepped down as associate dean of students, served as adviser. Mohammad Ihtisham Alam, president, wrote to King in October 1973:

> Under your guidance the international students could gain success during the year 1972-73, some of them being our affiliation with the Center for Ethnic Affairs, creation of an International Education Committee, dedication of McConnell Hall as the International House, creation of an office of International Students Association, and a Reading Room in McConnell Hall.[7]

At times, international students brought to the campus their concerns for political and social issues in their home country. In 1978 North Texas had admitted a number of students from Middle Eastern nations that were benefiting from their petroleum industry. In the case of Iran, students who supported the Shah and those who supported the revolutionary movement posted signs and painted slogans around the campus. The Iranian Students Association in September 1978 was given permission to hold an on-campus rally on a weekday between 11:00 A.M. and 2:00 P.M. They were advised to work with the approval of the international programs director, to avoid loudspeakers, and to avoid disturbing classes.[8]

Encountering "Gay Liberation"

In 1975 Jane Gentry Smith, vice president for student affairs, alerted the President's Cabinet to the plans of a "gay liberation" group to apply for official campus organization status. At a November meeting, the cabinet "took the matter under study."[9] On March 12, 1976, Ruben Salinas of the Denton Gay Alliance asked the President's Cabinet for official recognition by the university. On March 23, the request was denied by the cabinet. Nolen subsequently wrote the group that "We are in the process of seeking a formal opinion from the Attorney General of Texas which concerns all student organizations on campus."[10]

Alcohol on Campus?

For most of the twentieth century, Denton was known as a "Dry City," forbidding the sale of alcohol. State law permitted such sale, however, to members of licensed private clubs. A number of such businesses appeared on the traditional "Corner" of the campus at Hickory and Fry Streets.[11] Nevertheless, students sought the sale of beer and wine in the University Union. There was some administrative resistance to this and considerable opposition from the Board of Regents. After much discussion and legal investigation, the board on January 14, 1977, approved, 6–2, seeking a license for the sale of beer and wine for on-premises consumption in the Rock Bottom Lounge of the union. Sale was to begin at 5:00 P.M. on weekdays and 1:00 P.M. on Saturdays.

Employment of Students' Attorney

The student association asked that an attorney be added to the staff to service the legal needs of students, endorsed by the student services division staff. This met with resistance from the regents, especially "Judge" Carroll Sullivant of Gainesville. A board committee was appointed in the fall of 1973, and Nolen negotiated with Sullivant to bring the attorney's post under the direct authority of the dean of students.[12] Nolen subsequently got Sullivant's approval to name C. J. Taylor as assistant dean of students for legal services starting January 15, 1974.

Representing Student Views

The *Campus Chat* had gone to four-day publication as the *North Texas Daily* in 1970 and became more involved than ever in coverage of student issues. The *Yucca* experimented in magazine format and attempted to represent serious political and social concerns of students. But publication costs were forcing the student purchase price upwards and the Student Service Fee committee was becoming less willing to allocate fee support to the yearbook. On page sixty-four of its 1974 edition, the staff announced that this would be the last *Yucca*.

Since World War II the United Students of North Texas had worked with varying degrees of effectiveness in bringing change to student life. In the spring of 1971 a group of students called for an election to adopt a new constitution for a replacement group to be known as the Student Government Association. The USNT Senate opposed the election, but voters approved it, 1,226 to 507.[13] It was to be the following year before final approvals could be worked out to create the new organization.

STUDENTS ORGANIZE TO HELP

Students of the normal and teachers college had built a strong tradition with service groups. The Green Jackets had been led by Miss Beulah Harriss through four decades. Lindsay Keffer, a graduate of NT who had been active in student affairs and student union administration, credits the women students in Green Jackets with creating the friendly atmosphere for students on the campus. A later service group for men, the Talons, formed in 1963 to build school spirit and athletic support. They mounted the old normal bell on a trailer and took it to games as "The Victory Bell." When the bell became cracked, it was retired to a place of honor in the University Union.

The women of Meritum, a local scholastic honor society, achieved their long-time dream by becoming a chapter of Mortar Board. This group led in the establishment and development of Honors Day as a student-run program. Another new organization, Blue Key for men, joined in this effort. (Both groups later became coeducational.)

President Nolen invited students to become interested in supporting university development and created the NT 40 in 1974 to assist him as hosts for events for prospective university donors. Later it became the North Texas Forty Student Foundation to promote "the pride, spirit and positive image of the university." These student leaders expanded their service areas to work with the Admissions Office, Alumni Office, and the president's office. One of their major successes has been hosting NT Previews, which brings high school juniors and seniors to the campus each semester to become acquainted with the university.

When the Student Union Building was closed for expansion in the early 1970s, its activities shifted to Crumley Hall, which became known as the Temporary Union Building (the TUB). An otherwise minimal facility was made livelier by the work of the Student Activities Union, which scheduled programs and events to keep students tied to the Union concept. It later became the Union Program Council.

ARE WE A COMMUTER SCHOOL?

The rapidly concentrating urban population of the Metroplex was creating a new class of commuting students. In fall 1971 the commuting population had risen to 37.4 percent of the student body.[14] (Students living outside of Denton were counted as commuters.) The percentage was even higher among graduate students—58.8 percent compared to 31.2 percent of undergraduates. Men tended to commute only slightly more than women, 39.5 percent to 34.3 percent. What was of significant difference in living patterns was the continuing lag in representation of Fort Worth and its suburbs. Only 560 students (3.6 percent) lived in Tarrant County. The overwhelming majority, 87.7 percent, lived either in Dallas County or Denton County. The commuting pattern reflected the increasing age of North Texas students, the lack of student housing in the city of Denton, and the existence of far more part-time job opportunities at better pay in the metropolitan centers.

In the fall of 1971, the ratio of men to women students remained as it had since World War II at about sixty percent men and forty percent women. Starting in 1966, the number of freshmen and sophomores declined steadily as enrollments ballooned at the new Dallas and Tarrant County community college campuses. Out-of-state enrollment had increased to 7.7 percent. International students were still not numerous, but they had increased from eleven in 1954 to 123 students from twenty-seven countries in 1971.

ATHLETICS: A NECESSARY KEY TO BUILDING?

As it moved to obtain legislative separation from the teachers college system in 1949, North Texas left the Lone Star Conference. In 1948–49 a new group, the Gulf Coast Conference, was formed with Trinity University, the University of Houston, and Hardin College (later Midwestern). Unfortunately, the early departure of the University of Houston left only a few schools small in enrollment and financial strength. Supporters of North Texas wanted "big-time" athletics.

What About the Missouri Valley?

The Missouri Valley Conference looked like a life-saving means of escape from the Gulf Coast. North Texas entered the MVC in 1956 and began competition with the 1957 spring meet in Tulsa. In football, the two nearby MVC members, Oklahoma State and Houston, appealed to North Texas fans and drew large crowds on their first visits to Fouts Field. However, Oklahoma State soon joined the Big Eight and Houston left to seek Southwest Conference membership.

That left North Texas with good football opponents lacking geographical appeal in Denton: Tulsa, Wichita State, Drake, and Cincinnati. Basketball was a different story. One or more MVC teams could frequently be found in the national rankings. Large crowds often filled the 4,500-capacity Men's Gymnasium for Cincinnati, Bradley, St. Louis, and Drake. When a future All-American, Oscar Robertson, came to town with Cincinnati, control of overflow crowds became a problem. The Eagles almost never ranked near the top of the MVC standings, but the games in Denton were a major attraction. Plans moved ahead to replace the Men's Gymnasium with a new 10,000-seat coliseum.

Records in the Missouri Valley

In football, the Eagles finished second in the MVC standings in their first season, 1957, and won their first title with a 9–1 record in 1959. They lost to New Mexico State in the Sun Bowl in El Paso that year. North Texas tied for first in football three times, placed second four times, and tied for second two other times during the eighteen years of Valley competition. The football zenith for NT in the MVC could be found in Odus Mitchell's final season, 1966, and in Rod Rust's first three seasons, 1967–1969. In those four years, North Texas had a 30–8–1 record, won one title outright, tied for another, and had two second-place finishes. In all, the Eagles finished second or better eleven times in eighteen years in the Missouri Valley.

North Texas had its best Valley basketball years under Coach Dan Spika. His 1968–69 team was 15–10 overall, 8–8 in the conference, and had the first winning record since 1953–54. The 1969–70 team posted the best record of eighteen years in the MVC, going 18–8 for the season and 11–5 to place third in the MVC.

In golf NT achieved its greatest conference dominance. Coach Herb Ferrill led the Eagles to eighteen championships in nineteen years. The golfers were invited to the NCAA tournament sixteen times, finishing in the top ten each time. Kenneth Bahnsen was the only tennis coach in the team's nineteen years in the MVC, winning four championships beginning in 1966 and finishing in second place six times.

Veteran track coach Winton "Pop" Noah had track championships in 1967 and 1970 before retiring in 1971 after twenty-four years as head coach. He was succeeded by Carl Babcock, who was killed in an auto accident in 1973. John McKenzie took over in April of that season and a month later his athletes won the conference title and repeated in 1974. The Eagle track team had four first places, and seven runner-up places.[15]

In his first three years as football coach, Rod Rust's teams had great success. However, after he was named athletic director as well as coach and as the Eagles began playing in Dallas at the Cotton Bowl and at Texas Stadium, his next three seasons were disastrous. The team went 7–26, with the absolute bottom being the 1972 mark of ten losses and one victory.

The Regents Want Improved Athletics

Within six months after President Nolen arrived, the regents named a committee "to study the athletic program in depth" and report in May 1972. Dean Davis, a North Texas graduate, was named chairman, with Hugh Wolfe and Bruce Street as members.[16] At the June 1972 board meeting, regents voted unanimously:

> That the Board of Regents of North Texas State University commit itself and this university to an intercollegiate athletic program of excellence within its available fiscal capacity.
>
> That the administration be instructed to institute immediate, strict

> budgetary controls over the athletic budget and that such controls be rigidly and fairly enforced.[17]

The regents asked that Nolen dismiss all football coaches and the athletic director. The new athletic director would be responsible directly to the office of the president, maintaining tight budgetary control and instituting a "public relations" program for alumni, students, faculty, and Denton citizens and business people. This marketing campaign would be expected to increase attendance and to hold the community leadership to achieving a minimum goal of selling 5,000 season tickets for football. The president and athletic director would be expected either to improve membership in the Missouri Valley Conference by bringing in members closer to North Texas in geography and tradition, or to plan to leave the MVC and better the NT position in another conference. The regents also wanted to abandon Texas Stadium and to play most games in Fouts Field with a maximum effort to fill the stadium. The new athletic director would be expected to restructure the entire athletic program.

The Hayden Fry Era

Rod Rust and his coaches were dismissed. On December 16, 1972, Hayden Fry came to North Texas football. He had just been fired by Southern Methodist University after a 7–4 season. Fry, forty-three, had been head coach at SMU for eleven years and athletic director for nine years. Shortly after his arrival at North Texas in early January 1973, he was named athletic director.

Fry brought a dynamic personality. His goals were clear: build North Texas into an independent power outside of the MVC, worthy to join the Southwest Conference. He added many major-college opponents that could build national recognition for North Texas. SMU was already on the schedule. He arranged games with Houston, Tennessee, Mississippi State, Auburn, New Mexico, Kansas, Oklahoma State, Florida State, and Texas. In Fry's first season after NTSU left the MVC, 1975, his team won seven and lost four games, gaining special attention because Tennessee and Houston were two of the teams beaten.

After the Tennessee victory, United Press International named Fry the national coach of the week. For the same game, Eagle running back Sears Woods was named the national offensive player of the week by *Sports Illustrated*. Woods scored all three NT touchdowns, including the game-winning ninety-eight-yard kickoff return. Earlier, Walter Chapman had been named the Associated Press defensive player of the week in the North Texas 28–0 upset of Houston. In the 1977 season, United Press International ranked NT fourteenth in its national poll.

Southwest Conference, Here We Come

Fry's teams played out existing contracts and competed in the MVC in 1973 and 1974, his first two years. After Board of Regents action in November 1974,[18] North Texas withdrew from the Missouri Valley Conference effective August 31, 1975.[19]

However, independent status brought disadvantages. One came with a proposed change in status: NCAA plans to divide "major college" teams into two divisions, Division I and Division IA. Nolen wired the NCAA in October 1975, saying it was "Imperative that North Texas State University be considered for top major division status in order to accomplish our goal of becoming Number One major independent in the southwest."[20] Fry's team helped the cause by winning seven and losing four in that 1975 season. One of those victories was the upset 21–14 win against Tennessee in Knoxville.

Let's Change Our Name

Fry had another proposal: change the name of the school to Texas State University. In other states, this type of change had gone to the land-grant campus, one that was frequently called "A&M." At NTSU, there was an institutional fondness for the "North Texas" designation, which had been in all five names in use from 1894 to the 1970s. Fry argued that "TSU" would give the school a national recognition like that of Ohio State, Penn State, Michigan State, Florida State, and others. The idea was submitted to the Board of Regents, which discussed it but did not act.

Fry, Basketball, and Conflict

North Texas opened a new 10,000-seat coliseum for the 1973–74 basketball season, and for that year and the following one, the school was the host for the first round of the NCAA regional basketball tournament. In March 1975, at the end of the first independent basketball season, the North Texas record was six wins and twenty losses. Gene Robbins resigned as coach. Athletic Director Fry named Bill Blakeley to succeed him.[21]

In his first season, Blakeley set out with only one player added to the previous year's squad. His team finished with a 22–4 record, the sixteen-game turn-around being described as the best improvement among all NCAA colleges. The team ranked second nationally in team scoring, and only five teams in the nation had fewer defeats. The Texas Sports Writers Association named Blakeley as senior college coach of the year for winter sports.[22] North Texas supporters expected an invitation from the NCAA selection committee for the postseason basketball tournament. None came, and Blakeley was outraged. A *Houston Post* columnist, Mickey Herskowitz, offered an explanation:

> Blakeley knows the reason North Texas was kept out of the playoffs—it was the school's "penalty" for leaving the Missouri Valley Conference. NCAA selectors did not want to reward a deserter. Dropping the MVC was football coach Hayden Fry's idea, so he could shoot for big-time success and eventual inclusion in the Southwest Conference.
>
> Now Blakeley has put together a tougher schedule for next season—Kansas State, Missouri, Illinois, Syracuse, Baylor, SMU, TCU, Oral Roberts, Pan American—and is trying to get back into the MVC on a basketball-only basis.[23]

A Houston graduate wrote the alumni association about the Herskowitz column, and Fry fired off an immediate response:

> I can assure you NTSU was not selected for the NCAA basketball playoffs because of a "penalty" brought about because we terminated the MVC. . . . My personal opinion. . . is very simple: Our schedule included only 16 Division I teams from a 26 game schedule. . . . The selection committee realized that we had no previous history of playoff experience and with the obvious weak schedule they would be taking a chance on NTSU. . . . Obviously everyone that watched NTSU believes that they made a big mistake.
>
> Yes, I did ramrod NTSU's withdrawal from the MVC. It was perhaps the best decision ever made for the athletic program at NTSU. We nearly tripled our income the first year over the previous record in the MVC. . . .
>
> We have no intention of going back into the MVC in basketball or any other sport. As an independent in one year we have achieved the most success in the history of the school. . . .[24]

Blakeley continued his success in the next two seasons. In February 1976 the Eagles landed in the number twenty spot in Associated Press rankings. After three years Blakeley's record was 65–16, achieved with three consecutive twenty-win seasons. He told the *Dallas Morning News* that other major schools "didn't want to play such a strong independent team." Then, he made a controversial statement: "Hayden (Fry) has the same problem with his football program that we have," added Blakeley. "He's 9–2 this year and can't get a bowl bid anywhere. Frankly, I don't think he'd been invited to a bowl even if they'd been 11–0."[25] Fry was dissatisfied with this reference to the football team and asked Blakeley to discus the issues with him before taking them to the news media.[26]

Wooing the Southwest Conference

One year earlier, the NTSU Athletic Council had voted to seek membership in the Southwest Conference. Early in 1977, Dr. W. A. Miller, the faculty athletic representative, spoke to and wrote to faculty representatives of the Southwest Conference schools about the North Texas interest. In March, Nolen asked that NTSU membership be considered at the conference's May meeting. This wasn't the correct approach, so his staff had to learn the criteria for being considered.[27]

Nolen pressed for full support of conference membership at the fall 1977 faculty meeting, but the conference was not ready for public action. Nolen wrote each prospective athlete in February 1978 that "Our goal is to be No. 1 in the nation while achieving Southwest Conference membership." The university printed an elaborate brochure including two pages that listed the academic accomplishments of North Texas. The rest presented an elaboration of recent records.

The Associated Press reported in April that the May conference meeting would not consider the NTSU bid. Finally, on August 22, 1978, Fry announced at a press conference in Dallas that North Texas would get a hearing before the winter meeting of the SWC. "We have been invited to attend the meeting by a Southwest Conference school and the motion to allow our presentation will be seconded by another school," Fry said. An SWC spokesman said he was not yet aware of any school's plan to invite North Texas to the meeting,[28]

After a Denton visit in October, an Austin sportswriter wrote that he doubted the North Texas membership would be voted on, even though it appeared that the University of Texas was one of two schools willing to get NTSU on the agenda. "It is doubtful," the writer said, "that the four private schools in the SWC are in favor of admitting NTSU, a state university." [29]

Fry Heads North

In late November, Fry was giving up hope. Instead of wooing the Southwest Conference, he began attacking it. Statements at a Dallas-Fort Worth media luncheon revealed his disappointment:

> Fry has coached at North Texas for five years and has lobbied loud and long for more recognition. He said he was particularly bitter that ABC-TV had chosen not to televise the Eagles game with Memphis State last week and that his team was overlooked in the bowl selections.
>
> "If it wasn't for my obligation to the youngsters at our school I would leave in a New York minute," Fry said.[30]

In not much more time than that New York minute, though, the campaign for Southwest Conference membership ended in irony. On the December day in 1978 when it had appeared that the North Texas hearing would come up, Hayden Fry was off taking the job as head football coach at the University of Iowa. And North Texas membership was not discussed at the meeting.[31]

Were Fry and the North Texas leaders tilting at windmills? An NTSU journalism graduate wrote in *Texas Sports* magazine two years later:

> Whereas Fry's drive pleased some, however, it offended others—most notably SWC athletic directors. Privately, there were those who said they would never let North Texas join as long as Fry was there. As one athletic director put it, "nobody (in the SWC) cared for the way Hayden was going around mouthing off about getting into the conference. He was making it sound like we'd be making a big mistake not to admit them, and that turned a lot of people off."[32]

Whither Athletics?

Immediately after Fry left, NTSU named his assistant athletic director, Andy Everest, as athletic director. Basketball Coach Blakeley revealed on a radio interview that North Texas was looking for another conference to join. This forced Everest to defend that position earlier than he had wanted. He was helped out when the new president, Frank Vandiver, spoke up:

> "It's awfully hard to be an independent in college athletics today, unless you're Notre Dame," Vandiver said. "And North Texas is not Notre Dame." Vandiver said North Texas didn't have "a snowball chance in hell" of getting into the SWC. That not only backed up Everest, but it carried a high degree of credibility since the new president was from a SWC school, Rice.[33]

The Campus Wants Brashier

When Fry resigned, every member of the football team signed a petition, urging the selection of their defensive coordinator, Bill Brashier, to replace Fry. The twelve members of the Athletic Council voted unanimously to endorse Brashier, and President Nolen did the same, recommending the appointment to the Board of Regents. However, the board released a statement that it wished to employ an athletic director before hiring a football coach. Upon learning of these developments, Brashier issued a statement that said, "If the Board of Regents cannot concur with the unanimous endorsement of the Athletic Council, the president, and the vice president, then I am no longer a candidate for the position of head football coach at North Texas State University."[34] Brashier then left for Iowa and a position there as Fry's defensive coordinator. The regents drew a surprisingly harsh attack from the *Denton Record-Chronicle* editorial page, decrying the board action.[35]

The committee and the president moved swiftly after that, and on January 8, 1979, Jerry Moore was named head football coach. He came from six years at the University of Nebraska, where he had been offensive coordinator for Coach Tom Osborne.

Nothing but problems lay ahead for North Texas football. After Fry's 9–2 record in his final season of 1978, none of the six coaches who tried in the next twenty years would have a North Texas career record with more wins than losses. Fry also left behind a mounting deficit in athletic budgeting.

chapter 35

Joining the Osteopaths

We shall take whatever steps are necessary to enhance the physical presence of North Texas in Fort Worth and in Dallas. We will go there and provide whatever physical facilities are required.

C. C. Nolen
Speech to the faculty, 1974

During C. C. Nolen's last year as TCU vice chancellor, a fledgling private medical school opened its doors. Twenty students began classes in Fort Worth Osteopathic Hospital. Administrators occupied a nearby four-room house, and the gross anatomy lab was set up in a garage apartment. Thus began the Texas College of Osteopathic Medicine, which had been chartered in 1966. For its second year, the college bought and renovated a bowling alley on Camp Bowie Boulevard, in a block next to the hospital. This structure contained 18,000 square feet, enough to house a second freshman class of 32.[1]

The legislature authorized the Coordinating Board to contract with TCOM for instruction to prepare doctors of osteopathic medicine and appropriated $100,000. The amount was raised to $300,000 in 1972.

In the fall of 1971, Nolen thus took to Denton an acquaintance with this new venture, and he was receptive to a proposal that North Texas develop a relationship with TCOM. In a 1974 *President's Bulletin*, he recounted the chronology of how that came about:

> On November 8, 1971, a committee of the Coordinating Board with consultants from the allopathic and osteopathic professions, the Texas State Board of Medical Examiners, the Texas Legislature, some 15 persons, visited TCOM in Fort Worth. During that visit Dr. G. V. Brindley [an M.D. and member of the coordinating board] suggested that TCOM consider "the feasibility of relating to another institution as an academic partner." Dr. George Luibel [chairman of the TCOM Board of Directors] concurred. . . .
>
> Dr. J. K. G. Silvey, chairman of the Biology Department, North Texas State University, made first contact at the Annual Convention of the American Osteopathic Association, November 14–21,1971.
>
> Dr. Luibel, Dr. Henry Hardt [dean of TCOM], President Nolen, Dr. Silvey and others met in Fort Worth on December 21, 1971, to discuss the possibility of North Texas State University providing teaching services for Texas College of Osteopathic Medicine.[2]

First Step: Teaching Contract

In February 1972, NTSU and TCOM announced a contract to cooperatively teach forty-eight first-year osteopathic students on the Denton campus beginning in September 1972. North Texas was to receive $24,000 at the start of each semester for the use of classrooms, laboratories, faculty offices, and other facilities. The equivalent of six full-time faculty members would teach gross anatomy, microanatomy, neuroanatomy, biochemistry, physiology, and immunology. Nolen told news people, "This is just another way in which we intend to provide cooperative service for agencies and persons in the metropolitan area and the state."[3]

In August of that year, the TCOM Board of Directors met on the NTSU campus, dining with the NTSU Board of Regents but holding its own meeting to approve the TCOM budget for fiscal 1972–73.[4] Dr. Silvey was named to head the program at North Texas.[5] North Texas administrators soon discovered that their costs for the TCOM operation were double what had been estimated and sought to modify the contract with TCOM. Nolen explained to the TCOM board chairman, Dr. George J. Luibel, that the contract had been made based on TCOM receiving $150,000 in state funds. When in the summer of 1972, the osteopaths succeeded in getting $300,000 in state funds during a special session of the legislature, Nolen asked that TCOM payments to North Texas be doubled.[6]

Providing Facilities in Denton

Specialized instructional and laboratory space was needed for the Denton TCOM classes. Regents in February voted to construct TCOM space in the unfinished attic space of the NTSU Biology Building with $160,000 from a federal grant to TCOM. NTSU would make the space available to TCOM for five years.[7]

Coordinating Board Urges Merger Study

Experience made clear that the expense of medical education would be too great for a state-assisted private school. What was needed was full state support. The Coordinating Board became instrumental in fostering a union between the two schools. Nolen explained:

> On March 10, 1973, the Medical Education Advisory Committee recommended Coordinating Board approval of a request from [NTSU] in conjunction with [TCOM] for a Department of Basic Health Sciences and a new degree program in Basic Health Sciences, ". . . provided that TCOM and NTSU agree to study a plan for consolidation of all educational activities of these two institutions into a School of

Osteopathic Medicine as a part of NTSU and to report the results of their study to the Coordinating Board by January 1, 1974."

On May 24, 1973, a new contract was made between TCOM and NTSU for the academic year 1973–74. This was approved by the Coordinating Board. It called for teaching 102 Texas resident students at $5,625.00 per student and a maximum amount of $573,750.00.

At the regular meeting of the Coordinating Board on April 13, 1973, the proposal for a Department of Basic Health Sciences at North Texas State University was approved.[8]

As stipulated by the coordinating board, the TCOM Board of Directors voted to study the feasibility of a permanent affiliation with North Texas, and the NTSU board voted to take part in the study.[9]

Seeking Permanent Affiliation

President Nolen, Vice President Gus Ferré, and Silvey in January 1974 met in Fort Worth with a visiting team from the American Osteopathic Society. TCOM President Marion Coy arranged the meeting to discuss the merger of the two institutions. That led to a joint meeting of NTSU regents and TCOM trustees to discuss the merger.[10] The final formal action came on October 14, 1974, when the regents voted unanimously for TCOM to become an integral part of the university with one board of regents and one chief executive officer, the president.[11] On behalf of the osteopathic physicians and their college, President Coy endorsed the consolidation plan before the Coordinating Board.[12]

Final approval came from the Coordinating Board on December 6, 1974. (A full account of the development of TCOM from 1960 to 1975 may be found in a doctoral dissertation by Richard Rafes.[13])

Dr. Guinn's Medical School

The coordinating board at the same time had yet another request for a medical school in Fort Worth. That request came from President John Guinn of Texas Woman's University. Dr. Guinn had helped build the health professions as a major emphasis for TWU, including the development of nursing education centers in Dallas and Houston. It was clear that he also wanted to get a center in Fort Worth. Having two medical school requests before the Coordinating Board created a public appearance (probably justified) of major competition between the two Denton universities. Not apparent to the public was the reawakening of questions among NTSU regents about the possibility of formal joint action with or outright merger with TWU.

TWU asked the Coordinating Board on January 26, 1973, to approve a medical school in Fort Worth. The *Dallas Morning News* later wrote that "an existing medical school" opposed this action, noting that the closest medical school to the proposed school was the University of Texas Southwestern Medical School in Dallas. The Coordinating Board did not act on that proposal.[14]

Guinn and the TWU regents got busy building support and prepared what Guinn called a new plan centered on a school in Fort Worth. On June 20, the *Fort Worth Star-Telegram* carried a front-page story reporting that Sears, Roebuck & Co., American Manufacturing Co., and Woodbine Development Corp had donated a sixty-acre tract for the TWU medical school. The land was located in north Fort Worth at Spur 280 and Riverside Drive near Interstate 35W and was valued at $1.5 million. Dr. Guinn optimistically told newspapers that the program was to begin in the fall of 1974 on the Denton campus, with the first class of about fifty potential physicians admitted for the 1975–76 academic year. He announced at a press conference in Fort Worth that science and administration buildings would cost $9.5 million, financed by contributions, federal grants, and state appropriations. Construction would begin "sometime after fall 1974."[15]

Governor Dolph Briscoe at first said he "heartily approves" of the project. His public attitude changed once the proposal came before the Coordinating Board on October 18, 1974. That was the same day that the board approved the concept of the TCOM-NTSU merger. The Coordinating Board staff recommended against creating any new medical school, whereupon the board deadlocked in a 7–7 vote on the TWU proposal, leaving Chairman Harry Provence to vote no and defeat the measure.[16] The governor subsequently pronounced the measure dead unless the Coordinating Board changed its mind.

TWU then moved to the legislature with an added feature: consolidate TWU's plan for a Fort Worth medical school with one calling for a medical school in the Lower Rio Grande Valley. The house voted 108–30 on May 16 to give the measure final passage. On May 29, the Senate State Affairs Committee voted 8–0 to authorizing the bill, but Senator Bill Moore of Bryan refused to sign the committee report and kept the proposal off the senate floor.[17]

TWU had one more move to try for Fort Worth. In the fall of 1976, President Guinn asked President Nolen to consider a joint site for TCOM and a TWU medical school, using the sixty acres donated to TWU. That led to further discussions between NTSU Chairman Willis and the chairman of the TWU Board of Regents, Mrs. Marcella Perry. From Fort Worth, TWU board vice chairman John Shivers wrote to Willis in October with this formal request for a joint site feasibility study:

> The joint study will encompass the potential sharing and cost saving between the TWU School of Medicine and the Texas College of Osteopathic Medicine on a site in Tarrant County. Such a study will look into the joint use and sharing of streets, parking lots, security and perhaps dormitories, food services and auditoriums. However, in no way is the above to be construed to suggest any type of merger or combining of the TWU Medical school and/or TCOM.[18]

Willis responded that TWU had already chosen a site and made decisions that would require NTSU to regard the study as unwise unless both parties agreed to start over from scratch. He also said it would be inadvisable for NTSU to enter into a study until the proper state agencies had approved the TWU request for an additional medical school.[19]

The Legislature Approves

The President's Cabinet and Nolen's staff repeatedly urged that the new institution carry the name of the university as an integral part of its title. Indeed, in his fall 1974 *President's Bulletin*, Nolen wrote that on September 1, 1975, we would see the establishment of "NTSU College of Osteopathic Medicine." He later told his administrative group that the pressure from the osteopathic physicians and their association was too great and that he had to agree to legislation retaining the name of the private school.

The enabling legislation was carried in the 1975 legislature as S. B. 216. The senate passed the bill on March 17, 1975, and the house on May 15. Governor Briscoe signed the bill May 22 to create a separate "Texas College of Osteopathic Medicine" governed by the Board of Regents of North Texas State University under the supervision of the Coordinating Board.

Managing a Medical School

As noted in Chapter 31, Nolen wanted an experienced university administrator to report directly to him on medical school affairs. He judged that the physicians now on staff lacked that administrative background. However, the regents could not officially assume legal control of TCOM until September 1. On June 6, Chairman Willis initiated a telephone conference call meeting of the executive committee of the board to "approve certain administrative changes."

Ferré Sent to Fort Worth

This put Gus Ferré on a one-year leave from his NTSU post to become vice president for medical affairs, ad interim, TCOM, from September 1, 1975, through August 31, 1976. At the same time Dr. Miles Anderson, associate vice president for academic affairs, was named to become vice president ad interim during Ferré's absence. This committee action was ratified by the full board at a meeting on June 13. At the same time, the board stated its intention to appoint C. C. Nolen as president and chief executive officer of both NTSU and TCOM. This instructed him "to implement the transition of Texas College of Osteopathic Medicine from private to state status. . . ."[20]

Nolen had not waited for official action to inform Ferré of his expected duties. He wrote on May 27 that Ferré would work with Nolen as TCOM president in a direct-line relationship and handle the usual duties of a vice president. Ferré was assigned to help the medical dean establish himself as the academic leader so that he would become capable of assuming the vice president spot himself.[21]

In June Nolen appointed Ferré to head a "Transition Implementation Task Force." Members were Dr. Marion Coy, who had been named in March 1972 as the first and only president the private college was to have, NTSU Vice President Carter, and NTSU attorney Jack Barton. Nolen asked for immediate action on a number of pending matters "even though the official budget change will not begin until September 1."[22] Liaison was further strengthened by having Carter named vice president for fiscal affairs and treasurer for TCOM as well as for NTSU.

The Board of Regents on August 30 named Dr. Ralph Willard, D. O., as dean of TCOM, and authorized acceptance of a $4.8 million federal grant, employed an architectural firm, and started plans for Medical Education Building 1.

Working With the Teaching Hospital

Nolen confirmed with the executive vice president of the Fort Worth Osteopathic Hospital that it would remain as the teaching hospital for the college. The two entities would enter joint planning efforts and begin major remodeling to accommodate the impact of a growing TCOM on the hospital.[23]

Delegating More Local Control

Within a few months, Nolen began to delegate more control to those physically located in Fort Worth, noting that Dean Willard had rapidly become familiar with TCOM and that Carter's enlarged responsibilities required more assistance in Fort Worth. On December 23, 1975, Nolen advised the transition task force that in January 1976 Jack Robason would be assigned to represent Carter on the task force and to be responsible at TCOM for business management, purchasing accounting, budget preparation, and other fiscal areas assigned to him by the president. At the same time Dr. Willard would assume operational responsibility under the policy direction from the president through the vice president for medical affairs (Ferré) for all duties related to academics, clinics, basic sciences, hospitals, and students. The dean was also given a strengthened relationship in dealing with the hospital administrator. Vice President Ferré remained as chairman of the task force, but was now seeing many of the tasks he had undertaken being delegated to staff members.

In January 1976, Nolen directed that on June 1, Dean Willard would "assume full responsibility for daily operations of TCOM." In a January 29 memorandum to Ferré, Nolen directed that Willard would report directly to the president and the transition task force would no longer be needed. He noted that it would be important to raise "the level at which the Dean is perceived by those who are greatly concerned with TCOM such as those in the hospital, the D. O. profession, and the Fort Worth community."[24]

Although the memo suggested that Ferré would continue in an important role at the medical school, it appeared that Ferré was at odds with the persons or groups characterized by Nolen as "those who are greatly concerned with TCOM," and that this had created still further regent anxiety. In just twelve days, Nolen told Ferré that his relationship with TCOM was at an end and that his only option would be to return to Denton with a one-year appointment as consultant to the president. Nolen also said that he didn't plan to name another vice president for medical affairs.

Thus, the TCOM fiscal year began on September 1, 1976, with the dean in clear control of internal operations and reporting to Nolen as president of TCOM. The regents endorsed this arrangement on October 14, 1976, asserting it "looks to the president for the implementation of this organizational policy." Six months later, the board voted to reaffirm its policy of October 14, 1976.

In the meantime, Regent E. E. Stuessy had developed a proposal to relocate the TCOM campus elsewhere in Fort Worth. The concept greatly alarmed the osteopathic groups. His plan was not supported by his colleagues, however, and on November 18, 1977, the board emerged from an executive session to report that the board had voted 7 to 1 to build the second medical building "within the presently approved site boundaries provided adequate land and funds are available." [25] The regents then proceeded to vote unanimously for yet another statement of policy that had been moved by Kenneth May, chairman of the board's Role and Scope Committee. This declared again that the legislature had mandated that NTSU and TCOM "be operated as sister institutions under the governance of the board and the administration of the president." This vote instructed the president to establish a permanent joint group to include the TCOM vice president for medical affairs and the NTSU vice president for academic affairs and such others as he considered appropriate from each institution. The resolution suggested monthly meetings alternating between campuses, and asked the group to recommend and implement ways in which the sister institutions could cooperate in educational programs and share facilities, personnel, and resources. The board then went further in seeking to emphasize this "oneness" of governance:

> All sites utilized for osteopathic medical education or for any other health care professions which are or may be brought under the governance of this Board shall be designated and be referred to as a "North Texas State University Health Sciences Center."
>
> Campus graphics at the TCOM site(s) shall identify it (them) as North Texas State University Health Sciences Center/Texas College of Osteopathic Medicine."

> Letterheads and news releases shall likewise use this identification. The correct abbreviated form is "NTSU/TCOM."[26]

The planning and construction of the first medical building moved along under the general supervision of the task force, with Larry Luce being assigned from the NTSU planning office to supervise the liaison work with TCOM staff and the architects. Medical Education Building 1 opened in 1978, having been financed with $8 million in state appropriations and $4.8 million in federal funds. In the meantime, though, the U. S. Office of Education declared that the Biology Building attic space being used for basic health science instruction was ineligible for use for medical education because of the source of federal funds used in its original construction. With this dilemma, TCOM leased 38,000 square feet in an office park and moved most of the basic science program from Denton in 1977.

Peat, Marwick Makes Recommendations

The uncertainty in the board members' minds about TCOM management became part of a larger concern about relationships between the board and the president. As will be seen in more detail in Chapter 37, the regents in January 1978 retained Peat, Marwick, Mitchell & Co. of Austin to study these relationships. They also requested a parallel study of the relationship between TCOM and NTSU. A final draft was delivered in June 1978.[27]

The consultants recommended that the Board of Regents abandon the practice of assigning one regent as the liaison to the medical school, correct the scheduling that led to only two meetings of thirty being held on the TCOM campus, and create greater visibility for the entire board of regents before the TCOM faculty and staff.[28] The report also suggested a more equitable means of prorating to TCOM those costs incurred at NTSU in support of TCOM. Perhaps even more dramatic in its potential impact was the recommended change in the organizational structure. This called for creation of three new administrative positions: executive vice president and dean of the college, associate dean for academic and student services, and vice president for financial and administrative services. This was intended to identify "the direct line of authority and responsibility for TCOM's administration from the regents to the president and directly to the executive vice president and dean of the college."[29]

Before any direct moves could be made toward adopting any of the Peat, Marwick agenda, immediate crisis management was required on the political front.

Osteopaths Seek Transfer

Campus development plans called for the construction of Medical Education Building 2 immediately after the first building. The Board of Regents had voted to build this on a site less crowded than the one originally planned but one that would require the purchase of more land. The 1977 legislature had appropriated $15 million for the structure, but Attorney General John Hill ruled that none of that money could be used to purchase land for the building. The regents decided to delay construction until the land purchase could be provided by the 1979 legislature, thus further straining unhappiness with the NTSU situation, especially on the part of the Texas Osteopathic Medical Association (TOMA).

TCOM supporters had become disturbed not only by delays in construction on the Fort Worth campus, but also with the medical school's lack of a president of its own, and with the fear that TCOM gift funds might have been misapplied. Each of these concerns helped lead to an effort to remove the Texas College of Osteopathic Medicine from NTSU control.

TOMA Wants Liberation

TOMA supported H. B. 1100, which was introduced in the house on February 15, 1979, by Representative Gib Lewis of Fort Worth. Lewis proposed to transfer control of TCOM from NTSU to the University of Texas System. Lewis told the *North Texas Daily* that the transfer would be more efficient and would save tax money. He explained that the bill was recommended by the Texas Osteopathic Medical Association. [30]

Meeting the day after the Lewis statement appeared in the *Daily*, the regents voted unanimously "to exert every effort within our power" to block the transfer. The resolution, drafted by Kenneth May of Lubbock, said the board was "surprised and dismayed to learn after the fact" that the bill had been introduced. The statement continued:

> There are problems with any new institution, especially a medical school, but NTSU/TCOM has made tremendous progress since it

> came under the governance of this Board of Regents. We are well along toward assembling an outstanding faculty and staff. We have occupied the first buildings on our permanent campus, and our plans are to begin construction on Medical Education Building II this year.[31]

Rep. W. T. (Tip) Hall of Denton said Lewis told him he had been receiving pressure from some of his constituents to introduce the bill. By this time, it was clear that the issues had been thoroughly politicized. Lewis told the *Daily* that he had no intention of giving up the fight for the TCOM transfer but acknowledged that the board's unanimous vote would hurt chances for the bill's passage.[32]

Lewis tipped off his hand, however, by pointing out that he didn't like the NT delays in starting construction on the second medical education building. If the regents would show him they could provide the facilities promptly, he said, then he would take a different attitude toward the transfer.

Compromise: Create an Independent President

The next step by TOMA was to propose a substitute bill that would allow TCOM to have its own president, who would report directly to the Board of Regents. The substitute bill passed unanimously through the House Committee on Higher Education on April 17. At first, a spokesman for the osteopathic association said the group continued to back H. B. 1100, but then told legislators that the replacement bill was satisfactory. An unnamed source told the *Daily*, "As soon as we presented this new bill, we put that one aside and tabled it."[33] The move for an independent president was made just as Nolen announced his resignation as president of NTSU and TCOM on April 12, 1979. The *Daily* reported that Tex Roberts, executive director of the Texas Osteopathic Medical Association, said discussions with legislative leaders and NTSU regents led to the decision to remain in the NT system. [34]

The NTSU board did not, however, prefer this approach. Writing as chairman of the Role and Scope Committee, Regent Kenneth May advised Gib Lewis that the Board of Regents had never discussed the concept of separate presidents for the two institutions. May said that "the board must have one person to whom it can look and hold responsible for the management of both schools, whether that person be called the president, the chancellor or by whatever title."[35]

Creating a Chancellor and a President

The first step from the Board of Regents was to name Dr. Ralph Willard as vice president for medical affairs, NTSU, and dean of TCOM. This helped allay some of the concerns of the osteopathic community. The goal that the osteopaths sought awaited the selection in November 1979 of the president to succeed Nolen. At a meeting in Fort Worth on February 27, 1981, the board voted for a resolution establishing a chancellor over the two schools, with a president for TCOM. The vote was hardly a ringing endorsement: four ayes, one no, and two abstentions.[36]

The regents' choice for NTSU/TCOM president was Dr. Frank E. Vandiver, who was to serve on a part-time basis until completing duties at Rice University in August 1981. After necessary details had been worked out, the regents voted on May 1, 1981, to name Vandiver as chancellor and chief executive officers of the two institutions and Dr. Willard as president of TCOM. Vandiver continued with a dual role, serving also as president of NTSU.[37]

chapter 36

Expanding the University

At North Texas we stand ready to serve every institution in the area to the maximum of our capability. We cannot be all things to all people, but we can be more things to more people.

C. C. Nolen
Inaugural Address, 1971

President Nolen was by nature enthusiastic and attracted to the new and interesting directions in which the university might be taken. Here are some of the ideas that caught his attention and, in some cases, came into existence:

• Create a medical school, a Law School, and a Pharmacy School at NTSU.

• Merge with Texas Woman's University or bring it under the same board of regents.

• Acquire a permanent Dallas center for instruction and public service.

• Build a center for fashion marketing and design in the Dallas Market Center.

• Lease the university golf course property to a private developer to build a hotel-conference center.

• Construct two more phases of the new library building, doubling the first phase to its intended size.

• Complete the closing of city streets within the campus planning area, and develop a new major entrance to the campus by curving Avenue D around to Avenue E northward from the interstate highway.

• Join a "New Town" development in Flower Mound to create a community instruction and fine arts center.

• Join other Denton agencies to put a VHF television station on the air, using an early Federal Communications Commission allocation for Denton.

• Bring North Texas intercollegiate athletics into the Southwest Conference.

• Acquire from the federal government some twenty acres of land formerly used as a Nike missile launch site and convert it to a "north campus" for science programs.

• Move a historic one-room schoolhouse to the campus and develop a museum of educational history.

• Create an incentive and awards program to recognize the work of nonfaculty staff employees.

• Pull together various units in Dallas, Fort Worth, Flower Mound, and Denton into a system under a single chancellor.

• Purchase the papers of Arturo Toscanini from New York for the Music Library.

• Employ a recently released convict as a resident poet-artist.

• Implement a full-scale university planning and budgeting system.

• Create a major educational foundation that would bring in large gift income.

NEW PROGRAMS, NEW UNITS

The Nolen team moved early and successfully to establish Texas College of Osteopathic Medicine under control of the NTSU regents. Not so fortunate was the hope expressed for a School of Law. One approach in this direction was an early request for a Department of Legal Studies, to be followed by an NTSU School of Law.[1] The Coordinating Board turned down both proposals in March 1973.

A number of degree programs were added in the 1970s. The Department of Basic Health Sciences was approved in July 1973, a contractual tie to TCOM. The master's degree program in home economics was restored in April 1974. The Coordinating Board in July 1974 approved Ed.D. and Ph.D. degrees in adult-continuing education and master's degrees in adult-continuing education and vocational-technical education, all through the Federation of North Texas Area Universities. In May 1975 the federation also gained a doctorate in reading. In April of that year, board approval created the bachelor of applied arts and sciences degree, which was designed for a community college transfer who had already completed a two-year specialization. In 1977, a major in biochemistry, a bachelor of social work degree, and a bachelor's degree in computer science were added.

Another "college" was acquired with a name change in March 1979. The School of Education became the College of Education.

Yet another school would soon be added because of the work of faculty members in moving into new areas. Some of the most significant new programs came from the late 1960s. The areas included studies in aging, rehabilitation studies, economic education, industrial relations and applied economics, and community service programs. These were built on strong external support, at first from federal and later from state and private sources. They also had a strong continuing education component, much of it offered off-campus. Most of these programs were also offering credit courses through host departments in the College of Arts and Sciences.[2]

Correspondence and Extension

State teachers college attendance was heavily oriented toward summer sessions, meeting the needs of the public school teachers. But enrolling only in the summer for twelve semester hours took too long. Students wanted credit classes brought to them in some fashion. The first such instruction came in correspondence courses by mail and extension courses taught by faculty members who drove once a week to the site of instruction. Extension classes were typically taught for three hours a night in a local public-school classroom. Distances of one hundred miles to cities like Wichita Falls were not uncommon for extension locations. The Division of Extension and Correspondence administered all work.

Extension Work Thrives

The first institutional self-study for the Southern Association in 1962 indicated that these off-campus programs were still active. In fall 1960 North Texas conducted twenty-six extension classes in eight cities, most of them within a forty-mile radius of Denton. These enrolled 535, of whom 179 were graduate students. Faculty evaluation of this instruction found it to be of satisfactory quality but was often skeptical of its use for graduate credit.[3]

The 1971–73 self-study showed that extension work had grown considerably. In the 1971–72 long session sixty-two courses were taught in cities ranging from El Paso to Houston. Most of the classes were in education. They enrolled 1,762 students, of whom 1,399 were graduate students.[4]

Resident credit could not be awarded for extension work, but in the spring of 1972, the Coordinating Board approved an experimental program for resident credit in Dallas. That fall the College of Business Administration offered four regular graduate classes taught at Richland College in Dallas. Regular faculty members taught these as part of their normal class load.[5]

Study by Correspondence

No graduate work was ever offered by correspondence, but as many as eighteen semester hours of study-by-mail could be applied to a bachelor's degree, the maximum allowable under a policy of counting thirty hours of extension and correspondence work. This was still in effect at the time of the 1971–73 self-study; the 1983–85 self-study noted a decline in faculty interest in teaching correspondence courses.

The Concept of Continuing Education

Conferences for teachers and administrators were an established practice, at first conducted on the campus and then extended to public school campuses, especially after the state began requiring in-service training for teachers. The School of Business Administration also offered noncredit instruction in fields such as preparation for CPA examinations and in petroleum accounting. Other conferences were conducted in a variety of business fields, public administration, librarianship, and some scientific areas. This function generally had to be financed by fees or by external grants.

A Federal Stimulus

The Higher Education Act of 1965 and other federal programs stimulated other community service and continuing education activities. Encouraged by the Coordinating Board, NTSU and TWU established a Joint University Center for Community Services in May 1966 with partial federal funding. The first director was Dr. Mary Evelyn Huey, NTSU government professor who later became TWU president. The center eventually became the sole responsibility of NTSU and offered credit and noncredit instruction in many Texas cities with financial assistance from the Higher Education Act, the Law Enforcement Assistance Administration, the State Department of Mental Health and Mental Retardation, and the Texas Education Agency.

Professional Development Institute

The Professional Development Institute was created in 1972 as the continuing education extension of the College of Business Administration. PDI was administered by the dean of the college through a director, who was a business faculty member. NTSU faculty members and other professionals taught courses and each was paid an hourly fee for the service. Fees sustained the program and generated revenue that could be returned to the College of Business and to the university. PDI developed courses and seminars for accounting and management professionals in petroleum industry accounting, insurance, and personal/professional management. CPA review classes were offered in locations in several states.

Center for Economic Education

The Joint Council on Economic Education sponsored the creation in 1968 of a summer institute for public school teachers that evolved into the Center for Economic Education. It was directed by Dr. Kendall Cochran and then continued by Dr. Bill Luker. Early support came from the Sears, Roebuck Foundation and the Texas Council for Economic Education.[6] The center grew during the next thirty years in programs designed to serve public schools with teacher training, material distribution, and curriculum development. By the end of the century the program was training between 700 and 1,000 teachers a year.[7]

Center for Studies in Aging

The critical political factor that brought North Texas into this field was the passage in 1965 of the Older Americans Act, which authorized the support of training for persons to work with the elderly. The head of the Department of Economics and Sociology, Dr. Hiram Friedsam, taught and did research in this field and initiated application for funds and secured approval from President Matthews for the formation of a Center for Studies in Aging. The emphasis at first would be on administration of long-term care facilities. He was aided by an adjunct faculty member, Dr. Herbert Shore, then director of Golden Acres, the Dallas Home for Jewish Aged. The Administration on Aging began a series of grants that enabled the starting of degree programs in sociology. The 1970 allocation from the Social and Rehabilitation Services Administration was $193,443 for training in the administration program in aging.[8] Friedsam was able to recruit Dr. Cora Martin, who was later to become codirector and then director of the Center. She was a nurse who had received a master's degree in sociology at North Texas.

School of Community Services

Service programs continued to develop. In October 1968 Vice President J. J. Spurlock reported staff discussions on the possibility of a school of public service. He asked President Kamerick to appoint a study group chaired by Graduate Dean Robert B. Toulouse.[9] That group recommended creation of a School of Continuing Education and Community Services, hoping to locate it in Marquis Hall, which would be freed from dormitory assignment.[10]

Directors of the affected units continued their discussions. As Dr. Friedsam pointed out, their shared characteristics of external funding, continuing education, and applied orientation resulted in:

> uneasy relationships between the units and the host departments. To a considerable extent their academic objectives were different; the types of students enrolled and the course content offered were different; and, although external funds provided some latitude, the programs were theoretically subject to departmental control and, at the extreme, rejection.[11]

The unit directors in April 1972 asked Vice President Ferré for creation of a School of Community Service in April and the Coordinating Board approved in July.[12] Dr. Hiram Friedsam was named dean. Units included were:

Center for Studies in Aging
Center for Public Administration
Manpower and Industrial Relations Institute
Center for Community Services
Extension and Correspondence
Rehabilitation Services Training Program
Center for Minority Enterprises
Communication Research and Training Center.

OTHER PROGRAM DEVELOPMENTS

Intensive English Language Institute

The arrival of international students in significant numbers for the first time led to the need to provide instruction in a new language. Sixty-five students enrolled at the Intensive English Language Institute during its first semester in 1977. Almost half were from Saudi Arabia. Enrollment also included seventeen Iranians, eight Venezuelans and a few students from Algeria, Bahrain, Greece, Guatemala, Iraq, Jordan, Korea, Mexico, and Thailand. In the next twenty years, the institute was to enroll more than 2,000 students. About eighty-four percent of IELI graduates eventually studied at UNT.

International Accelerator Conference

In 1974, 300 scientists and engineers came from around the world to NTSU for a three-day international conference on the application of small accelerators. Dr. Jerome L. Duggan of the physics faculty started the biennial conference in Oak Ridge, Tennessee, in 1968 and 1970, and moved it to NT in 1974. It continued to grow in international participation, becoming the International Conference on the Application of Accelerators in Research and Industry. By the time of the fifteenth conference in 1998, attendance had grown to more than 1,000, and more than 7,000 scientists from forty-seven countries had come to the North Texas campus.

Cooperative Education

A federal grant supported the placement of eighteen students in a cooperative education program in 1976–77. This provided academic credit for paid, career-related work experience. By 1979 there were 126 students enrolled, 340 by 1982,[13] and 678 in 1983.[14]

Institute of Applied Sciences

The Institute of Environmental Studies was formed in 1970 under the direction of Dr. J. K. G. Silvey, chairman of biological sciences, to coordinate interdisciplinary environmental research. Dr. William H. Glaze, professor of chemistry, became director in 1973. The institute was housed in the General Academic Building from 1978 to 1998. In 1975, the institute was renamed the Institute of Applied Sciences and in 1976 became a unit of the School of Community Service. In September 1979, the directorship was assumed by Dr. Kenneth L. Dickson. The IAS received the President's Award in 1985 for bringing significant recognition to the University. In 1986 the institute moved to the College of Arts and Sciences to facilitate close alignment with other academic departments there. The institute had a major role in developing the Environmental Education, Science and Technology Building, which it occupied in 1998.

Seeking a Television Channel for Denton

Channel 2 for the North Texas region was assigned to Denton in the 1950s as an educational channel. On several occasions the channel was sought for commercial use, but Presidents J. C. Matthews and John Guinn and others in Denton protected it by maintaining that Denton universities and public schools hoped to build the educational station.

However, in 1976 the public television group that operated KERA-TV, Channel 13, in Dallas asked to start up Channel 2 as a second educational station. At first, President Nolen indicated that NTSU wanted to participate in programming and endorsed the foundation's application for Channel 2.[15] This did not satisfy others in Denton, however. Just before the May 23, 1977, deadline for applications, an ad hoc group, the Denton Channel 2 Committee, petitioned the Federal Communication Commission to deny the Dallas application and give Denton ninety days to prepare its own application.[16]

The Denton Channel Two Foundation was formed to represent the community and the schools. Dr. John Horvat of the NT education faculty delivered the foundation's application to the FCC in Washington on August 23, 1977.[17] After years of legal maneuvering in Washington, the rival foundations agreed in January 1985 to merge to create North Texas Public Broadcasting. The FCC approved a new joint application. The result was Channel 2, KDTN, "Dallas, Fort Worth, and Denton." Yet, it was not until September 1, 1988, that the station went on the air.[18]

Doctoral Development Suspended

A number of departments planned to begin offering doctoral programs and others wished to expand existing offerings. The Coordinating Board on January 26, 1977, declared a moratorium on requests for additional doctoral programs at Texas public universities. This automatically turned down seventeen proposals that were on the board agenda. A federation program of NT and ETSU for a Ph.D. in Computer Science was denied by this action. The moratorium ended in 1980 with the initiation of comprehensive reviews of all academic degree programs offered in the state's public colleges and universities, beginning at the doctoral level.[19]

Expanding Computing Power

Many faculty members saw the need for bringing the greatest possible computing power to the campus for instruction and research as well as for administrative applications. Computerization began when President Matthews authorized a faculty-staff committee to plan for a centralized facility, one that led to adoption of the IBM System 360 mainframe platform. Upon occupancy of a new Library Building in 1972, the existing building was remodeled to accommodate an expansion of the Computing Center.

Modest academic entry into the field came in 1971–72 with the creation of a Department of Computer Sciences with two full-time faculty. The only degrees offered were master's degrees, but there was an eighteen-hour undergraduate minor. Classes were held in the science buildings and a computer laboratory was created from former dormitory rooms in Marquis Hall.[20]

But it had become clear that North Texas lacked the means for continued development of computing power. Nolen appointed Library Science Dean Dewey Carroll chairman of a Task Force on Future Funding and Operation of the University Computer Center. It included a TCOM representative and had liaison with TWU. The task force report appeared August 9, 1978, a nineteen-page document that called for major systems acquisitions and development. It awaited the arrival of the next administration for significant implementation.

In the late 1970s the first personal computers appeared in several campus offices—models such as the Apple II, Radio Shack TRS-80, and the Osborne.

WORKING WITH THE FACULTY

After the revolutionary introduction of faculty participation by President Kamerick, faculty members expected to continue making gains in their status in the 1970s. One of Nolen's first moves was to ask the Faculty Senate to amend its charter to remove the designation of the university president as the senate chairman.[21] The senate obliged by passing a proposed amendment providing for the senate to elect a member as chairman. This was subsequently ratified by a faculty election.[22] While Nolen worked amicably with most faculty members, Vice President Gus Ferré worked to retain more power in administrative hands. He was, however, sympathetic to most moves for betterment of faculty salaries and benefits.

Growth in Salaries

Nolen quickly learned that for the start of his first year in office there had been no salary increases budgeted "because of the political problems in Austin."[23] The situation did show some improvement in the next few years. Here's the way faculty nine-month salaries compared in fiscal 1974 and fiscal 1978:

Average Salaries for Nine Months, 1973-74

Rank	NTSU	State Weighted Avg.
Professor	19,203	19,452
Associate Professor	14,993	15,061
Assistant Professor	11,058	12,482
Instructor	10,095	9,556
All Ranks	12,746	13,187

Average Salaries for Nine Months, 1977-78

Rank	NTSU	State Weighted Avg.
Professor	25,311	25,312
Associate Professor	19,949	19,762
Assistant Professor	16,335	16,170
Instructor	13,481	12,741
All Ranks	20,261	19,040

This took place in a framework provided by the Board of Regents: don't give across-the-board raises but base them on merit. The regents typically petitioned the legislature to build this policy into the appropriations bill because "mandated across-the-board cost-of-living increases deprive the institution of effective personnel management controls."[24]

Recognition for Employees

Nolen began two programs planned to extend recognition for service to all employees, both faculty and staff. One was an annual service program at which awards were handed individually to each person on an anniversary year of his employment at North Texas—five, ten, fifteen, twenty, twenty-five, thirty, and thirty-five years. Similarly, an annual university retirement banquet was given to honor those who were retiring.

John Carrell of the business faculty worked for several years at the statewide and the campus levels to implement a program of early retirement for faculty members starting at age sixty. This was strongly supported by Vice President Miles Anderson and by Nolen and implemented in the later 1970s to the extent that funds made possible. This permitted a faculty member to begin retirement, draw full benefits through the Teacher Retirement System, and be permitted to be paid to teach up to one-half time without reduction in retirement benefits.[25]

Where's the Faculty Club?

Faculty members had long sought the establishment of a physical site on or near the campus for a Faculty Club, citing the existence of such at a number of other campuses. Ad hoc committees had been formed to try to establish a club. One such venture was realized briefly when Resident Tenor Eugene Conley undertook a private venture to establish a private club and dining facility for the community on University Drive. A special faculty membership was offered there and it briefly became a type of "Faculty Club."

Back on the campus, many of the benefits of faculty association had been provided in Marquis Hall, the first women's dormitory. Many university and community dining, tea, and social functions were provided in its Crystal Room and reception hall. The cafeteria and dining hall served residents of Marquis Hall and adjoining Terrill Hall—plus larger numbers of faculty and staff members who joined them for lunch. When both Marquis and Terrill Halls were withdrawn from dormitory service in the late 1960s, the cafeteria-dining hall continued as a popular faculty luncheon area. Nolen also arranged for the former living room and game room areas to be set up for table-service lunching areas for employees.

As the time neared for an expanded University Union to open with major dining facilities in 1976, the status of Marquis Hall came into question. Faculty members in the local TACT chapter requested the operation of a faculty dining area, coffee lounge, and faculty club in the game room-living room area. Nolen asked University Food Service and Marquis Hall staff to investigate such provisions, including the continuation of the Crystal Room, and the group presented a procedure for doing this on May 15, 1975. This was opposed by Jane Smith, student affairs vice president, who saw this both as competition for income for union dining services and as an expense to be subsidized from student fees.[26]

When Nolen supported the closing of Marquis facilities, the Faculty Senate resolved in January 1976 that it "expects the NTSU Administration to provide separate and appropriate facilities for a faculty lounge in the new building."[27] Senate Chairman Cliff Hardy asked Smith to provide an official response to explain why they had been told that their request was "impossible." The lack of faculty dining facilities on the campus remained a faculty grievance for a good many years.

MOVING OFF CAMPUS

Interest increased in activities to extend the university presence into the metropolitan community. An interesting insight into this change can be found in the 1971–73 self-study, which reported that "At the same time that NTSU correctly described itself as the major state-supported institution of higher education in the North Texas area, the university was surprisingly insulated from the area, except in terms of origin of its student body."[28] The report noted the increasing presence of community colleges in Dallas and Tarrant Counties, the transformation of Arlington State into the University of Texas at Arlington, and the political pressure to build the University of Texas at Dallas. By 1970, "it seemed clear that the future of this university depended upon its taking a more aggressive initiative in broadening its relationship to the metropolitan area."

What this meant in terms of strategic development in the struggle to maintain metropolitan leadership was that the university wanted permanent centers in Dallas and in Fort Worth in which to teach classes *for resident credit.* This became part of a competitive struggle among the colleges and universities of the region, and the legislature and the Coordinating Board soon sought to curb these territorial impulses.

Search for a Dallas Site

TWU had facilities for Dallas instruction in its nursing center adjacent to the Parkland Hospital and the University of Texas Health Science Center. NTSU gained a similar potential in Fort Worth with Texas College of Osteopathic Medicine. However, in Dallas, North Texas relied on rental of educational space.

Just as North Texas was trying to strengthen its operations in Dallas, the 1975 legislature gave the Coordinating Board expanded powers to attempt to halt off-campus expansion by Texas public institutions. At that point Carter alerted Nolen to the provisions of SB 706: "No off-campus courses for credit may be offered by any college or university without specific prior approval of the board." Carter said that all courses offered for credit at all off-campus locations would need prior approval from the Coordinating Board, "particularly the Dallas facility."[29] Nevertheless, later that year the Board of Regents voted unanimously to instruct the president to establish official instructional centers in both Dallas and Fort Worth.[30]

When Southern Methodist University closed its downtown evening college in the Easterwood Building, NT in 1975 leased this for evening classes for resident credit. When SMU sold the building to First Baptist Church in Dallas, North Texas rented the space at night from the Baptists for another year, then taught in classrooms rented at night from Jesuit Preparatory School and later in various spaces rented from the Dallas Independent School District.

A Home in Flower Mound New Town?

In 1973, the federally assisted "new town" concept came to Denton County, and Nolen saw in it an opportunity for North Texas. The project was planned for the small community of Flower Mound, just north and west of Lewisville, where two Dallas businessmen sought to create a planned community called Flower Mound New Town. One, Edward Marcus of the Neiman Marcus specialty store family, owned a ranch that was to become the nucleus of the development. His partner was Raymond Nasher, who had developed the NorthPark shopping center in Dallas.

A copy of the general development plan reached President Nolen in March 1973. Nolen asked James L. Rogers, director of institutional analysis, to meet with a Flower Mound representative to discuss involving NTSU in the new town plans.[31] This led to meetings involving North Texas faculty and staff and the new-town group. At the end of November, Nolen proposed that NTSU coordinate higher education activities in Flower Mound, that a facility be provided as NTSU headquarters, and that North Texas scientists undertake an archaeological studies program early in 1974.[32]

On January 14, 1974, Nasher brought three staff members to the campus to discuss specific North Texas proposals.[33] An exuberant news release was issued that spring, telling of a major partnership agreed upon for NTSU at Flower Mound New Town. It described the celebration of a joint agreement at "a champagne affair at 10 A.M. on a grassy park by a pond to the strains of a string quartet." The agreement designated North Texas to coordinate all credit and noncredit courses for residents of the new town and to initiate or coordinate all research for Flower Mound New Town.[34]

At the time of the announcement, two projects had already begun: a cooperative community arts program with Southern Methodist University, funded in part by a $10,000 grant from the National Endowment for the Arts, and an archaeological site evaluation to identify sites which showed promise for preservation and future excavations. Dean Hiram Friedsam of the School of Community Service became the coordinator for NTSU. By July 4, 1974, Nolen was writing enthusiastically to Marcus of progress on a summer enrichment program, further archeological studies, an oral history project, community recreation program, and plans for facilities construction.[35]

Almost one year to the day, Nolen again addressed Marcus, this time not with enthusiasm or good news. The tide in Washington turned against funding the New Town concept. The Flower Mound project was canceled.[36] It would be a quarter of a century before a major Dallas development arrived.

DEVELOPMENT OF THE DENTON CAMPUS

Implementation of the campus plan continued during the acting presidency of John Carter in 1970–71. In September the Social Science Building (later

Wooten Hall) was completed, and the new library building stood ready for occupancy except for a contractual disagreement with the carpeting contractor.

The Street-Closing Dilemma

On October 7, 1970, NTSU requested the closing of Avenue A for three blocks, Mulberry to Chestnut and Prairie to Highland. It also asked to close Sycamore between Avenue A and Welch between the Speech Building and the upcoming Art Building. The City Council on November 10 voted immediate abandonment of Sycamore. It also voted for a renewed traffic study to develop alternate routing so that Avenue A could be closed. The problem was serious for the pedestrian goals of the university: the campus plan located three major buildings east of Avenue A.

In March, four city staff members, three NTSU representatives and planning consultants for the city and for the university conducted a major planning session. The group reported these agreements to the Denton City Council and to the board of regents: The city and university would jointly develop the major perimeter roads of Avenue E, Hickory, Bernard, and Eagle Drive. It was agreed that "creation of Avenue E as a perimeter road will lead to the closing of Avenue C within a very few years" and "creation of Bernard as a perimeter road would lead to the ultimate closing of Welch in the more distant future." This action also designated the major north-south thoroughfares on either side of the campus as Carroll Boulevard to the east and Bonnie Brae to the west.[37]

This agreement opened the way for the council to vote to quit-claim title to the three blocks of Avenue A. The result was a wide pedestrian mall running two blocks between the new art and speech buildings on the east and the older physics-mathematics and business administration buildings on the west. A block to the south, university workers developed a similar landscaped area between the Social Science Building and the Education-Home Economics Building.

The Nolen Team Picks Up

Nolen knew as he was preparing to take office that campus expansion was creating a problem with the city of Denton. He hoped to assign this to his new staff and smooth some of the feelings of resentment over university growth into private territory. In October 1971, the regents engaged Caudill Rowlett Scott to return to the campus for a fifth-year update of the campus plan. In

May 1972, CRS presented a campus-planning workbook to administrators as a guide to development.[38]

Progress in Buildings

The new library was occupied in May 1972. The old library, now renamed the Information Sciences Building, became the home of the science library, the library science library, and several other collections.[39]

The university acquired the 19.92 acres of the former Nike missile launch site in January 1972, and this became a north campus for programs in astronomy and some other science programs. In April and July of 1972, the Art Building and the Coliseum were completed, the Coliseum having been delayed for redesign after 1970 bids were far higher than budgeted. A contract for a nearly $6 million expansion of the University Union was awarded in May 1973. Nolen and staff thus had visible evidence of the fruits of five years of planning. They moved on to other physical plant planning areas, launching a city-university transit study, a utility master plan, and design of a campus graphics system in 1974. Development continued in 1975 and 1976 with renovation of the old library as the Information Sciences Building, start of construction on a general academic building, bids for a Music Building and two music practice buildings, and renovations of a portion of the Sam Houston School building, the Auditorium Building, and the Chemistry Building.

Street Problem Goes to Court

The NTSU campus plan called for the closing of Avenue C and Avenue D. This created major problems in the minds of many Denton interests. Avenue C (over President Matthews's objections) had become a connecting thoroughfare all the way to University Drive in north Denton, and it moved from the campus southward through the center of a major shopping center, Carriage Square. Avenue D reached a dead end at Hickory Street, the northern campus boundary, but it provided the access to Interstate 35E for both north- and south-bound traffic and fed much southwest Denton traffic into the campus area and beyond.

President Nolen asked on July 29, 1975, for the closing of Avenue D between Chestnut and Highland on November 1, 1975, and of Avenue C between Chestnut and Highland by September 1, 1976. The new health, physical education, and recreation center would be built astride Avenue D and Prairie Street, he wrote; the Avenue C area would be developed as a pedestrian site interconnecting five buildings of the "music center." Bids would be opened on the HPER building and an additional music building in November 1975.[40]

After a public hearing on August 20, 1975, the Planning and Zoning Commission unanimously recommended approval to the City Council. However, an unexpected complication emerged: three of the five council members were employees of NTSU and announced they would abstain because of potential conflict of interest. This left the council without a quorum to act on the NTSU request. The university then moved reluctantly to file a condemnation suit to acquire the Avenue D property so that construction could begin on the physical education building. The case was assigned to the 158th district court in Denton, and in March 1976, Judge Bob Scofield issued a summary judgment blocking the street closing. The university appealed, but in September 1976, the Fort Worth Court of Civil Appeals affirmed the Scofield decision ruling that the city of Denton had exclusive dominion over its streets and that a state university did not have power of eminent domain over public streets.[41]

Nolen and staff tried again on July 23, 1976, with a request to close Avenue D and to exclude the Avenue C closing at that time. Two university employees on the council tried to get the motion tabled so that the council could move to executive session for conferences with attorneys. They got no support, though, and the other council members carried a vote to table pending outcome of the condemnation suit. Thus it was that on August 28, 1976, Nolen wrote to Mayor Elinor Hughes proposing a cash settlement with the city in order to obtain the closing of Avenue D and two blocks of Prairie Street.[42] The council accepted the offer, and the Board of Regents voted to ratify the agreement to pay $400,500 to the city. The board also stipulated that the university would not seek the closing of Avenue C by any means other than by action of the City Council.[43]

Revised Plan for New Fund Decade

For many years, most new education and general buildings had been financed by the state ad valorem tax. Renovations were provided by special items in the appropriations bill, and student fees backed the sale of bonds for land purchase, campus site development, and some buildings. In 1973, for example, the regents sold $15 million in student general fee building bonds.[44] Another major ad valorem-tax allocation was planned for September 1, 1978.

In the fall of 1977, the university sought another campus-plan review by retaining Omniplan, architects and planners, of Dallas. That group produced a document in

February 1978 to provide the basis for establishment of funding priorities.[45]

New Campus Entrance

A principal feature of the updated plan was the creation of a major entrance from the interstate highway. This would use the Avenue D interchange from I35E and curve a widened access around to Avenue E on the western edge of the campus. The board voted the following February to approve the purchase of necessary land after gaining approval from the Coordinating Board.[46] This block was bounded by Avenue D on the east, Avenue E on the west, Interstate 35E access road on the south, and Eagle Drive on the north.

Finish the Library Building

At that same February 1978 meeting, the regents heard a recommendation from the president and his cabinet "as the highest priority need in facilities development" the provision of the Phase II portion of the library at the earliest possible time. In 1967, a schematic design had been completed for a library to meet the program space requirements. Funding permitted the development of construction documents for only half of this plan. Completion of a Phase II and Phase III were scheduled for arrival of constitutional funds in 1972 and in 1978. The regents responded to this renewed request by voting unanimously to approve the Phase II project of about 88,000 square feet at an estimated cost of $7 million to be funded from the 1978 sale of ad valorem tax bonds.[47]

Constitutional Fund Lost

These moves seemed to set the stage for additional significant progress. But state politics intervened. State Representative Wayne Peveto of Orange filed a lawsuit in an Austin federal court to abolish the twenty-cent ad valorem tax because it was inequitably assessed and unconstitutional. The outcome was the abolition of that fund source and the delay of planned construction.[48]

In late April Vice President Miles Anderson wrote to David A. Webb, director of libraries, to report that the regents had delayed selection of an architect for Phase II of the Library. Anderson attributed the decision in part from the ad valorem tax issue that was still in the courts, but declared, "it became clear to me in some subsequent discussions that there has arisen in the minds of some members of the Board some uncertainty regarding the actual need for the project."[49] Later efforts were made, but more than twenty years later the task had not been completed. Other moves had been made to try to solve library space problems.

chapter 37

Some Coalitions Crumble

I submitted my resignation as President of North Texas State University because I am aware of the responsibility of that position for any questions involving the management or operation of the University. My sincere hope is that the air can be cleared soon concerning the many allegations which often times have been based on inaccurate or misleading information. I welcome any thorough investigation, because to my knowledge each allegation thus far presented has a valid answer.

My intention always has been to serve the university to the best of my ability and with the best interest of the university in mind. I believe I have done that. It is unfortunate when innocent individuals are involved needlessly when their only desire is to serve the university in an honest manner.

Unfortunately, there is an air of distrust within society which allows character assassination to come about more readily than it should. North Texas State University is a finer institution than it was eight years ago, and I am very proud of the part that I played in that progress. I know the future is bright for the university because it is strong enough to withstand any allegations against any individual related to it.

C. C. Nolen
April 12, 1979[1]

When C. C. Nolen resigned in April 1979 and wrote that he hoped the air could be cleared soon, he was trying for a faster, happier resolution to a troubled period than was to happen. After an emergency meeting of the Board of Regents in Austin that April 12, a written statement said that "The board received and accepted the resignation of C. C. Nolen as president of North Texas State University effective immediately. The board has asked Mr. John L. Carter, vice president for fiscal affairs, to be acting president of North Texas until the next board meeting."[2]

All nine regents were present that morning for an executive session and an open session in Room 241 at the old Supreme Court Room of the State Capitol Building in Austin. Also present were Lt. Gov. William P. Hobby, House Speaker Bill Clayton, and Rep. Richard C. Slack, chairman of the House General Investigating Committee. The presence of those twelve men testified to the fact that a tragic moment in North Texas history was taking place.

WHAT IS GOING ON IN DENTON?

Questions were widespread around the state. Statements in public speeches by government leaders suggested that the president of a major state university might be guilty of criminal misconduct. The public was exposed to a major investigative series from the *Dallas Morning News* and to reports of investigations by the State Auditor's Office, the House General Investigating Committee, and a grand jury.

What really went on? That question is not easily answered, and not all the necessary evidence can be found to provide an impartial, definitive answer.

State auditors said NTSU had not followed correct procedure in separating the NTSU Educational Foundation from the university and in financing it entirely without public funds—and in the process appeared to have misdirected some gifts to purposes for which they were not intended. The Dallas newspaper articles alleged criminal misuse of public funds and diversion of gift funds to illegal purposes. A continuing study by the house committee led eventually to an official report eleven months later, detailing at great length twelve "irregularities" and instances of "improper conduct." Five months after that, a Denton grand jury voted not to indict Nolen on any charges—in the words of the *Dallas Times Herald* "clearing Nolen of criminal allegations" and in the phraseology of the *Dallas Morning News* deciding "not to indict Nolen and other NTSU officials."

Two years later Nolen told the *Denton Record-Chronicle* that he resigned because he got caught in a power play with one of the NTSU regents and saw resignation as the only way to protect the university from further damage.

THE FOUNDATION UNDER INVESTIGATION

The area in which Nolen seemed most vulnerable to attack was in the conduct of the affairs of the fledgling educational foundation—ironically, the area in which Nolen enjoyed the greatest experience and expertise.

Nolen brought to Denton his experience with two quite different university fund-raising environments. At Texas Christian University, he knew the freedom from state regulation that is enjoyed by a private institution. At the University of Texas System, he enjoyed an operating budget provided by private funds that did not come under the same controls as appropriated dollars.

At NTSU, though, he undertook to implement a development program that was forced to raise itself by its own bootstraps. Every dollar of appropriated funds that was spent in the development area was liable to criticism and intervention by the state auditors. This came at a time when the State Auditor's Office had undertaken a review of foundations at several other state universities.

An Early Warning Signal

As director of development, Jim Reid recognized several difficulties in the North Texas position. He noted that since the foundation was maintained as an entity legally separate from NT and independent of the supervision of the auditor's office, strict interpretation of legislation could hold that no state funds could be used to provide campus space, utilities, and supplies. (The activities were then housed in offices in the Administration Building.) State employees might be barred from contributing any effort to the foundation, even from drawing travel expenses, Reid warned.[3]

The development director outlined several alternatives, including total off-campus independence for the development and alumni affairs staffs at a cost of $200,000 a year. Another choice would be transferring foundation assets to university fund accounts, bringing it under full state supervision. Concluding that the existing procedure provided "an adequate working relationship between the NTSU Educational Foundation and the university. If no further inquiries or objections are raised by the auditor's office, the situation should be allowed to continue as is." One year after Reid's letter, the very "inquiries or objections" he cited became real.

Auditors Request Changes

A management letter from the State Auditor's Office in September 1977 pointed out areas that needed managerial attention.[4] The auditors warned that the Professional Development Institute should send funds it collected to the State Treasury instead of depositing them in a local bank; when NTSU billed TCOM for goods and services, it should include proper supporting documentation. These were matters that could be handled without serious difficulty.

A third item posed a bigger problem: a directive to halt expenditures on behalf of the NTSU Foundation. Legislative appropriations were used to pay salaries and operating expenses of the foundation in 1974, 1975, and 1976, in amounts totaling more than $270,000. In addition, the Foundation paid no charge for a suite of offices in the Administration Building. This was held to violate Article 3, Section 51 of the state constitution. The auditors instructed, "All such gifts and expenditures should be recouped and no further diversions of State Funds should be permitted."[5]

On June 30, 1978, auditors listed some of the same concerns. Vice President Carter met shortly after that, on July 11, with Mike Ferguson in the State Auditor's Office. In a memo to Nolen, Carter said, "I pointed out to Mr. Ferguson that the management letter sent out June 30 left the impression with the regents that we were having some errors in magnitude similar to the University of Houston. Mr. Ferguson said we definitely were not having those problems." Carter wrote to Nolen:

> Mr. Ferguson said there were a lot of places that had many more problems than NTSU and if there had been anything wrong of a critical nature the State Auditor would not have certified to our report. There is a difference in sending out a management letter and in taking an exception in the certification letter such as the one sent to Houston.[6]

Carter explained in a letter to regents that the funds collected by the Professional Development Institute and deposited in a Denton bank had subsequently been transferred to the State Treasury on February 8, 1978, as desired by the auditor. Regarding the requirement by the auditor that North Texas cease expenditures on behalf of the NTSU Foundation, Carter said he told the auditors that the elements of cost as defined by the Coordinating Board listed an area of permissible expenditures as "Development Activities." Carter said that "On the basis of this definition, we have been paying the expenditures of that office from state funds." And Carter wrote that the relationships between NTSU and TCOM regarding interagency contracts had been "somewhat clouded for approximately two years because of duplication in personnel and the fact that there was some question concerning some of the interagency activities."[7]

The Problem Grows

In February 1979 Vice President Roy Busby asked Jim Reid and his staff to move the foundation, development activities, and alumni relations to self-sufficiency immediately. He cited increasing scrutiny by the public and by state officials of monies used for these activities at state universities and "continuing pressure to control in Austin all funds that are generated at the local campus level." His letter gave Reid a tough collection of assignments to handle, calling for the group

> to move as fast as possible to attain as much self-sufficiency as we can under the law to control the destiny of our alumni and development programs, while at the same time adhere to State requirements.
>
> I believe these moves include:
>
> 1. Physically moving the NTSU Educational Foundation, Development, and Alumni functions from the Administration Building as soon as possible to houses owned by the University, at which time appropriate rent will be paid to the University. . . .
>
> 2. Begin immediately a campaign to raise the money to build an Alumni Center on campus. . . to house the. . . Foundation, Development, and Alumni functions.
>
> 3. Formulate and put into effect *immediately* a planned fund effort by which [these] functions will eventually pay their own way. . . .
>
> 4. Enlist the immediate support of the appropriate. . . boards and support groups to accomplish the above moves. . . .
>
> I would like to have a plan to achieve the above steps by February 15 and begin implementation of the plan by March 1.[8]

Reid's response to the assignment was both immediate and troubled. He saw the possibility that independent fund-raising and alumni activities could work at cross-purposes to university objectives. He said that financial independence could not be soon achieved under existing university policies and that the university would have to contract to pay both the Alumni Association and the foundation for services rendered to the university, including alumni records, donor records, donor research, foundation research, and gift accounting and acknowledging.[9]

Reid's February memo also suggested that "much further thought must be spent" on this problem. But time was running out. On March 22 an assistant state auditor who was working on the NTSU campus received a telephone call from Earl Golz, a reporter for the *Dallas Morning News.* Thus was launched a major public inquiry that brought the collapse of the Nolen administration.

Golz's first telephone call reached Jim Rackley, assistant state auditor who worked on NTSU records on the campus. Rackley explained that he referred the reporter either to John Carter or to his supervisor, Mike Ferguson. Rackley told a member of Carter's staff that Golz was inquiring about foundation expenditures, possible political contributions, and alteration of checks made payable to the university to be payable to the foundation.[10]

Golz talked to Carter by telephone on March 27. His questions are instructive in foretelling the direction that his newspaper articles would take. Carter reported to Nolen:

> [He] inquired about the use of the Coliseum for a John Hill rally. He asked if any of the expenses were absorbed by the university. I told him we were investigating the matter but the investigation was not complete.
>
> Has the foundation paid to the university any of the amount set forth in the auditor's letter?. . . I replied none had been repaid but we are in the process of reorganizing the Foundation. . . .
>
> His next question concerned the changing or altering of checks made payable to the university by the foundation. I had to admit there was some evidence of this. . . . He wanted to know how much the altered checks amounted to and I told him I did not know since we were still in the process of reviewing the deposits.

> Mr. Golz asked if I was approached about making a contribution to the John Hill campaign. I told him I was but this was not unusual. . . .[11]

The *Dallas Morning News* Moves Ahead

The lead story on page one of the *Dallas Morning News* on April 6, 1979, brought major attention to the NTSU problems. The *News* continued its story by Golz to cover the entire top half of Page 6A. Here are some excerpts:

> State auditors are examining the diversion of donations to North Texas State University into the school's private foundation, a fund used in part to benefit athletics and supplement salaries of some NTSU officials.
>
> The channeling of the funds, without the donors' knowledge, was accomplished by altering the checks, making them payable to [the] foundation. . . .
>
> The nonprofit foundation already has been ordered by the state to return $393,217 illegally spent from state funds appropriated for NTSU. The money principally went to pay salaries of foundation officials for four fiscal years beginning in 1974. . . .
>
> As a result [of state auditors' revelations], the university's internal auditor, in cooperation with state and private auditors, launched the investigation.
>
> A. M. Willis Jr., chairman of the NTSU board of regents, recently instructed John L. Carter Jr., university vice president of fiscal affairs, to conduct the investigation and report back to Willis.
>
> Willis, one of two regents on the foundation's board of directors, said he intends to resign soon because the state auditor's office views the regents' presence on the 10-member board as a conflict of interest. . . .
>
> Willis said he "instructed him (Carter) to get to the bottom of it."
>
> "I don't give a damn who it hits," he said. "I want to know what the story is."[12]

This became the major focus of pressure on an already troubled administration that was within a week of collapse.

REGENT DISCONTENT BRINGS CONSULTANTS

In January 1978, in the middle of Nolen's seventh year in office, the board had hired a consulting firm to study the relationship between the regents and the president. Peat, Marwick, Mitchell & Co. of Austin interviewed twenty-one individuals: each regent and all key NTSU and TCOM administrators. A final draft was delivered in June 1978, although the final version is dated in September.[13]

Four Organizational Problems

The report faulted Nolen's organizational approach and his managerial style and assigned to him the blame for regent intervention in internal operational matters. A letter to Chairman Willis accompanied the report, and it identified four organizational problems:

> 1. The significant, necessary commitment by the President to development and communication activities disrupts coordination and management of NTSU and TCOM operational matters. In addition, an apparent reluctance to act on certain decisions has led to active involvement, on occasion, of individual Regents in Administrative matters.
>
> 2. The emerging planning and budgeting system does not appear to fully describe the mechanisms and formats to deliver and portray actual results to the Regents.
>
> 3. The grouping or definition of budgetary administration, facilities planning and usage, and internal audit are inconsistent.
>
> 4. The position responsibilities assigned to each of the six organizational areas are unclear, resulting in the use of an "informal" organization structure to facilitate operational matters.[14]

That letter identified as the key to recommended improvements a new organizational structure that "features an Executive Vice President and Provost position with overall NTSU operating responsibility."

In recent years, the report noted, the regents had become more involved in operating details of the university as a result of campus construction difficulties, TCOM organizational and operational matters, and personnel assignments and decisions. The regents' committee structure, the consultants noted, put them in a working relationship with each vice president rather than primarily with the president. They found that commitments to development and communication off campus had disrupted organizational effectiveness. That plus the president's unwillingness to make certain important, necessary decisions had brought members of the policy body (the regents) into involvement in regular administrative operations. This "close and direct interaction" of board members in daily affairs:

• Precludes assigning the responsibility and the accountability for performance of the management function of NTSU to the chief executive officer (the President);

• Diffuses the distinction between the decision-making process and the policy-making process;

• Establishes the precedent of vice president level position turning to the Regents for guidance and counsel on operational matters; and

• Places the Regents in the position of providing operational coordination and direction.[15]

The report then went into great detail as to how information systems should be designed, how auditing functions should be handled, and ways in which the board should carry out its responsibilities to the State of Texas.

QUESTIONS ABOUT AUSTIN

Once it became clear that Nolen's record was under scrutiny by the state auditors and by some members of the house, including Speaker Billy Clayton, rumors surfaced on the campus about even closer ties between the speaker and the North Texas campus. When Vice President Miles Anderson appeared before the Faculty Senate in 1979, he was asked by Senate Chairman Don Smith about the truth of rumors that Vice President Hermas Miller and University Attorney Jim Neill "are on the payroll of House Speaker Billy Clayton to the amount of 20 percent of their salary." As to the truth of that report, Anderson responded:

> Well, as you know NTSU has had considerable involvement with the Speaker of late. . . . I have not personally talked to Mr. Miller about that matter, but I understand that it is true, that he is now serving as a consultant part-time to the Speaker of the House, on what matters I do not know. Most of you know that Mr. Miller served for a half dozen

> years or more as a member of the staff of the Legislative Budget Board, and he is very knowledgeable about the state fiscal procedures and the politics thereof. So although the arrangement might be an unusual one, it could be understandable from that point of view.[16]

When Smith asked if Neill had that same expertise, Anderson responded, "Mr. Neill is an attorney." Smith then asked what was going on, what that meant to NTSU, and "Are they investigating North Texas from the inside?" Anderson replied, "I have no knowledge that it is the case. I do not know that it is not the case." To that, the senate chairman declared "That is a unique or unusual arrangement I never heard of before. I did not know that this is any kind of standard practice. I'll bet it is not. That is a very curious kind of thing that puzzles me very much."[17] On May 13, 1979, the *Dallas Morning News* reported that the two NTSU administrators had been appointed to help Speaker Clayton as special investigators for the house investigating committee.[18]

PHYSICAL PLANT PROBLEMS BOTHER REGENTS

Coordination Problems Created

As noted in Chapter 31, Carter and Resident Engineer John Matt Howard did not work well together and suffered personality conflicts during the Kamerick term and while Carter was acting president. This led to what Carter described to the Building Committee chairman, Regent E. E. Stuessy, as "reorganization of the physical plant division" after Nolen became president. This action transferred Howard to report to the Office of Institutional Analysis as resident engineer and brought in Delbert Overstreet as director of physical plant operations. This split in authority with almost no clarification of responsibility and authority division, led inevitably to territorial jurisdictional disputes ("turf wars") and divided recommendations being brought to the president's office. This added further coordination problems, especially in the matter of working with an engineering firm that had been contracted to prepare a master plan for campus utilities.

A Major Break: Nolen vs. Stuessy

In this environment, Regent Stuessy soon determined that strong intervention by the regents was required. As chairman of the building committee,

Stuessy told Nolen of "insubordination" by Howard during a review of utility plans. Nolen several years later said this launched a series of struggles between the president and the regent. The Nolen version of this conflict appeared in the *Denton Record-Chronicle* in 1981, two years after Nolen left the office. This is part of that story:

> Nolen said his problems with Stuessy began in 1975, when Stuessy wanted to directly influence construction projects.
>
> "I didn't take his advice on some things. He wanted to do things directly without going through the normal administrative process. He wanted to work directly with the staff on building projects. He didn't like the staff that I had built," Nolen said.
>
> Nolen's deteriorating relationship with Stuessy began with a dispute Stuessy had with NTSU's engineer, John Matt Howard, on one construction project in 1975 over the number of manhole covers in a city block. Nolen said Stuessy wanted Howard fired over it, but Nolen disagreed.
>
> "It was just a classic power struggle," Nolen said. While it was a struggle with Stuessy only, Nolen said, he was able to withstand the pressure. It was after A. M. "Monk" Willis Jr., who was chairman of the board at the time, apparently began siding with Stuessy that, Nolen said, he lost his effectiveness.[19]

In an executive session of the Board of Regents to discuss personnel matters, the board decided that Howard must be fired, and their decision was communicated to Nolen. Some board members also became dissatisfied with Jack Barton, a former Denton City attorney who had become the NTSU police chief and subsequently was named university attorney. In the summer of 1977 Barton was dismissed by Nolen upon instructions from regents.

MOVE TCOM TO UT CONTROL?

The cloud that covered the educational foundation spread to TCOM as well. TCOM supporters were already dissatisfied with delays in construction on the Fort Worth campus and with the fact that the medical school had a dean rather than a president of its own. (See Chapter 34.) A problem with a bequest to TCOM aggravated the discontent.

A woman who died in 1974 bequeathed $14,000 to be used for student loans to osteopathic medical students, but the money was instead diverted to the NTSU Educational Foundation. A TCOM attorney said that when he first read the will, he did not realize the gift had any restrictions on it, and Foundation Director Jim Reid subsequently deposited it into an unrestricted account "because no one told me it was for student loans." The attorney said that two years later he sent Nolen a letter dated June 21, 1976, to notify him that the money was designated for student loans. Then a state auditor in 1979 told the estate executor that the check was made payable to TCOM and might have been improperly endorsed by the foundation. The money was subsequently returned to the executor in April 1979 and was rerouted to serve its intended purpose at TCOM.[20]

Although it was not publicly stated, there is a strong presumption that incidents such as this contributed to an effort to remove the Texas College of Osteopathic Medicine from NTSU control. As seen in the previous chapter, the regents withstood the legislative challenge, but it put one more source of strain in their relationship with the president.

THE ATTACK ON PRESIDENT NOLEN

All of these matters were boiling throughout the 1978–79 academic year. Newspapers throughout the state carried many of the stories about alleged wrong-doing on the campus, especially when the charges originated in Austin or when they were originated in stories by Earl Golz in the *Dallas Morning News*. Most of his more serious allegations against Nolen and the operation of NTSU were attributed to unnamed sources. Two years later, Golz testified in a civil trial that his source was Jim Neill, the university's legal counsel, and that it was Neill who had first talked to him about anything concerning NTSU. Golz said, "I told him that his identity would remain confidential, and he in turn agreed to continue supplying me with information that he had heard about the university situation." He also testified that after Neill left the university's staff, Neill no longer desired or required confidentiality.[21]

Political Rally Challenged

A copyrighted story in the *News* in early April 1979 alleged that NTSU had wrongfully used $1,100 in state funds to support a political fund-raising rally in the Coliseum sponsored by the Young Democrats for gubernatorial candidate John Hill on the previous August 5. Letters were mailed to about 160 persons in the Denton area, the implication being that this was directed by Nolen and done by state employees on state time. This was challenged by the director of the university news and information service, Keith Shelton, whose statements appeared in a lead story in the *Daily* on April 10:

> Shelton said that. . . the *News* was "wrong in saying that it was a fund-raising event.
>
> "It was intended as a rally and speech. It was not intended as a fund raising event."
>
> . . . . Under state law, it is unlawful to use the state money to influence any election.
>
> "The $1,100 figure," Shelton said, "was generated for our internal auditor by Delbert Overstreet, physical plant director, and it represents all the costs that could conceivably be attributed to the event in the Coliseum.
>
> "The story gave the impression that the $1,100 figure was generated at the time (of the event), and that's not correct," Shelton said.
>
> The Young Democrats paid a $383 rental fee for the Coliseum.[22]

Claiming Mileage for a State Car

News stories also said that Nolen submitted mileage reimbursement claims on travel vouchers for use of a state-leased car. He had two letters signed by Chairman Willis authorizing him to claim this expense. The *Denton Record-Chronicle* subsequently reported that Nolen had written the letters and sent them to Willis for his signature. A state auditor told the newspaper that the state should pay only for gasoline used in this car. By the time of this story, Vice President John Carter was again acting president, and he told the *Record-Chronicle* that he had told Nolen that the mileage payments would be "questioned" and suggested that the costs be figured on the same basis as other leased cars used at NTSU.[23]

NOLEN'S ACCOUNT OF TROUBLED TIMES

Nolen kept silent for two years about the attacks that he felt had been orchestrated in order to force him out of office. He had resigned April 12, 1979; on April 16, 1981, Janie Leigh Frank wrote of an interview with Nolen when he returned to Denton to testify in a lawsuit filed against NTSU in another matter.

Nolen Tells Board of Resignation Plans

Revealed for the first time was Nolen's report that he had advised the regents in the fall of 1978 that he would be starting to look for another job. Regent Stuessy, he said, persisted because he wanted to be sure to get Nolen out of office before Stuessy's term on the board expired in May 1979. This is the account of that sequence:

> At the October 1978 board meeting in executive session, Nolen said he told the regents he thought his term at NTSU had run its course.
>
> "I wanted some time to begin to look for other opportunities. I wanted to take the pressure off, too, so Stuessy would say, OK, we don't have to fight any more."
>
> The regents told him that was fine, Nolen said. "But Mr. Stuessy apparently couldn't wait. He knew his appointment was coming up in May (1979) and so I presume he assumed that I was trying to outwait his appointment.
>
> Nolen said he did not make his plans known outside the board because the Legislature was to convene in January 1979 and he did not want to appear before budget hearings and in other matters as a lame duck president.[24]

The *Record-Chronicle* reporter next turned to unnamed regents as a source for reporting that the regents held another executive session during their meeting of February 1979. According to some regents, the story said, Stuessy tried to convince the board to fire Nolen. Willis joined the movement, raising the question with regents of Nolen's improper claiming of mileage expenses for a state-leased car.

The sequence of events from there on was explained this way by reporter Frank:

> "That was all that came up at that time because that was all Mr. Stuessy had," Nolen said. The regents were reportedly furious, but,

before voting to fire Nolen, decided to call him in to account for his behavior.

Nolen produced two letters signed by Willis that authorized him to do his travel expenses that way. The board split 7 to 2 , in support of Nolen on a vote of confidence, according to some regents.

At this point, Nolen said, he had already accepted a job with the Christian Church's foundation to open its southwest regional office in Fort Worth, whenever he felt like he could leave NTSU. He said he was also negotiating with a university in Missouri for the presidency and that Willis knew that. After Nolen resigned, he did take the job with the Christian Church for awhile, until he went to work for the Oklahoma Medical Research Foundation in Oklahoma City, where he is now.

In November 1979, after the Missouri university officials had conducted its own investigation into the charges against Nolen, they offered him the presidency, although Nolen did not accept it. The university had determined that the controversy was just "Texas politics," Nolen said.

After the February regents meeting, however, Nolen said he began to hear that Stuessy was seeing regents individually and telling them he had collected evidence and was going to seek Nolen's indictment.

"It became a personal matter," Nolen said. Stuessy had lost in February and could not lose again; he had acted similarly in past disputes with other people, Nolen said. "Stuessy wants you not only out, but hung and drawn and quartered," Nolen said.

Also, he said, "With the state auditor trying to get at how the things were handled in the foundation, there was enough question about the way some of our management practices were conducted that was timely and played into his hands. . . ."

He [Nolen] did not know until. . . April 11 that. . . a hearing [was] to be conducted by the House General Investigating Committee.

Two people Nolen trusted, one a regent at the time and the other a former regent, told him that the only thing that could help NTSU was to go to Austin and "make the best deal that I could with Stuessy," he said.

Nolen went to Austin. . . April 10 with his resignation in hand, he said. Stuessy had been out of town, so Nolen waited at Stuessy's house until he returned about midnight. They talked until 12:30 A.M.

"My approach to Stuessy was 'Call this off. I don't know what's coming, but I hear stories that this is harmful only to the university. You don't believe I'm in negotiation with another university, you don't believe I'm going to leave. OK, if you don't believe me, here's my resignation,'" Nolen said he told him.

"As far as I was concerned I had resigned only to him, which was not resigning to the board. It's to let Stuessy know that I was sincere in my effort to resign.

Then I was vulnerable to him. He put his arm around my shoulder and said, 'We've differed in the past, and I will do what I can to stop this because you've done the right thing." And something to the effect of, "Now that you've done the right thing, I will show you that I can work just as hard for you as I have been against you.'"

The next day, Wednesday, subpoenas came for Nolen and Stuessy to appear Thursday at the House General Investigating Committee hearing. . . . [Jim] Reid and Mrs. [Jane] Smith had also been subpoenaed. . . .

"I thought Stuessy hadn't had time to cut it off," Nolen said. He thought therefore that it would be friendly, which it was, and that the controversy would die after the hearing.

But he came to believe later that Stuessy never meant to "call off the dogs," because of the subsequent investigation, publicity and firings, he said.[25]

A CHEERLEADER DEPARTS

Nolen did not leave the campus without expressions of appreciation. Members of the Council of Deans adopted a resolution expressing "a very real sense of loss on his departure." The resolution was signed by a dean or associate dean from each of the colleges and by Vice President Miles Anderson and Associate Vice President Howard Smith. It said in part:

> The Council of Deans notes with genuine regret the resignation of President C. C. Nolen, who had given effective and inspiring leadership to this university for a period of eight years.

> [Nolen] has worked energetically and unceasingly for the transformation of the institution from a good one to a great one, and has achieved a marked degree of success in his unstinting efforts.[26]

Just before the Nolens moved away from Denton, a group of faculty and Denton friends and supporters held a farewell rally for the family at a private club west of Denton. Several informal speeches thanked the former president for his work and praised his efforts for North Texas. They concluded by presenting a new car that had been purchased for the Nolens by individual private donations.

Finding a New Location?

As early as the spring of 1978, Nolen had begun considering alternate career futures. In March he wrote the chairman of the presidential search committee at Phillips University in Oklahoma that he would be unable to pursue a position there because "the next two months in Austin are very crucial to the future of both NTSU and TCOM and will require my utmost attention."[27] Later that same month, however, Nolen submitted a biographical data sheet to the chairman of the chancellor search committee at Texas Christian University. He expressed thanks for the chance to be considered as TCU chancellor.[28] Nothing materialized from that overture, however. In April 1979 he advised the search committee at the University of Oklahoma that he would be pleased to be considered for the presidency there. He said he had advised the board chairman of the submission of his résumé and asked that the committee contact no one except Willis.[29]

But another university job was not in the cards. On June 7 the student newspaper ran a picture of a smiling Nolen with a story under the headline, "Cheerful Nolen readies to begin new position." The Nolens were packing to leave the President's Home for two future addresses: Fort Worth and Santa Fe, New Mexico. He had accepted a position as president of the Christian Church Foundation of the South Central Zone. His job was to raise funds for the general body of the Christian Church (Disciples of Christ). However, his plans for the church job did not develop, and Nolen soon moved on to Oklahoma City to become vice president for development of the Oklahoma Medical Foundation.

chapter 38

Carter: Act Two

You and the Board of Regents of North Texas State University are to be commended for taking action to correct the problems which have occurred at North Texas State University. We feel the board is fulfilling its legal responsibilities in allowing the acting president to implement changes that should prevent future problems within the university.

Chairman Richard Slack
House Investigating Committee
August 6, 1979

Just six days after becoming acting president of the university for the second time, John L. Carter, Jr., spoke optimistically to a Denton audience, "Everyone is alive and well at North Texas State University despite the discussion of our auditing problems in the newspapers. About ninety-nine percent of the university is functioning just as it always has."[1] Remarkably, most of the faculty and staff had indeed been accomplishing a great deal, by focusing on their jobs in spite of the many distractions. Nevertheless, some of the headlines were destined to stay large for a while.

SEARCH FOR A NEW PRESIDENT

Faculty members wanted to restore a sound educational environment to the campus. They were aware of external intrusion in internal academic affairs and of a statewide perception that North Texas State University had a big mess on its hands. The faculty wanted a respected academic leader to help them restore collegial order. On the day that Nolen resigned, April 12, 1979, the NTSU chapter of the Texas Association of College Teachers met and sent a message to the Board of Regents: please reaffirm the principle of faculty participation in the selection of the University's President.[2]

The Board Responds

Regents responded on May 18, 1979, with a statement on "Organization for the Selection of a President." This called for a University Advisory Committee to assist the board in a presidential search. It was to have twenty members, including eight UNT and two TCOM faculty members elected by the faculty, five appointees of the acting president, an alumni representative, presidents of two student groups at NTSU, and the president of the Texas Osteopathic Medical Association.[3]

Swift Committee Action

The advisory group was formed quickly and met June 8 and 12, electing as its chairman Dr. Howard Smith, associate vice president for academic affairs. By July 5 desired qualifications of the next president were adopted unanimously. This was presented in a handsome brochure, *A President for North Texas State University and Texas College of Osteopathic Medicine*. The publication also listed the search and screening committee that would take over the task from that point forward. A. M. Willis chaired the selection group and other regent members were Winfree L. Brown, Harrell E. Chiles, and William

W. Jamar, Jr., Other members were Dr. Charles Ogilvie of TCOM and Dr. J. B. Smallwood and Dr. Smith of NTSU.

The brochure defined the critical issues of NTSU/TCOM, with academic leadership as the most important presidential attribute.[4] Also stressed was the need for a change in the operating style of the Board of Regents, calling for clearly established lines of communication from campus units through the president to the board and from the board back through the president. In order to "reduce misunderstandings that can lead to divisiveness."[5]

The campus community was regaining a sense of direction, but Austin investigations still cast shadows on the campus. Earl Golz of the *Dallas Morning News* reported on July 17 that the chairman of the House General Investigating Committee, Rep. Richard C. Slack, might recommend to the Board of Regents the removal of some more NTSU administrators. Slack attributed this to "the improper diversion of a very substantial amount of university funds through the university's private foundation."[6] On a Friday afternoon three days after that news story came the startling news of the elimination of a large part of the core central administration.

THE FRIDAY MASSACRE

On Friday, July 20, as the Board of Regents went into executive session, the NTSU Public Information Office received a telephone call from Golz at the *Dallas Morning News*. He asked for information about the firing of three NTSU vice presidents that had taken place in a board meeting that day. This was shocking news to the staff in that office—the board had excluded all nonmembers of the board from its executive session.

It was verified that three vice presidents would be removed from their offices at the end of the current fiscal year, August 31, 1979. They were Dr. Miles Anderson, vice president for academic affairs; Jane Gentry Smith, vice president for student affairs; and Dr. Busby, vice president for university relations. There was no record of any formal board action. Among many campus veterans, the whole affair became known as "The Friday Massacre."

An Official Explanation

Acting President Carter explained the actions as a reorganization plan in a "Special Issue" of *UPDATE,* an internal university newsletter, on July 27. He began by announcing that Howard Smith would act as academic vice president, Dean of

Students Joe Stewart would consolidate student affairs, and university relations would report to the president. This resulted from what Carter called a premature announcement by the *Dallas Morning News.* Carter said state agencies had informed him that the NTSU administration was top-heavy. He also said he reported his plan of reorganization to the board of regents in executive session July 20. They received the report favorably but took no action, Carter said.[7]

The *North Texas Daily* attempted to pick up more details by publishing a statement from Willis that said "The Board of Regents did not take any formal vote because it was within the authority of the president to do what he did."[8]

Campus critics of the firings said that the idea was actually to respond to the house investigating committee. Confirmation of this view came when committee chairman Slack, who had suggested administrative firings in July, returned in August with a letter of praise to the Board of Regents, a portion of which appears at the head of this chapter.[9]

"Climate of Uncertainty, Rumor, and Counter-Rumor"

In spite of customary inactivity in summer sessions, strong reaction to the July 20 dismissals came from three NTSU faculty organizations.

The Faculty Senate called a special meeting July 30, but could muster only thirty-one members, one short of the thirty-two required for a quorum. However, Senate Chairman Don Smith opened voting on a resolution to some one hundred individuals in the gallery. He said the packed gallery was a first in the history of the senate. "Informal" action by the senators and by the visitors in the gallery was unanimous for the resolution. The document set forth the causes of deep concern felt by the NTSU faculty. These were listed as removal of an academic vice president without faculty consultation, absence of substantive faculty participation in university decision making, lack of adequate faculty representation in the presidential screening committee, and lack of clear explanations of the recent administrative firings, resulting in a "climate of uncertainty, rumor and counter-rumor." The Faculty Senate document urged the governing board "to stand firm against pressures that politicize the academic procedures of the university" and to insure that political pressures would not impede or unduly hasten the presidential selection process.[10]

On the same date, the executive committee of the Texas Association of College Teachers addressed to John Carter "comments regarding certain events of Friday, July 20, 1979," with copies to the governor and the regents. The comments said, "We know that the manner of the removal has caused a further erosion of faculty morale." The TACT leaders further declared that "organization of a university should primarily reflect the ideas of the permanent chief executive," and "this sudden reorganization will seriously impair the flexibility of the new president," and could "cause a truly capable candidate to hesitate to accept the position."[11] The local chapter council of the American Association of University Professors on August 2 endorsed the statements by TACT and the faculty senators regarding retention of administrators.[12]

The leaders of the academic departments in the College of Arts and Sciences on August 13, 1979, issued a "Statement by Departmental Chairpersons," which sent to Carter and the Board of Regents the view that academic integrity and credibility had been damaged by "the abrupt and largely unexplained dismissal" of the academic vice president. Of Miles Anderson, the statement wrote, "His removal from his role of academic leadership has had a devastatingly adverse effect on faculty morale and threatens the quality and continuity of current academic programs, while at the same time it endangers the orderly development of new programs."[13]

"Blow to a Demoralized Campus"

Possibly the harshest public criticism of Carter came from a source not usually heard from in such a style, the editorial page of the *Denton Record-Chronicle* on July 24. The editorial said in part:

> Friday's wholesale firings at North Texas State University were another blow to the already-demoralized campus. . . .
>
> What it amounts to is that the regents, led by Chairman A. M. Willis Jr., [E. E.] Stuessy, and Vice President Hermas Miller, are acting to secure their control over the university before a new president arrives.
>
> The removal of Mrs. Smith and Busby seems premature until a new president can assess their abilities and their value to him or her.
>
> The removal of Anderson seems like a slap in the face of the faculty, most of whom respect Anderson as the man who has administered the rise toward quality on the academic side while Nolen was working in the political, public relations and fund raising areas.
>
> If the removals were necessary, the way it was done was shoddy. . . .
>
> A tremendous amount of damage has been done to the university, not

only by the adverse publicity, but also to the morale of the campus. There have been hints of something more than has been made public. . . .[14]

INVESTIGATIONS CONTINUE

The investigation by the House General Investigation Committee had been requested by Representative Frank Gaston of Dallas, who now told the *North Texas Daily* that he would not be surprised if indictments were issued as a result of the investigation. Gaston said he provided the committee with "documented evidence" that the NT Educational Foundation violated state law.[15]

The Carter View of the Investigations

As the chief fiscal officer, John Carter had brought his objections out into the open after NTSU accounting procedures were challenged in Austin.

On the date that Nolen resigned as president and the House Investigating Committee began meetings to scrutinize NTSU financial practices, Carter gave the *North Texas Daily* a particularly strong indictment of Jim Reid, the development director, concerning charges of transferring NTSU checks into the foundation. He said Reid should have deposited checks made out to the university in the school account and not with the foundation.[16]

Then, on June 17, 1979, the house committee released the state auditor's report on the NTSU Educational Foundation, Inc., declaring that thousands of dollars originally donated to the university for scholarships had wound up in the private foundation accounts. Carter reacted by saying, "I'm glad to see all this straightening out. Unfortunately, I've been telling the board and president Nolen for years that this wasn't the correct way to do things."[17]

The Board of Trustees of the foundation reported to the Board of Regents on July 20, expressing compliance with the state auditor's wishes. As submitted by Willis, the statement read, "The NTSU Educational Foundation will become an active arm of the University, with the Vice President for Fiscal Affairs assuming the accounting responsibilities."[18]

The release of the auditor's report led to consideration of criminal prosecution in the case. The district attorneys from Travis County (Austin) and Denton County met in closed session with the House committee and said they would look into possible criminal charges of abuse of public funds, bid-rigging, and perjury involving past and present NTSU administrators. Representative Slack issued an August 8 statement that his committee would look to the district attorneys to study criminal charges and the state attorney general to check possible civil charges. He wrote the Board of Regents encouraging them to take "full control and to run the school in a way that would make the people proud of it and to serve the best interest of all, and especially the students."[19]

The regents picked up on that cue and on August 14 passed a resolution calling for "swift justice."

> Be it resolved that those. . . charged with enforcement of our laws be invited to aid the Board of Regents in fully investigating all matters of concern. . . to this university to the end that justice may be honestly and expeditiously served.
>
> Those persons found to have violated the law should be appropriately punished, no matter the size or degree of the transgression. . . .[20]

CHARGES RENEWED IN 1980

The house investigating committee renewed public hearings on the NTSU accusations to hear further witnesses from January 14 to 17, 1980. The report of the committee was released on February 28. The *Denton Record-Chronicle* reprinted the complete text of the report in nearly two full pages of the newspaper.[21]

The report found wrong-doing in the areas of use of university facilities for political purposes, misuse of state personnel and supplies for political purposes, use of state funds in support of petition to obtain Channel 2 television license for Denton, irregularities in administration of educational foundation funds (seven instances), improper transactions by the physics department, improper donations to political candidates, improper automobile expense payments, and improper collection of travel expenses.

Grand Jury Examines Charges

A Denton County grand jury began its examination of the case on April 10, 1980, and its findings were published on August 16. The *Dallas Times Herald* reported that the jury cleared Nolen of allegations of criminal mishandling of funds. The *Dallas Morning News* story wrote that the grand jury "decided not to issue indictments." According to the *Times Herald*, District Attorney Cobb and defense attorneys "harshly criticized the house investigating committee and called the report politically motivated." The grand jury probe also cleared James A. Reid, the former foundation director. Cobb was quoted as saying, "I think it was the idea of the committee to have it appear some criminal activity had occurred to justify the time they spent on the investigation."[22]

A CHAIRMAN STEPS DOWN

Toward the end of the troubling summer of 1979, the Board of Regents met in regular session on August 24, the final item being the election of officers. Regent Neuhaus moved that Willis be re-elected chairman of the board, seconded by a new member, Harrell E. Chiles of Fort Worth. The motion passed with a 9–0 vote. The minutes show that Willis then "thanked his colleagues for the confidence expressed in him, but resigned the chairmanship and asked that the floor be reopened for nominations." Regent Hugh Wolfe moved that the board accept the resignation and that Winfree L. Brown be elected chairman and Chiles be named vice chairman. This, too, passed with a 9–0 vote. Another unanimous vote was recorded for a resolution of appreciation for "his long, unselfish, and great service to the university while he served as the chairman."[23]

FOUND: A SCHOLAR FOR PRESIDENT

At the end of his first term as acting president, John Carter expressed the hope that he would not be remembered as the president who was in office during the Elizabeth Ann Duke protests. He no doubt thought much the same thing about the whole Nolen investigation problems and the dismissal of three of his colleagues. Yet when the next president was named, Carter was not yet freed of all of his "acting" responsibilities as his successor could assume the office on a part-time basis only for some months.

The advisory committee stipulated that the next president must have solid academic credentials. The protests filed with the regents about the administrative firings all stressed the importance of selecting a true academic scholar of outstanding reputation. So it was with great relief and hopeful optimism that the North Texas academic community on December 9, 1979, greeted the news that the Search and Screening Committee had recommended and the Board of Regents had approved the selection of Dr. Frank Vandiver, prize-winning historian and vice president and provost of Rice University in Houston.

Vandiver was unable to leave his commitments at Rice immediately, so his first term of employment as president of NTSU and TCOM was part-time at a salary of $1,000 per month until August 1, 1980. The regents stipulated that while Vandiver was away from the campus, "Acting President John Carter will perform all the duties of the president at the direction of the president."[24]

chapter 39

Hunkering Down—Briefly

I began toying in late November with an idea for a radical shift in NTSU's situation—radical in that the University would undergo fundamental organizational and programmatic changes. I thought of turning the University toward the two emerging interests of the Metroplex and the Southwest—international and future outlooks. If NTSU can shift more toward an international focus and toward concern for the future. . . we will serve our purposes, our neighbors, our state, our nation, and, I believe, the world, in a truly unique way.

. . .I urge your support of a new program: "NTSU—The New Dimension for the Future." Under this program, NTSU will be reorganized into Centers whose activities will mesh with traditional, current, and foreseeable concerns in the Greater Southwest and the nation. The focus of the reorganization will be on the future with major attention to: expanding human potential; preparing the citizens of this region to interact with the world at large; enhancing resource development; and creating strategies to cope with change in individual and organizational lives.

Frank E. Vandiver
Letter to the Faculty and Staff , January 5, 1981

The NTSU regents made it clear that they wanted Frank Vandiver to sweep the central administration clean. They had reached a consensus to that effect at a meeting November 9 and confirmed it at a meeting December 9, 1979. Even before they voted to elect a new president, they voted "that all vice presidents be asked to resign immediately as a condition of the employment of a new president and that Acting President John Carter be asked to immediately obtain the resignations." On the Denton campus, there was only one NTSU vice president remaining other than Carter, Hermas Miller. Carter had made clear his intention to retire once his latest "acting" assignment was complete, so Vandiver was ready to install another "new team." The regents confirmed his election as president by a vote of 9–0, effective immediately on a part-time basis, with his term of office as full-time president to start August 1, 1980.

COUNTING ON A SCHOLAR

Regents and faculty alike felt that the new president fully met the regents' announced determination to employ "an outstanding scholar/administrator who will command respect, inspire confidence, and provide decisive leadership as the University addresses the challenges of the eighties."

How did Frank Everson Vandiver earn his distinguished reputation?

His official biography from the NTSU Public Information Office said he "followed an unconventional scholastic path to achievement, leaving formal school after the seventh grade to pursue independent study." This became more formal when he was named a Rockefeller Fellow in the Humanities at the University of Texas in 1946–47 and in American Studies in 1947–48, leading to the master of arts in history in 1949. He earned the Ph.D. degree from Tulane University in 1951.

Most of Vandiver's career as a teacher and administrator was spent at smaller private institutions: Washington University in St. Louis, 1952–55, and Rice University, 1955–80. At Rice he became the Harris Masterson Jr. professor of history, chairman of history, acting president in 1969–70, provost from 1970 and vice president from 1975. In the 1963–64 academic year he went to Oxford University as the Harmsworth professor of American history.

Vandiver was born December 9, 1925, in Austin. His curriculum vitae filled several pages. It included his authorship of several prize-winning books, including *Black Jack: The Life and Times of John J. Pershing*, which was a National Book Awards finalist, and *Mighty Stonewall*. He was a past-president of the Texas Institute of Letters and the Texas Philosophical Society, and an elected member of the Society of American Historians.

GETTING STARTED

Vandiver had secured several agreements from the Board of Regents as a condition of his employment. He met in executive session with the board in Fort Worth on November 9 to discuss his acceptance of the position. Chairman Brown and Regent Chiles were instructed to negotiate an agreement. They invited Willis to join them so that the full executive committee would be present. A letter of agreement was signed by members of that committee and by Vandiver on November 14. It agreed to a salary of $75,000 a year, with private gift funds to provide any portion not covered by appropriations. The document also agreed to eleven perquisites that were to be provided for the new president. The regents agreed to provide these items, using private gift money for any item not covered by state appropriated funds:

1. An appropriate home for his need as an individual and as president. The board would consider either buying or building a suitable home. In the meantime, private funds would pay any added costs for temporary housing above the $4,800 housing allowance from the state. (This led to the purchase of a home at 3300 Santa Monica in Denton at a total cost of $303,377.80. The acquisition was approved by the Coordinating Board on an 8 to 7 vote.[1])
2. Moving expenses from Houston to Denton.
3. Utilities.
4. Maid service.
5. An automobile.
6. Up to twelve percent retirement contribution to TIAA-CREF.
7. Membership in three clubs (at least one each in Denton, Dallas, and Fort Worth).
8. An appropriate expense account for entertainment.
9. Appointment as distinguished professor of history beginning August 1, 1980.
10. An appropriate location on campus for the Jefferson Davis papers.
11. A research fund so that Dr. Vandiver could continue research that had been "in progress for many years."[2]

While this probably was not too different from the perquisites afforded chief executives at many American universities at that time, critics later used it to fault the scholar from a prestigious private university as being too elitist in his personal requirements in a campus with a seriously inadequate budget. Others were quick to classify this as a necessary and justifiable price to pay for getting the kind of leadership that would lift the university to a better status.

First Meeting With Faculty

The new president's appointment came right on top of final examinations, so he chose to delay his first faculty convocation until after the Christmas break on January 9, 1980. His prepared remarks were fairly long, detailing his philosophy for a major university, the role of the faculty as "the heart of the university," the importance of being a research-dominant campus, and his personal operating methods. This served both to reassure almost all in the audience that the movement of the university toward stability was resuming and to signal to many that there were fundamental differences of opinion to be adjusted in setting the future course of North Texas. His comments surely defined the philosophical struggle that would preoccupy much faculty deliberation and decision-making for the next fifteen years or more.

To some of the older, more instructionally oriented faculty, Vandiver appeared to go too far in asking them to leave the past behind; many younger faculty welcomed his call for an elite approach to building a fine university. He began by asserting that of all the public universities in Texas, this university had a special opportunity to be excellent. The faculty had established NTSU as "a good middle-range public institution," he said, "but it is still dogged by the teachers college label."

Vandiver declared that North Texas had a chance to rank with the University of Texas and Texas A&M as one of the top three public universities in the state. He called for increasing medical science programs, keeping good faculty, tightening the curriculum, and never settling for mediocrity. North Texas, he told the faculty, can and should be "a university of at least national repute." Although not referring directly to the investigations into NTSU administrative operations, Vandiver asserted the need for better management with more accountability to the public: public and private universities "ought to get their administrative houses in order to strengthen their claim to being distinctive and their right to special favoritism." The new president then moved into the evangelical mode, calling for strengthening North Texas by recognizing that "our most important function is as researchers."[3]

Building an Administrative Group

The combination of the firing of three vice presidents, the retirement of another, and the mandated resignation of another left the new president with no administrators on hand except Carter as acting president/fiscal vice president for a brief time, Dr. Howard Smith as acting academic vice president, and Dean of Students Joe Stewart handling coordination of student affairs.

As noted in Chapter 34, the regents moved to try to reassure the medical community of their support of TCOM by creating the post of chancellor over both schools, with a president over each campus, reporting to the chancellor. Vandiver became both chancellor of NTSU/TCOM and president of NTSU in May 1980.

On June 20, 1980, the still part-time president announced the appointment of Dr. Alfred F. Hurley as vice president for administrative affairs beginning on September 1. Dr. Hurley had been head of the Department of History at the U.S. Air Force Academy since 1966 and also chairman of the academy's Humanities Division since 1977. He began work in September while on terminal leave from the Air Force as a brigadier general. He was a summa cum laude English graduate of St. John's University and received master's and doctoral degrees from Princeton University in history and philosophy.

Vandiver asked for faculty evaluation through their departmental units and from the Faculty Senate of Dr. Howard Smith. He notified Smith on September 24, 1980, that upon recommendation from the senate, he had named Smith as the new vice president for academic affairs. Before his year's service acting in that position, he had been named associate vice president by Dr. Miles Anderson.

The remaining early Vandiver appointments were of Dr. Eddie J. Davis as vice president for fiscal affairs and treasurer, and Richard S. Rafes as university attorney, on October 10, 1980, and of Fred Pole as executive assistant to the president. In a December memo to his personal staff the president announced that Pole would be given responsibilities for management of the staff in the presidential office suite and in addition would speak for Vandiver in contacts with the directors of athletics, institutional advancement, news and information service, and the university general counsel (the new title for the university attorney).[4]

The position of vice president of student affairs remained unfilled for several years. The following July saw Vandiver recommending the creation of a new position: vice president for external affairs. He selected Pole for that job to "direct efforts to create broad public awareness of program requirements and financial needs and stimulate alumni and community interest in the University's activities to meet those needs." This assigned to Pole the responsibility for advancement and alumni affairs, athletics, government relations, and a renamed information service office: Public Affairs and Information Services. A director of that office and of the advancement program was still to be named.[5]

An Impressive Beginning

Even before Vandiver was in residence in Denton and at work on the campus full time, he created a group to plan a major inauguration, a traditional formal ceremony in the Coliseum. On November 13, 1980, some 350 delegates, including thirty-eight university presidents and chancellors, came to Denton for the observance. Among those present were Lieutenant Governor William Hobby and five regents. The inaugural address was given by Daniel J. Boorstin, librarian of Congress, with a response by President Vandiver. The celebration stretched over two days to include academic symposia by Dr. James O. Breeden of SMU; Dr. Patricia McFate, deputy chairman of the National Endowment for the Humanities; and Dr. Norman Hackerman, president of Rice University.[6]

The amount of money to be spent for that inauguration (about $40,000) was criticized in advance by some faculty members, leading Vandiver to defend it in remarks to the Faculty Senate on April 9, 1980. He told senators the university would get money back from the two-day inaugural festival. "We can showcase the university," he said. "It will be beneficial to have outsiders come here to see what we are doing."[7] But continued negative reactions apparently influenced him when he left NTSU to become president at Texas A&M. The *Austin American-Statesman* ran a photograph with this caption:

> Thrifty Aggie
>
> Texas A&M University President Frank Vandiver saves A&M the cost of a formal inauguration by accepting a medallion before commencement. Vandiver said he preferred the money be spent on university operations rather than an inauguration.[8]

Working on Communication

As his inauguration date approached, Vandiver sent an eight-page letter to the faculty and professional staff members on November 5, 1980. He complained of the bureaucratic situation that kept him from arranging adequate personal meetings with faculty. The letter began by referring to some concerns of the regents, who had just met. The board, he wrote, had been concerned for many months with the "late unpleasantness" with the foundation and other financial matters. He said that things had improved dramatically and that the attorney general had written that no further legal actions were contemplated by state or local agencies and that "clears the past from our path." Vandiver wrote that the news came at a critical time since it impinged directly on fund-raising. He announced that the newly established Office of Advancement would make a major campaign in the spring.[9]

The letter also suggested that remarks made at his first speech to the faculty the preceding January had not been completely well received, especially in his assertion, "But I think our most important function is as researchers." Now his words suggested that he was shifting positions somewhat: "It's always seemed to me that the most stimulating teaching is done by active researchers. By this I don't mean to imply that good teaching can't happen without research. It can, and often does. And I do think the dedicated teacher who works long years without doing research ought to be rewarded as an important contributor to the University's purpose."[10] This question related also to concerns over Coordinating Board pressures to cut programs and reduce expenditures. He noted that Commissioner Kenneth Ashworth

> in his proposed new plan, cautions against "the halo effect of the 'research university'" and suggests that pursuit of this artificial benchmark of excellence is possibly damaging. That may, in part, be true. NTSU, though, is on the threshold of that status. We ought to attain it; we will not if we tolerate "Mickey Mouse" courses in various schools or if we fail to upgrade steadily our admission standards.
>
> We will also fail to attain it if we do not steadily improve faculty and staff quality by internal stimulus and external recruiting.[11]

PLANNING FOR CHANGE

When John Carter became acting president again in the summer of 1979, he sent a memo to all budget units on the campus to cease work on their plan documents under the planning and budgeting system established by Nolen. He suggested that everyone wait to see how the next president wanted to approach the problems. In that first January 1980 talk to the faculty, Frank Vandiver indicated his dissatisfaction with recent planning efforts. In their place, he suggested that to change the image of North Texas there must be a clear institutional self-image, and he didn't find that in the previous planning statement. A new self-conception would be needed to plan a realistic but visionary program for the 1980s.[12]

Ten months later, Vandiver had moved toward activating such a plan, writing in a November letter to faculty that a "Special Committee" would be formed to assess "our own situation, our special needs and ambitions, and recommended priorities for funding, and enhancement, as well as retrenchment."[13]

This was a clear statement of his intention for a major campus review of university direction. It appeared to outline for the community exactly what they could expect in the way of a planning process. But few were prepared for the rumors that began to circulate about that plan.

The "Hunker Down" Surprise

The manner of introduction of the concept of a restructured university almost guaranteed that it would create a major controversy. When he talked to individuals or small groups, Vandiver explained that he has awakened at 4:00 A.M. and "hunkered down" to come up with a vision of a different kind of North Texas. He even signed his first major report to the faculty, "Hunkering down and hoping." That phrase was to be used in derision by those who opposed his ideas.

The president discussed his ideas with his vice presidents and his staff members and assigned Dr. Howard Smith, academic vice president, to meet with the Council of Deans to discuss the plan. On the day before Christmas Eve, 1980, the president's staff was considering ways to make the plan palatable to the campus. Dr. Smith said the deans were "cautiously optimistic." Education Dean Jim Muro and his associate dean, Jim Miller, volunteered to write a proposal to the Fund for Improvement of Postsecondary Education for a grant on "Innovative Restructuring of an Institution." The deans were reported as concerned over the reaction of department chairmen and how they would be notified. Dean Hiram Friedsam was reported by Smith as urging immediate involvement of faculty. As a result of the report, Vandiver asked Smith to monitor how Dean Mark Myers "marshals music alumni against it." The degree to which Vandiver envisioned the elimination of existing departmental structure was revealed in the suggestion that "*Beyond Academic Departments* is a book the staff might have to read." Smith had already established fiscal and personnel working groups to draw up internal structure and present a model by February 1. Smith recommended to the group that the faculty should be invited to a winter convocation where they could be informed immediately upon their return from the Christmas break. But, it was noted at the staff meeting, a convocation "may not be possible because of Dr. Vandiver's schedule."[14]

An outside evaluation of this process came in the *Denton Record-Chronicle* some nine months later, just before Vandiver announced his resignation:

> Perhaps his most serious error was the way he informed the faculty of his idea for reorganizing NTSU's academic structure. Vandiver came up with a plan, discussed it with top administrators and showed it to the deans. Before he was ready to present it to the faculty, word of the plan's existence and contents leaked out. During the 1980 Christmas holiday party circuit, rumors of the plan's contents spread like wildfire. By the time Vandiver left for a Caribbean cruise the first week in January, he had decided to end the rumors and send the faculty a letter explaining the plan. The fact that it was midsemester break and not all the faculty members were in town to receive their letters hurt too.
>
> Many faculty members thought Vandiver should have consulted more people, like them, before making a pronouncement that NTSU will reorganize. They do not like his tendency in general for not consulting knowledgeable people before announcing a decision.[15]

International and Future Roles

It was an eight-page, single-spaced document prepared on January 5, 1981, that introduced faculty and staff to the details of the Vandiver vision. The president told the faculty that in deciding what ought to be done here, one issue overshadowed all others: "How can NTSU meet the needs of higher education best, while competing with other universities in the Metroplex?"

He pointed out that no systematic effort had been made "to educate people in this area for the international and future roles the region is beginning to play." This was his notion of a responsive and innovative organization:

> While maintaining traditional program strengths, we must organize to meet the problems of contemporary society across the traditional subject matter boundaries.
>
> We need to encourage new thinking and new instructional techniques which will include the use of flexible faculty teams and assignments to interdisciplinary and multidisciplinary programs. . . .
>
> I began toying in late November with an idea for a radical shift in NTSU's situation—radical in that the University would undergo fundamental organizational and programmatic changes. . . . If NTSU can shift more toward an international focus and toward concern for the future, then, I think, we can go to the public with a legitimate appeal for partnership. . . and serve. . . in a truly unique way.
>
> To achieve this partnership, I urge your support of a new program: "NTSU—The New Dimension for the Future." Under this program NTSU will be reorganized into *Centers* whose activities will mesh with traditional, current, and foreseeable concerns in the Greater Southwest and the nation. The focus of the reorganization will be on the future with major attention to: expanding human potential; preparing the citizens of this region to interact with the world at large; enhancing resource development; and creating strategies to cope with change in individual and organizational lives.[16]

The letter then took about a page and a half to show examples of new centers for American and International Business Enterprises, Study of Science, Health Services, Administration and Activities of American Governments, Culture, English and Foreign Languages, Controlled Change, Study of Values Toward 2000, Learning Resources, Education of Future Generations, Strategic Planning, and Human Services.

How would such a system manage to function? Vandiver's answer suggested strongly that departments as then existed would disappear into centers, a factor that accounts for much of the organized opposition that appeared. This was the explanation:

> the proposed reorganization focuses on redeploying the academic elements of the institution. "Schools" and "departments" as currently known would be absorbed by one or more Centers; the new alignment would reduce the current line organization and offer a greater degree of autonomy for the basic academic units. Budget and resource management would be vested in Center Directors, with Program Leaders assuming responsibility for more direct curricular and instructional matters. Faculty governance matters, curriculum planning, and other academic activities would be focused in Centers, whose directors would have authority to function rather freely within broad institutional policies and management guidelines.[17]

Vandiver noted that his ideas had been tested on his staff, the deans, some faculty and staff members, the governor, lieutenant-governor, commissioner of higher education, and the Board of Regents. He reported enthusiastic responses. He did write that he had told the regents that this was a high-risk proposal, one that would require all of us to "hunker down" through the transition period. He also acknowledged that the proposal "will not work if you—the faculty and staff—don't want it to." He then called for a campus task group to work with a committee of distinguished citizens to meet with the Board of Regents in February to "announce our intention to move into our New Dimension at a special press conference."[18]

Trial by Faculty Forum

The first real give-and-take between faculty and the president came at a called meeting of the Faculty Senate on January 21. Preliminary business was conducted in the usual meeting place, the Forum Room of the Speech and Drama Building, but it was quickly moved next door to the University Theater so that all of the faculty attending (estimated at 200) could be seated. The full meeting lasted from 2:00 P.M. to 4:00 P.M. and was one of the livelier sessions seen on the North Texas campus involving a president and the faculty. Twenty-one faculty members addressed questions and critical comments to Vandiver, and many more could have been heard had time not run out. It was not a session that could have been viewed with much satisfaction by the president.

Many of the questions asked for a listing of the bad things that made it necessary to change the organization (answer: to compete for a better class of student and faculty), the role of existing departments (answer: the departments *per se* have to disappear), an explanation of how matters such as faculty evaluation for promotion and tenure would work (answer: it's up to the faculty to work that out), and some serious challenges of the method of introducing the proposal to the faculty. The most direct example of the latter came from Dr. Clovis Morrisson, a respected political science professor and veteran Faculty Senate leader. Referring to the method of proposing change, Morrisson said the faculty saw this:

> as a distressing beginning of what we hope to be a very successful presidency for you here. As yet you seem not to have demonstrated a strong willingness to share your ideas in any kind of organized fashion, with any organized faculty arrangement. . . . I think the fire was touched off by your proposal. It was touched off because we took that as set in concrete—you included the governor, you included the Coordinating Board and the Board of Regents. But as far as any of us could determine, no faculty were consulted and certainly no organized faculty group was consulted. Now that you have said that is not true. . . I am much relieved. But can a lesson be learned that it is very important to consider how you, and we, the faculty, can get together on things like this and start doing them in an organized fashion so that the initial reaction is not negative simply because of the way that it was done?[19]

The meeting was ended at 4:00 P.M. because the president had an appointment. Some twelve pages of small type, single-spaced, with narrow margins, recorded the many critical comments but revealed no resolution to the problem. Six days later Vandiver wrote Vice President Smith and Faculty Senate Chairman J. B. Smallwood to give the charge to a "Steering Committee for the Reorganization of North Texas State University." The committee was to be composed of ten members appointed by Smith and ten members elected by the senate. The charge indicated some softening of the Vandiver position. The committee's reorganization plan "should be presented to the broader University community for review before we proceed to an implementation phase."[20]

The Study Begins

The senate convened on January 28 to consider ten persons nominated by the Committee on Committees. After a number of efforts to change the purpose of the committee (including one motion for the senate to decline to name committee representatives), the ten nominees were elected, one from each senatorial district and two at-large.

Howard Smith read Vandiver's memo giving the charge to the steering committee, and the senate turned to questions of not accepting the charge as given. A substitute motion stated that the senate supported those portions of the president's charge to the steering committee that "promote an open-ended investigation of options which might be recommended for NTSU's reorganization." The substitute motion passed on a 20–10 vote, but when the new main motion came up for a vote, a quorum call disclosed that a quorum had been lost. The item was held over for a February 11 meeting.[21] On that date the new main motion passed the senate on a voice vote with no dissent.

A rather bland announcement of the committee appointments appeared in *Update*, the campus newsletter, on February 9. It named the members of the committee and reprinted the presidential charge but said nothing further. Smith's ten appointees included two vice presidents, Dr. Ed Davis and Dr. Al Hurley, the director of libraries, two center administrators, and two student representatives, the president of the Graduate Student Council and the president of the Student Association, and two faculty members.

The steering committee met February 9 and 16 with Smith as chairman and developed proposed procedures for the study.[22] This was approved by the Board of Regents on February 27 in a resolution carefully avoiding endorsement of the Vandiver proposal for abolishing departments and creating centers. Instead the board sanctioned a "process for examining the necessity for and the methods of reorganizing the administration."[23] The Steering Committee and its subcommittees accomplished a great deal in their first six months of labor. In August Smith agreed to slow the process down to permit several members to draft some specific ideas. The group promised to meet again in September.[24] By that time Vandiver had resigned. On November 20 Howard Smith sent a memo to the faculty and staff as president ad interim, reporting that the steering committee had agreed to suspend activities until a new president had been selected.

A SUDDEN DEPARTURE

Frank Vandiver of necessity could be only a part-time president while maintaining his obligations to Rice University in late 1979 and the first seven months of 1980. That was enough to maintain a presence, but it put him at a handicap in moving into a new position with the normal momentum that accompanies a change of leadership. Once here after August 1980 he built a new staff, established much improved relationships with Austin leaders, and launched the campus on a drive toward a dramatic reorganization.

But once he was inaugurated, the new president still was conspicuously absent from campus in a way that the faculty had not expected. Just as the faculty was getting wind of the proposed structural changes, Vandiver left for a midwinter Caribbean cruise. As the steering committee on reorganization picked up speed, Vandiver was again gone, this time for nearly a month as a delegate to the People's Republic of China for the American Association of State Colleges and Universities. He was gone from June 17 to July 13, 1981.[25] Before leaving for China, he arranged to present a paper at the University of Montpellier in France and to conduct research at the National Library of Scotland, Oxford University, and the Imperial War Museum in London. The Council of Deans was notified on August 12 that President Vandiver "is now in Europe on a research study trip and will be presenting a paper. It is anticipated that he will be out until Sept. 12, with a return to the campus for part of the week of Aug. 24. This would allow him to be present for the general faculty meeting on Aug. 25 and the Regents meeting on Aug. 27."[26]

Surprise Announcement

That faculty meeting referred to at the dean's meeting was actually held on August 26. Instead of seeing Vandiver at the lectern in the Music Recital Hall, the group saw the chairman of the Board of Regents, Winfree L. Brown. By that time the rumor mills on campus had led to an expectation that Brown would announce the resignation of Vandiver and his appointment as President of Texas A&M University. His announcement was reported in a special edition of the student newspaper, which also reported that he named Dr. Howard Smith, vice president for academic affairs, as acting president.[27]

> Smith was met with prolonged applause as he stood to address the gathering. . . .

> "I know that you are anxious to get out of here and discuss this situation to its fullest," Smith said.
>
> He said Vandiver was partially responsible for factors that will contribute to university growth, such as "excellent" rapport with the Texas Legislature, recent Coordinating Board approval of campus construction and plans to streamline the NT fiscal administration.
>
> He called Vandiver a "visionary, charismatic leader," and credited him with the addition of university services, such as the reinstatement of winter commencement, a computing council and steering committee for NT and the Texas College of Osteopathic Medicine.[28]

A&M regents had received 550 nominations for the presidency there and had narrowed the field to thirty-five. The selection committee had approached Vandiver two weeks earlier, he said. The A&M System chancellor and selection committee members met the Sunday before the announcement and agreed on terms of his appointment effective September 1. Those terms, Vandiver told the *Daily*, included acceptance of the existing Texas A&M administrative system. As the paper put it, "He said because the university had been run along the same lines for many years, no reorganization would be attempted."[29]

Mixed Evaluations

The student paper subhead probably characterized fairly the attitudes on campus: "Faculty reaction ranges from jubilation to disappointment." Some said that the fact that A&M wanted Vandiver would enhance the NTSU reputation and that "we did not have a bad decision to begin with." One said "the administrative leadership is a lot better than when he came," while another was quoted as saying "His leaving can only help NT's image. This is one of the most wonderful things that could happen to NT." One of the more thoughtful analyses was delivered by Dr. Charldean Newell, an experienced teacher of political science and public administration and an experienced academic administrator. This is the *Daily* account:

> Dr. Charldean Newell. . . said, "Any institution that has had three presidents in the past three years doesn't look like a good place to go. . . ."
>
> Newell said confusion in Vandiver's administration resulted because Vandiver saw himself as a change agent.

"From 1979 to the present, there hasn't been much stability to this institution," she said. "And there is a strong feeling among the majority of the faculty and the townspeople that the university didn't get its money's worth."

"I don't think the president very fully appreciated the strengths and traditions of this university, thus it is no wonder he has had difficulty making the changes he wanted," Newell said. "In short, communication simply wasn't very good."

"I'm sorry in one sense. He had some good ideas, and I don't want this institution to be regarded as one that couldn't accept new ideas."[30]

Probably the most directly antagonistic evaluations came from the two local newspapers. The *North Texas Daily* editorial declared that its knight in shining armor now had tarnished armor. It reviewed his inaugural pledges and said he wouldn't be here to help fulfill them. "Now the bubble has burst. Promises were made that Vandiver can't keep," the student viewpoint said. As NT's knight rides on to Texas A&M, the *Daily* called for selection of a president "who will serve the university rather than serving himself at the expense of NT."[31] The *Denton Record-Chronicle* editorial lashed out at Vandiver for a commitment "about as deep as the thickness of the paper his paycheck was printed on." As part of a full column of criticism and of calls for a new president of different characteristics, the editorial said:

> The future of the university was in his hands more than most universities ever are in the hands of one man. Whether he was about to make it great or ruin it remained to be seen. . . .
>
> So, should Vandiver have turned down the A&M job? Yes. He had a commitment to North Texas State that was not fulfilled; he plowed up a lot of fields without replanting them. He done us wrong.[32]

Vandiver spoke at a news conference that Wednesday afternoon just after his appointment was confirmed by the Texas A&M Board of Regents at a meeting in Dallas. He expressed regrets at leaving North Texas and said "NT is in better shape than it was two years ago. NT was never in any really deep trouble. Most of the trouble was more fancied than real. NT's future is going to be perfectly fine."[33] Vandiver also expressed confidence in the North Texas future in an interview with a *Dallas Morning News* writer, saying, "It's going to take a big selling job, but when they get started, the rest of the universities in Texas better watch out."[34]

At the first fall meeting of the Faculty Senate, Chairman J. B. Smallwood offered a hopeful assessment: "Dr. Vandiver put together a very solid administrative team that can help maintain stability during the interim. It certainly is a quite different situation than. . . we had at the time President Nolen resigned."[35]

At College Station, Vandiver found a warm welcome. Almost 3,000 students marched to the president's home and held a yell practice "to welcome him to Aggieland and show him that the student body is behind him," one of the cadet leaders said. The Associated Press reported that Vandiver was obviously pleased with the demonstration and led the group in one yell.[36]

Vandiver remained in the A&M presidency for seven years. During that time he was nominated to be considered for the posts of chancellor of the A&M system and president of the University of Texas at Austin. He declined to be considered for those. He resigned the A&M presidency in the summer of 1988 to become head of a new national defense think tank, the Mosher Defense Studies Institute, with the rank of distinguished university professor.

IN THE INTERIM, CARRY ON

The Board of Regents on August 27 accepted Vandiver's resignation and appointed Howard Smith to serve as ad interim chancellor of NTSU and TCOM and president of NTSU while continuing as academic vice president. Dr. Smith had come to NT as assistant professor of education in 1961. He had served as acting dean of the College of Education in 1972–73, became associate vice president for academic affairs from 1976 to 1979, and acted as vice president until appointed to that post by Vandiver in October 1980.

Interim President Smith pursued his multiple jobs vigorously, leading the committee on organization to suspend operations until the next president could give direction to the group. He spoke to the first fall meeting of the Faculty Senate on September 9, 1981. He declared that Vandiver's "staying or his leaving is not and does not foretell either the doom or the resurrection of this institution. We are not dependent on any one person or personality for our existence. . . . I think we can move toward some of our aspirations that we already put forth, and I am sure that we will." His remarks were well received by the faculty as indicative of the course of the university.[37]

part VIII

Regaining Momentum

1982–2000

The shortcomings of NTSU which require long-term and very patient attention include: no consensus throughout the University as to who we are and where we are going; repeated instances of budgets and other major actions undertaken without educating the university community, causing insufficient grass roots support for essential programs and an attitude of indifference or worse, a concentration on petty complaints; insufficient attention to developing the leadership and managerial qualities of our many good people, with the price being that we have not used as effectively as possible the marvelous resources in money and facilities given us by the state; minimal attention to development of the faculty, a process that has to be individualized to meet the needs of people hired under widely varying standards across the past thirty years; neglect in meeting the needs of the NTSU student body that is quite different from the student bodies in residential universities; and last, but not least, a failure to develop an institution-wide commitment to excellence in all that we do.

Alfred F. Hurley
First Annual Report, February 1983

chapter 40

Managing for Stability

During the final interview before my appointment, one of the Board members asked me an especially good question: "How long would it take you to achieve all your goals, if you were selected?" My response, "ten years," seemed to surprise some of you, but I went on to explain that my greatest contribution should be to change attitudes among all associated with NTSU/TCOM. I am all the more aware now that it will take nine more years to achieve this goal. By "changing attitudes," I mean that we must end the shortcomings of the past which generate attitudes that could outlast any administration.

Alfred F. Hurley
February 1983

Winfree L. Brown must have felt that he had stepped into one of the highest pressure spots in higher education when he was elected chairman of the Board of Regents in August 1979. Nevertheless, he led the group that set out to find a president who could return stability to the campus, leaving behind the public outcry that followed the Nolen presidency and the frustration and disappointment that accompanied the unexpected departure of President Vandiver.

YET ANOTHER PRESIDENTIAL SEARCH

A twenty-eight-member advisory committee, headed by Vice President Ed Davis, set guidelines for the search. This group included regents, administrators, faculty and staff members, alumni, and student leaders of both NTSU and TCOM. A twelve-member screening committee subsequently reviewed the eighty-five applications received, interviewed candidates, and presented a list of four finalists to the Board of Regents. These four included Dr. Alfred F. Hurley, vice president for administrative affairs; Dr. Howard Smith, Jr., the academic vice president who had served as interim president and chancellor since Vandiver's departure; Dr. Donald Zacharias, president of Western Kentucky University; and Dr. G. Robert Ross, chancellor of the University of Arkansas at Little Rock. Dr. Marvin Berkeley, dean of the NTSU College of Business Administration, was among the final six candidates.

The full board then interviewed the finalists and on February 1, 1982, voted to name Dr. Al Hurley as the next chancellor and president. He took office immediately.

Early Reception

As chronicled by the *Fort Worth Star-Telegram*, a faculty convocation reaction to Hurley's introduction was considerably different from that afforded the public announcement of the Vandiver resignation:

> His appointment as NTSU's 12th president, announced by the university's board of regents Monday, was greeted with a standing ovation from faculty and senior staff members, one professor said.
>
> "I'm sure that Hurley caught the significance of that, because that ovation was from people who know him," said Don Smith, an assistant biology professor and former chairman of the faculty senate. "I do know that Hurley's stock was pretty high among the faculty."

> . . . After the publicity and turmoil of recent years, Smith said, the faculty appears glad to see NTSU return to business as usual.[1]

Many were still concerned over the fate of the Vandiver proposal for the replacement of academic departments with special centers. The new president told the reporter that he did not support the radical reorganization of the university proposed by Vandiver and viewed with skepticism and disapproval by many faculty members. Hurley said he hoped to see some interdisciplinary centers on a voluntary basis, "but not for the entire university."[2] Hurley, who had been a member of the committee on reorganization, asked Howard Smith to reconvene that group to examine further questions of organization and to report its recommendations.

The Residue of Problems

A graduate wrote the alumni publication, the *North Texan*, to ask why the university was unable to keep qualified people in office. The answer came in a May 1982 letter from Board Chairman Win Brown, who wrote that the regents sought a stable administration: Regents chose Dr. Al Hurley as an individual who already had demonstrated his commitment to NTSU as Vice President for Administrative Affairs and who "made clear to us his willingness to be with us for a long time." [3]

Hurley presented a hopeful view while acknowledging previous problems. He told a Denton group that "I have been tremendously impressed by the many dedicated professionals at the university. Many good things have gone on despite what was going on in the higher reaches of the administration."[4] In his 1983 personal Christmas letters to his principal administrators Hurley wrote that "we are going to put this institution on the solid footing it has badly needed for an incredibly long time."[5] He wrote Daniel J. Boorstin, the librarian of Congress who had spoken at the Vandiver inauguration, that in his first one hundred days in office he had visited every one of the fifty-one academic departments and each administrative area. "The visits persuaded me all the more that this university's strengths have gone unrecognized for too long a time. I have told our Board of Regents that I want to devote the next 10 years of my life to waking this sleeping giant."[6]

The *Dallas Morning News* chose the occasion of the university name change in May 1988 to give a brief assessment of how Hurley had been fitting into the academic community. This appeared as the Sunday feature, "High Profile."

Noting that Hurley had been sought for higher-paying, more prestigious jobs, the writer referred to Winfree Brown

> who's part of the crowd that calls Hurley, "one of the best things that ever happened to the University of North Texas."
>
> "Al believes in all the corny things, an honest day's work for an honest dollar. . . Al lives and breathes that university," adds former regent Wayne Stockseth. . . .
>
> "Hurley is very regimented. But we needed that, really, at that particular time," reflects Brown, who initially saw Hurley as "a little abrupt" in his style of politicking.
>
> "When we found him, he was a diamond in the rough. He sure polished out to be a pretty good diamond."[7]

AN IRISHMAN FROM BROOKLYN

Hurley and Vandiver, both military historians, had met at a professional seminar. Vandiver named Hurley as vice president for administrative affairs on June 20, 1980, and in September Hurley moved from the Air Force Academy to North Texas. He was assigned responsibility for physical plant, planning, new construction, affirmative action, utility systems, security, and service operations including maintenance. Hurley said one factor deciding him to make the career switch was the opportunity to work with Vandiver, described as "such a distinguished educator and scholar." When Vandiver resigned a year later, Hurley described his reaction as "total shock."[8]

The Son of Immigrants

Alfred Francis Hurley was born in Brooklyn on October 16, 1928, the son of Irish immigrants. His parents worked in menial jobs to support a family of four children in Brooklyn during the Depression. They lived in an ethnic neighborhood that reflected national origin and religious background; there were 55,000 residents and seven Catholic churches.

Hurley received a bachelor of arts in English and philosophy at St. John's University in Brooklyn a few weeks before the outbreak of the Korean War in June 1950. He enlisted in the U.S. Air Force as a private and spent the next thirty years in the Air Force as a navigator, planner, administrator, and educator. Under Air Force sponsorship, he earned his M.A. and Ph.D. in history and philosophy at Princeton University to prepare for duty on the history faculty at the Air Force Academy, where he first served from 1958 to 1963 and again beginning in 1966 as a permanent professor. Hurley headed the History Department at the academy from 1966 to 1980 and served as chairman of its Humanities Division as well as a member of the Academy Board from 1977 to 1980, when he retired as a brigadier general.

Hurley was the author of the first scholarly biography of General Billy Mitchell and a contributor to other works on the history of air power. He won a Guggenheim Fellowship in the Humanities in 1971–72 and served as a fellow in the Eisenhower Institute of the Smithsonian Institution in Washington in 1976–77. Once at North Texas as a professor of history as well as administrator, he taught graduate history classes from time to time. Each fall Hurley conducted a Military History Seminar for Executives from the metropolitan area and the state and beyond. The ninth occurred in 1991.

"My Wife, Joanna, and I"

At the time of his vice presidential appointment, the Air Force officer said, "My wife, Joanna, and I are delighted to come back to Texas." Those first five words formed a phrase that would soon become as familiar to the North Texas family as the appearance of the two Hurleys together at almost every public gathering in the years ahead.

Joanna (Leahy) Hurley and fellow Brooklynite Al Hurley married in 1953. They shared thirty years of military service while raising four sons and a daughter. Mrs. Hurley majored in French at St. John's University, was an airline stewardess for Pan American Airways, taught elementary school in New York, Texas, and Colorado, and earned her M.A.T. at Colorado College in 1971.

When they first moved to Denton, Joanna Hurley began studying toward a master of business administration degree. But when her husband became chancellor, as the *Dallas Morning News* put it:

> "I had to make a decision: whether to enjoy a once-in-a-lifetime experience or remain in school."
>
> She became part of a "twofer package," as she calls it, a full-time partner in Hurley's university work. In her trim St. John knits, the sociable Mrs. Hurley is a staple at university functions, keeping a schedule that rivals her husband's. All without pay.[9]

In his seventeen months as administrative vice president, Dr. Hurley had brought a structured discipline to his administrative support units. From this diverse group came the university's first staff evaluation system, a thousand additional campus parking spaces, a new campus-wide outdoor lighting system for better security, completion of the fifth floor of the General Academic Building for computer science and Computing Center equipment and services, a contract for a radically new computer-controlled telephone system, and achievement of an especially difficult goal: Coordinating Board approval of a 30,000-square-foot Science Research Building.

That kind of mission-oriented, goal-seeking management would be intensified in the office of chancellor and president. It could have been predicted by those who knew him in Colorado Springs. Hurley told the *Dallas Morning News* that his theory of leadership is "to be out front and to work harder than everybody else. . . . Leadership means the eager acceptance of responsibility."[10]

Energizing the Regents

In his first meeting with the board in February 1982, Hurley used the technique of briefing to outline the strengths and serious shortcomings of North Texas. He then told the regents his proposals for short-range and long-range initiatives to overcome these shortcomings. He told Board Vice Chairman H. E. Chiles of Fort Worth, "Your willingness, and that of the other members of the Board, to face up to the key issues and to address them in a no holds barred, yet supportive, manner reinforces my optimism about the future of NTSU/TCOM."[11]

Hurley's briefing[12] identified the strengths as "many good people, many effective facilities, excellent locations, high quality of life, fine academic reputation in several fields, and a new emphasis on management." The serious shortcomings for both TCOM and NTSU, he identified as "fragmented leadership and weak on fundamentals essential to outstanding organizations." For NTSU only, these were "limited financial resources and faceless students." Perhaps immodestly but nonetheless staking out his intention to take charge, he listed the key solution as "leadership by a builder." He proposed immediate initiatives for those shortcomings:

For fragmented leadership, he would maximize visibility of the chancellor, make clear decisions about ties between NTSU and TCOM, and reinforce the university's ties to Denton and the Metroplex. As to weaknesses on organizational fundamentals, he proposed creating a sense of mission, promoting the image of NTSU/TCOM, establishing firm expectations as to performance, upgrading the planning office, systematically auditing all activities, and stepping up managerial innovations.

To deal with NTSU's limited financial resources, he told the board he would prioritize objectives, strengthen relationships with state agencies, hire a fundraiser, lead a grassroots buildup of alumni, and step up student recruitment. He proposed a regular analysis of the student body for better service.

For long-range initiatives, the chancellor proposed to set NTSU/TCOM on these tracks: develop interim, intermediate, and long-range plans, develop full potential of faculties and staffs, systematically hire even better qualified faculty, grow with Denton and the Metroplex, and make the most of the one hundredth anniversary in 1990.

Creating a Management Group

Hurley took office with three vice presidential colleagues, all Vandiver appointees: Dr. Howard Smith, academic affairs; Dr. Eddie J. Davis, fiscal affairs; and Fred Pole, external affairs. All three were to change soon. Smith returned to teaching in the School of Education. Davis followed Vandiver to Texas A&M. Pole, a retired army colonel, succeeded Hurley as vice president for administrative affairs effective March 1, 1982. Walter E. Parker, special assistant to the president for external affairs, became vice president for external affairs, and Tom C. Purdy was named director of institutional advancement to head the private fund development effort.[13]

Within two more months, the new chief executive had selected two women as administrators. Dr. Aline Arnold, of the business administration faculty, became executive assistant to the chancellor. She served until 1984, to be succeeded by Dr. Peter B. Lane, a former faculty member at the Air Force Academy.[14] Dr. Charldean Newell was named special assistant to the chancellor for planning, a new function being merged with the position of director of the University Planning and Analysis Office. Dr. Newell was a member of the political science faculty who had served as departmental chairman and as an associate academic vice president.

During the search for a new academic leader, Dr. Robert B. Toulouse, dean of the Graduate School, became vice president for academic affairs ad interim.[15]

When it became clear that the academic post search would continue through the following year, Dr. Toulouse was named to the position for the academic year 1982–83 while his associate graduate dean, Dr. Hugh L. Kirkpatrick, became acting dean. Toulouse's interim appointment was subsequently made permanent in 1983, and he served until retirement in the summer of 1985 after thirty-seven years with the university. After several committee searches over a three-year period, the regents in June 1985 named as vice president of academic affairs and provost, Dr. David E. Golden, chairman of the department of physics and astronomy and distinguished professor of physics at the University of Oklahoma, effective August 27, 1985.[16] One month later, the position of vice president for development was created, to be filled on an acting basis by Dr. James Muro, dean of the College of Education.

From Reorganization Committee to Planning Council

The new president found a new approach for the committee on organization, the one born of the Vandiver proposals. He told the faculty in August 1982 that this study group, which had at first focused on total reorganization, had changed to include specific recommendations for organizational adjustments. Before any recommendations could be carried out, he said, "we first must more precisely define our mission and goals." This was to be the first task of the new University Planning Council. The council would soon create task forces to study ideas other than organizational that had been posed by the study.[17]

Ties to Southern Association Self-Study

Hurley found two valuable roles for Howard Smith: continue as chairman of the steering committee on organization, whose report would help begin the self-study report for the coming reaccreditation review by the Southern Association of Schools and Colleges."[18] Smith was named in May 1983 to lead that institutional self-study.

Recommendations from the organization panel became part of the agenda for the planning process developed through the spring and summer of 1982 and begun that fall. In appointing Newell, Hurley returned the reporting base of the Office of Planning and Analysis from the vice president for academic affairs to the office of chancellor/president. The move emphasized the planning function and gave a support role to the analytical processes.[19]

The New Planning Structure

Newell developed a planning structure that created two central groups. One was the University Planning Council (UPC), made up of the academic vice president as chairman, the Faculty Senate chairman and two other faculty members, the Student Association president, the academic deans, and one representative each from administrative, external, fiscal, and student affairs. The other group was an executive subset of the UPC, the Planning Steering Committee, made up of the vice presidents and the dean of students.

The University Planning Council was named in September, and a task force on mission and goals was created. Existing bodies were asked to examine decentralization of the Graduate School, faculty governance, international programs, core curriculum and related matters, enrollment management, computer needs and policies, degree and course requirements, and academic advising.

EXAMINING ORGANIZATION

The main document from the study of organization was twenty-five tightly spaced pages of single-spaced typing, accompanied by thirteen more pages of exhibits. Much of its content helped shape the course of North Texas.[20]

Educational Values

For the following five to ten years a set of educational values would guide development. These included emphasizing both high-quality teaching and excellence in research; improving degree program quality by deflating faculty grading patterns and raising entrance standards; building student mastery of a common core of knowledge; supplementing traditional learning with interdisciplinary, honors, and experimental courses, encouraging both traditional and interdisciplinary research, and developing faculty professional and community service.

Internal Thrusts

Fifteen thrusts to deal with implementation of goals were presented, including a long- and short-range planning system; more effective use of human, financial, and physical resources; merit salary increases for faculty; a faculty and staff incentive fund to reward good teaching, outstanding research, and significant service; continued emphasis on faculty and staff development programs; and recruitment of faculty who have the potential to exceed the performance of the best scholars now serving in each discipline.

Also proposed were higher priority for significant research, creative production, and scholarly publication, with external support, much of it obtained by the individual researcher. Computer capability would be improved in all areas of institutional life, there would be more effective cultivation of the partnership between NTSU and TCOM, and aggressive recruitment of graduate scholars.

External Thrusts

First on a list of external thrusts was to mount a campaign to convey an accurate image of NTSU. "The university should consider adopting a name which more nearly reflects its stature among other institutions of higher education."

Others were to seek the good will, advocacy, and financial support of alumni; involvement with business, industry, commerce, and government, with special emphasis on the Metroplex; solicit permanent external funding and other resources from the private sector; establish an aggressive program of student recruitment and retention; work closely with community college systems; develop strong ties to the university by commuting students; build on the cooperative education program to provide visibility and liaison with business and industry; and commit to international education and seek funding for its support.

Becoming an Urban University

The organization committee identified the school's location on the periphery of the Metroplex in the path of population expansion, and concluded that NTSU would become an urban university. This presented such challenges as an increasing vocational orientation among students, large numbers of commuter students, large numbers of part-time and other nontraditional students, generally weaker student academic preparation, and increased participation by the university community in the life of the metropolitan area served.

Minimum requirements for meeting these challenges include an increasing emphasis on remedial education programs, development of work-study programs such as cooperative education, development of transportation alternatives for commuting students, reassessment of the formats and locations in which instruction and services are delivered, and development of a set of services designed to meet the needs of commuting and nontraditional students.

Proposals for Organizational Change

The steering committee on organization stated that radical reorganization was not feasible. It found no compelling support or justification for replacing existing academic units with free-standing centers. Its report did endorse the idea of centers that complement existing units and programs.

The most significant structural change was the proposal to create a College of Applied Sciences and Technology (CAST). This would include three existing schools—Community Service (somewhat realigned), Library and Information Sciences, and Home Economics. In addition a new School of Mass Communication would include the Division of Radio, Television, and Film and the Journalism Department, all to be moved from Arts and Sciences. CAST would also include aerospace studies, industrial technology, and computer sciences.[21]

BECOMING A RESEARCH UNIVERSITY

Support for research was still rather small as the 1980s began. As reported to the Southern Association, there were 182 sponsored grants for $401,418 in 1981, 171 for $346,981 in 1982, and 191 awards for $424,418 in 1983.[22] The self-study in 1984 showed a strong set of goal statements for research but a lack of financial support, inadequate facilities and equipment, and faculty teaching loads that would not encourage heavy research activity.

Positive Research Aspects

On the positive side, the self-study said the university had made a significant commitment to increasing the quality and quantity of its research efforts. Of promising impact was the opening of the new Science Research Building in late 1984. Computing capacity and services had "dramatically increased." New faculty member selection gave increasing weight to research qualifications. Additional funds were provided to encourage faculty travel to present research results at national and international conferences.

A major step came with the reorganization of the research office. The Office of Research and Academic Grants had been established in March 1969 as an adjunct to the office of the graduate dean, where it remained until 1981. The director was also an associate dean of the Graduate School. In the fall of 1981, the office became an adjunct of the office of academic vice president, and in May 1983, an associate vice president for research and academic grants was appointed. Establishment of this office and administrative position, the self-study committee said, "makes clear and explicit the key role of research and academic grants in the overall mission of the university.[23]

The Need to Improve Research Effort

In spite of an increase in research funds obtained in recent years, the 1984 report complained that appropriations for capital equipment and operating costs had not kept pace and were "clearly insufficient to maintain the base level of excellence necessary in a graduate research university." Evident at North Texas, it said, was the national epidemic of training students on obsolete equipment and operating departments with subsistence-level funding. "Any significant reduction in research funding would make a bad situation intolerable," the study said.[24]

Surveys of faculty members and departmental administrators found that more than half of the departments said they emphasized teaching more than research but nevertheless placed a great deal of weight on research and publication in deciding on merit raises, promotion, and tenure. But morale was damaged, the committee wrote, for faculty members with large teaching loads being put under pressure to carry out research and to publish. Teaching load standards were regarded as "especially onerous for faculty members from whom research expectations are high." Failure to correct these problems led faculty to view the university research commitment as "less than total."[25]

The strongest statement from the committee came in its first research goal statement urging a stronger administrative commitment to research, backed by funding priorities. This was stipulated in the broadest sense to include basic and applied research, sponsored programs, and performing and visual arts.[26]

REGAINING PUBLIC CONFIDENCE

Hurley and staff worked with the Board of Regents to create an "Executive Summary" that would communicate the salient points of progress at North Texas. This document was sent by Brown to Governor Clements on September 30, 1982.[27] The board stated that it had "taken extraordinary measures to operate a quality educational institution." The statement listed the variety of goal-setting, planning, and effective management techniques that were being developed.

As a graduate of North Texas and as one of the first appointees to the Board of Regents by the then new Republican governor, Win Brown clearly wanted Governor Clements to realize that the regents were responsive to the governor's concerns. Chairman Brown wrote this to Clements:

> As you know, NTSU had more than its share of problems for several years, and I am pleased to report that this excellent university is now solidly on its way to becoming the most outstanding university in the North Texas region. TCOM is a very new institution, but, with the completion of its second major building, it stands even more ready to serve the primary medicine needs of the people of this state.[28]

The response from the governor the following month was encouraging: "I am very pleased that the University seems to have turned the corner in overcoming its problematic past. The new administrative team that you have in place seems to have the ship well on course. I commend you and the other regents for your diligent work in turning things around."[29]

IT WILL TAKE A LONG TIME

Nevertheless, Chancellor Hurley showed no complacency in his first annual report to the Board of Regents in February 1983 after one year in office. This presented the commentary on shortcomings that appears on the title page of Part VII of this history.[30] Hurley reminded the regents that in the final interview before his appointment he had explained that his greatest contribution should be to change attitudes among all associated with NTSU/TCOM. By "changing attitudes," he said he meant that "we must end the shortcomings of the past which generate attitudes that could outlast any administration."

Hurley declared that his objectives would be to win board approval for a revised mission and goals statement, have a successful legislative session, strengthen standards of performance by everyone in the NTSU/TCOM communities, exploit opportunities we have neglected, and step up external relations work. He concluded his report by telling the board, "you know full well how fortunate I am to have inherited situations at NTSU/TCOM where so many good people have achieved a great deal. With their help. . . we will do even more."[31]

chapter 41

Centennial Decade: New Outreach

Much has been done to reshape North Texas. Fortunately, this change has neither disrupted campus affairs nor damaged traditional strengths. . . .

In its one hundredth year the university is living up to the name it assumed in May 1988. In programs and people it is truly the University of North Texas.

La Forte and Himmel
Down the Corridor of Years, 1989

In the first week of the ninetieth year, on January 5, 1981, Frank Vandiver issued his controversial reorganization call to maintain traditional program strengths while organizing "to meet the problems of contemporary society across the traditional subject matter boundaries." He visualized interdisciplinary and multidisciplinary centers.[1] Vandiver's centers would have "redeployed" the resources of existing schools and departments to manage their educational goals. This feature helped rouse the opposition that kept the reorganization from taking place.

However, the concept of centers that did *not* threaten existing units was attractive to many faculty members. The years leading up to the centennial year saw an acceleration of the development of new centers, institutes, and credit and noncredit programs that had begun in the 1960s and 1970s. La Forte and Himmel call it "The Centennial Administration, 1982-2000."[2] Hurley told his first faculty meeting that the committee on organization had originally focused on a total reorganization but had changed "to include specific recommendations for organizational adjustments and many promising ideas that surfaced."[3]

PROMISING IDEAS MATERIALIZE

The full report of the Steering Committee for the Study of the Organization appeared in August 1982. Its one major reorganizational proposal, for the College of Applied Sciences and Technology, did not materialize. However, it identified major directions for university development that fed into the work of the new University Planning Council and helped provide the impetus for a great deal of innovative change.

Faculty members began working with the new president in 1982 on two programs for faculty improvement: (1) early retirement to teaching on modified service and (2) faculty development leaves.

In 1977 John Carrell of the business law faculty had submitted a proposal for early retirement that was considered but not adopted. In February 1982, Hurley learned of that proposal and submitted it to the Board of Regents. It was adopted by the board the following September. The plan evolved with Coordinating Board support and was widely used thereafter. It enabled a full-time tenured faculty member to take early retirement at age fifty-five or thereafter and continue teaching at reduced load and proportional salary for five years.

In December 1982 the Faculty Senate reactivated a Faculty Development

Committee to consider faculty development leaves. Such a program was developed with administrative encouragement and was approved by the Board of Regents. It provided for paid leaves at full pay for one semester or for half pay for two semesters for a faculty member to conduct research or creative activity or for activities for renewal and enrichment of academic skills. Six such leaves were recommended by a faculty committee and approved by the regents in August 1984.

Texas Academy of Mathematics and Science

In 1986, Dean Jim Miller of the College of Education proposed a specialized mathematics and science program for high school students at UNT. The Texas Legislature authorized the creation of the Texas Academy of Mathematics and Sciences (TAMS) in 1987. Participants in this two-year program simultaneously complete what would have been their junior and senior high-school years, as well as the first two years of college while in residence on the UNT campus.

TAMS was created strictly as a residential program, with all students required to live in a university residence hall, McConnell Hall, which was enlarged to accommodate their numbers. Admission requirements are strict. Although a minimum SAT score taken as a tenth grader was set at 1000 with at least a 550 on the mathematics portion, the average SAT of admitted students was 1200 with 660 on mathematics. By 1998, 1,100 students had graduated through the program. The class of 1998 included sixty-four National Merit Scholarship finalists and twenty-eight graduates with perfect 4.0 GPAs. TAMS had more students—eleven—accepted to Stanford than any high school in the nation.[4]

Meadows Foundation: Excellence in Teaching

The Meadows Foundation of Dallas gave $850,000 in 1982 to start an imaginative five-year program to provide exceptional graduates to enter teaching. Led by Dean Jim Muro, the Excellence in Teaching Program designed a curriculum to enrich the education and the practical supervised teaching experience of students leading to a master's degree.

Classic Learning Core

In 1986, with a grant from the National Endowment for the Humanities, the UNT College of Arts and Sciences began an innovative humanities program called the Classic Learning Core (CLC). Based upon classic texts, the program sought to create a coherent sense of wholeness among the liberal arts courses required for a bachelor's degree. In 1991, the CLC was merged with the college's honors and great books programs to create Academic Core Programs within the College of Arts and Sciences. Students in honors enroll for the honors core curriculum rather than the university core curriculum. The Great Books Program offers an interdisciplinary exploration of some of the great books of history. Another option offered is the opportunity for an undergraduate student to spend a semester or a year on exchange at one of more than 150 colleges and universities that are members of the National Student Exchange. The student remains in continuous enrollment at UNT while studying at the other campus.[5]

Business Administration Additions

The Institute of Petroleum Accounting began operations in 1980 to serve the oil and gas and other extractive industries through research, publications, and education. The institute became the conduit through which academic research in the oil and gas industry reaches the working professional. In conjunction with the UNT Professional Development Institute, the institute conducts seminars in petroleum accounting for working professionals.

The Information Systems Research Center began in 1986, combining instruction, research, and service to support economic development and industrial opportunities in Texas. It was sponsored by seventeen business firms.

In 1990, the College of Business Administration received a grant from the Accounting Education Change Commission to begin a program known as the Professional Learning Core (PLC). This is a five-year program in accounting leading to the MBA degree, with special courses in the humanities and CLC.

University Press

The University of North Texas Press was created in August 1987, the result of discussions initiated by Dr. David Golden, vice president and provost, with Dr. James Lee and A. C. Greene. Lee was chairman of the English Department and director of the Center for Texas Studies, which brought Greene to the campus. Lee began the press operations, and Fran Vick came to the campus to be full-time director of the press. Its first book was *Out of Dallas*, a collection of fourteen short stories by faculty and staff of Dallas County community colleges published in March of 1989.[6] Publishing some sixteen to twenty books a year, the press had more than 140 books in print in 1998.[7]

University presses face difficult financial situations, and to help cut expenses, the UNT Press joined six Texas institutions in a publishing consortium. The original consortium members were Texas A&M, Southern Methodist University, Rice University, TCU, the University of Texas at El Paso, and the Texas State Historical Association. Each operates independently, and when the books are printed they are sent to A&M, which takes care of marketing, shipping, billing and collecting. The seven presses produce a joint catalog and share use of sales representatives.[8]

OTHER NEW VENTURES

Economic Development and Research

North Texas's heavy involvement in the educational and economic development of the Metroplex led to the creation of the Center for Economic Development and Research in 1989. It serves to conduct economic analysis and public policy research and provide forecasting and strategic planning services to businesses, governments, and nonprofit agencies with an interest in economic development. Dr. Bernard L. Weinstein was the founding director. Interdisciplinary by design, the center usually undertakes studies with some public policy dimension, and its clients often release reports into the public domain.[9] The center is not an instructional unit but works closely with the Institute of Applied Economics, which offers master's degree programs in public policy and economic development.

Experimental Music and Intermedia

The Electronic Music Center had been established in 1963 by composer Merrill Ellis, and was renamed CEMI in September 1983 in recognition of the development of the Merrill Ellis Intermedia Theater in the new Music Building and of its expanded activities. These include composition with several types of computers, research and software design in composition, research in sound diffusion techniques with a multispeaker sound system, and intermedia composition with dance and visual projection systems.

North Texas Community and Junior College Consortium

A new education faculty member from Florida, Al Smith, helped found a consortium in the summer of 1989, joining UNT and several nearby community and junior colleges. It aimed to provide staff development and research projects to nine or ten community colleges. The organization began operation from the North Texas campus in September 1989 with fifteen community colleges from nine districts.

Center for Network Neuroscience

The Center for Network Neuroscience was established January 1, 1987 to facilitate a pioneering effort — research on how neural networks process and store information.

TRIO Center for Student Development

Congress established three programs under the TRIO name in 1965 and there are now seven. The UNT center houses five programs. Two-thirds of students served by TRIO must come from families with taxable income under 150 percent of the poverty level and where neither parent graduated from college. UNT established these programs:

Upward Bound, which helps students in grades nine through twelve prepare for higher education; Upward Bound Math and Science, a five-week summer residential program for high school students; Talent Search, which counsels students in grades six through twelve on college preparation; Ronald E. McNair Post-Baccalaureate Achievement, which encourages undergraduates to consider careers in college teaching as well as prepare them for doctoral study; and Student Support Services, designed to increase retention, academic performance, and graduation rates.

North Texas Institute for Educators on the Visual Arts

NTIEVA was established in 1988 through a grant from the J. Paul Getty Trust and is one of six national institutes that are part of a national reform movement in art education. This is a consortium of art museums, K-12 schools, arts agencies, and the UNT School of Visual Arts. It provides training for school district teams of art specialists, art supervisors, classroom teachers, principals, superintendents, and school board members. NTIEVA also administers the Marcus Fellows Program in art education graduate study.

Consortium members include the Amon Carter Museum, the Dallas Museum of Art, the Kimbell Art Museum, the Meadows Museum, the Modern Art Museum of Fort Worth, the University of North Texas, the Greater Denton Arts Council, the Texas Commission on the Arts, and the independent school districts of Denton, Fort Worth, Hurst-Euless-Bedford, Pilot Point, and Plano.

chapter 42

Crisis in the Oil Patch

The way things are going in Texas, college students at state schools will soon see their tuition triple, professional wrestlers will pay $15 instead of $10 for their licenses and paroled convicts will have to pay the state $10 a month to supervise their parole.

These are the lengths to which the Texas Legislature is going to balance the state's budget in the face of continuing recession in the petroleum industry, which has long been the state's main source of revenue and has given Texans a kind of free lunch as far as taxes go.

It is the stark irony of the spring of 1985 that Texas, whose once-booming economy has been dampened by falling world oil prices, is struggling to make ends meet at a time when once-distressed Northern industrial states like New York and New Jersey are suddenly enjoying comfortably balanced budgets and even cutting taxes.

The New York Times
May 22, 1985[1]

In the 1980s Texas continued to move toward becoming a highly urbanized state but at the same time lost much of its principal tax base—the petroleum industry—and suffered an agonizing reappraisal of its tax and public expenditure policies. An inordinate amount of time would be spent by North Texas leaders in anticipating, analyzing, and responding to a variety of threats (and opportunities) that arose during this decade. It was the decade that led the university to its Centennial Year celebration in 1990.

OIL PATCH FINANCIAL WOES: 1984-85

The alarm bell sounded clearly as legislators gathered in January 1983. State Comptroller Bob Bullock announced that he was cutting his estimate of state income by $1.5 billion over the next three years. Nevertheless, the legislature still had $4.1 billion more to work with in developing the 1984–85 appropriations bill.[2] Bullock warned Hurley in a letter that a crisis was at hand:

> Texas has lived on Easy Street for 12 years. . . .
>
> That day is gone, As your State Comptroller I will collect every dollar of tax money legally due the state, but I cannot "create" tax money where none exists. . . .
>
> The Legislature has options but they are limited—cut the budget, raise taxes or risk deficit spending.[3]

Oil revenue for Texas peaked in 1982, and the following year the oil and gas industry paid thirty percent of all state taxes. Just two years later, that share had fallen to twenty percent. The severe consequences of the collapse in world oil prices became convincingly evident in 1984, just as budget proposals were being prepared for the 1985 Texas Legislature. Texas ranked forty-seventh among the fifty states in tax burden per person and was one of only four with neither a corporate nor a personal income tax. Furthermore, the state provided one of the lowest levels of state services. The *New York Times* pointed to the two-year budget of about $36 billion in Texas, less than half the $39 billion budget for just one year in New York State.[4]

NTSU Cites Savings Initiatives

Governor Mark White wrote state agencies in May 1984, asking that they take any steps to save state funds. NTSU Board Chairman Win Brown wrote the governor of "major initiatives to make the best possible use of resources." These included holding down staff size in spite of a fifteen percent enrollment increase from 1980 to 1983, scheduling weekend classes for better classroom use, and developing energy management programs. Brown noted, however, that NTSU utility costs per square foot had only been about half of the state-wide average. He also proposed quarterly management reviews to monitor goals and expenditures, staff development programs, and staff and student surveys to identify ways to do a better job.[5]

The price of Texas oil had reached thirty-five dollars a barrel in 1981, was down to twenty-seven dollars in 1986 and headed still lower. State revenue estimators noted that for every drop of one dollar in the price of a barrel of oil, the state lost $100 million. The 1985 estimates of the budget shortfall ranged as high as $900 million and would reach $1.1 billion by the following May.[6] The Legislative Budget Board in December 1984 recommended that higher education budgets be cut by an average of twenty-six percent. One obvious countermove, raising taxes to restore the lost oil revenue, was generally regarded as politically impossible. However, Lieutenant Governor Bill Hobby suggested that it would be necessary to increase tuition to avoid new taxes. His proved to be a prophetic voice.

A new tax bill was made even more unlikely because the legislature in the summer of 1984 had passed a three-year, $4.8 billion tax measure for public school reform and for highways. Most of that came from an increase in the state sales tax.

Impact of Budget Cuts

The commissioner of higher education, Dr. Kenneth Ashworth, told reporters in December 1984 that fifteen years of improvements in Texas universities could be wiped out by the state financial crisis. This came just three years after the legislature had raised Texas above the national average in faculty salaries and some other spending categories. Ashworth suggested that this was not a temporary condition but one that might last as long as six years.[7] The *Dallas Times Herald* reported on December 13 that the LBB proposal for NTSU for the 1986–87 biennium was $82.7 million, a cut of 21.8 percent.

Meantime, internal planning for budget cuts produced the expected stress among budget units. In January 1985 a memo went to Hurley and Vice President Toulouse from Dean Tom Preston on behalf of the chairs of arts and sciences. He said that any cuts in the primary mission of teaching, research, and service should occur "only after all other areas of the University have been reduced as much as possible."

> A particularly frustrating issue is the use of auxiliary enterprise monies to support non-academic areas, particularly athletics, instead of academic programs and faculty salaries. It does not seem reasonable to continue pouring money into what is apparently a very limping football program while cutting back on the primary elements of the University. . . .
>
> I cannot convey to you the depth of resentment and anger that surface about these matters.[8]

The Governor's Role

Party politics was now a stronger factor. Democrat Mark White had replaced the first Republican governor of the century, and he faced certain and strong Republican opposition in his stand for re-election. Advocacy of any form of income tax would be political suicide for a candidate.

White called a summit meeting in December 1984 with state agency heads, including those from higher education. The governor had his leaders lined up to commit to keeping state spending within estimated revenue. Comptroller Bob Bullock told them there would be a downturn in funds for several years to come. Treasurer Ann Richards expressed concern about cash flow patterns. Speaker Gib Lewis said there would be no new taxes but some higher fees, including higher tuition. Lieutenant Governor Hobby delivered a commitment to a legislative session without a tax bill.[9]

The governor stressed that higher education would have to absorb a fair share of budget reductions but argued: "Those reductions should be limited to administration and maintenance; they should not and need not extend to classroom instruction or reductions in faculty positions." The governor declared that "every campus cannot be all things to all people" and urged each university to enhance only those programs "that are of the highest quality or for which the need is most pressing." He urged the Coordinating Board to promote greater cooperation among campuses and declared that "Now we must ensure even more firmly that one institution does not duplicate the efforts of another, particularly where the two schools are in close proximity.[10]

STRUGGLE FOR APPROPRIATIONS (AND REVENUE)

By mid-April of 1985, three parallel efforts moved toward completion in the legislature. These were each house's appropriations bill, a tuition-increase bill in each house, and a proposed constitutional amendment to establish a Higher Education Assistance Fund for schools outside of the University of Texas and Texas A&M systems. Popularly referred to as Proposition 2, this amendment would create the equivalent of the Permanent University Fund for these schools. This was vital to schools like North Texas, which lost its construction funds when the old constitutional ad valorem tax fund was cut off in 1979.

Shifting the Burden to Students

The legislature sought to place more of the burden on students with major tuition increases. This was opposed by Governor White. Nevertheless, on the last possible day, June 16, 1985, the governor signed the appropriations bill that included the first tuition increase in twenty-eight years. White pointed out that even with the increase, Texas would still rank fiftieth in state tuition levels. Nevertheless, Texas led the nation in size of recent tuition increases with hikes more than seven times higher than the national average for home-state students.[11] In nonresident tuition, Texas jump from fiftieth to twenty-first in the nation.[12]

The bill tripled tuition for Texas residents to twelve dollars per semester hour beginning in the fall of 1985 and from forty dollars to $120 for out-of-state students. This was estimated to bring in $275 million over the next two years, avoiding dramatic appropriations cuts.

The Select Committee

This same legislature also created the Select Committee on Higher Education to examine the direction that Texas universities should take. Work of this committee and its impact on NTSU are examined in Chapter 40.

Prop 2: Salvation?

From 1966 to 1980, North Texas received line-item appropriations for major repair and rehabilitation of buildings of $11,840,582 and an ad valorem tax allocation for new construction of $33,585,582. The ad valorem tax was established in the state constitution, but the legislature killed it in 1979 by rewriting the Property Tax Code. Any possibility of restoration of the property tax vanished in a 1982 election, when voters formally repealed the tax through adoption of a constitutional amendment.[13]

Hobby and Clements Propose Funds

In 1981, Hobby proposed a new constitutional fund for construction—a Higher Education Available Fund, similar to the Available University Fund, which is created by the income from the Permanent University Fund. President Frank Vandiver wrote in May 1981 to Hobby suggesting that its scope be enlarged to allow financing of repair and rehabilitation of buildings and to give the universities "the option to plow these funds into their academic programs, rather than build edifices. . . by adding the authorization and otherwise enhancing the institutional programs. . . ."[14] The NTSU fiscal vice president, Eddie J. Davis, encouraged Vandiver in this move, estimating that North Texas could gain somewhere between $50 and $100 million in a ten-year period. He told Vandiver that "with the appropriate flexibility as proposed in your letter to Bill Hobby, this could be the most valuable financial decision ever made for North Texas State University."[15]

The Hobby proposal got nowhere in the 1981 legislature but reappeared early in 1982 as a proposal by Governor Bill Clements. The NTSU regents and Hurley endorsed the concept of a fund from general revenue of at least $80 million a year with legislative discretion to increase this fund, approval of construction to come either from the Coordinating Board or the legislature but not both, issuance of bonds backed by the fund, and expenditure of the proceeds for purchase of land, repair and rehabilitation of existing buildings, new construction, purchase of equipment, and purchase of library books and equipment. The North Texas proposal also asked for "support of excellence in educational programs." Hurley also urged insurance "that proceeds from this fund do not act as a substitute for appropriations that currently exist."[16]

The Council of Presidents Endorsement

The Council of Presidents of the Public Senior Colleges and Universities of Texas voted unanimously in September 1982 to ask that the constitution be amended to provide for a dedicated annual appropriation from general revenue to the non-PUF schools excluding junior colleges to be allocated by "an equitable formula." Each university could sell bonds for at least a ten-year bonding period; individual boards should exercise control over their portion.

The Permanent University Fund should be expanded to include all components of the University of Texas and Texas A&M Systems, some of which had been receiving funds from the constitutional ad valorem tax fund.[17]

The Legislative Response

The 1983 legislature overwhelmingly approved a proposed amendment that would create a $2 billion endowed fund for the twenty-six state universities outside of PUF. After a strong campaign by the institutions with the support of the Coordinating Board, the amendment received a seventy-two percent approval in the election.[18] The task from then on was for continued negotiation with the legislature for fund allocation and with the Coordinating Board for approval of construction projects using these funds.

Prop 2 at NTSU

Proposition 2 helped North Texas attain goals that had been out of reach with the dedicated ad valorem tax funds, which could be used solely for the construction and original equipping of buildings. Here is a summary of the allocations of Higher Education Assistance funds (HEAF) at NTSU in millions of dollars over the first five fiscal years:

	FY 1986	FY 1987	FY 1988	FY 1989	FY 1990
Bond payment	0	2.268	2.210	2.234	2.255
Repair/renovat	4.429	9.617	3.277	3.558	4.35
Instr Equipment	4.249	4.459	3.73	3.73	3.15
Library Mater	1.364	1.379	1.39	1.393	1.677
Admin.Equipm	1.352	.823	.5	.65	.41
Computing	1.6	.764	.7	.7	.8
Contingencies	2.382	.7	0	.250	.245
TOTALS	14.950	20.01	11.807	12.515	12.887

Barriers to Campus Development

NTSU still had on hand a fair balance of ad valorem bond funds, but the Coordinating Board took on a new watchdog role, challenging the need for further construction. This attitude reached its strongest point during the early years of Hurley's administration. The board commissioned two studies that reinforced this attitude and greatly influenced the course of development at North Texas. One was a study of space needs on Texas campuses, the other a study of the condition of existing campus facilities.

The Coordinating Board Space Study

A panel of eight consultants from out-of-state universities analyzed data on Texas higher education facilities. Their report in April 1980 led the board to discourage (and disapprove) a great deal of university construction in the 1980s. The panel's study paper argued that most space needs could be met with more efficient use of existing facilities. Even when specialized space was needed, the panel recommended conversion of underused space.[19]

In February 1980, the NTSU Board of Regents authorized Phase I of a Science Research Building for $3.5 million.[20] It was July 1981 before the Coordinating Board authorized only a 30,000 square foot facility, half of what was planned. The university was also denied permission to construct a University Services Building at Fouts Field. Hurley and Provost David Golden continued to write justifications for the full research facilities. It took action in the legislature to accomplish this. After a bill to cover construction and renovation died in the 1981 legislative session, a special session in May 1982 approved Phase II of the research building and the services building, the money to come from ad valorem tax reserves.[21] The attorney general ruled that Coordinating Board approval was not required for these. Finally, a bid was awarded on February 4, 1983, for $5.2 million for a two-story, 60,000-square-foot Science Research Building. This was later altered by change orders to $6.2 million. Regents authorized additional research equipment and increased the project budget to $8 million on May 25, 1984.

The regents in July 1981 authorized $1.5 million to complete the fifth floor of the General Academic Building, which had been left uncompleted. This was to become the new home of the central processing equipment for the Computing Center. The Coordinating Board approved a project budget of $4,175,000 in October 1981 from ad valorem tax funds.[22] An additional $550,000 was subsequently added in order to provide two central processing units: one for academic use and one for administrative.[23]

Enter Page Southerland Page

The other state study dominated a great deal of capital funding decision-making in the next decade on every Texas campus. This was the building quality survey by Page Southerland Page of Austin, commissioned by the 1981 legislature and reported in October 1983. This reported that twenty-five Texas public colleges and universities needed $301 million in building repairs, including about $63.5 million just to meet fire and life safety codes. The consultants found that Texas Tech needed the most for repairs, about $46 million, and NTSU the next most, about $38 million. The survey did not include the University of Texas at Austin or Texas A&M University's main campus at College Station.[24]

The Coordinating Board moved quickly to establish a policy of giving priorities to renovations that followed the building quality survey.[25] The Coordinating Board would also deny any new construction project "that would increase space that generates state funding for operation and maintenance. . . unless the same amount of space is removed for purposes of formula funding."[26]

Renovation Becomes the Byword

The first response of North Texas and other universities was to include renovation costs to meet Page Southerland Page quality goals in biennial appropriations requests. The presidents' council recommended an initial dedicated annual appropriation amount of $60 million to meet the major repair and rehabilitation needs of twenty-three state-supported institutions.[27]

HEAF Money Goes for Remodeling

For the decade starting in 1986, the Page Southerland Page recommendations would dominate the building activity on the North Texas campus.[28] In the first five years, major renovations included the following:

1986 Add quantity food production laboratory in College Inn for hotel and restaurant management program, $260,000.

Renovate and enlarge Terrill Hall for psychology, others, $2.9 million,

1988 Upgrade and expand Power Plant, $1.8 million.

1989 Renovate and expand Chilton Hall for School of Community Service and others, $7.8 million.

Renovate Matthews Hall (Education-Home Economics Building, no longer home economics), $1.9 million.

Board approved renovation of TWU building, Bralley Annex, for $500,000 to serve as remote library storage for NT.

Construct addition to McConnell Hall to increase housing capacity for Texas Academy of Mathematics and Science, $3 million.

1990	Renovate Women's Gymnasium, $1.6 million.
	Renovate Historical Building (once the Library, Museum) for business administration, $2 million.
	Remodel Oak Street Hall (former dormitory) for art facilities, $1.65 million.
	Replace Clark Hall plumbing, $240,000.
1991	Upgrade Bruce Hall electrical system, $238,450.
	Remodel Journalism Building as a clothing and costume design facility, $928,000.
	Renovate Willis Library, $2.7 million.
1992	Repair Music Building roof, $349,000.
	Renovate Men's Gymnasium, $2 million.
	Renovate Auditorium Building, $1.48 million.
	Complete installation of fiber optic communication network among campus buildings, $593,000.
1993	Install sprinkler system in Kerr Hall, $779,250.
1994	Renovate Biology and Chemistry Buildings, $4.47 million.

Renaming the Renovated Buildings

Renovation of several buildings made their names obsolete. A policy was adopted to name such structures for former academic deans, in this case those first named when schools and colleges were created in 1946. Thus the Historical Building became Curry Hall, for Dr. O. J. Curry, business administration; the Journalism Building, Scoular Hall, for Dr. Florence I. Scoular, home economics; Quad 1, Bain Hall, for Dr. Wilfred Bain, music; Women's Gymnasium, Stovall Hall, for Dr. Floyd Stovall, arts and sciences.

At the same time, the Men's Building (former laboratory school) became the Music Annex and the Pupil Appraisal Center became Matthews Hall Annex.

Bringing in Private Partners

With inadequate funds available, the university arranged for private investors to build and operate service facilities on campus. Two such ventures were a hotel on the golf course and a parking garage at the eastern campus entry point across the street from the University Union.

The Board of Regents had turned down President Nolen's proposal for a golf-course hotel back in 1977. However, in July 1983, the board approved the lease of approximately five acres of land on the NTSU Golf Course to the Sumner, Greener, Fussell Group for the construction of a Sheraton Hotel at no cost to the university. The remainder of the golf course land was leased to the same group to operate, manage, and maintain the course. The agreement also provided office space in the conference center for the Professional Development Institute.[29]

In 1985, regents approved a contract to lease land to Stone and Teague Joint Venture for constructing a three-story parking garage and lot at no cost to NTSU. The university was to operate the facility, which would occupy the site of the former Sam Houston Elementary School. The original agreement called for demolition of the newer part of the Sam Houston structure, which had been converted to the College of Education's Pupil Appraisal Center. After much protest from center supporters, the size of the parking garage was scaled back and the center building remained.[30] Regents subsequently leased to Stone and Teague land for three parking lots to be upgraded, the costs to be amortized from revenues from metered parking spaces.[31]

Original investors for the two ventures experienced financial difficulties and other companies took over and continued operations. The hotel became a Radisson Hotel.

Other Partnerships

Fouts Field needed extensive improvement and the Denton Independent School District wanted a larger and better athletic site for its athletic activities. In January 1986, the Board of Regents made a ten-year contract with the school district to use Fouts Field, for which the schools would pay $500,000. The university would place artificial turf on the field and improve the seating.[32] The Coordinating Board had earlier approved the new artificial playing surface, to cost $1.2 million from auxiliary enterprise funds.[33]

Adequate housing for social fraternities and sororities had long been a problem. Sororities had occupied Chilton Hall and then the dormitory on Avenue D, the College Inn. In 1985, however, the university bought the inn from Bass Brothers Enterprises of Fort Worth, paying $3 million plus closing costs for property, appraised at $4.75 million. The purchase would be paid for totally by income from room rentals.[34] The next step was to try to help fraternities to build their own housing units on land leased from North Texas. The land selected was a block on the southeast corner of the campus, one that had been designated in the first campus plan for university dormitories. After the university and sororities could not agree on terms in 1986, the Interfraternity Council approved a plan for fraternities to lease the land. Sororities could do the same if they later desired.[35]

Tackling the Library Problem

Since 1972, the problem of building Phases 2 and 3 of the Library Building had faced administrators. The ad valorem tax fund had been expected in 1972 and in 1978 to finance the library construction, at first listed by the Board of Regents as the number-one priority. But inaction left the project dangling until that fund source was abolished. Equally damaging was the Coordinating Board policy against new construction. In 1989, the university had turned to renting remote library space in the Bralley Annex at TWU, but this did not prove satisfactory.

On August 27, 1993, the Board of Regents selected an architect to design an addition to the Willis Library. However, just a few months later, the course was changed. It was decided to buy a vacant factory in an industrial district on the road to the Denton airport in far west Denton. The board voted to buy the Kolmar Building on December 3, 1993. For its next meeting, Vice Presidents Fred Pole, Blaine Brownell, and Phillip C. Diebel proposed selection of an architect to renovate the two existing libraries, Willis and Science Technology, at a cost of $3 million, and to design renovations at the Kolmar Building.[36] The vice presidents' proposal as approved by Hurley said the move would eliminate the near-term need for expanding the Willis Library. They said "purchase of the Kolmar Building has avoided adding expense to the state at this time by not having to build a far more expensive facility for library storage and staff functions."[37] The cost of adapting the factory building to library use was $1.5 million, plus another $144,494 for repair of a leaking roof.[38] Thus, the near-term library solutions cost about $4.5 million.

Another Street-Closing Effort

Early in his administration, Chancellor Hurley attempted to tackle the remaining problems created by penetration of city streets into or through the main campus area. He had become involved in these problems because of his responsibilities as administrative vice president. There was no immediate result, but Hurley's 1982 letter to the city manager is of considerable historical interest:

About two years ago members of our staffs discussed informally a proposal for us to accept the streets forming a horseshoe near the Union Building. Their consensus was that it was a good idea. I agree but feel there are other streets that would also be mutually beneficial if they were deeded to us.

Accordingly, I recommend the city grant us a quitclaim deed for the following streets:
West Mulberry from Avenue A [*sic*, should be B] to Avenue C
Avenue B from West Mulberry to West Hickory
West Prairie from Welch to Avenue A
Avenue A from West Prairie to Chestnut
Chestnut from Avenue A to Welch
Highland from Central to Avenue C
Avenue A from Maple to Highland
Avenue B from Eagle to Maple

These streets are all internal to the campus. The only two parcels of private property adjoining these streets are the Baptist Student Center at the corner of Prairie and Avenue A and the University Ministry Center at Maple and Avenue B. These streets are not required as a part of the thoroughfare system of the city and carry a very limited amount of traffic other than directly university related.[39]

1986: IT MAKES 1985 LOOK GOOD

Comptroller Bob Bullock in February 1986 said that Texas tax income would be $1.3 billion less than he had projected when the appropriations bill was passed the previous year. This was caused by a drop of oil prices from $31.80 a barrel in November to the $15 range in mid-February.

Executive Order Directs Budget Cuts

Gov. Mark White on February 18 directed all state agencies and universities to cut their two-year budgets by thirteen percent. He gave agency heads two weeks to outline their proposed budget cuts that should be made without laying off employees, halting essential services, or cutting a scheduled three percent pay raise for state workers. Only the legislature could alter appropriations amounts, but Hobby and Speaker Gib Lewis supported the order. The governor said that self-imposed austerity measures would enable legislative action to await the regular session in January 1987.[40]

White's order asked all agencies and universities to reduce spending and impose a hiring freeze. White said he did not intend for the freeze to apply to university faculties.

> The executive order calls for a hiring freeze at state agencies and prohibits most promotions and merit pay raises, forbids new professional and personal service contracts and the purchase of non-essential supplies. Out-of-state travel would be allowed only if approved by the head of the agency, and in-state travel should be reduced by 20 percent.
>
> It also requires officials to review and renegotiate existing contracts, defer building construction and renovation except for prisons and other critical areas, and conserve utility costs by reviewing the operation of all. . . equipment. . . .
>
> Asked where in higher education, for example, the state could reduce spending, White said, "The state of Texas, without reducing its thrust in higher education, might be in a position to reassess the fact that we have the second-highest administrator-to-faculty ratio of any university in the country. Maybe there is where we start."[41]

Reaction to the Executive Order

In public, at least, most agency heads pledged full cooperation with the governor's request. The chairman of the Coordinating Board, Larry Temple, acknowledged the "unpleasant fact of life" that there would have to be some reductions in expenditures. Lt. Gov. Hobby argued that the cuts should be directed "at less essential programs so that critical human services can be maintained at or near the current level."[42] Gary Hughes, executive director of the Texas Public Employees Association, accused the governor of "talking out of two sides of his mouth." Hughes said, "It will cut state services, and it will cause employees to be laid off.[43]

A staff paper from Comptroller Bob Bullock's office said that the governor's plan would save no more than $300 million rather than $1.3 billion. Whereas White had announced that $10.2 billion of the current state budget was available for cutting, the comptroller's staff report said that only $4.2 billion was available, a figure that would require a thirty-one percent reduction to prevent the deficit.[44]

Moratoriums From the Coordinating Board

In March 1986 Chancellor Hurley received a letter from Commissioner Ken Ashworth notifying him that "I have decided that the most appropriate course of action is for us to delay board consideration" for the time being of any requests either for new programs or for administrative changes. The only exception would be if the university could demonstrate "unquestionable savings" or could show that it had new funds to pay for the change "at the same time it is trying to reduce overall general appropriations expenditures by 13%."[45]

On April 25 the board resolved:

> The Coordinating Board will limit consideration of new construction of educational and general space only to projects clearly justified as critically and demonstrably essential to protecting the existing educational or research role of the institution. This policy will remain in effect until the Select Committee on Higher Education has made its report to the Legislature, and the Governor and the Legislature have had an opportunity to address the financial condition of the state and higher education.[46]

SPECIAL SESSION TO THE RESCUE

On July 25 White called a thirty-day special session of the legislature to begin August 6 to make cuts in the state budget. It was reported that the deficit was expected to reach $3.5 billion by August 31, 1987. Speculation arose on the possibility of action to create new taxes, establish a state lottery, or allow gambling in the state.[47]

It Takes Two to Tangle

The thirty-day session started August 6, 1986, and the house and senate adjourned at noon September 4 with house members voting to cut spending by $740 million and senators agreeing on a figure of $418 million. The governor, lieutenant governor, and the senate favored a tax bill, but this was blocked on the house side by Speaker Gib Lewis. Within less than an hour after adjournment, Governor White called a second special session.[48]

The second session took a bit less than its thirty days to produce an appropriations bill that reduced spending and a temporary tax bill, effective January 1 to August 31,1987, raising the sales tax by 1⅛ cents to a total of 5 ¼ cents on the dollar, and the motor fuels tax by a nickel to fifteen cents a gallon on gasoline and diesel fuel. Most of the budget cuts were placed on higher education, a fact rued by Lieutenant Governor Hobby, who said it would take years for universities to recover from these cuts.[49] Governor White put a much rosier outlook on the proceedings, declaring "We have assured funding for essential state services and, above all, reaffirmed our commitment to educational excellence."[50]

Not So Fast, Governor

A different view is found in an Associated Press story run in the *Dallas Morning News* at the end of October:

> Texas is one of only five states that cut higher education appropriations for this school year and ranks next-to-last in how well it treated colleges and universities compared with two years ago.
>
> These were among the findings in an annual survey published Wednesday in the *Chronicle of Higher Education*.
>
> Higher education leaders in Texas said the survey underreported the state's appropriations and they cautioned that the diverse funding methods among the states can make comparisons difficult, if not impossible.
>
> But they did not dispute that the state has one of the poorest showings in the degree to which support for higher education has increased or decreased since 1984.
>
> "I don't think there is any question that Texas is at the bottom in terms of support for higher education," said Kenneth Ashworth, Texas commissioner of higher education.

Hobby continued to advocate more funds for Texas higher education. In mid-October, he pointed out that some forty percent of the more than $500 million in budget cuts made by the two special sessions came at the expense of higher education.[51] Hobby referred to a survey reported by the Coordinating Board:

> Survey results show 217 faculty resignations were reported by mid-July before the full extent of the fiscal crisis was known. At least 220 prospective faculty members declined offers from Texas universities. . . .
>
> Reasons cited for resignations and refusals included higher salaries at out-of-state institutions, ranging from $4,000 to $10,000 depend-

ing on the file. Other reasons included better fringe benefits, greater research support, lower teaching loads, fear that Texas will not support higher education, and general economic conditions of the state. Another reason given for resignations was that starting salaries for new faculty often exceed that of faculty with years of service to the state.

Of those resigning many faculty took positions in major public and private universities in other states. Very few moved to other Texas universities. Some accepted positions in industry or government.[52]

SURVIVING AT NTSU

The special session appropriations action cut deeply into the annual NTSU budget that had been planned. North Texas had avoided "severe layoffs of faculty and staff. . . by using up virtually all our reserve dollars drawn from earnings in housing, food service, and the Union," Hurley later told the faculty.[53] Without additional reserves, NTSU faced almost certain layoffs unless the 1987 appropriations act at least equaled the amount of the supplemented 1987 budget.

The 1987 Session: Another Deadlock

The five-month regular session in January 1987 faced a $1 billion deficit left hanging by the special session and would have a fresh deficit of between $5 billion and $7 billion to cover. Furthermore, the temporary tax cut would expire before the next appropriations biennium got started.[54] And once again a Republican governor, Bill Clements, was in office and talking strongly against new taxes. An added significant influence would be the Select Committee on Higher Education, which released its final report on February 25.[55] (The Committee's work is discussed more fully in Chapter 40.)

Higher education would be the major center of interest before the lawmakers. And North Texas State University had a highly individual center of interest in one bill—the one that proposed to change the name of the institution to the University of North Texas.

Governor vs. Lieutenant Governor

From January to May the legislative budget struggles looked pretty much like those of the 1986 special sessions. The governor had repeatedly announced that he would be calling a special session. It was agreed in news reports that this was inevitable because legislators "have given up in their efforts to pass a balanced state budget for the next biennium."[56] A rift between the governor and lieutenant governor became worse, aggravated especially by proposals for permanent extension of the sales and gasoline tax increases.

Once Again: a Special Session

As expected, the 70th Legislature became the third in modern history to fail to pass a biennial appropriation in regular session. As expected, one day before adjournment, Clements on May 30 called a special session, to begin June 22. His call was accompanied by a public plea for constituents to voice no-tax sentiments to their lawmakers during the three-week recess.[57] Hobby outlined the need for keeping the state competitive for new industry and staying in the current race to be the site of a supercollider. Of higher education Hobby said that faculty salaries had fallen to nine percent below the national average, making faculty flight to other states a major problem. [58]

Starting on June 22, the house, the senate, and the governor again went on divergent paths, with the senate providing the most money in the budget and the governor still fighting to hold down taxes. But on July 15 a two-hour private session broke the deadlock. The governor, lieutenant governor, and speaker of the house agreed on a $38.1 billion budget that would require a $5.7 billion state tax hike and an average 3.5 percent increase in school district property taxes. The budget agreed on by Hobby and Lewis provided $1 billion less than the spending plan passed in the senate and $180 million less than that in the house. For higher education, Hobby and Lewis had agreed to give universities $500 million more than they currently received; at Clements' insistence, this was reduced to $430 million.[59]

At the Bottom of the Nation

In national terms, the downward slide was not over. In 1984 the Texas per-capita higher education appropriations was $145.15, sixth in the nation. But by 1990 that figure had risen only to $154.45, and the rank had slid to twenty-fourth. The picture looked even worse when the dollar change and the percentage change in per capita appropriations was calculated—in 1990 Texas ranked forty-seventh in dollar difference and forty-eighth in percentage change.[60]

Hurley Upbeat With Faculty

At the annual fall convocation, Hurley was decidedly upbeat, saying that "we have emerged from a year-long struggle in better shape than many. . . had anticipated." The senator in whose district Denton was located, Bob Glasgow, drew praise as the North Texas "champion." Hurley also saluted the "unwavering leadership" of Hobby and the constant involvement of former board chairman Wayne Stockseth and other board members.

Hurley said that not only had severe layoffs in faculty and staff been avoided, but the legislature had provided more funds, including a five percent pool for merit increases in FY 1988 and eight percent for FY 1989. This round, he asserted, "went to those of us who believe that education is the key to that future."[61]

Evolution of a New Name

The need for yet another name for North Texas resurfaced in August 1982 in the report of the Committee on Organization, which wrote, "The University should consider adopting a name which more nearly reflects its stature among other institutions of higher education."[62] The struggle for appropriations and for recognition from the Select Committee made the strategy appealing. Hurley brought the question before an executive session of the board in August 1986. He then wrote three board members:

> During the executive session of the Board meeting last Friday, I asked the members present to consider our looking into the possibility of a name change for NTSU.
>
> During my six years here, alums and friends of the University have argued to me that NTSU has developed to the point where the word "State" in its title does not properly describe our role as a significant graduate and research institution. For example, Robert Dedman of Dallas, the head of Club Corporation of America, has argued to me that NT should consider such a change for marketing purposes.
>
> The members present last Friday agreed to my floating a trial balloon by asking our University Planning Council to study the possibility. You may be sure that, within five minutes after the Council finishes its meeting, the whole world will know that we are considering the possibility of a name change. I should have enough feedback for you by the time of our November meeting to make a recommendation to you in this matter.[63]

When that trial balloon went to the University Planning Council and emerged into public view, support was far from unanimous among students, faculty, and alumni. The Faculty Senate heard a report in October 1986, that the University Planning Council had voted on "a motion to recommend changing the name of North Texas State University to the University of North Texas," with 7 for, 5 against, and 1 abstention.[64] But otherwise, the trial balloon didn't draw as much attention as predicted. Hurley wrote board members in December 1986 that the *North Texas Daily* had finally come out with an editorial, leading the chancellor to comment that "To my surprise, I had to leak it more than once, but the student leadership is now heavily in favor of the idea. There has been very little feedback so far from the faculty or staff."[65] A surprisingly lukewarm, almost completely negative, viewpoint came from an editorial in the *Denton Record-Chronicle* in February 1987, just before the proposal came before the regents. It commented in part:

> An institution of higher education builds on its reputation and its alumni. Therefore, changing its name is a major matter. It should not be done lightly, and it should be done for very sound reasons.
>
> Friday the regents of North Texas State University will consider endorsing a change in the name to the University of North Texas. The proposed designation of the university by the state as an emerging national research institution has prompted the proposal, according to the university.
>
> NTSU has had a Rodney Dangerfield complex for a long time—like the comic, the university thinks it "don't get no respect."
>
> . . . . Whether a change of name would give NTSU the respect it deserves, and whether or not the loss of the identity and alumni affection for the name NTSU would be offset thereby are major questions. . . .
>
> Changing the name also would be very expensive, at a time when universities are hurting financially. . . .
>
> If the proposal gains some attention to the university and some statewide discussion about it, so much the better. However, the value of actually making the change does not seem to be worth the losses involved at this time.[66]

The proposal on the board agenda sheets referred to six names for the institution, saying that:

> Each of the names appropriately reflected the role and scope of the institution at the time of its designation. The recent action of the Select Committee on Higher Education in recommending the designation of North Texas State University as an "emerging national research institution" recognizes a new stage in the evolution of this University. In order to reflect more accurately the expanded role and scope of this institution, whose service to this region has vastly increased, it is appropriate to act to change its name to University of North Texas.[67]

The Board approved 9–0. Soon thereafter the *Fort Worth Star-Telegram* editorial page joined the approval parade:

> The name has a nice ring to it—the University of North Texas. . . . The proposed new name for the university does have a certain flavor that connotes prestige befitting its impending designation as a graduate-research university with a state and national scope. North Texas has, indeed, come a long way since its last name change from North Texas State College in 1961. At that time, it had only 8,100 students. The university now has 21,000 students and boasts a broad complement of doctoral programs. What has happened is that North Texas has simply outgrown another name.[68]

The matter was introduced in the legislature and emerged successfully as Senate Bill 84. On the last day of the regular session, the legislature sent the bill to the governor. The occasion of the signing of the bill was used to emphasize the position of the university, as reported in the *Dallas Times Herald*:

> It's official: In May, North Texas State University in Denton will change its name for the seventh time in 98 years to become the University of North Texas.
>
> Gov. Bill Clements ceremoniously signed the bill into law Tuesday. The name change becomes effective May 15, 1988.

The new name is an attempt by educators to raise the university to another class, one of more stature intended to generate more research funding. NTSU, with 200 graduate and 100 undergraduate programs, is gaining research clout and deserves a name to represent the change, said Chancellor Alfred Hurley.

"We're in a very competitive economic battle to get outside dollars," said Wayne Stockseth, chairman of the university's Board of Regents. "In general, the perception of the public and the people that grant the dollars is that the big-name universities that you think of generating a lot of research money begin with the word 'university'."[69]

FORWARD UNDER A NEW NAME

On May 15, 1988, North Texas State University would become the University of North Texas. The campaign to enhance the reputation and gain greater support would be keyed to that name change and to the designation of North Texas as an emerging national research university. The chancellor told the 1987 faculty meeting:

> It will be my objective to continue to bring here representatives of every significant community between the Red River and the southern edge of the counties making up the Metroplex. The scheduled visit here in November of the Board of Directors of the Fort Worth Chamber of Commerce is but one example of this work which already has involved ten communities. The purpose of these visits is two-fold:
>
> —To permit these visitors to see first hand all that is being accomplished here so as to raise their comfort level as taxpayers about their new investment in education *and*
>
> —To prompt them to adopt this institution as their university (in keeping with all that our new name is intended to convey to everyone in this region).
>
> To carry out this work, we will be calling on more and more of you to lend a hand or to give us your ideas and suggestions.[70]

Renewing the Lease

Hurley then asked the meeting to permit him to sound a very personal note: he announced that he had just notified the Board of Regents that he would exercise his option to extend his contract with the board for five more years beginning in February 1988. This came from his public commitment in 1982 to serve here for at least ten years to help give the university "the stability it so clearly lacked at the beginning of this decade." Further, he told the faculty that the decision also reflected the immense satisfaction that he and his wife had received from being part of "this very special place." It stemmed, too, he said, from "our admiration for all that you so often do out of a sense of professionalism that goes far beyond any possibility of a material reward."

Perhaps the most important factor in his decision to extend his term for five years was the factor that brought the Hurleys here and that also kept them here: "our continuing sense of the potential of this place."

A Transition to Full Recognition

The chancellor concluded his report to the faculty with this summation of the progress made by the university:

> North Texas State University, soon to be the University of North Texas, is now well into its transition from obscurity and limited support to full recognition and proper support.
>
> —With your continued help and your unfailing good ideas that have included this year the Center for Information Sciences Research in the College of Business; the new NTSU Press; the joint venture with SMU in neuro-science, the Gerontology Assessment Program, the Classic Learning Core Program for non-traditional students, and many other marvelous ideas.
>
> —With the continued flexibility on the part of this institution that has brought the Boeing Electronics plant to Corinth and helped us to take the lead in Texas higher education by creating the Texas Academy of Mathematics and Sciences.
>
> —With our continued determination to raise admission and performance standards that have led to a decided improvement in student quality (while we keep an eye on demographic changes that could dramatically affect every university in the State by the year 2000).
>
> —With continued growth in external fund-raising that has seen this support increase to more than $2 million this year compared to the $300,000 we recorded for 1982.

—With continued advances in research funding that have brought us from $4 million two years ago to $10 million this year, not to overlook the major opportunity held out to us by gigantic, new improvements in this state's moral and financial support for research,

—And, with a little luck

All of us *together* will help this university complete its transition very soon to full recognition and proper support.[71]

chapter 43

Echoes of Perot: Reform Higher Education

There is no more critical issue that will go before the Legislature in the upcoming session than that of reforming this state's hodgepodge system of higher education.

Not only is the system lurching forward without clear-cut goals or a vision for the future, it also is inextricably linked to the economic fortunes of the state and unduly driven by politics.

The good news is that somebody has noticed. The Legislature last year created the Select Committee on Higher Education to take a comprehensive look at the state's public colleges and universities. . . .

The select committee is expected to ask the Legislature to reduce the number of governing boards. . . from 15 to five, and to group the colleges and universities into five systems based loosely on academic missions.

Carolyn Barta
Dallas Morning News, January 5, 1987

After battling the impacts of the declining state economy, legislators and leaders in the executive branch sought revolutionary changes in Texas higher education. They were mindful of the two-year-old example of the Select Committee on Public Education, more commonly known as the Perot Commission, and the drastic legislative changes that it produced. These were popular views: Texas has too many campuses with too many degree programs; our resources are spread too thin and quality is suffering; colleges and universities are not efficiently managed; we need to find ways to reduce costs. There were, typically, calls to abolish some campuses and to merge others. And as had happened many times in the past, fingers were pointed at Denton as the model of program duplication with "two state universities a mile apart."[1]

CREATING THE SELECT COMMITTEE

The hectic 1985 legislature created the Select Committee on Higher Education. House Concurrent Resolution No. 105 created a special interim committee to "make a comprehensive study of all issues and concerns relating to higher education in Texas, covering all components of the higher education system, including junior colleges." Subjects of the study were to include "financing, cost-effective alternatives to maintaining the higher education system, curriculum requirements, [degree] programs, and technology." Emphasis was to be placed on "long-term enrollment projections; the distribution, production, and excellence of academic programs; projected appropriations; and the projected needs for higher education programs, research, and facilities in Texas."

Members of the committee were the governor, lieutenant governor, speaker of the house, chairmen of the senate and the house education committees, five members appointed by the governor, four by the lieutenant governor, four by the house speaker, and the chairman of the Coordinating Board. The governor was designated the chairman but was authorized to appoint someone to carry out that function on his behalf. As the bill moved toward passage, Governor White gave his directions to the committee, repeating his call to eliminate duplication of education services and create "centers of excellence" instead.

A Dual Chairmanship

As chairman of the select committee White named Larry Temple of Austin, the chairman of the Coordinating Board. His public statements upon appointment featured a quotation, "I don't think there's anything sacred," indicating that no area of higher education would be off limits to the committee.[2]

Some were reminded of Governor Connally's Committee on Education Beyond the High School, whose work led to the creation of the Coordinating Board in 1965. Dick Cory, the sponsor of the bill that launched the Coordinating Board, criticized the board for allowing new programs to multiply like rabbits. As evidence, Cory cited the growth from twenty state universities to thirty-nine, approval of 1,100 new degree programs with only seventy-seven disapproved, and vetoing of only $116.5 million worth of construction while approving $629.4 million.[3]

The feeling was strong that the Coordinating Board must be strengthened and given more responsibility and authority. The committee itself wrote of the magnitude of the tasks it had been given:

> We find that public higher education in Texas is a massive enterprise—37 universities, 449 community colleges, 4 technical institutes and 8 medical and health-related institutions. Those 98 institutions are housed in a $7 billion investment in physical plant. Sixteen boards of regents and 49 boards of trustees govern the system, which includes 830,000 students, faculty and staff. It costs almost $4.5 billion annually to operate. Out of economic necessity we must find a better way to manage the entire enterprise more effectively and efficiently.[4]

Executive director for the committee was Victor Arnold, director of the Bureau of Business Research at the University of Texas in Austin. Arnold, who took a leave of absence from his university post, had served from 1979 to 1982 as director of Texas 2000, a state commission looking at the state's future.[5]

Select Committee Tasks Debated

Government leaders and committee members offered more reasons for a university to be fearful than for it to look toward an improved future. This was intended to be "a hard look at higher education in Texas." Chairman Temple promised there would be "no sacred cows" in streamlining and improving the universities and colleges.

Legislative comments suggested that campuses might have become "glorified high-class trade schools" that produced qualified workers but not a well-rounded education. Others suggested that, to the contrary, some college programs were irrelevant to the state job market. Others attacked the overemphasis on intercollegiate athletics. A popular question: which campuses could be closed and which could be merged in the name of efficiency? Which universities have too many degree programs and which are trying to develop too wide a scope and too many doctoral programs and professional schools? Spokesmen from large cities thought there were too many campuses in predominantly rural areas, inviting the closing of a number of them and redevelopment of metropolitan campuses. A ground swell was developing in South Texas, especially among Hispanic organizations, who would soon be seeking university systems, law schools, and medical schools in "deprived" sections of the state.[6]

An editorial in the *Fort Worth Star-Telegram* prepared its own set of key questions, asking if it is wasteful "to have two competing universities (competing for students and competing for funds) in the same city, almost within a stone's throw of each other, as is true in Denton and Houston?" and are fundamental changes needed in the Coordinating Board?[7]

FINDING A PLACE FOR NTSU

In this turbulent environment, NTSU confronted its own set of basic threats:

1. Will NTSU be combined with a number of other universities and have to give up its own independent Board of Regents? Will it have to merge with TWU?

2. Will concern over degree proliferation threaten its graduate programs, especially doctorates?

3. Will state support be shifted to other campuses in Dallas-Fort Worth, diminishing the dominant role that NTSU was in the process of staking out for itself?

4. Can NTSU show an important role in serving the burgeoning minority population in the metropolitan area and state?

The Urban University Strategy

Larry Temple invited Chancellor Hurley to submit comments on higher education needs and information that would help the committee. Hurley responded in January 1986 with a four-page single-spaced statement. This repeated the call for separate consideration of the North Texas region, recognizing increasing collaboration among universities and among higher education, business, and government. Specifically, he argued that NTSU was the most comprehensive institution in the region with an extraordinarily high level of graduate education and direct ties to a medical school partner. He pointed out that North Texas had become an urban university drawing most of its 21,000 students from the area.[8]

What Kinds of Systems?

The select committee held public hearings throughout the state, bringing out many proposals for the role and scope of universities in each area and for what kind of governing board should control them.

On May 9, 1986, the committee employed Coopers & Lybrand to conduct a $400,000 management audit of Texas higher education. The contract called for the accounting firm to examine the efficiency and cost effectiveness of the fifteen separate boards of regents that governed thirty-seven state-supported colleges and universities.[9] The Coopers & Lybrand report in November 1986 called for the grouping of higher education units into five categories: major research and teaching universities, limited scope doctoral universities, baccalaureate teaching universities, health study institutions, and community and technical colleges.[10]

THE ETERNAL PROPOSAL: NTSU/TWU

It is hard to maintain an accurate count of all proposals that have been made over the decades to merge North Texas and TWU. A new dimension to the merger movement this time around was added by the South Texas movement for more higher education facilities for Mexican-American citizens. In October 1985, Corpus Christi attorney Ruben Bonilla, chairman of the Mexican American Democrats of Texas, urged creation of regional university systems and specifically asked to combine the two Denton schools.[11]

Temple also told reporters in November that a former NTSU regent told him, "I might not have said this when I was on the board, but you're right on target." Temple acknowledged that was an exception to what he had been hearing.[12] An editorial in the Austin paper suggested considering that NTSU and TWU become one institution with a new name.[13]

TWU Takes the Lead in Protesting

One of Al Hurley's first actions upon becoming president was to call on Dr. Mary Evelyn Huey, the former NT faculty member who was president of TWU.

At that time, he told her, he knew of no individual—board, administration, or faculty—at NTSU who had any desire to merge with TWU or to bring TWU into a tighter formal alignment with North Texas.[14]

Speaker Gib Lewis raised the possibility of an NTSU-TWU merger. The Fort Worth paper received an adamant "no" from Huey, when a reporter asked, "Is it too expensive for a state that expects a $1 billion deficit to pay for two separate universities located about a mile apart in Denton?" She said a merger not only would not save money but would destroy the reputations the schools have built over the years. "We need differences in Texas," she declared.[15] Across town, Hurley declined to discuss the merits or disadvantages of any merger, telling the *Star-Telegram* that "we certainly will do whatever the legislature tells us to do."

Early reaction from Hobby expressed doubt that a merger of Texas Southern and the University of Houston would take place in his home town. He also predicted that the Denton merger would not happen "despite the planned retirement next year of President Huey."[16]

After President Huey retired, the new president, Dr. Shirley Chater, carried on the opposition. At one hearing in October 1986, TWU brought 600 students in a delegation to fill the senate gallery.[17] President Chater said at a November meeting of the select committee, where 1,000 Texas Southern students rallied against merger of its campus with the University of Houston, that TWU decided not to repeat the large delegation to Austin. Instead, she said in a written statement, "We believe that responsibility and accountability can be more quickly and effectively demonstrated by remaining as an autonomous institution providing a unique market niche for women and men."[18] Chater did give the committee a folder with signatures of 6,000 alumnae urging that the school remain open.

NTSU Regents Make a Surprising Counter Offer

Since several governance possibilities listed by the committee in June 1986 involved relocating NTSU into one proposed system or another, the NTSU Board of Regents and the administrations of North Texas and TCOM sent a response to Arnold. It was a radical departure from all previous North Texas policy: a proposal to create a new governing board for all the units of both schools and a chancellor to administer that cluster.

Backed by a unanimous vote from the board, Chairman Wayne O. Stockseth sent a five-page letter plus appendices, explaining why many of the system alignments were unsuitable. He wrote that if both universities, the TWU nursing centers, and TCOM were placed under one board, "one major focus of the new arrangement could be better integrated medical and allied health programs for the North Texas region."[19]

BEYOND A TWU MERGER

Beyond the TWU issue, however, lay an offer in response to proposals for realignment of state universities under various boards of regents. One possibility was to reorganize governance on a regional basis rather than on common programs. The regents' plan was presented this way in Stockseth's letter:

> A logical arrangement would be a Universities of the Metroplex System or a Universities of North Texas System. . . . Such a system would include NTSU, TCOM, TWU, UT-Arlington, UT-Dallas, UT Health Science Center at Dallas, TWU Nursing Center at Dallas, and possibly, East Texas State University. . . .
>
> . . . a new regional system would afford the state through a single governing board the opportunity to reallocate resources, to assist in the further economic development of the largest metropolitan region of the state, and to assure educational quality and access in the region. . . . The NTSU-TCOM Board fully recognizes the political and legal difficulties of this proposal since UT System institutions are involved. Certainly, a prestigious, decisive, and tough-minded governing board would be needed to make this rearrangement work. Nevertheless, we urge the Select Committee to consider this possibility.[20]

At least one influential state organization, the Texas Research League, reacted favorably to the North Texas letter. The league president, Jared E. Hazleton, wrote to Stockseth:

> It is indeed heartening to see one of Texas' major university systems making a rational proposal with regard to organization of the state's higher education system rather than merely defending the status quo.

> Your Board's position is indeed bold, but it appears to me to be an approach with a great deal of merit—and one which should receive serious consideration by the Select Committee.[21]

Not surprisingly, the University of Texas system was not pleased with the North Texas proposal. In a letter to an alumnus, Hurley reported the UT reaction:

> The Chancellor of the System has told me that he and his Board will fight to keep control of The University of Texas at Dallas and at Arlington. I, for one, believe that we have reached the point in the development of the region whereby we must unify our efforts to get the maximum advantage of the strengths of all of the area institutions.[22]

At the November 1986 select committee hearing, Chairman Stockseth delivered "Remarks to the Select Committee on NTSU-TWU Merger." He told the committee that he was missing a regular meeting of the Board of Regents in order to emphasize their desire for a single system for all of higher education in the North Texas region. He told the committee, "Our Board believes so strongly in the merits of this idea that it stands ready to step aside to permit the creation of the new single board."[23] Hurley wrote Temple on the same date as Stockseth's testimony. Referring to that occasion, the chancellor wrote that implementation would take a minimum of five years. [24]

Select Committee: Five Systems

During fall 1986 hearings, committee members were given seven different organizational charts showing ways in which campuses might be combined. Some were based on geography, proposing regional clusters. Others were mission-oriented, attempting to bring together universities of similar degree structures and general purpose. Some included mergers or closing of "problem" schools. Some showed a response to local or area political pressures to "upgrade" the availability of degree programs. Few dared tamper seriously with the two politically entrenched systems of the University of Texas and Texas A&M, although one proposal split off some UT campuses.

In November Temple mailed Select Committee members specific recommendations: merge NTSU and TWU, merge Texas A&I in Kingsville with Corpus Christi State, and merge the University of Houston downtown into

Texas Southern University. He also asked for the creation of four tiers: University of Texas and Texas A&M as comprehensive graduate research universities, the state's undergraduate and master's degree institutions, community colleges and technical schools, and a cluster of comprehensive regional research universities made up of North Texas State, University of Houston, Texas Tech, TWU, and the UT campuses at Arlington, Dallas, San Antonio, and El Paso.[25]

Temple's November plan aroused angry responses from many of the institutions and from communities involved. Governor White stepped in after a week of public controversy, writing to Temple opposition to the Denton and Houston mergers. The governor did say that the Corpus Christi/Kingsville plan might have some potential. The latter proposal divided Kingsville and Corpus Christi backers, but it was seen by many as the means to increase the number of doctoral programs available to South Texas students.[26] Of the A&I merger plan, Attorney Tony Bonilla said it was needed to correct past neglect of the education system in South Texas. "The history of South Texas particularly among Mexican-Americans is one of high unemployment, underemployment, and poverty," he told the Corpus Christi newspaper.[27]

On December 11, as the time drew near for a show-down vote, Temple withdrew the Denton and Houston merger proposals and the committee agreed to create one state-wide comprehensive system of Texas Tech, NTSU, TWU, Texas Southern, University of Houston, and an undesignated school in South Texas. But the next day the committee scrapped that plan and voted to table the Corpus Christi plan and substitute a strengthened Pan American University in Edinburg.[28] The committee voted that same day to realign state-supported universities into five systems.

For North Texas/TCOM, that would mean joining in a "Texas Comprehensive University System of the North and West" with TWU and Texas Tech. A similar comprehensive grouping "of the South and East" would contain four University of Houston campuses, three Lamar University sites, Texas Southern University, and two Pan American University campuses in the Rio Grande Valley. The UT and A&M systems continued their structures, and eleven other four-year campuses were grouped in a "Texas State University System." Each of these systems was to have a twelve-member "super board" of regents instead of the existing nine members, and there would be no boards for any individual schools.

The *Dallas Morning News* reported that this grouping had the approval of the boards of regents of both TWU and NTSU and quoted TWU President Chater as saying that this would help both schools promote further cooperation. Real trouble was foreshadowed, however, when Temple and four legislator-members of the committee voted against the recommendation and a fifth abstained.[29]

Role and Mission Statements

The University of Texas at Austin and Texas A&M University at College Station had the advantage of constitutional designation and legislative backing to be designated major research universities of the state. A lot of political activity was necessary on behalf of any other university that sought to be linked in stature to the top two, and there was much speculation about naming half a dozen or more campuses to the major research designation. Interestingly, Governor White injected himself into the deliberations by writing Temple this position:

> The designation of two statewide comprehensive research universities and a number of regional comprehensive universities is unduly restrictive for those regional institutions with major and rapidly developing programs. The University of Houston, Texas Tech University, and North Texas State University must have access to the resources and support which will further their progress and rise to the first tier. Our major urban centers and West Texas area are equally deserving of prominence.[30]

Earlier, Hobby had also called for recognition of those three universities as suitable candidates for status as major universities. This, of course, supported the repeated personal and written pleas by the NTSU board and chancellor for a major research designation. The Select Committee also had before it a plea from Chairman Stockseth, arguing that NTSU must be included in any organization of comprehensive research and graduate institutions.[31] Also, Hurley wrote Temple to suggest some modification of "points raised in your proposal to the Select Committee" and suggesting that it would be in the best interests of Texas to allow for more than two top-tier universities in the state.[32]

Temple and Arnold had prepared the drafts of a "Charter for Texas Higher Education" being circulated in late November, indicating that the final charter would not include North Texas at the level it sought. Stung somewhat by wide criticism and by comments from the governor and lieutenant governor, Temple told reporters on December 5 that his November proposal had "resulted in a misunderstanding of what I have been saying all along. It's more important that everyone understands what their role and scope should be rather than who is in the first tier and the second tier and so on."[33]

However, on December 8 Hurley wrote to the regents, "Some excellent news: in case your local paper missed the item, the Select Committee decided last Friday to amend the draft Charter for Texas Higher Education to designate North Texas State University, along with Texas Tech and the University of Houston, as 'emerging national research universities.'"[34]

When it was released, the report of the Select Committee introduced five universities with the same phrase: "a comprehensive, graduate research university offering an array of undergraduate, master's, doctoral and special professional degrees." To that extent, NTSU gained its goal of inclusion among the top five. The committee, however, used one key phrase only with UT Austin and Texas A&M: each was assigned "emphasis on maintaining a nationally and internationally recognized research institution." NTSU, Texas Tech, and the University of Houston shared a phrase that research "would be conducted with emphasis on maintaining momentum as an emerging national research university."[35]

LEGISLATIVE RESPONSES TO THE SELECT COMMITTEE

Virtually every detail of the report of the select committee was made public in December, although it was February 25, 1987, before the official printed version was delivered. That document consumed eighty-one typewritten pages covering virtually all of the areas that the group had set out to study. A surprisingly large number of them were adopted by the legislature.

No Mission?

The designation of NTSU, Tech, and Houston as "emerging national research universities" ran into trouble in the legislature. Hurley and the regents continued to use the executive summary proposing North Texas as one of five major graduate and research universities. Hurley asked his colleagues on the North Texas Commission for "understanding and help" in getting this enacted.[36] The North Texas Commission, however, felt an obligation to represent all of the institutions in its area. Its officers wrote Temple to seek the equal endorsement of the Select Committee for the two UT schools at Arlington and Dallas.[37]

Gib Lewis, speaker of the house, who was from Fort Worth, decided to drop from the Select Committee bill the designation of missions for each university, largely because of pressure from the Tarrant County and Bexar County delegation (on behalf of the University of Texas at San Antonio). Hurley explained in a memorandum to board members:

> A legal issue also was raised about putting mission statements into law because of the subsequent difficulty of changing those statements, but the overriding issue appears to have been the political storm generated by those communities that did not want limitations on the mission statements for their local institutions. Of course, we will continue to use the recommendation of the Select Committee to our advantage, and we will go before the Coordinating Board with the strong support of individuals such as Larry Temple.[38]

Although Temple had advocated views that ran counter to the stated positions of NTSU on some Select Committee issues, Hurley in general held Temple in high regard. Much later, Hurley stated that the Select Committee had been a significant force in changing Texas higher education and that much of this came about because of the strength of Larry Temple as chairman of the committee and of the Coordinating Board. Temple was viewed as having the "political savvy" necessary to both of those positions because of his experience in working with Lyndon Johnson and John Connally. Hurley said that "in my experience" Temple had been the best Coordinating Board chairman of all.[39]

No Reorganization?

As widely forecast, the reorganization of the colleges and universities under just a few boards of regents proved to be politically unattainable. There was no new system of higher education for North Texas or for the Dallas-Fort Worth Metroplex. In Denton, NTSU and TWU retained their individual identities under their own governing boards. Neither did the legislature adopt the role and mission statements for each senior college and university; the Coordinating Board was judged to have the authority to adopt such statements and this task was left to that board. One legislator, however, did introduce legislation to eliminate some of the multiple boards. Representative Wilhelmina Delco, of Austin, sought unsuccessfully to create a "University System of the North" and a similar one for the south. North Texas would have been placed under control of the northern board along with Midwestern State, East Texas State, and TWU.[40]

The legislature did follow the committee report to establish a basic skills test to diagnose academic weaknesses of entering freshmen, to require all universities to have a core curriculum, and to abolish the undergraduate education degree, requiring instead that candidates for teaching certificates major in the academic field or fields in which they planned to teach.[41] A major change was also made in the breakdown of appropriations to universities: the legislature was directed to appropriate base funding in a lump sum for institutions to spend among the various funding elements of the formula used to determine base funding; also to appropriate to institutions the unexpended balance of appropriations made for the preceding year. Beyond those items, the real significance of the select committee's work would show up in new state approaches to the support of university research and in an important set of powers added to those already possessed by the Coordinating Board. Here, a major impact was made on Texas higher education.

New State Research Programs

Most observers agreed that the research proposals, even though they carried an estimated cost of $85 million, had broader support in the legislature than most other recommendations. These were based on competitive funding to encourage research tied primarily to the state economy, and legislators saw these as an aid in attracting federal and private funding and moving the state away from reliance on the sagging oil industry.[42]

For some years, the elements of cost on which appropriations formulas had been based included "organized research." A line item in the appropriations bill for North Texas specified an amount in this category, and distribution of these funds was recommended by the Faculty Research Committee. This item was replaced by one of the four research programs recommended by the select committee and passed by the legislature. North Texas was faced with a major problem in being regarded as eligible for advanced research program funding: as legislation creating this program moved through the legislative processes, it was written so that only the University of Texas and Texas A&M would be able to apply for these research grants. Hurley later credited the North Texas Austin representative, Walt Parker, for staying in Austin and working to the final vote, successfully persuading the vote to permit the non Permanent University Fund schools to compete for thirty percent of the research dollars, which were required to be allocated outside of the favored "big schools."[43] The NTSU chancellor wrote to one senator to thank him for his efforts to balance the research effort in the state:

> perhaps none of your achievements may ever exceed in educational and economic value to our state your success in putting into law the principles that govern the research work of higher education.
>
> Some weeks ago, a reporter tried to get me to say something negative about the work of the committee. When I tried to turn the question around by pointing to its achievement in recommending. . . such forward-looking action in research, the reporter said: "My editor does not think that research principles are very exciting to our readers." The reporter then had to listen to my lecture on the enormous importance of what you were about to do. Unfortunately, no story was printed.[44]

The legislature created four research programs.[45]

1. Research Enhancement Program. This program replaced the organized research formula for public general academic institutions. The formula was a relatively simple one based on the number of full-time equivalent faculty. The funds are distributed by competitive peer review procedures on the campus, quite similar to those already in use.

2. Advanced Research Program. This was created to support basic research at all public institutions of higher education by faculty members in astronomy, atmospheric science, biological and behavioral sciences, chemistry, computer sciences, earth sciences, engineering, information science, mathematics, material sciences, oceanography, physics, and social sciences. The Coordinating Board appoints an advisory committee to recommend priorities, guidelines, and procedures for making awards. A separate committee conducts a peer review of proposals.

3. Advanced Technology Program. For this fund, independent colleges and universities are allowed to join public institutions in applying for funds in agriculture, biotechnology, biomedicine, energy, materials science, aquaculture, telecommunications, and manufacturing science. The two-committee system is also followed for this category.

4. Research Assessment Program. The Coordinating Board uses two committees here to conduct merit reviews of special university programs that had been funded by line-item appropriations rather than by formula. The law requires that the programs be evaluated for their "intrinsic merit, research performance, and the potential contribution of the research to the development of knowledge and instruction in advanced and emerging technologies and the economic growth of the state."

Power to the Coordinating Board

The Coordinating Board was given a new name: the Texas Higher Education Coordinating Board. Its new powers were intended to concentrate more control of higher education affairs in Austin. The board was required or authorized to develop a five-year master plan for higher education in Texas to include role and mission statements for public senior institutions and maximum enrollment limits for each institution. The board was told to complete a sunset review of all doctoral programs at public institutions by December 1992.

New coordination efforts were to include free transferability of lower-division course credit among institutions; a management information system appropriate to planning, financing, and decision-making; publication of material on admission policies, course transferability, and financial assistance programs; and encouragement of cooperative agreements among institutions.

Student-oriented assignments were to develop guidelines for institutions to report student performance and to report first-year academic performance of entering students to their respective high schools and junior colleges. The Coordinating Board was assigned much greater involvement in financial matters. This included analysis of appropriations requests for the governor and legislators, allocation of initiative funding among institutions to promote academic excellence and to reward institutions that achieved goals set by the board in minority recruitment, graduation rates, meeting planning goals, and energy conservation. The board would study faculty compensation across the nation and gather data to use as a basis for a comparable compensation package in Texas.[46]

chapter 44

"Bring Back the Eagles"

It is a fact of life in higher education that an institution's identity often is linked to the status of its athletic program. Athletic excellence placed in its proper perspective should be a source of great pride for us all.

But the challenge we face is not to be won simply for the glory of football. UNT's return to Division I-A status has profound implications for the entire university community in our efforts to broaden the base of support of all that we do.

Alfred F. Hurley
October 6, 1993[1]

After Hayden Fry left for Iowa, the new president, Frank Vandiver, publicly renounced Southwest Conference ambitions. However, Vandiver did assert that any university hoping for recognition has to have a good athletic program to get regional and national identification. He said in his early newspaper interviews that people identify with an athletic program and then they may identify with the university.

Recognizing the difficulties in maintaining independent status, Vandiver tried unsuccessfully to interest half a dozen other universities in forming a new athletic conference.[2] North Texas remained an athletic independent. Bill Blakeley continued with winning basketball seasons, but produced nothing like the twenty-one or twenty-two victories as in each of his first three seasons. In football, Jerry Moore tried for two seasons and Bob Tyler for one year, but neither with any success.

CLASSIFICATION: I-A OR I-AA?

In 1978 the National Collegiate Athletic Association placed its "major colleges" into two divisions for football, putting the less ambitious and less costly schools into a lower subdivision. The NTSU Board of Regents voted to authorize a request for Division I-A status.

When it appeared that NTSU would succeed in that effort, the rules got tougher. Just as Al Hurley took office, the NCAA on February 2, 1982, reclassified North Texas and thirty-eight other schools as division I-AA. This was done because of new NCAA regulations that football teams must have averaged 20,000 fans per game for the prior four years to retain Division I-A status. This resulted in NT being allowed twenty fewer football scholarships in the 1982 season.[3]

FINANCIAL PROBLEMS MOUNT

The NCAA reported that in 1977, eighty percent of colleges and universities with football programs were losing money on the football operation. In the fall of 1980, Frank Vandiver encountered major money problems with athletics. He told an alumnus that the school could not continue with an athletic deficit like that year's $825,635 shortfall—he sought to build a viable athletic program and to reduce the "horrendous deficit."[4]

Personnel changes soon became a part of the financial difficulties. Football Coach Jerry Moore and six assistants resigned on January 4, 1981, to take similar jobs at Texas Tech. Athletic Director Andy Everest was forced to resign two days later after refusing to assume coaching duties, saying he couldn't do justice to both jobs.[5] Vandiver and the regents search committee moved rapidly, announcing on January 19 the appointment of Bob Tyler as athletic director and head football coach. He had held a similar post at Mississippi State.

However, Tyler's record that fall was two wins and nine losses. He was also having serious problems in financial management. On June 9, 1982, Tyler resigned, saying he needed to spend more time with his family.

Fred McCain, former assistant football coach and for nine years director of the coliseum, was named athletic director on July 1 and undertook an immediate review of the budget status. McCain presented to the Board of Regents on July 15 "evidence of previous overestimation of income, underestimation of expenditures." The board found it necessary to add as much as $325,000 to the current budget.[6] A subsequent audit showed a $1.6 million deficit.[7]

HURLEY INHERITS ATHLETIC HEADACHES

Just after taking office, Al Hurley told a meeting with seventeen Denton leaders that abolishing football was "a possibility." An analysis sent to Vice President Eddie Davis by Comptroller Phillip C. Diebel showed how few options the university had—and not solely in athletics.

Diebel observed that after the education and general surplus was gone sometime early in the 1983 fiscal year, the sinking fund was the only source of reserve funds. If athletics continued at the existing pace, Diebel estimated it would use not only all of the earnings of the sinking fund but would begin to "eat away" rapidly at the designated fund balance. His projection was that by the end of FY 1985 athletics would have to operate entirely within student service fees and income generated by athletic events.[8]

Prescription: Join a Conference

Having lost its I-A status, North Texas looked for a conference affiliation within which to begin a rebuilding process. Regents voted in February 1982, to join the Southland Conference as its eighth member.[9]

The Southland Conference lost two members in December 1986, when Lamar University and Arkansas State University withdrew to join other schools in creating a new Division I-A conference. The Southland subsequently added four Texas state schools: Southwest Texas, Sam Houston, UT-Arlington, and Stephen F. Austin.

Prescription: Make Immediate Cuts

Hurley received board approval to reduce the athletic budget by one-third, so he immediately assigned the faculty Athletic Council the task of applying this to the proposed budget for 1982–83. The committee tried to enable North Texas to be competitive in eight sports in the Southland Conference, to be a serious contender for football and basketball champions, guarantee equity for women's programs, and not emasculate any one program to the point of extinction.[10]

Prescription: Bring Back the Eagles

The Hayden Fry era had brought new school colors, a rather brilliant yellow-green. Fry had also emphasized the nickname of "Mean Green" and downplayed the traditional eagle symbol. Now, to try to win back more of the traditional supporters, both of these efforts were reversed. Hurley explained his emphasis to an alumnus:

> Tradition is a major factor in any outstanding university, and it is my goal to continue to emphasize those traditional elements that will enhance our university. We have painted the stadium in the traditional dark green; and we are using "Eagles" in all of our press releases. In time we hope the press media will emphasize "Eagles" instead of "Mean Green Eagles." Also we are about to push several other programs to reorient everyone to using "the Eagles."[11]

Prescription: Share Fouts Field

Another costly problem was the need to improve the condition of Fouts Field, the football and track stadium. Partial help for this came in a contract with the Denton Independent School District whereby the school paid for the use of the stadium and the money helped defray the cost of artificial running and playing surfaces.[12] Denton voters in 1985 approved a $500,000 school bond issue that would pay a share of the stadium improvements.[13]

FACULTY AND STUDENT CONCERNS

Faculty attitudes toward athletics remained divided during this time span. The committee on university organization in August 1982 wrote that alumni support was given as a reason for giving high priority to football but that alumni did not support the program. The committee feared that football would "continue to be a major financial drain on other financial areas."[14] Faculty Athletic Council Chairman John Thornton reported that the 1983–84 athletic budget was just over $1.7 million, containing a deficit of half a million dollars. He compared that deficit to $1.4 million and $800,000 for the two preceding years.[15]

A survey in 1984 reported that staff members viewed athletics more favorably than faculty, and the faculty, in turn, found athletics somewhat more important than did students.[16] 1982, in fact, the survey reported that the least-liked aspects of NTSU included athletics, especially football. Much attention was attracted in November 1985 when the University of Texas at Arlington announced it would no longer compete in football. UTA President Wendell Nedderman said that it was costing almost $1 million a year with no success in winning or in attendance. His statement declared that "the top priorities of the university, teaching and research, must take precedence."[17] Some faculty members read into this action of a nearby fellow Southland member a close parallel to the North Texas situation, and there was a fairly sizable antifootball feeling within the faculty from that time forward.

PROBLEMS IN STAFF CONTINUITY

North Texas had difficulty in maintaining continuity in staff. The *North Texas Daily* noted that six men had been athletic director in the 1980s. Fred McCain provided stability at the post for five of those ten years.[18] Corky Nelson had success in his early years as football coach and was also made athletic director in June 1989. This tenure lasted only through 1990, and Steve Sloan came in as athletic director in February 1991. Craig Helwig served as athletic director from January 1994 to December 2000.

After Hayden Fry completed six years as football coach in 1978, his successors were Jerry Moore, 1979–80; Bob Tyler, 1981; Corky Nelson, 1983–90; Dennis Parker, 1991–93; Matt Simon, 1994–97; and Darrell Dickey from 1998. There was slightly less turnover in basketball, with Bill Blakeley coaching for eight seasons until 1983, Tommy Newman for three seasons, Jimmy Gales for seven seasons until 1993, and Tim Jankovich for four seasons until 1997. Vic Trilli began his tenure with the 1997–98 season.

BRINGING WOMEN INTO ATHLETICS

Title IX of the Education Amendments of 1972 prohibited sex discrimination by institutions receiving federal financial assistance. Its impact on athletics was not immediately apparent at NTSU. The 1972 *Yucca* allocated fifty-eight pages to sports; exactly one page covered women's athletics. The next year's yearbook also had a single page with two photos and a description of extramural tournaments in badminton, basketball, tennis, and gymnastics. In the 1974 *Yucca*, two pages appeared under a heading, "Women's Extramurals: Success on a Shoestring." This revealed that the university provided $10,000 to support seven different sports. Pat Caldwell of the physical education faculty was quoted in a forecast of things to come: "The time has come that we should receive our equal amount in proportion to what has been put into men's athletics."[19]

When Hayden Fry was named athletic director over both men's and women's sports, President Nolen asked him to develop an intercollegiate program for women. Nolen received notice in 1978 that the regional Office for Civil Rights planned to conduct a preliminary inquiry into two complaints charging North Texas with discriminating against women in its athletic program.[20] The complaints contained nine allegations of discrimination. The allegations claimed that funds for women's athletics were less, that scholarships favored men, that there were inequities in the number of sports offered to female students and less satisfactory travel accommodations for women, and that there were fewer dollars per woman athlete for training and equipment.

At the time, men could compete in football, basketball, track and field, soccer, tennis, and golf. Women were offered volleyball, basketball, track and field, and tennis.[21] The wheels of civil rights compliance turned slowly and the matter was inherited by Hurley as the new president. He and his staff engaged in discussion with the civil rights officers and issued a letter in August 1983 describing changes in the women's program: more equipment and supplies, uniform travel provisions, equal access to all facilities, and increased funds for recruitment.[22] The regional director declared that these actions corrected the violation.[23]

In October 1996 Athletic Director Helwig worked with a national consultant to develop a Title IX action plan for the university. This was submitted to the Board of Regents, which voted 8–0 to approve it.[24] Nevertheless, in 1996 the National Women's Law Center filed a complaint against twenty-five schools, including UNT, alleging that scholarships for female varsity athletes were worth less than those for male athletes. Helwig told the *Dallas Morning News* that North Texas offered six men's and eight women's sports, having added women's soccer in the fall of 1996 after eliminating men's soccer and men's tennis. Helwig reported that UNT fully funded its women's sports, offering the maximum number allowed by the NCAA for each sport.[25]

THE SOUTHLAND CONFERENCE EFFORT

For thirteen years NT worked to build a successful program in the Southland Conference. In football, the national category as to "level" of play was Division I-AA; in basketball, the Southland Conference champion might be invited to compete in the NCAA Division I-A tournament, but that post was not automatic. The football team under Coach Corky Nelson won the Southland championship and went into the NCAA I-AA playoffs in 1983, 1987, and 1988. In his first year as football coach in 1994, Matt Simon's team won the conference championship. All four of these teams lost in the first round of NCAA playoffs. Coach Jimmy Gales had basketball championships in 1987–88 and 1988–89; the Eagles were invited to play in one NCAA postseason tournament, in 1988, and were eliminated in the first round.

Women achieved their first intercollegiate successes in the Southland. On March 8, 1986, the women's basketball team won its first-ever conference championship, then lost in the first round of the NCAA playoffs in Seattle. Their record was 20-10. In 1989 the women's cross country team won its first Southland Conference title.[26]

BACK TO I-A

The Eagles competed at a 50-50 level in football in the Southland Conference, winning sixty-four, losing sixty-three, and tying three. This was not enough to arouse great interest. The rationale for spending large sums on athletics was not being supported by results.

Student Assembly Backs I-A Conference

The Student Association assembly voted 42 to 1 in the fall of 1990 to campaign for membership in a Division I-A athletic conference. Public questions were still being raised about football support at UNT. And in November 1990 this appeared in the *Dallas Morning News*:

> The Eagles had gone through five [athletic directors] in the previous seven years. . . . The "experiment" flopped. North Texas' athletic program continued to operate at a deficit, and attendance declined. Even worse, so did the football team. A group of seniors, ranked No. 1 in the nation as sophomores, finished 6-5 this season. A crowd of 6,800 watched Saturday as the Eagles completed a second consecutive 2-4 Southland Conference finish.
>
> Such numbers do not make North Texas an attractive candidate for a Division I-A invitation, a bid the Eagles so desperately crave. Hurley knows they won't get in the SWC, or any other big league, until they climb to the top of Division I-AA. . . .
>
> To move up. . . the Eagles need solid financial management. They also need a greater monetary commitment than the $2.8 million allotted to men's athletics, which would be a pittance in the SWC.[27]

An interview published three days later in the same newspaper gave Hurley an opportunity to speak more positively of athletic plans. The story had a revealing headline: "UNT Thinks Big Despite Financial Losses in Football." Hurley advised that not only would the university not drop football, it would one day return to Division I-A.

> "Having a broad-based athletic department is very important, I believe, to a Texas university," UNT chancellor Alfred Hurley said. "I've been able to convince our people that we can withstand deficits because of the many benefits the athletic programs bring to North Texas . . . ."
>
> But until UNT's football program becomes more competitive in the SLC, in which the team has finished fifth and sixth the last two years, those plans must remain on hold.[28]

The student government campaign didn't build momentum immediately, but it was greatly helped the following February by the hiring of Steve Sloan as athletic director. Sloan was a head football coach for fourteen years at Vanderbilt, Texas Tech, Mississippi, and Duke, and had served for a year and a half as athletic director at his alma mater, Alabama, in 1989 and 1990. Sloan told his first news conference that his concentration on finances and increased fan support would prepare "for a possible move from NCAA Division I-AA to I-A."[29]

Stadium Capacity the Key

The key to I-A status was paid attendance. Schools with stadiums seating 30,000 or more were required to average 17,000 in home attendance in one of four years. Those with smaller stadiums needed to average 17,000 for four consecutive years. That latter figure seemed unrealistic on the basis of the record, so UNT was left with two choices: designate Texas Stadium in nearby Irving as the home stadium or enlarge Fouts Field to at least 30,000 seats.

Sloan told the Athletic Council in late 1991 that metal bleachers to seat an additional 10,000 could be built for about $1 million. Student Association President Bill Miller conceived the idea of a student-financed stadium expansion.[30] Miller persuaded the student assembly to set a student referendum to increase fees to finance the expansion. Despite opposition from the *North Texas Daily*, the issue narrowly passed. Voters numbered 1,217, fewer than five percent of enrolled students, and of these, 661 voted for the referendum and 556 opposed it. The supporting vote thus constituted 2.6 percent of the student body.[31]

Regents responded with a two dollar per semester increase in the eight dollar general use fee in June 1992. Vice President Phil Diebel estimated that this would generate $1.2 million for Fiscal Year 1993, and $1 million of this would be set aside for the Fouts expansion.[32]

After considerable planning and discussion with the Coordinating Board, it was agreed that the university would have to solicit private funds to repay half of the student fee money. The Coordinating Board gave final approval on October 28.

Westward Ho!

Athletic Director Sloan had not waited to work toward the I-A conference goal. While still a member of the Southland Conference, Sloan had made overtures in 1992 to the Big West Conference, a consortium of California and mountain-state schools. He followed up conversations with a letter to the commissioner writing that North Texas would like to participate in the Big West starting with the 1995 season.[33] Thus began a successful move westward into Division I-A.

But Sloan Moves Eastward

However, Sloan resigned in July 1993 to become athletic director at the University of Central Florida. Craig P. Helwig took over the post on January 4, 1994. He left a job as executive director of the John Hancock Bowl and the Sun Carnival Association in El Paso. He had been assistant director of athletics at the University of Texas at Austin from 1982 to 1991 and had had the same title at Kansas State from 1978 to 1982.

Big West Beckons

On July 1, 1996, UNT became an official member of the Big West. Members were Boise (Idaho) State University; California Polytechnic, San Luis Obispo; California State, Fullerton; California State, Long Beach; University of California, Irvine; University of California, Santa Barbara; University of Idaho; University of Nevada, Reno; Utah State; University of the Pacific; New Mexico State University; and UNT. Arkansas State University was voted in as a football-only member starting in 1999.

The NCAA Says Okay

Metal bleachers were installed in 1994, adding 10,500 seats by curving around in either end zone from the student stands on the east side of Fouts Field. With this done, the other NCAA condition became the achievement of a single-year attendance average of at least 17,000. Fortunately for UNT, the count was made on paid attendance, not actual attendance at games. Thanks to several enthusiastic donors who bought large blocks of season tickets, the average was attained and the NCAA approved a I-A status for the Eagles' 1995 football season. The following year they began Big West competition.

WHAT FUTURE IN THE SECOND CENTURY?

After nearly a decade into the second North Texas century, the future of intercollegiate athletics remained uncertain. The university had attained its goals of regaining I-A status and of membership in a I-A conference. There had been a few successes in terms of wins and losses, but overall the program still struggled for recognition as a frequent winner. The financial problems had deepened rather than improved.

Criticism Continues

Two consistent public questioners of the North Texas position in athletics continued to point to the problems: the *North Texas Daily* and the *Dallas Morning News.* In the Eagles' first two years in the Big West Conference, these headlines indicate the nature of this public pressure:

"Can NT afford Division I-A football?" This was a banner headline atop page one of the *Daily* on October 4, 1996.

"Is It Worth It? A look at the decision to enter Division I-A football." This occupied the entire editorial page of the *Daily* on April 18, 1997.

"No Rooting Interest: UNT's toughest opponents are identity and indifference." The *Dallas Morning News* gave this the top half of three pages in its football preview section on August 28, 1997.

An identity crisis drew the emphasis in a 1997 *Dallas Morning News* football preview feature:

> For one, the Denton school has had almost as many name changes—seven—as football conferences—eight. The official mascot is the Eagles, but some years, the unofficial nickname "Mean Green" is emphasized. It's hard to root for a school whose identity keeps changing. And longtime conference rivalries? Forget it. . . .
>
> The commuter-school image hurts school spirit, the lifeblood of an athletic department. Students don't identify with a place they see only on weekdays. . . .
>
> Perhaps the reason few people identify with North Texas is few people know the correct name. In May 1988, North Texas State University became the University of North Texas. But not everyone was paying attention. . . .
>
> Changing a name doesn't always change perceptions.[34]

The Legislature Gets Interested

The general financial condition of athletics at Texas state-supported institutions caught the attention of the House Committee on Higher Education in Austin. That group noted that UNT ranked second in the state with a $3.4 million operating loss in its athletic program before transfers in from student service fees.[35] Texas schools were directed to submit reports to the 1997 legislature. For North Texas, this took the form of a document, "Benchmarks for

Athletics," presented to the Board of Regents on November 12, 1996. After explaining the goals of its I-A football program, the document reported this way:

> The move to I-A level in football, along with increased emphasis on women's sports (Title IX), rising costs of scholarships, and other cost factors have led to a significant increase in the Athletic Department's expenditure budget. Revenues have also increased during this period, but not to the same level as expenditures. Therefore, more funds from other University resources have been required to support the Athletic program. . . .
>
> The University has developed a set of benchmarks using the following considerations:
>
> • 1995 is the base year. . . .
>
> • One of the primary reasons UNT moved to I-A level in football was to promote more giving to the University. Accordingly, the University should expect giving to the University to increase at a rate significantly greater than that of any additional resources going into the Athletic program.
>
> • The University does not believe that Athletics at UNT will become self-supporting in the near future. In addition, Title IX will require the University to add another women's sport, related staff, and scholarships. We do, however, expect the gap between revenues and expenditures to begin closing after Title IX obligations have been met.
>
> • The Athletic budget should be capped as a percentage of the University's overall budget. Doing so will maintain the Athletic budget at a reasonable level.[36]

Regents voted 8-0 to approve this document for submission to the legislature and for guidance in future athletic decisions.

By 1998–99, some improvement in performance was noted, especially in golf and in women's basketball. "Hopeful" signs were seen in the conference performances near the end of the season in football and basketball. Track and field performers placed well in a number of meets. But the turn in the financial fortunes still lay ahead. The annual budget began carrying a line under auxiliary enterprise funds headed "Designated fund supplement for athletics." This amount kept rising as the institution tried to gain some attention for its athletic efforts. The figures in the annual budgets look like this for the athletic supplement:

1996	$1,529,722
1997	$1,885,879
1998	$2,170,428
1999	$2,370,428

In 1999 shifts were taking place in collegiate conference affiliations. In June the University of Nevada at Reno withdrew from the Big West Conference. A different conference affiliation could be attractive for UNT if it included more member schools closer to Denton.

On to the Sun Belt

It was thus really no surprise when alumni read in their magazine, "Eagles head for the Sun Belt Conference."[37] UNT joined New Mexico State and Middle Tennessee as the conference's newest full members. The University of Louisiana–Monroe signed on as a football-only member. Most of the changes were scheduled to start in 2001, although UNT and NMSU were given permission from the Big West members for early withdrawal to speed up Eagle participation in Sun Belt title competition. UNT won the Sun Belt conference championship in 2001 and went on to play in the inaugural New Orleans Bowl, thus ending the longest bowl drought of any Division I-A school.

chapter 45

Toward the Second Century

Even as the university celebrates its Centennial Year, a course has been plotted for the Centennial Decade. By the year 2000, the University of North Texas seeks to become an institution whose students have exceeded the academic achievements of today's student body. The faculty will be more distinguished in both research and teaching. The staff and physical plant will have grown sufficiently to meet increased responsibilities and demands. A continued sense of community will have allowed the university to move forward with a spirit of unity within diversity. And finally, the university's excellence as a metropolitan university closely tied to the economic, social and cultural future of the Dallas-Fort Worth Metroplex will have been recognized by the region, state and nation.

Centennial Convocation Program
January 31, 1990

In his briefing to regents at his first board meeting in February 1982, Al Hurley set forth as a long-range initiative, "make the most of the 100th anniversary in 1990." In his list of immediate initiatives, he declared his intention to "create a sense of mission" and to "prioritize objectives." It was not surprising, then, that over time these ideas would emerge in the form of a "Centennial Agenda" to guide efforts at institutional improvement.

THE CENTENNIAL AGENDA

In August 1984 the regents received a study draft and approved it in principle. A final recommended draft was submitted at the board meeting of October 29. It was recommended by Vice President Robert B. Toulouse, who commented that the strategies would "allow the administration to develop specific tactics and determine their costs, before the Centennial Advancement Campaign is launched in 1985–86."[1]

Centennial Agenda in Brief
University of North Texas, 1984–1990

By 1990 North Texas State University seeks to become an institution:

—whose academic excellence is acknowledged regionally, statewide and nationally

—whose students are highly qualified at entry, thrive in a positive educational environment, and are prepared to make a significant contribution to society

—whose faculty are prominent in scholarly and creative activities, excellent in teaching, and enhanced through endowed chairs and professorships

—whose staff have achieved an optimum delivery of vital services on campus

—which displays an effective commitment to affirmative action in its recruitment of students, faculty, and staff

—whose cooperative relationships with area institutions, especially Texas College of Osteopathic Medicine, have enhanced academic programs, increased educational opportunities for students, and maximized the use of resources

—whose alumni and friends have rallied to provide endowment, capital, and athletic funding as well as strong involvement in recruiting and programmatic efforts

—whose facilities can fully meet instructional, research, and support needs.[2]

LET THE CELEBRATION BEGIN

As a new president in 1982, Al Hurley had begun thinking of means of capitalizing on the one hundredth year's arrival. A preliminary committee to make plans was headed by Dr. Tom Preston, dean of the College of Arts and Sciences. This group proposed a schedule of events for the calendar year 1990.[3] As the end of the decade drew closer, yet another committee was formed, and in December of 1988 Hurley reminded the faculty and staff of the nearness of special events and announced that Dr. William Luker would work as director to see that the Centennial "becomes the occasion for both a rededication and a renewal of our University."[4]

Flag Day, Convocation Open 1990 Events

Under the headline, "Banner Year," the *North Texas Daily* noted in pictures and stories the first official event, Flag Day, on January 15. President George Bush sent congratulations. State and federal officials presented flags that had flown over the capitol buildings, and the official centennial flag was introduced. All three were raised ceremoniously at the flagpole by the University Union.[5]

A convocation in the Coliseum offered the grand opening for the year's celebration on January 31. Dr. Margaret Hudnall of the music faculty chaired a group of thirty-seven faculty and staff members arrayed in eight committees to stage the program. Dr. Allan W. Ostar, president of the American Association of State Colleges and Universities, gave the convocation address.

Musical presentations created the atmosphere of pride and excitement, starting with the fanfare by the UNT Trumpet Ensemble and academic processional music by the combined university bands. All of the university bands and university choral ensembles came together for the national anthem and later were joined for "The Battle Hymn of the Republic" by the Texas Woman's University choral ensembles and choirs from Denton High School and two Denton junior high schools. The featured music after the address was the premiere performance of Regents Professor Martin Mailman's specially commissioned centennial march, "Toward the Second Century." Yet another North Texas composer, Distinguished Professor Emeritus William Latham, was represented with the recessional, "Proud Heritage," by the combined university bands.

Centennial Extravaganza

The major spectacle of the one hundredth year was reserved for Homecoming, a three-day celebration that started with the Centennial Extravaganza staged in Fouts Field on Thursday night, October 18.

Regents Lucille Murchison and Billie Parker served as cochairmen for the big show, and an anonymous donor underwrote the production with a pledge of $500,000. Starlight Entertainment of Dallas, which had produced bowl-game half-time shows, closing ceremonies for the Olympics, and Cotton Bowl parades, was employed as production coordinator. Bob Blocker, dean of the School of Music, served as campus coordinator for the event. This show was reported to have drawn 25,000, 2,000 more than could be accommodated, the largest crowd ever for Fouts Field.

It featured a fireworks display by the family that had coordinated the Statue of Liberty rededication in 1986, a caravan of ten 1955 Thunderbirds, a laser light show, elaborate floats and costumes, and more than 1,000 student participants. About 325 students recorded a musical journey from the 1890s to the present, directed by Dennis Fisher, the extravaganza music director. The musical review was presented as some eighty student dancers performed. Choreography for all the dance routines was created by faculty members and students in the Division of Dance and Drama. Some 2,700 costume pieces and the stage props were constructed by costume design students and others in the division.[6]

The occasion was the setting for announcement of the school's first major capital campaign, a $35 million fund-raising project, toward which "we have quietly raised more than half," Chancellor Hurley reported. He said the money would be used mostly to fund scholarships and faculty chairs, to supplement academic programs, and to build a new performing arts building.[7]

Scholarships Awarded

Revenue from the extravaganza provided scholarships to the units whose students and faculty participated in the production. All such grants were named "Lucille Murchison Scholarships" in recognition of Mrs. Murchison's leadership in conceiving, planning, and executing the Fouts Field celebration.

Capital Campaign

Dallas banker and UNT alumnus Roy Gene Evans joined Hurley to announce the Centennial Capital Campaign as the first such drive ever conducted by the university. Dr. Clovis Morrisson, the political science professor now working in the Advancement Office, was in charge of the gift operations.

Just seven months after the campaign kickoff at the Extravaganza, Morrisson was able to report to former regent Grace Cartwright that "We have raised a little over $37,000,000, beyond our $35,000,000 goal, and still with over a year to go. My estimate is that we will top out at about $42,000,000."[8] The following December the figure had surpassed $40 million.[9]

Centennial Special: a New Eagle

On the afternoon after the Extravaganza, a fifteen-foot bronze sculpture of a soaring eagle, "In High Places," was unveiled on a knoll between the Administration Building and the University Union. The $150,000 sculpture was created by Gerald Balciar, a wildlife artist. Led by graduate Larry Jobe, sixty alumni and friends donated the money for the project.

And a Light-Hearted Salute

The Centennial Year was drawing near a close, but one smash production remained to punctuate the year's observances. That was "Forever Green," a historical review presented in the Main Auditorium on November 30. With words written to popular melodies by Denton satirist Donna Trammell, it was billed as a light-hearted musical salute to the North Texas spirit. The cast included 121 townspeople (many of them alumni), 108 students, and fifty-eight faculty, staff, and administrators. Chancellor Hurley portrayed the founding president, Joshua C. Chilton. The second president, John J. Crumley, was played by James Laney, an education faculty member and grandson of former President J. C. Matthews. Bob Castleberry, then the mayor of Denton, appeared as the 1890 mayor. And the cast included staff from many campus areas, deans and vice presidents and faculty, and a member of the Board of Regents, Topsy Wright. Probably the most rousing reception came just before the intermission when the full marching band, "The Green Brigade," marched down the auditorium aisles playing the North Texas Fight Song at full volume. It was, several observers commented, a stirring occasion, providing a memorable cap to the Centennial Year.

UNT AT THE CENTURY

Four days before the Extravaganza, an advertising section appeared in *Dallas Life Magazine* of the *Dallas Morning News,* on October 14. Under a subhead declaring "A decade of record growth has expanded the university's scope and importance," Hurley explained that "Many people don't realize that we're the most comprehensive university in the region as measured by the breadth and depth of the programs we offer in the fine arts, business education and the sciences." The section was designed to salute "the school's 100-year evolution from a small teachers college to the fourth largest university in the state."[10]

A more enduring record of the status at one hundred years came in the publication of *Down the Corridor of Years: A Centennial History of the University of North Texas in Photographs, 1890-1990*, by Robert S. LaForte and Richard L. Himmel.[11] The authors concluded that the university was living up to the name it adopted in 1988, and that in programs and people it had truly become the University of North Texas. "Having begun as a normal school," they wrote, "It is now an important research university in Texas and the Southwest. This, then, is the promise of the future."[12]

part IX

From 100 Years: A New University

Texas Normal College

It will be our aim to become leaders in the education of the young men and women of Texas, fitting them to creditably fill the most important positions in business and professional circles.

Joshua C. Chilton

Opening day speech, September 16, 1890

North Texas Normal College

During the fall term each year—until cotton picking was over—the Normal. . . had a good many school teachers enrolled carrying on their studies. When the little country schools opened, these student-teachers dropped out and went to teaching. They taught till plowing time came in the Spring when the country schools closed and then they came back for the Spring term and continued their studies.

Recollection of a young student

North Texas State Normal College

My conception of the work of this institution was the preparation of teachers of all grades of elementary and high schools of the state. . . . Graduates from this institution, instead of being admitted to the freshman class in the universities, should be admitted to the graduate work in them.

W. H. Bruce
First faculty meeting, October 1906

North Texas State Teachers College

The North Texas State Teachers College is superior as an institution, academically, professionally, and in general organization and administration. [It] is the largest, and in many respects the best, of the teachers colleges of Texas. It has a better qualified instructional staff; it has the same admission standards, but higher scholarship standards. . . ; it has a better internal organization than most such colleges; it has a better organized curriculum.

The Griffenhagen Report
to the Texas Legislature, December 1932

North Texas is now training teachers, is offering to many of its students who do not plan to enter the teaching profession a broad cultural education, and is offering to many others preprofessional training in such fields as medicine.

L. A. Sharp, Graduate Council chairman,
On new statement of aims, October 17, 1941

North Texas State College

. . . enrollments and appropriations for the North Texas State Teachers College have increased rapidly in the last several years to the point that said College is now one of the leading educational institutions in Texas and the great Southwest.

Bill creating new Board of Regents
for North Texas State College, May 23, 1949

North Texas State University

All the factual evidence indicates that by all odds North Texas State University is the public institution most logical for adoption by the region in its search for the greatly needed expansion of public higher education programs.

J. C. Matthews
75th Year Statement, 1965

The Faculty Senate is the primary voice of the faculty in expressing convictions or opinions on a wide range of topics of campus-wide significance.

John Kamerick, May 1969

The university which does not make clear choices about what it will be and what it will not be will, at the same instant, not make progress and will begin to die at the core.

C. C. "Jitter" Nolen
Faculty address, August 1974

North Texas State University is a finer institution than it was eight years ago, and I am very proud of the part that I played in that progress. I know the future is bright for the university because it is strong enough to withstand any allegations against any individual related to it.

C. C. "Jitter" Nolen
April 12, 1979

University of North Texas

By the year 2000, the University of North Texas seeks to become an institution whose students have exceeded the academic achievements of today's student body. The faculty will be more distinguished in both research and teaching. . . . A continued sense of community will have allowed the university to move forward with a spirit of unity within diversity.

Alfred F. Hurley
Centennial Convocation, January 31, 1990

chapter 46

The Legacy of a Century

UNT has emerged as the leading university of the Dallas-Fort Worth area. We are also one of Texas' "Big Five" universities, the state's largest and most academically challenging. With the North Texas region's largest student enrollment and faculty base, the largest number of degree programs and the most comprehensive offerings, UNT has become an enterprise with great potential in a location of dynamic economic growth. We are poised to become one of the nation's top metropolitan-focused research universities.

Alfred F. Hurley
North Texan, Fall 1998

The self-examination that came with the celebration of the University Centennial Year dramatized the magnitude of a century of change. This chapter will use that as a starting point, observing the nature of that change.

FIRST DECADE, SECOND CENTURY

Early in the second North Texas century, in 1992 and 1993, another ten-year self-study for the Southern Association came due. The committee in charge noted extensive changes in the decade since the last reaffirmation in 1985.

Administrative Changes

The position of vice president for student affairs was reinstated and filled in 1990. Two other vice presidents were added: one for development and another for legal affairs and general counsel.

Athletics was moved from external affairs to report directly to the president. Public Affairs and Information Services was moved from external affairs to report to the president, led by an associate vice president for marketing and communication. The planning director for a time had a dual reporting line to the president and the provost, later moving back to reporting to the president as associate vice president for planning and special assistant to the president. In 1994 the executive assistant to the chancellor became the associate vice president for university and Health Science Center affairs, and executive assistant to the chancellor. Also named were an assistant vice president and director of the office of equal opportunity. A new position on diversity was created to report to the president, as was an assistant vice president and director of the Office of Multicultural Affairs.

The number of upper-level administrative titles continued to grow. A 1985 organizational chart showed four vice presidents, two associate vice presidents, and no assistant vice presidents. A 1995 chart listed seven vice presidents, four associate vice presidents, and two assistant vice presidents. And in 1998, there were seven vice presidents, eight associate vice presidents, two vice provosts, and one assistant vice president. Another post was proposed in late 1998—that of executive vice president and provost, with plans that this individual would become president as Hurley moved to the sole capacity of chancellor. After an extensive search process, a committee recommended Dr. Norval Pohl from the University of Nevada-Las Vegas. He started in that capacity in January 1999 and did, indeed, become president in the fall of 2000.

Changes in Academic Organization

North Texas in 1995 had nine colleges and schools. The School of Music became a college. The Department of Art became a free-standing School of Visual Arts. The School of Home Economics went through several changes in academic emphasis and titles, becoming the School of Human Resource Management for a time and then the School of Merchandising and Hospitality Management. The graduate school was renamed the Robert B. Toulouse School of Graduate Studies. The graduate dean was also the associate vice president for research (in 1997 the latter position was separated as the vice provost for research).

These departmental changes took place: public administration and sociology departments moved from Arts and Sciences to the School of Community Service. The sociology department included social work but no longer covered anthropology, which became a part of the Center for Public Services in the School of Community Service. Courses in religion became part of a new Department of Philosophy and Religion Studies. The Department of Speech and Drama was divided into four departments in Arts and Sciences—dance and drama, communication studies, speech and hearing sciences, and radio-television-film. The Department of Industrial Technology was moved from the College of Education to the College of Arts and Sciences and renamed Engineering Technology.

Notable Buildings Added

In the decade of the 1990s, there was less than consensus on the best way to alleviate the shortage of space on the campus. In the previous ten years, North Texas had moved from a position where the Coordinating Board called it greatly overbuilt to a new status: the second largest shortage in Texas public higher education. Recommendations for building development came from both the University Planning Council and the space committee. As often happens, the UPC members supported the university's listed goals but differed on priorities to be assigned to efforts for better service to students.

Unifying Student Services

In January 1994, the chancellor asked Provost Blaine Brownell as chair of the UPC for a careful examination of recommendations for a new student services building. This building was planned to renovate the former Laboratory School Gymnasium and incorporate it into a new structure that would link with the University Union. Hurley asked for a planning group to accommodate student advising functions and include the offices for admissions, financial aid, the bursar, and the registrar. [1]

The result was the Eagle Student Services Center. This embodied the philosophy of a one-location service for new and returning students. It also included the graduate admissions office and the Toulouse School of Graduate Studies. The one-time gymnasium area became a large lecture hall/auditorium.

Environmental Education, Science, and Technology

The Science Research Building in 1985 established the viability of a large interdisciplinary facility. This concept was developed still further in the design of the Environmental Education, Science, and Technology Building, which opened in the fall of 1998. It is located on the west side of Avenue C between Hickory and Mulberry Streets. It contains offices and work space for faculty in the natural sciences, social sciences, and humanities. The EESAT Building also serves for public education on the environment with exhibition space, a sky theater (planetarium), and an outdoor environmental learning area.

Home for Performances, New Campus Entrance

The first campus plan in 1966 had called for a major entrance to the campus, one that would relate the university to the interstate highway. A 1978 planning effort called for the acquisition of property west of Avenue D at the freeway, with a broad entry thoroughfare to be created by curving the road around to Avenue E and thence northward. This was not done at that time.

In 1999, however, the university saw the fruition of three decades of hoping with the opening of an Avenue D to Avenue E campus entry. This coincided with the completion of a major new showcase building: the Lucille G. (Lupe) Murchison Performing Arts Center. The grand opening in February 1999 fulfilled a long dream of the College of Music.

Gateway Center: Emphasizing the Welcome

The campus entry area gained added emphasis in May 2000 with groundbreaking ceremonies for a state-funded $17.5 million University Gateway Center. The 116,000 square-foot complex was designed to serve as the primary gateway for visitors to the UNT campus and persons attending special events.

The design accommodated twenty-two classrooms with audio-visual-video systems; a visitor center; a conference center and exhibit hall; distance learning facilities; a hospitality management program training restaurant; and offices for the North Texas Exes, development, and the UNT Foundation.

The Health Science Center

After eighteen years of public operation Texas College of Osteopathic Medicine sought to broaden itself into a health science center. In a 1992 document, the staff reported to regents that eighty percent of the nation's 141 medical schools fit the definition of a health science center. This asserted that "the organizational structure of an HSC is virtually a prerequisite to accomplish the tripartite mission originally vested in individual U.S. medical schools."[2]

In 1993 the legislature created the University of North Texas Health Science Center with a college of osteopathic medicine. Basic health science programs had earlier become biomedical sciences and moved from direction of the academic vice president to the Biological Sciences Department. In 1993, biomedical science programs (not including biochemistry) were phased out at the university and transferred to the Health Science Center.

SOME KEY QUESTIONS CONTINUE

We have seen that certain pivotal questions occupied North Texas faculty, staff, and students during the first century. Others, such as how to expand into greater research and service efforts, arose more recently. Here are some of those issues:

1. Who shall attend North Texas?
2. Where shall we teach our students?
3. How do we attain national research status?
4. How shall we provide special service?
5. How shall we finance all of this?

1. Who Shall Attend North Texas?

In 1995 graduate students made up twenty-five percent of the enrollment. Characteristic of urban universities, sixty-one percent were enrolled part-time, most of them employed full-time. Another urban characteristic has been the large number of transfer students who enroll to work toward bachelor's degrees. In the fall of 1995 more than fifty-seven percent were admitted originally as transfer students, the largest number having come from community/ junior colleges.[3]

Ethnic Diversification

For more than half a century, North Texas students were predominantly white, Protestant Texans. With the admission of Black undergraduates to NTSC in 1956, service to the Black population became significant. The Spanish-speaking population for much of the century lived primarily in South Texas, a condition reflected in North Texas enrollment in the 1970s. Comparisons of undergraduate students showed 646 Black and 74 Hispanic in 1970, 703 and 162 in 1971, 847 and 239 in 1972, 881 and 256 in 1973, 1,040 and 272 in 1974, 1,172 and 329 in 1975, 1,244 and 359 in 1976, 1,252 and 369 in 1977, 1,283 and 288 in 1978, and 1,323 and 440 in 1979.

The number of undergraduate Hispanics passed 500 for the first time in 1986 at 531, and that number shot up rapidly by the centennial year of 1990 to surpass a thousand at 1,022. By 1997 the undergraduate number was 1,346, compared to 1,608 Blacks. At the graduate level, Hispanic enrollment didn't reach 200 until 202 enrolled in fall 1992. In 1996 and 1997 the Hispanic graduate students outnumbered graduate Black students for the first time, 288 to 249 and 299 to 263.

How Representative of the Metroplex?

The 1990s brought into play the phenomenon of "Political Correctness" in dealing with racial and ethnic questions, of awareness of "multiculturalism," and of "diversity" workshops to train faculty and staff. Several functions were combined in a new organization in 1995, reporting directly to the vice president for student affairs: the Center for Cultural Diversity. Its purpose was "to support and enhance a welcoming environment at UNT which fosters communication across cultures and honors all people." [4]

Questions arose as to how well the university recruited a diverse student body representative of the nearby population. One answer could be to compare enrollment for 1997[5] with 1997 population estimates as reported by the *Dallas Morning News* in 1998.[6]

Area	Total Population	Percent White	Percent Black	Percent Hispanic	Percent Am. Ind.	Percent Asian/Pac.
Texas	19,128,261	57	12	29	0.5	3
Dallas County	2,000,192	56	21	20	0.6	4
Collin County	372,445	83	4	4	0.5	4
Denton County	348,453	83	5	5	1	4
Rockwall County	34,153	88	4	4	0.4	1
Tarrant County	1,305,185	70	13	14	0.6	4
UNT	25,013	77.8	7.5	6.6	0.8	3.2

Actual numbers rather than percentages for the fall of 1997 were White 19,426, Black 1,871, Hispanic 1,645, Asian/Pacific Islander 806, and American Indian/Alaskan Native 198. In the fall of 1998 the number of African American students rose to 2,039, Hispanic to 1,769, Asian/Pacific Islander to 875, and American Indian/Alaskan Native to 201. In part because students in 1998 were able to check an "other" category for the first time, the number identified as White dropped to 18, 873, a decline from 77.8 percent to 73.9 percent. [7]

Adding an International Flavor

Students from other nations were virtually nonexistent in the state normal college, teachers college, and state college. North Texas State College had fall semester international enrollments from 1954 to 1959 of eleven, ten, fourteen, ten, and ten. The numbers and percentages began to pick up in the 1970s.

International enrollment climbed from four percent in 1976 to 7.2 percent in 1980, and eleven percent in 1984. A tuition increase bill in 1985 led to a steady decline from the 1984 peak of 2,375 to 1,552 in 1997. In 1984, the greatest number of students were from South Korea 109, Hong Kong 124, Malaysia 175, Iran 213, Thailand 241, Nigeria 255, and Republic of China (Taiwan) 318. In 1997, the only countries with more than one hundred students enrolled at UNT were the People's Republic of China, India, Japan, Korea, and Taiwan. [8]

Protest in the 1990s

In June 1995 Black Student Alliance students appeared before the Board of Regents to accuse administrators of condoning racism. They complained of unequal spending on Black student programs and a lack of recruitment of Black students, faculty, and administrators. They demanded the resignation of Hurley as chancellor. At that time, UNT had twenty Black faculty members on a staff of 788, and Blacks made up 6.8 percent of UNT's fall enrollment of 25,114.

The regents appointed a "blue-ribbon committee" of thirteen Black business people, alumni, students, and faculty. Regent Joe Kirven, the only Black member of the board, chaired the committee. The committee reported in December 1995,[9] recommending a zero-tolerance policy toward racism and asking for a grievance procedure for racism complaints. The group also sought better recruiting and retention of minority faculty and students. The report stated, "The area of greatest deficiency and concern is campus climate. Specific instances of insensitivity and incivility were noted. A campus-wide program consistently and continually administered, supported by words and actions from the chancellor and his administrative staff, must be implemented."[10]

Regent Kirven told the *Dallas Morning News* that he was dismayed that racism is an issue at the university, declaring that issues of fairness and equal opportunity should have been dealt with earlier. But he defended North Texas by saying, "This is not a racist school, and this chancellor is as fair a man, and maybe even the fairest, that you are going to find anywhere." The panel recommended formal mechanisms for student redress of grievances, with departmental ombudsmen set up to hear complaints. [11] Chancellor Hurley told the regents he would begin implementing the recommendations by the time of the next board meeting in two months. James Guillory of the Black Student Alliance told the *Dallas Morning News* he was encouraged by the report but wouldn't say that everything would be all right.

In just one week a related complaint came from the Denton League of United Latin American Citizens. A spokesman said the regents had conducted an "exclusionary review of minority concerns that contributed to ethnic divisions and tensions" on the campus. He said regents had acted improperly by naming only Blacks to the blue-ribbon panel. He added that the group would ask Governor George W. Bush to appoint a Hispanic to the UNT board. [12]

2. Where Shall We Teach Our Students?

As Texas became predominantly urban, higher education institutions sought to serve people where they lived. In the 1980s this led the Coordinating Board to impose stringent limitations on competition for off-campus sites among public institutions.

North Texas wanted to maintain metropolitan leadership, aided by permanent centers in Dallas and in Fort Worth offering resident credit. The Coordinating Board imposed a financial penalty on any institution that offered more than two percent of its total semester credit hours in a semester outside of its main campus. Minimum class sizes were also specified to be larger than for those on campus.

For North Texas, this meant direct orders to delete proposed course offerings. In 1983 Commissioner Kenneth H. Ashworth told Chancellor Hurley that the proposed 327 courses for 1983–84 would be cut back to 275. In addition, he complained, even then NTSU would have only one other school within one hundred courses of the number approved for North Texas. [13] That same year, the penalty reduction from formula appropriations because of spring semester classes was $102,215 for faculty salaries and $15, 613 for departmental operating expenses.[14]

New Approach for a Dallas Site

A different strategy was taken in 1994 with a new partnership arrangement in downtown Dallas. With approval from the Coordinating Board, the Dallas Downtown Education Center was created in a building once known as Titche's department store. Original partners in this enterprise were UNT, TWU, ETSU, UT-Arlington, and UT-Dallas. The Alliance for Higher Education, a consortium of twenty-six area colleges and universities coordinated the center's programming. El Centro College, one of the Dallas community colleges, occupied space in the center while its downtown campus was being renovated. [15]

Unfortunately, the consortium conducted its first classes in the summer, and the June 1994 registration was an embarrassing failure: "barely anyone showed up for the courses offered by five universities." The number was actually twenty, signed up for sixteen courses, most of which were canceled. Of those twenty, only three enrolled for a UNT course.[16] Fall efforts fared only a little better with 175 students, twenty-eight of them from North Texas.[17]

In 1997, the Federation of North Texas Area Universities assumed the management of the newly renamed Universities Center of Dallas. In 1998, the Dallas County Community College District bought the center from a group of business investors. The district assumed control of the facility, with the federation overseeing academic offerings. Five universities offered upper-division undergraduate and graduate courses. The University of Texas at Dallas and the

University of Texas at Arlington became affiliate members of the federation, whose regular members are UNT, TWU, and Texas A&M University-Commerce (formerly East Texas State University). A master's degree in business administration could be completed entirely at the Dallas center.[18] Enrollments rose substantially under this arrangement. For the 1999-2001 biennium, UNT as fiscal agent for the federation received a continuing special item appropriation of $700,000 for the Universities Center. [19]

A New Campus for South Dallas?

In 1998 a coalition of minority interests, with State Sen. Royce West as spokesman, campaigned for a new state university campus in South Dallas. Here, they argued, in one of the state's largest minority population centers, public higher education beyond the community college was essentially unavailable—for reasons of economics and lack of personal or public transportation.

At a public hearing, three state universities made presentations: Texas Tech University, Texas A&M University, and the University of North Texas. News accounts suggested that the best-prepared and most detailed proposal was presented by Chancellor Al Hurley for UNT. It also seemed agreed that considerations from that point forward would be given to A&M and North Texas. [20]

The UNT Board of Regents on August 28, 1998, voted unanimously to state that North Texas was interested in creating a new campus in southern Dallas. "This affirms the long-standing mission of the university to meet the higher education needs of anybody in this region," Chancellor Hurley said.[21]

The ad hoc citizens' committee voted at a September 17 meeting to recommend that UNT pursue building a full-scale four-year campus, including a law school, in southern Dallas County. After a hearing in Lancaster on September 24 a Coordinating Board committee recommended that the board take a gradual approach. Rather than building a freestanding campus immediately, upper-level courses should be taught at existing community college sites.[22] UNT regents asked the Coordinating Board in January 1999 to approve a UNT system center to operate on three community college campuses in southern Dallas County. Based on student demand, this could lead to a UNT campus in that area. [23]

The Coordinating Board approved the North Texas proposal on January 28, 1999. UNT could begin offering course work as early as the fall of 1999. The Coordinating Board listed fourteen degree or certificate programs that could be started, some of them in 2000 and 2001. The next step was for

Senator West to secure appropriations for start-up funds.[24]

The biennial legislative appropriations bill that passed in May 1999 included $4.2 million to fund the UNT center for southern Dallas and northern Ellis counties. The needed amount to operate the center as proposed was $6.8 million, so UNT and its Dallas supporters began a campaign to raise $2.6 million in addition to the appropriations. Plans were made to begin offering a limited number of courses in the fall of 1999 at two campuses of the Dallas community college district.[25]

For the spring semester of 2000, space was leased in a building in Stoneridge Business Park on South Hampton Road near Interstate 20 in South Dallas. The structure was built by Trammel Crow Co. with UNT leasing about half of the space for the first year and then moving into full occupancy. The venture got a major public boost with a ground-breaking ceremony attended by Governor Bush, Senator West, and many other state and local officials. Private fund-raising efforts found success among Metroplex-area corporations and foundations to supplement the state appropriation.

Senator West later recalled that he had never considered North Texas for that role in southern Dallas County. "I believed we needed the muscle of a Texas Tech or an A&M to get it done," he told the *Dallas Morning News.* "UNT didn't have the wherewithal to get it done politically or financially." But the newspaper declared that Hurley proved him wrong, and West agreed, pointing to the attendance of 2,000 people at a fund-raising program for the center in September 2000. "I think UNT is poised to move to the next level as a system with the Denton campus as the mother ship," the senator said.[26]

The move to formalize this next level came sooner than anticipated. In April 2001 Senator West and Rep. Jesse Jones of Dallas moved through both houses of the legislature with unanimous votes a bill establishing the University of North Texas at Dallas as a component institution in the UNT system. A campus was to be planned on the south side of the city near Interstate 20. Gov. Rick Perry signed the bill on May 8, 2001, at ceremonies at the system center at 8915 Hampton Road, three blocks south of Interstate 20. As soon as the Coordinating Board certified that enrollment at the center reached 2,500 full-time equivalent students, UNT-Dallas would begin offering courses and granting degrees. In the interim, the system center continued to offer courses leading to UNT degrees and certificate programs.

North Texas Locations Elsewhere

In Fort Worth and the mid-cities area, North Texas expanded night classes in public schools, community colleges, and a few corporate sites. In the fall of 1998, classes were scheduled in public schools in Fort Worth, Carrollton, Dallas, Garland, Denton, Hurst/Euless/Bedford, Irving, Plano, Flower Mound, Mineral Wells, and North Richland Hills. Community college facilities were used in Frisco, Dallas, Denison, and Arlington. Classes were also placed at Comanche Peak Power Plant in Glen Rose, Electronic Data Systems in Plano, and Sheppard Air Force Base in Wichita Falls. Cooperative programs also placed UNT credit instruction at Midwestern State University, Texas State Technical College, Texas Tech University, University of Houston, University of Texas at Arlington, and the UNT Health Science Center.

An Electronic Approach

In the 1990s, they started calling it "distance learning," referring to various forms of telecommunication to take instruction out to the student. It was not an entirely new concept. As early as the 1960s, North Texas had the example of the TAGER microwave television network at the Graduate Research Center of the Southwest. Primary users then were SMU, TCU, Austin College, and UT Arlington. In the 1980s, North Texas experimented with a few classes taught by microwave TV transmission. In the 1990s, UNT used a network operated by the Association for Higher Education to transmit and receive a limited number of graduate courses. In 1997–98, the system transmitted courses in business administration and computer science to selected industrial sites and business locations in the metropolitan area.[27]

Distributed Learning

Dr. Philip M. Turner was named in 1996 as dean of the School of Library and Information Sciences and associate vice president for distance learning. The 1998–99 undergraduate and graduate catalogs carried a formally worded paragraph under the heading of "Distributed Learning," noting that UNT "offers a limited selection of undergraduate and graduate courses via distributed learning, which includes courses delivered via the World Wide Web and via videoconference." These could be taken from any location in the world where Internet access was available.[28]

The Center for Distributed Learning began operation in August 1998, offering help in course design and production of distributed-learning courseware. For fall 1998, the center listed ten graduate videoconference courses. UNT joined TWU to conduct two-way video courses leading to the master's degree in library science. This instruction was available to students at Midwestern State in Wichita Falls, Abilene Christian University, Texas A&M at Texarkana and the University of Texas-Pan Am in Edinburgh. TWU and North Texas each offered half the courses needed for the degree, with students choosing the school from which to receive the degree. Students did not ever have to come to a Denton campus for the program.[29]

Also noted in February 1998 were 200 courses using Internet web pages to provide interactive content, course outlines, and class notes. Metroplex-area students telephoned free to the UNT computing center to access various computing capabilities. Students with Internet access could reach their course materials and communicate with the instructor from anywhere in the nation.

3. How Do We Attain National Research Status?

Broad regional and national recognition of North Texas required the development, expansion, and improvement of research programs throughout the campus. Inadequate financial support was the obstacle. Vastly increased external support was the key to progress.

Growth of Extramural Funding

The extent of support was still rather small as the 1980s began. There were 182 sponsored research grants in 1981 for $401,418; 171 for $346,981 in 1982; and 191 awards for $424,166 in 1983.[30] It is helpful to look at a ninety-one-page white paper by Dr. Rollie Schafer, vice provost for research, presented in May 1999. The Schafer White Paper shows the development of the research function and relates external funding to enrollment and graduate degrees awarded.

Enrollment, Graduate Degrees Awarded, and External Funding, 1976–1998 [31]

Fiscal Year	Enrollment	Master's	Doctorates	External Funding
1976	17,016	992	130	$2.6 million
1977	17,151	1,039	125	$2.1 million
1978	17,300	997	118	$4.2 million
1979	17,228	981	131	$4.5 million
1980	17,158	896	151	$4.3 million
1981	17,487	863	143	$5.8 million
1982	18,782	918	163	$5.6 million
1983	20,234	923	158	$4.8 million
1984	21,414	1,028	163	$4.9 million
1985	20,996	1,064	161	$4.7 million
1986	21,271	1,093	148	$8.1 million
1987	22,380	1,130	194	$10 million
1988	24,498	1,088	157	$13.1 million
1989	26,519	1,103	157	$15.2 million
1990	27,160	1,159	184	$19.4 million
1991	27,020	1,225	176	$16.5 million
1992	26,433	1,172	213	$18.5 million
1993	25,759	1,251	168	$20.7 million
1994	25,605	1,152	193	$20.3 million
1995	25,114	1,205	188	$23.8 million
1996	24,957	1,165	177	$20.6 million
1997	25,013	1,156	190	$20.6 million
1998	25,514	1,168	161	$25.5 million

For the Centennial Decade

The Centennial Decade Agenda for 1989-99[32] identified immediate strategies to encourage research: seek more organized research appropriations; develop with external funds the existing Institute of Applied Sciences and the Center for Networks Neuroscience; and continue development with external financial support the Centers for Texas Studies, Materials Characterization, Economic Development, Research on Biological and Chemical Bases of Learning; and Marketing and Design. (Two that did not survive were Texas Studies and Marketing and Design.)

Medium-range strategies included: increase external research funding to $20 million a year; use external financial support to build Centers for Public and International Affairs, Computational, Mathematical and Information Sciences, Humanities and Social Sciences, Innovation in Performing Arts, and Applied Life Science; enhance library collections appropriate to a research university; and enhance computing resources consistent with a research university.

Purpose number one in a 1992 strategic plan was strong research emphasis. The plan acknowledged problems with lack of financial support and the pressures to subordinate research to teaching but predicted that applied research would grow in importance along with basic research. The report foresaw that the slow rate of library growth, limited capital expenditures, and inadequate funds for nationally competitive salaries would affect North Texas's ability to achieve a national research reputation. The document further acknowledged that teaching would be a major priority for parents and legislators, and that individual faculty members would face conflicting demands between teaching and research.[33]

Two years later, the strategic plan for 1997–2001 again asserted that "With changes in public priorities, more research funding must be found in private sources," and "Doctoral institutions that fail to maintain a research profile will have difficulty attracting top quality faculty."[34] The document asserted the significance of the link between research and strong undergraduate and graduate instructional programs:

> UNT views the presence of over 40 doctoral programs as a way to provide undergraduates with a high-quality educational experience not available at universities that do not have strong graduate offerings. Faculty who teach at the doctoral level must remain current in their disciplines through their research and professional activities. At UNT these same faculty generally also teach undergraduates, thus, providing top professors to teach at the baccalaureate level.[35]

Other Research Initiatives

In the *North Texan* in 1997, Chancellor Hurley reviewed faculty success in obtaining external funds, more than quadrupling research funding in the decade from 1985 to 1995. He noted that research was increasingly interdisciplinary: "Our three newest doctoral programs are research-oriented, interdisciplinary programs: information science, environmental science, and materials science. This is a signpost of the future, as many believe that the problems of the 21st century can be solved only through the teamwork of experts from various fields."[36]

Developing a Joint Venture

In October 1998, Texas Instruments made an equipment gift that would join four area universities to work on semiconductor research. UNT joined SMU and the University of Texas units at Dallas and Arlington to create the Metroplex Research Consortium for Electronic Devices and Materials.[37]

4. How Shall We Provide Special Service?

Through the 1980s and the 1990s the impetus toward organized service units accelerated greatly. In 1998, the *Fact Book, University Planning* listed a major array of organized research and service units. The listing offers dramatic contrast with approved campus functions of the early North Texas decades:

Provost and Vice President for Academic Affairs

North Texas Community/Junior College Consortium
Texas Institute for Research and Education on Aging
University Center for Economic Development and Research

College of Arts and Sciences

Center for Economic Education
Center for Environmental Economic Studies and Research
Center for Environmental Philosophy
Center for Inter-American Studies and Research
Center for Network Neuroscience
Center for Nonlinear Science
Center for the Advancement of Psycholegal Studies
Center for Research in Parallel and Distributed Computing
Center for Spatial Analysis and Mapping
Center for Sport Psychology and Performance Enhancement
Center for the Study of Diplomatic & Military History
Center for Transportation Studies
Institute of Applied Sciences

Center for Environmental Archaeology
Center for Remote Sensing and Land-use Analysis
Institute of Public and International Affairs
Interdisciplinary Center for Study of Work Teams
Labor and Industrial Relations Institute
Laboratory of Forensic Anthropology
University Writing Center
UNT Psychology Clinic
UNT Speech and Hearing Center

College of Business Administration

Center for Educational Technology in Accounting
Center for Quality and Productivity
Information Systems Research Center
Institute of Petroleum Accounting

School of Community Service

Center for Public Management
Center for Public Service
Cultural Sensitivity, Training and Research Center
Institute for Studies in Addictions
Minority Aging Research Institute
National Academy for Teaching and Learning about Aging
National Academy for Victim Studies
Survey Research Center
College of Education
Center for Higher Education
Center for Parent Education
Center for Play Therapy
Center for Sport Psychology and Performance Enhancement
Center for the Study of Education Reform
Child Development Laboratory
Counseling and Human Development Center
Educational Research Laboratory
Investigations of Talented Students

Maturational Assessment Clinic
Office of Field Services
The Child and Family Resource Clinic
TRIO Center for Student Development
UNT Institute for Behavioral and Learning Differences

Robert B. Toulouse School of Graduate Studies

Industry/University Cooperative Research Center for Nanostructural Materials Research

College of Music

Center for Experimental Music and Intermedia

School of Visual Arts

North Texas Institute for Educators on the Visual Arts

5. How Shall We Finance All This?

The story of North Texas is dominated by the struggle for adequate funds. For seventy years this was almost exclusively a matter of persuasion of the Texas Legislature and of the governor and his budget staff. Income from tuition and fees was a minor factor for most of this time; the federal government had not become a major partner in support of higher education activities; there was no tradition of organized alumni giving; private fund solicitation was virtually nonexistent.

Matthews: For Federal Funds, Against Private

President J. C. Matthews was widely known as being opposed to private giving to North Texas. Matthews did agree that some nongovernmental groups were appropriate sources of support. A key example was the Robert A. Welch Foundation of Houston for research in basic chemistry. This became the first major source of external funding for research in the sciences at North Texas.

With the Higher Education Act of 1965 and the Higher Education Facilities Act came many opportunities for federal grants. President Matthews encouraged the formation of committees that would seek such support. He faced major opposition for a time from ultraconservative regents, but federal funding did become significant in the latter years of the Matthews administration.

In 1969 the university's financial reports began to show sources of research funds as separate items, and federal participation was shown in these amounts:[38]

Fiscal Year	Amounts
1969	$107,000
1970	$356,977
1971	$153,221
1972	$123,348
1973	$119,931
1974	$159,948
1975	$228,191
1976	$426,168
1977	$576,624
1979	$2,282,831
1980	$2,533,065
1981	$3,527,012
1982	$3,669,068
1983	$3,249,118

Growth of the Federal Dollar

Here are yearly records of total federal funds received in the category of sponsored projects awards:[39]

Fiscal Year	Total
1993	$8,430,341
1994	$7,322,621
1995	$10,298,487
1996	$6,177,483
1997	$5,808,743

SEEKING THE PRIVATE DOLLAR

Importing a Fund-Raiser

A major motive of the Board of Regents in selecting President Nolen was to make private fund-raising a major factor in building North Texas. Foundation efforts included these results in building gift support in the first half of the 1970s:

1970–71	$246,500.00
1971–72	$361,768.00
1972–73	$516,271.00
1973–74	$541,727.00
1974–75	$598,106.00

In spite of problems with the state auditors and with public perceptions of private fund giving, Nolen's group did build up nonpublic revenue. In the last two years of his presidency, private gifts, grants, and contracts yielded $2,018,585 and $2,075,600.

In the Carter and Vandiver interregnum years, private income was $2,0027,557 and $1,755,209.[40]

Private Giving Builds

After the success of the Centennial capital gifts campaign, income from private sources continued to build. Private giving for sponsored projects, for example, was reported this way for the middle fiscal years of the 1990s:[41]

FY 93	$10,086,267
FY 94	$10,750,276
FY 95	$11,461,293
FY 96	$10,874,552
FY 97	$13,093,571

A group of deans who met to discuss the 1999 white paper on extramural funding endorsed the institution's progress in this area. That document reported their consensus: "In the past ten years, UNT has done an excellent job in attracting private dollars, to the extent that approximately half of our extramural funding is from private sources."[42] In July 2000 UNT received a 2000 Circle of Excellence in Educational Fund-Raising Award from the Council of Advancement and Support of Education. The school was one of twenty-seven chosen from 1,289 competitors. Reports cited a ten-year gift increase of forty percent.[43]

Total Budget Grows Rapidly

For many years, annual budgets portrayed the planned expenditures at North Texas in terms of two major elements: education and general and auxiliary enterprises. Annual budgets did not factor in capital expenditures for construction of buildings. Those limited funds from gifts and contracts were generally handled outside of the budget process. These were the annual total budget figures for these years:

1983	$88,585,258
1984	$92,526,735
1985	$98,107,187
1986	$99,342,482
1987	$100,591,608
1988	$108,731,756
1989	$123,725,295
1990	$131,787,429

From that point forward, however, other kinds of funds were included in the annual budget, some of them being previously nonexistent or inconsequential in size. The legislature had created the Higher Education Assistance Fund to appropriate special funds to the universities outside of the University of Texas and Texas A&M systems. This was expended for new buildings, remodeling, library purchases, instructional equipment, and other education and general purposes. HEAF funds were included in the annual budget starting in 1992. In addition, the legislature authorized regents to collect a variety of instructional fees and other fees collected from student registrations. As private funds grew, these were included in "restricted funds" in the budget. Plant funds were also added in. The result was that the fiscal year budget reflected a great deal more in expenditures than had once been the case. After 1995, for example, the annual budget totals were approved in these amounts:

1996	$226,923,197
1997	$254,512,400
1998	$269,738,866
1999	$271,237,666

SEEKING "CARNEGIE RESEARCH II" STATUS

North Texas had enjoyed the official designation as an emerging national research university and had several times been classified with "Doctoral Universities I" by the Carnegie Foundation for the Advancement of Learning, the last such designation coming in 1994.[44] The university would have preferred to be classified with Research Universities II but failed to do so in the 1994 classification because it did not meet the threshold for external funding: schools in this group receive annually between $15.5 million and $40 million in federal support.[45] Chancellor Hurley proposed that UNT consider committing to a systematic effort to qualify as a Carnegie Research II university.

Necessary to Credibility

Indeed, this concept became central to the Schafer White Paper in 1999. As mentioned above, a group of deans discussed the white paper issues and concluded that Carnegie Research II status was necessary to the credibility of the UNT claim to be regarded as one of the flagship research universities in Texas. The deans noted that in master's and total graduate semester credit hours UNT ranked in the top four universities, although Texas Tech was ahead in doctoral hours. Their report emphasized that UNT "should clearly differentiate the institution from the other Carnegie Doctoral I institutions in the state, which incidentally are located in the North Central Texas region (Texas A&M at Commerce, Texas Woman's University, UT-Arlington, and UT-Dallas)."[46]

Recognition for a Research Library

Dean of Libraries Donald Grose reported on the importance of membership in the Association of Research Libraries in the white paper on national recognition of research. Membership became yet another goal for the next century. Grose noted that Carnegie Research II status was essential to an invitation to join the ARL. He said that the university could achieve membership by using a newly approved library fee, continued increases in the library's HEAF allocation, and convincing the association to accept a combined application from UNT and UNT Health Science Center. [47]

Joining Internet 2

UNT was an early participant in the Internet when it was an academic/governmental computer networking system—one that was not accessible for commercial ventures. Beginning in 1987, the National Science Foundation backbone known as NSFnet provided connectivity for the United States research community and expanded globalization of research. The Internet was privatized in 1995, and academic users were forced to compete with commercial users of Internet resources. The Schafer white paper noted that, "Frequent congestion of the network, sluggish responses, and the competition for bandwidth has had a negative impact on the university research community."[48]

This led thirty-four research universities to follow a government-led Internet-

2 initiative and to establish a charter for a University Corporation for Advanced Internet Development in 1997. Regular membership was restricted to universities. Of 130 members in 1998, those in Texas were UT-Austin, Texas Tech, Houston, SMU, Rice, and Texas A&M. The white paper pointed to "obvious benefits" to UNT in keeping up with those Texas universities, "but pursuing membership in UCAID would have practical benefits as the university and its faculty actively participated in the development of a national high-speed network infrastructure." The document then listed reasons for North Texas to consider membership in the Internet-2 initiative: (1) access to new applications, (2) cutting-edge technology that would lead to new research endeavors, (3) membership as a precursor to external funding, (4) favorable impact in improving the campus network, and (5) benefits to the image and reputation of a research university.

In fact, said the white paper, "Failure to make a commitment to global high-speed connectivity may cause UNT to be ranked at a level that does not reflect its scientific and educational capabilities." The document then outlined a plan for joining Internet-2.[49] This was successful, and the university began operating on the Internet-2 connections in the spring semester of 2001 as one of 180 universities in the consortium.

PUTTING IT ALL TOGETHER: THE SYSTEM

In 1981 the Board of Regents added the title of "chancellor" to that of "president" to indicate oversight of Texas College of Osteopathic Medicine. This moved the enterprise toward becoming a system. The movement became reality when TCOM expanded to become the University of North Texas Health Science Center in Fort Worth and the UNT South Dallas Center was established.

The Texas Legislature in the spring of 1999 authorized the formation of the University of North Texas System, conditioned upon approval of the Higher Education Coordinating Board. That approval came on July 23, 1999, designating UNT as one of six public university systems in the state. Approval was given at the same time to Texas Tech University. Existing systems were Texas A&M, University of Texas, University of Houston, and the Texas State University system (including universities remaining in what was once the state teachers college system).[50]

This change opened the way to a planned formal division of the title and the responsibilities of chancellor and president. In September 2000 Hurley nominated Dr. Norval Pohl to become president, a move that had been envisioned when he became executive vice president and provost the preceding January. The Faculty Senate and the Council of Deans endorsed him for the position. The regents named Pohl to the post on October 10, 2000.[51] Pohl had served four years as vice president for finance and administration at the University of Nevada, Las Vegas, after service from 1986 to 1994 as dean and professor of the College of Business and Economics there.

Pohl's responsibility as the university's chief operating officer began October 15. At the same time, the regents approved a period of transition between October 15 and December 31 before the formal UNT System structure was initiated on January 1, 2001.

When this administrative development was announced in September, the *Dallas Morning News* editorially saluted Hurley with a headline that called him "the unsung hero of higher education." The paper noted that during his presidency, North Texas had grown from an enrollment of 18,782 to 27,132 in the current semester; the university endowment had grown from $850,000 to $45 million. But, said the *News*, "North Texas' greatest debt to Dr. Hurley is for his clear vision of the educational needs of the entire region. His willingness to take risks to expand the higher education choices for everyone will serve as his strongest legacy."[52]

Chancellor Hurley saw the emergence of a statutory system as the logical culmination of the story of North Texas:

> Achieving system status reflects the growth of our two institutions, the university in Denton and the Health Science Center in Fort Worth. The formal establishment as a system makes it easier for our institution to help make the people of this region aware of our readiness to serve them and their communities. The addition of the new System Center in South Dallas will increase that awareness even more.[53]

Final Note from the Author: North Texas Proud

In the forty-eight years since this writer joined the North Texas faculty, he has spent much of his professional life believing in and being an advocate for the institution. He unashamedly believes that the 1894 forecast of President Menter B. Terrill has been justified by events of more than a century: "Our work shall prove our worth." He is convinced that this record shows that North Texas is far more than just another teachers college that happened to grow larger with the passage of time and the growth in American college attendance patterns.

Much of this story has focused on the efforts of its leaders, but no one should fail to notice that in the course of the first 110 years, there has worked a faculty of exceptional talent and energy. Chancellor Hurley declared in September 2000 that "we have had an extraordinary commitment to the university from administrators and faculty and staff members who have worked tirelessly over the years to make this institution what it is today."

W. H. Bruce said that his chief merit was "the faculty I assembled." President Marquis agreed, calling the teachers college faculty Bruce's finest contribution to the college and to the state. A little after that, a visiting examiner from the University of Texas described the faculty as young, vigorous, and progressive, signaling that "this school is bound to develop into a very strong college." Faculty progress led the *Campus Chat* in 1928 to proclaim a first ranking among the nation's state-supported teachers colleges. This was based on a U. S. Bureau of Education survey that ranked NTSTC first in teacher qualifications, first in the reduction of percentage of lower degrees during the previous decade, first in the amount of progress made, and first in the meeting of standards of "general practice" over the United States.

In 1933 it was the work of the faculty that led the Joint Legislative Committee on Organization to single out North Texas as superior as an institution, academically, professionally, and in general organization. In the later 1930s, faculty committees led the development of more broadly based curriculums that built on the teachers college strengths to move to a general college status. And strong faculty action created the multiple colleges of the university style of organization in 1946.

When the Texas Legislative Council reported in *Public Higher Education in*

Texas in 1950, it found that many teachers in state colleges were teaching in fields in which they had no degree. The best record in Texas belonged to NTSC, with a low of 7.5%. The University of Texas had 19.7% and there were highs of 47.8% and 52.1% at one university and one college. Of the state total of faculty, 34.4% held the doctor's degree, but the two leaders were 57.8% at the University of Texas and 45.9% at North Texas. There were 292 bachelor's degree teachers in the state, only three at North Texas.

During the rest of the century, the North Texas faculty built even more remarkable contributions. They are so numerous that it has become impossible in this space to enumerate all of those worthy of recognition.

That white paper mentioned above noted that "Recently, a proprietary study of prospective Metroplex students revealed that UNT has a neutral image and should campaign to achieve an active, positive appeal to attract the most talented students." It noted that such a marketing campaign had begun.

The institution in 1998 began presenting its review of achievements and status under the heading, "UNT Proud." This appeared in brochures, handout packages, the university web page on the Internet continuing into the year 2001.

The university offerings now included ninety-one bachelor's, 121 master's, and forty-seven doctoral degree programs and it had been designated a Class I Doctorate-Granting Institution by the Carnegie Foundation. Entering freshmen were now scoring higher: 1075 average SAT scores compared to a national average of 1016 and a Texas average of 995. North Texas was noted as the largest, most comprehensive university in the Metroplex and fourth-largest university in Texas. UNT had become the largest residential campus in the North Texas region, public or private. Since 1987 its enrollment had grown 11.8%; African American enrollment up 28.5%, Hispanic enrollment up 109%.

Impressive progress was made in the naming of UNT students to major national academic awards. In his fall 2000 convocation address, Hurley praised "the work of some 30 volunteer faculty members associated with Dr. Jim Duban, head of the Office of Postgraduate Fellowships, in the extracurricular work of preparing promising students to compete for national scholarships and fellowships." In the five years ending in 2001, national scholarships won by UNT students included three Goldwater, six Rotary Ambassadorial, five Fulbright, five Intel Science Talent Search semifinalists and two finalists, two Harry S. Truman, two James Madison, two Morris Udall, and one Phi Kappa Phi, and one National Science Foundation and one Jacob K. Javits fellowship.

The school had been named one of America's Best College Buys, one of America's 100 Most Wired Colleges, one of the nation's top 100 colleges for Hispanic students, and one of the nation's 100 best colleges for African American students. The counseling psychology program was ranked sixth nationally in research activity by an American Psychological Association journal. The library system was designated as a major research library by the U.S. Department of Education with 2 million cataloged holdings.

Other marketing items noted statistical evidence of program leadership: more computers per student than other comparable Texas institutions, the region's largest hotel and restaurant management program, the state's largest master's degree program in engineering technology and the third largest in the country, fourth in the nation in the number of professional educators graduated each year, city management and urban policy field in the master of public administration program ranked first in Texas, eleventh nationally, and one of the nation's largest visual arts schools at a public university,

It reads as though written in response to Joshua C. Chilton's 1890 pledge, "It will be our aim to become leaders in the education of the young men and women of Texas, fitting them to creditably fill the most important positions in business and professional circles." Indeed, in his inaugural speech on May 4, 2001, President Norval Pohl did acknowledge Chilton's vision, echoing some of his words:

> I echo Chilton's call today. We open the 21st Century with the desire and steadfast determination to become one of our state's top-tier universities. Our vision challenges us to gain new and renewed recognitions as the premier educational, intellectual research, and cultural resource for our North Texas region. At the same time, we aspire to play an increasingly responsible role in creditably serving the higher education needs and meeting the expectations of the entire State of Texas.
>
> UNT *is* a great university. It is great because of the vision of its founder and because each succeeding administrator believed in the power of a vision to shape our future. At UNT we can shape our future.

On that May afternoon, this writer heard another voice, that of President Terrill calling out from the past, "Our work shall prove our worth. Try us."

Dr. John J. Kamerick
President, 1968–70.

(below) Hundreds of North Texas students and faculty members marched through Denton in May 1970 in memory of the students who died at Kent State University.

A hallmark of the administration of President John Kamerick was the introduction of widespread faculty participation in campus decision-making and the creation of the Faculty Senate. Here Dr. Clovis Morrisson, an early chair of the senate, leads a faculty discussion.

Working in a university-owned residence, Merrill Ellis of the music faculty developed this electronic music studio in the 1960s. This work continues today in the Center for Experimental Music and Intermedia.

(above) Opening of Interstate 35 East to Dallas in 1958 and Interstate 35 West to Fort Worth in 1968 helped stimulate major growth in the number of commuting students. A private bus company started daily service in 1975 from metropolitan points to this bus stop opposite the University Union.

C. C. "Jitter" Nolen
President, 1971–79.

A new library building arose on the site of the old Eagle Stadium in 1971, Phase I of an intended three-phase construction project. The second and third phases were never built.

Osteopathic physicians were operating a new private medical school, the Texas College of Osteopathic Medicine in Fort Worth, when the legislature voted to place it under the North Texas State University Board of Regents. The TCOM campus became the nucleus of the UNT Health Science Center, a major unit of the UNT System.

Another long-standing tradition for Homecoming each fall is the parade around the campus to downtown Denton and around the courthouse square.

Students operate a 100,000-watt FM radio station, KNTU. It began broadcasting with only 450 watts in 1969 from the Speech and Drama Building, then developed its own quarters in Smith Hall, a converted home. When fire struck those studios on June 22, 1989, staff members like this went back on the air in twenty-four hours in temporary quarters until Smith Hall was rebuilt in 1990. In 2000 the station got new quarters in the former Speech Building, now remodeled as the Radio/TV/Film & Performance Building.

(below) Peer counselors—students from many majors—get ready to greet new students for one of the three-day freshman orientation sessions that offer an introduction to student life, academic counseling, and class registration. This became a feature of assistance to freshmen in the 1970s and was later extended to include transfer students.

Frank E. Vandiver
Chancellor and President, 1980–81.

Alfred F. Hurley
President, 1982–2000; Chancellor, 1982– .

Joanna Hurley was an active partner with her presidential husband in many campus activities. Here, in 1988, she branched out to take a role (third from left) in *The Women,* a drama scholarship benefit performance in the UNT Theater.

Three commencements per year fill the Coliseum floor with candidates for bachelor's, master's, and doctoral degrees. More than 4,500 degrees were awarded each year from 1995 to 2000.

The one-time Texas Normal College took its seventh name on May 15, 1988, becoming the University of North Texas as this sign was dedicated at the Avenue C and Chestnut Street entrance to the inner campus.

Ron Skillens and Lisa Watson won the annual student election in 1989 as Homecoming king and queen. Tradition brings the winning pair onto the Fouts Field gridiron for presentation at halftime of the Homecoming football game.

(middle) Engineering technology faculty members and students began demonstrating alternative fuel vehicles with a UNT Centennial project, the Solar Car. This was followed in later years by a liquid-nitrogen powered CoolN2Car.

Student dancers join the pageantry at Fouts Field for the Centennial Extravaganza in 1990.

Among major research installations added in the 1990s was this tandem electrostatic pelletron-type accelerator for physics research. It was the largest in Texas.

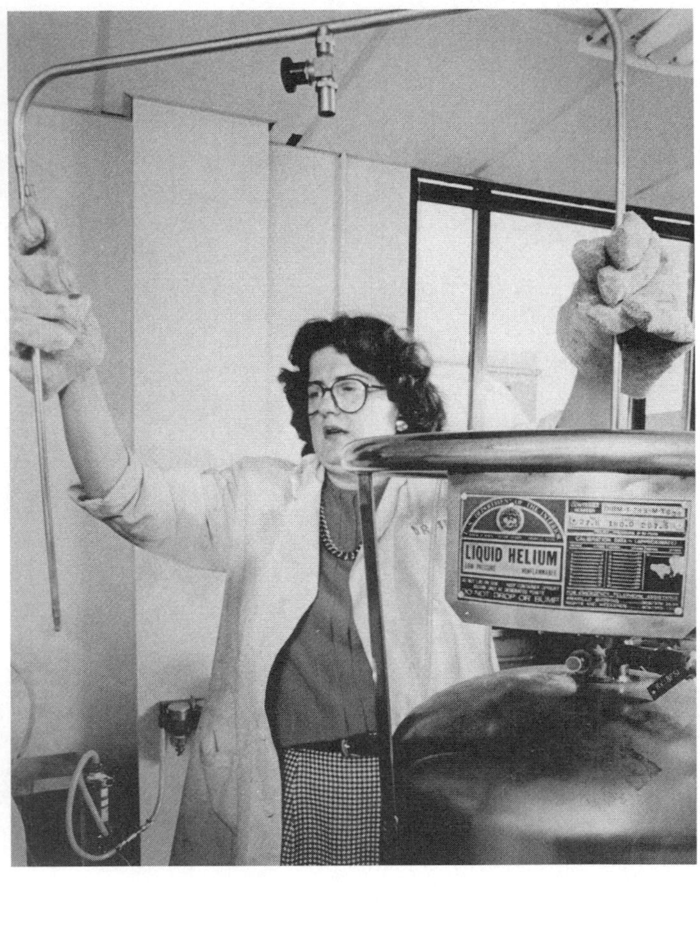

In the 1990s, faculty research grew in extent and importance in the university mission. Here, in 1993, Dr. Ruthanne Thomas, Chemistry Department chair, works with liquid helium for a superconducting magnet.

(above) Drs. Samuel Atkins and Bruce Hunter work on a satellite remote sensing project in the Center for Remote Sensing and Land-use Analyses in the Institute of Applied Sciences.

Students from drama, dance, and music joined in recent years to present major Broadway stage productions such as this 1999 *A Chorus Line* and the 1999 *Fiddler on the Roof.*

North Texas has for some time been the largest residential university in the North Texas region. For thousands of students like this woman in her room, the residence halls have been a significant part of student development.

Cheerleaders present acrobatic support for Eagle athletic teams, like this group at work at a basketball game in the Coliseum. North Texas cheerleaders won the NCAA Division I-A national championship in 2000.

Students come to the Help Desk, part of a better way to arrange for their educational needs. This is in the Eagle Student Services Center, which opened in 1997. It houses undergraduate admissions, graduate admissions and studies, financial aid and scholarships, registrar, and student accounting. The building connects to the University Union on the former site of the Swimming Pool.

The UNT System Center opened in a leased building in January 2000 to provide upper-level and graduate courses leading to bachelor's and master's degrees. Located on Hampton Road just south of Interstate 20 in Dallas, it offered the first public higher education access beyond the community college level in Dallas and Ellis counties.

Gov. George W. Bush spoke at groundbreaking ceremonies in September 1999 for the new UNT System Center in Dallas. Here, Board of Regents Chairman Bobby Ray watches as Dallas Mayor Ron Kirk and State Sen. Royce West join the governor with shovels.

Where Eagle football players once played their games, students stream along what is now the Library Mall and around the Administration Building.

A student chef exercises culinary skills in laboratory training in the School of Merchandising and Hospitality Management.

A student at work on a laptop computer in the University Union dining area illustrates the extent of UNT studies based on use of computers.

Students transferred the name of the former student newspaper, the *Campus Chat*, to the newest dining area in the University Union. The Chat became a special service for nonresidential students.

Art students bring their pottery craft to a tent at Fouts Field for a Homecoming Day picnic and demonstration of campus activities for returning exes.

International students became a significant part of the university population from the 1970s forward. Here, a parade of flags with an African Drum Ensemble opens another celebration of International Week.

The Art Department became the School of Visual Arts in 1992. Here faculty member Annette Lawrence works with students in a painting class.

Dr. Frank Kemerer, regents professor of education law and administration, works with students on campus and in remote sites connected by television and computer networks. "Distributed learning" became a major outreach technique of the university in the 1990s.

Shrader Pavilion, just west of the University Union, became a new center for campus performance and special events with its dedication at Homecoming in 2000.

They called it the fulfillment of a dream: the Murchison Center for the Performing Arts, which opened in 1999 to critical acclaim. It is located on the new entrance to the campus at Avenue E and Interstate 35E.

The UNT Symphony Orchestra performs in Winspear Hall, the 1100-seat performance hall in the Murchison Center. Groups performing there include the numerous university bands, orchestras, and choruses and a variety of visiting programs.

Earth Day 1999 draws participants to the Environmental Education, Science, and Technology Building, a 117,000 square foot environmentally friendly facility. The building houses interdisciplinary programs for environmental science, applied geography, environmental ethics, community journalism, and a planetarium.

President Norval Pohl receives the UNT mace during his inauguration May 4, 2001. Provost and Vice President for Academic Affairs David Kesterson, right, presents the traditional symbol of the office.

As the university entered the twenty-first century, the campus had grown to include 134 structures on 500 acres.

Notes to Chapter 1

1. C. A. Bridges, "The Denton Story" (Denton: np., nd), 280.

2. This statement, like the material on early Denton schools, comes from Bridges.

3. Oscar H. Cooper, *Seventh Biennial Report of the Superintendent of Public Instruction* (Austin: np, 1890), vii.

4. Frederick Eby, *The Development of Education in Texas* (New York: Macmillan, 1925), 182.

5. "Teacher Training in the U. S.," downloaded from http://encarta.msn.com, January 23, 2001.

6. B. M. Baker, *Fifth Biennial Report of the Superintendent of Public Instruction* (Austin: np, 1886), 16.

7. Oscar H. Cooper, *Sixth Biennial Report of the Superintendent of Public Instruction* (Austin: np, 1888), 31-32.

8. Oscar H. Cooper, *Seventh Biennial Report,* xix.

9. *Pilot Point Post-Mirror,* August 2, 1890.

10. Baker, 105, 112, 184.

11. *Pilot Point Post-Mirror,* issues of 1890.

12. M. E. Hall, "The Development of North Texas State College, 1890-1949" (Ph.D. diss., New York University, 1954), 21.

13. *Pilot Point Post-Mirror,* March 22, 1890

14. *Campus Chat,* April 18, 1935.

15. Harvey M. LaFollette, January 25, 1890, letter located in 1963 in the North Texas State University Museum.

16. Bridges, 288; Hall, 22.

17. W. N. Masters, *Campus Chat,* April 18, 1935.

18. *Pilot Point Post-Mirror,* April 18, 1890.

19. *Pilot Point Post-Mirror,* May 10, 1890.

20. City of Denton, *Minute Book,* vol. IA, 67.

21. Ibid., 68-71.

22. Ibid.

23. Ibid., 80.

24. *Pilot Point Post-Mirror,* May 24, 1890.

25. *Pilot Point Post-Mirror,* June 21, July 19, 1890.

26. Hall, 29; Bridges, 288; Robert Louis Higginbotham, "A History of North Texas State Teachers College" (master's thesis, North Texas State Teachers College, 1936), 3.

27. City of Denton, *Minute Book,* vol. IA, 77. This source is cited by Hall.

28. Ibid., 125.

29. Ibid., 126.

30. *Campus Chat,* April 18, 1935.

31. City of Denton, *Minute Book*, vol. IA.

32. *Denton Record-Chronicle,* February 1, 1948, Sec. 7; Bridges, 288.

33. City of Denton, *Minute Book,* vol. IA.

34. Bridges, 288; Hall, p.28.

35. City of Denton, *Minute Book,* vol. IA.

36. Bridges, 288.

37. Ibid.

38. Ed F. Bates, *History and Reminiscences of Denton County* (Denton: McNitzky Printing Co., 1918), 196.

39. *Pilot Point Post-Mirror,* December 13, 1890.

40. *Pilot Point Post-Mirror,* February 21, 1891.

41. Ibid.

42. Bates, 196.

43. Sam P. Allison, Kansas City, to R. C. Sherman, Denton, February 9, 1963.

44. City of Denton, *Minute Book,* vol. IA, 168.

45. Ibid., 196.

46. Ibid., Vol. IB, 19.

47. Ibid., vol. IA, 192.

Notes to Chapter 2

1. Manuscript originally found in the North Texas State University Museum. The NTSU Museum collection is now part of the University of North Texas Archives.

2. Pamphlets from the Orleans school in the North Texas State University Museum.

3. *Pilot Point Post-Mirror,* September 20, 1890.

4. Ibid.

5. Manuscript of speech by J. C. Chilton, September 16, 1890, in the North Texas State University Museum, now the UNT Archives.

6. *Pilot Point Post-Mirror,* September 20, 1890.

7. City of Denton, *Minute Book,* vol. IA, 126.

8. *Pilot Point Post-Mirror,* October 4, 1890.

9. *Pilot Point Post-Mirror,* December 13, 1890.

10. Jane F. Smith, National Archives and Records Service, to the author, August 22, 1963; Theda Wammack, the Creek Indian Memorial Association, to the author, September 18, 1963.

11. J. M. Carlisle, *Eighth Biennial Report of the State Superintendent of Public Instruction* (Austin: np, 1893), 62–66, 125.

12. Quoted in George Kimball Plochmann, *The Ordeal of Southern Illinois University* (Carbondale, IL: Southern Illinois University Press, nd, Preface dated July 1957), 522.

13. The material in this section is drawn from *Announcement of the Faculty and Course of Study of the Texas Normal College and Teachers' Training Institute,* 1890–91.

14. M. E. Hall, "The Development of North Texas State College, 1890–1949" (Ph.D. diss., New York University, 1954), 44.

15. Jessie M Pangburn, *The Evolution of the American Teachers College* (New York: Teachers College, Columbia University, 1932), 117.

16. W. W. Wright, quoted in the *Denton Record-Chronicle,* April 16, 1940.

17. *Campus Chat,* May 10, 1940.

18. *Campus Chat,* May 23, 1935.

19. *Campus Chat,* January 28, 1937.

20. W. H. Bruce, "Data Concerning the Establishment and the Development of the North Texas State Teachers College, 1901–1939" (Office of the President, North Texas State University), 19.

21. *Pilot Point Post-Mirror,* September 20, 1890.

22. *Campus Chat,* December 5, 1931, referring to the gift of a copy of the first year's catalog from Charlton, then living in Dallas; April 18, 1935, in one of a series of historical articles written by W. N. Masters.

23. *Campus Chat,* April 18, 1940.

24. "City of Dallas," downloaded February 23, 2001, from http://encarta.msn.com.

25. *Catalogue of Texas Normal College,* 1893–4, 10–11.

26. Ibid., 15, 17.

27. J. J. Crumley to W. N. Masters, reprinted in *Campus Chat,* May 2, 1935.

28. Ibid.

29. Transactions referred to in this section may be located in City of Denton, *Minute Book,* vol. 1B, 52-74. A discussion of this period was first reported in Hall, 59–61.

30. J. C. Matthews to Foster Crumley, May 10, 1962.

31. Unless otherwise indicated, material in this section is drawn from a dedicatory statement by the author on the occasion of the dedication of Crumley Hall on May 9, 1962.

32. *Pilot Point Post-Mirror,* August 23, 1890.

33. *Campus Chat,* May 2, 1935.

34. *Campus Chat,* May 9, 1935.

35. Clipping File, undated and unidentified, originally in the North Texas State University Library. This appears from the wording to come from a contemporary Denton newspaper.

Notes to Chapter 3

1. Material in this section is based on Hall's work with the City of Denton, *Minute Book*, Vol. IB.

2. *Catalogue of North Texas Normal College*, 1894–95, unpaginated.

3. Holman H. Terrill to the author, February 19, 1964.

4. *Campus Chat*, April 18, 1940.

5. W. N. Masters in *Campus Chat*, May 16, 1935; interviews with W. W. Wright and A. S. Keith in *Campus Chat*, April 18, 1940.

6. *Catalogue,* 1894-95.

7. Sam P. Allison, Kansas City, to R. C. Sherman, Denton, February 9, 1963.

8. O. C. Charlton to W. N. Masters, in *Campus Chat*, July 16, 1927.

9. *Denton County News*, April 13, 1893, quoted in C. A. Bridges, "The Denton Story" (Denton: np., nd), 292.

10. *Texas School Journal*, vol. XI, March 1893, 123–124.

11. *Denton County News*, January 31, 1895, quoted in Bridges, 292.

12. City of Denton, *Minute Book*, Vol. IB, 319.

13. Ibid., 324.

14. Ibid., 326.

15. Original document located in the North Texas State University Museum, now in the UNT Archives.

16. City of Denton, *Minute Book*, Vol. IB, 337.

17. Ibid., 352.

18. *Eleventh Annual Announcement of the North Texas Normal College, 1900–1901*, 10, 26.

19. S. B. McAlister, "History of the Senate Bill No. 145," unpublished manuscript in the possession of the author. Unless otherwise indicated, all the material in this section is drawn from Dr. McAlister's work, which he based on Senate records and interviews with A. C. Owsley, who as secretary of the Board of Regents in 1899 had been in Austin to engage in the struggle for support of the bill.

20. *Campus Chat*, November 5, 1936.

21. Bridges, 294.

22. Ibid.

23. Allison.

24. City of Denton, *Minute Book*, vol. lB, 377.

25. *Terrillian. The Yearbook of the Terrill School.* Vol. I, 1914.

26. Bridges, 344.

27. This section was drawn in part from Bridges, 344.

28. *Denton County News*, September 3, 1903, quoted in Bridges, 345.

29. Ibid., 348.

30. Ibid., 345.

31. Ibid., 346.

Notes to Chapter 4

1. *Announcement of the North Texas State Normal College for the Annual Session Beginning September 18, 1901, and Ending May 27, 1902* (Denton: np, 1901), 5.

2. Ibid.

3. *Catalogue of the North Texas State Normal College for the Annual Session Beginning September 18, 1901, and Ending May 27, 1902 With Announcements for 1902–3* (Denton: np, 1902), 7.

4. Ibid.

5. Robert Louis Higginbotham, "A History of North Texas State Teachers College" (master's thesis, North Texas State Teachers College, 1936), 11.

6. M. E. Hall, "The Development of North Texas State College, 1890-1949" (Ph.D. diss., New York University, 1954), 21.

7. W. H. Bruce, "Data Concerning the Establishment and the Development of the North Texas State Teachers College, 1901–1939" (Office of the President, North Texas State University), 9.

8. *University of Texas Bulletin No. 14*, May, 1902, 2.

9. *University of Texas Bulletin No. 212*, December 22, 1911.

10. *Announcement, 1901*, 8.
11. *Catalogue, 1902,* 16.
12. "Minutes of the Faculty," May 22, 1917.
13. *Announcement, 1901*, 5
14. "Minutes."
15. *Catalogue, 1902*, 16.
16. Ibid.
17. Arthur Lefevre, *Thirteenth Biennial Report of the State Superintendent of Public Instruction, Austin, 1902* (Austin: np, 1902), 2.
18. C. E. Evans, *The Story of Texas Schools* (Austin: The Steck Company, 1955), 111–12.
19. J. S. Kendall, "Biographical," June 2, 1902.
20. Ibid.
21. *Announcement, 1901*, 10.
22. *North Texas State Normal Journal*, October 1906, 14.
23. W. H. Bruce to J. A. Sanders, August 17, 1912.
24. Bruce, "Data," 24.
25. J. S. Kendall, *Twelfth Biennial Report of the State Superintendent of Public Instruction, Austin, 1900* (Austin: np, 1900), table facing lix.
26. *Eleventh Annual Announcement of the North Texas Normal College, 1900–1901* (Denton: np,nd), 2.
27. W. H. Bruce to R. A. Deen, June 20, 1911.
28. W. H. Bruce to David Kennedy, July 29, 1912.
29. W. H. Bruce to F. L. Prichard, August 3, 1912.
30. This quotation and the material that follows on the opening year of the state normal are drawn from Kendall's first annual report to the State Board of Education, September 1, 1902.
31. Arthur Lefevre to J. S. Kendall, October 14, 1902.
32. Arthur Lefevre to J. S. Kendall, October 23, 1902.
33. *Normal Journal* (October 1906): 14.
34. Ibid., 16.

Notes to Chapter 5

1. W. H. Bruce, "Data Concerning the Establishment and the Development of the North Texas State Teachers College, 1901–1939" (Office of the President, North Texas State University), 10.
2. "Minutes of the Faculty," May 22, 1917.
3. Bruce, "Data," 23–24.
4. Ibid., 10.
5. Ibid.
6. Arthur Lefevre, *Fourteenth Biennial Report of the State Superintendent of Public Instruction* (Austin: np, 1905), 29.
7. *First Preliminary Report of the Educational Commission of the Conference for Education in Texas* (Austin: np, 1909), ii.
8. *Proceedings of the Fourth Annual Session of the Conference for Education in Texas* (Waco: np, 1910), 43–44.
9. F. M. Bralley, *Seventeenth Biennial Report of the State Department of Education* (Austin: np, 1911), 33.
10. "History of the 'Uniform Course' for the State Normal Schools," undated. This was apparently written by Dr. Bruce. From the type of letterhead used, the date appears to be either 1908 or 1909.
11. Normal principals to the State Board of Education, January 13, 1908.
12. T. G. Harris to R. B. Cousins, April 16, 1908.
13. *General Laws of Texas*, 31st Legislature, Chapter 113, 221.
14. *Bulletin No. 35*, July 1911, 13–15.
15. W. H. Bruce to H. F. Estill, July 18, 1910.
16. Ibid.
17. General Laws of Texas, 32nd Legislature, First Called Session, 1911, Chapter 5. Cited in C.

E. Evans, *Laws Establishing and Maintaining Texas State Teachers Colleges* (San Marcos: Southwest Texas State Teachers College, 1943), 21.

18. *First Biennial Report of the State Normal School Board of Regents* (Austin: np, 1913), 3–5.

19. Ibid., 5–6.

20. *Normal Journal* (February 1912): 183.

21. *Second Biennial Report of the State Normal School Board of Regents* (Austin: np, 1915), 5.

22. Ibid., 7.

23. *Bulletin No. 39*, July 1912, 14.

24. *Second Biennial Report*, 6.

25. *Fourth Biennial Report of the Texas State Normal Schools* (Austin: np, 1919), 9.

Notes to Chapter 6

1. Charles A. Harper, *A Century of Public Teacher Education* (Washington, D. C.: American Association of Teachers Colleges, 1939), 38.

2. Jessie M. Pangburn, *The Evolution of the American Teachers College* (New York: Teachers College, Columbia University, 1932), 73.

3. R. B. Cousins, *Fifteenth Biennial Report of the State Superintendent of Public Instruction* (Austin: np, 1906), 19.

4. R. B. Cousins, *Sixteenth Biennial Report of the State Superintendent of Public Instruction* (Austin: np, 1909), 24.

5. F. M. Bralley, *Seventeenth Biennial Report of the State Department of Education* (Austin: np, 1911), 60.

6. F. M. Bralley, *Eighteenth Biennial Report of the State Department of Education* (Austin: np, 1912), 24–25.

7. *First Biennial Report of the State Normal School Board of Regents* (Austin: np, 1913), 16–17.

8. W. H. Bruce, "Data Concerning the Establishment and the Development of the North Texas State Teachers College, 1901–1939" (Office of the President, North Texas State University), 25–26.

9. *Second Biennial Report of the State Normal School Board of Regents* (Austin: np, 1914), 14.

10. *Bulletin No. 45*, July 1914, 9.

11. Robert Louis Higginbotham, "A History of North Texas State Teachers College" (master's thesis, North Texas State Teachers College, 1936), 46.

12. *Bulletin No. 45,* July 1914, 7–8.

13. Ibid., 29–30.

14. *Bulletin No. 48*, July 1915, 57–58.

15. C. E. Evans, *The Story of Texas Schools* (Austin: Steck Company, 1955), 408.

16. Ibid., 105.

17. J. S. Kendall, *Twelfth Biennial Report of the State Superintendent of Public Instruction* (Austin: np, 1900), xxii.

18. *Suggestive Course of Study for Summer Normals,* State Department of Education Circular No. 28C, Austin, December 1892.

19. J. S. Kendall, *Twelfth Biennial Report of the State Superintendent of Public Instruction.* (Austin: np, 1900), xxiii.

20. Ibid., xxiv.

21. Cousins, *Fifteenth Biennial Report*, 21.

22. Arthur Lefevre, *Thirteenth Biennial Report of the State Superintendent of Public Instruction* (Austin: np, 1902), 7.

23. Ibid., 6.

24. Cousins, *Fifteenth Biennial Report*, 19–20.

25. Harper, 117.

26. *Catalogue of the North Texas State Normal for the Annual Session of 1901–2 With Announcements for 1902–3* (Denton: np, 1902), 46, and subsequent bulletins through 1908.

27. *Campus Chat,* May 28, 1927.

28. J. S. Kendall to State Superintendent R. B. Cousins, February 8, 1906.

29. Ibid.

30. *Bulletin No. 27*, July 1909, 28.

31. *Bulletin No. 38,* April 1912, unpaginated.

32. W. H. Bruce to F. M. Bralley, June 12, 1912.

33. W. H. Bruce to Norah Smith, undated, presumably 1912.

34. W. H. Bruce to W. C. Caldwell, October 18, 1912.

35. *Bulletin No. 42*, July 1913, 8.

36. *Normal Journal* (November 1957): 40.

37. W. H. Bruce to Superintendent J. M. Glass, January 13, 1911; to Superintendent E. C. Grady, March 1, 1911.

38. W. H. Bruce to J. C. Coit, July 27, 1912.

39. Registration figures are taken from bulletins of the appropriate years.

40. *Bulletin No. 55*, January 1918, 335

41. *Bulletin No. 74,* July 1923, 229.

Notes to Chapter 7

1. Jessie M. Pangburn, *The Evolution the American Teachers College* (New York: Teachers College, Columbia University, 1932), 12.

2. Charles A. Harper, *A Century of Public Teacher Education* (Washington, D. C.: American Association of Teachers Colleges, 1939), 105.

3. Based on figures from the bulletins of each year.

4. Harper, 107–8.

5. Pangburn, 33–34.

6. A. Linscheid, in N. E. A. Proceedings, 863, quoted by Pangburn.

7. *Bulletin No. 55*, January 1918, 322.

8. "Minutes of the Faculty,"May 22, 1917.

9. Arthur Lefevre, *Thirteenth Biennial Report of the State Superintendent of Public Instruction* (Austin: np, 1902), 18.

10. W. S. Sutton, "What Should Be Done by Universities to Foster the Professional Education of Teachers?" *Bulletin No. 50*, January 15, 1905 (Austin: The University of Texas).

11. Ibid., 9.

12. Ibid., 10–11.

13. *Proceedings of the Fourth Annual Session of the Conference for Education in Texas, Waco, 1910*, 115–16.

14. Arthur Lefevre, *The Organization and Administration of a State's Higher Learning* (Austin: np, 1914), 26.

15. Ibid., 28.

16. Frederick Eby, *The Development of Education in Texas* (New York: Macmillan, 1925), 51.

17. Texas State Board of Education, *Statewide School Adequacy Survey* (Washington, D. C.: Works Progress Administration, 1936), 6.

18. W. F. Doughty, *Twenty-First Biennial Report of the State Superintendent of Public Instruction* (Austin: np, 1918), 643.

19. Harper, 119.

20. Ibid., 120–30.

21. Ibid., 138–39.

22. Ibid., 140–41.

23. *Catalogue of the North Texas State Normal for the Annual Session of 1901–2 with Announcements for 1902–3* (Denton: np, 1902), 41.

24. W. H. Bruce to R. A. Davis, January 5, 1910.

25. *Bulletin No. 39*, July 1912, 12.

26. W. H. Bruce to ten schools, June 11, 1912.

27. W. H. Bruce to Presidents H. B. Cousins, H. F. Estill, C. E. Evans, June 15, 1912.

28. *Bulletin No. 42,* July 1913, 37.

29. W. H. Bruce to L. D. Moore, March 1, 1911.

30. Ibid.

31. *Bulletin No. 45,* July 1914, 24–25.

32. General Laws of Texas. Thirty-Second Legislature, First Called Session, 1911, Chapter 5. Cited in Evans, *Laws Establishing and Maintaining Texas State Teachers Colleges* (San Marcos: Southwest Texas State Teachers College, 1943), 21.

33. "Faculty Minutes," November 7, 1916.

34. Ibid.

35. "Faculty Minutes," December 13, 1916.

36. "Faculty Minutes," May 22, 1917.

37. Ibid.

38. Ibid.

39. "Minutes of the Board of Regents," December 17, 1917.

40. W. M. Thornton, "How Texas Trains Its Teachers," 33. Reprinted from *Dallas Morning News,* November 11 through 25, 1928.

41. C. E. Evans, *The Story of Texas Schools* (Austin: Steck Company, 1955), 150–51.

42. "Faculty Minutes," September 13, 1917.

43. "Faculty Minutes," April 2, 1918.

44. "Faculty Minutes," April 4, 1918.

45. "Faculty Minutes," April 30, 1918.

46. *Bulletin No. 57,* July 1918, 12–13.

47. *Bulletin No. 64,* July 1920, 21.

48. Ibid., 44–48.

49. *Bulletin No. 64,* 39.

50. *Bulletin No. 58,* August 1918, 105.

51. *Bulletin No. 62,* August 1919, 105.

52. *Campus Chat,* June 12, 1919.

53. James Wm. Smith, "A Survey of the Development and the Needs of the North Texas State Teachers' College" (master's thesis, Southern Methodist University, 1925), 30.

54. *Sixth Biennial Report of the Board of Regents,* 11.

55. Ibid., 17.

56. "Minutes of the Council of Normal College Presidents," April 25–26, 1921.

57. Smith, 30.

58. Letter from I. P. Comer, secretary of the association, cited in Smith, 30.

59. Paul Woodring, "The Short, Happy Life of the Teachers College," *Saturday Review.*

60. U. S. Bureau of Education, *Statistics of Teachers Colleges and Normal Schools, 1921–22, Bulletin No. 10* (Washington, D. C.: Government Printing Office, 1924), 33.

61. Ibid., 34–37.

62. W. H. Bruce, "Report to the Legislative Committee Making a Survey of Higher Education in Texas," April 15, 1922.

63. *Campus Chat,* August 12, 1920.

64. *Campus Chat,* March 18, 1922.

65. W. H. Bruce, "Data Concerning the Establishment and the Development of the North Texas State Teachers College, 1901–1939" (Office of the President, North Texas State University), 30–31.

66. C. M. Mizell, "Dr. W. H. Bruce, His Contribution to Public Education" (master's thesis, Southern Methodist University, 1926), 113.

67. *Campus Chat,* April 10, 1923.

68. General Laws of Texas, 38th Legislature, 1923, Chapter 160.

Notes to Chapter 8

1. C. M. Mizell, "Dr. W. H. Bruce, His Contribution to Public Education" (master's thesis, Southern Methodist University, 1926), 113.

2. C. E. Evans, *Laws Establishing and Maintaining Texas State Teachers Colleges* (San Marcos: Southwest Texas State Teachers College, 1943), 1.

3. *General Laws of Texas,* 27th Legislature, 1901, Chapter 10, 10.

4. *Announcement of the North Texas State Normal College*, 1901, 8.

5. Arthur Lefevre, *Thirteenth Biennial Report of the State Superintendent of Public Instruction* (Austin: np, 1902), 180.

6. Arthur Lefevre, *Fourteenth Biennial Report of the State Superintendent of Public Instruction* (Austin: np, 1905), 32. These figures vary slightly from those reported in Bruce, "Data," 6. See note 14 in this chapter for full citation.

7. Ibid.

8. Copies of the circulars referred to are in the University Archives.

9. J. S Kendall, "First Annual Report to the State Board of Education," September 1, 1902, 4.

10. Figures taken from Kendall's annual reports.

11. *Bulletins No. 1 and 2.*

12. W. H. Bruce to F. M. Bralley, January 13, 1910.

13. See, for example, his annual reports to the board.

14. W. H. Bruce, "Data Concerning the Establishment and the Development of the North Texas State Teachers College, 1901–1939" (Office of the President, North Texas State University), 21.

15. *Normal Journal* 8 (November 1908): 33.

16. Lefevre, *Fourteenth Biennial Report*, 31.

17. *Proceedings of the First Annual Session of the Conference for Education in Texas, Austin, 1907*, 14.

18. Cree T. Work to T. G. Harris, January 8, 1909.

19. W. H. Bruce to F. F. Hill, January 13, 1910.

20. W. H. Bruce to H. F. Estill, January 13, 1910.

21. *First Preliminary Report of the Educational Commission of the Conference for Education in Texas* (Austin: np, 1909), 12–13; and *Proceedings of the Fourth Session of the Conference for Education in Texas* (Waco: np, 1910), 149.

22. F. M. Bralley, *Seventeenth Biennial Report of the State Department of Education* (Austin: np. 1911), 43.

23. E. D. Shurter, *A Constitutional Tax for the Support of Higher Educational Institutions in Texas, Bulletin 30* (Austin: Univ. of Texas, 1915), 13–16.

24. F. M. Bralley, *Eighteenth Biennial Report of the State Department of Education* (Austin: np, 1912), 18.

25. Organization for the Enlargement by the State of Texas of Its Institutions of Higher Education, *The State Institutions of Higher Education in Texas* (Austin: np, May 1, 1912), 25–27.

26. Arthur Lefevre, *The Organization and Administration of a State's Institutions of Higher Learning* (Austin: np, 1914), 25–27.

27. Ibid., 38.

28. Shurter, 12.

29. *Second Biennial Report of the State Normal School Board of Regents* (Austin: np, 1914), 2.

30. Ibid., 3.

31. "Minutes of the Council of Normal College Presidents," December 31, 1921.

32. Letter, March 2, 1918, in University Archives.

33. *Campus Chat,* January 17, 1931.

34. W. H. Bruce to C. C. McDonald, June 6, 1911.

35. W. H. Bruce to F. M. Bralley, March 13, 1911.

36. W. H. Bruce to Governor O. B. Colquitt, September 1, 1911.

37. W. H. Bruce to F. M. Bralley, September 11, 1912.

38. "Minutes of the Faculty," May 22, 1917.

39. "Minutes of the Board of Regents," April 14, 1917.

40. "Minutes of the Board of Regents," July 2 and 3, 1917.

41. "Faculty Minutes," May 22, 1917.

42. "Faculty Minutes," November 7, 1917.

43. "Faculty Minutes," June 4, 1914.

44. "Faculty Minutes," March 27, 1917

45. "Faculty Minutes," September 15, 1917.
46. "Faculty Minutes," October 17, 1917.
47. "Minutes of the Council of State Normal Presidents," September 9, 1920.
48. Mizell, 113.
49. "Faculty Minutes," April 24, 1923.
50. "Minutes of the Board of Regents," May 26, 1923.

Notes to Chapter 9

1. This quotation and the information immediately following are taken from the Kendall circular, located in the University Archives.
2. *Normal Journal* 2 (February 1903): 12.
3. *Normal Journal* 3 (November 1903): 3.
4. *Normal Journal* 3 (April 1904): 38.
5. *Bulletin No.* 7, July 1904, 25–26.
6. *Normal Journal* 3 (November 1903): 4.
7. *Normal Journal* 5 (January 1906): 27.
8. *Normal Journal* 6 (October 1906): 37.
9. *Normal Journal* 5 (January 1906): 36.
10. *Normal Journal* 6 (January 1907): 33.
11. *Normal Journal* 7 (November 1907): 27–29.
12. *Normal Journal* 7 (October 1907): 47.
13. *Normal Journal* 7 (November 1907): 41.
14. Typewritten manuscript, undated, in the University Archives.
15. *Bulletin No. 39*, July 1912, 9.
16. W. H. Bruce, "Data Concerning the Establishment and the Development of the North Texas State Teachers College, 1901–1939" (Office of the President, North Texas State University), 27.
17. *First Biennial Report of the State Normal School Board of Regents* (Austin: np, 1913), 12.
18. *Second Biennial Report of the State Normal School Board of Regents* (Austin: np, 1915), 17.
19. *Normal Journal* 10 (October 1910): 36.
20. *Bulletin No. 39*, July 1912, 9.
21. W. H. Bruce to F. M. Bralley, February 28, 1910.
22. *Normal Journal* 10 (October 1910): 47.
23. C. A. Bridges, "The Denton Story" (Denton: np. nd), 333.
24. Ibid., 356.
25. Ibid., 357.
26. Ibid.
27. W. H. Bruce to F. M. Bralley, August 22, 1910.
28. W. H. Bruce to F. M. Bralley, January 13, 1910.
29. W. H. Bruce to C. C. McDonald, January 30, 1911.
30. W. H. Bruce, "Report to the State Board of Education," June 5, 1911.
31. *Bulletin No. 42*, July 1913, 43.
32. Bruce, "Data," 37-38.
33. W. H. Bruce, "Report to the State Board of Education."
34. W. H. Bruce to Governor-elect O. B. Colquitt, January 4, 1911.
35. *Bulletin No. 39,* July 1912, 9; *Bulletin No. 45*, July 1914, 9.
36. *Normal Journal* (December 1915): 15.
37. W. H. Bruce to F. M. Bralley, undated.
38. *Bulletin No. 44*, April 1914, 14–15.
39. Ibid., 10; *Bulletin No. 45*, July 1914, 9.
40. *Bulletin No. 51*, July 1916, 11.
41. "Our Most Pressing Needs," *Campus Chat,* January 24, 1917, 2.
42. *Bulletin No. 54*, July 1917, 13.
43. *Campus Chat,* January 9, 1919.

44. *Fourth Biennial Report of the Texas State Normal Schools (*Austin: np, 1919), 19.

45. *Campus Chat,* December 11, 1919; June 19, 1920; February 7, 1931; April 18, 1940.

46. *Sixth Biennial Report of the Board of Regents of the Texas State Normal Colleges* (Austin: np, 1922), 12.

47. *Campus Chat,* June 11, 1920.

48. *Sixth Biennial Report of the Board of Regents of* the *Texas State Normal Colleges,* Austin, 1922, 11–12.

49. *Campus Chat,* December 19, 1922.

50. *Seventh Biennial Report* of *the Board of Regents of the Texas State Teachers Colleges* (Austin: np, 1924), 13.

51. "Faculty Minutes."

Notes to Chapter 10

1. Figures on the makeup of the student body may be found in the annual catalogs of the state normal.

2. *Normal Journal* 2 (October 1902): 4.

3. W. H. Bruce, "Data Concerning the Establishment and the Development of the North Texas State Teachers College, 1901–1939" (Office of the President, North Texas State University), 29–30.

4. These figures were taken from the annual catalogs. They do include subcollege but not training school students.

5. *Campus Chat,* December 10, 1921.

6. C. A. Gill to J. S Kendall, December 23, 1904.

7. *Normal Journal* 5 (December 1905): 16.

8. *Normal Journal* 11 (March 1912): 212.

9. *Normal Journal* 5 (November 1905): 34.

10. *Campus Chat,* November 11, 1929.

11. This quotation and the other material on disciplinary regulations comes from *Bulletin No. 39,* April 1912, 23–24, supplemented by material from a printed sheet of regulations given to students by Dr. Bruce during the early years of his administration.

12. "Faculty Minutes," October 13, 1914

13. "Faculty Minutes," December 31, 1913.

14. "Faculty Minutes," May 21, 1914.

15. *Bulletin No. 45* (July 1914): 26–27.

16. *Normal Journal* 2 (October 1902): 12.

17. Ibid., also *Normal Journal* 2 (May 1903): 54.

18. Ibid., 59.

19. *Normal Journal* 2 (November 1902): 19.

20. W. N. Masters, quoted by Davis, "A Survey of the Growth and the Development of Extra-Curricular Activities in North Texas State Teachers College, 1919–1939" (master's thesis, North Texas State Teachers College, 1940), 16.

21. Ibid., 17.

22. *Normal Journal* 2, (October 1902): 17; (December 1902): 19.

23. *Normal Journal* 2 (February 1903): 19.

24. Ibid., 10.

25. *Normal Journal* 3 (February 1904): 38.

26. *Normal Journal* 4 (February 1905): 36; (April 1905): 40.

27. *Normal Journal,* Vol. 8, April 1909, 41.

28. *Yucca,* 1922, 168.

29. Ibid.

30. *Normal Journal* 6 (February 1907): 25.

31. W. H. Bruce, "Data," 38–39.

32. W. H. Bruce to W. H. Wilson, October 8, 1908.

33. *Campus Chat,* October 19, 1929.

34. "Faculty Minutes," October 23, 1913.

35. *Campus Chat*, February 27, 1919. The handwritten comments appear in the microfilm copy in the UNT Library.
36. *Normal Journal* 8 (April 1909): 44.
37. *Normal Journal* 3 (February 1904): 35–36.
38. *Normal Journal* 4 (October 1904): 33.
39. *Normal Journal* 12 (March–April 1913): 36–37.
40. *Normal Journal* 14 (November 1914): 30.
41. *Yucca,* 1922, 14.
42. "Faculty Minutes," April 24, 1923.
43. "Faculty Minutes," December 10, 1913.
44. *Normal Journal* 15 (April 1916): 21.
45. *Campus Chat,* February 11, 1922.
46. *Campus Chat,* November 8, 1916.
47. *Campus Chat,* November 6, 1919.
48. Ibid.
49. "Faculty Minutes," November 7, 1917.
50. "Faculty Minutes," November 19, 1918.
51. "Faculty Minutes," March 13, 1923.
52. "Faculty Minutes," April 24, 1923.
53. Ibid.
54. *Normal Journal* 4 (November 1904): 37–38.
55. W. H. Bruce to F. M. Bralley, January 13, 1910.
56. *Bulletin No 45*, July 1914, 26.
57. Mildred Wilkerson Vick, "The History of the Growth and Development of the Health Service Program of North Texas State Teachers College from November 1918 Through August 1941" (master's thesis, North Texas State Teachers College, 1942), 11–13.
58. "Faculty Minutes," September 22, 1910.
59. "Minutes of the Council of Normal School Presidents," August 18, 1919.
60. "Faculty Minutes," October 7, 1919.
61. "Faculty Minutes," October 10, 1919.
62. *Normal Journal* 2 (October 1902): 7, 24.
63. *Normal Journal* 2 (January 1903): 16.
64. *Normal Journal* 3 (October 1903): 32.
65. Ibid., 24–25.
66. *Normal Journal* 5 (October 1905): 41.
67. *Normal Journal* 5 (January 1906): 34.
68. *Normal Journal* 6 (April 1907): 33.
69. *Normal Journal* 7 (October 1907): 7–11.
70. *Normal Journal* 7 (November 1907): 34.
71. *Normal Journal* 12 (December 1912): 39–40.
72. *Campus Chat,* January 24, 1931.
73. See various athletic brochures in the files of the university athletic office.
74. *Campus Chat,* December 17, 1921.
75. Reminiscence by a former student, Miss Julia Lucker, quoted in *Campus Chat,* May 7, 1932.
76. *Normal Journal* 8 (October 1908): 15.
77. *Campus Chat,* January 21, 1922; *Yucca,* 1922, 11.
78. *Campus Chat,* November 6, 1919, and November 20, 1919.
79. *Campus Chat,* November 18, 1922.
80. *Yucca,* 1922, 140-41.
81. *Campus Chat,* February 20, 1923.
82. "Faculty Minutes," November 7, 1917.
83. "Faculty Minutes," November 27, 1917.
84. *Bulletin No. 64,* July 1920, 31–32.
85. "Faculty Minutes," January 2, 1922; *Bulletin No. 71*, July 1922, 37–38.

Notes to Chapter 11

1. C. M. Mizell, "Dr. W. H. Bruce, His Contribution to Public Education" (master's thesis, Southern Methodist University, 1926), 87.

2. Ibid., 87–88,

3. Ibid.

4. "Minutes of the Council of Normal School Presidents," August 18, 1917.

5. Ibid., February 26, 1922.

6. W. H. Bruce, "Data Concerning the Establishment and the Development of the North Texas State Teachers College, 1901–1939" (Office of the President, North Texas State University), 39–40.

7. Mizell, 88.

8. "Report to the State Board of Education," undated but appears to have been submitted in the summer of 1903.

9. "Faculty Minutes," September 13, 1913.

10. "Faculty Minutes," February 27, 1914.

11. "Faculty Minutes," September 11, 1915.

12. "Minutes of the Council of Normal School Presidents," July 1 and 2, 1917.

13. "Faculty Minutes," May 21, 1914.

14. *Bulletin No. 50*, June 1916, 4.

15. Ibid.

16. "Bulletin Giving Data Concerning the Work of the North Texas State Normal College," 1901–1921, 22–24.

17. W. H. Bruce to A. W. Ore, January 30, 1911.

18. W. H. Bruce to J. H. Beveridge, March 2, 1910.

19. *Normal Journal*, March 1912, 234.

20. C. A. Bridges, "The Denton Story" (Denton: np., nd), 420.

21. Unless indicated otherwise, the material in this section is drawn from Mizell.

22. *Campus Chat*, August 13, 1932.

23. *Bulletin No. 45*, July 1914, 3.

24. *Campus Chat*, May 29 and June 19, 1923.

25. "Minutes of the Board of Regents," May 26, 1923.

26. *Campus Chat*, September 23, 1937.

27. *Denton Record-Chronicle*, December 31, 1943.

28. Mizell, 104.

Notes to Chapter 12

1. All statements in this section have been drawn from a report by University of Texas staff members. File was located in 1963 in the Office of the President, North Texas State University.

2. C. E. Evans, *The Story of Texas Schools* (Austin: Steck Company, 1955), 227–28; Frederick Eby, *The Development of Education in Texas* (New York: Macmillan, 1925), 314–19.

3. "Faculty Minutes," August 6, 1923.

4. "Minutes of the Council of Presidents of State Supported Colleges," April 16–17, 1926.

5. George M. Crutsinger, *Survey Study of Teacher Training in Texas, and a Suggested Program* (New York: Teachers College, Columbia University, 1933), 203.

6. "Minutes of the Board of Regents of the State Teachers Colleges," December 28, 1924.

7. J. A. Hill to A. B. Martin, January 7, 1925.

8. "Minutes of the Council of Presidents of State Supported Colleges," January 15, 1926.

9. Ibid., March 19, 1926.

10. Ibid., May 10–11, 1926.

11. "Minutes of the Texas Council of Teachers College Presidents," June 10, 1925.

12. R. L. Marquis to William Thornton, September 28, 1928.

13. R. L. Marquis to Joe Moore, January 30, 1929.

14. "Minutes of the Board of Regents of the State Teachers Colleges," May 31, 1933.

15. Ibid., August 22, 1925.

16. Ibid., March 19, 1926.

17. Ibid., May 9, 1932.
18. "Faculty Minutes," August 19, 1929.
19. The American Association of Teachers Colleges, *Yearbook*, 1928.
20. Crutsinger, 104.

Notes to Chapter 13

1. Association of Colleges and Secondary Schools of the Southern States, *Proceedings of the Twenty-ninth Annual Meeting*, 1924, 225.
2. Ibid., 52.
3. "Faculty Minutes," August 6, 1923.
4. *Bulletin No. 79*, 1925–26, 113.
5. This letter and all others not otherwise annotated in this section may be found in the Southern Association correspondence file, Office of the President.
6. "Minutes of the Texas Council of Teachers College Presidents," July 12, 1923.
7. "Faculty Minutes," January 9, 1924.
8. "Minutes of the Texas Council of Teachers College Presidents," January 5, 1924.
9. Ibid., April 4, 1924.
10. Ibid., May 9, 1924.
11. Ibid., August 25 and November 1924.
12. Ibid., December 26, 1924.
13. Ibid., April 13, 1925.
14. Ibid., June 10, 1925.
15. Ibid., October 16, 1925.
16. Association of Colleges and Secondary Schools of the Southern States, *Proceedings of the Thirtieth Annual Meeting*, 1925, 336–343.

Notes to Chapter 14

1.The Joint Legislative Committee on Organization and Economy, *The Government of the State of Texas* (Austin: np, 1933), 125–26.
2. R. L. Marquis to the Presidents of the Texas State Teachers Colleges, August 25, 1925.
3. S. M. N Marrs to R B. Cousins, September 23, 1925.
4. R. L. Marquis to H F. Estill, September 15, 1926.
5. H. F. Estill to the Presidents of the Texas State Teachers Colleges, September 11, 1926.
6. R. L. Marquis to H F. Estill, June 8, 1927.
7. *Campus Chat,* July 1, 1927.
8. R. L. Marquis to the Presidents of the Texas State Teachers Colleges, April 19, 1928.
9. George M. Crutsinger, *Survey Study of Teacher Training in Texas, and a Suggested Program* (New York: Teachers College, Columbia University, 1933), 15.
10. The Joint Legislative Committee on Organization and Economy, Part X, 47.
11. Ibid.
12. Ibid., 51.
13. Ibid., 58.
14. Ibid., 75.
15. Ibid., 98.
16. Ibid., 121.
17. Ibid., 122.
18. Ibid., 127.
19. Ibid., 88.
20. Ibid., 87.
21. Ibid., 352.
22. R. L. Marquis to the Presidents of the Texas State Teachers Colleges, April 15, 1932.
23. *Campus Chat,* January 5, 1933.
24. Ibid., January 19, 1933.
25. "Faculty Minutes," January 13, 1933.

26. "Minutes of the Board of Regents of the State Teachers Colleges," February 15, 1933.

27. J. A. Hill to J. M. North, December 15, 1932.

28. Sam H. Whitley to the Presidents and Regents of the Texas State Teachers Colleges, December 23, 1932.

29. *Austin Statesman,* January 13, 1932.

30. "Minutes of the State Board of Education," December 17–18, 1932.

31. A. W. Birdwell to A. B. Mayhew, February 7, 1933.

32. "Minutes of the Board of Regents of the State Teachers Colleges," May 9, 1932.

33. H. F. Estill to the Presidents of the State Teachers Colleges, March 12, 1934.

34. "Minutes of the Board of Regents of the State Teachers Colleges," November 26, 1934.

Notes to Chapter 15

1. All figures are from the biennial reports of the Board of Regents of the Texas State Teachers Colleges. Amounts for buildings are excluded.

2. J. A. Hill to M. O. Flowers, August 20, 1926.

3. R. L. Marquis to Mrs. Bob Barker, September 28, 1928.

4. "Minutes of the Council of State Teachers College Presidents," February 5, 1932.

5. Accounts of construction described in this section are taken from contemporary news stories and maps in the *Campus Chat* unless otherwise indicated.

6. John H. Bartlett to R L Marquis, October 1, 1924.

7. Robert Louis Higginbotham, "A History of North Texas State Teachers College" (master's thesis, North Texas State Teachers College, 1936), 28–30.

8. *Bricks and Mortarboards* (New York: Educational Facilities Laboratories Inc., 1964), 149.

9. *Campus Chat,* June 22, July 21, 1928.

10. *Campus Chat,* July 4, 1931.

11. *Campus Chat,* March 29, 1930, March 14, 1931.

12. "Minutes of the Board of Regents of the Texas State Teachers Colleges," May 31, 1933.

13. "Minutes of the Board of Regents of the Texas State Teachers Colleges," June 24, 1927.

14. *Campus Chat,* June 24, 1927.

15. R. L Marquis to Ben E. Brooks, January 22, 1929.

16. "Minutes of the Council of Presidents of State Supported Colleges," October 15, 1929.

17. R. L. Marquis to S. M. N. Marrs, November 10, 1925.

18. R. L Marquis to Harrold Kayton, January 23, 1929.

19. "Minutes of the Council of Presidents of State Supported Colleges," November 7, 1930.

20. R. L Marquis to J. W. E. H. Beck and Phil L Sanders, February 14, 1931.

21. "Minutes of the Board of Regents of the Texas State Teachers Colleges," February 13–15, 1933.

22. "Minutes of the Council of Presidents of State Supported Colleges," January 21, 1933.

23. *Campus Chat,* February 2, 1933.

24. "Minutes of the Council of Presidents of State Supported Colleges," March 18–19, 1932.

25. "Minutes of the Board of Regents of the Texas State Teachers Colleges," August 7, 1933.

Notes for Chapter 16

1. Charles A. Harper, *A Century of Public Teacher Education* (Washington, D. C.: American Association of Teachers Colleges, 1939), 153.

2. J. A. Hill to R. L. Marquis, June 25, 1928.

3. R. L. Marquis to J. A. Hill, June 28, 1928.

4. R. L. Marquis to J. A. Hill, July 7, 1928.

5. "Minutes of the Board of Regents of the State Teachers Colleges," October 8, 1929.

6. "Minutes of the Board of Regents of the State Teachers Colleges," February 10, 1930.

7. This interchange is from several letters: H. F. Estill to R. L. Marquis, February 18, 1930; J. A. Hill to Marquis, February 18, 1930; Marquis to Estill and Hill, February 21, 1930.

8. "Minutes of the Board of Regents of the State Teachers Colleges," October 16, 1930.

9. "Minutes of the Board of Regents of the State Teachers Colleges," January 26, 1931.

10. *Eleventh Biennial Report,* 1932, and *Twelfth Biennial Report,* 1935, Board of Regents of the Texas State Teachers Colleges, Austin.

11. R. L. Marquis to H. F. Estill, January 18, 1932.

12. Sam H. Whitley to the Presidents, Texas State Teachers Colleges, January 21, 1932.

13. H. F. Estill to H. W. Morelock, January 28, 1932.

14. S. H. Whitley to Presidents, Texas State Teachers Colleges, September 5, 1932; J. A. Hill to Whitley, September 8, 1932; R. L. Marquis to Whitley, September 17, 1932.

15. Joint Legislative Committee on Organization and Economy, *The Government of the State of Texas*, "Part X–Education, Teachers Colleges" (Austin: np, 1933), 65.

16. Ibid., 66–67.

Notes to Chapter 17

1. *Bulletin No. 74,* July 1923, 46.

2. *Campus Chat,* January 6, 1925.

3. *Campus Chat,* January 23, 1932; August 2, 1934.

4. *Campus Chat,* June 29, 1929.

5. *Campus Chat,* July 21, 1933; January 17, 1935.

6. *Campus Chat,* July 4, 1941.

7. *Campus Chat,* November 2, 1929.

8. Dorothy Marie Davis, "A Survey of the Growth and the Development of Extra-curricular Activities in North Texas State Teachers College 1919-1939" (master's thesis, North Texas State Teachers College, 1940).

9. *Campus Chat*, May 6, 1927

10. *Campus Chat,* February 1, 1930.

11. *Campus Chat,* April 5, 1930.

12. *Campus Chat,* May 10, 1930.

13. *Campus Chat,* July 26, 1934.

14. *Campus Chat,* May 2, 1931.

15. *Campus Chat,* May 28, 1927.

16. *Campus Chat,* June 16, 1925.

17. "Minutes of the Texas Council of Teachers College Presidents," June 10, 1925.

18. *Campus Chat,* October 1, 1927.

19. *Campus Chat,* November 11, 1929.

20. *Campus Chat,* May 10, 1930.

21. *Campus Chat,* June 21, 1930.

22. *Campus Chat,* July 26 1930.

23. *Campus Chat,* May 3, 1930.

24. *Campus Chat,* December 9, 1924.

25. *Campus Chat,* January 11, 1930.

26. *Campus Chat,* April 12, 1934.

27. Mildred Wilkerson Vick, "The History of the Growth and Development of the Health Service Program of North Texas State Teachers College From November 1918 Through August 1941" (master's thesis, North Texas State Teachers College, 1942), 10–22.

28. "Minutes of the Board of Regents," May 11, 1928. For a detailed account of early placement procedures see Jack L. Coppage, "A Study of the Teacher Placement Service of the North Texas State Teachers College" (master's thesis, North Texas State Teachers College, 1939).

29. R. L. Marquis to D. A. Penick, November 4, 1924.

30. *Campus Chat,* November 11, 1924.

31. George M. Crutsinger to D. A. Penick, May 17, 1925.

32. *Dallas Morning News*, July 12, 1925.

33. Kern Tips to R. L. Marquis, June 19, 1925.

34. R. L. Marquis to Kern Tips, July 25, 1925.

35. T. S. Clyce to R. L. Marquis, August 18, 1925.

36. R. L Marquis to T. S. Clyce, August 21, 1925.

37. This material appears in an unidentified newspaper clipping, identifiable only as that of a Dallas newspaper of December 1925.

38. W. D. Hooper to R. L. Marquis, December 18, 1928.

39. "Minutes for North Texas State Teachers College Athletic Council, (November 30, 1921–January 13, 1945)," January 18, 1932.

Notes to Chapter 18

1. *Campus Chat,* June 26, 1923.
2. *Campus Chat,* October 14, 1926.
3. *Campus Chat,* June 9, 1925.
4. *Bulletin No. 74,* July 1923, 9.
5. C. E. Evans, *The Story of Texas Schools (*Austin: The Steck Company, 1955), 353.
6. *Campus Chat,* July 3, 1923.
7. *Campus Chat,* August 19, 1924.
8. All the references in the matter of thc Texas A&M presidency were contained in a correspondence file, Office of the President, North Texas State University.
9. "Minutes of the Board of Regents of the State Teachers Colleges," May 10, 1926.
10. *Campus Chat,* April 11, 1931.
11. *Campus Chat,* June 13, 1931.
12. "Minutes of the Board of Regents of the State Teachers Colleges," June 17–18, 1931.
13. *Campus Chat,* April 19, 1934.
14. Ibid.

Notes to Chapter 19

1. The statistics on enrollment and student characteristics may he found in *North Texas State Teachers College Statistics,* Vol. I-III, September 1901 to September 1937.
2. "Minutes of the Board of Regents," May 14–15, 1934.
3. "Some Immediate Objectives of the Teachers Colleges of Texas," Office of the President, North Texas State University, written sometime in March 1937.

Notes for Chapter 20

1. "Minutes of the Board of Regents," June 14, 1935.
2. "Minutes of the Board of Regents," February 28, 1936.
3. Figures obtained from the biennial reports of the Board of Regents of the Texas State Teachers Colleges.
4. *Bulletin No 111,* August 1935, 10–15.
5. "Report to the Board of Regents," August 27, 1937.
6. C. E. Evans, San Marcos, to W. J McConnell, Denton, January 9, 1936.
7. W. J. McConnell, Denton, to C. E. Evans, San Marcos, January 30, 1936.
8. "Minutes of the Board of Regents," October 16, 1936.
9. W. J. McConnell, "Report Made to the State Board of Education," November 19, 1936. Quoted in M. E. Hall, "The Development of North Texas State College, 1890-1949" (Ph.D. diss., New York University, 1954).
10. *Campus Chat,* November 25, 1936.
11. J. A. Hill, Canyon, to W. J. McConnell, Denton, March 15, 1937.
12. W. J. McConnell, Denton, to J. A. Hill, Canyon, March 19, 1937.

Notes to Chapter 21

1. H. B. Masters to the President of Teachers' College, undated but presumably written in February 1933.
2. W. J. McConnell and R. L. Marquis to H. B. Masters, et al., February 1933.
3. "Report of the Committee on Research in Teacher Training," May 16, 1933.
4. Ibid.
5. *Bulletin No. 104,* March 1934, 10–11.

6. *Campus Chat,* February 28, 1935.
7. W. J. McConnell to J. C. Matthews, et al., March 4, 1935.
8. J. C. Matthews to Members of the Staff, April 2, 1935.
9. *Bulletin No. 118*, October 1936, unpaginated.
10. "Minutes of the Board of Regents," November 25, 1937.
11. "Minutes of the Faculty," October 17, 1941.
12. *Campus Chat*, October 24, 1941.
13. *Campus Chat,* November 29, 1940.
14. *Campus Chat,* December 5, 1941.
15. "Faculty Minutes," December 8, 1941.
16. "Minutes of the Board of Regents," May 14–15, 1942.
17. "Minutes of the Board of Regents," November 24, 1942.
18. "Faculty Minutes," November 12, 1945.
19. "Faculty Minutes," November 15, 1945.
20. "Faculty Minutes," December 15, 1945.
21. "Final Report of the Committee on Reorganization," November 6, 1945.

Notes for Chapter 22

1. "Minutes of the Teachers College Board of Regents," August 7, 1933.
2. "Minutes of the Teachers College Board of Regents," February 5, 1934.
3. Ibid., 29.
4. Ibid.
5. *Campus Chat,* November 15, 1934.
6. *Campus Chat,* August 1, 1935.
7. "Minutes of the Board of Regents," June 14, 1935.
8. *Campus Chat,* May 9, 1935.
9. *Campus Chat,* June 20, 1935.
10. "Minutes of the Board of Regents," December 12, 1935.
11. *Campus Chat,* October 10, October 17, November 21, 1935.
12. *Campus Chat,* November 27, 1935.
13. "Minutes of the Board of Regents," February 28, 1936.
14. *Library Handbook of the North Texas State Teachers College*, 1938; *Campus Chat*, May 28, 1927, April 13, 1929, February 14, 1931, May 12, 1938.
15. Robert M. Lester to W. J. McConnell, December 15, 1938.
16. W. J. McConnell to Mrs. Pearl McCracken, August 1, 1939.
17. William Stanley Houle to W. J. McConnell, October 23, 1939.
18. William Stanley Houle to J. Henry Highsmith, August 23, 1941.
19. William Stanley Houle to W. J. McConnell, January 26, 1942.
20. William Stanley Houle to W. J. McConnell, February 14, 1942.
21. *Campus Chat,* February 13, 1936.
22. *Campus Chat,* January 30, 1936.
23. *Campus Chat,* February 20, 1936.
24. *Campus Chat,* October 28, 1937.
25. *Campus Chat,* September 23, 1938.
26. "Minutes of the Board of Regents," November 24, 1937.
27. "Minutes of the Board of Regents," May 16–17, 1938.
28. Ibid.
29. "Minutes of the Board of Regents," July 5, 1938.
30. "Minutes of the Board of Regents," August 17, 1938.
31. *Campus Chat,* September 23, 1938.
32. *Campus Chat,* September 23, 1938; April 18, 1940.
33. *Bulletin No. 131*, July 1939, 45-47.
34. "Minutes of the Board of Regents," September 30, 1938.
35. *Campus Chat,* May 18, 1939.

36. "Minutes of the Board of Regents," August 16, 1940.
37. *Campus Chat,* October 11, 1940, March 21, 1941.
38. "Minutes of the Board of Regents," November 21–22, 1940, May 5, 1941.
39. *Campus Chat,* September 26, 1941.
40. *Campus Chat,* November 28, 1941.
41. Report to the Board of Regents, May 17, 1940.

Notes to Chapter 23

1. Salary figures are drawn from the biennial reports of the State Teachers College Board of Regents for the years mentioned.
2. "Minutes of the Board of Regents," April 15, 1935.
3. "Faculty Minutes," September 15, 1937.
4. "Faculty Minutes," November 2, 1939.
5. "Minutes of the Board of Regents," May 2, 1939.
6. *Campus Chat*, May 4, 1939
7. *Campus Chat,* May 21, 1932.
8. R. L. Marquis to L. A. Sharp, Harold Brenholtz, and V. Y. Craig, June 1, 1932.
9. Report to the Board of Regents, November 16, 1931.
10. Report to the Board of Regents, May 16, 1936.
11. Report to the Board of Regents, August 27, 1937.
12. Report to the Board of Regents, May 16, 1938.
13. *Campus Chat*, July 26, 1934.
14. *Campus Chat,* September 23, 1938.
15. "Faculty Minutes," November 2, 1939.
16. *Campus Chat*, October 2, 1942.
17. *Campus Chat*, January 9, 1942.
18. *Campus Chat,* August 2, 1934.
19. *Campus Chat,* October 18, 1934.
20. *Campus Chat*, February 14, March 28, April 25, 1935; March 5, 1936.
21. *Campus Chat*, January 16, 1936.
22. *Campus Chat,* September 23, 1938.
23. *Campus Chat,* February 3, 1939.
24. *Campus Chat*, May 12, 1938.
25. *Campus Chat*, April 25, 1940.
26. *Campus Chat*, October 18, 1940.
27. *Campus Chat*, October 24, 1941
28. *Campus Chat,* May 3, 1934.
29. *Campus Chat,* May 23, 1935.
30. *Campus Chat,* November 7, 1935.
31. *Campus Chat,* November 20, 1937.
32. *Campus Chat,* October 6, 1938.
33. *Campus Chat,* November 10, 1939.
34. *Campus Chat,* November 7, 1941.
35. *Campus Chat,* October 6, 1939.
36. *Campus Chat,* April 18, April 25, 1940.
37. *Campus Chat,* December 17, 1936.
38. Lee Hinton, *Athletic Records of Major N.T.S.T.C. Sports,* North Texas State Teachers College Library, 1941. Mimeographed, unpaginated.
39. Ibid.
40. Ibid.
41. C. E. Evans to the Lone Star Conference College Presidents, August 25, 1938.
42. W. J. McConnell to Marvin S. Pittman, November 4, 1937.
43. "Minutes of the Board of Regents," August 16, 1940.
44. Ibid.

45. Ibid.
46. *Campus Chat,* July 19, October 18, 1940.
47. *Campus Chat,* September 20, 1940.
48. *Campus Chat,* July 25, 1941.
49. *Campus Chat,* December 12, 1941.
50. *Campus Chat,* December 19, 1941.
51. *Campus Chat,* January 9, 1942.
52. Ibid.
53. *Campus Chat,* January 16, 1942.
54. *Campus Chat,* March 27, 1942.
55. Report to the Board of Regents, August 20, 1942.
56. *Campus Chat,* September 25, 1942.
57. *Campus Chat,* September 25, 1942; Report to the Board of Regents, October 12, 1942.
58. W. J. McConnell to H. A. Turner, March 20, 1943.
59. Report to the Board of Regents, August 5, 1943.
60. Ibid.
61. Report to the Board of Regents, May 15, 1944.
62. Report to the Board of Regents, November 26, 1943.
63. "Faculty Minutes," June 25, 1943.
64. "Minutes of the Council of Presidents of the Texas State Teachers Colleges," January 17, 1943.

Notes to Chapter 24

1. Texas Legislative Council, *Public Higher Education in Texas* (Austin: np, November 1950).
2. "Minutes of the Board of Regents of the State Teachers Colleges," October 1–2, 1945; Report to the Board of Regents of the State Teachers Colleges, October 1, 1945.
3. "Minutes of the Board of Regents of the State Teachers Colleges," November 23–24, 1945.
4. "Faculty Minutes," September 9, 1946.
5. "Minutes of the Board of Regents of the State Teachers Colleges," November 29–30, 1946.
6. "Minutes of the Council of Presidents of the State Teachers Colleges," June 17, 1945.
7. "Faculty Minutes," April 8, 1947.
8. *Eighteenth Biennial Report of the Board of Regents of the Texas State Teachers Colleges,* 12.
9. Report to the Board of Regents, June 16, 1947.
10. Report to the Board of Regents, August 21, 1947.
11. The comments in this section were drawn from a group of responses to a memorandum directed to deans and department directors by President McConnell on February 26, 1948.
12. Report to the Board of Regents, May 3, 1948, not presented at the board meeting as planned.
13. "Minutes of the Board of Regents of the State Teachers Colleges," April 11, 1949.
14. Report to the Board of Regents, August 6, 1946, November 18, 1946, May 9, 1947.
15. "Minutes of the Board of Regents of the State Teachers Colleges," February 8–9, 1946.
16. Ibid.
17. "Faculty Minutes," April 8, 1947.
18. Report to the Board of Regents, May 9, 1947; March 5, 1948.
19. Report to the Board of Regents, March 5, 1948.
20. "Minutes of the Board of Regents of the State Teachers Colleges," July 5–6, 1948.
21. "Minutes of the Board of Regents of the State Teachers Colleges," November 26–27, 1948.
22. E. N. Jones, Lubbock, to the Council of Presidents of State-Supported Colleges, March 23, 1945.
23. "Minutes of the Council of Presidents of State-Supported Colleges," February 11, 1946.
24. "Faculty Minutes," May 13, 1946.
25. *Dallas Morning News*, December 9, 1948.
26. *Texas Constitution,* Article 7, Section 17.
27. *Dallas Morning News*, April 24, 1948.
28. *Denton Record-Chronicle*, May 21, 1948.
29. *Dallas Times Herald*, October 20, 1948.

30. *Denton Record-Chronicle*, January 5, 1949.
31. *Dallas Morning News*, January 8, 1949.
32. Office of the Attorney General of Texas. Opinion No. 0-6932, January 18, 1946.
33. Telegram, William L. Kerr to Bullock Hyder, July 30, 1948.
34. Price Daniel to William L. Kerr, August 5, 1948.
35. "Minutes of the Board of Regents of the State Teachers Colleges," February 8, May 6–7, 1946.
36. "Faculty Minutes," October 8, 1945.
37. "Minutes of the Board of Regents of the State Teachers Colleges," May 5–6, 1948.
38. "Faculty Minutes," May 29, June 2, 1948.
39. "Minutes of the Board of Regents of the State Teachers Colleges," November 26–27, 1948.
40. "Minutes of the Council of Presidents of State Teachers Colleges," March 1, 1949.
41. News release, NTSC News Service, March 11, 1949; *Denton Record-Chronicle,* March 15, 1949.
42. *Denton Record-Chronicle*, May 10, 1949.
43. William G. Woods to W. J. McConnell, February 1948.
44. *Bulletin No. 201*, January 1949, 69–76.
45. *Bulletin No. 195*, May 1948, 68.
46. Theron J. Fouts to W. J. McConnell, May 7, 1947.
47. *Dallas Morning News*, October 8, 1947.

Notes to Chapter 25

1. J.C. Matthews, Denton, to Garth Carroll, Houston, January 26, 1967.
2. J. C. Matthews, Denton, to Alonzo Jamison, Austin, February 9, 1967.
3. Ben H. Wooten, Oral History Collection, OH Number 9. Interview November 11, 1969, 11.
4. Ibid., November 10, 1969, 16.
5. "Minutes of the Board of Regents," February 19, 1964.
6. "Minutes of the Board of Regents," October 19, 1964, 11-12.
7. This action is recorded in the minutes of the Board of Regents. The words are reconstructed from the memory of the author, who was present and keeping those minutes as secretary to the board.
8. "Minutes of the Board of Regents," February 18, 1965, 43-44, 62.
9. "Minutes of the Board of Regents," July 16, 1964, 182.
10. "Minutes of the Board of Regents," April 15, 1965, 70.
11. "Minutes of the Board of Regents," November 4, 1965.
12. *North Texas State University Design Study* (Houston: Caudill Rowlett Scott, May 1966).
13. "Minutes of the Board of Regents," February 10, 1966.
14. *North Texas State University Comprehensive Campus Plan* (Houston: Caudill Rowlett Scott, May 1967).
15. John L. Carter, "Loan Management Report for Year Ending August 31, 1967."
16. Report of the Southern Association Visiting Committee, North Texas State University, Denton, March 4-7, 1962, 37-38.
17. J. C. Matthews, Denton, to Ray A. Fowler, Austin, May 18, 1966.
18. "Minutes of the Board of Regents," May 8, 1968, 119.
19. North Texas State University, *Institutional Self-Study, 1971-73.* V-78.
20. Report of the AAUP-TACT Joint Committee on Faculty Organization, April 17, 1961.
21. Ibid.
22. Meeting notes preserved in the papers of Jack Scroggs, University Archives.
23. "The Faculty," *Report of North Texas State University for the Institutional Self-Study and Periodic Visitation Program of the Commission on Colleges and Universities*, Denton, 1962, VI-14.
24. J. C. Matthews, "Commencement," January 1962.
25. Report of the Southern Association Visiting Committee, 39.
26. North Texas State University Chapter, AAUP, "Minutes of the Meeting of May 17, 1962."
27. Martin Shockley, to the Executive Council, AAUP Chapter, May 29, 1962.

28. Gordon W. Sweet, Atlanta, to J. C. Matthews, Denton, December 14, 1962.

29. Second Follow-Up Report, North Texas State University. The document found in the Archives is undated, but a draft copy has penciled in "September 1963."

30. Second Follow-up Report, North Texas State University, September 30, 1964, 3.

31. Gordon W. Sweet, Atlanta, to J. C. Matthews, Denton, January 15, 1965.

32. Gordon W. Sweet, Atlanta, to J. C. Matthews, Denton, November 3, 1965.

33. 1965 Follow-up Report of North Texas State University, November 17, 1965.

34. Gordon W. Sweet, Atlanta, to J. C. Matthews, Denton, December 20, 1965.

35. Fifth-Year Report of North Texas State University, May 1967.

36. Office of the Attorney General, State of Texas, Opinion No. M-16, January 31, 1967.

37. Report of the Southern Association Visiting Committee, 38-39.

38. Ibid., 5-6.

39. Ibid., 14.

40. Second Follow-up Report, 3.

41. 1965 Follow-up Report of North Texas State University, 2.

42. "Minutes of the Board of Regents," August 17, 1967, 277–78.

43. Ben H. Wooten, Oral History interview.

44. *Yucca*, 1968, 33.

45. J. C. Matthews, Commencement Remarks, August 1968.

46. David A. Webb, to J. C. Matthews, July 26, 1968.

47. James L. Rogers, "Confidential Report of Conversation with Dr. Jack K. Williams," August 1, 1968.

48. J. C. Matthews, Commencement Remarks, August 23, 1968.

49. *Yucca*, 1968, 141.

Notes to Chapter 26

1. *Texas Almanac and State Industrial Guide (1986-1987)* (Dallas: A.H. Belo Corporation), 443.

2. Ibid., 442.

3. Ibid., 565.

4. University Planning and Analysis, *Fact Book* (Denton: North Texas State University, 1978), 1.7-3.

5. Coordinating Board, Texas College and University System, *Enrollment Projections for Texas Colleges and Universities, (Staff Draft Number 3),* May 29, 1968.

6. Texas Legislative Council, *Public Higher Education in Texas* (Austin, Texas, November 1950).

7. "Minutes of the Board of Regents of North Texas State College," August 28, 1951.

8. *Denton Record-Chronicle*, March 10, 1961.

9. *Dallas Times Herald*, April 11, 1961; *Dallas Morning News*, April 11, 1961.

10. *Fort Worth Star-Telegram*, April 20, 1961.

11. Ibid.

12. *Denton Record-Chronicle*, May 11, 1961.

13. Ibid.

14. J. C. Matthews, Commencement Remarks, June 2, 1961.

15. *Report of North Texas State University for the Institutional Self-Study and Periodic Visitation Program* (Denton: np, 1962).

16. Helen B. Callaway, "Graduate Education," *Goals for Dallas* (Salado, TX: Goals for Dallas Conference, 1966), 189.

17. Ibid.

18. Ibid., 186–87.

19. Ibid., 187–88.

20. Ibid.

21. *Goals for Dallas* (Salado, TX: Goals for Dallas Conference, 1966).

22. Ibid. , 18.

23. Ibid. 171–172.

24. Callaway, 191–192.

25. *Public Higher Education in Texas 1961–1971* (Austin: Texas Commission on Higher Education, March 25, 1963).

26. "Minutes of the Board of Regents," August 14, 1959.

27. J. C. Matthews, Commencement Remarks, January 31, 1965.

28. *Bulletin of North Texas State University, 75th Anniversary, 1890-1965,* 1965, 10.

29. Much of the material in this section is excerpted from the mimeographed document: Request for Legislative Appropriations, Fiscal Years Ending August 31, 1966 and 1967 (Denton: North Texas State University, nd).

30. Callaway, 193.

31. *Bulletin*, 1965, 2.

32. Quoted in James L. Rogers, *The Story of North Texas* (Denton: North Texas State University, 1965), 358.

33. Described in a policy document, "A Program of Cooperation in Graduate Studies for North Texas State University and Texas Woman's University," approved and recorded in "Minutes of the Board of Regents," February 17, 1966.

34. Jack K. Williams, interview with the author, August 1, 1968.

35. J. C. Matthews, conversations with the author, various dates, 1964–1968.

36. H.S.R. No. 375. (May 27, 1967). Austin: House of Representatives, The Texas Legislature.

37. "Staff Draft Number 3," (Austin: Coordinating Board, Texas College and University System, May 29, 1968), 16–17.

38. Ibid., 24.

39. J. C. Matthews, conversations with the author, various dates, 1964–1968.

40. Statement of the Chancellor, University of Texas System, June 21, 1968, referenced in Memorandum for the Coordinating Board, August 21, 1968.

41. Ibid.

42. Ibid., 1–2.

43. "Proposed Policy and Administrative Design." 1–2. In Memorandum (August 21, 1968).

44. "Principles for the Transfer of The Southwest Center for Advanced Studies to the University of Texas System." 1. In Memorandum (August 21, 1968).

45. Jack K. Williams, interview with the author, August 1, 1968.

46. Ibid.

47. Coordinating Board, Texas College and University System, August 5, 1968, "A Preliminary Staff Recommendation to Establish an Urban Multi-Campus University in the Dallas-Tarrant-Denton County Area," (Staff Draft Number 6).

48. "The Systems Approach to University Education for the Dallas-Fort Worth Urban System," Manuscript prepared August 16, 1968, Revised August 28, 1968. Initials on one copy indicate the author to be James L. Rogers. University Archives. (This copy shows a handwritten note by John Kamerick: "This seems excellent to me.")

49. Ibid.

50. "A Preliminary Staff Recommendation," 8–10.

51. "Moudy Backs UT Plan for Acquiring SCAS," *Fort Worth Star-Telegram*, September 26, 1968.

52. John Kamerick, Denton, to Harry Ransom, Austin, September 20, 1968.

53. Harry Ransom, Austin, to John Kamerick, Denton, October 4, 1968.

54. John Kamerick, Denton, to J. M. Moudy, Fort Worth, November 1, 1968.

55. All statements of Kamerick in this section are from a duplicated document handed out at the Coordinating Board meeting on November 11, 1968: "North Texas State University Position Paper."

56. "A Recommendation to the Coordinating Board, Texas College and University System. Presented Jointly by the Following State Universities: East Texas State University, North Texas State University, and Texas Woman's University," November 11, 1968.

57. Ibid.

58. "Proposal concerning U.T. Arlington, U.T. Southwestern Medical School, and the Center for Advanced Studies," Austin, University of Texas System, November 11, 1968, 2–4.

59. "Analysis of the Prospective 1980 Needs for Higher Education in North Central Texas," November 11, 1968.

60. "Minutes of the Coordinating Board, Texas College and University System," December 3, 1968, 13–21.

61. Ibid.

62. Transcript of KRLD broadcast, April 2, 1969, cited in letter, James L. Rogers to H. G. Wells, April 2, 1969.

63. John Kamerick, Denton, to Governor Preston Smith, Austin, June 6, 1969.

Notes to Chapter 27

1. J. C. Matthews, interview by Robert Mangrum, February 18, 1977, University of North Texas Oral History Collection, Number 360.

2. University Planning and Analysis, *Fact Book*, 1978 Edition, 1.11.

3. C. E. Evans, compiler, *Laws Establishing and Maintaining Texas State Teachers Colleges* (San Marcos: Southwest Texas State Teachers College, 1943).

4. Oral History Collection, Number 360, 1–2.

5. J. C. Matthews, Denton, to John Ben Shepperd, Austin, September 3, 1953.

6. Ronald E. Marcello, "Reluctance versus Reality: The Desegregation of North Texas State College, 1954–1956," *Southwestern Historical Quarterly* (October 1996): 159.

7. Oral History Collection, Number 360, 6-7.

8. A. T. Miller, Port Arthur, to J. C. Matthews, Denton, undated.

9 Notes for telegram, undated, J. C. Matthews, Denton, to A. T. Miller, Port Arthur.

10. "North Texas State Admits First Negro," *Dallas Times Herald*, July 21, 1954.

11. A. Tennyson Miller, interview by Michele Glaze, January 11, 1992, Oral History Collection, Number 857.

12. Oral History Collection, Number 360, 4–5.

13. Marcello, "Reluctance," 166.

14. Ibid., 153–85.

15. Joe L. Atkins, interview by Ronald E. Marcello, June 29, 1995, Oral History Collection, Number 1057.

16. Arthur M. Sampley, Denton, to Joe L. Atkins, Dallas, June 22, 1955.

17. Oral History Collection, Number 360, 18.

18. Marcello, "Reluctance," 170–71.

19. Oral History Collection, Number 360, 45.

20. Arthur M. Sampley, Denton, to Joe L. Atkins, Dallas, July 18, 1955.

21. Atkins.

22. J. C. Matthews to members of the Board of Regents, December 2, 1955.

23 .J. C. Matthews, Denton, to Billy E. Lee, Austin, December 15, 1955.

24. *Joe L. Atkins v. James Carl Matthews et al.* Civil Action No. 1104, in the District Court of the United States for the Eastern District of Texas, Sherman Division, December 2, 1955.

25. Marcello, "Reluctance," n. 3.

26. "Civil Rights Chronology," Accessed April 16, 1999, from http://library.advanced.org12111/chrcivil.htm.

27. Based on the author's personal recollections as NTSC News Service director at the time.

28. Marcello, "Reluctance," 155.

29. *Denton Record-Chronicle*, August 30, 1956, cited in Ronald E. Marcello, "Integration of Texas Intercollegiate Athletics: A Peaceful Transition," manuscript in the University Archives.

30. Nancy Anderson, "Coming Together: A Retrospective Look at Integration on Campus," *North Texan* (June 1994): 6–10.

31. Marcello, "Integration of Texas Intercollegiate Athletics," 16.

32. Ibid.

33. Ibid., relying on Abner Haynes, interview by Ronald E. Marcello and Randy Cummings, various dates in 1983 and 1984, Oral History Collection, Number 620, and on Kenneth Bahnsen, interview by Ronald E. Marcello and Randy Cummings, March 5, 1984, Oral History Collection,

Number 305.

34. Ibid., 26.

35. J. C. Matthews, Denton, to Richard Morehead, Austin, March 17, 1958.

36. Morehead to Matthews, October 28, 1965; Matthews to Morehead, October 29, 1965.

37. Southern Regional Council, "Desegregation in Higher Education," January 24, 1961.

38. Marion Ruhland to J. C. Matthews, October 12, 1967.

39. Jess Cearley to J. C. Matthews, October 16, 1967.

40. Urcie Timblin to J. C. Matthews, June 1, 1957.

41. J. C. Matthews, Denton, to Theodore R. Chatham, Houston, January 11, 1961.

42. Informal memorandum, apparently from Virginia Briscoe, president's secretary, to J. C. Matthews.

43. Andersen, 10.

44. Ibid., 10.

Notes to Chapter 28

1. *Time 1968: The Year That Shaped a Generation.* Special Collector's Edition, Spring 1989.

2. University of North Texas Oral History Collection, Number 145, "Interview with Professor Miles Anderson, June 27, 1968." Interviewer, Dale Odom.

3. "A New President for North Texas State University: A Report to the Board of Regents, Special Committee on the Selection of a President" (Denton: The Faculty Advisory Committee, November 15, 1967).

4. Anderson, 55. Five of the candidates were from out of state, two from Texas. The Texans included one member of the NTSU staff, the author of this book, who was at that time vice president for administrative affairs.

5. *Campus Chat*, Sept. 20, 1968, 6.

6. "Minutes of the President's Cabinet," September 9, 1968.

7. Ibid.

8. "Minutes of the President's Cabinet," September 23, 1968.

9. "Minutes of the President's Cabinet," October 14, 1968.

10. Ibid.

11. *President's Bulletin*, November 1968, No. 2.

12. "Minutes of the Board of Regents," March 14, 1969, 208.

13. "Statement on Academic Freedom, Tenure, and Responsibility for Faculty Members in Texas Public Colleges and Universities" (Austin: Coordinating Board, Texas College and University System, October 1967).

14. "Minutes of the Board of Regents," March 14, 1969, 208–209.

15. Ibid., 220-27.

16. "Instructors Air Complaints, Express Ideas in Senate As Faculty Caucus Seeks to Modify NTSU Policy," *Yucca,* 1970, 36.

17. John Kamerick to University Committee, June 20, 1969.

18. *President's Bulletin*, December 19, 1969, No. 14.

19. *President's Bulletin*, June 16, 1970, No. 20.

20. "Minutes of the Faculty Senate," May 18, 1970.

21. "Minutes of the Faculty Senate," October 8, 1969.

22. "Minutes of the Administrative Council," October 16, 1968.

23. "Minutes of the Board of Regents," February 6, 1969.

24. Ibid.

25. *President's Bulletin*, February 5, 1970, No. 16, and "Minutes of the Faculty Senate," January 14, 1970, and April 8, 1970.

26. John Kamerick to James J. Spurlock, June 20, 1969.

27. "Minutes of the Council of Deans," October 22, 1969.

28. John Kamerick to Jack Cross, October 24, 1969.

29. *President's Bulletin*, January 1970, No. 1.

30. Jack Cross to John Kamerick, February 12, 1970.

31. John Kamerick to J. J. Spurlock and the Council of Deans, March 10, 1970.
32. John Kamerick to J. J. Spurlock and the Council of Deans, April 28, 1970.
33. "Minutes of the Council of Deans," May 1, 1970.
34. AAUP Committee on Salary and Merit, "Report," August 13, 1968.
35. Harry F. Snapp to John Kamerick, October 15, 1968.
36. John Kamerick to Harry F. Snapp, October 21, 1968.
37. Committee on Faculty Participation to John Kamerick, January 16, 1969.
38. John Kamerick to Interim Review Committee, December 11, 1969.
39. *President's Bulletin*, January 12, 1970, No. 15.
40. John Kamerick to Council of Deans and the Interim Review Committee, April 27, 1970.
41. Sam Barton to John Kamerick, May 18, 1970.
42. John Kamerick to Sam Barton, July 20, 1970. (At this time, Kamerick had already announced his resignation from his position.)
43. First Annual Report of the University Review Committee, undated.
44. "Minutes of the President's Cabinet," February 24, 1969.
45. "Minutes of the Faculty Senate," March 11, 1970.
46. "Minutes of the Faculty Senate," September 23, 1969.
47. "Minutes of the Faculty Senate," October 8, 1969, and April 28, 1970.
48. "Minutes of the Faculty Senate," March 25, 1970.
49. John Kamerick to Jack Cross and James Sybert, October 20, 1969.
50. John Kamerick to the Faculty Election Committee, May 1, 1970, and *President's Bulletin*, June 16, 1970, No. 12.
51. "Guidelines for Faculty Participation in Instructional Units."
52. Ibid.
53. James J. Spurlock to Dwane Kingery, August 15, 1969.
54. *President's Bulletin*, February 1969.
55. Application to Coordinating Board, June 15, 1970.
56. *President's Bulletin*, June 16, 1970.
57. *Campus Chat*, February 28, 1969, 1.
58. *North Texas State University Comprehensive Campus Plan* (Houston: Caudill Rowlett Scott, May 1967).
59. "Campus Planning at NTSU: A Twelve-Year Chronology, 1964–1976," Prepared as a discussion paper in 1976 by James L. Rogers at the request of President C. C. Nolen. Copy in the files of the author.
60. John Kamerick, Notes to Bob Veteto, undated, apparently December 1969 or January 1970.
61. John Kamerick to James L. Rogers, January 14, 1969.
62. Frantzreb and Pray, North Texas State University Development Planning Audit, June 1970.
63. *President's Bulletin*, February 5, 1970, No. 16.
64. *Campus Chat*, February 14, 1968, 1.
65. John Kamerick, Denton, to Lieutenant-Governor Preston Smith, Austin, September 20, 1968.
66. John Kamerick, Denton, to Governor Preston Smith, Austin, January 7 and February 27, 1969.
67. Governor Preston Smith, Austin, to John Kamerick, March 17, 1969.
68. John Kamerick, Denton, to Governor Preston Smith, Austin, April 15, 1969.
69. John Kamerick, Denton, to Governor Preston Smith, Austin, September 25, 1969.
70. "Minutes of the Board of Regents of North Texas State University," August 28, 1969.
71. John J. Kamerick to the Board of Regents, May 26, 1970.
72. "Minutes of the Board of Regents," February 6, 1969, 205.
73. Harry F. Snapp, Roscoe C. Adkins, and Maxine Turnage, Denton, to Ben H. Wooten, Dallas, May 16, 1969.
74. "Minutes of the Board of Regents," May 28, 1970, 281.
75. *President's Bulletin*, No. 21, July 27, 1970.
76. "Minutes of the Board of Regents," May 28, 1970, 282.

Notes to Chapter 29

1. Joe Belden, "Crackdown on Campus Militants Favored," *Dallas Morning News*, April 25, 1969.

2. William C. Lindley, et al., to John Kamerick, October 11, 1968.

3. John Kamerick, to the Board of Regents, October 23, 1968.

4. Robert P. Wallis, "History and Recommendations Concerning North Texas State University Campus Police, Parking and Traffic," submitted to John Kamerick September 23, 1968. University Archives, Box 585, Folder 4.

5. *Campus Chat*, September 20, 1968, 1; "Kamerick Initiates Changes," *Yucca*, 1969, 473.

6. John Kamerick to Troy Phillips, October 15, 1968.

7. Troy Phillips to John Kamerick, November 19, 1968.

8. John Kamerick to William Lindley, September 30, 1968.

9. "Minutes of the President's Cabinet," November 25, 1968.

10. James L. Rogers to John Kamerick, November 13, 1968.

11. John Kamerick to William C. Lindley, November 15, 1989.

12. William C. Lindley to John Kamerick, November 26, 1968.

13. John Kamerick to the President's Cabinet, December 6, 1968.

14. Paul Smith, to John Kamerick, December 20, 1968.

15. Ibid. Attachment to Smith letter.

16. John Kamerick to Paul Smith, December 20, 1968.

17. James L. Rogers to John Kamerick, January 20, 1969, with attachment, "Code of Student Conduct and Discipline." Copy located in Box 583, Folder 3, University Archives.

18. "Minutes of the Board of Regents," March 14, 1969. 228.

19. John Kamerick to John Carrell, April 29, 1969.

20. "Minutes of the Board of Regents," March 14, 1969, 238.

21. *Campus Chat*, March 7, 1968, 1.

22. *Campus Chat*, March 12, 1968, 1.

23. Don Beck to John Kamerick, December 4, 1968; Kamerick to Roy Busby, December 11, 1968; Beck to Kamerick, January 15, 1969.

24. "Minutes of the President's Cabinet," April 7, 1969.

25. "Minutes of the President's Cabinet," May 13, 1969.

26. William C. Lindley to John Kamerick, May 20, 1969.

27. William C. Lindley to John Kamerick, September 24, 1968.

28. "Minutes of the Board of Regents," February 6, 1969, 73.

29. John Kamerick to the Board of Regents, April 23, 1969.

30. *President's Bulletin*, February 5, 1970, No. 16; and "Minutes of the Board of Regents," January 29, 1970, 152.

31. John Kamerick to Jack Cross, July 16, 1970.

32. John Kamerick, Denton, to A. M. Willis Jr., Longview, July 23, 1970.

33. North Texas State University, "Compliance Report of Institutions of Higher Education Under Title VI of the Civil Rights Act of 1964 (Fall, 1968)," November 15, 1968.

34. North Texas State University, "Report to Governor Preston Smith," October 30, 1968.

35. *Campus Chat*, September 27, 1968, 1.

36. *Campus Chat*, October 2, 1968, 1.

37. John Kamerick to Leonard G. Benson, Chairman, Campus Clubs Committee, October 22, 1968.

38. John Kamerick to Leonard Benson, November 18, 1963.

39. David A. Webb to John Kamerick, October 6, 1969.

40. Undated document filed with undated handwritten note, apparently January 14, 1969, John Kamerick to James L. Rogers.

41. James L. Rogers, "Statement Relating to 'Racism' as an Institutional Policy," January 14, 1969.

42. John Kamerick to James Frank Wyman, January 15, 1969.

43. "Afro-American Student Union Demands upon the University Administration,"

Mimeographed page, undated. Filed with "Minutes of the Administrative Council," February 19, 1969.

44. "Minutes of the Administrative Council," February 19, 1969.

45. John Kamerick to Frank Wyman, February 21, 1969.

46. *Campus Chat*, February 12, 1969.

47. James Frank Wyman, Letter to the Editor, *Campus Chat*, February 12, 1969, 2.

48. *Campus Chat*, February 12, 1969, 1.

49. *Campus Chat*, March 26, 1969, 1.

50. *Campus Chat*, June 6, 1969, 1.

51. John Kamerick to Leonard G. Benson, November 24, 1969.

52. Clarence A. Laws to John Kamerick, June 24, 1969.

53. John Kamerick to Cabinet, Administrative Council, and Department Directors, June 26, 1969.

54. John Kamerick to Clarence A. Laws, July 12, 1969.

55. John Brooks to Roy Busby, April 2, 1969.

56. *Campus Chat*, November 6, 1968, 1.

57. John Kamerick to Members of the Board of Regents, November 6, 1968.

58. *Campus Chat*, November 22, 1968, 1.

59. *Campus Chat*, November 15, 1968, 1.

60. *Campus Chat*, November 20, 1968, 2.

61. *Campus Chat*, December 11, 1968, 1.

62. *Yucca*, 1969, 132.

63. *Campus Chat*, May 14, 1969, 1.

64. *Campus Chat*, May 16, 1969, 1.

65. *Campus Chat*, March 12, 1969.

66. John Kamerick, Denton, to Governor Preston Smith, Austin, January 14, 1970.

67. Ibid.

68. James L. Rogers to John Kamerick, August 29, 1969.

69. "Minutes of the Board of Regents," January 29, 1970.

70. "Survey of Some Areas of Importance in the Successful Operation of the Intercollegiate Athletic Program at North Texas State University," submitted to Dr. Jess Cearley, director of athletics, November 19, 1968.

71. *Campus Chat*, April 2, 1969, 1.

Notes to Chapter 30

1. Bob Campbell, "Campus Issues, Problems Concern Regent," *North Texas Daily*, February 16, 1971, 1.

2. John L. Carter to Jerry Jordan, August 28, 1970.

3. John L. Carter to John Hargrove, Jan. 12, 1971; John L. Carter, Denton, to Tom Sealy, Midland, December 15, 1970.

4. John L. Carter to James J. Spurlock, Dec. 11, 1970.

5. John L. Carter to James J. Spurlock, Jan. 25, 1971.

6. Virginia Briscoe to John L. Carter, March 16, 1971.

7. Bob Bain, "Regents Urged To Crack Whip," *Fort Worth Star-Telegram*, January 6, 1971.

8. "School Control Hit by Godfrey; Faculties Faulted," *Fort Worth Star-Telegram*, January 6, 1971.

9. Ernest Stromberger, "Austin Report: The Senate vs. Smith's Appointees," *Dallas Times Herald*, November 29, 1970, 26A.

10. "Kennard Seeking Help to Block NTSU Regent Pick," *Fort Worth Star-Telegram*, undated clipping in the University Archives.

11. "Senate Rejects Regent Godfrey," *North Texas Daily*, March 26, 1971, 1.

12. "Summer Changes Transform Campus," *North Texas Daily*, September 1, 1970, 1.

13. Bronson Havard, "Crackdown on Campus," *Dallas Times Herald*, October 21, 1970.

14. Dick West, "A Shocking Start for a Freshman." *Dallas Morning News*, August 30, 1970.

15. Ibid.

16. Candy Chestnut, "English Mentors Rebut Criticism of 'Phase Blue' As Controversy Grows," *North Texas Daily*, September 10, 1970, 1.

17. Berl E. Godfrey, Fort Worth, to James L. Rogers, Denton, September 4, 1970.

18. E. Bruce Street to Mrs. A. L. Pharr, September 21, 1970.

19. Letter to John Kamerick, August 3, 1970.

20. John L. Carter to parent, August 11, 1970.

21. Don Smith to John L. Carter, November 16, 1970.

22. "Minutes, Board of Regents," November 19, 1970.

23. E. Bruce Street, Graham, to A. M. Willis, Longview, September 21, 1970.

24. E. Bruce Street, Graham, to John L. Carter *et al.*, Denton, October 21, 1970.

25. AAUP Committee on the Betty Duke Case, memorandum to Executive Council, North Texas Chapter, AAUP, April 2, 1972.

26. lbid.

27. Ibid.

28. "Dialogue: Elizabeth Ann Duke," *North Texas Daily*, October 6, 1970.

29. Personal recollection of the author, who was serving as secretary of the President's Cabinet at that time.

30. Terry Kelly, "Students Protest Firing of Teacher," *North Texas Daily*, September 24, 1970, 1.

31. Ibid.

32. Ibid.

33. Personal recollection of the author, who participated in the day's events as a member of the Cabinet.

34. "USNT Senate Votes Confidence in Five Suspended Students," *North Texas Daily*, October 15, 1970, 1.

35. "Committee Finds Five Guilty of Student Code Violations," *North Texas Daily*, October 22, 1970, 1.

36. Terry Kelly, "Regents Extend Facility Policy Against Non-Student Activity," *North Texas Daily*, October 23, 1970.

37. University Committee to John L. Carter, October 21, 1970.

38. Jack Cross to John L. Carter, November 25, 1970.

39. "USNT Endorses Policies, Demonstration Proposal," *North Texas Daily*, October 27, 1970.

40. James L. Rogers to Members of the Board of Regents, November 13, 1970.

41. Ibid.

42. "Daily Supports COPE Questions," *North Texas Daily*, November 12, 1970, 2.

43. Ellen Moore, "Carter To Give Regents Students' Six Proposals," *North Texas Daily,* November 13, 1970,1.

44. "Board Hears Deming, Forms Liaison Group," *North Texas Daily*, November 20, 1970, 1.

45. "Minutes of the President's Cabinet," November 23, 1970.

46. Terry Kelly, "Duke To Take Dismissal to Court Following Board Action on Appeal," *North Texas Daily*, February 26, 1971.

47. "Senate Approves Bill To Call Student Strike," *North Texas Daily*, February 10, 1971, 1. David Lewis, "Organizers Say Today's Rally Designed To 'Educate the People'," *North Texas Daily,* February 17, 1971.

48. Ellen Moore and David Lewis, "Rally Speakers Defy Court Order," *North Texas Daily,* February 18, 1971, 1.

49. "Two Jailed; One Freed," *North Texas Daily,* February 19, 1971, 1.

50. Tracy Mesler and Jo Murphy, "Prosecutor Uses Film In Duke, Haylon Case," *North Texas Daily,* February 25, 1971, 1; Jo Murphy and Tracy Mesler, "Permanent Injunction Set Against Mrs. Duke, Haylon," *North Texas Daily,* March 5, 1971, 1.

51. Jo Murphy, "Duke, Haylon File Federal Suit Seeking $150,000 from State," *North Texas Daily,* March 2, 1971, 1.

52. "Duke, Haylon Case Delayed," *North Texas Daily,* March 11, 1971, 1.

53. George Foster, "Duke Files Suit for Reinstatement," *North Texas Daily,* June 10, 1971, 1.

54. Ibid.

55. "Betty Ann Duke Wins Reinstatement Following Drawn-Out Court Battle," *North Texas Daily,* September 8, 1971, 1.

56. Ibid.

57. Doug Swanson, "Betty Ann Duke: From 'Prom Girl' to Fugitive," *Dallas Morning News,* July 10, 1988, 1A, 22A.

58. Ibid., 22A.

59. Ibid.

60. Bettye Megason, "John L. Carter Says Nolen 'Good,' Calls Year 'Enjoyable, Privilege'," *North Texas Daily,* May 7, 1971, 1.

61. Transcript of tape recording, public assembly at 11:30 A.M. May 7, 1970, at North Texas State University Music Recital Hall.

Notes to Chapter 31

1. Transcript of tape recording, public assembly at 11:30 A.M. May 7, 1971, at North Texas State University Music Recital Hall. Located with the Nolen papers, University Archives.

2. Kara Lee Selman, "Committee Picks Nolen," *North Texas Daily,* May 7, 1971, 1.

3. Derro Evans, "Jitters in the Halls of Ivy," *SUNDAY Magazine, Dallas Times Herald,* November 28, 1971, 28.

4. May 7, 1971, transcript.

5. Evans, 29.

6. C. C. Nolen, Denton, to Jim Wright, Washington, October 27, 1971.

7. C. C. Nolen, Denton, to Logan Wilson, Washington, May 31, 1971.

8. C. C. Nolen, Fort Worth, to LeNoir Dimmitt, undated, apparently May or June 1971.

9. C. C. Nolen, Denton, to A. Dale Fiers, April 9, 1973.

10. C. C. Nolen, Denton, to Herbert L. Polinard, Denton, September 23, 1971.

11. *President's Bulletin,* Vol. 8, No. 5, August–September 1977.

12. "Board Hears Deming, Forms Liaison Group," *North Texas Daily,* November 20, 1970, 1.

13. Bob Campbell, "Campus Issues, Problems Concern Regent," *North Texas Daily,* February 16, 1971, 1.

14. Evans, 28.

15. A. M. Willis, Longview, to Cecil C. Humphreys, Chancellor of the State University and Community College System of Tennessee, March 20, 1973.

16. "Minutes of the Board of Regents," May 7, 1971.

17. C. C. Nolen, Fort Worth, to A. M. Willis, Longview, May 6, 1971.

18. Evans, 29.

19. Evans, 30.

20. C. C. Nolen, Denton, to Art Frantzreb, New York, June 7, 1971.

21. Ibid., 5-6.

22. Ibid. 7.

23. Gustave A. Ferré, Denton, to C. C. Nolen, Denton, undated copy 1975, attachment to memorandum from Ferré to Alfred F. Hurley, November 20, 1984.

24. "Institutional Progress Report, (1971-Present)," August 26, 1976.

25. Gus Ferré, November 20, 1984, 4.

26. North Texas State University, *Institutional Self-Study 1971-73,* Report to the Southern Association of Colleges and Schools, September 1973, II-11.

27. Ibid., II-12-16.

28. Rollie Sininger to Gus Ferré, July 20, 1973.

29. Gus Ferré to C. C. Nolen, September 13, 1973.

30. North Texas State University, *Report of the Visiting Committee,* The Southern Association of College and Schools, Commission on Colleges, October 7-10, 1973, 36.

31. *President's Bulletin,* Vol. 5, No. 1, September 1973.

32. *Report of the Visiting Committee,* 8-9.

33. C. C. Nolen to Vice Presidents Carter, Ferré, and Sininger, March 28, 1974.
34. C. C. Nolen to members of the President's Cabinet, November 19, 1976.
35. John L. Carter to C. C. Nolen, June 7, 1973.
36. *President's Bulletin*, Vol. 5, No. 7, June, July, August 1974.
37. C. C. Nolen to Gustave A. Ferré, May 27, 1975.
38. C. C. Nolen to Gustave A. Ferré, February 10, 1976.
39. C. C. Nolen to Gustave A. Ferré, April 5, 1976.
40. Joyce Hopkins, "Return to Pulpit 'Surprises' Ferré," *Denton Record-Chronicle*, May 30, 1976, 4A.
41. "Regents Name Library After Board Chairman," *North Texas Daily*, August 31, 1978, 1.
42. "Senate Opposes Library Naming," *North Texas Daily*, October 19, 1978, 1.
43. C. C. Nolen to members of the Board of Regents, September 8, 1971.
44. Jim Reid to C. C. Nolen, November 4, 1971.
45. C. C. Nolen, Denton, to Dean Davis, Austin, April 27, 1972.
46. John L. Carter to Miles Anderson, September 22, 1976.
47. C. C. Nolen, Denton, to E. E. Stuessy, Austin, October 4, 1976.
48. Jane Gentry Smith, Denton, to A. M. Willis, Longview, November 8, 1974.
49. *Report of the Visiting Committee,* 6.
50. A. M. Willis, Longview, to Kenneth May, Lubbock, July 8, 1974.
51. C. C. Nolen to Members of the Board of Regents, September 11, 1975.
52. C. C. Nolen to Members, President's Cabinet, September 11, 1975.

Notes to Chapter 32

1. C. C. Nolen, Denton, to A. M. Willis, Jr., Longview, May 6, 1971.
2. *President's Bulletin*, Vol. 5, No. 7, June–August 1974.
3. "Minutes of the Faculty Senate," September 12, 1973.
4. North Texas State University, *Institutional Self-Study 1971-73*, Report to the Southern Association of Colleges and Schools, September 1973, XII-21.
5. Ibid., I-7.
6. Ibid., 36–37.
7. North Texas State University, *Report of the Visiting Committee,* The Southern Association of Colleges and Schools Commission on Colleges, October 7–10, 1973.
8. Ibid., 3.
9. Ibid., 57.
10. Ibid., 61.
11. Ibid., 67.
12. Gordon W. Sweet, Atlanta, to C. C. Nolen, Denton, December 16, 1974.
13. President's Report, North Texas State University, 1971–1975, 7.
14. W. H. Glaze to C. C. Nolen, June 10, 1975.
15. Ibid., 2-6.
16. C. C. Nolen to Marvin Berkeley, et al., July 1, 1975.
17. "Minutes of the Board of Regents," November 21, 1975.
18. C. C. Nolen, Denton, to Bevington Reed, Austin, August 5, 1974.
19. "Role and Scope Project," *President's Bulletin*, Vol. 7, No. 2, October 1975–February 1976, 3–9.
20. President's Report, 23.
21. "Role and Scope Project," 4–5.
22. Ibid., 7-9.
23. Ibid., 6.
24. "Minutes of the Board of Regents," November 21, 1975.
25. "Minutes of the Board of Regents," February 27, 1976, 80.
26. "Presidential Evaluation: An Assessment of Institutional Leadership," June 3, 1976.
27. Ibid., 1.
28. Roy Busby to the President's Cabinet, June 8, 1976.

29. *Institutional Progress Report* (1971–Present), August 26, 1976.

30. "Text of President Nolen's Remarks to the Planning and Budgeting Task Force Conference September 29, 1976," *President's Bulletin*, Vol. 7, No. 5, August–September 1976, 1.

31. C. C. Nolen to the University Community, "Program Plans and Priorities," February 16, 1978.

32. Miles Anderson to Richard Harris, June 27, 1977.

33. Miles Anderson to C. C. Nolen, May 18, 1978.

Notes to Chapter 33

1. Transcript of tape recording, Public Assembly at 11:30 A.M., May 7, 1971.

2. "Town and Gown Meeting, May 13, 1971." Attachment to memorandum, Roy Busby to C. C. Nolen, August 11, 1971.

3. Jim Reid to C. C. Nolen, August 23, 1976, 1.

4. Jim Reid, "Development Report for September, 1971."

5. "Minutes of the Board of Regents," November 3,1971.

6. "Rules and Regulations of the Board of Regents of North Texas State University for the Operation and Program of Private Fund Development," November 3, 1971.

7. News Release, Public Information Office, November 30, 1971.

8. "Minutes of the Board of Regents," April 6, 1972.

9. "Minutes of the Board of Directors," North Texas State University Educational Foundation, Inc., August 24, 1972.

10. "Minutes of the Board of Regents," November 9, 1973, 10.

11. Articles of Incorporation, North Texas State University Educational Foundation, June 27, 1972.

12. Roy K. Busby, "Prexy 'Needs Patience of Job'," *Dallas Morning News*, March 26, 1972.

13. "Minutes of the North Texas State University Development Board," October 5, 1972.

14. "Minutes of the Board of Regents," November 22, 1974, 29.

15. North Texas State University Alumni Association, Status Report, May 24, 1974.

16. Community Service Bureau, Inc., Report and Recommendations, November 21, 1975, 1-2.

17. Ibid., 13.

18. Ibid., 17.

19. Jim Reid to Roy Busby, James Rogers, Janice Odom, December 5, 1975.

20. Jim Reid to C. C. Nolen, August 23, 1976.

Notes to Chapter 34

1. Photograph, *North Texas Daily*, September 15, 1971, 1.

2. *Yucca*, 1972, 118, and 1973, 14-18.

3. "The Student Vote," *Yucca*, 1973, 66-75.

4. "Energy Crisis," *Yucca*, 1974, 6-7.

5. *Yucca*, 1973, 36-41.

6. *Yucca*, 1974, 8-9.

7. Mohammad Ihtisham Alam to Harve D. King, October 9, 1973.

8. C. C. Nolen to Police Chief Robby Robinson, September 14, 1978.

9. "Minutes of the President's Cabinet," Nov. 4, 1975.

10. C. C. Nolen to Michael W. George, Denton, April 1976.

11. "Students and Alcohol," *Yucca,* 1973, 27-29.

12. C. C. Nolen to Carroll Sullivant, October 9 and October 17, 1973.

13. *North Texas Daily*, March 19, 1971, 1.

14. "Figures on Student Cost, Density," *Update*, November 3, 1971, 1.

15. Bruce Howard, "Football Closes MVC Chapter," *North Texas Daily*, July 24, 1975.

16. "Minutes of the Board of Regents," February 18,1972, 25.

17. "Minutes of the Board of Regents," June 21, 1972, 72.

18. "Minutes of the Board of Regents," November 22, 1974, 38.

19. C. C. Nolen, Denton, to Mickey Holmes, Tulsa, November 25,1974.

20. C. C. Nolen, Denton, to Walter Byers, Kansas City, October 22, 1975.
21. *North Texas Daily*, March 18, 1975, 1.
22. "Blakeley Honored by Press," *Dallas Morning News*, July 18, 1976, 8B.
23. Mickey Herskowitz, "North Texas Paid 'Desertion' Penalty," *Houston Post*, April 13, 1976.
24. Hayden Fry, Denton, to Arnie B. Deaton, Houston, April 20, 1976
25. Randy Galloway, "New year, old problem," *Dallas Morning News*, November 20, 1977.
26. Hayden Fry to Bill Blakeley, January 25, 1978.
27. C. C. Nolen, Denton, to Cliff Speegle, Dallas, March 29, 1977.
28. "NTSU Gains Hearing with SWC," *Dallas Morning News*, August 22, 1978.
29. Carter Cromwell, "North Texas State Steadily Improves Goal of SWC Membership," *Austin American-Statesman*, October 8, 1978.
30. "No Bowl Offers Disappoints Fry," *Lubbock Avalanche-Journal*, November 21, 1978, D-3.
31. "AP Analysis: Fry Falls Short Of Goals," *Temple Daily Telegram*, December 10, 1978.
32. David Moore, "Hayden Leaves North Texas in *Frying* Pan," *Texas Sports*, October 1980, 23.
33. Ibid.
34. Bill Brashier, statement read to news media by John Carrell, December 17, 1978.
35. "NT Regents Renege on Coaching Vacancy," *Denton Record-Chronicle*, December 17, 1978.

Notes to Chapter 35

1. Texas College of Osteopathic Medicine, *A 20th Anniversary Celebration*, 1990, 2.
2. "NTSU-TCOM Consolidation Plan," *President's Bulletin*, September-October 1974, 4-5.
3. "Osteopathic Study Planned at NTSU," *Dallas Times Herald*, February 18, 1972, 31A.
4. "Medical School Budget Approved by Osteopaths," *Fort Worth Star-Telegram*, August 25, 1972, 4D.
5. C. C. Nolen, Denton, to Dr. George Luibel, Fort Worth, November 6, 1972.
6. C. C. Nolen, Denton, to Dr. George Luibel, Fort Worth, July 31, 1972.
7. "Minutes of the Board of Regents," February 8, 1974, 59.
8. "NTSU-TCOM Consolidation Plan," Ibid., 5.
9. "Minutes of the Board of Regents," August 20, 1973, 190.
10. C. C. Nolen, Denton, to members of the Board of Regents, March 26, 1974.
11. "Minutes of the Board of Regents," October 14, 1972, 3.
12. Marion E. Coy, Fort Worth, to Bevington Reed, Austin, September 16, 1974.
13. Richard Rafes, "The Historical Development of the Texas College of Osteopathic Medicine as a State Medical School, 1960–1975" (Ph.D. diss., University of North Texas, 1990).
14. "Fort Worth Campus: TWU Unveils Plans for Medical School," *Dallas Morning News*, June 20, 1974, 1A.
15. Ibid.
16. "Minutes of the Coordinating Board, Texas College and University System," October 18, 1974.
17. Various stories in *Fort Worth Star-Telegram*, January 31, April 9, May 17, and May 30, 1975.
18.John Shivers, Fort Worth, to A. M. Willis, Longview, October 20, 1976.
19. A. M. Willis, Longview, to John Shivers, Fort Worth, undated draft response in the Nolen collection, University Archives.
20. "Minutes of the Board of Regents," June 12–13, 1975, 97.
21. C. C Nolen, Denton, to Gustave A. Ferré, Fort Worth, May 27, 1975.
22. C. C. Nolen to Gustave A. Ferré, June 15,1975.
23. C. C. Nolen, Denton, to Claude Rainey, Fort Worth, July 1,1975.
24. C. C. Nolen to Gustave A. Ferré, January 29, 1976.
25. "Minutes of the Board of Regents," November 18, 1977, 19.
26. Ibid.
27. Peat, Marwick, Mitchell & Co., "A Study of The Relationship Between Texas College of Osteopathic Medicine and North Texas State University," September 1978.
28. Ibid. I-2.

29. Ibid., II-3-4.

30. "UT-Austin may take over TCOM," *North Texas Daily*, February 22, 1979, 1.

31. "Minutes of the Board of Regents," February 23, 1979.

32. Allan Cook, "Regents Oppose TCOM Transfer to UT System," *North Texas Daily*, February 27, 1979, 1.

33. "TCOM Bill to Face House," *North Texas Daily*, April 25, 1979, 1.

34. "Committee Approves Bill to Change TCOM Control," *North Texas Daily*, April 18, 1979, 1.

35. Kenneth May, Lubbock, to Gibson Lewis, Austin, April 24, 1979.

36. "Minutes of the Board of Regents," February 17, 1981, 60.

37. "Minutes of the Board of Regents," May 1, 1981, 77.

Notes to Chapter 36

1. Bevington Reed to C. C. Nolen, October 17, 1972.

2. Hiram Friedsam, "Origin and Early Development of the Center for Studies in Aging at North Texas: A Memoir," downloaded July 2000 from the center's webpage at www. unt.edu.

3. *Report of North Texas State University for the Institutional Self-Study and Periodic Visitation Program of the Commission on Colleges and Universities, Southern Association of Colleges and Secondary Schools* (Denton: np, 1962), X 2-3.

4. *North Texas State University Institutional Self-Study, 1971-73* (Denton: np, September 1973), IX-4.

5. "College Offers NTSU Credits," *Denton Record-Chronicle*, August 27, 1972, 8A.

6. H. J. Friedsam to J. C. Matthews, July 2, 1968.

7. Stephen L. Cobb, "Center for Economic Education," July 2000 update to Web page at ww.unt.edu.

8. John G. Tower to John Kamerick, May 3, 1970.

9. J. J. Spurlock to John Kamerick, October 2, 1968.

10. "Minutes of the President's Cabinet," April 7, 1969.

11. Friedsam.

12. *North Texas Daily*, July 27, 1972, 1.

13. James J. Muro to Alfred F. Hurley, July 12, 1982.

14. D. Jack Davis to Cooperative Education Branch, U. S. Department of Education, August 11, 1983.

15. C. C. Nolen, Denton, to Ralph B. Rogers, Dallas, May 26, 1976.

16. "Channel 2 Petitions," *President's Bulletin*, July 1977, 2.

17. Nila Dunaway, "Group Seeks Control Of Dormant Channel," *North Texas Daily*, August 31, 1977, 1.

18. Charles Siderius, "Birth of KDTN No Easy Labor," *Denton Record-Chronicle*, October 20, 1988, 2D, 5D.

19. *Annual Report*, Coordinating Board, Texas College and University System, Austin, Aug. 31, 1981, 1.

20. *Yucca*, 1972, 73.

21. "Minutes of the Faculty Senate," October 13, 1971.

22. "Minutes of the Faculty Senate," February 9, 1972.

23. C. C. Nolen to Dr. and Mrs. Robert C. Cotner, Austin, June 22, 1971.

24. "Minutes of the Board of Regents," January 14, 1977.

25. Miles Anderson to John Carrell, November 18, 1977.

26. Jane Gentry Smith to C. C. Nolen, May 26, 1975.

27. Clifford Hardy to Jane Gentry Smith, January 20, 1976.

28. *North Texas State University Institutional Self-Study*, 1971–73., IX-1.

29. John L. Carter to C. C. Nolen, June 23, 1975.

30. "Minutes of the Board of Regents," Nov. 21, 1975.

31. C. C. Nolen, Denton, to E. Kent Meek, Dallas, April 4, 1973.

32. C. C. Nolen, Denton, to Marshall Kaplan, Dallas, November 30, 1973.

33. C. C. Nolen, memorandum to vice presidents, deans, and others, January 10, 1974.

34. News Release, Public Information Office, North Texas State University, April 8, 1974.

35. C. C. Nolen, Denton, to Edward Marcus, Dallas, July 5, 1974.

36. C. C. Nolen, Denton, to Edward Marcus, Dallas, July 1, 1975.

37. "Campus Planning at NTSU: A Twelve-Year Chronology, 1964-1976," prepared as a discussion paper in 1976 by James L. Rogers at the request of President C. C. Nolen. Copy in the files of the author.

38. *North Texas State University Campus Plan* (Houston: Caudill Rowlett Scott, 1972).

39. Velma Lee Cathey, Report on Library Moving Operation, July 1972.

40. C. C. Nolen, Denton, to Jim White, Denton, July 29, 1975.

41. "Street Ruling Upheld," *Denton Record-Chronicle,* September 24, 1976, 2A.

42. C. C. Nolen, Denton, to Elinor Hughes, Denton, August 28, 1976.

43. "Minutes of the Board of Regents," September 11, 1976, 1-2.

44. "Minutes of the Board of Regents," February 27, 1973, 52.

45. *North Texas State University Master Plan* (Dallas: Omniplan, February 1978).

46. "Minutes of the Board of Regents," February 23-24, 1978, 179.

47. Ibid., 178.

48. "Suit May Stall Building Projects," *North Texas Daily*, April 14, 1978, 1.

49. Miles Anderson to David A. Webb, April 28, 1978.

Notes to Chapter 37

1. "Minutes of the Board of Regents," April 12, 1979, 86.

2. Ibid.

3. Jim Reid to Bruce Street, August 25, 1976.

4. Mike Ferguson, Jr., Austin, to John L. Carter, ~~Jr.,~~ Denton, September 7, 1977.

5. Ibid.

6. John L Carter to C. C. Nolen, July 11, 1978.

7. John L. Carter, Denton, to Vernon F. Neuhaus, Edinburg, July 11, 1978.

8. Roy Busby to Jim Reid, February 9, 1979.

9. Jim Reid to Roy Busby, February 14, 1979.

10. George W. Hardin to John L. Carter, March 17,1979.

11. John L. Carter to C. C. Nolen, March 27, 1979.

12. Earl Golz, "NTSU Fund Probed for Diverting Money," *Dallas Morning News*, April 6, 1979, 1A, 6A.

13. Peat, Marwick, Mitchell & Co., "A Study of Organizational Relationships Between the Board of Regents and the President, North Texas State University," September, 1978.

14 Peat, Marwick, Mitchell & Co., Austin, to A. M. Willis, Longview, September 27, 1978.

15. Peat, Marwick. Mitchell & Co., "A Study," I-3.

16. "Minutes of the Faculty Senate," May 9, 1979, 2.

17. Ibid., 3.

18. Earl Golz, "NTSU Officials to Help Clayton," *Dallas Morning News*, May 13, 1979.

19. Janie Leigh Frank, "Nolen Says 'Power Play' with Regent Caused Resignation," *Denton Record-Chronicle*, April 16, 1981, 1A.

20. Javier Rodriguez, "Foundation Returns Money to Med School," *North Texas Daily*, April 25, 1979, 1.

21. No. 79-3356-A, *A. H. Belo Corporation, Earl Golz and Hermas Miller, Appellants, vs. J. Newton Rayzor, Appellee*, in the District Court, 16th Judicial District, Denton County, Texas, October 12, 1981.

22. Javier Rodriquez, "News Director Refutes Allegations of Misusing State Funds in Rally," *North Texas Daily*, April 10, 1979, 1.

23. Janie Leigh Frank, "Nolen Wrote, Willis Signed, State Car Use Letters," *Denton Record-Chronicle,* May 18, 1979, 1-2A.

24. Janie Leigh Frank, "Nolen Says," 1A.

25. Ibid., 1A-2A.

26. "Deans Voice Regret Over Resignation," *North Texas Daily*, April 26, 1979, 1.

27. C. C. Nolen to Robert Y. Empie, March 1978.
28. C. C. Nolen, Denton, to Bayard Friedman, Fort Worth, March 26, 1978.
29. C. C. Nolen to Eugene Kuntz, April 5, 1978.

Notes to Chapter 38

1. *President's Bulletin* 9, no. 7 (June 1979): 9.
2. William B. Warde, Jr., Denton, to A. M. Willis, Washington, April 13, 1979.
3. *President's Bulletin*, 9, 1–2.
4. *A President for North Texas State University and Texas College of Osteopathic Medicine.* July 1979, 8.
5. Ibid., 8.
6. Earl Golz, "House Panel May Seek NTSU Removals," *Dallas Morning News,* July 17, 1979, 1A, 6A.
7. "President Carter Announces Administrative Reorganization," *UPDATE* 9, no. 22 (July 27, 1979, "Special Issue"): 1.
8. Allan Cook, "Carter Discharges Vice Presidents." *North Texas Daily,* July 26, 1979, 1, 4.
9. *UPDATE* 9, no. 23 (August 13, 1979): 1.
10. Ibid., 1-2.
11. TACT Executive Committee to John Carter, July 30, 1979.
12. David H. Malone to Faculty Colleagues at NTSU, August 7, 1979.
13. "Statement by Departmental Chairpersons, College of Arts and Sciences, North Texas State University," August 13, 1979.
14. "NTSU Firings Cause Unnecessary Damage," *Denton Record-Chronicle*, July 24, 1979, 4A.
15. Javier Rodriguez, "Nolen Quits, Cites President's Duties," *North Texas Daily*, April 17, 1979, 1.
16. Javier Rodriguez, "Nolen Resignation Rumor Lingers after Talk with Regent Steussy [sic]," *North Texas Daily,* April 12, 1979, 1.
17. Ralph Frammolino, "District Attorneys Ready to Examine NTSU Charges," *Dallas Times Herald*, July 18, 1979, 1, 8.
18. "Minutes of the Board of Regents," July 20, 1979, 170.
19. Allan Cook, "Cobb Asks Prosecutors to Carry on Investigation," *North Texas Daily*, August 9, 1979, 1.
20. "Resolution Relative to Recent Events at North Texas State University," "Minutes of the Board of Regents," August 24, 1979, 207.
21. "Complete Text of NTSU Investigation Report," *Denton Record-Chronicle*, March 3, 1980, 4A, 5A.
22. Tim Jarrell, "No Indictments in NTSU Probe; Ex-President Cleared of Allegations," *Dallas Times Herald*, August 16, 1980.
23. "Minutes of the Board of Regents," August 24, 1979, 205–6.
24. "Minutes of the Board of Regents," December 9, 1979, 23–24.

Notes to Chapter 39

1. "Minutes," Coordinating Board, Texas College and University System, July 18,1980. Vandiver was the only president to occupy this house. On May 12, 1983, the board authorized the facilities committee to sell this house. This was done in July, but a condition of the sale was to accept a residence at 2141 Fairfax in trade. On August 26, 1983, the board authorized the facilities committee to sell that structure.
2. Winfree Brown to members of the Board of Regents, June 5, 1980, enclosing "Letter of Agreement Between the Executive Committee of the Board of Regents and Frank E. Vandiver," November 14, 1979.
3. Frank E. Vandiver, Convocation Speech, Faculty Convocation, January 9, 1980.
4. Frank E. Vandiver to My Personal Staff, December 8, 1980.
5. "Minutes of the Board of Regents," July 15, 1981, 129.
6. Frank E. Vandiver, "Regents Report," December 9, 1980.

7. Frank E. Vandiver, Speech to the Faculty Senate, April 9, 1980.

8. "Thrifty Aggie," *Austin American-Statesman*, May 8, 1983.

9. Frank E. Vandiver to Faculty and Professional Staff Members, November 5, 1980, 1-2.

10. Ibid., 2.

11. Ibid., 6.

12. Faculty Convocation, January 9, 1980, op. cit., 3.

13. Vandiver, November 5, 1980, 7.

14. Notes on President's Staff Meeting, December 23, 1980, #19.

15. Janie Leigh Frank, "Vandiver's Style Controversial after One Year," *Denton Record-Chronicle*, August 16, 1981, 1A.

16. Frank E. Vandiver to Faculty and Staff Members, January 5, 1981.

17. Ibid., 6.

18. Ibid., 7.

19. "Minutes of the Faculty Senate," January 21, 1981, 10.

20. Frank E. Vandiver to Howard W. Smith, Jr., and J. B. Smallwood, January 27, 1981.

21. "Minutes of the Faculty Senate," January 28, 1981, 3.

22. Howard W. Smith, Jr., to Frank E. Vandiver, February 16, 1981.

23. "Minutes of the Board of Regents," February 27, 1981, 44.

24. Clovis C. Morrisson, Jr., and J. B. Smallwood Jr. to the Faculty, August 11, 1981.

25. Frank E. Vandiver, Denton, to Paul Wrotenbery, Austin, May 15, 1981.

26. Summary, Council of Deans, August 12, 1981.

27. Carol Rust, Karen Ball, and R. Daniel Cavazos, "Vandiver Resigns to Accept A&M Post," *North Texas Daily*, August 27, 1981, 1.

28. Ibid.

29. Ibid.

30. Carol Rust, "Speculation Surrounds Departure," *North Texas Daily*, August 27, 1981, 1.

31. "Unfulfilled Promises," *North Texas Daily*, August 27, 1981, 2.

32. "Frank Vandiver: Here Today, and Gone to A&M," *Denton Record-Chronicle*, August 28, 1981, 4A.

33. Rust, et al.

34. Elna Christopher, "Vandiver Vows Not to Forget NTSU," *Dallas Morning News*, August 31, 1981, 14A.

35. "Minutes of the Faculty Senate," September 9, 1981, 1-2.

36. "3,000 Welcome New President to Texas A&M," *Fort Worth Star-Telegram*, September 10, 1981, 2B.

37. "Minutes of the Faculty Senate," September 9, 1981.

Notes to Chapter 40

1. Brian Howard, "Historian named NTSU president," *Fort Worth Star-Telegram*, February 2, 1982, 1,12.

2. Ibid., 12.

3. Winfree L. Brown, Brownwood, to Donna Lee Raley, Conroe, May 21, 1982.

4. Keith Shelton, "NT President Renews Community Bonds," *Denton Record-Chronicle*, March 12, 1982, 1-2A.

5. Alfred F. Hurley to Phil Diebel, December 26, 1983.

6. Alfred F. Hurley, Denton, to Daniel J. Boorstin, Washington, May 12, 1982.

7. Diane Reischel, "Alfred Hurley," *Dallas Morning News*, 1E, 3E.

8. Renee Schafer, "NTSU President Works to Create 'Sense of University,' Set Priorities," *Denton Record-Chronicle*, October 30, 1983, 1–2A.

9. Reischel, 3.

10. Reischel, 2.

11. Alfred F. Hurley, Denton, to H. E. Chiles, Fort Worth, March 3, 1982.

12. Discussion of this briefing here is based on copies of the material sent to Chiles March 3, 1982.

13. "Minutes of the Board of Regents," February 26, 1982, 100.

14. News release, June 8, 1984.

15. "Minutes of the Board of Regents," April 30, 1982.

16. "Minutes of the Board of Regents," June 14, 1985.

17. "Convocation Address, Faculty," August 24, 1982, 6–7.

18. Alfred F. Hurley to Members of the Faculty, August 26, 1982.

19. "Organization for Long-Range Planning," *North Texas State University Institutional Self-Study, 1983–1985*, November 1984, XII-11.

20. Report of the Steering Committee for the Study of the Organization of North Texas State University, August 1982.

21. Ibid., 15.

22. North Texas State University Institutional Self-Study, 1983-1985, November 1984, XI-4.

23. Ibid., XI-2.

24. Ibid., XI-13.

25. Ibid., XI-14,

26. Ibid., I-11.

27. "Executive Summary," September 30, 1982.

28. Winfree L. Brown, Brownwood, to William P. Clements, Jr., Austin, September 30, 1982.

29. William P. Clements, Jr., Austin, to Winfree L. Brown, Brownwood, October 29, 1982.

30. "Annual Report," February 1983, 1.

31. Ibid., 4.

Notes to Chapter 41

1. Frank E. Vandiver to Faculty and Staff Members, January 5, 1981.

2. Robert S. LaForte and Richard L. Himmel, *Down the Corridor of Years: A Centennial History of the University of North Texas in Photographs, 1890-1990* (Denton: University of North Texas Press, 1989).

3. "Convocation Address, Faculty," August 24, 1982, 6–7.

4. Nancy Holsti, "Whiz Kids," *North Texan*, Fall 1988, 23–25.

5. University of North Texas, *1998/1999 Undergraduate Catalog*, 100–1.

6. Stanford L. Semones, "New NT Press Begins Publishing to Reflect University," *North Texas Daily*, December 1, 1989, 10.

7. "About UNT Press," Accessed September 1998 from http:// www.unt.edu.

8. Olin Chism, "University Presses Move to Mainstream," *Dallas Morning News*, December 27, 1992, 8J.

9. "Center for Economic Development," downloaded from www.unt.edu July 2000.

Notes to Chapter 42

1. Robert Reinhold, "Texas Runs Short of Revenue as Oil Recession Continues," *New York Times*, May 22, 1985.

2. Comptroller of Public Accounts, News Release, January 10, 1983.

3. Bob Bullock, Austin, to Alfred F. Hurley, Denton, January 10, 1983.

4. Reinhold.

5. Winfree L. Brown, Brownwood, to Governor Mark White, Austin, May 24, 1984.

6. Ibid.

7. Laylan Copelin, "Cuts Threaten College Gains from 15 Years," *Austin American-Statesman*, December 16, 1984.

8. Tom Preston to Alfred F. Hurley and Robert B. Toulouse, January 25, 1985.

9. Council of Presidents of the Public Senior Colleges and Universities of Texas, *Informational Memorandum,* December 21, 1984, 1.

10. Ibid.

11. *Houston Post*, January 21, 1986.

12. Monty Jones, "Tuition Plan Unlikely Barrier," *Austin American-Statesman*, April 14, 1985.

13. Clay Robison, "Universities Begin Push to Sell Education Fund to Voters," *Houston Chronicle,* March 11, 1984.

14. Frank Vandiver, Denton, to Bill Hobby, Austin, May 11, 1981.

15. Eddie J. Davis to Frank E. Vandiver, May 11, 1981.

16. Alfred F. Hurley, Denton, to Leonard Rauch, Austin, March 31, 1982.

17. "Minutes of the Council of Presidents of the Public Senior Colleges and Universities of Texas," September 15, 1982.

18. Council of Presidents, *Informational Memorandum*, November 9, 1984.

19. Coordinating Board, Texas College and University System, *Space Use-Space Needs: The Availability and Use of Public Senior Higher Education Facilities in Texas. Study Paper 28* (Austin: np, April 1980), 65–66.

20. "Minutes of the Board of Regents," February 22, 1980, 21–22.

21. Fred Pole, Denton, to Gordon Flack, Austin, July 16, 1982.

22. "Minutes of the Board of Regents," April 28, 1982, 127–128.

23. "Minutes of the Board of Regents," May 13, 1983.

24. "State College Repair Needs Estimated," *Houston Post*, October 29, 1983.

25. Attributed to Jess Ben Latham III in undated 1988 clipping from the *Amarillo Globe-News*, University Archives.

26. Don W. Brown, Austin, to Fred Pole, Denton, December 20, 1991.

27. "Agenda," Council of Presidents of the Public Senior Colleges and Universities of Texas, November 10, 1982.

28. *Facility Evaluation Survey for North Texas State University* (Austin: Page Southerland Page, November 16, 1983).

29. "Minutes of the Board of Regents," July 8, 1983.

30. "Minutes of the Board of Regents," February 15, 1985.

31. "Minutes of the Board of Regents," August 22, 1986.

32. "Minutes of the Board of Regents," January 11, 1986.

33. Gordon Flack, Austin, to Alfred F. Hurley, Denton, October 22, 1985.

34. "Minutes of the Board of Regents," December 21, 1984. See also Alfred F. Hurley, Denton, to Sid Bass, Fort Worth, February 13, 1985.

35. "Minutes of the Board of Regents," June 27, 1986, and November 10, 1987.

36. "Minutes of the Board of Regents," December 20, 1993, 55-56.

37. Ibid., 55.

38. "Minutes of the Board of Regents," February 12, 1994.

39. Alfred F. Hurley, Denton, to Chris Hartung, Denton, May 7, 1982.

40. Edward M. Sills, "Governor Orders 13% Cut in Agency, College Budgets," *San Antonio Light*, February 19, 1986, 1.

41. Raul Reyes and Ann Marie Kilday, "White Asks State Agencies to Trim Spending by 13%," *Houston Chronicle*, February 13, 1986, 1.

42. Ibid.

43. Ibid.

44. Lee Jones, "White's Austerity Plan Shot Down," *Fort Worth Star-Telegram*, February 25, 1986.

45. Kenneth Ashworth, Austin, to Alfred F. Hurley, Denton, March 5, 1986.

46. "Minutes," Coordinating Board, Texas College and University System, April 25, 1986.

47. Jim Rich, "Texas Economic Rumblings," *Houston Chronicle*, July 26, 1986.

48. John C. Henry and Bruce Hight, "White Urges Compromise in New Session," *Austin American-Statesman*, September 5, 1986, 1.

49. Jorjanna Price, "Legislature Adjourns after Passing Tax Hike," *Houston Post*, October 1, 1986.

50. Mark White, Austin, to Alfred F. Hurley, Denton, October 1, 1986.

51. Joe Old, "Budget Cuts Cause Brain Drain for Higher Education in Texas," *El Paso Herald-Post*, October 16, 1986.

52. *Coordinating Board Report*, XXI:10, October 1986, 1–2.

53. "Chancellor's Message," *Update*, Vol. 18, No. 1, September 14, 1987, 6–8.

54. Fred Bonavita, "Come January, Lawmakers Get to Bite the Bullet Again," *Houston Post*, October 6, 1986.

55. State of Texas, *Report of the Select Committee on Higher Education*, February 1987.

56. G. Robert Hillman, "Bullock Issues Revenue Warning," *Dallas Morning News*, May 30, 1987.

57. Kenneth F. Bunting and Karen Hastings, "Clements Calls Special Session on Budget," *Fort Worth Star-Telegram*, May 31, 1987.

58. James McCrory, "Hobby: Income Tax for Texans possible," *San Antonio Express*, June 18, 1987.

59. Glenn Smith, "Clements, Hobby and Lewis Agree on $38.2 billion Budget," *Houston Post*, July 16, 1987.

60. Robert M. Sweeney, "Changes in State Higher Education Appropriations Ranking, FY 1984 to FY 1990" (Washington: AASCU, October 1991).

61. "Chancellor's Message."

62. "Report of the Steering Committee for the Study of the Organization of North Texas State University," August 1982.

63. Alfred F. Hurley, to Regents Lucille G. Murchison, J. Jack Hays, and Joe Greene, August 27, 1986.

64. "Minutes of the Faculty Senate," October 8, 1986.

65. Alfred F. Hurley to the Board of Regents, December 2, 1986.

66. "Changing School's Name Should Not be Done Lightly," *Denton Record-Chronicle*, February 26, 1987.

67. "Minutes of the Board of Regents," February 27, 1987, 41.

68. Editorial, *Fort Worth Star-Telegram*, March 3, 1987, quoted in Alfred F. Hurley to All Faculty and Staff, June 23, 1987.

69. Catherine Chriss, "Clements Endorses NTSU Name Change," *Dallas Times Herald*, June 24, 1987.

70. "Chancellor's Message."

71. Ibid. 8.

Notes to Chapter 43

1. Lee Jones, "Efforts to Coordinate Colleges Riddled by Politics," *Fort Worth Star-Telegram*, September 24, 1985.

2. Clay Robison, "Higher Education Panel Chief Promises No Areas are Sacred," *Houston Chronicle*, Sept. 25, 1985.

3. Jones.

4. State of Texas, *Report of the Select Committee on Higher Education*, February 1987, 1.

5. "Victor Arnold to Aid Committee Study of Future of Higher Learning," *Austin American Statesman*, November 8, 1985.

6. Clay Robison and Raul Reyes, "Panel to be Selective about Quality, Quantity," *Houston Chronicle*, September 29, 1985.

7. "College Panel Faces Task," *Fort Worth Star-Telegram*, September 29, 1985.

8. Alfred F. Hurley, "Summary of Statement on the Needs of Higher Education in Texas, Prepared for the Select Committee on Higher Education," attachment to letter, Hurley to Victor L. Arnold, Austin, January 30, 1986.

9. Ibid. Also, G. Robert Hillman, "Management Audit Set for Texas Colleges," *Dallas Morning News*, May 10, 1986.

10. Nancy Stancill, "Report Backs Overhaul of University System," *Houston Chronicle*, November 8, 1986.

11. "Hispanic Leader Calls for College Mergers," *Austin American-Statesman*, October 8, 1985.

12. Karen Potter, "College Merger Foes Wait to Speak," *Fort Worth Star-Telegram*, November 14, 1986.

13. "Higher Education Reform Well Worth Consideration," *Austin American-Statesman*, November 14, 1985.

14. Alfred F. Hurley, interview with the author, July 7, 1998.

15. Frank Trejo, "Location Could Close in on Denton Schools," *Fort Worth Star-Telegram*, (copy in university archives undated).

16. Clay Robison, "Education Reform, the Sequel," *Houston Chronicle*, Sept. 8, 1985.

17. A detailed account of the October 10 discussion of the TWU merger possibilities may be found in Council of Public University Presidents and Chancellors, *Informational Memorandum*, "Task Force on Funding, Governance, and Management," October 11, 1986, 5–7.

18. Connie Pryzant, "Backers of 6 Universities Speak Out," *Dallas Morning News*, November 22, 1986.

19. Wayne O. Stockseth, Corpus Christi, to Victor L. Arnold, Austin, June 27, 1986, 2.

20. Ibid., 3–4.

21. Jared E. Hazleton, Austin, to Wayne O. Stockseth, Corpus Christi, July 14, 1986.

22. Alfred F. Hurley, Denton, to B. B. Trotter, M.D., Abilene, September 2, 1986.

23. Wayne O. Stockseth, "Remarks to the Select Committee on NTSU-TWU Merger," November 21, 1986.

24. Alfred F. Hurley, Denton, to Larry Temple, Austin, November 21, 1986, 2–3.

25. Nancy Stancill, "Tempers Flare over UH-TSU Merger Proposal," *Houston Chronicle*, November 13, 1986.

26. "White: S. Texas Merger has Potential," *San Antonio Express*, November 23, 1986.

27. Dana Palmer, "White Slams University Merger Plan," *Corpus Christi Caller*, November 22, 1986.

28. Karen Potter, "Education Committee Scotches Third Merger Proposal," *Fort Worth Star-Telegram*, December 13, 1986.

29. Connie Pryzant, "Panel Calls for 5 Texas College Systems," *Dallas Morning News*, December 13, 1986.

30. Mark White, Austin, to Larry Temple, Austin, November 20, 1986.

31. Wayne O. Stockseth, Corpus Christi, to Victor L. Arnold, Austin, June 27, 1986, 3.

32. Alfred F. Hurley, Denton, to Larry Temple, Austin, November 21, 1986.

33. Monty Jones, "Panel Wants 3 Colleges Added to Research List," *Austin American-Statesman*, December 6, 1986.

34. Alfred F. Hurley to the Board of Regents, December 8, 1986.

35. State of Texas, Report of the Select Committee on Higher Education, February 1987, 22–31.

36. Alfred F. Hurley, Denton, to Harden H. Wiedemann, Dallas, February 17, 1987.

37. Harden H. Wiedemann and E. L. Langley, Dallas, to Larry Temple, Austin, February 16, 1987.

38. Alfred F. Hurley to Board of Regents, April 28, 1987.

39. Alfred F. Hurley, interview with the author, July 7, 1998.

40. "Lawmaker Balks at School Restructuring," *Fort Worth Star-Telegram*, March 13, 1987.

41. Connie Pryzant, "Education Panel's Impact Assessed," *Dallas Morning News*, June 8, 1987.

42. Nancy Stancill, "Higher Education May Take Leading Role in Legislative Session," *Houston Chronicle*, January 11, 1987.

43. Alfred F. Hurley, interview with the author, July 7, 1998.

44. Alfred F. Hurley, Denton, to Chet Edwards, Austin, July 7, 1987.

45. Larry Temple, Austin, to Presidents and Chancellors, June 26, 1987.

46. Adapted from a memorandum, Larry Temple to Presidents and Chancellors, July 10, 1987.

Notes to Chapter 44

1. Alfred Hurley, "To Soar, UNT Needs Denton," *Denton Record-Chronicle*, October 6, 1993.
2. Frank Vandiver, Denton, to Ray Thornton, State University, Ark., July 23, 1981.
3. "NT Sports in the '80s," 13.
4. Frank E. Vandiver, Denton, to Jim G. Plummer, Fort Worth, September 10, 1980.
5. "NT Sports in the '80s," 13.
6. "Minutes of the Board of Regents," July 15, 1981, 138.
7. Phil Rogers, "NTSU Official Expects Audit to Reflect Growth."
8. Phillip C. Diebel to Eddie J. Davis, February 23, 1982, 72.
9. "Minutes of the Board of Regents," February 26, 1982.

10. Bill Miller to Alfred F. Hurley, March 25, 1982.

11. Alfred F. Hurley to James W. Thomason, October 6, 1983.

12. Robert T. McGee, Denton, to Alfred F. Hurley, March 27, 1986.

13. "NT Sports in the '80s," 13.

14. Report of the Steering Committee for the Study of the Organization of North Texas State University, August, 1982, 18–19.

15. "Minutes of the Faculty Senate," April 13, 1983.

16. University Planning and Analysis, "University Staff Survey: A Report of the Findings for 1984," UPA No. 56-584.

17. Jacquielynn Floyd, "UTA Drops Football," *Dallas Times Herald*, November 26, 1985.

18. Joe Buie, "Athletic Department Enters 1990s with Financial Woes," *North Texas Daily*, December 1, 1989, 14.

19. "Women's Extramurals: Success on a Shoestring," *Yucca*, 1974, "Collegiate" Volume, 30–31.

20. Miles Schulze, Dallas, to C. C. Nolen, Denton, November 22, 1978.

21. Andy Everest, Denton, to Miles Schulze, Dallas, January 16, 1979.

22. Alfred F. Hurley, Denton, to Taylor B. August, Dallas, August 23, 1983.

23. Taylor B. August, Dallas, to Alfred F. Hurley, Denton, August 25, 1983.

24. "Minutes of the Board of Regents," October 25, 1996.

25. Keith Whitmire, "UNT among 25 Named in Title IX Complaint," *Dallas Morning News*, June 3, 1997, 11B.

26. "NT Sports in the '80s," 13–14.

27. Kevin Sherrington, "UNT Can Learn 2 Times as Much from SMU's Pye," *Dallas Morning News*, November 22, 1990, 1B.

28. Dan Noxon, "UNT Thinks Big Despite Financial Losses in Football," *Dallas Morning News*, November 25, 1990, 14B.

29. "Sloan Arrives at UNT," *Dallas Morning News*, February 23, 1991, 3B.

30. Henry Martinez, "Field of (student) Dreams?" *Denton Record-Chronicle*, March 1, 1992, 1A.

31. "Fouts Field Referendum," *North Texas Daily*, April 21, 1992, 1.

32. Jenny Lichtenwalter, " Fouts Field Expansion Issue Goes Before Board," *North Texas Daily*, June 18, 1992, 1.

33. Steve Sloan, Denton, to Dennis Farrell, Santa Ana, CA, September 7, 1992.

34. Keith Whitmire, "No Rooting Interest: UNT's Toughest Opponents are Identity and Indifference," *Dallas Morning News*, August 26, 1997, 69F–70F.

35. Garth Lewis and Lori Hawkins, "Is It Worth It? A Look at the Decision to Enter Division I-A Football," *North Texas Daily*, April 18, 1997, 2.

36. "Minutes of the Board of Regents," November 12, 1996, 32.

37. "Eagles Head for the Sun Belt Conference," *North Texan*, Winter 1999, 30.

Notes to Chapter 45

1. "Minutes of the Board of Regents," October 29, 1984, 10.

2. Ibid., 18.

3. Tom Preston to Alfred F. Hurley, April 8, 1985.

4. Alfred F. Hurley to all faculty and staff, December 14, 1988.

5. Kirsten Frederick, "Banner Year: Flag Day ushers in NT's Centennial," *North Texas Daily*, January 16, 1990, 1.

6. Sasha Koci, "Extravaganza to Honor NT's 100th birthday, *North Texas Daily*, Homecoming Supplement, October 18, 1990, 6.

7. Connie Pryzant, "UNT Centennial Celebration Ending with $35 million Capital Campaign," *Dallas Morning News*, October 18, 1990, 32A.

8. Clovis Morrisson, Denton, to Grace Cartwright, Weatherford, May 10, 1991.

9. Richard Dini, Houston, to Alfred F. Hurley, Denton, December 10, 1991.

10. "A Look at the University of North Texas," *Dallas Life Magazine*, October 14, 1990, 14.

11. Robert S. LaForte and Richard L. Himmel, *Down the Corridor of Years: A Centennial History of the University of North Texas in Photographs* (Denton: University of North Texas Press, 1989).

12. Ibid., 262.

Notes to Chapter 46

1. Alfred F. Hurley to Blaine Brownell, January 31, 1994.

2. "Rationale for a Health Sciences Center," a one-page document from the University Archives not labeled as to source but carrying page number 168.

3. University of North Texas, *Agency Strategic Plan for the 1997–2001 Period*, June 10, 1996, 10.

4. *1998/1999 Undergraduate Catalog*, 77.

5. "Enrollment by Race/Ethnicity and Level, Fall Semesters, 1984-97," *University of North Texas Fact Book 1997–98*, 5.

6. "By the Numbers," *Dallas Morning News*, August 2, 1998, 34A.

7. Richard Greene, "Minority Enrollment Increases." *North Texas Daily*, October 1, 1998, 1, 5.

8. Figures from various annual editions of the university's *Fact Book*.

9. Nita Thurman, "UNT Panel Urges a Zero-Tolerance Policy on Racism," *Dallas Morning News*, December 2, 1995, 35A, 40A.

10. Ibid.

11. Ibid.

12. Linda P. Campbell, "UNT Regents Left Hispanics off Panel, Group Says," *Fort Worth Star-Telegram*, December 9, 1995, np.

13. Kenneth H. Ashworth, Austin, to Alfred F. Hurley, Denton, June 22, 1983.

14. Alfred F. Hurley, Denton, to William A. Webb, Austin, August 2, 1983.

15. Linda Stewart, "Work Begins at Universities' New Downtown Site: Details Unveiled on Facility in Old Joske's Building," *Dallas Morning News*, January 19, 1994, 25A, 30A.

16. Linda Stewart and Stephen Lee, "Learning Center Looks to Autumn: Echoes, Few Students Fill Halls on 1st Day of Summer Classes," *Dallas Morning News*, June 7, 1994, 15A, 21A.

17. Linda Stewart, "175 Students Enroll at University Center: Officials Hope Late Signup Today is Boost," *Dallas Morning News*, August 31, 1994, 37A.

18. *1998–99 UNT Graduate Catalog*, Accessed September 24, 1998 from http://www.tsgs.unt.edu/guniversity.html#top, Internet.

19. Al Hurley to Members, Faculty and Staff, June 8, 1999.

20. Jayne Noble Suhler, "Universities Seeking Area Campus," *Dallas Morning News*, June 24, 1998.

21. Christian Bohmfalk, "Dallas Campus Planned," *Denton Record-Chronicle,* August 28, 1998, 1A.

22. Christian Bohmfalk, "Plans Postponed: UNT-Dallas Project May Not Materialize," *Denton Record-Chronicle*, September 25, 1998, 1A.

23. Colin Pope, "UNT Moves One Step Closer to Dallas," *Denton Record Chronicle*, November 14, 1998, 1A, 14A.

24. Jayne Noble Suhler, "UNT Gets Approval for Center," *Dallas Morning News*, January 29, 1999, 35A, 37A.

25. Jayne Noble Suhler, "State Gives UNT $4.2 Million for University Center," *Dallas Morning News*, June 3, 1999, 30A.

26. Linda K. Wertheimer, "Change at the Top for UNT," *Dallas Morning News*, September 18, 2000, 15A, 22A.

27. "Televised Instruction," *1997-98 Graduate Catalog*, 77.

28. "Distributed Learning," *1998/1999 Undergraduate Catalog*, 78.

29. Robin M. Smith, "Computers Shorten Distance for Off-Campus Students," *North Texas Daily*, September 22, 1998, 1.

30. North Texas State University, *Institutional Self-Study 1983-1985*, November 1984, XI-4.

31. Rollie Schafer, "Achieving National Recognition in Research and Graduate Studies Through Increased Extramural Funding at the University of North Texas: A White Paper," May 1999, http://www.unt.edu/ospa/whitepaper/whitepaper.htm

32. "Minutes of the Board of Regents," May 12, 1989, document unpaginated.

33. "Minutes of the Board of Regents," May 20, 1992, 122–23.

34. "Minutes of the Board of Regents," June 10, 1996, 111.

35. Ibid., 92.

36. Alfred F. Hurley, "University works to expand its research efforts," *North Texan*, Spring, 1997, 3.

37. Jayne Noble Suhler, "TI Giving Equipment to Colleges: $6 Million Deal Forms Research Consortium," *Dallas Morning News*, October 10, 1998, 33A.

38. North Texas State University, *Fact Book,* 1978, 4.2-1-2. University of North Texas, *1997–1998 Fact Book,* University Planning, 140.

39. University of North Texas, *1997–1998 Fact Book*, University Planning, 140.

40. North Texas State University, *Institutional Self-Study 1983–1985*, IV-4.

41. University of North Texas, *1997–1998 Fact Book*, University Planning, 140.

42. Schafer, 87.

43. "UNT Named Winner," *Denton Record-Chronicle*, July 3, 2000, 12A.

44. Schafer, 6.

45. Ibid.

46. Ibid., 87.

47. Ibid., 71–72.

48. Ibid., 73.

49. Ibid., 71–78.

50. Patrick M. Walker, "UNT Now a 'System'," *Denton Record-Chronicle*, July 23, 1999, 1A. 11A.

51. Karen Treat, "Regents Officially Appoint Norval Pohl," *Denton Record-Chronicle*, October 11, 2000, 1A, 10A.

52. "Dr. Al Hurley: He's the Unsung Hero of Higher Education," *Dallas Morning News*, September 20, 2000, 26A.

53. Jessica Jarrett, "Board Gives NT Formal System Status," *North Texas Daily*, July 29, 1999, 1, 3.

Index

** NOTE: Due to the many variations in the name of the institution, it is referred to as simply "NT."
** NOTE: Schools are listed under their most recent names noted in the text.

A

B

E

F

H

K

L

M

O

Q

R

S

T

U

V

W

Y

Z